| DATE DUE | |
|---|---|
| ~~468483~~ | ~~2/25/33~~ |
| | |
| | |
| | |
| | |
| | |
| | |
| | |
| | |
| | |
| | |
| | |
| | |
| | |

# Introduction to
# Personality

FOURTH EDITION

# Introduction to
# Personality

E. Jerry Phares

Kansas State University

William F. Chaplin

The University of Alabama

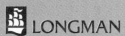 LONGMAN

An imprint of Addison Wesley Longman, Inc.

New York • Reading, Massachusetts • Menlo Park, California • Harlow, England
Don Mills, Ontario • Sydney • Mexico City • Madrid • Amsterdam

Editor-in-Chief: Priscilla McGeehon
Supplements Editor: Cyndy Taylor
Project Coordination and Text Design: Ruttle, Shaw & Wetherill, Inc.
Cover Designer: Nancy Sabato
Cover Illustration: Janet Atkinson
Photo Researcher: Diane Kraut
Electronic Production Manager: Christine Pearson
Manufacturing Manager: Helene G. Landers
Electronic Page Makeup: Ruttle, Shaw & Wetherill, Inc.
Printer and Binder: R. R. Donnelley & Sons Company
Cover Printer: Phoenix Color Corp.

For permission to use copyrighted material, grateful acknowledgment is made to the copyright holders on pp. 683–688, which are hereby made part of this copyright page.

Library of Congress Cataloging-in-Publication Data
Phares, E. Jerry
    Introduction to personality / E. Jerry Phares, William F. Chaplin. —4th ed.
      p.     cm.
    Includes bibliographical references (p. 000) and index.
    ISBN 0-673-99456-2
    1. Personality  I. Title.
  BF698.P48  1997
  155.2—dc20                  98-38681
                                      CIP

ISBN 0-673-99456-2

12345678910—DOC—999897

# Contents

Preface   xiii

# PART 1
## An Introduction to the Study of Personality   1

### Chapter 1
### Introduction to Personality   2

Informal and Formal Personality
  Theory   3
Personality as a Science   7
Defining Personality   8
  The Modern View of Personality   8
  The Field of Personality
    Psychology   10
  The Nature of Personality: Two
    Issues   14
Toward a Comprehensive Theory
  of Personality   15
Overview of Personality Determinants   18
  Biology   19
  Environment   20
  Cognition   22
Philosophy of This Text   23
Summary   24

### Chapter 2
### The Tools of Understanding   26

Theory: Proposing Explanations and
  Making Predictions   27
  A Diversity of Theories   27
  Personality Theory and Constructs   28
  Value of Personality Theories   30
  Dimensions of Personality Theories   32
  Evaluating Theories: Nonempirical
    Criteria   33
Research: Empirically Evaluating
  Explanations and Testing Predictions   35
  Research and Theory   35
  Observation: Unsystematic, Naturalistic,
    and Controlled   36
  Case Study Methods   38
  The Experimental Method   39
  The Correlation Method   44
  Statistical Versus Practical
    Significance   48
  Single-Subject Research   49
Assessment: Measuring Constructs and
  Describing People   50
  Issues in Personality Assessment   50
  Evaluating Measures   53
  Approaches to Personality
    Assessment   55
Nomological Network: Putting It All
  Together   59
Summary   61

# PART 2
## Theories of Personality　63

## Chapter 3
### Psychoanalytic Theory: The Freudian Revolution, Dissent, and Revision　64

The Beginnings of the Psychoanalytic Age　65
Basic Theory　68
　Psychic Determinism　68
　Unconscious Motivation　68
　Instincts　71
Structure of Personality　72
　The Id　73
　The Ego　74
　The Superego　74
Development of Personality　75
　The Oral Stage　75
　The Anal Stage　76
　The Phallic Stage　76
　The Latency Period　78
　The Genital Stage　78
Anxiety and Ego Defenses　80
　Anxiety　80
　Defense Mechanisms　80
Personality and Adjustment　81
Approaches to Psychotherapy and Behavior Change　81
　Goals of Therapy　81
　The Therapeutic Circumstance　83
　Free Association　83
　Dream Analysis　84
　Interpretation　84
　Resistance to Analysis　85
　Transference　85
　Working Through　85
Dissent　89
Adler's Individual Psychology　89
　Inferiority and Compensation　89
　Striving for Superiority　90
　Social Interest　90
　Style of Life　92

Development of Personality　92
Personality and Adjustment　94
Approaches to Psychotherapy and Behavior Change　96
Jung's Analytic Psychology　96
　Personality Structure　99
　Archetypes　99
　Psychological Types and Personality　102
The Neo-Freudians　103
　Karen Horney　103
　Erich Fromm　104
　Harry Stack Sullivan　104
　Ego Psychology　104
Contemporary Psychoanalytic Theories　108
　The Theory of Object Relations　109
　The Self-Psychology of Kohut　110
Summary　112

## Chapter 4
### Psychoanalytic Theory: Research, Assessment, and Evaluation　115

Psychoanalytic Research Methods　116
　The Case Study Method　116
　Associations, Dreams, Fantasy, and Behavior　118
　The Comparative-Anthropological Approach　122
　Psychobiography and Psychohistory　122
　Subjectivity and Objectivity in Scientific Research　124
　Experimental Research　124
Research on Freudian Concepts　125
　Repression　125
　The Unconscious　127
　Defense Mechanisms　129
　General Conclusion　131
Research on Jungian Concepts　131
Research on Adlerian Concepts　134
Research on Ego Psychology　135
Summary Evaluation　136

Strengths    137
Weaknesses    138
Summary    141

## Chapter 5
### Biological Influences: Behavior Genetics, Evolution, and Physiology    143

The Influence of Appearance and Body
Type    144
  Sheldon's Constitutional Theory    145
  Critique of Constitutional
    Psychology    145
The Genetic Basis of Personality:
  A History    147
  Gregor Mendel: Linking Characteristics
    to Genes    147
  Chromosomes and DNA    150
  Francis Galton: Heredity and Individual
    Differences    153
Behavior Genetics    161
  Basic Models    161
  Methods of Behavior Genetics    162
Mechanisms of Influence on
  Personality    169
  Biochemistry and Neuroscience    170
  Evolutionary Theory    171
  Uses and Limitations of Biology in
    Personality    176
Summary    177

## Chapter 6
### Biological Influences: Research and Summary Evaluation    179

Behavior Genetics and Personality    180
  Twin Studies    181
  Family Resemblance and Adoption
    Studies    183
  Reconciling Twin and Adoption Study
    Results    183
  Environmental Influences    185
Biological Influences on Personality    187
  Physique and Personality    187

Biochemistry and Personality    189
Brain Structure and Personality    193
Evolution and Personality Psychology    198
  Human Nature and Individual
    Variation    199
  Evolution and Personality
    Structure    200
  Animal Personality    201
  The Continuity Between Animal Behavior
    and Human Personality    202
Summary Evaluation    204
  Strengths    204
  Weaknesses    206
Summary    207

## Chapter 7
### Phenomenology and Social Cognition: The Self and Personal Constructs    209

The Nature of Phenomenology    210
The Self    211
  Components    211
  Development    212
  Function of the Self    213
Rogers: A Person-Centered Approach    214
  Basic Theory and Concepts    215
  Development of Personality    220
  The Nature of Adjustment    221
  Implications for Behavior Change    223
  The Humanistic/Existential/
    Phenomenological Approach    225
Maslow and Humanism    225
  Hierarchy of Needs    226
  Self-Actualization and Being    228
Existentialism    230
Kelly: A Personal Constructs
  Approach    231
  Basic Theory and Concepts    232
  Development of Personality    237
  The Nature of Adjustment    238
  Implications for Behavior Change    238
Social Cognition    239
  The Computer Metaphor as a
    Beginning    239

Human Cognition in Its Social
Context　240
Some Basic Concepts　241
Social Cognitive Theories of
Personality　242
Summary　244

## Chapter 8
## Phenomenology and Social Cognition: Research, Assessment, and Summary Evaluation　247

Idiographic Inquiry　248
The Nomothetic Emphasis in
Psychology　248
Idiographic Evaluation in Everyday
Life　249
Idiographic Measurement　251
The California Q-Set　253
The Rogerian Research Legacy　256
Empirical Investigation of Maslow's
Humanism　256
Needs Hierarchy　256
Self-Actualization　258
Peak Experience　260
Existential Research　260
Qualitative Data　262
Content Analysis　262
Research on Personal Constructs　264
The Rep Test　264
Change in Personal Constructs　266
Complexity of Personal Construct
Systems　267
Self-Schemata Research　267
Implicit Personality Theory　269
Features of Implicit Personality
Theory　270
Validity of Implicit Personality
Theory　270
Implicit and Formal Theories of
Personality　272
Phenomenology and Personality
Assessment　273
The Classic Semantic Differential Rating
Scale　273

Types of Personality Data　274
Problems with Phenomenological Self-
and Other-Reports　275
Formal Versus Implicit Theories and
Assessment　275
Accuracy of Global Ratings　277
Rating Agreement　278
Summary Evaluation　280
Strengths　280
Weaknesses　282
Summary　285

## Chapter 9
## The Behavioral Tradition　288

The Beginnings of Learning Theory　289
Classical Conditioning　290
Watson's Behaviorism　291
Thorndike and Hull and the Era of
Behaviorism　293
Skinner's Operant Conditioning　294
Basic Skinnerian Concepts　295
Structure of Personality　302
The Idiographic Method　302
Development of Personality　303
Nature of Adjustment　304
The Reinforcement Theory of Dollard and
Miller　305
From Animal Behavior to Human
Personality　305
Basic Concepts of Reinforcement
Theory　307
Structure of Personality　312
Development of Personality　312
Nature of Adjustment　313
Summary　317

## Chapter 10
## Behaviorism: Therapy, Assessment, and Summary Evaluation　320

Behavior Therapy　321
Counterconditioning　321
Systematic Desensitization　322

Aversion Therapy 322
The Operant Approach 324
The Engineered Society 326
Cognition as Behavior 327
Cognitive Restructuring 328
Stress Inoculation 329
The Hidden Goal of
Understanding 330
Behavioral Assessment 330
Sign Versus Sample 331
SORC Model 331
Interviews 331
Inventories and Checklists 333
Direct Observation 333
Controlled Settings 334
Role Playing 336
Self-Monitoring 336
Summary Evaluation 337
Strengths 338
Weaknesses 340
Summary 346

Chapter 11
Social Learning Theory 348

Rotter's Social Learning Theory 349
Assumptions and Basic Principles 350
Theory and Concepts 351
Development of Personality 359
Nature of Adjustment 359
Implications for Behavior Change 362
Bandura's Social Cognitive Theory 363
Two Theoretical Principles 364
Reciprocal Determinism 366
Observational Learning 366
Vicarious Reinforcement and
Conditioning 368
Self-Regulation 369
Self-Efficacy 369
Development of Personality 370
Nature of Adjustment 370
Implications for Behavior Change 371
Mischel: A Cognitive Social Learning
Reconceptualization of Personality 373

Competencies 374
Encoding Strategies 374
Expectancies 374
Subjective Values 375
Self-Regulatory Systems and
Plans 376
Summary 376

Chapter 12
Social Learning: Research, Assessment,
and Summary Evaluation 379

Research on Rotter's Concepts 380
Early Research Supporting Social
Learning Theory 380
Extensions of Social Learning Theory:
Response Expectancy 383
Generalized Response
Expectancies 384
Applications of Social Learning
Theory 387
Research on Bandura's Cognitive Social
Learning Theory 389
Observational Learning 390
Self-Efficacy 392
Goal Setting and the Immediacy of
Reward 395
Mischel and the Delay of
Gratification 397
Role of Expectancy 397
Effects on Reward Value 398
Imitating Delay Behavior 398
Personality Correlates 399
Social Learning Theory and
Assessment 400
Measuring Expectancies 401
Assessing Reinforcement Value 402
Projective Techniques 402
Incomplete Sentences 403
Measurement of Internal-External Locus
of Control (I-E) 403
Summary Evaluation 403
Strengths 404
Weaknesses 406
Summary 408

Chapter 13
Trait Theory: Personality Dispositions
and Personality Description    411

Personality Description and Personality
   Theory    412
     Trait Constructs    412
     Advantages of Trait Constructs    413
Traits: The Dispositional View    414
     Historical Beginnings of Dispositional
       Theory    414
     Traits and Types    415
Allport: A Trait Theory    415
     Basic Theory and Concepts    416
     Development of Personality    420
     Nature of Adjustment    421
     Implications for Behavior Change    422
Cattell: A Factor Theory of Traits    422
     Basic Theory and Concepts    423
     Development of Personality    428
     Nature of Adjustment    428
     Implications for Behavior Change    429
Eysenck: A Theory of Types    429
     A Hierarchical Personality
       Structure    430
     Basic Types    430
     Nature of Introversion-Extroversion
       432
Murray: A System of Needs    434
     Traits as Needs and Motives    434
     Basic Concepts    436
     Achievement Motivation    438
     Need for Power    440
     Need for Affiliation    441
The Trait-Situation Controversy    441
     Dispositional Traits and Situational
       Specificity    441
     Conclusion    446
Traits as Descriptions, Not Causes, of
   Behavior    446
     The Act-Frequency Theory of
       Traits    447
     The Big Five Model of Personality
       Description    448
Summary    451

Chapter 14
Traits: Assessment, Research, and Summary
Evaluation    454

Allport: The Search for Individuality    455
     Letters from Jenny    455
     Expressive Behaviors    457
     Assessment of Values    458
Cattell's Psychometric Approach to Trait
   Research    458
     Bivariate-Multivariate-Clinical
       Axis    459
     Factor Analysis    460
     Hypothetical Example of Factor
       Analysis    461
     Sources of Data    463
     Empirical Identification of
       Traits    465
     Analysis of Heredity and
       Environment    467
     Measurement of Similarity and
       Change    467
Eysenck's Search for Types    469
     Criterion Analysis    470
     The Biological Basis of Eysenck's
       Factors    470
Murray's Research Legacy    472
     Intensive Study of Individuals    472
     The Diagnostic Council    473
     The TAT    473
     Enhancing Achievement
       Striving    478
Descriptive Models: Research and
   Critique    479
     Act-Frequency Research    479
     The Category View of Personality
       Description    481
     Critique of the Act-Frequency
       Approach    482
     Research Based on the Big Five    483
Summary Evaluation    486
     Allport's Strengths    486
     Allport's Weaknesses    486
     Cattell's and Eysenck's
       Strengths    487

Cattell's and Eysenck's
  Weaknesses    488
Murray's Strengths    489
Murray's Weaknesses    489
Descriptive Theories: Strengths    490
Descriptive Theories: Weaknesses    490
Summary    491

Test Bias    514
Intelligence: Summary and
  Conclusion    517
Creativity    518
Cognitive Style    519
Need for Cognition    521
Absorption    522
Openness to Experience    522
Summary    523

# PART 3
## Applications of Personality Theory and Research    493

### Chapter 15
### Personality and Intellect    494

Personality and Intelligence    496
  Judgments Versus Sentiments    496
  Differences Between Measures of
    Intelligence and Personality    496
  Reconciling Intelligence with Personality
    Theory    497
Nature of Intelligence    497
  Definitions    498
  Prototype Approach    498
Formal Theories of Intelligence    499
  g Versus s Factors    499
  Hierarchical Models    499
  The Structure of Intellect Model    500
  Cognitive Theories    500
  Triarchic Theory    501
Assessment of Intelligence    501
  The Stanford-Binet    502
  The Wechsler Scales    504
Major Correlates of IQ    505
  Correlation and Explanation    505
Heritability of Intelligence    507
  Role of Heredity    508
  Studies of Adopted Children    508
  Environments, Genes, and Innate
    Potential    510
Group Differences in Intelligence    511
  Ethnic Differences    512
  Social Policy Implications    513

### Chapter 16
### Personality and Anxiety, Stress, and Health    526

Specific Versus General Psychological
  Causes    527
Anxiety    529
  Definitions of Anxiety    529
  Anxiety and Learning Theory    530
  Different Conceptions and Measures of
    Anxiety    531
Stress    534
  Definitions of Stress    535
  Phenomenological Appraisal    535
  Types of Stressful Events    537
  Responses to Stress    540
Type A Behavior Pattern    545
  The TABP Construct    545
  Measurement of TABP    546
  TABP and CHD    546
  Components of TABP    548
Personality Characteristics That
  Strengthen    550
  Optimism and Hardiness    551
  Self-Efficacy    551
  Ego Control and Ego Resiliency    551
  Motives    552
  Humor    552
  Personal Control    552
Critical Issues in Personality and
  Health    555
  Mechanisms    555
  Women and Minorities    556

Outcome Measures    557
Neuroticism and Negative
    Affectivity    557
Summary    558

## Chapter 17
## Personality, Occupations, and the Workplace    561

Personality and Occupational Choice    562
Strong Vocational Interest Blank    562
Holland's Theory of Vocational
    Choice    564
Motivation    566
Intrinsic and Extrinsic Motivation    566
Psychological Theories of
    Motivation    567
Motivation as a Personality
    Variable    567
Leadership    571
Theory X and Theory Y    571
Specific Theories of Leadership    573
Personality Characteristics    574
Honesty and Integrity    578
Polygraphs    579
Integrity Tests    580
Evaluation of Integrity Tests    581
Personnel Selection    583
Problems with Personality
    Measures    584
Contemporary Personality Assessment
    and Personnel Selection    585
Summary    587

## Chapter 18
## Personality and Gender Differences    589

Sex and Gender    590
Gender Stereotypes    591
Description of Gender Stereotypes    591
Stereotyping Among Psychologists    595
Factors That Promote Stereotypes    595
Variations in Stereotypes    596
Research on Gender Differences    596

Prediction Versus Explanation    596
Group Versus Individual
    Differences    597
The Politics of Gender Research    597
Psychoanalytic Theories and Gender
    Differences    599
Biology and Gender Differences    600
Differences in Infants    601
Animal Research    602
External Versus Chromosomal Sex    603
Gender Differences in Brain
    Structure    604
Social Cognition and Gender
    Differences    605
Cognitive-Developmental Theory    605
Gender Schema    605
Flexibility    606
Behaviorism and Gender Differences    606
Social Learning and Gender
    Differences    609
Imitation and Differential
    Attention    609
Consistency    611
Self-Regulation and Reciprocal
    Determinism    611
Gender Differences in Personality Structure
    and Description    612
Gender Differences and the Big
    Five    612
Androgyny    612
Summary    614

Glossary    616
References    639
Credits    683
Author Index    689
Subject Index    699

# Preface

## A Turning Point

This fourth edition of *Introduction to Personality* is a transition in the publication history of this textbook. Certainly, the most obvious change is the addition of a second author, William F. Chaplin, who brings a background in phenomenological/cognitive personality research and trait theory to complement the social learning and clinical orientation of E. Jerry Phares. With this co-authorship, we have reflected on the changes that have taken place in the history of personality psychology and have come to assess the field of psychology as it stands today. The result is a substantial revision of a classic text: the debut of a book that reflects the new directions in personality research and will continue to mature into the next century.

Faithful to previous editions, the authors cover the broad theoretical conceptions of human personality as defined by the preeminent psychologists of our time and emphasize their basis in psychological research. Now included in this framework are the most contemporary theories on biological factors in personality (encompassing behavior genetics and evolutionary psychology), the influence of the cognitive revolution in psychology on personality theory and research, and recent developments in trait theory and the Big Five. These chapters are placed alongside the classic theories and research that have prevailed, and still continue, in personality psychology.

## A Balanced Organization

This balance of classic and contemporary work is achieved through a division of the text into three parts.

- Part 1, consisting of Chapters 1 and 2, is an introduction to the field and methods of personality.

- Part 2, Chapters 3 to 14, is devoted to the major theoretical orientations within personality theory: psychoanalytic, biological, behavioral, phenomenological, social cognitive, social learning, and dispositional/descriptive. Balanced coverage is achieved through a twin-chapter format: each odd-numbered chapter is devoted to a theory, and the following, even-numbered chapter concerns the research, assessment, and applications of that theory.

- Part 3, including Chapters 15 to 18, applies personality theory to pertinent issues in the modern world: personality and intellect; personality, occupations, and the workplace; personality and anxiety, stress, and health; and personality and gender differences.

In this way, personality theory comes alive as a discipline that is rigorous scientifically as well as conceptually and is relevant to everyday life.

## Features of This Edition

We have aimed to present this breadth and depth of information in a way that is interesting and accessible to the student. We have taken care to highlight several areas that help build on, and contextualize, the theory and research that is presented in the main body of the text. See for example:

- *Case studies* (including one that illustrates psychoanalytic interpretations of the discontent of a 20-year-old college undergraduate, p. 86, and one, which describes the personality change in Phineas Gage after he experienced a severe brain injury, p. 195.)

- *Brief biographies of psychologists* (including Freud, pp. 66–67; Galton, pp. 154–155; Rogers, pp. 216–217; Skinner, pp. 296–297; Bandura, p. 365; and Allport, p. 417)

- *Close-ups* of issues under debate within personality theory (such as Box 4-4, on the reality of repressed memories, p. 126; Box 8-2, which summarizes the classic exchange between Rogers and Skinner on science and human behavior, pp. 257–258, and Box 17-4 on the use of personality measures in employee selection decisions, p. 586)

- More *technical discussions* of methods of personality research (see Box 2-4, on the analysis of aggregate and single-subject data, p. 51; and Box 5-5, on calculating heritability coefficients, p. 168).

Other features also enhance students' understanding of personality psychology and help them think critically:

- *Strengths and Weaknesses* sections conclude Chapters 4, 6, 8, 10, 12, and 14, summarizing the applications and research based on each of the major theoretical orientations and providing critical evaluations of the different theories.

- *Summaries* are presented at the end of each chapter to highlight the main points of the chapter and serve as a useful study aid.

## What's New: Chapter by Chapter

Several significant changes are apparent in this edition. They are based on feedback from professors as well as students:

- Chapter 1 has been shortened to provide a broad overview of personality that can complement the specific orientations of the individual instructors without imposing a particular point of view. We give a balanced description of the environmental, biological, and cognitive perspectives that, singly and in combination, form the major theories of personality.

- The discussion of psychoanalytic theories and research has been reduced from three to two chapters (Chapters 3 and 4) to make coverage of this approach more equal to that devoted to other approaches. In making this change, the discussion of psychoanalytic approaches to psychotherapy has been reduced and the application of cognitive research to the study of psychoanalytic concepts such as repression and the unconscious is emphasized.

- Two new chapters (5 and 6) on biological theories have been added to this section, reflecting the explosion of research in the field of behavior genetics. These chapters clarify how modern behavior genetic research has documented the influence of both genetic and environmental factors on personality. In addition, the intriguing but controversial application of evolutionary theory to personality psychology is discussed.

- Likewise, the chapters on phenomenology (7 and 8) have been extensively revised to reflect the influence of the "cognitive revolution" on personality theory and research. In particular, theories and research based on the constructs of social intelligence and self-schemata are emphasized. The role of implicit personality theory in personality assessment and research is also discussed.

- Behavioral or learning theory approaches to personality (Chapters 9 and 10), while appearing at present to be on a slow growth curve, have been revised to include the powerful influence of behavioral technologies on human behavior.

- Chapters 11 and 12, on social learning theory, incorporate some of the recent outgrowth of learning theory and cognitive theory. In addition to including the theories of Rotter and Bandura, the work of Mischel on delay of gratification and the applications to the concept of self-efficacy to a variety of domains are discussed.

- The chapters on trait theory (13 and 14) are now placed at the end of Part 2, reflecting the qualitative difference between modern trait theory, which emphasizes personality description, and the other major personality theories, which emphasize explanation. That is, after psychodynamic, biological, phenomenological, social cognitive, behavioral, and social learning forces have had their influence on a person, we are left with a personality to be described.

- The chapter on personality and intellect (15) discusses the traditional concept of intelligence, but also considers associated constructs such as openness to experience, need for cognition, and creativity.

- The chapter on personality and health (16) describes some of the most recent conceptual advances in this rapidly growing area of application and research. The negative impacts of such personality variables as hostility and anxiety on health, as well as the positive impacts of humor, optimism, and hope, are discussed.

- Chapter 17, Personality and the Workplace, is new to this edition. There is a long-standing belief that personality variables impact leadership effectiveness, employee satisfaction, and organizational productivity. This chapter provides an up-to-date summary of the research that is relevant to these beliefs.

- The final chapter, Gender Differences, has been structured to review each of the major theoretical approaches to personality discussed in Part 2 by illustrating how they are used to explain gender differences in personality. It now includes new research on cross-cultural gender stereotyping and sex differences in brain structures, as well as a discussion of the politics of gender research.

## Supplements

Dr. Jim Council, of North Dakota State University, has prepared a testbank for this edition, including over 2,000 questions written in multiple choice, true-false, short answer, and essay formats. The testbank will be available in printed form and on disk for DOS and Macintosh.

## Acknowledgments

The authors would like to acknowledge the following reviewers for their invaluable feedback during the preparation of this edition: Joel Arnoff, Michigan State University; Gordon Atlas, Alfred University; James F. Calhoun, University of Georgia; Barbara Chapman, State University of New York–Albany; Jim Council, North Dakota State University; Natalie Denburg, Michigan State University; Amerigo Farina, University of Connecticut; Lisa Feldman Barrett, Pennsylvania State University; Steven Funk, Northern Arizona University; Lee

Hansell, University of Virginia; Dorothy Hochreich, University of Connecticut; James Johnson, Illinois State University; Edwin Lawson, State University of New York–Fredonia; Charles Lord, Texas Christian University; Doug Needham, Redeemer College; Steve Nida, Franklin University; Frederick Rhodewalt, University of Utah; Richard Rakos, Cleveland State University; and Rasyid Bo Sanitioso, Colgate University.

E. Jerry Phares
William F. Chaplin

# Part 1
# An Introduction to the Study of Personality

This textbook is organized into three parts. Part 1 provides a general introduction to the issues, topics, and methods that characterize the contemporary study of human personality. In Chapter 1 we provide a general definition of personality that emphasizes the discipline's focus on the consistent and stable patterns of individuals' thoughts and actions that together provide the distinctiveness that makes each individual unique. The chapter also describes the major areas of interest to personality psychologists: development, adjustment, change, assessment, and research. The chapter concludes with a brief discussion of the three major perspectives that have been used to understand human personality: biological, environmental, and cognitive. The major theories of personality can be characterized as emphasizing one or more of these perspectives.

In Chapter 2 the focus is on the methods of personality research. In this chapter we consider the role of theory in guiding research, the various types of research designs and data analysis that are commonly used by personality psychologists, and the major approaches that are used to measure personality constructs. The goal of this chapter is to provide the student with a sufficient methodological background to understand and evaluate the research described in the subsequent chapters in this text.

# Chapter 1
# Introduction to Personality

Informal and Formal Personality Theory
Personality as a Science
Defining Personality
    The Modern View of Personality
    The Field of Personality Psychology
    The Nature of Personality: Two Issues
Toward a Comprehensive Theory of
   Personality
Overview of Personality Determinants
    Biology
    Environment
    Cognition
Philosophy of This Text
Summary

The concept of personality is basic to the study of people and their behavior. It is also a concept that is familiar to everyone, and scores of new books dealing with one or another facet of personality appear each year. Some ideas about personality can be found in even the most primitive of our ancestors in their recognition that although no two people are exactly alike, there are ways in which all people are the same. Likewise, in children, one of the signs of their growing maturity is their ability to recognize the sameness in all human beings while at the same time using their knowledge of the differences among people to effectively attain their interpersonal goals (see Box 1-1). Scientists, laypersons, and children all recognize and accept the seeming paradox of the similarity of humankind and the uniqueness of all individuals. Moreover, everyone uses this paradox to predict, understand, and explain their own and others' behavior and to cope with the demands and challenges of a complex social world. The study of personality is not merely an abstract scholarly exercise; it is rooted in the practical problems of social life.

## Informal and Formal Personality Theory

In many ways, then, all people are personality psychologists. Throughout our everyday lives we have all developed ideas about the important characteristics of people; the effect of those characteristics on how people behave, think, and feel; and how those characteristics are related to each other. These beliefs represent our **informal** or **implicit personality theory**, a term coined by Bruner and Tagiuri in 1954. For example, some people believe that good-looking men are vain or that people with close-set eyes cannot be trusted. Still others are convinced that creative people are likely to be emotionally unstable. These ideas are impressions we have about one another, and they help us to make sense of the world. Some of these impressions may be accurate and useful, whereas others may be inaccurate and cause problems. Some of our ideas are simple, whereas others are complex. But whether accurate or inaccurate, simple or complex, all these ideas influence how we think, feel, and act with respect to other people and events. The Brief Biography on page 6 illustrates how a world leader's implicit theory influenced his perceptions of other world leaders.

Personality psychology, as a scholarly discipline, is based on **formal** or **explicit theories**. It is not surprising that everyday implicit personality theories and the formal theories of personality psychologists show some similarity. After all, personality psychologists are also people, and they developed implicit theories about people long before they became personality psychologists. It seems likely that the ideas of personality psychologists would be influenced by their informal observations and interactions with people.

However, the formal study of personality, which is what this book and this course are about, goes beyond the informal, everyday beliefs people have about personality. Unlike informal personality theories, formal theories of personality

---

## BOX 1-1
# Learning That People Are All Different Yet Alike

Children learn at an early age that people differ from one another in many important ways. For example, little Ralph discovers to his chagrin one morning at day care that not all little girls are as placid as his sister Kim. Take, for example, that red-headed girl over there in the corner. She decked him when he tried to take her chocolate milk away from her. And what about Dorothy, his afternoon teacher? Unlike his mother, Dorothy promptly deposits him in "time-out" whenever he hits someone. After repeating this experience with many different people, Ralph learns that to deal with others he must recognize and use individual differences. It is not enough to be in a situation where someone else's chocolate milk is available. You must also know whose chocolate milk you are confronting.

But that is not the only lesson Ralph will learn. He will also learn that in many important ways, everyone is alike. All human beings have certain characteristics in common that set them apart from other objects in the environment. Everyone bleeds when cut, but rocks do not. People need to eat, but clouds do not. All of Ralph's teachers seem to be larger, smarter, and stronger than he. Some of his peers will be pushovers and some will not. But all of his teachers will outsmart him nearly every time. He will have to discover both the sameness and the diversity in those people with whom he would interact.

Of course, if Ralph grows up in a hut in a remote countryside, tends his goats, and never comes into contact with other human beings, chances are good that he will not need to learn much about personality (although knowing something about the personalities of goats would be a real blessing). But Ralph will most likely not tend goats. He will exist in a complex network of human interactions from the very moment he is born.

---

require that their descriptive and explanatory components be made explicit. In addition, formal theories tend to be more detailed, consistent, and complete then informal theories. Indeed, formal theories that contain inconsistencies or that leave relevant questions unanswered are generally sharply criticized and discarded. Finally, formal theories are accepted as legitimate only to the extent that they can be, and are, rigorously evaluated through scientific methods.

For some students, the detail, comprehensiveness, and scientific rigor of formal theories makes a course on the scholarly discipline of personality psychology disappointing. When the richness, complexity, and wonder of the individual are distilled into a series of detailed and precise theoretical propositions, it may seem

"I THINK YOU SHOULD BE MORE EXPLICIT HERE IN STEP TWO."

We are more tolerant of incomplete or unstated aspects in our informal theories than in our formal ones.

that personality scientists are ignoring many of the most intriguing aspects of people. The same has been said about watching a sunset with a physicist who can reduce the colors and patterns into wavelengths and light diffraction.

This criticism is, in part, well taken. Scientific models and explanations are necessarily simplifications of the phenomena that they characterize. The models and theories of personality that are presented in this text do not and cannot characterize and explain all the extraordinary complexity of human thought and behavior. However, this limitation is offset by the benefit that scientific approaches, though limited, can help us to find and even avoid some of the errors, overgeneralizations, and biases in our informal beliefs. The scholarly books on the study of personality may not seem as exciting, useful, or easy to read as the popular psychology books that dominate the shelves in book stores. However, these scholarly books can provide the dedicated reader with a far more detailed and rigorous understanding of human personality than the popular press.

## A BRIEF BIOGRAPHY OF

# Henry Kissinger

Henry Kissinger was Assistant to the President for National Security and Secretary of State in the Nixon administration. Swede and Tetlock (1986) report the results of a study in which they used a quantitative method to extract personality descriptions from Kissinger's 1979 book *White House Years*. They carried out a content analysis that resulted in 3,759 trait descriptions of 38 important world leaders based on Kissinger's words. From this analysis there emerged five consistent personality themes: *professional anguish, ambitious patriotism, revolutionary greatness, intellectual sophistication,* and *realistic friendship.*

Using these themes or concepts, Kissinger differentiated among various leaders throughout the world. For example, he believed that he, William Rogers, Melvin Laird, and Indira Gandhi were prone to experience professional anguish. Thus, Kissinger said of himself:

> I did my best, if with frayed nerves. I had been in motion for over two weeks rarely getting more than four hours of sleep and riding an emotional roller coaster from hope to frustration, from elation to despair. (Kissinger, 1979, p. 1395)

He perceived Mao Tse-tung, Leonid Brezhnev, Chou En-lai, and Anwar Sadat as having revolutionary greatness. For example, Kissinger described Chairman Mao as a "colossal figure, who challenged the gods in the scope of his aspirations" (p. 1064) and as a "the titanic figure who made the Chinese Revolution" (p. 1065).

Through such implicit personality themes Kissinger came to understand world figures. And it was through such understanding that he undoubtedly felt he could anticipate and interpret their behavior. As Swede and Tetlock (1986) note, "These themes provide a potential key for understanding how Kissinger structured the extraordinarily complex political environment that he faced in the first Nixon administration" (p. 639).

## Personality as a Science

As with any formal theoretical concept, personality has been closely examined to assess its scientific legitimacy. Over the years, many have directly challenged the status of personality as a scientific discipline. For example, Burnham (1968) noted that in the middle of the nineteenth century, most scholars believed that neither a science nor a theory of personality was possible. More recently, B. F. Skinner, one of the best-known psychologists of the twentieth century, argued that personality as a scientific concept is at best superfluous and at worst misleading. Likewise, Walter Mischel (1968) asserted that if we know in detail the nature of the specific situations in which individuals find themselves, information about the individual's personality is unnecessary for predicting their behavior.

But despite such assaults, the scientific study of personality continues. Of course, the ideas and methods used in personality research have changed, and, we may hope, advanced over the years. In classical Greece, Aristotle decided that the essence of the human being resided in the ability to reason and that human behavior is a proper subject for scientific study. In the same period of history, Theophrastus contended that people differ among themselves in the types of character they possess. Some of these same Greeks talked about a person's "soul" as the basis of personality; others talked about the mixtures of bodily "humors" as the cause of individual differences. Today, such concepts as reinforcement, ego, cognitive schema, factors, and observational learning are commonly used. An idea of the focus and breadth of contemporary personality research can be found by reading the titles of research articles in recent journals that concern personality. For example, in the December 1995 issue of the *Journal of Research in Personality* the following titles appeared:

> Sensitivity to conditioned and unconditioned stimuli: What is the mechanism underlying passive avoidance deficits in extroverts?
>
> Situation and personality correlates of psychological well-being: Social activity and personal control.
>
> Leader power motive and group conflict as influences on leader behavior and group member self-affect.
>
> The criterion validity of broad factor scales versus specific facet scales.
>
> Positive and negative valence within the five-factor model.
>
> Self-handicapping and dimensions of perfectionism: Self-presentation versus self-protection.
>
> Identity styles and the five-factor model of personality.

Although many of the concepts and issues in these titles may be unfamiliar now, after completing this book the student should have a good sense of what each of these papers is about.

## Defining Personality

The quest to understand personality has spanned several thousand years and has used vastly different methods of inquiry. Indeed, over the years, the best efforts of poets and philosophers as well as scientists have been enlisted in this search. But the essential insight on which the study of personality has been based throughout this time and across these methods is that all people are alike in some ways and yet different in others. Thus:

- We all learn, but we learn different things and in differing degrees.
- We each think, but our thoughts are often not the same.
- We all have feelings, but those feelings differ in kind and degree.

### The Modern View of Personality

The contemporary concept of personality was introduced in the 1930s and 1940s by such scholars as Gordon Allport, Henry A. Murray, and Gardner Murphy. Many specific definitions of personality have been offered over the years. Box 1-2 presents a very brief sample of such definitions. In general, however, a

People show distinct differences from one another. These differences are stable over time and situations.

definition of personality that is similar to many of those used by psychologists today would be as follows:

> Personality is that pattern of characteristic thoughts, feelings, and behaviors that distinguishes one person from another and that persists over time and situations.

Two aspects of this definition are of particular importance.

**Distinctiveness.** One emphasis of personality is **distinctiveness** or individuality. Some of this distinctiveness may be found in the way a person acts, thinks, or feels. However, there is also often some similarity between how two intelligent people think or how two aggressive people act. Thus, individual uniqueness comes from the overall pattern and combination of personality characteristics as reflected in each person's feelings, thoughts, and behavior. According to this view, people may possess differing degrees of intelligence, aggressiveness, or, say, sensitivity. But the critical feature is the unique way in which each person combines these traits. Of course, if we regard every person as a one-of-a-kind event, this can create problems in trying to study people scientifically. In searching for general principles that apply to all humans, how can we deal with uniqueness?

## BOX 1-2
## Some Definitions of Personality

1. Deceptive masquerade or mimicry
2. Superficial attractiveness
3. Social-stimulus value
4. The entire organization of a human being at any stage of development
5. Levels or layers of dispositions, usually with a unifying or integrative principle at the top
6. The integration of those systems or habits that represent an individual's characteristic adjustments to the environment
7. The way in which the person does such things as talking, remembering, thinking, or loving
8. The dynamic organization within the individual of those psychological systems that determine his or her unique adjustments to the environment. (Items 1–8 were adapted from those collected by Allport, 1937, pp. 25–50)
9. A person's unique pattern of traits (from Guilford, 1959, p. 5)
10. Those characteristics of the person or of people generally that account for consistent patterns of behavior (from Pervin, 1989, p. 4)

We can study an individual separately and exhaustively and then develop principles of behavior that apply to that specific person. But if we do so it will be difficult to derive a more general theory based on what we have discovered about that person. For this reason, the scholarly study of personality is not always about individuals but about characteristics that can be applied to, and used to differentiate among, people in general.

**Stability and Consistency.**  The second property of many definitions of personality is **stability** and **consistency**. In everyday language the terms *stability* and *consistency* have about the same meaning. Personality psychologists, however, use these terms differently. *Stability* refers to regularity of a person's behavior and personality across time. Stability is a developmental phenomenon and refers to the extent to which a person who is, say, friendly or intelligent during adolescence is also friendly or intelligent at age forty. *Consistency* refers to the regularity in behavior and personality across different situations. In the language of learning theory, consistency might be thought of as stimulus and response generalization and concerns the extent to which a person who is, say, conscientious at work is also conscientious with friends. Given that a person is never in two situations at precisely the same time, consistency implies some stability; likewise, because no two situations across time are ever precisely identical, stability implies some consistency. However, more generally, one can imagine a person who is consistently conscientious in high school and consistently unconscientious at age forty. Such a person would be consistent, but unstable, on conscientiousness. Finally, one can imagine a person who is friendly at home but unfriendly at work and has been that way for forty years. Such a person would be stable, but inconsistent in friendliness.

If people are unique, they must to some extent exhibit their particular patterns of characteristics in recognizable ways across time and over a variety of situations. This is not to say that there must be perfect consistency or that no one ever changes. There must, however, be a detectable degree of stability over time and consistency across situations so that we can say, for example, "Well, I haven't seen John in 25 years but he's still his old pessimistic self!" Or, "That's Mary all right; she's always there to help when she's needed!" The issue of personality consistency and stability has been a topic of concern and intense study among personality psychologists.

## The Field of Personality Psychology

The brief definitions of personality belie the breadth and complexity of the field of personality as a scientific discipline. People who call themselves personality psychologists often specialize in subfields of personality, and books and advanced courses are devoted to each of these specialties. There are six aspects of the field that will be used as themes for the discussion of the major theories of personality. These aspects are *assessment, theory, development, adjustment, change,* and *research.* The Case Study of Rick L., on page 12, will be used to introduce these points.

Assessment. Before theories to explain personality can be generated; before personality development, adjustment, or change can be studied; and before research in any of these areas can be designed; individuals' personalities must be described and measured. We must know what we are studying before we can study it. For example, in the case of Rick L. we may use a language of traits to describe him as possessing insecurity, guilt, depression, intelligence, and anger. Where do personality psychologists get the information that enables them to describe people, determine their patterns of adjustment, understand how they have become what they are, or alter their current modes of adjustment? The field of personality assessment concerns the measurement and description of personality and the types of data that are useful for that purpose. The material presented about Rick L. was autobiographical data. But many more types of data are available to the personality psychologist, including a variety of other life records and case history materials, numerous interview techniques, and many psychological tests.

Of course it is not sufficient to passively receive information to make judgments about personality. That information must be actively processed, combined, and interpreted before it is useful. Personality assessment also concerns how personality information is treated to make it useful and legitimate. Moreover, the types of questions we have to answer and the particular personality theory to which we are committed will determine the types of interviews or tests we employ and how they are interpreted.

Theory. Once a person's characteristics have been described, the question of how those characteristics originated becomes relevant. What forces contributed to Rick's becoming the person he is? His characteristics could be determined by deep-seated, unconscious urges. If we make this choice, some form of psychoanalytic theory would be appropriate. One could certainly say that Rick's concern with his mother seems intense, which could reflect unresolved problems. Or maybe his outbursts of temper reflect some unconscious instinctual force. Then, again, maybe we should look to a modification of psychoanalytic theory and focus on his feelings of incompetence, which may reflect an inferiority complex.

Many perspectives can be used to understand and explain an individual's personality: existential, behavioral, social learning, and biological, to name a few. Part II of this book is devoted to the major theories of personality. The choice of a theory has profound implications not only for research, assessment, and personality change but also for how we perceive people. One's view of human nature in general (and of Rick's in particular) is not something that has been decided forever and about which everyone will agree. Whether Rick's personality reflects a storehouse of unconscious impulses, a chain of behaviors, or someone searching for the meaning of life will be answered differently by different observers depending upon their theoretical orientations.

# CASE STUDY

*An excerpt from the case of Rick L.*

I was 47 last month. I live with my wife and oldest daughter. My two younger sons are both married. One lives here in town, and the other has a job in California. My mother is in her sixties now and lives in an apartment several miles from here. My parents were divorced a long time ago, and both remarried.

Dad remarried right away, and although I used to visit them, I never really felt comfortable, and then after they had a kid of their own, I just kind of felt like I was intruding. Don't get me wrong. They were nice, but it was just a feeling I had.

My mother worked for an insurance company after the divorce. She was a real competent gal, to say the least, and pretty soon she was an underwriter. We were really close. After awhile I felt like I had to get away, so I got an apartment of my own. We always seemed to be arguing about something. Mainly it was because I wouldn't go to college. When I decided to get married to this girl I knew in high school, Mom really hit the ceiling.

Then Mom married an engineer from Delaware, and they moved there. I got a job with the telephone company. Gradually I worked myself up so I was in charge of customer relations. I've done pretty good, but I suppose I should have gone to college. I just don't feel at ease around the other executives. It's like they have something I don't.

Mom and the engineer split up about ten years ago, and she moved back here. She still works part time in a clothing store. Since she moved back I have felt sort of uneasy. Maybe she spends too much time with us, I don't know. My wife—Emily—really clams up when she is around. Emily and I seem to be getting along pretty good these days. For awhile after we got married I was really happy. But when the kids started coming I felt . . . I know it sounds trite, but I felt trapped. I would see myself forever with the telephone company. We fought a lot I guess. She kind of lost interest in things, and those girls at the office started looking better and better. I played around a little, not much. Just enough to feel guilty as hell afterward. I don't think Emily ever realized what was going on. But Mom sure as hell did.

Well, everything has settled down now. The kids are all raised, and Mom isn't quite as demanding. I guess I have everything I should. The house is almost paid for, and we go to Colorado every summer for two weeks. We're thinking of buying a place out there. I don't get so mad at people anymore. In fact, things don't seem to bother me enough nowadays. I can just sit and stare at TV for hours. Sometimes I think I've mellowed, but at other times I think it's depression.

**Development.**  If personality refers to stable, enduring characteristics, it becomes more than a matter of idle curiosity to understand how such characteristics develop. Most of us are not content merely to see ourselves as happy, dependent, insecure, and so forth. We want to know how we became that way. We know intuitively that our understanding of ourselves or others will never be complete un-til we find out what caused us to be what we are. In the case of Rick, what made him subject to outbursts of temper? Why did he and his mother argue so often—was it simply his refusal to go to college, or were there deeper reasons? What was the real nature of his relationship with his father, and how did the divorce affect Rick's perceptions? No full understanding of Rick is possible until some of the earlier events in his life, especially those of his childhood, are understood. In ad-dition, can we better understand Rick's development into old age if we are aware of some of his current problems, aspirations, and thoughts?

If we know the critical conditions for certain events, we can work to provide the kind of environment that will foster the outcomes we want for children. In addition, personality development takes place throughout life, so understanding development will help us to cope more effectively with problems that arise in any part of the life cycle. If we know how personality develops, we will be in a stronger position to change it. Not everyone is satisfied with what he or she has become. There may also be compelling social reasons to want to alter the behav-ior of seriously maladjusted individuals. In either case, knowledge about how personality develops, or about the conditions that lead to one outcome rather than another, is a good reason for studying personality development.

**Adjustment.** Was Rick L. maladjusted? How serious should we consider his de-pression or his temper to be? Clearly, a case study of personality such as Rick's has implications for adjustment. Most theories of personality have addressed the issue of what constitutes the adjusted personality. For the behaviorist, adjust-ment may be defined as a satisfactory repertoire of behaviors. The psychoanalyst will assert that adjustment can be achieved only when a person is free of the tyranny of the unconscious. A social learning theorist may claim that adjustment exists when needs and expectations of fulfilling them coincide. It is therefore im-portant that we include under the study of personality the implications for ad-justment offered by each theoretical point of view.

**Change.** Modifying personality and conducting psychotherapy are often associ-ated with clinical psychology or psychiatry. To accomplish those ends, these pro-fessions depend upon ideas from the field of personality. For example, psycho-analysis as a theory of personality and as a technique of therapy developed almost simultaneously in Sigmund Freud's consulting rooms. The early client-centered counseling approaches of Carl Rogers carried with them particular conceptions about human nature and personality. Thus, behavior- and personality-change tech-niques are closely linked to different conceptions of personality (Phares, 1992).

Theories of personality not only have specific implications for adjustment but also have specific implications for accomplishing changes in personality. In-deed, one way to evaluate personality theories is to see whether they provide use-ful techniques for changing personality and behavior. In the case of Rick L. we would feel more confident in our analysis if we were able to recommend how his feelings of depression could be eliminated. Our ability to decrease his discomfort around his fellow executives would be evidence that we had a valid understanding of his personality.

**Research.** Without research we cannot have much confidence in our understanding of particular personality issues. With empirical research we put our theoretical speculation about how individual differences develop or how they affect behavior to the test. Also, we can study the specific conditions that give rise to behaviors such as aggression, sexual responses, and helping. That is, aside from learning how one person comes to behave more aggressively than someone else in a wide variety of situations, we can determine how certain conditions or situations promote or retard aggressive behavior. In addition, research can help us understand how particular personality characteristics interact with certain situational or environmental conditions to produce a given behavior.

There are many methods of research. Some are experimental and may be carried out in a controlled laboratory setting. Other research is based on the intensive study of a single case or individual. Some personality research involves testing a person for only a few minutes; other research means following the same person over a period of years. But whether research is conducted in a laboratory or in the field, or whether it consists of a brief encounter or sustained contacts over years, it is a fundamental component of scientific study.

## The Nature of Personality: Two Issues

There is some general agreement about the definition of personality and about the major subdisciplines that constitute the field of personality. However, when discussion turns to the determinants or causes of personality there are substantial differences of opinion. Indeed, there have been, and continue to be, long and heated debates on the determinants of personality.

**Nature Versus Nurture.** Traditionally these determinants have been classified as representing either nature or nurture, and the discussions about them have been called *nature versus nurture debates*. Is our personality largely a product of nature and the biological and genetic factors that constitute us? Or are we nurtured and molded by our physical and social environment? Is our behavior and personality determined by inherited, innate, biological forces or by learning, experience, and environment? Obviously, the answer is "Both of the above." I cannot jump as far as a kangaroo, and no amount of training or motivation is going to change that. And how far I actually can jump (and, indeed, whether I desire to jump at all) is heavily influenced by coaching, diet, and other environmental forces.

So it is with many personality traits and characteristics. Biology and genetics surely play an important role and are complemented by culture and experience. But which is more important: biology or experience? Well, the only proper answer is "It depends." It depends on what aspect of personality we are considering and the level at which we are considering it. For example, a preference for rock music over waltzes is most certainly influenced by culture or learning, but the mechanisms through which we hear the music are biological. On the other hand, the tendency to be aggressive is found in many species and thus appears to be influenced heavily by biology, but whether one is aggressive by throwing rocks or by swinging a stick depends upon whether sticks or rocks are available in the environment. Therefore, the question of how much of personality is biological and how much is environmental is really a silly question. They are often considered separately for the sake of discussion, but as we shall see, they really operate in concert. Box 1-3 illustrates how nature and nurture operate together as soon as a child is born.

**The Cognitive Influence.**  During the past several of decades, the field of psychology has been undergoing what some have termed the *cognitive revolution.* (Lachman, Lachman, & Butterfield, 1979). As a field, psychology has become increasingly sensitive to the importance of the mind in understanding how people act, think, and feel. That people can perceive, process, and remember events has an impact on their personalities that is as basic as their biology and their environment. Indeed, it is the extraordinary sophistication of our cognitive processes and abilities, relative to other species, that makes us more than the product of our biological heritage and our environmental experience. Our individuality comes from, and is reflected in, the fact that we perceive, process, and remember the same events differently. To appreciate this, just consider how often a close play in basketball is viewed as a flagrant foul by one side and a great defensive play by the other.

## Toward a Comprehensive Theory of Personality

Later in this book, a variety of theoretical and research topics will be examined. In each instance it will be useful for you to consider how issues of biological, environmental, and cognitive determinants of behavior and personality are handled. Figure 1-1 provides a general overview of how the major types of personality theories can be organized in terms of the importance they attach to these basic biological, environmental, and cognitive influences. In this figure the five major types of personality theories appear in the middle row of boxes. *Biological-genetic theories* concern primarily the biological influences. *Phenomenological* approaches emphasize the influence of cognition, and *behavioral* approaches emphasize the environment. Two other types of theories, *psychodynamic* and *social learning*, emphasize blends of cognitive with biological, and cognitive with environmental influences, respectively.

At the bottom of Figure 1-1 is a box labeled "Personality" as the end result of the three determinants and the five specific types of theories about how those determinants operate and combine to influence personality. Finally, below the

## BOX 1-3
## Personality and Parent-Child Interactions

According to Thomas and Chess (1977), some babies are cheerful and easy right away. They sleep regularly and adapt readily to new experiences and people. But other infants are difficult from the beginning. They start out as fussy babies and go on to be overactive and even difficult to toilet train. These seem to be built-in tendencies. Consider the following examples adapted from Babledelis (1984) and Meichenbaum et al. (1989):

> A baby is born one fine day. From the very start he is active and energetic—even a bit hyperactive. But he is not cranky or irritable—just very active. He quickly learns to sit up and just as quickly is crawling all over the place. He is into everything. No table, cupboard, or bookshelf is safe. He is delighted when he can manage to take things apart. Thus, disorder is his constant companion.

Given this brief description, how might his parents respond to him? Well, it all depends on the nature of the parents. But make no mistake. Their responses will ultimately affect that little boy's personality.

1. The Smiths are parents who do not like messes. They like an orderly house. They also believe that children should be obedient, and they are quite definite about what is proper behavior for little boys. So, punishment seems to follow their little boy everywhere. He is also constantly reminded that he is clumsy, disobedient, and a great bother to everyone.
2. The Martins are parents who can tolerate a mess. They are not exactly in love with disorder, but they can tolerate it as part of the price of being parents. But they do like what they perceive as their son's curiosity. They see this as a sign of an inquisitive mind. Maybe he will become an important scientist. As a result, their strategy becomes one of rewarding his curiosity and labeling him as good or smart even as they try to cut down a bit on the breakage.

What, then, is the likely outcome in these two scenarios? Although the following are undoubtedly an oversimplification, they are real possibilities:

1. The Smiths could produce a son who develops into a tense, overcontrolled person who constantly tries to suppress his own wishes so as to gain approval from others.
2. The Martins could produce a son who develops feelings of competence, is open with others, and seeks approval by striving to achieve. Had each set of parents been blessed with a child with a different temperament, personality development might have proceeded quite differently. At the same time, had each set of parents been able to respond differently to their child, his personality development would have followed a different course.

Adult personality is a product of genetic, cognitive, and environmental factors, and "environment" can be within one's household as well as one's culture.

box labeled "Personality" is a box labeled "Description/Dispositions." Historically, the term dispositional has been used to describe those theories of personality that concern the broad *traits*, such as friendliness or conscientiousness, that can be used to characterize an individual's personality. The term *dispositional*

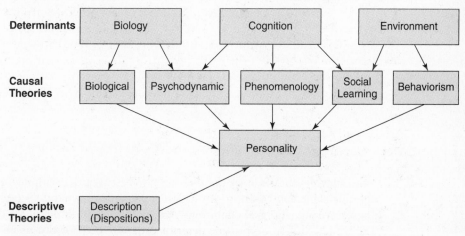

**Figure 1-1** ☙ An organization of the major types of personality theory on the basis of their biological, cognitive, environmental, and/or descriptive emphasis.

implied that these traits had a causal influence on behavior and personality in the same way biological, environmental, and cognitive variables did. Thus, those theories were typically included with the five types of theories listed in the middle boxes. However, the view taken by this text is that dispositional theories are qualitatively different from the other types of theories. Specifically, they are best viewed as describing the *result* of the forces discussed by the other theories rather than being treated as a force or cause themselves. Thus, we have labeled those theories "descriptive."

Biological, social learning, psychodynamic, behavioral, and phenomenological theories provide an explanation for personality. The focus of descriptive theories is how that personality might best be described. The view of trait-based theories as descriptive is not intended to imply that descriptive theories and research cannot also address the fundamental issue of whether or not our descriptions imply a disposition. That is, if I describe a person as friendly, does this also mean that the person has an underlying disposition or tendency to be friendly? However, the position in this text is that this dispositional issue is not a necessary part of descriptive theories because the description can simply be a label of how a person has acted, or how we think that person will act, without any dispositional implication. The issue is an important one: if descriptions are always presumed to imply dispositions we can end up making the scientifically meaningless statement "Bill is friendly because he is friendly."

One of the problems that has plagued personality psychology for much of its modern history has been the absence of a single, generally accepted theory of personality description. Instead, personality psychology has been characterized by many different theories for describing people, with the result that research based on one theory is difficult to compare with research based on another theory. At this point in history, one descriptive theory of personality psychology is as close to being generally accepted as has ever been the case. This theory is most commonly referred to as the **Big Five.** The Big Five and other descriptive theories will be described and evaluated in Chapters 13 and 14. However, use of the Big Five is so widespread that we will refer to it from time to time throughout the text. In essence the Big Five is a theory of personality description that organizes description into five broad areas: (1) extraversion, (2) agreeableness, (3) conscientiousness, (4) emotional stability, and (5) intellect.

## Overview of Personality Determinants

In the chapters that follow, the theories and research that emphasize one, or another, or some combination of the three major determinants of personality—biology, environment, and cognition—will be presented in detail. In this section a brief general description of the determinants will be provided as an initial foundation for the remainder of the text.

## Biology

It might seem shortsighted to ignore our biological heritage and attributes when trying to understand human personality. Historically, however, psychologists have been reluctant to use biological principles for understanding psychological characteristics. There are several possible reasons for this reluctance. Initial applications of biological and genetic principles to human behavior were oversimplified and ideologically motivated, and their influence was exaggerated (Kamin, 1974). Early biological theories seemed to imply that human characteristics such as intelligence, morality, and motivation were *determined* by a person's genetic heritage. This resulted in a pessimistic view of our ability to change people and their conditions. Even worse, it formed the basis for a *eugenics movement* that resulted in, and legitimized, many social injustices. These included restricting the immigration of some groups of people into the United States and justifying the sterilization and incarceration of some who were already here. Although these abuses seem to be behind us, the controversy that followed the publication of *The Bell Curve* in 1994 (Herrnstein & Murray, 1994) indicates that many are still concerned about how possible biologically based differences between people will be interpreted and used in formulating social policy.

Modern biological approaches to studying personality are more sophisticated and generally more appreciative of the additional influence of environmental and cognitive factors on the development of psychological characteristics. As a result of this maturation, biological-genetic factors on personality is more widely accepted now. The field of *behavior genetics* has shown tremendous growth in the numbers of students and researchers who are trained in the theories and methods of this field. Likewise, the methods of behavior genetic analysis have increased so much in power and sophistication that convincing evidence has now been offered for the genetic transmission of a variety of characteristics, including activity level, anxiety, alcoholism, dominance, criminality, locus of control, manic depressive illness; schizophrenia, sexuality, and even political attitudes (Holden, 1987). More anecdotally, there are striking reports of identical twins reared apart and separated for 40 years who, when they finally meet, are wearing virtually identical clothing and have similar haircuts and the same occupations and hobbies (Bouchard et al., 1981).

Although the methods of behavior genetics have convincingly established the heritability of many psychological characteristics, the specific manner in which these characteristics are transmitted from generation to generation is often unknown. That is, behavior genetic analysis may provide evidence that a characteristic is partly influenced by biology, but that analysis does not generally provide any information about the specific manner in which biological factors influence the characteristic. More complete biological theories must not only provide evidence of *some* unstated biological influence but describe the specific mechanism of that influence as well. Some biological mechanisms that may directly influence personality include biochemistry; physical characteristics, including appearance, body type, and gender; and the structure of the brain.

Separated at birth, the Mallifert twins meet accidentally

## Environment

In contrast to its uneasy relation with the genetic and biological determinants of personality, psychology as a field has long accepted the critical role of environmental forces in shaping behavior. In part, psychology's emphasis on environmental factors was a reaction to the early abuses that resulted from the naive biological theories that were proposed around the beginning of the twentieth century. Also, because the environment is viewed as easily altered, theories of personality based on environmental determinants seemed to hold more promise for improving both society and the lives of individuals through active interventions to change the environment. Whereas biological theories seemed to doom people to live out their lives under the innate conditions that nature dictated, environmental theories held out the optimistic possibility of intervention and change.

During much of its history, psychology was dominated by theories of learning, all of which were based on principles of *conditioning* such as *rein-*

*forcement* and *punishment. Learning theories* concern how a person or other organism responds to its environment. Thus, learning is the relatively permanent modification of behavior through the selective experiencing of environmental events. Whether we are talking about the psychoanalytic treatment developed by Sigmund Freud, the conditions of worth that Carl Rogers believed shape a person's self-esteem, or the ways in which Albert Bandura believed that observational learning affects behavior, we are really discussing the influence of the environment upon the person. Unfortunately, for a long time, psychology emphasized learning theory or *behaviorism* to the exclusion of any other points of view. The best example of extreme behaviorism is John Watson's infamous claim that *behavioral engineering,* through the manipulation of the environment, could create any type of personality in any type of person regardless of any other influences. That is, biology and cognition mattered little in determining behavior and personality. Modern psychology has adopted a more temperate view of the role of the environment, although radical behaviorists, whose best-known member was the late B. F. Skinner. continue to deny the importance of cognition and to downplay the role of biology in determining behavior.

There are many ways to conceptualize the environment, and each might affect personality and behavior. At the most basic level we can consider the surrounding physical world in which people live, interact, and try to survive. Consider the physical worlds of the Eskimos and the Temne people of Sierra Leone. In the barren, ice-covered northern regions, the Eskimo becomes a hunter—growing food is not an alternative. In contrast, the Temne people of Sierra Leone are able to depend on agriculture because of more benign climatic conditions. But contrasting methods of food accumulation also seem to require contrasting personalities in the people involved. For example, Barry, Child, and Bacon (1959) have contended that because the Eskimo culture relies on hunting and fishing, it requires individuals who are assertive, individualistic, and willing to take risks. As a result, there is leniency in disciplining children and individualism is encouraged so as to nurture the traits required in the adult. But the Temne people rely on growing their food, and such reliance requires a more conscientious, compliant, and conservative adult. Only a single crop is harvested each year and food is doled out carefully so that it will last until the next harvest. To produce such an adult, the Temne shower their infants with affection until weaning. At that point discipline is imposed, and even toilet training becomes harshly applied. Little or no individuality is permitted.

Berry (1967) tested this analysis of the Temne and the Eskimo by presenting groups of subjects from both cultures with a conformity task. This was a line-judging task in which subjects were subtly pressured to agree with the experimenter in making their judgments. As predicted, the Eskimo subjects virtually disregarded the experimenter's suggestions, while the Temne accepted them. Berry (1967) described the contrast in subjects this way:

[O]ne Temne (in Mayola) did offer the following spontaneous comment: "When Temne people choose a thing, we must all agree with the decision—this is what we call cooperation." On the other hand, Eskimo subjects, although saying nothing, would often display a quiet, knowing smile as they pointed to the correct one. (p. 417)

Environmental influences are not limited to our physical surroundings. We create a variety of *social environments* that also influence behavior and personality; indeed, the influence of the social environment on personality is probably greater than the influence of the physical environment. Also, psychologists have studied social environments far more intensively than physical ones. Some examples of social environmental variables are cultural and subcultural training, including child rearing practices and the differential socialization of men and women in most societies, and social class and circumstances, such as poverty that may create stress and lack of control that in turn may influence ability and well-being.

## Cognition

The influences of our biological heritage and environmental experiences can be powerful. However, people do not generally passively absorb their environmental experiences or automatically respond to their biological urges. Instead, people actively process the signals from their environments and the desires of their bodies, often reinterpreting, repressing, and overriding those signals and desires. A hungry person will wait patiently in line at a buffet. A tired person will stay awake to welcome in the new year. A fall from a swing will scare one child, but it will make another climb back on to try again. A score of 90 percent on a test would probably please most students, but some will focus on the 10 percent they missed. That human beings are sophisticated perceivers, processors, and rememberers of events appears to have important implications for understanding human behavior and personality.

As with biological influences, many psychologists have had difficulty incorporating cognitive processes into their theories. In particular, psychologists working in the behavioral tradition have historically rejected cognitive concepts and theories because a person's thoughts, and the processes that lead to those thoughts, are not directly accessible to outside observers. Behavioral psychologists did not deny that people think; rather, they argued that thoughts and cognitive processes could not be observed and therefore were not proper components of scientific theories. For psychologists working in the behavioral tradition, theories of personality were restricted to what could be directly observed. Thus, a psychologist could observe the event the subject experienced and could also observe how the subject reacted to the event. However, the psychologist could not directly observe how the subject perceived, processed, or remembered the event, so these cognitive "intervening" variables could not be incorporated into a theory of behavior, even though the subject undoubtedly "thought" about the event before responding to it.

Refusing to accept cognitive influences on human personality because those influences are difficult to study or observe seems as shortsighted as ignoring biological influences because they are ideologically disagreeable. However, the reluctance of behaviorally oriented psychologists to acknowledge cognitive influences is an important caution. It is all too easy to postulate unobservable cognitive structures to account for unexplained observations. Scientists find it necessary that cognitive models be accompanied by some evidence, however indirect, that those models are reasonable. Likewise, it is important to demonstrate that the cognitive variables contribute meaningfully to our ability to understand and explain people's actions. Contemporary philosophy of science has long abandoned the requirement that scientific constructs and processes be directly observed and "operationally defined," but it still requires that there be a convergence of indirect evidence in support of those constructs and processes (Suppe, 1977).

The emergence of **social cognition** as a dominant view in social and personality psychology (Schneider, 1991, Fiske, 1993) indicates that the cognitive revolution has now come to these fields. The application of cognitive models to understand how people organize and categorize their social worlds, how people evaluate themselves and others, and how biases and stereotypes operate to influence behavior, thought, and action has already been useful.

## Philosophy of This Text

This text reflects the view that human personality is a complex function of our biological heritage, our environmental experience, and how we perceive, process, and remember that heritage and experience. Although one or another theory of personality will emphasize one or another of these forces, ultimately all of those forces must be considered in the quest for knowledge of what we are. Individual personality psychologists will generally focus on one or another theory in their research, often with the implication that other theories and their associated determinants are inferior, weak, or wrong. Indeed, much good research is devoted to demonstrating the relatively greater importance of one force, say cognition, over another, say environment, for a understanding some specific personality phenomenon. It is important to remember that research and scholarly analysis that seem to demonstrate the superiority of one force over another are limited to the specific aspect of personality, subjects, and the context that was the focus of the research and analysis. To understand personality as a general phenomenon and as a field of study it is important to give each determinant and each theory based on those determinants full consideration. We have tried to do so in this text.

Also, individual personality psychologists conduct research in a variety of ways. Some focus on assessment, and study personality by developing and evaluating measures of characteristics. Others focus on personality development and change across both time and situations. Still others, often working as clinical psychologists, study issues of adjustment and how to change behavior and personality by applying techniques derived from one or another personality theory. All of these approaches to personality research are useful and important, although perhaps for different questions and in different contexts. As with the variety of personality theories, we have tried to describe the study of personality broadly by considering all of these approaches.

## Summary

- Personality is a sturdy, resilient concept that is embedded in the paradox that in some ways all people are alike and at the same time different from each other.
- In some sense we are all personality psychologists because we have all developed theories and beliefs about what people are like. However, the formal study of personality differs from everyday informal theories in terms of completeness, consistency, and testability.
- Personality is commonly defined as that pattern of characteristic thoughts, feelings, and behaviors that persists over time and situations and distinguishes one person from another. This definition emphasizes the elements of distinctiveness, stability, and consistency.
- Personality as a field of study is composed of six subfields, each an important branch in its own right. These six subfields are assessment, theory, development, adjustment, change, and research.
- Personality is determined by three forces: biology, environment, and cognition. All personality theories emphasize one, or another, or some combination of these basic determinants.
- An important group of personality theories, often called trait theories, concerns personality description. Historically these theories treated traits as causal dispositions, the theories were called dispositional, and they were included with the other theories based on the determinants.
- In this text, traits are treated as descriptive, and the view is that after biological, cognitive, behavioral, social learning, and psychodynamic forces have had their influence, we are left with a personality to be described.
- Descriptive theories concern how best to describe and structure personality. One descriptive theory, the Big Five, has had considerable influence on modern personality description.

- A brief overview of the three determinants and their historical position in personality psychology was provided.
- The philosophy of this text is that for specific personality phenomena that occur in a particular context, one or another determinant may be more important, one or another theory may be more useful or valid, and one or another approach to research may be more fruitful. However, a broad understanding of personality requires a knowledge of all three determinants, an appreciation of all the major theories based on those determinants, and a willingness to employ a variety of research methods.

# Chapter 2
# The Tools of Understanding

Theory: Proposing Explanations and Making
   Predictions
      A Diversity of Theories
      Personality Theory and Constructs
      Value of Personality Theories
      Dimensions of Personality Theories
      Evaluating Theories: Nonempirical Criteria
Research: Empirically Evaluating Explanations
   and Testing Predictions
      Research and Theory
      Observation: Unsystematic, Naturalistic,
        and Controlled
      Case Study Methods
      The Experimental Method
      The Correlation Method
      Statistical Versus Practical Significance
      Single-Subject Research
Assessment: Measuring Constructs and
   Describing People
      Issues in Personality Assessment
      Evaluating Measures
      Approaches to Personality Assessment
Nomological Network: Putting It All Together
Summary

I n contrast to our everyday interest in the personalities of ourselves and our friends, the scientific study of personality is based on formal theories, rigorous research methods, and explicit assessment procedures. Theory, research, and assessment together constitute the necessary tools that personality psychologists use to understand human personality.

## Theory: Proposing Explanations and Making Predictions

For many people a **theory** is the end product of research and measurement. That is, after careful observations are made and a series of studies is conducted, a theory will emerge. This view was the basis of a particular **philosophy of science** called **logical empiricism,** which was popular for a brief period of time in the 1920s. In essence, this philosophy viewed scientists as "gatherers of facts." Once enough facts had been assembled, an obvious theory to explain those facts would take shape; as more facts were collected theories would be revised to accommodate those observations.

This philosophy of science was rejected by most philosophers almost as soon as it had been proposed (Suppe, 1977). One problem is that there will always be more than one theory that is consistent with the observed facts. Another problem is that how a scientist designs a study or chooses a measure is necessarily based on some theoretical assumptions. The conduct of science must begin with a theory and can not simply end with one. Thus, theoretical development is the most basic tool of research that guides investigations and organizes thinking about personality.

### A Diversity of Theories

As a discipline, personality psychology probably has a greater diversity of theories than most other areas of psychology and certainly has more than most other sciences. This diversity reflects the complexity of the subject matter of personality; people's feelings, thoughts, and behaviors; and the reasons they feel, think, and act that way. Moreover, scientists are interested in personality for a variety of reasons, and these reasons influence how they think about personality. This influence is illustrated in the following example:

Suppose that three men, a realtor, a farmer, and an artist, are standing on a hilltop looking at the panorama of uncultivated land spread out below them. To the realtor, the scene represents an opportunity to develop a new housing project. To the farmer, the view suggests a chance to obtain arable soil for growing grain. To the artist, the vista is the embodiment of natural beauty. On descending, the realtor makes inquiries about the cost of the land, the availability of municipal utility services, and the supply of construction labor in the vicinity. The farmer takes soil samples for testing. The artist gets his easel and returns to the hilltop to paint a picture. All three men have "seen" the same thing, but each has responded in terms of a personal frame of reference, in terms of those aspects of the experience which were personally meaningful. (Shoben, 1954, pp. 42–43)

My interests, experiences, and goals will affect my understanding of people, places, and situations. This is true of personality theorists just as much as it is of realtors, farmers, and artists. Three of the most notable students of human nature have been Sigmund Freud, Carl Rogers, and B. F. Skinner. Each has made a contribution that is brilliant in its own way, but it would be hard to find three views of human nature that are more different from one another. Freud saw people as driven by sexual and aggressive impulses struggling for expression. Rogers, in contrast, saw within us a striving for self-enhancement and growth. Skinner seemed to view humans as little different from animals in the way they respond to rewards and punishments.

A consideration of the backgrounds of these men makes it easy to understand how they arrived at such opposing views of personality. Freud worked in the late 1800s with inhibited patients who were discouraged by a Victorian society from expressing their sexuality. What is more, he was educated in a scientific world that emphasized the role of instincts in guiding behavior. On the other hand, Rogers grew up in a religious family and for a while attended a theological school. Later he worked not with severely maladjusted patients but with young intelligent college students who had prospects for a bright future. Skinner, who spent his childhood designing everything from kites to perpetual motion machines, became a psychologist who worked with animals confined in a laboratory environment. The approach each of these theorists took to explaining and studying personality can be sensibly related to their separate backgrounds and experiences.

## Personality Theory and Constructs

Essentially, a **personality theory** is an organized collection of concepts and assumptions about how best to regard people and study them. A theory is represented by the concepts it employs, the manner in which those concepts are organized and related to each other, and the procedures through which those concepts can be measured and studied. The term **construct** is typically used to describe personality concepts. A construct is a theoretical concept that has no physical reality. The term *construct* was chosen to emphasize that most personality concepts can not be directly observed. For example, we can not see intelligence or self-esteem, we can only observe the effects of these attributes. Intelligence and self-esteem are abstractions that were *constructed* to summarize their observed effects. The use of constructs is not unique to personality psychology; atoms, black holes, quarks, genes, and gravity are all examples of constructs.

**Constructs as Descriptions.** A construct is a way of describing and perhaps explaining some portion of reality. However, we should not confuse the construct

How we understand complex human behavior is heavily determined by our theoretical perspective. Depending on why this individual is protesting, you may or may not sympathize with his getting dragged off.

with that part of reality it is meant to describe. If I describe someone as adjusted, this is not to say that adjustment is an inherent property of that person. Rather, it is a way I have devised to differentiate among people for some specific purpose. By observing many different people, I eventually construct in my head a notion of adjustment-maladjustment. But the person is just a person; the adjustment is a description I have *constructed* to better understand people.

Constructs and Reality. That constructs have no observable existence troubles some students and even a few scientists. However, any effort to make constructs real will either reduce them to triviality (e.g., friendliness is reduced to the mark I make on a rating scale) or be unsuccessful. Where, for example, should I look in the brain to locate your self-concept? Is the superego at the top of the head or at the bottom? The answer is that they are in *my* head, not yours. Psychoanalysts like to use descriptions such as *superego,* but when they do so they are really only asserting that such a concept has some purpose. Perhaps it helps the analyst understand why a patient keeps behaving in a self-destructive fashion. The superego has no existence, it is not *real,* but the construct of superego is useful. Constructs can not be used to answer the question "What is John really like?" but they can address the issue "What is the best way to describe John for certain purposes?"

Focus of Convenience. Theories and constructs are all limited by what George Kelly (1955) called a **focus of convenience**. This means that constructs do not apply to all things. We do not typically discuss the intelligence of a rock, neither do we describe the sandiness of a person. Theories also do not have unlimited application. Even the so-called **grand unified theories** ("theories of everything") that physicists have proposed are restricted to physical phenomena, and, as Hawking (1988) notes, do not actually even cover all physical events. A theory is restricted to a limited universe of situations or events; indeed, part of the complete statement of a theory provides information about the limitations on its applicability. Theories of economics may explain inflation, but they are not of much use for understanding stomachaches. Sociologists have much to say about the structure of society, but they are notably silent about how to fertilize wheat.

In a less overstated fashion, the same is true of personality theories. Freudian theory developed in the context of hysterical disorders in Vienna at the turn of the century, so it is a useful theory for explaining similar forms of neurosis. Likewise, a theory of conditioning may be useful for teaching new skills to some mentally retarded persons but not so useful for understanding the identity crisis of an adolescent. A theory, therefore, can not be legitimately rejected simply because it does not account for everything. On the other hand, theories that have broader ranges of application are generally preferred to the narrower theories they encompass.

## Value of Personality Theories

Levy (1970) has argued that the one overriding purpose for all theories of personality is that they provide the "organization of knowledge in a form that will make it usable and communicable" (p. 38). There are several aspects of a personality theory that determine how usefully and effectively it communicates knowledge.

Explicitness and Clarity.  Part of the charm—and frustration—of our everyday implicit theories is their vague and intuitive character. For example, when two people with different personalities are attracted to each other we "explain" this with the "theory" that "opposites attract." Conveniently, if the people have similar personalities we say, "birds of a feather flock together." Although these explanations are generally accepted in everyday conversation, it is easy to demonstrate their imprecision by asking the speaker "why?" after the explanation has been offered. In contrast, formal, scientific theories of personality are systematically formulated (ideally as assumptions, postulates, and corollaries) and organized so that they can be conveyed clearly. The rigid and detailed statement of formal theories helps ensure that the theory is interpreted reliably, in the sense that different people agree about what the theory predicts. If people can deduce contradictory hypotheses from a theory, the theory is considered scientifically invalid.

Organized Structure. Good theories offer a framework to help us explain what we have observed. They provide a system that will allows us to organize what we know about people, so that their behavior can be efficiently predicted and compellingly understood. Without a systematic framework, our knowledge would be reduced to a boring and overwhelming catalog or a list of facts. We need a framework to help identify and select the facts that are important. For example, in predicting aggression in a given situation, what should we know about the potential aggressors? Their size, strength, or height? their expectancies for success? their eye color? In any situation, many facts are available. Some are trivial or irrelevant, but others are significant and consequential. A good theory provides a framework for telling which are which.

**Expansion of Knowledge.** We never have enough knowledge. The more we know, the more we become aware of the gaps in our information. A good theory assists us in the search for new knowledge by providing specific guidelines. Our theoretical orientation serves to direct both our research and assessment: because we cannot know everything or pursue every question, a theory will help us decide what knowledge to seek. And, when evidence or data are lacking on a certain question, a theory can often provide hints about where to find those data.

**Consistency of Explanations.** It is generally easy to tailor explanations to fit any set of observations. Informal, everyday theories of personality are particularly prone to this **post-hoc explanation** (making up explanations to fit, rather than to predict, the facts). For example, if "opposites attract" is used to explain why one couple fell in love, "birds of a feather flock together" can readily be invoked to explain why this couple broke up and each fell in love with a more compatible person. In contrast to the inconsistency of informal theories, formal theories emphasize consistent explanations. Although it is appropriate to modify a formal theory as new data are collected, those modifications are limited to the extent that they do not lead to inconsistent explanations or predictions. The consistency of formal theories makes it easier to tell when our ideas are wrong. Indeed, a contradiction in a formal theory is strong evidence against that theory.

The emphasis on consistency often limits the phenomena, methods, and interpretations that a theory encompasses. Students sometimes feel that a theoretical commitment is overly restrictive because of these limitations. The alternative is an eclectic approach in which the parts of each theory that provide the most persuasive explanations and make the most accurate predictions are selected and combined. A fanciful recipe might read: Take a little self-concept, add a bit of superego and a pinch of reinforcement, mix them together in a bowl of humanism, and let simmer in a social learning pan. The problem with this approach is that the concepts, predictions, and methods from one theory often contradict those of another theory, primarily because the theories were developed for different purposes and have different ranges of convenience. The solution to this dilemma is to recognize that the different theories of personality may all contribute to understanding human behavior. However, when working within a specific theoretical framework one is limited to that theory's goals, methods, and range of convenience.

## Dimensions of Personality Theories

There are many different views, conceptions, and theories of personality. Likewise, there are many different dimensions along which personality theories can be categorized and compared. In their authoritative personality text, Hall and Lindzey (1978) devote 15 chapters to various personality theories, and several contain more than one theory. They also listed more than 20 dimensions along which personality theories may be compared. Rotter & Hochreich (1975) provide a more simplified scheme for characterizing personality theories that is based on five dimensions.

More and Less Systematic. Formal theories generally provide a more systematic view of personality than our informal everyday beliefs. However, the degree to which personality theories are relatively systematic or unsystematic varies. Some theories have a detailed set of propositions that are tightly organized and can clearly be related to one another. These systematic theories are generally easy to understand and evaluate because their structures are so clear. In addition, more systematic theories generally provide a clear set of methods for evaluating their predictions. Rotter's **social learning theory** (Chapter 11) is an example of a more systematic personality theory. In contrast, less systematic theories are often expressed as a loose collection of statements. The relations among these statements are often not specified, and the implications of one statement for another are often not clear. Also, the methods through which predictions derived from these theories can be tested are often not well defined. Maslow's **humanistic theory** of personality (Chapter 7) is an example of a less systematic theory.

More and Less Explicit Measures. Formal theories of personality that provide more explicit methods for measuring their constructs are generally clearer and more useful. For example, the assertion that "successful people will have actualized their potential in a more nearly perfect fashion" is harder to understand and evaluate if we have no agreed-upon means for measuring actualization (or potential, for that matter). The existence of accepted measures of constructs increases the likelihood that the theory will generate research and lead to testable hypotheses.

Description Versus Development. Some theories focus on the contents of personality, whereas others emphasize the processes through which personality develops and changes. For example, a theory may proclaim that personality is best described by traits 1 through 141, but there is little in the theory to suggest how these 141 traits are acquired or altered. By contrast, other theories concern how people develop a particular personality without devoting much attention to what that personality is. The **learning theories** described in Chapter 9 provide a detailed explanation for how personality might develop, but provide no information about the contents of personality. The Big Five model that was briefly described in Chapter 1 provides an extensive description of the contents of personality but has nothing to say about how that personality might develop or change.

Generality Versus Specificity. Theories vary in their breadth. Some theories focus on one or a few specific aspects of personality, whereas others attempt to provide broad coverage for nearly all aspects of individual differences and human nature. During the first half of this century, personality theories tended to encompass nearly all human behavior. The psychodynamic theory of Freud, for example, attempted to explain all aspects of human functioning in terms of underlying unconscious wishes and impulses. More recently the field of personality has moved to a *microtheoretical approach* (Chaplin, 1988), which emphasizes one specific construct such as locus of control, need achievement, or self-monitoring that is intended to explain a more limited domain of human behavior. One perennial issue in personality theory is deciding how to compromise between the unrealistic simplicity of general explanations and the overwhelming complexity of totally specific ones.

Person Versus Situation. Theories differ in the extent to which they emphasize the importance of factors inherent in the person or in the situation for influencing behavior. Some theorists view behavior as determined by internal forces, such as genetic factors or personal constructs, that operate consistently from situation to situation. Others emphasize that behavior is determined by external factors, such as threat and reward, that are specific to different situations. Although a more complete understanding of human behavior will require an appreciation of both person and situational factors, different theories may focus on one or the other.

## Evaluating Theories: Nonempirical Criteria

The crucial basis for evaluating a scientific theory is **empirical research,** which is discussed in the next section. However, theories can also be evaluated and sometimes rejected without any empirical study being done. Both Hall and Lindzey (1978) and Levy (1970) discuss important nonempirical criteria that can be used to evaluate theories.

Breadth, Significance, and Simplicity. These criteria are generally applied comparatively to pairs of theories. In general, a theory that deals with a broad range of events will be judged superior to one that deals with a narrow range. Likewise, a theory that concerns more important or significant events will generally be preferred to one whose focus is on more trivial matters. For example, a theory that provides an explanation of why men tend not to use middle urinals in public bathrooms may be viewed as less significant than a theory that explains why people get divorced, even if interesting psychological principles apply in both cases. Finally, if two theories each provide a reasonably complete explanation of some phenomenon, the simpler (more **parsimonious**) theory, such as one that uses a smaller number of constructs or makes fewer assumptions, will preferred

Human behavior is influenced by both situational and personal factors. Your behavior may be different when you are in a stressful situation than when you are in an unstressful one—even if that stress is a surprise party.

to the more complex theory. These criteria are generally applied subjectively, and they may conflict. For example, a broad theory may not be as simple as a more narrow theory. Thus, these criteria can not always be used to decide between two theories.

**Disconfirmation.**  Because scientific theories are evaluated by empirical research, an important criterion for a theory is that it generates predictions that can be tested. In particular, it must be possible to **disconfirm** a theory (Popper, 1962). For example, a theory that makes predictions that cover all possible outcomes can not be shown to be wrong. Likewise, a theory that uses constructs, such as beings from the future or different dimensions, that are beyond our current knowledge can not be tested. Theories that cannot be tested are not scientifically acceptable. It is not that these theories are wrong. For example, it could be true that mental illness is caused by beings from the sixth dimension performing experiments on human beings. But such a theory could never be shown to be wrong, or right for that matter, so it is rejected on that basis.

**Relative Utility.**  Ultimately, any theory will be disconfirmed, or at least revised. The reason is that theories are always simplified explanations and descriptions of the phenomena they are trying to illuminate (Chaplin, in press). There is always an additional condition or disclaimer that would improve a theory. As scientists we attempt to develop theories that are wrong because of errors of omission (leaving something out) rather than commission (saying something wrong). But, regardless of the type of error, any theory will necessarily and always be incorrect. For this reason we do not ever use truth to evaluate theories, nor do we ever state that a theory has been "proved." Instead, we evaluate theories relative to each other. We conclude that one theory is relatively more useful or accurate than another at accounting for the data we collected, while recognizing that neither of those theories is true in an absolute sense.

## Research: Empirically Evaluating Explanations and Testing Predictions

Without research, personality theories might be little more than speculation. The knowledge that their theories will be tested imposes a discipline on personality theorists to avoid idle speculation or wishful thinking in their formulations. Without research, personality theories might stagnate because they would not be improved or revised on the basis of new evidence. Testing theories and beliefs through observation and experiment is what distinguishes science from other disciplines.

### Research and Theory

Research, whether it involves observing naturally occurring events or manipulating events through experimentation to better observe a particular feature of that event, is the means by which we "collect data." Those data provide a systematic description of phenomena, and they also enable us to assess the relations among events and to establish principles. Research not only helps extend and modify theories but is also the road to evaluating the relative efficiency or utility of those theories. There is, then, an intimate and crucial relation between theory and research—or at least there ought to be. Theory serves as both a stimulator and a guide that precedes observation and experimentation. It helps put together, in a meaningful fashion, the various facts that we have gleaned from our research. But there must be something to put together; research provides that something.

The beauty of research is that it takes us out of the exclusive realm of argument, speculation, or appeal to authority. Issues become settled in the arena of observation. Endless discussions give way to **empirical** testing—determining by observation or experiment what the facts or relations are. To make this method work, our procedures need to be systematic and reliable so that others can verify them. This is the essence of the scientific method. This does not mean that empirical or scientific methods are fixed procedures that generate truth, for they do not. The scientific path is a difficult and often frustrating one that involves as much perspiration as it does inspiration. Most scientific research ends in failure because of a flaw in the methodology, or in the theory on which the research was based, or both. Many different methodological approaches may be used to answer most questions, and the methods sometimes yield conflicting results. But over the long haul, empiricism, through its public and verifiable procedures, is better fitted to grapple successfully with our questions than is simple appeal to reason, or worse, authority. How research can clarify speculation about the nature of certain events is illustrated in Box 2-1.

## Observation: Unsystematic, Naturalistic, and Controlled

Observation is the essence of empirical research. All research, whether it is experimental, naturalistic, or the study of individual cases, involves someone making observations of what someone else is doing or has done under some conditions.

Unsystematic Observation.  The ideas for research often begin with unsystematic **observation.** Simply observing one's own reactions or those of another may lead to the development of hypotheses. For example, one might casually observe two friends who, on separate occasions, each express a fear of dying. Intrigued, the observer notes that each is a self-centered individual. Could it be that self-love is associated with or even causes a concern about death? Such observations can provide the initial impetus to a more systematic and rigorous study of events.

Naturalistic Observation.  **Naturalistic observation** is a more rigorous and systematic form of observation. Here, observations and measurements are made of various aspects of people's behavior. However, no control is exerted by the investigator over the situations in which the behavior occurs. In effect, these are field studies. A classic example is the work of Barker and Wright (1951), who followed a 7-year-old for an entire day and systematically recorded every move he made. Naturalistic observation is often used in hospitals and other treatment settings to detect patterns in problem behavior so that treatments to change that behavior can be developed. Typically both the behavior and aspects of the situation in which it occurs are recorded at specified times.

Of course, naturalistic observations depend on freely occurring events. For this reason alone, they can be cumbersome, and observers are often at the mercy of events over which they have little or no control. A second problem is that observation is vulnerable to the biases and preconceived notions of the observer. A third difficulty, as noted by critics of this approach, is that it is questionable how far one can generalize from one's observations of a few people or situations. Thus, findings may have very limited application. Finally, it is sometimes true that in the process of observing or recording, observers actually interfere with the events under study. For example, suppose you are observing family interactions to study the effects of dominance patterns. Can you be sure that your presence is not a variable that subtly affects the family's interaction patterns?

## BOX 2-1
## Research on Expectancies

A 1950s study on expectancies illustrates how research can help settle disagreements about the role of reinforcement in determining behavior. Although this issue may not appear particularly complicated today, its present clarity is at least partially attributable to the answers provided by that early research.

**"If someone offers me a dollar today or five tomorrow, which should I choose?"**

Based upon both animal and human research, the conventional wisdom was that immediate rewards are preferred over delayed rewards and that both rewards and punishment are less effective when their application is delayed. For example, given a choice between a small piece of candy that is offered now and a large one that will be provided two days hence, most children will choose the former. Obviously, delay does something to the *value* of immediate versus delayed rewards.

However, Mahrer (1956) believed that something was amiss here. Could it be that the crucial factor was the child's *expectancy?* That is, perhaps children choose the immediate but lesser reward because they have learned through experience that delayed rewards are less likely to occur than immediate ones. But rather than simply *offering* this revised argument, Mahrer *investigated* the problem empirically.

He did this by training groups of second- and third-grade children to have low, moderate, or high expectancies for receiving a toy promised by the experimenter. His data from the experiment supported the reasoning that when the child trusts the promises of an adult, the child will choose a more valuable but delayed reward rather than an immediate but lesser one. The point is that no matter how logical or intellectually impeccable one's reasoning may appear to be, that reasoning must be followed by systematic and reliable observation or experimentation. Without empirical research, we can never be sure.

Recent advances in technology such as beepers and portable recording devices have improved the ability of psychologists to sample behavior, thoughts, and feelings in a representative and relatively unobtrusive manner. The **experience sampling method** (Hormuth, 1986) is used to sample randomly from a person's everyday experiences. A subject carries a pager and a dictation machine programmed to ask a series of questions about the subject's experience at that moment. The pagers can be programmed to beep randomly or in a prespecified pattern, and the subject can respond to the questions by punching in simple codes.

Controlled Field Observations. The frustration and inefficiency of having to wait for some conditions and behavior to occur naturalistically have led some investigators to use **controlled field observations.** In this approach, observation is carried out in naturalistic settings but with a manipulation component. The manipulation may be designed to increase the frequency of the target phenomenon, to increase the control over the conditions under which it occurs, and/or to select the types of individuals (e.g., men or women, old or young) who experience the phenomenon. For example, after naturalistic observation has been used in treatment settings to identify problem behaviors and the conditions under which they occur, controlled observation might be used to evaluate treatments. The introduction of the treatment is under the control of the observer, but the patient is still being observed in a naturalistic setting.

An excellent illustration of controlled observation is the work of Mathews and Canon (1975), who were interested in environmental noise level as a determinant of helping behavior. A hidden observer recorded the behavior of subjects who wandered into the following situation. As a designated subject walked down the street, a confederate spilled a box of books all over the sidewalk. The behavior of interest was whether the subject would help the confederate pick up the books. At the same time, another confederate in an adjacent yard was either (1) operating a very noisy lawn mower or (2) bending over a silent mower. What the observer noted was that 50 percent of the subjects helped the confederate when there was no lawn mower noise, whereas only 12.5 percent helped in the noisy condition. Such a study has the distinct virtue of investigating questions in real settings, giving us increased confidence that the results can be generalized to other settings.

## Case Study Methods

In **case study** methods, single individuals are studied. The result is a rich and detailed description of that person. Included are interviews, test responses, and even psychotherapy sessions. Also included would be first-person accounts such as letters, diaries, autobiographies, and the like. Third-person accounts—biographies, case history accounts, and so forth—would also qualify, as would certain naturalistic observations. For example, Rosenberg (1989) studied the organization of personality. He did so by analyzing the physical and psychological traits used by Thomas Wolfe to describe himself and others in the autobiographical novel *Look Homeward, Angel.*

A major value of case study methods is their richness as a source of hypotheses. They provide a basis for speculation that can later be translated into testable hypotheses and then subjected to careful scientific scrutiny. Sustained observation of real people and their productions is vital if for no other reason than as a prelude to scientific investigation. Computer simulation, statistical tables, and reviews of the literature are all useful, but we cannot afford to ever get completely away from looking at real people. If nothing else, analysis of case material and recourse to observation can serve to dampen the enthusiasm of those who deal exclusively, on one hand, in theoretical speculation or, on the other, in laboratory research.

## The Experimental Method

A major problem with observational and case study methods, or any other method that relies on naturally occurring events, is that we are at the mercy of those events. We cannot control or often even know the factors that affect the events we are studying. It is always possible—indeed likely—that causes other than those we have hypothesized are affecting our observations. The fundamental justification for the experimental method is its ability to control phenomena so that causes can be discerned and evaluated with greater confidence.

Consider the following hypothetical example. There is much evidence to suggest that aging individuals are cautious, have difficulty solving a variety of problems, and show learning deficits (Botwinick, 1984). Some of this evidence comes from observing older subjects complete tasks on small computers. Consequently, it has been argued that lack of experience on these computers is responsible for what appears to be learning deficits. Therefore, suppose we hypothesize that one aging group of subjects will take more trials to learn the stimulus material than will another group of aging subjects when the former are unfamiliar with computer equipment. Each group is treated in exactly the same way—that is, the stimuli are presented in the same fashion on the final test. Furthermore, we randomly assign subjects to groups so that any individual differences in characteristics such as intelligence, educational background, and gender will not differ systematically between the groups. The tasks are presented to all subjects on a computer screen, and subjects respond by pressing appropriate keys on the computer terminal. The only difference between the groups is that one is given some familiarization training and the other is not. There are 50 subjects in each group. The data analysis shows that as predicted, the group with familiarization training learned faster and also made fewer errors than did the other group.

The foregoing example illustrates the main features of the experimental approach. We started with an **experimental hypothesis**—a prediction about what we should observe if our theory of aging and learning is correct. In this case we predicted that a group of aging people with task familiarity would be better learners than a matched sample without such familiarity. We chose an **independent variable**—a factor that we could control through manipulation *independent* of the characteristics of our subjects or the situation—in this case, the prior experience of the subjects. Finally, we examined the effects of this independent variable on the subjects' responses—the **dependent variable,** which is the measured outcome that *depends* upon (that is, is caused by) the independent variable: in this example, the responses to the stimuli appearing on the computer screen. In this hypothetical study, we followed good experimental procedure by randomly assigning subjects to groups and controlling the situation. This made only one aspect—task familiarity—systematically different between the groups. Because the latter was the only thing different about the two groups, there is strong evidence that it is what was the cause of the observed performance differences between the groups.

In this example, task familiarity was treated as the independent variable. It was manipulated through use of a **control group,** which is a group that serves as a comparison against which the performance of the experimental group can be evaluated. For example, suppose we wish to determine whether assertiveness training works. To do this we randomly select a group of people who are about to undergo such training, and we measure in some fashion their initial level of assertiveness. Following their training we again measure their assertiveness level. Happily, we find they are more assertive! Does this prove that the assertiveness training works? No, it does not.

What we need is a control group that is measured before training but which, for example, is placed on a waiting list. After the same amount of time that characterized the training of the experimental group, they are measured again. Their before and after scores are then compared with the before and after scores of the experimental group to evaluate whether the training was effective. Without a control group, one could just as easily argue that the real cause of the increase in assertiveness in the first group was their decision to undergo training rather than the training itself. Inclusion of a no-treatment control group increases our confidence that it really is the training and not some other set of factors that is causing the posttreatment improvement. Members of the control group and the experimental group come from the same total population under study, but are randomly assigned to either the control or the experimental group.

**Experimentation and Personality Psychology.** Historically, there have been five periods in the development of personality research methods: (1) the pre-identity era (the period before personality was really established as a field of study), (2) the pre–World War II era, (3) the post–World War II era, (4) the contemporary era, and (5) the current situation, which is a part of the contemporary era (Craik, 1986). As Figure 2-1 illustrates, the experimental or laboratory approach has been used continuously across these periods. Indeed, the experimental approach to personality study became the dominant influence in the early 1960s. The focus of experimental personality research is on human nature rather than on the individual uniqueness of personality. Experimental research concerns laws of behavior that can be applied to people in general. Such research is called **nomothetic.** During the 1960s, research on individual uniqueness nearly disappeared, leading one personality psychologist to ask "Where is the person in personality research?" (Carlson, 1971).

**Limitations of Experimental Personality Research.** In commenting on the emphasis on experimentation in personality research Epstein (1979b) remarked:

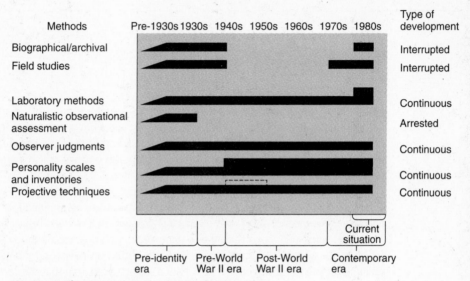

**Figure 2-1** &#x2773;&#x2774; Historical trends in personality research.

From "Personality Research Methods: An Historical Perspective" by K. H. Craik, 1986, *Journal of Personality*, 54 (1) pp. 18–51. Copyright © 1986 by Duke University Press.

"In our zealous pursuit of rigorous, experimental research models we have somehow lost track of our subject matter. Instead of . . . studying individuals in breadth and depth, we have pursued a narrow vision of science, one in which method has become more important than substance. As a result, our journals are filled with studies describing laboratory manipulations of variables of little significance to the people in the experiments. (p. 649)

These are strong but accurate words that reflect a growing dissatisfaction with the experimental approach to personality research.

Whereas we used to talk about the 50-minute therapy hour, we now have the 50-minute experiment. This research approach leads to a concentration on isolated bits of behavior that often have not been integrated very well with the larger framework of a subject's personality. Thus, there is little awareness of the coherence of personality. Box 2-2 shows a specific example of this phenomena.

In addition, it is not unusual to discover that a laboratory finding cannot be replicated. It is uncertain how common this failure to replicate is, for it is rare for laboratory studies to be repeated. Moreover, psychology journals do not routinely publish replication results unless there is some compelling theoretical reason to do so (see, for example Chaplin & Goldberg, 1984).

Also, laboratory studies are limited to independent variables that can be experimentally manipulated, and this eliminates the vast majority of personality variables from consideration. It is not possible, or if it were, ethically permissible,

BOX 2-2
## The 50-Minute Experiment

This study concerned the relation between learning and control (Phares, 1962). Specifically, it was hypothesized that when escape from a painful stimulus occurs only by chance, subjects will not learn to recognize other stimuli associated with the pain. However, when subjects find that escape depends on their skill in learning to recognize the associated stimuli, they will learn those stimuli.

Three groups of subjects—14 skill, 14 chance, and 14 nonshock—were used. Tachistoscopic thresholds for twelve nonsense syllables were determined for all subjects. Following this, the skill group was given 10 trials in which 6 of the syllables were always accompanied by shock and the other 6 were never accompanied by shock. By learning which shock syllable was associated with which button on their control panel, subjects could terminate the shock each time. Chance subjects were told that the correct button changed continuously so that no learning was possible, and thus that escape occurred only on a random basis. Chance subjects were matched with skill subjects with respect to number of escapes, syllables on which escape occurred, and sex. Following this procedure, thresholds were again determined for each of the 12 syllables. For nonshock subjects, the preexperiment and postexperiment thresholds were taken while, in between, the series of syllables was exposed for 10 trials without shock.

Results indicated that as predicted, threshold decrements were significantly greater for skill subjects than for chance subjects for both shock and nonshock syllables.

**Several Questions Might Be Raised About This Study**

1. Did subject selection have any influence? Subjects were paid volunteers, and all subjects fearful of electric shock were excused. Most subjects were college students.
2. How representative is the stimulus of electric shock? Are there specific qualities about shock that make it qualitatively different from other threatening stimuli?
3. Is learning nonsense syllables typical of learning in real-life situations? If so, how much so?
4. What were the needs that motivated the subjects, and were the needs possibly different from subject to subject? Was it money, a desire to please the experimenter, a wish to appear brave, a compulsion to achieve? Could each subject's results be replicated in another situation with different learning stimuli and different threats?
5. How significant was the overall laboratory setting to the subject? Would similar results be obtained in situations highly relevant to and typical of a subject's life?
6. Where, indeed, is the "personality" in this study? There are no measures of individual differences. Are all people, on the basis of this study, presumed to behave alike in all skill-chance settings? What about the subjects whose behavior did not follow the hypothesis?

to manipulate an individual's intelligence, depression, sociability, warmth, dominance, shyness, femininity, masculinity, and so on.

Yet another problem is that most laboratory studies concern a single behavior. But the expression of any specific behavior by a person is inherently unreliable and difficult to interpret. The behavior depends upon many things, including situational variables in the laboratory setting, the experimenter's characteristics, the subject's expectations, and the relation of the behavior to each subject's personality organization. All of this makes it hard to generalize a study's results to even a slightly different setting. Questions about the reliability and validity of the results of nomothetic studies that reflect averages and generalities are serious ones.

One strong critic of the traditional nomothetic emphasis of personality research is Jim Lamiell (1981, 1987). He has argued that conclusions based on studies that combine the scores of individual subjects so as to provide a group mean do not have any relevance for the prediction or explanation of the behavior of a single subject. Knowing how, on average, 40 subjects behave does not tell us how *one* subject behaves. Moreover, nomothetic research may not reveal anything about any of the individuals on which it is based. For example, consider the finding that the average American household contains 2.5 children. Although this is a perfectly understandable average, that average clearly does not characterize any household. So long as personality psychologists wish to reach conclusions about individuals it is important that we supplement the traditional nomothetic methods with more **idiographic** ones which emphasize the intensive study of single individuals.

The Popularity of Experimental Personality Research. Given that the experimental approach is of limited utility for addressing the important issue of individual uniqueness in personality psychology, why has the method been so popular? One reason has been the limitations of the idiographic method as commonly applied. The very strengths of the idiographic approach also result in some weaknesses. For example, how do we know that what is true for one person provides an adequate basis for generalization to others? The idiographic approach imputes unique characteristics to each person, which is fine if you are interested in that person but limited if you are interested in anyone else.

Another reason has been the success of the biological and physical sciences. Some observers believe that psychology decided to mimic the methods of physical sciences as a way of gaining respectability. Apparatus, control groups, and sophisticated methods of data analysis became associated with scientific status. This is understandable in a discipline that hardly existed before the 20th century and is striving for acceptance and identity.

Another factor is the "publish or perish" syndrome in the academic research establishment. Young investigators, learning early that promotions and salary increases are heavily dependent on the rapid accumulation of an impressive list of publications, tend to design studies that can be done quickly and easily. In addition, variables chosen for study are straightforward—ones that can be easily manipulated. Most researchers are not so deliberately Machiavellian. Indeed this general approach to research has become so institutionalized that many investigators are unaware of the problem. Unfortunately, one effect of this strategy may be an overabundance of trivial findings and uninteresting papers.

**Conclusion: A Balance of Approaches.** This critical evaluation of experimental methods is not intended to imply that the classic experimental methods of psychology are inherently wrong. Quite the opposite, the experimental method is a potent tool in our research arsenal, and we should continue to use it. The concern expressed in this critique is that the experimental approach has been used too much, often to the exclusion of other rigorous but nonlaboratory approaches to studying personality. In addition, experimental studies must be complemented by studies of people in their natural habitat (Tennen, Suls, & Affleck, 1991). Although naturalistic settings pose obvious difficulties in controlling variables, the gain is in using situations meaningful to subjects.

Fortunately, there is a growing interest in research based on non-experimental strategies and the intensive study of individuals and their unique constellations of characteristics (Bray, 1982; Epstein, 1979b). In particular, studies are now appearing that obtain a variety of measures on subjects over extended periods. These studies will help us to better address the complexity of personality and permit us to deal with issues of the organization of personality. The complementary nature of idiographic and nomothetic approaches is illustrated in Box 2-3.

## The Correlation Method

The most crucial observations in science concern the relations among variables. In classic experimental research, the question is whether the manipulated independent variable is related to the dependent variable. That is, is there a tendency for subjects in one experimental group to score higher or lower than subjects in a different experimental group. Relations are also the crucial issues in nonexperimental research. For example, is anxiety related to performance? Do IQ scores relate to school achievement? Is there a relation between obesity and unfulfilled needs for love and affection? The difference between experimental and nonexperimental research is whether or not one of the two variables whose relation is of interest is, or can be, manipulated. We cannot typically manipulate anxiety or IQ scores or obesity. The basic statistic for indexing the degree to which two variables are related is the **correlation coefficient.** Although this statistic can be used with both manipulated and nonmanipulated variables, it is common to refer to research on the relations between nonmanipulated variables as *correlational.*

To correlate two variables, we first obtain two sets of observations on each member of a group of subjects. For example, suppose we have ten subjects and

## BOX 2-3
## The Complementary Nature of Idiographic and Nomothetic Methods

Davis and Phares (1969) administered the 23-item I-E Scale. This is a forced-choice scale to determine the extent to which a person believes that his or her own behavior is the determinant of rewards (internals) or believes that fate, luck, chance, or powerful others (externals) are crucial. College students were administered this scale along with a 192-item questionnaire designed to reveal various parental behaviors. Internals reported their parents as showing less rejection, hostile control, and withdrawal of relations and more positive involvement and consistent discipline than externals.

Contrast these findings with the following quotation from R. W. White (1976):

> Bearing in mind that rejection involves interacting with the child as little as possible, it can be seen that such an attitude is not compatible with a real policy of close control and guidance. In his remarkable autobiography, John Stuart Mill describes in detail the manner in which his father, James Mill, undertook from the earliest years to control his education and preside over the forming of his mind. Clearly the elder Mill was committed to almost constant contact with his son in order to execute his strenuous plan for the shaping of character. The son describes studying his Greek lessons across the table from his father, who was writing a history of India, and interrupting him to ask the meaning of each new Greek word. He marvels that his father, naturally an impatient man, could have endured this constant breaking of his train of thought. It is indeed a marvel unless we assume that the son whose mind James Mill was shaping was in a true sense an object of love and esteem. The example makes it clear that high control need not imply rejection. Neither does low control necessarily signify love; it can go with indifference and with a desire to keep the child out of the way. (pp. 42–43)

Each of these disparate pieces, in its own way, contributes to our understanding of control. Each by itself is also incomplete as an analysis of the origins of control. Indeed, Hermans (1988) argues that psychology can only benefit from a combination of nomothetic and idiographic methods.

each is given two tests: one that measures friendliness and one that measures how trusting a person is. These hypothetical paired scores are presented in Table 2-1. The resultant correlation coefficient is +.76, which suggests a strong positive relation. Thus, as friendliness increases, so too does one's tendency to be trusting.

The full name of this statistic is the *Pearson product moment correlation coefficient,* and it is symbolized by *r.* An *r* may vary anywhere between –1.00 and

## &#x5352; Table 2-1
Hypothetical Data for the Correlation Between Friendliness and Trust

| Subject | Friendliness Score | Trust Score |
|---|---|---|
| Mary | 26 | 22 |
| Betty | 24 | 28 |
| Grace | 20 | 22 |
| Dorothy | 20 | 14 |
| Nancy | 16 | 18 |
| Esther | 12 | 22 |
| Paula | 12 | 6 |
| Ann | 10 | 14 |
| Juanita | 6 | 12 |
| Teresa | 4 | 2 |

Note: $r = +.76$ for the data above.

+1.00. An $r$ of +1.00 indicates that two variables are perfectly and positively related. An $r$ of −1.00 indicates a perfect negative correlation. The $r$ of .76 in Table 2-1 signifies a high positive correlation. A correlation of −.76 would mean a high negative relationship (i.e., as scores on Variable A increase, scores on Variable B decrease). A picture of relation between two variables can be obtained by plotting the pairs of observations. Such a picture is called a **scatterplot.** For example, the data from Table 2-1 have been plotted in Figure 2-2. Each data point corresponds to one subject's scores on both friendliness and trust. Thus, the data point nearest the lower left-hand corner represents Teresa's data (friendliness = 4; trust = 2).

Figure 2-3 presents scatterplots for several correlations. The more nearly perfect a relation is, the closer to a straight line will be the data points. When the $r$ approaches .00, there is no relation, and the data points are scattered randomly around the scatterplot.

The Problem of Causality.  We are prone to assume that because two variables are correlated, one causes the other. No matter how "logical" this may appear, we cannot assert, on the basis of a correlation alone, that a cause-and-effect relation holds. For example, we may find that in a third-grade class there is a correlation between IQs and teacher evaluations of intelligence. We might then assume that a child's intelligence is causing the teacher's evaluation (good or bad). But in a situation where the teacher is giving the IQ tests and also providing the evalua-

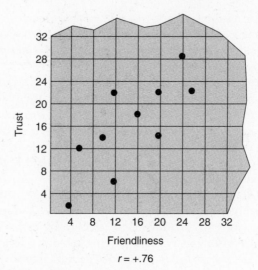

Figure 2-2 ᏮᎧ Scatterplot of data from Table 2.1

tions, it may turn out that the evaluations predispose the teacher toward a biased administration or interpretation of the IQ test. Thus, it is the evaluation that is "causing" the IQ outcomes.

It is a fact that among people who smoke there is a *positive* correlation between the number of cigarettes smoked across the lifetime and the number of years a person lives. That is, the more cigarettes smoked, the longer, on the average, a smoker will live! Does this mean a smoker should smoke more so that he or she will live longer? Hardly; the correlation reflects that a person who lives more years will have had more opportunities to smoke. Although inferences

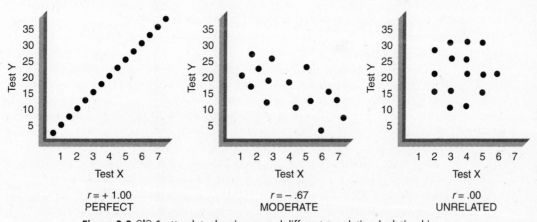

Figure 2-3 ᏮᎧ Scatterplots showing several different correlational relationships.

about causality are not possible from correlation coefficients, this is not to say that cause-and-effect relations do not exist in a given case. It only means that we must substantiate causal relations by use of experimental methods rather than by correlational ones.

Evaluation of Correlational Methods.  The inability to infer causality from correlations represents their chief weakness. But there are tangible strengths as well. It is generally easier and less time-consuming to correlate than it is to construct elaborate experimental variations and manipulations. Therefore, if we can determine right off that no relation exists between A and B, there is no point in experimentally investigating A as a cause of B.

There is no question that knowledge about relation can be useful. For example, everyone knows that cigarette smoking and lung cancer are correlated. The exact nature of any cause-and-effect relation may be debatable, but few people would advocate increased cigarette smoking on the basis of the correlation.

Finally, correlational methods permit us to study variables that cannot practically or ethically be manipulated. Variables such as gender, age, marital status, and birth order are not ones that can be manipulated experimentally. Nor can we ethically "train" someone to be a killer to study the effects of personality on crime.

## Statistical Versus Practical Significance

In the case of both correlation and experimental methods, the data are typically subjected to a **statistical analysis.** Statistical analysis is designed to assess whether the obtained correlation between two variables or the difference between the experimental and control group means is statistically significant. **Statistical significance** is a technical term that refers to the likelihood of obtaining the observed sample mean difference if the true (but unknown) difference between the experimental and control group means is zero. Traditionally, if the observed difference could be expected to occur by chance less than 5 times out of 100, the sample difference is called statistically significant. All other things being equal, the larger the correlation or the bigger the difference between groups, the greater the likelihood of significance.

However, statistical significance depends ultimately on the size of the sample rather than on the size of the correlation or difference. When large groups of subjects are involved, even small differences between groups, as well as relatively small correlation coefficients, will be significant. For example, with data from 180 subjects, a correlation of .19 will be significant. But if only 30 subjects were involved, a correlation of .30 would not reach significance.

This raises the issue of **practical significance.** Practical significance concerns whether the result of a study is large, useful, meaningful, or interesting. Statistical significance does not guarantee practical significance. For example, it might be that income correlates about .15 with the amount of gasoline purchased each month in a sample of five thousand people. But even though the observed relation is not likely to be a chance deviation upward from 0, the observed relation is small. Likewise, it is not clear that this result is useful or even very interesting. The point is that statistical significance is, at best, the beginning of the analysis and interpretation of results, not the end.

## Single-Subject Research

Both experimental and correlational research are nomothetic because they typically aggregate data across subjects and report results in terms of averages rather than individuals. In contrast, **single-subject research** is an idiographic approach that focuses on one individual so that the relevance of the findings for that individual can be evaluated. Single-subject research is similar to the case study method except that it is typically repeated (replicated) over several individuals, whereas the case study approach is usually restricted to one interesting case. Single-subject research is experimental because the experimenter observes a subject's behavior under several conditions that are controlled by the experimenter. This method has been most frequently used to evaluate the effectiveness of behavioral therapy.

An example of this approach is the case of Robbie (Hall, Lund, and Jackson, 1968). Robbie was a very disruptive third-grader enrolled in an urban poverty-level school. He spent only about 25% of his time studying. The rest of the time he spent laughing, throwing things, and generally being a nuisance. This is shown graphically in Figure 2-4 as the Baseline period. During Reinforcement period I, the teacher paid a great deal of attention to Robbie, and it can be seen that his study behavior increased markedly. During the Reversal period, the teacher reverted to her old level of attention, and Robbie's behavior deteriorated. With the reintroduction of attention by the teacher (Reinforcement period II), his behavior once again improved. The Reversal period, inserted as it was between the two reinforcement periods, effectively demonstrates a causal relation between the teacher's behavior and Robbie's behavior. However, the reason the teacher had this influence is not addressed by such research and remains unknown.

Broadly defined, single-subject research has the potential for combining the strengths of idiographic and nomothetic methods. Although the results that Hall et al. obtained with Robbie are applicable only to Robbie, similar patterns obtained across several children would provide more convincing evidence of the generality of the reinforcement value of a teacher's attention. Thus, a general (nomothetic) principle is derived from individualized (idiographic) data. Investigators are more often considering the extent to which a general (aggregate) pattern of results also characterizes the data from individual subjects. Box 2-4 provides an example of how the analysis of data in the aggregate and at the level of the individual subject can increase our understanding of a phenomenon.

Although single-subject research has long been associated with behavioral treatments, the analysis of the single case does not need to be limited to the evaluation of behavioral interventions. Technological innovations such as small recording devices, electronic pagers, and portable communications systems have

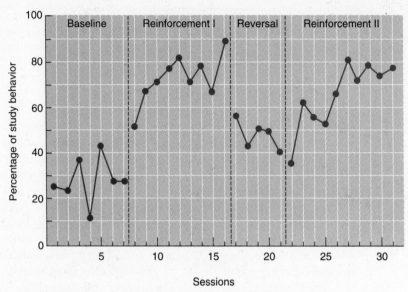

**Figure 2-4** Robbie: The giving and withdrawal of reinforcement.

From "Effects of Teacher Attention on Study Behavior" by R. V. Hall, D. Lund, and D. Jackson, 1968, *Journal of Applied Behavior Analysis, 1,* pp. 1–12. Copyright © 1968 by Society for the Experimental Analysis of Behavior.

allowed psychologists to intensively measure individual subjects' daily experiences and behavior and relate such measures to a host of personality and cognitive variables (Tennen, Suls, and Affleck, 1991; Stone, Kessler, and Haythornthwaite, 1991). In addition, quantitative methods are being developed to aid in the evaluation of data that have traditionally been treated more qualitatively (West & Hepworth, 1991).

## Assessment: Measuring Constructs and Describing People

Personality assessment or measurement provides the crucial link between theory and research. **Personality assessment** refers to the body of techniques, measures, and concepts that psychologists use to obtain and interpret information about people.

### Issues in Personality Assessment

Psychological assessment, and personality assessment in particular, is challenging. In the physical sciences, constructs such as height, weight, and time are clearly linked to their measures. Personality constructs are less easily related to the measures we use to assess them. In addition, the measurement of many psychological constructs requires the cooperation of the people we are measuring,

BOX 2-4
# The Aggregate and Single-Subject Analysis of Data

Chaplin and Buckner (1988) studied the extent to which subjects' self-evaluations are influenced by different standards of comparison, including comparing themselves with others and comparing their present selves with how they were in the past. In the aggregate, Chaplin and Buckner found that on the average, subjects tended to be more influenced by comparisons with their past rather than comparisons with others. In addition, however, they evaluated their data at the level of each individual subject. Their conclusion was strengthened by the finding that the average pattern in the data also characterized the data for the majority of individual subjects. However, for a substantial minority (25%) of subjects, comparison with others influenced self-evaluations more than a comparison with the past. Chaplin and Buckner wrote, "Also, if we approach the data idiographically, it is clear that the average results presented in Table 1 are not representative of all the subjects" (p. 519).

This idiographic finding means that the average (nomothetic) result should be interpreted with some caution. It also leads to many interesting questions, such as "Why are some people influenced more by different standards?" and "What are the consequences of evaluating oneself by these different standards?" These potentially interesting and important questions would not even have been raised if the nomothetic analyses had been the only treatment of the data.

and most psychological constructs have a substantial component of subjective meaning.

**General Versus Specific Measures.** Personality constructs may be broad or narrow. Consider "social interest," a construct that refers to an individual's willingness to be concerned with more than just self. This concern can be related to nearly all areas of life (work, marriage, and health, for example). However, "social interest" can be measured either in a broad sense or in a specific context, depending on our interests. To measure social interest broadly, we would sample a broad range of life situations and average the person's scores across those situations. Alternatively, items to assess this construct could be constructed so as not to refer directly to any specific situation. However, if the goal is to predict behavior specifically in the context of marriage, a specific measure would be desirable. This general versus specific assessment issue is illustrated in Box 2-5.

**Test-Taking Attitudes and Motives.** The psychologist always hopes that the person being assessed will respond in a straightforward, honest fashion. But this can be a vain hope. The point is, however, that regardless of what subjects' motives may

## BOX 2-5
## General Versus Specific Test Items for Predicting Narcissistic Behavior

### General

The following items (five-point agree-disagree scale) might be part of a scale that could be expected to predict moderately well over a number of different situations. Thus, the item content is not tied to specific situations but rather reflects general attitudes or beliefs.

1. If it feels right, it is right.
2. Thinking of yourself first is no sin in this world today.
3. It's best to live for the present and not worry about tomorrow.
4. It seems impossible to imagine the world without me in it.
5. I believe everyone has the right to live any damn way they choose.

### Specific

The following items (five-point agree-disagree scale) could compose part of a scale that could potentially predict well to the specific situations represented by the items but could not predict to other specific situations or be generalized:

1. Having children keeps you from engaging in a lot of self-fulfilling activities.
2. When choosing clothes I usually prefer style over comfort.
3. Having a career that permits a great deal of leisure time is not very important.
4. I would be willing to participate in a program of wage controls.
5. One cannot truly achieve sexual gratification unless one's partner is also gratified.

be, the psychologist may not be aware of them. When this happens, a subject's response can be misinterpreted. Objective tests can be vulnerable to these problems. Suppose a subject is asked to answer "true" or "false" to the following item: "I have terrible nightmares nearly every night." It is not very difficult to figure out how one should respond to create a good impression. Some objective tests have built-in detectors in the sense that certain items are designed to "trap" those being evasive or otherwise trying to "manage" their responses. But at best, these devices work imperfectly.

Other psychologists prefer projective tests—tests that are composed of ambiguous stimuli. Such tests make it more difficult for the subject to determine what is a correct or good response. But even here, ambiguous stimuli or not, the subject can, to some extent, manipulate the impression being conveyed. In short, the device has not yet been built that can totally defy a subject dedicated to misleading the examiner.

Subjective Meaning and Measurement.  In some instances, what we wish to measure is so poorly defined that measurement is inherently subjective. For example, if one can believe observers of the contemporary scene, a lot of us today are trying to "find ourselves" or looking to discover the "real me." But how can we measure this? What would those who have found themselves do or say on tests or in interviews that would distinguish them from those who are still looking? The problem results because the constructs are so vague and elusive that measuring them is next to impossible.

Another problem is that we are never sure that subjects will interpret the items as we intend (Chaplin & Panter, 1993). Consider again the item "I have terrible nightmares nearly every night." Even if a subject wishes to answer the question honestly, what exactly is a *terrible* nightmare? How often is *nearly* every night? A terrible nightmare to me may not be so terrible to you. This problem is one reason that most personality measures consist of many items; the assumption is that although a respondent may "misinterpret" one or two items, these errors of interpretation will be balanced across items and their impact will be reduced if a large number of items are used.

## Evaluating Measures

Because of the problems inherent in measurement, *psychometricians* have developed some basic standards for evaluating measures. These standards are generally of two types: reliability and validity.

Reliability.  Technically, measurement **reliability** refers to the extent to which a measure does not contain random error. The classic approach to assessing reliability is to determine how consistent subjects' scores are across time. This is commonly called **test–retest reliability,** and it is based on the assumption that scores that do not contain random error should be relatively stable across time. If a subject were administered the same intelligence test four months ago and then again today, a reliable test would produce scores that are similar. This outcome assumes, of course, that the testing conditions are comparable and that the subject has not undergone any serious changes in the meantime. Were the subject ill the second time, or in the grip of an emotional crisis, or even tested by an unskilled examiner, the scores could easily vary. But the fault would lie not in the test but rather in changes in testing conditions.

A second approach to assessing reliability is based on the consistency of subjects' responses to a set of similar items. This approach is called **internal consistency reliability,** and it requires that the items all measure the same construct.

The third aspect of reliability is the ability of different observers to agree among themselves when observing the same event. This is termed **interjudge reliability.** If different observers interpret an event differently, we have problems in deciding which observer to trust. Interjudge agreement has become a widely studied issue in psychology (Kenny, 1991). In addition to its measurement implications, the question why some observers agree more than others and the conditions that foster interjudge agreement is itself an interesting psychological question (Funder & West, 1993).

Validity. An assessment technique may be reliable, but that does not mean it is valid. A valid measure is one that reflects what it purports to assess. A valid test of anxiety should measure anxiety. A valid intelligence test should predict those who will be good problem solvers and those who will not. **Validity** is a complex concept that can be approached in a variety of ways. No one approach can fully establish a measures validity. Indeed, validation is akin to theory testing in that it is a dynamic and ongoing process.

**Content validity** is determined by observing whether the items of a given test appear to be sampling what is of interest. For instance, does a test of anxiety sample items congruent with our definition of anxiety? This is almost validity by inspection, and the difficulty, of course, is getting people of different theoretical persuasions to agree that the test items are indeed related to the construct in question.

**Criterion validity** is established by relating the scores on a test to an agreed-upon criterion. An example would be a test of creativity that predicted accurately creative accomplishments, such as music, art, or writing. Criterion validity may be of either of two kinds. The first is **predictive validity.** This involves the ability of the test to predict to some criterion in the future. An intelligence test shows predictive validity when it accurately predicts later grades in school. **Concurrent validity** is evident when a test correlates with another currently existing criterion. For example, when scores on an intelligence test are correlated with teachers' estimates of ability provided at the same time, concurrent validity exists. Of course, it is crucial that the teachers not have access to the scores. Otherwise, their judgments may be clouded or influenced by their knowledge, a situation called **criterion contamination.**

**Construct validity** refers to the extent to which a measure behaves empirically in a manner consistent with the theory of its construct. Evidence for construct validity can come from the more specific types of validity just described, as well as any other data we collect. Thus, any study that uses a measure can be thought of as a validation study. For example, if a well-established theory of anxiety suggests that anxiety will be related to performance, I can test the validity of a measure of anxiety by seeing whether it does relate to performance. Alternatively, if I have a well-established measure of anxiety, I can test the theory that predicts that anxiety is related to performance by doing that same study.

## ⚘ Table 2-2
Strategies for Determining the Validity of a Scale

| Strategy | Scale Is Valid If |
|---|---|
| Content validity | Items on the scale are representative of the trait being measured. |
| Predictive validity | Subjects respond the same way on the scale as they do on another measure taken some time in the future. |
| Concurrent validity | Subjects respond the same way on the scale as they do on another measure taken at about the same time. |
| Construct validity | Its scores behave in a manner consistent with the theory of its construct. |

How the study is viewed depends on our particular interest. Table 2-2 summarizes these approaches to evaluating a measures validity.

## Approaches to Personality Assessment

Interviews.  Nearly all of us have at some time been interviewed for one purpose or another. Most of us have also conducted informal or unobtrusive interviews of our own. As a result, there is an easy familiarity about interviewing that is actually deceptive. Good interviewing is a complex skill that involves both science and art. Still, assessment interviews are probably the most basic and serviceable of all assessment procedures.

An assessment interview is, of course, an interaction between at least two persons. Good assessment interviews are carefully planned, deliberately and skillfully executed, and goal oriented. The assessment interview is not used to achieve personal satisfaction or enhanced prestige. It is employed to elicit data and information.

Whenever interviews are conducted in a more or less freewheeling, unstructured format, the reliability and validity of the information gained from those interviews is in question. The impact of the interviewer can be significant, and the idiosyncratic mix between interviewer and interviewee can be an unpredictable one. When interviewers are free to use their own format, their biases can be overly influential in affecting their conclusions. To counteract some of these problems of bias, reliability, and validity, the structured interview is often employed. Here, the format of the interview and the role of the interviewer are standardized. There is less variability from interview to interview, and the interviewer is obliged to maintain a greater degree of constancy across subjects. Of

Interviewing remains the most widely used method of gathering information from people.

course, this can result in reduced rapport and sometimes in loss of information. But the advantage comes in enhanced reliability and validity.

Self-Report Tests. Students are familiar with objective (multiple-choice and true-false) tests and often feel they have been taking them forever. Basically, **objective tests** used by personality psychologists ask the subject to provide self-reports about feelings, motives, behavior, or cognitions. Two examples will illustrate typical objective personality tests.

The *Fear Survey Schedule,* a test widely used by behaviorally oriented clinicians, was developed by Wolpe and Lang (1964) to reveal the stimuli that provoke anxiety. There are items relating to fear of death, illness, noise, planes, and so on. Subjects respond to each item on a five-point scale, from "very much" to "not at all".

The *Minnesota Multiphasic Personality Inventory (MMPI)* (Hathaway & McKinley, 1951) is the best-known and most widely used self-report personality inventory. It contains 550 items that describe a variety of behaviors, feelings, preferences, and beliefs. The subject is asked to respond "true" or "false" to each item depending on whether or not he or she thinks the item is an accurate (true) or inaccurate (false) self-description. The MMPI was originally designed to assess ten aspects of psychopathology, such as depression. However, the large number of items on the test have led many investigators to combine those items into many different scales.

The prominent role of objective, self-report scales in personality research is due to several factors. Some of these are as follows:

1. Self-reports are economical to use. Group testing is sometimes feasible; administration and scoring by computer are possible.
2. Administration and scoring tend to be simple and objective. This, in turn, requires less interpretive skill on the part of the investigator.
3. Because of straightforward scoring, interscorer reliability is nearly perfect.
4. Self-report scales are often valid for specific purposes, particularly when large numbers of subjects are used. The prediction of a specific individual's behavior is less satisfactory.

There are also some disadvantages to self-report measures:

1. Because of the transparent meaning of so many of the items, it is relatively easy for subjects to manage the impressions they wish to present.
2. Because these are self-report devices, subjects are reporting on themselves. But there may be aspects of themselves of which they are unaware or about which they have distorted views.
3. Because objective tests provide a limited number of possible answers, subjects can not elaborate or qualify responses.
4. In some instances, the subject's limited ability to understand items, or even his or her level of literacy, may result in misinterpretation.
5. Many self-report scales ask subjects to report mainly on various aspects of their behavior. But the same behavior can occur in different people for different reasons. This may lead to lowered validity.
6. In certain cases, scales are a mixture of items relating to behavior, needs, and cognitions. Therefore, two subjects may get the same total score for different reasons. This may lower validity.

Projective Tests. Because objective tests are relatively transparent, many people believe they do not tap the deeper, more dynamic layers of personality. Therefore, they prefer to use **projective tests**—tests whose stimuli are relatively ambiguous.

Although the following criteria do not apply to every projective test, taken as a whole they provide a general description of projective devices:

1. The stimuli (e.g., inkblots, unstructured pictures) are ambiguous.
2. The method is indirect. That is, typically the subject is relatively unaware of the exact purposes of the test and thus finds it harder to slant responses.
3. There is freedom of response. Subjects do not have to respond "yes" or "no". An inkblot can represent anything.
4. As a result, scoring reliability does not approach perfection.

The *Thematic Apperception Test (TAT)* is a good example of a projective test. The TAT was introduced by Christiana Morgan and Henry Murray in 1935, and it is designed to reveal individuals' basic personality characteristics through the interpretation of their imaginative productions in response to a set of ambiguous pictures. Originally, the test was developed to investigate personality from a psychoanalytic point of view. The subject is asked to make up a story about each picture, indicating who the people are; what they are doing, thinking, and feeling; what led up to the scene; and how it will turn out. By and large, the scoring is subjective, although some scoring manuals do exist, especially for research purposes.

The published research on the reliability and validity of projectives such as the TAT is disappointing. Although their emphasis on the inner determinants of personality is thought to be their strength, the research indicates projective responses to be determined by situational, transitory influences as well. Thus, data obtained from projective measures tend to be controversial. Certainly this is true clinically. In the research sphere, projectives are still used, but not as frequently as in the past.

**Behavioral Assessment.** In behavioral assessment, the emphasis is on what subjects are observed to do in situations and less on what they say they do. Self-report is supplanted by observation of performance. From the behavioral viewpoint, all behavior is determined by the conditions that prevail in any given situation. Behavior is maintained by rewarding conditions in the situation, and it drops out when punishment or the failure of rewards occurs. The interest, then, is not in underlying, unobservable, hypothesized constructs (needs, self-concept, etc.) but in observable, overt behavior and the specific stimuli that maintain it. Our concern moves from underlying personality to behavior and stimuli.

What this reflects is a **sign versus sample** approach to assessment. The sign approach treats behavior as a sign of an underlying psychological condition; the behavior itself is not of interest except that it provides a sign. A psychoanalyst would attempt to determine the factors that underlie certain behaviors and would view responses and behaviors. The sample approach treats behavior as a sample of the phenomenon of interest. That is, the overt behavior or response, not an underlying condition is the focus of study. A behaviorist is interested in sampling the behaviors that occur in certain situations and how they are affected by specific changes in those situations.

Behavioral assessment has also borrowed from traditional self-report approaches. For example, subjects may be asked to monitor their own behavior and systematically record the occurrence of specific behavior or stimulus conditions. Sometimes this has involved keeping a diary. Various self-report inventories have also been adapted or developed to measure fears and anxieties. The emphasis, however, is on overt behaviors and the conditions under which they occur rather than on unobservable, mediating constructs.

Behavioral assessment is a loose collection of techniques. What binds them together is their emphasis on behavior and the conditions surrounding its occurrence. Many of these techniques have not yet been rigorously examined for reliability or validity. In particular, it is often unclear how much observers tend to affect what they are observing. An analogous problem exists when subjects monitor their own behavior. In addition, the presumption of behavioral assessment is that a particular behavior in a particular situation has the same meaning for everyone. This assumption is almost certainly not valid (Golding, 1978). For example, consider a behavioral measure of assertiveness that consists of counting the number of times a subject speaks in a group discussion. Suppose that one subject is participating in the study to fulfil a class requirement and is not happy about being there. So, the subject sits in the group for the required 50 minutes and does not say a word. Behaviorally, the subject would be assessed as very unassertive, but is that the case? Friends of the subject and the subject as well might report the subject as highly assertive. Which type of measure would be the more valid?

**Physiological Measures.** In some cases the investigator may wish to use physiological measures to assess the relation between psychological processes and physiological responses. Some common physiological measures are heart rate, blood pressure, and biochemical assays. For example, anxiety might be studied by relating scores on a self-report measure of anxiety with pulse rate or blood pressure. A specific example of this is a study with *Type A* subjects (Simpson et al., 1974). These are subjects who show intense competitiveness, aggressiveness, and a desire to do more in less time (see Chapter 16). In response to stress, Type A subjects had high levels of norepinephrine in the blood. Norepinephrine is a hormone that raises diastolic blood pressure and when released in large amounts can lead to arterial damage.

## Nomological Network: Putting It All Together

The study of human personality requires a combination of theory, research, and assessment. But how do these three components come together in personality psychology? In 1955 Cronbach and Meehl published a paper of fundamental importance to psychology that provides a framework for understanding how assessment, research, and theory work together as tools of understanding. In this paper Cronbach and Meehl presented the concept of a **nomological network,** which is a representation of psychological theories. A nomological network is diagramed in Figure 2-5. The circles connected by bold lines are personality constructs such as intelligence, conscientiousness, and self-esteem. The bold lines show that these constructs are theoretically related to each other. The circles between the dashed lines and double lines are **indicants,** or measures, of the constructs. It is through these indicants that theoretical predictions about the relations among these constructs are tested. This is represented by the connection of the indicants to reality by the double lines.

For example, a theory of self-esteem (C2) states that people who are intelligent (C1) and conscientious (C3) have higher self-esteem. The theory will also stipulate that a measure of intelligence (C'1) is the *Wechsler Intelligence Scale,* a measure of self-esteem is the *Marsh Self-Description Questionnaire,* and a measure of conscientiousness is the *Big Five Inventory.* To test this theory, the three measures could be administered to a group of individuals and the correlations among those measures computed. If the research provides data that result in positive correlations, and if the measures used to indicate our constructs are valid, then support for the theory of self-esteem will have been provided. A failure of research or of measurement can prevent us from testing our theories.

The nomological network illustrates the indirect links between research and theory. These links go through our measures and sometimes other theoretical constructs as well. In addition, the nomological network underscores the uncertainty of our research results. A breakdown anywhere in the network will compromise the validity of our conclusions. Personality psychologists try to understand human nature and individuality from brief observations of behavior or from marks subjects make on a piece of paper. It is a challenging and difficult task.

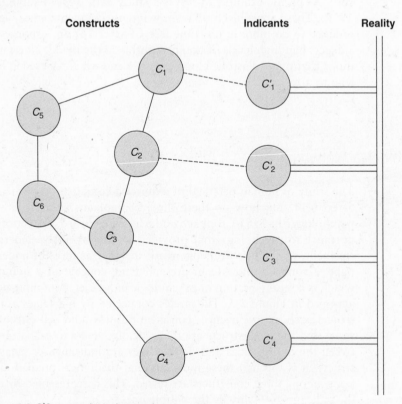

**Figure 2-5** ⟨⟩ A nomological network.

From *Personality and Prediction: Principles of Personality Assessment* (p. 399) by J.S. Wiggins, 1973. Reading, MA: Addison-Wesley.

# Summary

- There are many theories of personality that reflect different but equally reasonable interpretations of the same phenomena. Because human beings are complex, each theory captures only a part of that complexity.
- Constructs used in a particular personality theory represent the ways the theorist has chosen to describe reality. They are, however, just descriptions; they are not reality itself. Their purpose is to enhance our ability to predict and understand. As a result, they are judged by standards of verification and utility. Furthermore, each theory tends to have a focus of convenience. This means that a given theory will likely work better for some purposes than for others.
- The values of personality theory are several: they assist us in communication, they provide a framework for explanation, they help us expand our knowledge, and they encourage consistency in thinking.
- Theories tend to differ in numerous ways, including their systematic–unsystematic qualities, their explicit–implicit nature, whether they emphasize content or process, their general or specific application, and the degree to which they consider internal or situational factors as prime determinants of behavior. There are several dimensions that reflect the conflicting values within the field of personality.
- Typically, theories are evaluated by the extent to which they can deal with a broad range of important events. Parsimonious theories (those with an economical number of constructs) are usually preferred. Good theories were described as theories whose assumptions, propositions, and constructs are clearly and explicitly stated and that which fit together in a systematic way. Finally, good theories are useful theories.
- The importance of personality research resides in its capacity to take us out of the realm of rumination and speculation and into the arena of observation and experimentation.
- There are several forms of observation, including unsystematic observation, naturalistic observation, controlled field observation, and case study methods. Each approach has its strengths and weaknesses.
- In case study methods, qualitative studies are done on individuals, one at a time. Included are interview data, test responses, and autobiographical material. Of particular value in case studies is their ability to portray the richness and complexity of individuals.
- Experimental methods are a set of techniques employed in research. Some of their principal features including the control of the situation, random assignment of subjects, and use of control groups.
- For a time, the experimental-laboratory model of research was emphasized in the field of personality. The result was neglect of the organization of personality, emphasis on brief experiments that do not permit sustained contact with subjects, and problems replicating experimental findings.

- The reasons for an overreliance on the experimental method include the limitations of a purely idiographic approach, a desire to emulate the physical sciences, and the "publish or perish" syndrome in universities.
- The recognition that many methods, including experimental, correlational, and idiographic ones, can contribute to the study of personality will contribute to the growth of this discipline.
- We must distinguish between practical and statistical significance. Statistical significance is the beginning, not the end, of interpreting data.
- The analysis of single subjects has been found primarily in behavioral research. However, this method need not be restricted to the evaluation of techniques of behavior modification. Indeed, the analysis of the single case provides a basis for unifying nomothetic and idiographic perspectives in the same study.
- In approaching assessment, we must consider whether to view personality in general or specific terms. We must also keep in mind the test-taking attitudes of the subject. Finally, it was noted that poorly defined concepts lead to poorly conducted assessment.
- An important feature of test instruments is their reliability. Three forms of reliability were emphasized: test–retest reliability, internal consistency, and interjudge reliability.
- Validity of assessment techniques is essential and simply means that a test must measure what it purports to measure. Several forms of validity were discussed, including content validity, criterion validity, predictive validity, and construct validity.
- Interviews are still a common form of personality assessment. However, interviews are more likely to yield reliable and valid data if they are systematic and structured.
- Two examples of self-report tests were briefly discussed. Also, the general strengths and weaknesses of self-reports were addressed.
- The basic characteristics of projective tests were noted, and the TAT was briefly described.
- Behavioral assessment techniques focus less on what subjects say and more on what they actually do. The goal is to sample behaviors the subject uses rather than to seek signs of internal determinants. Several examples of behavioral assessment techniques were offered.
- A brief description of physiological methods was presented.
- The nomological network provides a framework for combining theory, research, and assessment. The nomological network highlights the indirect links between theoretical results and theoretical conjectures.

# Part 2
## Theories of Personality

art 2 is the longest and most fundamental section of this textbook. In Part 2 we describe and evaluate the major theoretical perspectives on personality and summarize the research that has been generated by each perspective. Each major theoretical perspective is represented by two chapters. The first chapter in each pair describes the major theories that have been developed within each perspective. The major implications for development, adjustment, and behavior change are also considered. The second chapter in each pair summarizes the research that each theory has generated and describes the major methods of personality assessment that characterize each theory. Finally, a critical evaluation of the strengths and weaknesses of each theoretical perspective is provided.

Chapters 3 and 4 concern the theories that have been developed out of the psychodynamic perspective that was pioneered by Sigmund Freud. The psychodynamic perspective emphasizes a combination of biological and cognitive influences on personality. Chapters 5 and 6, which are new to this edition, concern the theories that emphasize biological and particularly genetic influences on personality. Chapters 7 and 8 concern phenomenological, humanistic, and social cognitive theories of personality. These chapters emphasize the primary influence of cognition, self-awareness, and personal constructs on personality. In Chapters 9 and 10 we describe traditional behavioral theories of personality that emphasize the influence of the environment through classic learning theory on personality. In Chapters 11 and 12 social learning theories are considered. Social learning theories are based on a powerful combination of environmental and cognitive influences on personality and represent one of the most modern approaches to studying personality.

This section closes with a discussion of trait theories in Chapters 13 and 14. In previous editions these chapters were titled "dispositional" theories with an emphasis on the causal status of traits. The perspective in this edition is that after psychodynamic, biological, cognitive, phenomenological, environmental, and social learning forces have had their influence, we are left with an individual whose personality requires description. The emphasis in these chapters is on theories of how personality might be described and the major descriptive models that have been used to structure individual differences.

# Chapter 3
# Psychoanalytic Theory: The Freudian Revolution, Dissent, and Revision

The Beginnings of the Psychoanalytic Age
Basic Theory
    Psychic Determinism
    Unconscious Motivation
    Instincts
Structure of Personality
    The Id
    The Ego
    The Superego
Development of Personality
    The Oral Stage
    The Anal Stage
    The Phallic Stage
    The Latency Period
    The Genital Stage
Anxiety and Ego Defenses
    Anxiety
    Defense Mechanisms
Personality and Adjustment
Approaches to Psychotherapy and Behavior
   Change
    Goals of Therapy
    The Therapeutic Circumstance
    Free Association
    Dream Analysis

Interpretation
Resistance to Analysis
Transference
Working Through
Dissent
Adler's Individual Psychology
    Inferiority and Compensation
    Striving for Superiority
    Social Interest
    Style of Life
    Development of Personality
    Personality and Adjustment
    Approaches to Psychotherapy and
      Behavior Change
Jung's Analytic Psychology
    Personality Structure
    Archetypes
    Psychological Types and Personality
The Neo-Freudians
    Karen Horney
    Erich Fromm
    Harry Stack Sullivan
    Ego Psychology
Contemporary Psychoanalytic Theories
    The Theory of Object Relations
    The Self-Psychology of Kohut
Summary

Psychoanalytic theory, the creation of Sigmund Freud, has been the most influential contribution of the field of personality to scholarly thought. Hardly an area of life today has not been touched by this theory. It is reflected in our art, our literature, and our cinema. One is as likely (perhaps even more likely) to encounter psychoanalytic discussions and analysis in English departments as in psychiatry offices. Historians can be heard talking about prominent figures from a Freudian perspective. Many popular child-rearing beliefs have distinctly Freudian roots, and when we encounter psychological difficulties, we may consult a psychotherapist whose practice is influenced by Freudian ideas. Terms such as *ego, unconscious, death wish,* and *Freudian slip* are common in everyday conversation.

However, Freud's ideas initially received a rough reception. Psychologists of the time were accustomed to the ideas of Wilhelm Wundt, the founder of scientific psychology (Leahey, 1984). Wundt made the analysis of consciousness the centerpiece of investigation. Freud's ideas about the importance of unconscious forces in the mind, and his consideration of sex and aggressive urges to be the principal motivators of human behavior, earned him abuse and ridicule from the community at large. Remember that Freud wrote during the "genteel" Victorian era; "straitlaced" would not be an idle description of Vienna at the end of the nineteenth century. People perceived Freud as chaining the human mind to animal lusts. In relation to a society that could contemplate only conscious thought and the primacy of will, Freud was seen as a heretic. In addition, being a Jew, Freud was also subject to anti-Semitic attacks.

## The Beginnings of the Psychoanalytic Age

In 1885 Freud was awarded a grant that allowed him to travel to Paris to study hysteria with the famous French neurologist Jean Charcot. Hysteria was then regarded as a "female" disorder characterized most often by paralysis, blindness, and deafness. Charcot had found that some hysterical patients would, while under hypnosis, relinquish their hysterical symptoms and even at times recall the traumatic experiences that had generated them. Undoubtedly, the recall Freud observed in hypnotized patients played an important role in the development of his later ideas about the nature of the unconscious.

Some years earlier, Freud's curiosity had been aroused by Josef Breuer's experiences with a young hysteric, Anna O. This young woman had many of the classic hysterical symptoms, along with a double personality. The death of her father had apparently precipitated many of her difficulties. Breuer treated Anna using hypnosis, and during one session, in the midst of a trance, she told him about the first appearance of one of her symptoms. The curious thing was that when she came out of the trance, the symptom was gone! Realizing he was on to something, Breuer repeated the procedures over a period of time, with some success.

## A BRIEF BIOGRAPHY OF

## Sigmund Freud

Sigmund Freud was born in 1856 in Austria and grew up in Vienna, the oldest of seven children. After completing a classical education, he studied medicine at the University of Vienna. He received his medical degree in 1881 and soon took a research position. Although he was not particularly interested in private practice, three things conspired to make him relinquish his research appointment. First, he recognized that as a Jew he stood little chance of achieving advancement in the academic research environment, which was full of anti-Semitic sentiment. Second, his research work showed scant promise of ever allowing him to make much money. Third, he had fallen in love with Martha Bernays; marriage takes money, and Freud had none. As a result, he opened a practice as a neurologist. His marriage (in 1886) to Martha produced six children; one, Anna Freud, became a famous psychoanalyst.

About the time of his marriage, Freud began a brief but productive collaboration with Josef Breuer, a well-known physician in Vienna. Together they followed up Breuer's discovery of the "talking cure," a method by which the patient alleviates neurotic symptoms by talking about them. In 1895, Breuer and Freud published *Studies on Hysteria*. Then the two men had a falling-out. Some suggest money as the problem; others believe that Breuer became alarmed over Freud's emphasis on the role of sex in

Freud's interest in Anna O., coupled with his experiences with Charcot, led him to expand his practice. Many of his new patients presented hysterical symptoms with no organic basis. (Although hysterical symptoms are not so common now, they were quite prevalent in the emotionally repressive environment of Vic-

"Anna O." Bertha Pappenheim was identified by Ernest Jones (1953) as Breuer's patient Anna O. She carried out a remarkable career as a pioneer in the feminist movement and as a social reformer. In 1954, 18 years after her death, West Germany issued a stamp honoring her achievements.

hysteria. Whatever the cause, their collaboration had served its purpose: the foundation for psychoanalytic theory had been established.

Freud's most acclaimed work, *The Interpretation of Dreams,* was published in 1900, capping a remarkably productive decade. With the dawn of the twentieth century his work began to attract adherents. The Vienna Psycho-Analytical Society was founded, and followers began to flock to his side. However, a few years later several of these converts left the orthodox Freudian camp to develop their separate theories. Notable among them were Alfred Adler, Carl Jung, and Otto Rank. In 1909 Freud was invited to the United States to lecture at Clark University. The whole world now knew about Sigmund Freud.

Numerous books and achievements followed. But as the 1930s began, so too did Nazi harassment. Freud's books were burned, and he became a popular anti-Semitic target. Eventually Freud was allowed to emigrate to England. His last years were not pleasant. He suffered great pain from cancer of the jaw, undergoing 32 operations. A heavy cigar smoker, he periodically gave up cigars, although never completely. He died in September 1939.

An excellent biography of Freud was written by his longtime friend and fellow analyst, Ernest Jones (1953, 1955, 1957). A brief and readable account of the life of Freud may be found in Geiwitz and Moursund (1979).

torian Vienna.) Freud treated many of these patients with hypnotic procedures. Some patients, however, were difficult to hypnotize; others had the annoying tendency to awaken from a trance with no memory of what had transpired, thus cancelling many of the positive features of the method. A case in point was Elisabeth, a patient Freud saw in 1892. Rather than hypnotize Elisabeth, Freud asked her to concentrate on her ailment and remember when it began. He had her lie on a couch while he pressed her forehead with his hand. Although it took years to perfect the technique, this was the beginning of what later became the method of free association.

Freud's ideas did not come only from his experience with patients. Using himself as a subject, he spent long hours in self-analysis because he firmly believed that his theory applied not only to others but to himself as well.

These were the beginnings of psychoanalytic approaches to personality as well as a therapeutic method for treating neurosis. Breuer's work with Anna O. had led to the "talking cure," and this, in turn, was transformed into free association during Freud's work with Elisabeth. **Free association** meant simply that the patient was to say everything that came to mind; nothing was to be censored, no matter how silly, dull, revolting, or irrelevant it might appear. Freud also had realized that Anna had transferred to Breuer many of her feelings toward significant males in her life. This concept of **transference** would ultimately prove to be a valuable diagnostic tool in understanding the nature of the patient's problems, especially unconscious ones. By employing hypnosis, Freud learned that patients could relive traumatic events associated with the onset of their hysterical symptoms. In some cases, reliving the event released what could be described as "bottled-up energy." This became known as **catharsis**, a process often producing therapeutic effects.

In his work with Elisabeth, Freud also observed **resistance**, a general obstinacy toward discussing, remembering, or thinking about especially troubling or threatening events. Initially he saw this as a kind of defense, but later he called it **repression**, the involuntary banishment of a thought or impulse to the unconscious. The **unconscious** was the area of the mind not accessible to conscious thought.

## Basic Theory

Psychoanalytic theory (Freud, 1938) is based on two important assumptions: **psychic determinism** and **unconscious motivation**. In addition, human motivation is viewed as instinctive.

### Psychic Determinism

Psychic determinism is Freud's assumption that everything we do, think, or feel has meaning and purpose. From seemingly inconsequential actions such as slips of the tongue or gestures to major life decisions such as career choices—all have meaning and specific origins in the experience of the individual. Strictly speaking, of course, most behaviors have multiple determinants. For example, the decison of who to marry is influenced by the opportunity to meet the person, feelings of attraction, and, of course, that person's willingness to marry. Freud's early scientific training led him to seek causes of any and all behavior. Events were never chance occurrences or the result of free will. The assumption of psychic determinism allows the analyst to use a wide array of data in the search for an explanation of a patient's behavior. Often this search took Freud into the depths of the unconscious.

### Unconscious Motivation

Freud was convinced that a major portion of our behavior, thoughts, and feelings is determined by motives about which we are completely unaware. The idea of unconscious motivation did not originate with Freud but with the experimental psychologist Hermann Ebbinghaus, who published the first study on "inten-

Freud's office

tional forgetting" in 1885. However, Freud made the most extensive use of this concept in his theorizing. It is easy to see why Freud used this concept as he struggled to explain Anna O.'s ability to remember certain events while hypnotized and her inability to recall them in the waking state. Box 3-1 illustrates how our motives may remain unknown to us.

Freud conceptualized the mind as consisting of conscious, preconscious, and unconscious components. The **conscious** component represents everything of which an individual is aware at any given moment, such as sensations, perceptions, experiences, and memories. Freud believed the conscious component to be a small fraction of our mental life.

The **preconscious** component represents those things accessible to the person at any given time. The memories and material stored there are not immediately conscious but with some effort can be recalled. For example, I cannot at this moment recall the first psychology text I read, but with a little concentration and a few associations I could probably remember it.

The **unconscious** component is a largely inaccessible repository of urges and drives, or what might be viewed biologically as instincts. Although the individual is unaware of their existence, these drives or instincts are active forces that seek expression and are the major determinants of behavior. The vast majority of the contents of the mind are unconscious.

B O X   3 - 1
## Are We Always Aware of the Motives for Our Behavior?

Hypnosis played an important role in the early development of psychoanalysis. It has also been used by some to demonstrate the role of unconscious motivation. Take the following example:

> To illustrate how sincerely the subject believes in the authenticity of his posthypnotic experiences, I may cite an example of a posthypnotic negative hallucination induced in a man in the presence of one of my colleagues, Dr. S. The latter physician, skeptical about hypnosis, entered my office unexpectedly at a time when an experimental subject, known to both of us, was in a hypnotic trance. I suggested to the subject that when he woke up he would neither be able to see nor hear Dr. S. Upon awakening, the subject engaged me in a conversation regarding the pennant possibilities of the Dodgers, in the middle of which he casually asked if I had seen Dr. S. recently. I rejoined by asking him the same question. During this conversation, Dr. S. was leaning up against a window. I informed the subject that I was expecting Dr. S. and asked him to look out of the window to see whether he was in sight. The subject looked directly at Dr. S. and said, "No, he isn't." Inquiring as to what he saw, he remarked that he noticed the usual trees, grass, and buildings. At this point, Dr. S. addressed the subject directly. The latter interrupted him in the middle of a sentence with a remark pointed at myself. Dr. S. continued talking, but the subject paid absolutely no attention to him as if he were not in the room. At this point, I held an inkwell in the air and asked him if he saw it. Perplexed, he admitted that he could and wondered why I had asked him so silly a question. I then handed the inkwell to Dr. S. and asked the subject again if he could see the inkwell. He looked intently at the inkwell and exclaimed, "My God, you will think I am crazy, but the inkwell is floating around in space." He appeared to be genuinely alarmed. I took the inkwell from Dr. S. and he said, "You have the inkwell now." Even though I insisted that Dr. S. was in the room and pointed him out, the subject continued to believe that I was joking. He remarked that fortunately he had not yet lost his mind. He was certain that there was no other person in the room until I rehypnotized him and removed the suggestion.
>
> The most compulsive nature of the posthypnotic act is one of its most characteristic features. This is not to say that the suggestion cannot be resisted. Usually, however, resistance takes a tremendous effort. (Wolberg, 1948, pp. 56–57)

*(continued)*

BOX 3-1 (*continued*)

The exact explanation for hypnotic phenomena is still controversial. Some, such as Hilgard (1978), regard hypnosis as a state of altered consciousness in which people are more suggestible, show enhanced imagery and imagination, more uncritically accept distortions of reality, and believe firmly that they are in an altered state of consciousness. Others, such as Spanos (1991), explain hypnosis as a state in which the person is merely enacting a role or responding to the hypnotists expectations. Subjects behave in a fashion they believe to be characteristic of a hypnotized person.

Whatever the explanation for hypnosis, one thing does seem clear. Hypnotized individuals have great difficulty expressing the "real" motives guiding their behavior in the trance and, indeed, even acknowledging their trance behavior in many cases. Although scientific agreement here is elusive, hypnosis has, and will continue to be, an important tool for studying the nature of consciousness.

From *Medical Hypnosis* by Lewis R. Wolberg, M.D. Copyright © 1948 The Psychological Corporation. Reprinted by permission.

## Instincts

Reflecting his medical and biological training, Freud viewed human motivation as the result of the needs of the physical body. How these basic biological needs are translated into unconscious motives, and how these, in turn, are manifested in the myriad of activities in which humans can engage has yet to be solved satisfactorily by psychoanalytic theory. In general, however, states of psychic arousal brought on by needs are thought to give rise to mental representations, or wishes. Collections of wishes are termed **instincts**. The aim of these instincts is the reduction of tension, which is experienced as pleasure. Therefore, instincts have (1) a *source*, which is a state of arousal within the body, (2) an *aim*, which is the removal of that arousal, and (3) an *object,* which is either within the person's body or, more commonly, something in the external environment that will satisfy the aim.

Life Instincts.  The **life instincts** (**eros**) are the bases for all positive or constructive aspects of human behavior. The life instincts originate in bodily urges such as sex, hunger, and thirst but ultimately may be reflected in the creative components of culture such as art, music, literature, cooperation, and love. The energy responsible for the life instincts is called **libido**. The most important parts of the body from which libido arises are the **erotogenic zones**. These are parts of the skin or mucous membranes that are extremely sensitive to irritation and which, when manipulated in certain ways, remove the irritation and produce pleasurable sensations (Hall and Lindzey, 1978). For example, drinking water removes the irritation of a dry throat and produces the pleasurable sensation of quenching thirst.

Psychoanalysts suggest that many adult activities, whether ordinary or extraordinary, are determined by unconscious motivation.

Death Instincts. Initially, Freud relied on the life instincts as the basic human motivator. However, he found it difficult to use life instincts to explain the dark, destructive side of behavior. Freud was especially appalled by World War I and its crushing costs in human life and dignity. As a result, he introduced the concept of the **death instincts** (**thanatos**). However, the concept of death instincts has never been well developed. For example, the source of psychic energy for these instincts that would correspond to libido for the life instincts was never specified. In addition, the death instincts were not differentiated from each other. Freud simply argued that we are all born with the urge to return to an inanimate state.

## Structure of Personality

As Freud continued to see more patients, his initial theory proved to be insufficient. The ideas of a conscious and an unconscious mind seemed to account for hysterics but not for patients who were paranoid or who experienced an overwhelming sense of guilt. Freud's solution was to add to his theory by introducing the concepts of the id, the ego, and the superego. Which further subdivided the conscious, preconscious, and unconscious components of the mind (see Figure 3-1).

| OUTER WORLD | | |
| --- | --- | --- |
| Conscious | Super | E |
| Preconscious | E | g |
| Unconscious | g<br>o | o |
| | | Id |

**Figure 3-1** ∞ A representation of Freud's structural model of the mind. The ego and the superego make up a relatively small portion of the mind, although they have conscious, preconscious, and unconscious components. The majority of the mind is unconscious and dominated by the id.

Adapted from *The Structure and Meaning of Psychoanalysis* by Healy, W., Bronner, A. F., and Bowers, A. M., 1930. New York: Alfred A. Knopf.

## The Id

The **id** represents the deep, inaccessible part of the personality. It is in direct contact with biological needs and bodily processes and is the repository for everything inherited and fixed in the person's constitution. The id has no connection with the external world and therefore is the true psychic reality. We learn about the id indirectly through the analysis of dreams and various forms of neurotic behavior. Within the id reside the instinctual urges, in particular the sexual and aggressive instincts. The id is devoid of values, ethics, and logic. Its sole concern is the immediate and unhampered gratification of the instincts.

The reigning goal of the id is the achievement of an excitation-free state or, if that cannot be done, the lowest possible level of excitation. The id is said to obey the **pleasure principle,** which means that pleasure is good and nothing else matters. To reduce excitation and achieve pleasure, the id uses the **primary process**. This means that during early infancy, tension is discharged as quickly as it reaches the id. At first, this is done by immediately expending energy in motor activity (e.g., a swelling bladder leading to immediate urination). Later the id turns to another form of the primary process, in which it manufactures a mental image of whatever will reduce the tension. Thus, hunger results in a mental representation of food. This kind of thinking is neither logical, organized, nor mature. Failing the immediate attainment of an object that will satisfy the urge, the person may well hallucinate. Dreaming is an excellent example of primary-process thinking in which reality and logic fade and the most improbable and contradictory events occur together.

Unfortunately for the id, dreams and hallucinations do not completely satisfy the needs of the organism. It is the failures of the id's primary-process mode of operation to provide real gratifications that leads to the development of the ego.

## The Ego

The director of an individual's personality might be the most apt description of the ego. The **ego** is the organized, rational, reality-oriented system of the personality. It operates according to the **reality principle** in that it defers gratification of instinctual urges until a suitable object and method are found. To accomplish this it uses the **secondary process**, which involves perception, learning, memory, and reality testing.

The ego is pragmatic and also without values; it simply does what will work. This does not, however, mean that the ego always takes the immediate, most direct route to satisfying needs. It is also responsible for maintaining the integrity of the organism by any means possible. Although its goal is to satisfy the id, it will do so only in the context of the demands of reality. This means that the ego must juggle the often outrageous demands of the id, the constraints of the real world, and the prohibitions of the conscience.

## The Superego

The **superego** develops from the ego and out of the resolution of the child's unacceptable sexual attraction to the parent of the opposite sex. The superego represents the ideals and values of society as they are presented to the child through the words and actions of parents or parental surrogates. These ideals and values are also fostered in the child through systematic rewards and punishments. That which is punished generally becomes incorporated into the part of the superego known as the **conscience**. Rewarded behavior becomes represented in the superego as the **ego-ideal**. Eventually the conscience comes to serve the purpose of punishing individuals by making them feel worthless or guilty. The ego-ideal rewards the individual by conveying a sense of pride and personal value. In summary, the job of the superego is to inform the ego of the value of morality rather than lust or expediency and to remind the person to strive toward perfection.

As a way of recalling the character and functions of the three components of the personality, consider the following description from Geiwitz and Moursund (1979):

> Imagine a sex-starved hedonist, a black-frock-coated Puritan minister, and a totally humorless computer scientist chained together and turned loose in the world, and you have a good approximation of what Freud was trying to show us about the personality.

Because they are chained together, the id, ego, and superego cannot decide to go their separate ways. They have no alternative but to adjust to one another. And the result, for better or for worse, is the adult human personality. (p. 27)

## Development of Personality

 Freud's patients frequently talked about their sexualized encounters with their parents, including seductiveness, rivalries, and attractions, and Freud had similar memories about his own life. Freud's descriptions are similar to the recent highly publicized phenomenon of repressed memories (Loftus, 1993), in which patients, often after years of psychotherapy, report recovering memories of early abuse by their parents. These memories have provided the basis for some controversial legal actions and public accusations. For example, the actress Roseanne Barr Arnold's story of abuse by her mother when she was an infant made the cover of *People* magazine ("A Star Cries Incest," 1991). Likewise, a former Miss America, Marilyn Van Derber, reported repressing memories of sexual violation by her father until she was 24 years old, and went public with her story only after her father died (Darnton, 1991).

What Freud realized, but what has apparently escaped many contemporary psychotherapists, reporters, lawyers, and judges, is that these patients, and Freud himself, may not have been recalling real history. Instead, they were remembering fantasies or were constructing memories to explain their current anxiety and psychological distress (Ganaway, 1992). Thus, sexual instincts and the unconscious joined to produce fantasies, and these fantasies are the basis of Freud's stage theory of psychosexual development.

### The Oral Stage

It is evident that a newborn infant is totally dependent on others. Just as evident is that the infant's mouth, lips, and tongue are the center of its existence and are intimately associated with survival. At this time, libido is largely distributed in the oral region, and sucking and swallowing become the chief methods of reducing biological needs and therefore achieving pleasure. This stage lasts from birth to roughly 8 months of age and is known as the **oral sucking** period. At about 8 months, weaning begins, the breast is withdrawn, and other foods are offered. This can be a traumatic time, especially if the weaning is done abruptly and in an uncaring fashion. In such an event, vestiges of the oral sucking period may stay with the person throughout life.

From about 8 to 18 months the child is in what is called the **oral biting** period. The teeth have erupted, and the child now has a weapon with which to vent frustration. During this period aggression begins to develop, and the child realizes his or her separateness from the mother.

## The Anal Stage

As a result of weaning, pressure to develop habits of cleanliness, and possibly the birth of a sibling, the child begins to face the intrusions of the external world. The ego is beginning to differentiate itself from the id, and the reality principle begins to arise. This is the **anal stage** and lasts from about 6 months to 4 years of age. The chief mode of pleasure is in expelling feces and urine. During this stage the battle of wills between parents and child occurs. Toilet training is a major socialization event. The parents reward the child for urinating or defecating at the right time—for deferring gratification. They also punish or express disappointment at the child's accidents. All of this creates in the child the crude beginnings of the superego.

The child may also learn how to manipulate the parents by using elimination processes as aggressive weapons. Thus, he or she may demand "potty" when none is available or sit for hours while an impatient parent waits for the ultimate present from a socialized child. This period is usually appropriately called the **anal expulsive stage** (approximately 6 months to 3 years of age). During the **anal retentive stage** (approximately 12 months to 4 years of age), the child learns the importance of controlling, retaining, and possessing feces. The realization of the ability to do all this can lead to a feeling of omnipotence. After all, the child can present feces to the parents almost as gifts—gifts that are greatly appreciated when they occur at the right time and in the right place. They can also serve as punishment by angering parents or disrupting their routine when presented at inappropriate times or places.

## The Phallic Stage

Somewhere around 4 years of age, the genital region becomes the focus of erogenous interest. This marks the beginning of the **phallic stage**, which typically lasts until about the age of 7 or 8. During this time the child's interest shifts to a narcissistic preoccupation with genitals. The child may touch, rub, and exhibit his or her own genitals and may show interest in the anatomy of brothers, sisters, and parents. The child is beginning to formulate some ideas about sex and birth. These ideas are often naive or incorrect, but the child is becoming aware that babies are made not by some remote magic but rather by activities that occur at home. The child is also learning that sex involves making choices among potential sexual objects. It is natural that in the limited world of the child, his or her choice for sexual interest becomes a readily available member of the opposite sex: mother, father, or a sibling.

The male child's burgeoning interest in his mother begins to annoy both his father and mother. Interrupting her bath, wanting to be around her all the time, climbing into bed (on the mother's side) in the middle of the night—these and other behaviors result in warnings from the father to stop. This makes the father appear to be a fearsome rival, and threats of castration may be imagined. At this point the family is in the midst of the **Oedipus complex**. To ward off conflict and the threat of castration (a real source of worry, since he has already discovered that the little girl down the block has no penis, and worries that could happen to him!), the child begins to employ a process called **identification with the aggressor**. He resolves the Oedipus conflict by identifying with his father—adopting his values, goals, and even mannerisms. In an indirect fashion, by identifying with his father he can vicariously possess his mother. The final resolution of the Oedipus conflict brings with it, through the identification process, a more fully developed superego.

The Oedipus complex is characterized by the male child's attachment to his mother.

For the female child, the process is different. How different is not clear because the nature of the phallic-stage process for girls, called the **Electra complex,** was never as fully explicated by either Freud or subsequent analysts as it was for boys.

In essence, Freud's description of the Electra complex centered on the girl's lack of a penis. Therefore, she cannot fear castration; it has already happened. Instead, she sets about deciding who did it. She decides it was her mother and begins to hate her for what has been done. (Many analysts believe that this attribution is ultimately responsible for the ambivalence many females have toward their mothers for the rest of their lives.) At the same time she starts blaming her mother, she increases her love for her father. Psychoanalysts often assert that her love for her father is heavily dependent on **penis envy.** Some believe that a woman, therefore, goes through life behaving in ways that reflect her dismay over having lost the penis: search for power, envy of the male role, or personal devaluation because of "imperfect" anatomy (even having a baby becomes symbolic of regaining the lost penis). Eventually, however, the girl realizes that her loss is permanent and shifts her identification to the mother. Not surprisingly, this aspect of Freudian theory has been strongly criticized by feminist scholars (see Box 3-2).

## The Latency Period

Somewhere between the ages of 5 and 6, the child enters the **latency period,** which will last until about 12 or 13 years of age. This is an asexual period, during which all things sexual are inhibited or even repressed. The resolution of the Oedipus/Electra situation has been traumatic, and the child wants to forget those experiences. There is little interest in the opposite sex. Boys play with boys, girls with girls; and any interest in the opposite sex is likely to take the form of teasing and tormenting. Boys in particular want no displays of affection.

## The Genital Stage

The biochemical and hormonal changes that usher in puberty mark the beginning of the **genital stage,** the final stage of psychosexual development as described by Freud. Both the aggressive and sexual instincts become active, and there is again a focus on the opposite sex. Now, however, sexuality is less auto-erotic and narcissistic. Thus, increased sexual interest and excitability are accompanied by the "ethereal" love and romance of adolescence. When the genital stage first dawns, however, the threat of castration is still present, so initial experiences are often homosexual. This may be seen in such a phenomenon as mutual masturbation. Gradually, however, the focus shifts to a concern with heterosexual relationships, courting, marriage, and raising a family. Thus, from a Freudian

BOX 3-2
## Feminine Psychology—Freudian Style

Freud's ideas about women have focused almost exclusively on the *fact* that they lack a penis and on the *hypothesis* that this leads to penis envy. He claimed that because the woman never adequately resolves her Oedipal problems, her superego fails to develop properly. It is almost as if she remains angry and unfulfilled because of her presumed castration. She becomes narcissistic, vain, and envious. If she is lucky she will later marry and have a baby (ideally a boy), which is really a penis substitute. As Bootzin and Acocella (1988) summarize the Freudian view:

> [the] woman is morally feeble, culturally unproductive, and somehow "other"—a variation on the standard of masculinity, a deviation from the norm. Thus, the little girl's perception of herself as castrated, and her consequent envy, is responsible for her inferiority. (p. 45)

But as early as 1926, Karen Horney sarcastically suggested that Freud was not in a good position to understand little girls. Furthermore, she argued that little girls do not see their lack of a penis as being evidence of inferiority. It is little boys who react that way. And they grow up to be men who then try to force this idea of inferiority onto women (Horney, 1967). More recently, theorists such as Nancy Chodorow (1978) and Carol Gilligan (1982) concede that the child's attachment to its mother is critical for the development of masculine or feminine outlooks. But boys and girls show differing patterns of attachment, even though in the beginning they both regard the mother as the primary love object during early infancy. Later, the girl must adopt the feminine role and the boy must become masculine. For boys, an enduring value becomes a sense of being separate from others. For girls, there is not nearly so strong a need to see themselves as separate. Thus, the girl does not grow up to see herself as inferior or enmeshed in an eternal search for a penis. Rather, she becomes an adult with a stronger need for, and better ability to develop, close attachments to others than is true for many men.

perspective the ultimate aim of the genital stage is mature, adult sexuality. The narcissism, autoeroticism, and continuous seeking of immediate pleasure must be exchanged for loving and caring for others, for work, for postponement of gratification, and for responsibility. In this way, the expression of the sexual instincts that begins with sucking and swallowing culminates in the maturity of adulthood—at least ideally. This may not be the outcome for those persons who have been over- or under-gratified during earlier psychosexual stages.

# Anxiety and Ego Defenses

 **Anxiety**

Although the concept of **anxiety** has always been a central concept in psychoanalytic theory, Freud revised his views on it several times. His final notion was that anxiety is a warning to the ego of impending danger. The danger may come from several sources.

**Reality anxiety** is a response to a threat from the real world. For example, if I become anxious as I see a car bearing down on me, this is reality anxiety. This type of anxiety is basically the same as fear and serves to warn me that I had better do something to evade the danger. Of course, in some instances the anxiety can be so strong as to actually impede the individual's ability to cope.

**Neurotic anxiety** is a response to the threatened eruption of an id impulse into consciousness. Very early we learn that expressing our sexual or aggressive instincts directly will lead to punishment from our parents. Initially this is a reality kind of anxiety, but as development proceeds we may become apprehensive whenever the ego discerns instinctual impulses from the id. For example, a teenaged boy's avoidance of social interactions with girls may be the result of the anxiety he feels about the sexual feelings those girls arouse in him.

**Moral anxiety** stems from threat of punishment from the superego. It is expressed in feelings of guilt or shame. As an id impulse threatens to gain gratification in an "immoral" fashion, the superego responds accordingly. For example, when people who are brought up believing that alcohol is evil are given alcoholic drink, their anxiety may make them stammer and appear socially awkward.

All these forms of anxiety are experienced similarly by the ego; the difference lies in the source and not in the quality of the emotion. In addition, it may be obvious that reality anxiety, unless it is overwhelming, can help us deploy perception, memory, learning, and action in the service of avoiding the environmental threat. But what about threats from within—that is, moral and neurotic anxiety? Internal threats can be difficult to manage. Id impulses never go away; they leave only when the organism dies. Therefore, how does the ego handle the constant and contradictory demands of id and superego?

## Defense Mechanisms

Freud decided that id impulses can either be prevented from reaching awareness or distorted so that the superego is fooled. A variety of ego defenses or **defense mechanisms** can be used to accomplish this deception. All defense mechanisms distort or falsify experience and use psychic resources that could be used more constructively. Also, defense mechanisms are employed unconsciously. Most of us resort to one or another of these defenses at various times, but neurotic individuals use them more frequently. An individual's personality is, in part, a function of the particular defensive strategies that he or she favors, although most individuals employ different defense mechanisms in response to different threats. The major defense mechanisms listed in the diagnostic manual (DSM-IV) of the American Psychiatric Association (1994) are summarized and illustrated in Table 3-1.

## Personality and Adjustment

Freud, like most other personality theorists, regarded the ability to take pleasure in love and work as the mark of the adjusted personality. The realization of one's potential depends heavily on experiences during psychosexual development. The particular stage at which difficulties are encountered will leave specific marks on the adult personality. As a general rule, the earlier the level at which difficulties are experienced, the more severe the effects on personality. For example, frustrations at the oral stage will likely influence personality more than problems that occur at the phallic stage.

Many of the character traits of the adult are a function of the stage at which problems developed and the particular defenses used to deal with these problems. Table 3-2 provides some examples of the relations among psychosexual stages, defense mechanisms, and adult personality. Remnants of the psychosexual stages exist in all of us; achievement of the total maturity that characterizes the genital stage is only an ideal.

## Approaches to Psychotherapy and Behavior Change

Freud's psychoanalytic theory was intimately linked to psychotherapy and the process of behavior change. An unreasonable fear, an excessive character trait, a propensity for rationalization—all are signs of a deeper problem. Thus, the fear itself is not the problem but rather a superficial manifestation of an underlying conflict. It is not the reaction formation (see Table 3-1) of someone with puritanical attitudes toward sex that is of interest, but what the reaction formation signifies about the nature of the unconscious conflict of which it is symptomatic.

### Goals of Therapy

It would be wrong to assume that the ultimate goal of psychoanalysis is the simple removal of discrete symptoms, although that is part of it. Rather, what Freud tried to accomplish in therapy was a general strengthening of a person's ego so that instinctual impulses could be brought under control. The broad goal, then, became one of facilitating the sublimation of aggressive and sexual impulses. In psychoanalysis, one can learn about the nature of inner needs. But more than that, one can learn to direct those needs rather than be directed by them.

## Table 3-1
## Major Defensive Reactions

| Mechanism | Example |
|---|---|
| **Denial of reality**. Protecting self from an unpleasant reality by refusal to perceive or face it. | A smoker concludes that the evidence linking cigarette use to health problems is scientifically worthless. |
| **Fantasy**. Gratifying frustrated desires by imaginary achievements. | A socially inept and inhibited young man imagines himself chosen by a group of women to provide them with sexual satisfaction. |
| **Emotional insulation**. Reducing ego involvement by protective withdrawal and passivity. | A child separated from her parents because of illness and lengthy hospitalization becomes emotionally unresponsive and apathetic. |
| **Intellectualization (isolation)**. Preventing affect in hurtful situations by separating incompatible attitudes into logic-tight compartments. | A prisoner on death row awaiting execution resists appeals on his behalf and coldly insists that the letter of the law be followed. |
| **Undoing**. Atoning for, or magically trying to dispel, unacceptable desires or acts. | A teenager who feels guilty about masturbation ritually touches door knobs a prescribed number of times following each occurrence of the act. |
| **Overcompensation**. Covering up felt weaknesses by emphasizing a desirable characteristic or making up for frustration in one area by overgratification in another. | A dangerously overweight woman goes on eating binges when she feels neglected by her husband. |
| **Acting out**. Engaging in antisocial or excessive behavior without regard to negative consequences as a way of dealing with emotional stress. | An unhappy, frustrated sales representative has several indiscriminant affairs without regard to the negative effects of the behavior. |
| **Splitting**. Viewing oneself or others as *all* good or bad without integrating positive or negative qualities of the person into the evaluation. That is, reacting to others in an "all or none" manner rather than considering the full range of their qualities. | A conflicted manager does not recognize individual qualities or characteristics of her employees. Instead, she views each of them as entirely good or entirely bad, seeing most of them as all bad. |
| **Repression**. Preventing painful or dangerous thought from entering consciousness. | A mother's occasional murderous thoughts toward her hyperactive two-year-old are denied access to awareness. |
| **Projection**. Attributing one's unacceptable motives or characteristics to others. | An expansionist minded dictator of a totalitarian state is convinced that neighboring countries are planning to invade. |
| **Reaction Formation**. Preventing the awareness or expression of unacceptable desires by an exaggerated adoption of seemingly opposite behavior. | A man troubled by homosexual urges initiates a zealous community campaign to stamp out gay bars. |

(continued)

Table 3-1 (continued)

| Mechanism | Example |
|-----------|---------|
| **Displacement**. Discharging pent-up feelings, often of hostility, on objects less dangerous than those arousing the feelings. | A woman harassed by her boss at work initiates an argument with her husband. |
| **Rationalization**. Using contrived "explanations" to conceal or disguise unworthy motives for one's behavior. | A fanatical racist uses ambiguous passages from Scripture to justify his hostile actions toward minorities. |
| **Regression**. Retreating to an earlier developmental level involving less mature behavior and responsibility. | A man whose self-esteem has been shattered reverts to child-like "show-off" behavior and exhibits his genitals to young girls. |
| **Sublimation**. Channelling frustrated sexual energy into substitute activities. | A sexually frustrated artist paints wildly erotic pictures. |
| **Identification**. Increasing feelings of worth by affiliating oneself with a person or institution of illustrious standing. | A youth-league football coach becomes excessively demanding of his young players in emulation of an authoritarian pro-football coach. |
| **Fixation**. Attaching oneself in an unreasonable or exaggerated way to some person, or arresting emotional development at a childhood or adolescent level. | An unmarried, middle-aged man still depends on his mother to provide his basic needs. |

From *Abnormal Psychology and Modern Life*, 10th Edition by Robert C. Carson and James N. Butcher. Copyright © 1996 by HarperCollins Publishers Inc.

## The Therapeutic Circumstance

Traditional psychoanalysis has always been a time-consuming, lengthy process. Typically, the patient is seen four or five times per week, and the analysis can last for two or three years. The patient often reclines on a couch and is instructed to relax while the analyst sits in a chair behind the patient. However, modern analysts often dispense with the couch and have the patient sit in a chair.

## Free Association

The principal technique of psychoanalysis is **free association**. The patient, to remain in therapy, must say anything and everything that comes to mind, no matter how obscene, embarrassing, illogical, or seemingly trivial. Free-associating is not easy and often takes some time for the patient to learn. It is from this uncensored stream of consciousness that Freud believed insights into the patient's problems to be possible.

## ᘏ Table 3-2

Some Potential Relations Among the Psychosexual Stages, Defense Mechanisms, and Adult Personality

| Stage | Adult Extensions | Defensive Mechanisms | |
| --- | --- | --- | --- |
| | | Sublimations | Reaction Formations |
| Oral | Smoking, eating, kissing, oral hygiene, drinking, chewing gum. | Seeking knowledge, humor, wit, sarcasm, being a food or wine expert. | Speech purist, food faddist, prohibitionist, dislike of milk. |
| Anal | Notable interest in one's bowel movements, love of Bathroom humor, extreme messiness. | Interest in painting or sculpture, being overly giving, great interest in statistics. | Extreme disgust with feces, fear of dirt, prudishness, irritability. |
| Phallic | Heavy reliance on masturbation, flirtatiousness, expressions of virility. | Interest in poetry, love of love, interest in acting, striving for success. | Puritanical attitude toward sex, excessive modesty. |

## Dream Analysis

A technique related to free association is **dream analysis**. When a person sleeps, the ego relaxes its control over unconscious material. As a result, dreams are often especially revealing of the unconscious. Patients are encouraged to report their dreams. They will then be asked to free-associate to the dreams, and depending upon the point therapy has reached, the analyst may discuss or interpret the meaning of the dreams.

## Interpretation

Later in therapy, once the analyst believes the nature of the patient's problems is clear, the process of **psychoanalytic interpretation** by the therapist will begin. Through the therapist's interpretations the patient is able to recognize the unconscious meaning of certain thoughts, actions, or wishes. Interpretation is a way of facilitating the recognition of that which the patient had formerly not recognized and which was creating problems. Interpretation helps provide some connection, meaning, or reason that was not conscious but which was guiding the patient's thoughts, feelings, or behavior.

## Resistance to Analysis

Insight—the realization of the relation between one's current problems or behaviors and their unconscious origins—never comes easily. The same forces that have led to neurotic problems will also conspire to make the patient resist the therapeutic process. As the patient's unconscious is stirred and as defenses are threatened, **resistance** arises. Resistance is expressed in many ways—some patients begin to miss appointments or forget to pay their bills. Others start having difficulty free-associating or dismiss interpretations as trivial or silly. They may spend a great deal of time discussing inflation, the oil shortage, or supply-side economics—all weighty topics, but hardly what they are paying for. When the resistance begins to interfere with therapy, it must be handled by the therapist and resolved.

## Transference

**Transference**, an important element of nearly every successful analysis, occurs when the patient responds to the analyst as if the latter were some figure out of the patient's childhood. Both positive and negative feelings can be transferred. The therapy room, then, becomes an arena where old reactions and conflicts come alive. Transference provides important clues to childhood difficulties and also allows the therapist to interpret them to the patient. Statements of admiration, anger, or dislike are examples of transference. A patient may attack the usefulness of therapy or, conversely, express admiration for the analyst's skill.

The patient's transference reactions to the analyst or to the current situation are influenced by the patient's biases. These reactions often appear unrealistic to an outside observer because they reflect emotional residues from the patient's past. The analyst's task is to search out such reactions to achieve a deeper understanding of the patient's problems, but not to take them personally. When the therapist begins to respond to the patient's reactions on a personal level, the phenomenon of **countertransference** is occurring. Countertransference is a source of serious problems in therapy. It can appear in many forms, including sexual attraction toward the patient, anger or frustration toward the client and the client's behavior, or undue sympathy toward the client. Good therapists are aware of the possibility of countertransference and continually monitor their feelings to minimize these reactions.

## Working Through

Interpretation is not a one-time thing. The analyst must often repeat interpretations and identify, in many life areas, the conflicts and motives that are fueling the patient's neurotic adjustment. Resistance and transference must also be worked through repeatedly. Thus, insight comes not as a flash but as a result of laborious, repetitive working through.

# CASE STUDY

**The following case study of David W. is presented to illustrate Freudian theory and therapeutic practice. Although the individual described was seen for a series of therapy sessions, he would hardly be considered any more neurotic than most of us. He was seen in a university counseling center, and his stated reason for requesting the initial appointment had to do with vocational testing and career information. However, during the screening interview the counselor decided that he seemed to be seeking some sort of personal insight rather than just vocational counseling. Consequently, he was referred to a clinical psychologist on staff.**

**Although this case will be interpreted psychoanalytically, the actual therapy is not representative of classical psychoanalysis. It is, instead, what might be called a short-term, problem-oriented therapy. Rather than a strict Freudian form of analysis, it is what most professionals would describe as psychoanalytically oriented.**

David W was a 20-year-old chemistry major with a 3.7 grade point average. He was vaguely discontented and had a sense of foreboding about the prospect of becoming a chemist. The field was easy for him, but he somehow did not feel right about it. The following information was elicited as the clinician and David explored the bases for David's discontent.

David was an only child. His parents were both college graduates who married when both were 34. His father was a chemical engineer. His mother had been the office supervisor with the same engineering firm at the time of their marriage. She quit work immediately and set about having a family and running the home. Prior to David's birth she had suffered two miscarriages. Subsequently she was advised by her physician not to have any more children.

David's childhood was typical and uneventful. He grew up in the suburbs of a large midwestern city, graduated third in his high school class, and dated frequently, although never the same girl for any length of time. He was a second-string guard on the basketball team and was president of the science club. He attended the state university because "It was just assumed that I would go to school where Dad did." Similarly, "I always knew I would major in chemistry. That's the way I grew up." But once David was in college, things began to unravel a little. Although he did well in his chemistry and related classes, he was most excited by the courses in literature and art history. He got a job on the school paper and soon began writing a column of reviews on movies and local plays. His mother was pleased, but he sensed that his father was upset. That "sense" crystallized one weekend when David indicated he was moving out of his father's old fraternity and into an apartment with some friends on the paper. His father was furious and screamed, "If you have to work on that damned paper, at least you could be a sportswriter!"

*(continued)*

Case Study (*continued*)

There seemed to be a growing conflict in David's life, symbolized by his ambivalence about a chemistry major and reflected in his parents' differing views about his interests. But what lay behind all this? David, although obviously bright, was at a loss to explain his conflicting interests and his developing problems with his father.

Clearly, there must have been psychic determinants of David's conflicts and discontent. His inability to come to grips with them even after much thought over the past several months suggests they were unconscious. Although a little simple encouragement enabled him to recall some animosity toward his father and a few earlier episodes of disagreement (preconscious material), those events seemed inconsequential. As the sessions continued, however, a clearer picture began to emerge.

During the first 18 months or so following David's birth, his mother was extremely supportive. She devoted herself to his care and well-being. He was breastfed, and she was quite tolerant and flexible during the weaning period. She approached the beginning of his toilet training with a similar attitude. In fact, David's earliest memories were of sitting on a potty while his mother read stories to him. She would also go through the comic pages or show him reproductions of paintings. David recalled these first four or five years with a real sense of warmth and security. His memories of his father during this period were vague. Apparently, this was a time of financial struggle for the family, and his father worked long hours and was frequently on the road troubleshooting company problems. This meant that David's primary interactions were with his mother. It is also interesting to speculate about some of the origins of David's artistic and literary interests—interests that later figured prominently in his conflict with his father. David's mother was interested in art and literature. These interests, along with David, occupied her life during the early years when her husband was so often gone. The warm, sympathetic relationship between David and his mother explains how David's aesthetic inclinations could have taken root. Recall that his earliest memories were of toilet training, mother, happiness, stories, and pictures. From a child's point of view, these first few years were probably very nearly idyllic.

But when David was 5 or 6, his father assumed an executive position at the home office. This meant fewer trips, more time at home, and a generally more visible family role. David's father became someone who actively intruded into his life, not just someone who brought presents after a trip or who played with him but almost never seriously punished him. All of this took place just about the time David was beginning the phallic stage.

David recalled how his father would insist he go outside and play rather than stay indoors and thumb through books or magazines. He also remembered a few arguments his parents had over his being a "mamma's boy." His father would demand that he go to bed on time and not pester his mother to read him stories. David likewise dimly recalled a scene where he had apparently been playing with his genitals while lying in bed early in the morning. Normally his mother awakened him, but this time his father came into the room. When he saw what David was doing, he exploded with anger and threatened, "I'll cut that damn thing off if you ever do that again!"

(*continued*)

Case Study (*continued*)

David also remembered that he would cry when the babysitter came over on the few nights when his parents went to a party or to the movies. His mother would want to stay home, but his father always insisted they have some time alone. A final episode that David recalled had a clear Oedipal theme. He and his mother were taking a nap on her bed in the middle of the afternoon. His father came home early and found David snuggled up against his mother. That led to a stormy scene that terrified David. His father loudly proclaimed that his mother was turning him into a little "fairy"—that he should be out playing football or something like that.

From roughly this time onward, David's memories were of typical childhood activities. His relationship with his father improved, and he could recall playing on a Little League team his father coached. He also began to show an interest in his father's work and wanted to go with him to the plant so he could "see what Daddy did." It would seem, then, that David had resolved the Oedipus complex in the classic fashion by identifying with the aggressor.

Until the therapy sessions, David had generally repressed most of his early life. Repression is a relatively simple ego defense. Because the conflicts that surfaced mainly in the phallic stage were not overpowering, his ego did not find it necessary to resort to more complex defenses such as projection or reaction formation. His ego was relatively strong. He obviously was above average in intelligence, and his development had been marked by security and love. It was not until the phallic stage, with his discovery of genital urges coupled with the struggle with his father, that unconscious id impulses began to pose a threat. Given that strong ego and a generally supportive family milieu, David was able to cope for some time. Only during his college years did the repression begin to dissolve a bit, resulting in feelings of alienation, discontent, and misgivings about his chemistry decision. It was as if the reality and finality of his career choice now confronted him. The repressed longings for literary, aesthetic experiences that had been submerged as a way of solving the Oedipal situation began to break through. Some moderate pangs of neurotic anxiety signaled the return of the conflict.

Blessed with a relatively strong ego, David sought therapy, not as a debilitated neurotic but as a coping person striving to control his future realistically. His ego, cautious executive that it was, eased him into therapy obliquely by first seeking vocational counseling. Parenthetically, it turned out that his mother had sensed his conflict and had subtly urged him to talk things over with an "adviser."

With therapy (which lasted roughly six months), David was able to achieve insight into his conflicts. This, in turn, allowed him to face his father and, through some rocky discussions, ultimately resolve matters. David decided to remain in chemistry. It appeared that once the unconscious determinants of his feelings had been fully aired and understood, his commitment to science was strengthened, and his literary flair became the foundation for a rewarding set of secondary interests.

## Dissent

When Freud broke with Breuer in 1894, he began a period of intellectual loneliness and isolation, which did not end until 1902 when a group of young doctors started meeting with him to learn the practices of psychoanalysis (E. Jones, 1955). This marked the beginning of the famous Vienna Psycho-Analytical Society.

The people Freud attracted were people of considerable intellectual power. As time went on, several of them detected what they regarded as weaknesses, omissions, or errors in orthodox Freudian theory and practice. Freud tolerated a great deal of "discussion" from his colleagues, but members who presented notions that departed "too far" from psychoanalytic doctrine were asked to leave.

Revisionists attacked Freud on many fronts. In particular, his ideas about the reigning importance of libido and sexuality were disputed. Some attempted to reinterpret his description and explanation of the Oedipus complex. Others wished to alter his notions about the unconscious. To Freud, these were key concepts that could not be revised without seriously impairing the integrity of psychoanalysis. Two of the most famous of these early dissenters were Alfred Adler and Carl Jung.

## Adler's Individual Psychology

Alfred Adler had strong opinions. He was impressed by Freud's work, and this prompted him to become a charter member of the Vienna Psycho-Analytical Society. But in 1911 his views were vehemently criticized by the other members. He subsequently resigned as the group's president, and a few months later he officially ended his affiliation with Freudian psychoanalysis.

Much evidence suggests that the break between Adler and Freud was wide and bitter. His reasons for breaking with Freud centered on what he perceived as Freud's overemphasis on the sexual instincts and underemphasis on the ego defenses. Adler saw the individual as shaped by social and familial factors. Basically, Freud accepted biological determinism as reflected in instinctual energy. In recent years there has been renewed interest in the value and utility of Adler's **individual psychology** (Adler, 1924).

### Inferiority and Compensation

Adler's earliest theoretical contributions were the concepts of **organ inferiority** and resultant **compensation**. Adler was interested in the reason a person becomes afflicted with one illness rather than another and why a specific area of the body is affected rather than another. Initially, he felt that the site of illness was determined by a basic inferiority or weakness in that region that perhaps resulted from an inherited abnormality of development. Adler also noted that many individuals afflicted with an inferior characteristic eventually compensated for their weakness. For example, the person with a minor speech impediment becomes a speech major or an announcer. The frail, muscularly weak person takes up weight lifting. Basically, then, an inferior organ system can lead to psychological compensations. Although all of this may sound organic, Adler was more concerned with a person's attitude toward a defect than with the defect itself.

Adler later specifically considered psychological or social inferiorities in addition to inferiorities resulting from organic or bodily defects. Thus, being born into a family of limited financial means could set the stage for feelings of inferiority. A belief that one is not intelligent could likewise cause inferiority reactions. Adler also asserted that all of us are prone to develop feelings of inferiority. We are born weak and helpless, and without a prolonged period of dependence on others we would die. For a relatively long time during infancy and childhood, our world is peopled by "superior" adults who carry us around in the most powerful of ways. Even more important, they can outthink us. Is it any wonder, then, that we learn to perceive ourselves as inferior and then set about compensating for our weaknesses? In many instances, compensation is a healthy reaction that serves to move us toward the achievement of our potential. Unfortunately, the inability to develop successful compensations can lead to an **inferiority complex**.

## Striving for Superiority

Adler came to the conclusion that the basic motivation we all share is a **striving for superiority**. This is a drive that propels us toward perfection. It grows out of our need to compensate for our feelings of inferiority and is an attempt to attain power or strength so that we can better control our environment.

It is interesting to trace Adler's thinking about the essential human motive. Originally, he emphasized aggression. Later, this was replaced by the "will to power." This, in turn, evolved into a striving for superiority, which actually meant a striving for perfection, completion, or overcoming. Adler's theorizing went from aggression to power to superiority. He considered this striving for superiority as innate and universal, although each person strives in individualized ways.

## Social Interest

A later addition to Adler's theory that was influenced by his political views was the concept of social interest (Adler, 1939). Adler regarded **social interest**

## A BRIEF BIOGRAPHY OF

# Alfred Adler

Alfred Adler was born in 1870 in Penzig, Austria, a sub-urb of Vienna. He was the second son in a family of six children. His father was a grain merchant, and the family was comfortable financially. During his childhood, he experienced chronic illness and was a weak, physically inept child. His early years were also marked by hostile sibling relationships and mediocrity in school. All these elements undoubtedly played a strong role in the subsequent development of his theoretical ideas and in his conflicts with Freud.

Adler was an independent thinker, and he loved to discuss the social and political issues of the day. He was also argumentative and could be a formidable advocate for the weak and downtrodden. His distaste for running with the crowd was perhaps symbolized by his conversion from the Jewish faith to Protestantism.

Adler received his medical degree in 1895 and for a time practiced ophthalmology. He soon began to practice as a psychiatrist and about 1902 joined Freud's circle. In 1911 he severed his relationship with Freud. As his professional stature grew he was able to found his own psychoanalytic group, the Society for Individual Psychology. Subsequently, he became a leader in the child guidance movement and therefore could be regarded as one of the first community psychiatrists.

In the 1920s he lectured extensively in Europe and the United States. In 1934 he moved to New York City and continued to influence numerous social workers, clinical psychologists, and psychiatrists. He died in 1937 in Aberdeen, Scotland, while on a lecture tour.

An excellent source book of Adlerian concepts and methods is the edited volume by Ansbacher and Ansbacher (1956). Biographical material may be found in Bottome (1957). A succinct description of the man and his ideas has been written by Ansbacher (1977). Manaster and Corsini (1982) have written an introductory-level work.

as a predisposition, nurtured by experience, to contribute to society and to be concerned for others. Adler's original belief that people are driven by a need for power and domination was revised by his awareness of their wish for personal superiority and finally of their desire to subordinate their own needs for the good of society. We have, then, the socialization of superiority into a goal of a perfect society. Social interest develops in the context of family relationships and other formative experiences. In some cases these experiences thwart the development of social interest. Indeed, the neurotic person has not yet learned to substitute interest in others for the compensatory striving for superiority.

## Style of Life

To overcome feelings of inferiority, a person develops a **style of life**. Adler's definition of style of life varied over the years to include, self or ego, one's own personality, the unity of personality, individuality, the method of facing problems, and the wish to contribute toward life (Ansbacher and Ansbacher, 1956). This principle of style of life gives uniqueness to each personality. All of us struggle to overcome our feelings of infantile helplessness. We all pursue the same basic goal, but no one uses the same approach.

Adler felt that by about the age of 5 years, the individual's style of life has been determined. Our family relationships and other important experiences have by then provided us a basic style that will characterize us throughout life. New experiences may add embellishments, but the basic structure has been molded. Whether we shall be aggressive or passive, intellectual or athletic, or whether we shall depend on a weak stomach to get us out of trouble has been determined. Our inferiorities, either real or fancied, and our compensations have a crucial impact on our style of life.

## Development of Personality

In another important departure from traditional Freudian theory, Adler emphasized not only the relationship between parents and child but also such variables as family size, relationships among siblings, and the child's ordinal position in the family. Any of these factors can, in certain instances, lead to psychological problems.

The Pampered Child. Adler saw pampering as a major source of maladjustment. A pampered child may learn only to make demands without acquiring the ability to cope with frustration. Such a child develops a style of expecting others to meet his or her needs. When eventually there is no one to meet those needs, the child (or adult by then) may react by retreating. Not having learned to overcome, the individual withdraws to avoid feelings of inferiority. Such people do not learn to cooperate, to plan, or to become responsible. They often become egocentric, and their immaturity is reflected in their neurotic style.

**The Rejected Child.** Rejected children perceive the world as a hostile, threatening place. Fighting for their rights becomes the preferred style of life. Such people are often antagonistic and it is difficult to live with them. They frequently defeat their own purposes by being hostile and uncooperative. The basis of rejection may vary; it may be a physical defect, an unhappy marriage, or financial problems in the family. The rejection may be overt or it may be subtle; there may be physical brutality or psychological abuse. A sense of distrust may plague the child throughout life. Often such children become delinquents or criminals.

**Ordinal Position.** Adler believed that whether one is an only child, the eldest child, or a middle child affects the style of life. Only children are especially vulnerable to pampering. They are likely to receive much attention and concern. There are no siblings with whom to compete, and being the central focus of parents may lead to self-centeredness. This can become a problem later in life when the person is no longer the center of attention.

The oldest child is like a dethroned monarch. Once the pampered and protected only child, this child must make way for a newcomer. This situation can be threatening. To recoup his or her losses, the child may regress to a more childish phase or become demanding and destructive. As this child gets older, however, conformity to parental dictates may become the style. Consequently, the oldest child often becomes the upholder of family standards. Given a place of maturity and responsibility by the parents, the individual may well develop a conforming style of life in response to authority figures.

The upbringing of the second or middle child tends to be more relaxed. The parents have been through it all before and are less concerned about being good parents this time around. The second child has never been the sole center of attention and is, therefore, not as sensitive about encroachments from younger siblings. Skills of cooperation and compromise come more easily because the child has at least one other sibling. In some cases, however, a middle child may become concerned about the rights and prerogatives of that older, superior sibling. This can lead to feelings of inferiority that are compensated by striving, competitive behaviors.

The youngest child may also be pampered and overprotected much as an only child is. The pampering may be by older siblings as well as by the parents, especially if the youngest child is considerably younger than the other siblings. However, the youngest child has several siblings with whom to compete, and this may lead to strong feelings of competitiveness and a desire to show that he or she is just as good as the others.

These sibling styles are not inevitable or immutable. The dynamics of each family and situation are different. It was Adler's intention only to show that one's ordinal position in the family determines that certain problems rather than others are likely to be confronted.

## Personality and Adjustment

Because of the inevitability of experiences that lead to feelings of inferiority, everyone attempts to compensate and strive for superiority. But there will be obstacles in the path toward the goal of superiority. According to Adler, how the individual responds to these obstacles reflects his or her personality and determines whether he or she is adjusted or maladjusted.

Adler believed that the adjusted person responds to problems with courage. There is no fear of failure or unwillingness to confront the truth about oneself. Adjustment also means approaching life with common sense. Finally, the ultimate level of adjustment is the expression of social interest by relinquishing goals

According to Adler, the order of birth significantly affects psychological development. Older siblings, for example, may conform to the parents' values and act as role models for younger siblings.

of personal superiority in favor of contributing to the welfare of others. Adler used three concepts to describe how individuals may respond to life's obstacles.

Distance. Adler used the concept of **distance** to describe the neurotic's manner of handling potential failure. People do not like to experience failure because it reinforces their feelings of inferiority. Consequently, they guard against situations that could result in failure by setting up a distance between themselves and the goal. This psychological ploy is defensive because it demonstrates neither courage nor common sense. For example, the male who is fearful of being rejected by females psychologically distances himself from females. He says, in effect, "I would get involved if only I could find someone who is sensitive, pretty, and intelligent." This defensive scheme allows him to reject women before they reject him.

Masculine and Feminine Protest. Adler did not give sexual urges a central motivating role in his theory. To Adler, sexual problems were simply another manifestation of the striving for power and superiority. For example, he considered the Oedipus complex less a sexual matter than a struggle to achieve dominance. That is, sexual gratification from the mother is less important than having power over her.

One Adlerian concept that is related to gender is **masculine protest.** In many societies and families, masculinity is equated with power, dominance, and security. In families of male domination, both girls and boys may be impressed with the association between the masculinity of the dominant male and strength, assertiveness, and dominance. For some girls the goal of superiority may become translated into a *protest,* or striving for strength and dominance. Rather than being seen as superior and worthy of deference, men become rivals. But masculine protest can characterize males as well, as witnessed by the swagger, the macho outlook, and the male chauvinist. Of course, not every family is male dominated. When the mother is obviously in control, a **feminine protest** may occur. In this case, both boys and girls may develop such traits as femininity and nurturance. Later, Adler downplayed the dual concepts of masculine and feminine protest in favor of a more general striving for superiority, and he never suggested that men are innately superior.

Three Problems of Life. Adler argued that the problems of life can generally be grouped into three areas. There are problems of (1) sex and marriage, (2) school and occupation, and (3) family and social life. If a person is maladjusted in one life area, there is a tendency for the difficulty influence the other areas. The degree of influence depends upon the severity of the problem. Adler's emphasis was not on specific systems but on the extent to which the problem impacts each of the areas of life. For example, problems with a marriage may impact one person's effectiveness at work; however, for another person the marital problems may be unknown to co-workers because the person's work behavior is unchanged.

## Approaches to Psychotherapy and Behavior Change

Adlerian theory was not as closely associated with a set of psychotherapeutic techniques as was Freudian theory. There was little emphasis on dream interpretation and free association. As with Freud, childhood experiences and feelings were explored. The assumption, however, was that the patient's problems stem from a mistaken style of life. Therefore, there was a focus on sibling rivalry, pampering and rejection, and methods of coping with inferiority feelings.

Getting the patient to discuss such matters allows the therapist to determine the style of life. Adlerians would be encouraging and reassuring, to help patients face their feelings of inferiority, and find the courage and common sense to confront their problems. Adler, of course, believed that lack of social interest was the ultimate defect. Therefore, he would attempt to break down the patient's self-preoccupation and increase his or her attention to others and society.

Adler's therapy was more directive than Freud's. The therapist was an active figure rather than one who passively listened and made occasional interpretations. Adler not only made interpretations but also attempted to persuade the patient about various matters. Moreover, he was likely to make explicit suggestions for changes in behavior. And, although he talked about the past with patients, he also placed much emphasis on changing the present along with choosing and pursuing future behavior and goals.

Adler is perhaps best known for his treatment methods for children experiencing psychological and behavioral problems. His methods in these cases often involved the use of direct suggestions for changes in the behavior of significant adults (parents and teachers) in the child's life. Adler's ideas and methods for his work with children provide a historical foundation for contemporary therapeutic practice. For example, modern treatments for children with disruptive behavior often include **parent effectiveness training,** which is designed to teach parents more effective methods for disciplining their children and for having positive interactions such as playing or reading with their children.

## Jung's Analytic Psychology

Carl Jung was another follower of Freud who grew disenchanted with classical psychoanalysis. He could not accept Freud's narrow sexual definition of libido. This objection was not due to prudishness (Munroe, 1955). Rather, for Jung, libido was a creative life force with an almost spiritual quality. This conceptualization is consistent with Jung's wide-ranging interests, which included archaeology, spiritualism, mythology, Eastern as well as Western philosophy, astrology, and religion. This breadth of intellectual study gave his theory of personality a much wider base than could be offered by the dreams and free associations of patients on the couch. It led to a different approach to psychoanalysis called **analytic psychology.**

# CASE STUDY

**The following excerpts from a case study of Z. (Disher, 1959) illustrates several features of Adlerian theory and therapy. It is an account of a patient treated over a comparatively brief span of time, who showed decided improvement without, however, effecting any basic psychological change**.

Miss Z., 48 years old, contacted the Alfred Adler Consultation Center and Mental Hygiene Clinic in New York City, in December 1956, having been referred by a psychotherapist with whom she had been in treatment for ten months and who dismissed her because he had to reduce his case load.

The patient was average in appearance, except for a slight limp due to polio when she was a child. She was extremely self-conscious, however, and wore long dresses to hide her "bad" leg.

Miss Z. had a ten-year history of depression. She reported that she spent about nine months of every year in a depressive state, although she was able to go to work every day, work which she hated, and seemed to be functioning adequately in other areas. The diagnosis was "reactive depression."

During the years of her illness, Miss Z. had nine different therapists. At the initial interview Miss Z. complained that she had been shifted from the "best" therapist to one of lesser reputation and skill. She also complained that she had no occupation, having had only informal education and training. She boasted that her parents were well-known people who travelled a great deal. Her spasmodic schooling was due to frequent moves as a child. She was always in conflict with her mother, but was strongly attached to her father, in whose reflected glory she basked and who had assumed the role of a boyfriend until her "marriage."

Her first "husband" (this is the patient's word; she had never married) was a man of some reputation, of her father's age. In this relationship, and in all her subsequent relationships with men, she continued to be the cared-for and admired child. When the man ceased "courting" her, she lost interest. She stated that she could only be happy when she was with people of consequence. She also recognized that she had to be in "control" of a situation.

The patient felt that if she had the security of a profession in which she was successful, her depression would lift. This would have to be a position in which she controlled other people, not one in which she provided menial service. (She considered being a secretary or a nurse, for example, menial and therefore not really good enough for her.) After her third interview Miss Z. seemed to emerge from her depression and was able to accept her clerical job as a possible stepping stone to better opportunities. She also accepted the relationship with her current gentleman friend to a degree, although he, too, was not really suitable, being dependent, unknown, and socially inept.

*(continued)*

Case Study (*continued*)

However, after only two months she was again in a depressive state, having received a rebuff in her office, which she interpreted as an obstacle to her ever achieving the kind of position she wanted in life. Simultaneously, the man in her life became "completely impossible." She complained of not bathing, not eating, not sleeping, and of having to force herself to go to work each day.

During the course of her long treatment with her former therapists she had worked on her relationships with her parents and with her various men friends, and she had been made to recognize the use she was making of her depression. She had all the concepts; she knew all the words. Rather than persist in these attempts to increase her intellectual understanding, the therapist tried to emphasize her value as a person; the therapist stressed the fact that therapy is a situation in which two people work on a problem together; that neither was superior to the other. It was also pointed out that if she conceived of her therapy as being solely the therapist's responsibility, she could prove herself superior to the therapist simply by not getting well. At this point she became impatient, said she was not satisfied with the way things were going, and suggested termination. The therapist, in turn, suggested that she work through their relationship, even though she thought she was not being helped, instead of following her old pattern of running away.

There followed five months of depression in which things were "worse than they have ever been." Three events of importance then occurred, quite by accident. First, the drug marsilid came to her attention. She made inquiries which led her to a well-known psychiatrist at a state hospital, who generously gave her some time and prescribed the drug. She took this drug for a week without side effects. Secondly, matters took a turn for the better in her office, and she moved quickly into a coveted management position, which brought her into contact with world-famous people. Thirdly, a well-known man came into her life as a suitor. She was then "well" for six months, with the exception of two days. At the end of these two days she took another dose of marsilid and her depression lifted. At this point Miss Z. terminated her therapy; she felt that "marsilid was responsible" for her cure. Actually, we are not certain to what extent this drug contributed to the patient's improvement. We are sure, however, of the role of certain other forces in her life, forces which make it possible for her to function successfully in spite of, or perhaps because of, her neurotic needs:

1. She was valued as a person at the Clinic. She was made to feel that she was important to the therapist—she was encouraged to continue with her therapy, etc.
2. One of the "greatest" psychiatrists gave her his time and thus proved that he valued her as a person.
3. She was able to achieve some status in a profession at which she had served her apprenticeship. Her present job enables her to come into contact with important people; and she plays a dominant role at her office.
4. A well-known man, very much like her father, has come into her life, is courting her, and is charmed by her little-girl ways.

(*continued*)

Case Study (*continued*)

Although Miss Z. has not changed basically (unless marsilid has worked some change at the chemical level), she is now meeting life with greater courage because her environment has shifted. Still a child emotionally and sexually, she is performing well in her occupation, which has contributed to her self-respect. There has been improvement in the patient's life-style, without, however, any real change in social feeling.

From "Improvement Without Fundamental Change" by D. R. Disher in *Essays in Individual Psychology: Contemporary Application of Alfred Adler's Theories,* edited by Kurt A. Adler and Danica Deutsch. Copyright © 1959 by Grove Press, Inc. Reprinted by permission of Grove Weidenfeld.

## Personality Structure

For Jung, there were three basic components of the personality: the ego, the personal unconscious, and the collective unconscious.

**The Ego.** The **ego** is the conscious mind. It is composed of all those feelings, thoughts, memories, and perceptions of which we are conscious. It represents the "I" feeling and is responsible for getting us through the day. It is similar to Freud's concept of ego.

**The Personal Unconscious.** The **personal unconscious** is roughly equivalent to Freud's preconscious because its contents can be made conscious without much effort. The material may have been repressed or forgotten, or perhaps it was not vivid enough to have been remembered initially.

**The Collective Unconscious.** The **collective unconscious** is Jung's radical contribution to psychoanalytic theory. The collective unconscious is composed of memory traces from our ancestral past, including prehuman ancestry. The collective unconscious is the "deposit of ancestral experience from untold millions of years, the echo of prehistoric world events to which each century adds an infinitesimally small amount of variation and differentiation" (Jung, 1928, p. 162). Because the collective unconscious arises out of the common experiences of all our ancestors, its contents are similar for all of us. The collective unconscious has a strong influence on our thoughts and behavior. It is a set of predispositions to perceive and process information in ways that, if ignored by the ego, can disrupt our conscious, rational processes by gaining control of them and distorting them into symptoms of various sorts.

## Archetypes

Jung called the structural elements of the collective unconscious archetypes. **Archetypes** are universal, collective, primordial images. Since the beginning of time, our ancestors have seen the rising sun, experienced a mother, learned of death, admired a hero, and endured pain. These experiences predispose us to react in

# Carl Jung

Carl Gustav Jung was born in 1875 in the village of Kesswyl, Switzerland, the son of a pastor of the Swiss Reformed Church. Jung (1961) described himself as a lonely child who grew up in the midst of his parents' marital problems. His mother had a dominating personality; his father spent much time thinking about being a failure and questioning the sincerity of his religious beliefs. Some of Jung's childhood experiences influenced his later theorizing. For example, he was preoccupied with dreams, visions, and fantasies. He felt he possessed secret information about the future and also had the fantasy he was two different people.

Jung's first love was archaeology, and this interest also influenced his later work. However, he was convinced by a dream to become a doctor and received his medical degree in psychiatry in 1900. After reading Freud's *The Interpretation of Dreams*, he became interested in psychoanalysis. In 1906 the two men began corresponding regularly, and the following year Jung visited Freud. Jung and Freud greatly admired each other and in 1909 traveled to the United States together to lecture. Indeed, Freud designated Jung as his successor and convinced the members of the International Psychoanalytic Association to elect Jung as their first president.

certain ways to similar situations. Thus, to understand a child's terror of the dark, we must consider the archetypal content. But at the same time, that child's fear must also be examined in the context of his or her own life experiences.

When we fail to recognize our archetypes, their meaning unfolds in our dreams and fantasies. Primitive art, myths, and even the hallucinations of the psychotic are often symbolic representations of the archetypes. Indeed, understanding the archetypal meaning of symbols is fundamental to Jungian psychology. Archetypes are not trivial images; they elicit strong emotional reactions. Although Jung discussed many different archetypes, he focused on four: the persona, the anima and animus, the shadow, and the self.

**The Persona.** From the Greek word meaning "mask," **persona** is the public face presented by the individual in response to social demands. It represents our conventional role as defined by the expectations of others. This is separate from our real self, and its purpose is to impress others or to conceal our real self from them. When we identify too closely with our persona (e.g., if I begin to believe that my professorial role is the real me), psychological difficulties arise.

**The Anima and Animus.** The concepts of anima and animus reflect Jung's view of the essential bisexuality of human nature. The feminine side of men is the **anima**, and the masculine side of women is **animus**. These archetypes have arisen over

In 1912 their friendship began to cool, and in 1913 they ceased all correspondence. Jung resigned as president of the psychoanalytic group in 1914 and a few months later withdrew his membership. Freud and Jung never saw each other again. The split was probably based on both personal and theoretical grounds. However, the most obvious reason was their differing views of the libido and the nature of sexuality. The break was debilitating for Jung. For three years he could not bring himself to read a scientific book. He spent the time deeply exploring his own dreams and fantasies. Some believed that he was near the edge of madness.

A strange aspect of Jung's life involved accusations of pro-Nazi sentiments. He became president of Hitler's International General Medical Society for Psychotherapy. The society was based on the "truths" of *Mein Kampf* and was organized to separate the "true" Aryan psychology from "false" Jewish propaganda. Jung was condemned for giving substance to Nazi delusions, but it is possible that he accepted the position to help block the rising tide of anti-Semitism in Europe. He may have been politically naive rather than an ardent Nazi sympathizer.

Jung died in 1961 in Kusnacht, Switzerland.

eons of time in the collective unconscious as a result of experience with the opposite sex. Men have become a bit "feminized" by living with women over the ages, and the reverse holds true for women. Failure to recognize the archetypal "other side" of the opposite sex can lead to difficulties in interpersonal relations.

**The Shadow.** The **shadow** represents the unrealized possibilities in a person's life. A significant portion of the shadow is the threatening, animalistic component of personality. It accounts in part for our aggressiveness, our cruelty and immorality, and our passion. Manifestations of the shadow are the monsters and devils of our dreams and in primitive art and mythology. However, the unrealized possibilities in the shadow may also be constructive and good. Our perception of events and our reactions to others can be influenced by shadow images in the collective unconscious.

**The Self.** The **self** is the archetype that propels us to search for unity, harmony, and wholeness among all elements of the personality. It is the master that directs and organizes all the other archtypes and their shadows. Religion, according to Jung, can be a great facilitator of this integration. Because development of an integrated state takes time, the archetype of self is not fully achieved until perhaps middle age. When the self archetype is realized, the individual is balanced between the conscious and the unconscious.

The archetypal image of a circle persists across cultures in conveying the cycle of life and death. This is an example of a Hindu mandala, or "magic circle." Where else have you heard life referred to as a circle?

## Psychological Types and Personality

One of Jung's more influential contributions to personality psychology was his theory of **psychological types**. These types represent the typical manner in which an individual processes information and relates to the world. Initially, Jung proposed two opposite types, called introversion and extraversion, that concerned a person's general attitude toward the world. **Introversion** refers to a subjective attitude. The introvert is likely to be reserved, withdrawn, and interested in ideas rather than in social relations. **Extraversion** describes an attitude of interest in the outer world. The extravert is the more sociable person who is friendly and involved in events outside the self. Preference for one of these attitudes is likely rooted in inborn temperament, although experiences in life can encourage or discourage one's predisposition toward one orientation or the other.

Subsequently Jung realized that one pair of types was insufficient to characterize the diversity of personalities. He proposed two additional pairs of types to characterize an individual's preferred modes of perceiving and evaluating the world. One pair, **thinking versus feeling,** concerns a person's preferred mode of knowing the world. A thinking type of person wants to define the objects or events in the world, whereas a feeling person emphasizes the emotional reactions elicited by those objects and events. Jung referred to this pair as the rational types. The other pair consists of the nonrational types, **intuition versus sensation.**

These types concern how a person perceives the world. A sensing person focuses on the existence of objects and events, whereas an intuitive person emphasizes the origin and purpose of events. "*Sensation* (i.e., sense perception) tells you that something exists; *thinking* tells you what it is; *feeling* tells you whether it is agreeable or not; and *intuition* tells you whence it comes and where it is going" (Jung, 1964, p. 49).

In addition to being introverted or extraverted, people tend to be characterized by one rational and one nonrational type. For example, some people are thinking-intuitive-extraverts; others may be feeling-intuitive-introverts. Jung's theory of psychological types is the basis for a widely used personality inventory, the Myers-Briggs Type Indicator (Myers, 1975).

## The Neo-Freudians

Several psychoanalysts began to argue for the essential social nature of the human being. In particular, this group focused on interpersonal issues as the source of human distress and resulting coping strategies. Thus, they revised the orthodox Freudian doctrine of instinctual, sexual motives as the source of human personality. The principal members of this revisionist group are usually considered to be Karen Horney, Erich Fromm, and Harry Stack Sullivan. In addition, the school of ego psychology is considered to be neo-Freudian.

### Karen Horney

Karen Horney's work provides a feminist revision of Freudian theory. Horney rejected penis envy as a dominant motive in women and also rejected the idea that "anatomy is destiny." Instead, she argued that many of the feelings of inferiority and inadequacy experienced by some women are a function of the way our culture regards women in general.

To understand the individual's conflicts, we must understand how personality is shaped by the texture of society. It is within this broader context that she placed one of her primary concepts, **basic anxiety** (Horney, 1937). In a competitive culture such as ours, the child feels helpless, alone, and menaced by others because the child is small relative to adults. The child must develop ways of coping with this basic anxiety.

Horney (1945) discussed three basic strategies that are commonly employed: **moving toward people,** or protecting oneself by overtures of affection, dependency, and submission to others; **moving against people,** or protecting oneself through aggression, hostility, and attack; and **moving away from people,** or protecting oneself by isolation and withdrawal. The particular manner in which an individual combines these strategies is the basis of that person's personality. Neuroticism arises when we rigidly adopt only one strategy.

## Erich Fromm

The social theme is also found in the views of Erich Fromm. Our compelling need, according to Fromm (1941), is the need to belong. A basic fear results from feeling alone and insignificant. The human being is defined by a search for significance and relationship to others. Fromm outlined several orientations that individuals use to cope with their loneliness. An individual's personality is based on the orientation or combination of orientations employed. The first four are nonproductive and result in psychological problems.

- *Receptive:* The individual expects and requires support from the environment—from parents, friends, authorities, and God.
- *Exploitative:* The person takes from others by force or cleverness. Everything becomes an object of exploitation, and the prevailing attitude is one of hostility and manipulation coupled with feelings of envy, jealousy, and cynicism.
- *Hoarding:* Security is defined by acquisitions. Love becomes nothing more than possessiveness. There is no faith in the future.
- *Marketing:* Personal qualities have no intrinsic value; they are commodities of exchange. Personality is something to sell, and the "right" personality is whatever is in vogue. Such people are basically empty, anxious individuals.
- *Productive:* These are the healthy types whose ability to employ their talents and temperament and personal attributes to achieve everything possible for them make them productive members of society.

## Harry Stack Sullivan

For Sullivan (1953, 1964), every situation is **interpersonal**; even when alone, the individual is in tune with past experiences with others. Sullivan also used the concept of self—not an inborn self but one that grows out of the "reflected appraisals" of others. This means that the manner in which we are evaluated by others comes to be the manner in which we evaluate ourselves. Positive interactions with significant adults as the child is developing will lead to a positive view of the self; negative interactions will produce negative self-esteem. The major aspects of the self and personality are therefore firmly established through interactions with others. Like Freud, Sullivan emphasized stages of development, but the emphasis was interpersonal rather than psychosexual.

## Ego Psychology

Within Freudian theory, every function that the ego performed, such as thinking, acting, and repressing, was motivated by the demands of the id. Freud never relinquished his views about the supremacy of the id, but many more contemporary psychoanalytic theorists disagreed with this view. Foremost among these re-

## Table 3-3

Erikson's Eight Stages or Crises and Associated Emerging Traits

| Stage | Age | Succsessful Resolution Leads to: | Unsuccessfull Resolution Leads to: |
|---|---|---|---|
| I. Trust vs. Mistrust (Oral)* | Birth–1 year | Hope | Fear |
| II. Autonomy vs. Shame and Doubt (Anal)* | 1–3 years | Will power | Self-doubt |
| III. Initiative vs. Guilt (Phallic)* | 4–5 years | Purpose | Unworthiness |
| IV. Industry vs. Inferiority (Latency)* | 6–11 years | Competency | Incompetency |
| V. Ego Identity vs. Role Confusion | 12–20 years | Fidelity | Uncertainty |
| VI. Intimacy vs. Isolation | 20–24 years | Love | Promiscuity |
| VII. Generativity vs. Stagnation | 25–65 years | Care | Selfishness |
| VIII. Ego Integrity vs. Despair | 65 years–death | Wisdom | Meaninglessness and despair |

*Roughly corresponding Freudian stage.

visionists were Erik Erikson (1963), Heinz Hartmann (1958, 1964), David Rapaport (1959), and Ernst Kris (1952). These theorists did not regard the activities of the ego as solely a function of conflicts within the personality, nor did they see how psychoanalysis could continue to develop as a major theoretical force if it focused exclusively on unhealthy personalities.

These ego psychologists developed the concept of a **conflict-free sphere** of the ego: a part of the ego whose processes of thinking, perceiving, and learning are not in conflict with the id, the superego, or the real world. Hartmann (1958) described an **autonomous ego** that did not grow out of the id but arrived with its own predispositions and continued to develop independently. Erik Erikson, the most influential member of the ego psychology movement, presented the most comprehensive theory of ego development.

Psychosocial Theory and the Eight Stages of Development. **Psychosocial theory** was introduced in Erikson's first book, *Childhood and Society,* published in 1950 and revised in 1963. In this book he described the eight stages of human development.

According to Erikson, the eight stages unfold in a fixed and determined sequence. This sequence is guided by an **epigenetic principle**, which means that the growing personality moves through these stages in an orderly fashion and at an appropriate rate. The organization of society contributes to the systematic un-

A
BRIEF
BIOGRAPHY
OF

# Erik Erikson

Erik Erikson was born in 1902 near Frankfurt, Germany. His parents, who were Danish, separated prior to his birth, and when he was 3 years old his mother married Dr. Theodor Homburger, the pediatrician who had treated Erik for a childhood disease. Not for several years was Erik told that Homburger was not his real father, and Erikson used the name of his step-father for quite a few years, even on his first published papers. Not until he became a United States citizen in 1939 did he use the name Erikson. Even though his mother and stepfather were Jewish, he was sometimes taunted by his Jewish peers for being gentile, perhaps because of his Scandinavian blond hair and blue eyes. These kinds of experiences probably contributed to a feeling of not belonging, which is reflected in his later writings about confusions and identity crises (Coles, 1970).

Erikson finished high school, but that was all. Although he was interested in art and history, his was a generally mediocre school career. Thus, he decided, after a brief stint of studying art, to travel. He wandered about Italy until, at age 25, he accepted the offer of a friend from his high school days to become a teacher at a small American day nursery in Vienna. Here,

folding of development. Although the details vary from one culture to another, the basic elements of the psychosocial stages are universal.

Each stage presents the individual with a **crisis**—a point at which personality development can go one way or another. In essence, the person's level of physiological development, combined with society's expectations for a person of that age, brings about a crisis characteristic of each stage. If the crisis is resolved negatively, adaptation and the likelihood of a successful resolution of the crisis in the next stage will be diminished. A positive resolution has the opposite effect. Of course, rarely is a resolution completely positive or negative. Instead, each resolution has some positive and some negative aspects, and it is the balance and nature of these aspects that is important for the individual's personality. Table 3-3 summarizes these stages.

Although Erikson, like Freud, emphasized the concept of stages, there are important differences. As with the neo-Freudians, Erikson emphasized the social rather than the sexual developments at each stage. In addition, Erikson's stages span the entire life of the individual, with special emphasis on adolescence and adulthood. His willingness to address the crises of adulthood has made his work useful in the field of gerontology.

**Ego Identity Versus Role Confusion.** Erikson is best known for the attention he gave to the crisis faced during the adolescent years. The age of 12 to about 20

Erikson became acquainted with the Freud family, and this culminated in an invitation to undergo psychoanalytic training under the tutelage of Anna Freud and August Aichhorn. This training lasted from 1927 to 1933.

Erikson married in 1929. With his wife and two sons, he moved to Copenhagen in 1933. Shortly thereafter, the family moved again, this time to Boston, where Erikson became a practicing children's analyst and also held an appointment at the Harvard Medical School. From 1936 to 1939, he occupied a position at the Yale Medical School. In 1939 he resumed his psychoanalytic work with children after a move to San Francisco. He became a professor of psychology in 1942 at Berkeley but was discharged in 1950 along with other faculty who refused to sign the infamous loyalty oath. Later, he was asked to return but refused on ethical grounds.

From 1951 to 1960, Erikson served as a senior consultant to the Austen Riggs Center in Massachusetts, a residential treatment center for disturbed adolescents. He was also a part-time faculty member of the University of Pittsburgh Medical School and was affiliated with several other institutions. In 1960, he returned to Harvard. He died in 1994.

marks the close of childhood and the beginning of adulthood. Erikson attached particular importance to this period, and he invented the term **identity crisis** to help explain it.

In this stage the child must consolidate the information and skills acquired in previous stages and finally establish a personal identity. Children in this period become very concerned about the image others have of them and how they match up with that image. They must also develop a plan for the future. Establishing an **ego identity** is the work of this stage. It involves developing a confidence that one's self corresponds with how others perceive one, and that this can form the foundation for one's niche in life.

This is a stressful period. "Finding" oneself can be hard work and often involves experimenting with a variety of roles and aspirations. Idealism, vandalism, falling in love, studying, or having anxiety attacks may all occur. Role confusion, the danger at this stage, happens when the individual is unable to make a firm choice about an identity. Often this occurs because of insecurity over skills, sexual identity, or personal values. The turbulence of this period, with its accompanying role confusion and identity crisis, may explain the attraction of rock groups, movie stars, and other charismatic figures. Such figures provide an idealized image to which the individual can relate and thereby achieve some sense of personal identity. To fall in love, as is typical of adolescents, is another method of attaining identity by projecting one's own ego

People are pressured to conform with others throughout their lives, but Erikson observed that this pressure is particularly strong during adolescence.

qualities onto the other person and then seeing them clarified as they are reflected by that other person.

## Contemporary Psychoanalytic Theories

It is common in academic psychology departments for psychoanalytic theory to be criticized. In scientific circles psychoanalytic theory is generally criticized because its concepts are often vague and its theories are difficult to evaluate. However, psychoanalytic theory is also criticized in the pages of the poplar press, often because it portrays people in unflattering ways or because of its uncomfortable emphasis on sexual issues to explain human behavior. With all this criticism it is easy to get the impression that psychoanalytic theory is no longer taken seriously as a theory of personality. Indeed, many students seem distressed that they are asked to learn about what their professors and much of society describe as an outmoded approach. However, this impression is a mistaken one. Virtually every issue of *Contemporary Psychology*, a journal of book reviews, contains one or more reviews of new books on some aspect of psychoanalytic theory. Moreover, the March 1994 issue of *Psychoanalytic Abstracts* contains 192 abstracts of books and chapters on psychoanalytic theory and practice. Regardless of one's views of psychoanalytic theory as a basis for the scientific study of personality, it is certainly premature to pronounce it dead. The two most influential contemporary psychoanalytic theories are object relations and self-psychology.

## The Theory of Object Relations

**Object relations theory** focuses on people's relations to those "objects" that give meaning to their lives. The term *objects* refers to both people and things that have had an important impact on the individual, often during the earliest stages in his or her life. Object relations theory emphasizes that the way in which the individual relates to other people is of more interest than internal conflicts among the id, ego, and superego. The attachments of the infant to the mother and to other environmental figures shape the development of the ego and enable the individual to move from intense maternal attachment to a separate, autonomous state. This development process establishes the foundation for the style of later interpersonal relationships.

A crucial aspect of object relations theory is the importance of representations or cognitive images of important environmental objects such as the mother or father. These representations are considered to be internalizations of object relations. In the beginning, the child is attached to the mother and does not differentiate between the self and the mother. This primitive period is referred to as **symbiosis** (Mahler, 1968).

Later, as the sense of separateness develops, the child comes to depend on **object representations:** the individual's internalized images of an important object (e.g., the mother). Through such representations the child becomes able to handle the absence of the mother and to delay gratification. As the child matures it is these abilities that foster the growth of thinking and the related element of symbolism. So, regardless of the absence of an object or its varying appearance, the child learns to develop a constant image of that object. The father who plays with the child is the same person who becomes angry or impatient with the child. The mother who stands before the stove is the same object that sits before the computer and balances the checkbook. For object relations theorists, it is disturbances in object relations and the inability to develop adequate images of consistency that contribute to maladjustment. Indeed, extreme disturbances in object relations can lead to psychosis. Box 3-3 illustrates how environmental objects can help foster adjustment.

An example of the usefulness of object relations theory is the work of Josephine Klein (1993). She described the case of René from the perspective of object relations theory. René was a very disturbed young woman of 18 when she began therapy. She exhibited schizophrenic-like behaviors and suffered from eat-

## BOX 3-3
## The Nature of Transitional Objects

Winnicott (1953) discussed the importance of **transitional objects**. These are the objects (blankets, stuffed toys, diapers, etc.) that enable the child to tolerate separation from significant others. The toddler who is to stay overnight with the grandparents and arrives clutching a rumpled diaper is coping with separation. The diaper is a piece of security. In times of stress, the child may return to a transitional object and find solace in it. For example, the 6-year-old may feel too old to cry upon learning that grandmother is to babysit while mother is out to a movie. So, the child walks in grandma's front door bearing that old tattered blanket everyone thought was gone.

The transitional object is a calming force that provides a needed sense of comfort while helping the child deal with a widening world. Sometimes, even adults can find comfort in familiar objects. Gerontologists routinely advise that when it is necessary to move an elderly person to a residential or nursing home, for example, one should allow that person to bring along some personal household furnishings—pictures, dressers, and so on. Then, too, how many freshmen arrive at the dormitory carrying familiar objects from home? Obviously, excessive attachment to objects can signify problems. But like most other things, transitional-like objects in moderation can help people of all ages.

ing disorders. The eating disorders were interpreted as symbolic of mistreatment she had received or imagined she had received during feeding as an infant. One of the breakthroughs in her treatment occurred when her therapist offered her an apple. That the apple was nourishment offered by the nurturing figure of the therapist led to the interpretation that it was a representation of her mother's breast and milk. The apple was accepted and became the symbolic object that eventually resulted in a cure of the eating disorder and the schizophrenic-like symptoms.

## The Self-Psychology of Kohut

For Heinz Kohut (1971, 1977), the critical task is not the successful negotiation of the psychosexual stages but rather the development of an integrated self. Such a self will allow the individual to appreciate who and what one is so that life will have direction and meaning. To self-psychologists, the drive of the self to develop its full potential is innate and is called narcissism (Cooper, 1989). If this drive is thwarted, then a **narcissistic personality disorder** may result.

## Table 3-4
### Personality Disorders Associated with Narcissism

**Narcissistic Personality Disorders**

Involve thought processes more than action.

The *understimulated self* (resulting from lack of parental response) will do anything (e.g., promiscuity, perversion, gambling, drug and alcohol abuse, hypersociability) to create excitement and ward off feelings of deadness.

The *fragmented self* (resulting from lack of parental response) is extremely vulnerable to setbacks, responding with sharp decrease in self-esteem and disorganization.

The *overstimulated self* (resulting from excessive parental response) shies away from creative and leadership activities for fear of being flooded by unrealistic fantasies of greatness.

The *overburdened self* (resulting primarily from frustrated idealizing need) perceives others as hostile, reacting with irritability and suspicion to hardly noticeable events as frustrations or attacks.

**Narcissistic Behavior Disorders**

Expressed primarily in action rather than in thought.

The *mirror-hungry personality* (resulting from failure to mirror parental response) is famished for admiration, leading to incessant displays in an insatiable attempt to get attention.

The *ideal-hungry personality* (resulting from lack of parental response) can experience self as real only when related to others who conform slavishly to the person, though full satiation of the hunger is never really achieved.

From *Personality Theories: A Comparative Analysis,* 5th Edition, by Salvatore R. Maddi (The Dorsey Press, 1989). Reprinted by permission of Brooks/Cole Publishing Company.

Children have the desire for their expressions and achievements to be recognized, approved, and admired, most notably by the mother. The child also needs to admire and identify with more powerful figures such as the father. When these needs for recognition and identification are not fulfilled, the child's development will be at risk.

Ideally, the person will develop an **autonomous self**. This is a type characterized by self-esteem, self-confidence, and ambition. One's talents and skills become developed in the service of ambition and the establishment of goals (Maddi, 1989). Many of Kohut's insights arose out of his therapeutic work with narcissistic patients. Narcissistic patients express vague dissatisfactions with life. They see themselves as futile with no aims in life. They experience feelings of emptiness and depression or else lament a loss of "selfness." While they often function quite well, there is no sense of happiness, accomplishment, or meaning. Table 3-4 presents some of the common disorders associated with narcissism. Traditional psychoanalytic approaches were not effective with these patients. Therefore, Kohut developed techniques that conveyed the therapist's understanding of the patient's emotions and perceptions. For example, the technique of **mir-**

**roring** is used to reflect the patient's feelings back to him or her. The purpose of this technique is to make the patient aware of the emotions he or she is expressing because these emotions are often inappropriate for the events the patient is describing. By showing the patient how he or she is feeling, the patient may learn more appropriate affect.

## Summary

- Psychoanalytic theory and practice grew out of the brilliant insights of Sigmund Freud in the late nineteenth century in Victorian Vienna. Freud's collaboration with Breuer and his clinical work in treating hysterics were critical to the development of psychoanalysis.
- Two crucial assumptions of Freudian theory are psychic determinism (the idea that everything we do, think, or feel is determined) and unconscious motivation.
- Freud viewed the basis of all activity as motivated by two sets of instincts. The life instincts (Eros) are responsible for everything positive in our lives, whereas the death instincts (Thanatos) represent the destructive side of our personalities.
- The structure of the personality consists of the id, the ego, and the superego. The id is the primitive, unconscious aspect that demands immediate gratification. The ego develops out of the failures of the id to guide the individual toward gratification. The ego serves an executive role in the personality by mediating between the demands of the id, the conscience, and reality. The superego is the conscience and represents the influence of cultural values and prohibitions as conveyed by the parents.
- The individual's personality is shaped by a series of psychosexual stages. Each stage is characterized by an emphasis on a particular erotogenic zone (oral, anal, phallic, or genital). The latency period, a stage of little apparent sexual interest, precedes the genital stage. The specific experiences the individual undergoes in each stage shape his or her personality and help determine the degree of adjustment or neurosis.
- Anxiety was viewed by Freud as a signal to the ego of impending danger. Reality anxiety is a signal of danger from the environment. Neurotic anxiety suggests that an impulse from the id is about to erupt into consciousness. Moral anxiety is experienced as feelings of guilt or shame prompted from the superego.
- The ego may use any of many defense mechanisms to cope with neurotic anxiety. All ego defenses are employed unconsciously and are ways of thwarting the impulses of the id.
- Psychoanalytic theory has several implications for adjustment and personality. The particular manner in which one negotiates the psychosexual stages

and the subsequent pattern of ego defenses employed are the basis for the adult personality

- Psychoanalysis is also a method of treatment based on the view of symptoms as signs of an unresolved internal conflict. The ultimate goal of psychoanalysis is to provide the person with insight into the nature of the unconscious conflict.

- The methods of psychoanalytic therapy were briefly described, including free association, dream analysis, interpretation, analysis of resistance, transference, and working through.

- The revolutionary and brilliant ideas of Freud attracted adherents who did much to further the psychoanalytic cause. Several of these followers developed theoretical conceptions that differed from those of Freud and ultimately led to their alienation from him. In general, their ideas revised the role of sexuality and the ego.

- Adler, the first to depart, emphasized the part played by inferiority feelings and the resulting tendency to compensate for them. Eventually, he concluded that the basic human motivation is a striving for superiority. Still later, he developed the concept of social interest and defined it as a predisposition to contribute to society.

- A prominent Adlerian concept is style of life. This refers to the specific means the person employs to overcome his or her sense of helplessness.

- Adler wrote extensively on the role of the family in shaping the person's style of life. For example, he discussed both pampering and rejection as parental reactions that can lead to a mistaken style. He also considered ordinal position in the family to be a potent determinant of different styles of life.

- For Adler, adjustment meant facing problems with courage. An example of a maladjusted response is the tendency to put distance (either psychological or physical) defensively between oneself and other people or goals. The compulsive search for power (masculine protest) is another example of a maladjusted style.

- Jung also broke with Freud over issues of sexuality and libido. In the process, he gave psychoanalysis a broader intellectual base by drawing upon diverse fields such as archaeology, mythology, religion, and philosophy.

- The structure of the personality, Jung asserted, contains the ego, the personal unconscious, and the collective unconscious. Jung gave special emphasis to the last as a repository of the cumulative experiences of our ancestors. The structural elements of the collective unconscious are called archetypes.

- Four archetypes—persona, anima and animus, shadow, and self—were discussed as especially important ones that exert a powerful influence on behavior.

- Jung is noted for his descriptions of the ego orientations of introversion and extraversion, that is, interests that are, oriented toward the self or directed toward the outer world, respectively.

- Jung also introduced the concept of psychological types. In addition to being introverted and extraverted, individuals could be typed as being predominantly thinking or feeling and sensing or intuiting. Thus, individuals could be of eight general types, based on combinations of members of each of these three pairs.
- The neo-Freudians—including Horney, Fromm, and Sullivan—continued the Adlerian trend in emphasizing the role of the social context. Several of their principal concepts were noted, including ways of coping with basic anxiety (Horney), mechanisms for dealing with basic loneliness (Fromm), and stages of development from an interpersonal vantage point (Sullivan).
- Ego psychology was discussed as a further elaboration of the Freudian concept of ego. The ego psychologists gave a greater role to the ego and also saw it as being more autonomous.
- The psychosocial theory of Erikson was described as a prime example of the ego psychology movement. Erikson is particularly noted for his eight stages of psychosocial development. He saw these stages as genetic predispositions that unfold according to a plan. Each stage presents the individual with a crisis, and how each crisis is resolved, for good or ill, markedly affects the person's capacity to cope successfully with the next stage.
- In contrast to Freud's stages, Erikson's stretch across the entire lifespan, with an emphasis on adolescence and adulthood.
- Contemporary psychoanalytic theories include object relations and self-psychology.
- The focus of object relations theory is the important objects, including people, in the person's life. The most potent objects are those from infancy.
- The self-psychology of Kohut concerns the narcissistic drive of the self to develop its full potential. Thwarting this drive can result in the psychological disorder called narcissism.

# Chapter 4
# Psychoanalytic Theory: Research, Assessment, and Evaluation

Psychoanalytic Research Methods
    The Case Study Method
    Associations, Dreams, Fantasy, and
      Behavior
    The Comparative-Anthropological
      Approach
    Psychobiography and Psychohistory
    Subjectivity and Objectivity in Scientific
      Research
    Experimental Research
Research on Freudian Concepts
    Repression
    The Unconscious
    Defense Mechanisms
    General Conclusion
Research on Jungian Concepts
Research on Adlerian Concepts
Research on Ego Psychology
Summary Evaluation
    Strengths
    Weaknesses
Summary

Sigmund Freud exerted a lasting effect on personality theory because he could explain behaviors that had previously been incomprehensible. Not only did he have a theory to explain such phenomena as the phobic's fear of heights or the hysteric's physical symptoms, but he was, in many cases, able to remove these symptoms by applying his theory in therapy. The success of psychoanalytic therapy appears to be strong empirical support for Freud's theory.

Yet, many psychologists dismiss psychoanalytic concepts and observations. For many, the concepts of psychoanalytic theory are bizarre, poorly defined, and impossible to measure. Some of you may have had this feeling when you first encountered descriptions of the id or the psychosexual stages in Chapter 3. In this chapter these concepts will be presented and evaluated in the context of psychoanalytic research and methods of assessment.

## Psychoanalytic Research Methods

### The Case Study Method

For much of its history, the method of choice for investigating psychoanalytic theory has been the intensive study of an individual client by an individual therapist. Historically, there were no test tubes or tachistoscopes, no experimental or control groups, and certainly no statistics or computer printouts. What Freud and his followers did was listen carefully to their patients. Their laboratory became the consulting room. Their instruments were their senses and their ability to detect consistency in apparent incoherence and to abstract the similarities from the superficial differences among patients. The test of significance became the frequency with which patients relinquished their debilitating behaviors or fears. The case of Little Hans illustrates this method of investigation.

**The Case of Little Hans.** Freud's (1955) analysis of a phobia in a 5-year-old boy has become a milestone in the psychoanalytic method of case investigations. Actually, the analysis was based on letters the boy's father wrote to Freud; Freud saw the child only once. Nevertheless, the case illustrates the type of data upon which Freud built his notions of infantile sexuality, the Oedipus complex, and castration anxiety.

At the age of 3, Hans showed a noticeable interest in his penis, which he called a "widdler." He liked to touch it, wondered about the widdlers of others, and asked whether his mother had one. He noted the very large size of a horse's widdler and then remarked to his mother that he expected she had one as large as that. He observed that animals have widdlers but that tables and chairs do not. When Hans was 3 and a half, a sister was born, and he remarked on how small her widdler was but that he expected it would grow as she did. Eventually, his mother warned him about touching his widdler and even threatened to have it cut off. When Hans was about 4 and a half, his mother was powdering the area around his penis after a bath when he asked why she did not touch his penis. His mother explained that it was not proper, whereupon Hans exclaimed, "But it's great fun."

One day, about six months later, Hans was out for a walk with his nursemaid. When a horse-drawn van turned over, he began to cry and wanted to go home to be with his mother. Shortly thereafter, he developed strong anxiety over leaving the house, fearing that a horse would bite him if he did. Even before that, he was having bad dreams, and as a result his mother often took him to bed with her. He began to fear that a horse would enter his room. Soon his dread of horses escalated into a rather typical horse phobia. Another aspect of this fear was his preoccupation with the "black things around horses' mouths and the things in front of their eyes." In addition, prior to the onset of the phobia he was with his mother when the father of one of his friends remarked to her that there was a white horse nearby that bit, and that she should not hold her fingers up to it.

This account is a brief description of the case of Little Hans. You will find many additional details in Freud's (1955) lengthy description. After considering these details, Freud provided an explanation of Hans's phobia of horses. Briefly, there was Hans's interest in his (and everybody else's) penis. There was his apparent sexual attachment to his mother—his wanting her to touch his penis and their frequent sleeping together. There was the biting horse and its relation to castration. And there was the likelihood that horses' black blinders and muzzles were representations of his father's glasses and mustache. From these elements and many others, Freud concluded that Hans was in the midst of a severe Oedipus complex. His sexual attraction for his mother was strong, and his fear of punishment for these desires equally so. Although he loved his father, he also feared him, and this fear was then converted into a fear of horses. Even though it was his mother who threatened him with castration, Hans was unconsciously trying to avoid his fear of castration by his father by staying away from horses (which also made it more likely that he could spend time with his mother). There are, of course, alternative explanations for the behavior of Little Hans, but this case illustrates the psychoanalytic investigation of the single case.

Criterion of Internal Consistency. Without question, Freud's patients provided the material from which he built his theory. As Hall and Lindzey (1978) observe, "Inferences made from one part of the material were checked against evidence appearing in other parts, so that the final conclusions drawn from a case were based upon an interlocking network of facts and inferences" (p. 59). Freud sought verification of his hypotheses by repeatedly looking for consistency in his patients' verbalizations or reports. Much like the anthropologist or folklorist, he continually searched for the underlying thematic structure or recurrences in what his patients told him. Only when he found strong evidence for consistent, recurrent themes did he feel satisfied that he had discovered the basis of a patient's problems.

He would apply the same strategy to the data from many subjects when hypothesizing about a general principle. He would pursue evidence in case after case until he was convinced the principle held. A particularly revealing example of this procedure involves Freud's original belief that many of his patients had been seduced as children by their parents. Later, he became painfully aware (through careful analysis of the case data) that these patients were really reporting their fantasies, not reality. He had built so much of his theory on what turned out to be a fantasy! Thus, he set about revising his theory on the basis of his observations.

However, some scholars of Freudian thought now proclaim that Freud relinquished his seduction theory of neurosis prematurely. They suggest that the childhood seductions reported by his patients were often real and that Freud's motivation for his revision was his desire for fame rather than scientific objectivity (see Masson, 1985). Regardless of Freud's motivation for revision, the ideal of continually checking one's beliefs against new data is good scientific practice.

To many, this intensive study of the single case seems "unscientific" because the data on which the analysis is based are obtained from the subjective impressions of an individual investigator. The extent to which the investigator's biases, misperceptions, and unknown motivations influence his or her observations and their consistency is a potential problem. Although concern about the subjectivity of the data is appropriate, the subsequent analysis of that data is exemplary. Freud spent hour upon hour searching for consistencies in the pattern of data, both within a single patient and across many patients. This search for consistency within the data provided by a subject and the effort to replicate findings across subjects is the hallmark of good scientific practice. Thus, although the validity of the data might be questioned, it would be wrong to dismiss the entire approach as fundamentally flawed. Also, there is no guarantee that data gathered by more objective means are any more valid than the subjective appraisals of psychoanalytic theorists.

## Associations, Dreams, Fantasy, and Behavior

Free Association. **Free association** was Freud's major investigative tool. It continues to be a prime psychoanalytic method of inquiry, both clinically with the individual client and as a broader research approach. It is assumed that as one association leads to another, the person gets closer and closer to unconscious thoughts and urges. In one sense, free associations are hardly "free" at all. They are the outgrowth of unconscious forces that determine the direction associations take. Frequently, these associations lead to early childhood memories, as was the case with Freud's self-analysis. Such memories of long-forgotten experiences provide the analytic investigator with clues to the structure of personality and its development. Because it is rare to have detailed, objective accounts of development, free association can help the psychoanalyst reconstruct the vital elements of the patient's past. Box 4-1 provides an example of where free association can lead.

---

### BOX 4-1
## An Example of Free Association

In the following description, Munroe (1955) offers an example of how free association works. What is interesting is the contrast between the pedestrian opening and the emotionally tinged closing. Such is the value of free associations.

The patient begins with a brief report on the previous day—a sort of routine in his analytic sessions. Nothing special: he had a conference with his boss about a project. He didn't quite like the boss's policy, but it was not too bad, and who was he, in the hierarchy of his institution, to contradict the boss? By now this was an old issue in the analysis: did he habitually give in too easily, or did he evaluate correctly the major contours of his job? In any event, the conference was just a conference like any others. He'd had a dream—something about an ironing board, but that was as far as he could go. Associations to ironing board? Well, we have one. "Matter of fact, my wife said our maid irons badly. She could iron my shirts better herself, but I don't think she could and I'm sure she wouldn't. Anyhow, my shirts look alright to me. I wish she wouldn't worry so much. I hope she doesn't fire that maid." The patient suddenly hums a bit from *Lohengrin* and has to hunt for the words on the request of the analyst. It is the passage where Lohengrin reveals his glorious origin. ("My father, Parsifal, wears his crown and I am his knight, Lohengrin.") Patient: "Now I think of that last report X (his boss) turned in. That was *my* work—only I can't say so. That ironing board—my mother was ironing. I jumped off the cupboard, wonderful jump, but I sort of used her behind as support—she was leaning over. She told father I had been disrespectful and he gave me a licking. I was awfully hurt. I hadn't even thought about her old behind—it was just a wonderful jump. Father would never let me explain. My sister says he was proud of me. He never acted that way. He was awfully strict. I wish he hadn't died when I was so young—we might have worked things out." (p. 39)

(It should be noted that Munroe telescoped the reconstruction of these associations.)

---

**Dream Analysis.** Dreams are viewed as another window on the unconscious because they are assumed to represent unconscious wishes in symbolic form. Typically, dreams are construed as symbolic wish fulfillments that, as with free associations, often provide important clues to childhood desires and feelings. Patients are encouraged to give free associations to their dreams. Thus, the techniques of dream interpretation and free association are related.

Of course, not all psychoanalysts have viewed the role of dreams exactly as Freud did. Adler, for example, regarded dreams as more than elements or residues from the day combined with infantile wishes. He saw them as purposeful attempts to solve problems in a way that corresponds to the person's style of life. Jung also had a different view of dreams. He placed great emphasis on the role of archetypes. He believed that these archetypes become known principally through dreams and their interpretation. For example, according to Jung, a dream has specific personal associations for the dreamer. But beyond that is a meaning that comes from the collective unconscious.

Fantasy. Fantasies and daydreams are close relatives to free associations and dreams and are therefore also thought to provide information about the unconscious. In particular, psychoanalytically oriented therapists have contended that the fantasies, play, and make-believe of children can reveal much about child development. In addition to its diagnostic value, play has been employed for many years as a therapeutic device with children who are experiencing psychological difficulties. Some investigators believe that fairy tales have been employed by cultures throughout history not only to teach children but to help them confront their own developing emotions (Bettelheim, 1976). Box 4-2 expands on this latter point.

Psychopathology of Everyday Life. A further source of data for the psychoanalyst is everyday slips of the tongue (**Freudian slips**), memory distortions, and strange

Make-believe and fantasy are important components in a child's development.

## BOX 4-2
## Children and Fairy Tales

Critics often condemn the terror and violence that is found in fairy tales. Yet, Bettelheim (1976) wrote persuasively that there are benefits from those frightening symbols in fairy tales. Although that horrible old witch threatens to eat children alive, it is that same witch who winds up burning in the oven. Within the framework of fairy tales, children can confront their greatest fears and resolve them.

The fairy godmother is a symbolic way of telling the children that their real and loving mother will always be there to help when needed. Or it could be that the fairy godmother symbolizes the child's own inner strength. Even the "littlest" brother or sister can deal with or overcome an older, smarter sibling. Also, kindness can become a magical tool with which to confront impossible odds. And in the end, the child achieves the impossible.

What is more, Bettelheim believed that fairy tales personify the good versus evil theme that pervades our lives. Fairy tales can, then, help the child find a moral meaning to life. Whereas teaching and preaching will often fail to sway a child, a good fairy tale can successfully convey the moral message that not only *should* goodness triumph over evil, but it *will*. Although children know that such stories are not real, they learn constructive lessons from them (Crain, 1980):

1. In "Hansel and Gretel," the children are abandoned, but they learn to overcome that calamity and to be independent and intelligent.
2. Although Cinderella's mother died at her birth and Cinderella was given a menial place in her stepmother's home, the prince and happiness eventually arrived.
3. In "Jack and the Beanstalk," Jack learns to be strong and daring. In the process he overcomes the giant and brings comfort and help to his mother.

behaviors (Freud, 1938). Such mistakes are regarded by the analyst as originating in the unconscious.

For example, there is the man who persists in calling an old girlfriend by her maiden name or who cannot remember her married name. This would indicate that the attraction still lives. And there is the egotistical person who rises at a scientific meeting to comment on the paper of a friend and says, "May I offer a few brilliant remarks on this very modest paper?" Leaving objects such as umbrellas, hats, briefcases, or books in someone's office or home provides a convenient opportunity to return (J. F. Brown, 1940). Heckhausen and Beckmann (1990) have introduced the term **action slips** to describe behaviors other than verbal expressions that may be unconsciously motivated. An example might be an otherwise punctual person who is always late when meeting her mother.

## The Comparative-Anthropological Approach

Although the case study has served as a major tool for the psychoanalytic investigator, further evaluation of psychoanalytic hypotheses has been based on cultural and societal manifestations of psychodynamic phenomena. The work of Carl Jung is a notable example. Jung sought evidence for the nature of archetypes in a variety of places, including religion, mythology, and the occult. And, like Freud, he analyzed his own dreams and visions. Although many psychologists regard Jung's methods as unorthodox and controversial, there is always some utility in testing the limits of one's ideas, and Jung certainly did that—from Kenya to Arizona, from theology to alchemy, from literature to mythology. In these scholarly wanderings he found what he regarded as evidence for the universality of archetypes.

Erich Fromm was another who moved his research outside the consulting room. In one study, he went to a Mexican village seeking verification of his ideas about the nature of personality. He used interviews, questionnaires, and a projective test called the **Rorschach** (the well-known set of inkblots that people are asked to describe and interpret) to show how personality is affected by social structure and change (Fromm and Maccoby, 1970). Also, Erik Erikson (1945) studied several North American Indian tribes to evaluate his beliefs about the relation between adult personality and childhood experiences.

## Psychobiography and Psychohistory

**Psychobiography** refers to the study of individuals. The related field of **psychohistory** also concerns individuals but emphasizes the influence of his or her historical context on the individual's development and actions. Erikson's essays on Hitler's childhood and Gorky's youth and his books on Luther and Gandhi were psychobiographical, but they provided a powerful impetus to the growth of psychohistory as a field (Erikson, 1958, 1963, 1969). In Box 4-3 Erikson's psychohistorical treatment of Gandhi is illustrated.

Freud is credited with developing the technique of psychobiography, and the first genuine psychobiography is Freud's (1910/1957) *Leonardo da Vinci and a Memory of His Childhood*. Freud also delved into the lives of other historical figures, including Dostoevsky and Moses (Freud, 1961, 1964). These psychobiographical studies served both to evaluate his theory and to clarify the psychodynamics of these figures. This tradition continues with, for example, Liebert's (1983) psychoanalytic study of Michelangelo. Freud's approach to psychobiography is now viewed as naive, biased, and methodologically flawed (Elms, 1988).

BOX 4-3
# Erikson on Gandhi

Identity is a key concept in Erikson's writings. Nowhere did Erikson more clearly use this concept than in his book *Gandhi's Truth*, published in 1969. Identity became Erikson's key concept in understanding Gandhi, but also Gandhi's life became a way for Erikson to better understand the concept of identity. In an analysis of Erikson's description of ideology and identity in Gandhi's life, Scroggs (1985) makes several points. Among them is the description of how clothing came to symbolize Gandhi's struggle to achieve an identity. The little brown man in the cotton loincloth became universally associated with Gandhi and his cause, the freedom of colonial people. In the beginning, he tried to find his own identity by identifying with his oppressors, the British. Thus, as a young man in England he wore clothing (silk hat, black coat) that would proclaim his "English" identity. He even took dancing lessons to solidify his image. Later, in South Africa, it would be his clothing that would lead a South African judge to refuse to allow Gandhi to remain in his courtroom.

If the foregoing signified a definite identity crisis on the part of Gandhi, it was South African racism that pushed him toward a resolution of that crisis. Scarcely a week after being tossed out of the courtroom, he was thrown off a train when he refused to give up his compartment to a white man. It was this experience that led him to resolve that he would lead a movement to eradicate such discrimination. His identity crisis was over.

Twenty years later, he returned to India to be met by dignitaries in their finest formal attire. Gandhi, in contrast, stepped off the gangplank dressed in his customary shawl and loincloth. As Scroggs (1985) puts it, "Gandhi learned the hard way that you are what you wear; but once he had learned this lesson, he applied it with great effectiveness" (p. 104). In searching for and establishing his own identity, Gandhi restored India's identity. To understand India, we must, then, understand Gandhi and his struggle for a personal identity. To understand Gandhi, we must, in turn, learn about India. The influences are reciprocal ones.

However, techniques such as using established personality measures to guide the personality interpretations and approaching the biographical information with specific questions (Alexander, 1988) have made psychobiographical analysis more rigorous, and the value of psychobiography is again being recognized by personality psychology (McAdams, 1988; Runyan, 1988). In introducing an issue of the *Journal of Personality* that was devoted to psychobiography, McAdams (1988) noted, "Today, personality psychologists seem less ashamed than they did twenty years ago to admit that the subject of their study is human lives" (p. 1).

## Subjectivity and Objectivity in Scientific Research

The typical criticism of the traditional psychoanalytic study of the individual case, whether done in person or through biographical and historical documents, is that it is "too subjective." But what does it mean to refer to research as "subjective," and why does psychoanalytic research suffer from this problem more than so-called experimental studies? The term *subjective* means that two scientists who are looking at the same phenomenon may observe different aspects of the phenomenon and/or may interpret what they observe differently. The difference in interpretation of an observation is true of all scientific research. One need look no further than any of the heated debates published in scientific journals to appreciate this. So, at the level of interpretation, all science is subjective.

However, most scientists try to introduce some objectivity into their work. This objectivity is sought at the stage of making the observations. Although scientists may reasonably disagree about the meaning of an observation, the ideal is that at least they will all be making and interpreting the same observation. Of course, the decisions of who to study and what measures and procedures to use are also inherently subjective, but once those decisions are made, the resulting data are objective. The traditional psychoanalytic method of case study is viewed as too subjective because there is no guarantee that two different scientists will make the same observations when using this method. The experimental method, with control groups, standardized measures, and well-defined manipulations, was introduced in part to insure that any two scientists who viewed the same event using the same procedures and the same measures would obtain the same data.

## Experimental Research

Objective experimental methods have not been widely used by psychoanalytic practitioners. The training of psychoanalytic practitioners rarely provides them with either the skills or the inclination to use these methods. The attitude of Freud contributed to this resistance. In an often-cited exchange, Rosenzweig (1941) wrote to Freud about his experimental research on repression. Freud responded that psychoanalytic concepts had developed out of a host of clinical cases and thus did not require experimental proof. This succinctly states the prevailing attitude that verification of psychoanalytic concepts is best accomplished by intensive study of individual cases, by self-analysis, and by events that transpire during the therapy session. The assumption is that the intensive training of psychoanalysts will insure their ability to make valid, if not objective, observations.

In recent years there has been a growing effort to use objective measures and procedures to evaluate a number of psychodynamic concepts. Moreover, several investigators suggest that such testing of psychodynamic hypotheses is not only possible but promising (Masling, 1983, 1986).

## Research on Freudian Concepts

Ernest Hilgard (1952) commented that even though laboratory studies often provide support for psychoanalytic concepts, those studies are often trivial demonstrations that do little to advance understanding. Furthermore, the research often addresses superficial aspects of the theory. As a result, experimentally oriented critics are left unimpressed, and the psychoanalysts dismiss the research as silly demonstrations of what is already known from clinical experience. Moreover, in many studies, psychoanalytic phenomena such as the activation and creation of unconscious desires are manufactured in the laboratory so that greater experimental control can be exerted. It is possible that such transient and artificially created phenomena are of little relevance to the powerful forces described in psychodynamic theory. Nonetheless, the application of experimental methods to the study of psychoanalytic phenomena has attracted a growing number of scientists.

### Repression

Because repression is a concept so basic to psychoanalytic theory, it has been the subject of widespread investigation (e.g., Singer, 1990). However, the status of repression as a legitimate scientific phenomenon remains unclear. Some respected scholars (e.g., Erdelyi & Goldberg, 1979) have argued that clinically, "the evidence for repression is overwhelming and obvious" (p. 384). Other, equally respected scholars (e.g., Holmes, 1990) who have reviewed the experimental evidence for repression have argued that the concept remains unsupported and that use of the concept should be accompanied by a warning that "The concept of repression has not been validated with experimental research and its use may be hazardous to the clinical interpretation of behavior" (p. 97). Research generally suggests that material associated with threatening thoughts or experiences such as a mild shock is not well remembered or is relearned poorly. This finding is consistent with the interpretation that the material has been repressed because of its unpleasant associations. However, it is not clear that repression is the best explanation for these results. And in other cases, it is not clear that Freud would have agreed that repressive mechanisms were operative. Regardless of the scientific status of repression, the concept of repression has recently received widespread public attention and, in at least one case, legal acceptance (see Box 4-4).

An illustration of laboratory research on repression is a study by Zeller (1950). He asked subjects to study a list of nonsense syllables until they were recalled perfectly. Three days later, subjects were asked to relearn the list until they

BOX 4-4
## Convicted by a Repressed Memory

"In 1990, a landmark case went to trial in Redwood City, California. The defendant, George Franklin, Sr., 51 years old, stood trial for a murder that had occurred more than 20 years earlier. The victim, 8-year-old Susan Kay Nelson, was murdered on September 22, 1969. Franklin's daughter, Eileen, only eight years old herself at the time of the murder, provided the major evidence against her father. What was unusual about the case is that Eileen's memory of witnessing the murder had been repressed for more than 20 years" (p. 518).

Eileen's memory did not return all at once, but during psychotherapy, more and more details of the murder returned until the memory was rich and detailed. "Eileen's memory report was believed by her therapist, by several members of her family, and by the San Mateo County district attorney's office, which chose to prosecute her father. It was also believed by the jury, which convicted George Franklin, Sr., of murder" (p. 518). "It was apparently the first time that an American citizen had been tried and convicted of murder on the basis of a freshly unearthed repressed memory" (p. 519).

From Loftus, E. F. (1993). The reality of repressed memories. *American Psychologist, 48,* 518–537.

again had perfect recall. They also performed a psychomotor task that was manipulated by the experimenter so that half the subjects were led to believe they were succeeding and half that they were failing. Both groups had done equally well in their initial recall of the nonsense syllables. According to the theory of repression, it was expected that the effects of ego threat would affect the subjects ability to remember the nonsense syllables. Thus, the group that believed it did poorly on the psychomotor task was expected to forget (repress) the syllables to a greater extent than the group that believed it succeeded. This did happen. Indeed, the difference in recall for the two groups carried over to three days later. After this, all subjects were again administered the psychomotor task and allowed to succeed. This latter step presumably eliminated the ego threat. Under this condition, no difference in recall of the nonsense syllables between the two groups was found. Thus, Zeller seems to have demonstrated that ego threat leads to repression and that the lifting of that threat erases the repression. However, some people have argued that this experimental analog of repression is trivial compared with what happens in real life. Still others have contended that it was not repression that produced lowered recall. Rather, failure may have led subjects to become so preoccupied with that failure that they no longer concentrated on the syllable task. So what do we have: repression or an attentional deficit? Such is the problem with research on repression.

A recent and more naturalistic approach to studying repression is the use of subjects' responses to questionnaires to assess individual differences in a **repressive coping style** (Weinberger, 1990). Repressive coping style refers to a habitual tendency to repress feelings of anxiety and distress as a way of managing stressful situations. Individuals who are characterized by a repressive coping style show discrepancies in their responses to different measures (e.g., Davidson, 1993). For example, such individuals may self-report feeling little or no distress in a situation, yet show signs of distress on physiological measures. The interpretation of this discrepancy is that the individuals are coping with the distress that is affecting them physiologically by repressing it from consciousness. An assumption of this approach is that repressive coping style is a general tendency that is typical of how the individual responds to distress in most situations. Thus, after people's repressive coping style is assessed, the validity of this theory can be tested by determining whether the measure of repressive coping style is correlated with other measures and behaviors that are also indicative of repression. For example, Myers and Brewin (1994) found that individuals who were classified as repressors by means of this approach recalled fewer negative childhood memories than individuals classified as nonrepressors. Also, the age of the first negative memory was older for repressors than for nonrepressors. Such a result provides some support for the validity of the measure of repressive coping style and thus, indirectly, for the theory of repression from which the measure was derived.

## The Unconscious

The **unconscious** is the most basic construct in psychoanalytic theory. The term *unconscious* is a broad expression that refers to a variety of phenomena in both everyday discourse and scientific discussions. Within psychoanalytic theory the term has a more limited meaning. In particular, psychoanalytic theory views the unconscious as containing the large majority of cognitive activity and as being capable of complex and consequential mental operations. In addition, some form of repression is assumed to be operating to place or keep the target material in the unconscious. The scientific study of the unconscious has historically been difficult, and evidence for the psychoanalytic unconscious is controversial (Erdelyi, 1992).

Most approaches for studying the unconscious as it is viewed by psychoanalytic theorists require presenting material to subjects in a way that prevents them from becoming consciously aware of the material (Klein, 1987). The typical device for accomplishing this is the **tachistoscope**. The tachistoscope allows the experimenter to expose the subject to material for very brief periods of time and at low levels of illumination. The subject's only conscious perception is generally a flash of light. One approach is the **percept-genetics method**. Pictures or other stimuli that are threatening to the subject are presented through a tachistoscope under gradually increasing illumination levels. The subject must describe or draw the stimulus, and the time it takes the subject to do so is measured. A famous study by McGinnies (1949) exemplifies this approach. He flashed neutral or "taboo" words (e.g., *house, flower* versus *whore, bitch*) on the tachistoscope. He found that a longer flash interval was necessary for subjects to perceive the taboo words and that anxiety measured by a physiological index (**galvanic skin response**) was heightened when the subject did not correctly describe a taboo word. As the physical process of perception was the same for both taboo and non taboo words, the explanation for these differences is that the subjects repressed the taboo word into their unconscious before they consciously perceived it.

Another approach is the **drive-activation method**. Using this method, the experimenter presents stimuli that according to psychoanalytic theory should arouse unacceptable drives, activate the unconscious, and create symptoms of psychopathology. The stimuli must be presented subliminally (unconsciously) because if the subject becomes consciously aware of the material the ego can intervene and prevent the material from activating the unconscious.

The work of Silverman (1976) illustrates the drive activation method. This work has inspired numerous doctoral dissertations and has received much attention despite several serious failures in replication by other investigators. Silverman's research concerns the relation between psychopathology and unconscious libidinal and aggressive wishes. Silverman assumes that there are powerful unconscious wishes for a state of oneness with the "good mother of early childhood." He further assumes that if these wishes are gratified, an enhanced level of adjustment will be achieved. A variety of samples have been studied, ranging from schizophrenics to psychotherapy candidates, smokers who wish to quit, and adolescents with personality disorders (Silverman & Wienberger, 1985). The typical procedure is to use a tachistoscope to project stimuli such as "MOMMY AND I ARE ONE" to the subjects for four milliseconds (a short exposure time). Preexperimental and postexperimental assessments of various indications of neurotic anxiety or other forms of pathology are obtained. Consistent with the Oedipal theory, for males the typical finding is a reduction in pathology following the exposure to "MOMMY AND I ARE ONE." Consistent with the Electra complex, for females the message "DADDY AND I ARE ONE" produces comparable results.

Research on the unconscious as it is viewed by psychoanalytic theorists has led to some provocative results. However, this research is controversial, and these results are often not persuasive to psychologists who work outside the psychoanalytic tradition. Some of the reasons for the lack of acceptance are the difficulties many have in replicating the results, the necessity for making a large number of untested assumptions to interpret these results psychoanalytically, and the availability of alternative, nonpsychoanalytic explanations for many of the findings.

Perhaps the most damaging criticism of psychoanalytic interpretations of these results is recent work that suggests that the unconscious is not capable of performing the cognitive tasks required by psychoanalytic theory. After decades of neglect, the unconscious has become the target of research by contemporary cognitive psychologists (Kihlstrom, 1987; 1990). In 1992 Loftus and Klinger asked the question, "Is the unconscious smart or dumb?" The psychoanalytic view is that the unconscious is "smart"—that is, capable of purposeful and complex cognitive activity such as reconstructing memories. The cognitive view of the unconscious is less flattering. The consensus among cognitive psychologists is that although the existence of unconscious cognition is no longer an issue, the unconscious is relatively unsophisticated and is capable of only limited cognitive analysis, such as counting the frequency with which events occur (Greenwald, 1992). Thus, although the existence of the unconscious is now generally accepted by cognitive psychologists, the nature of that unconscious is different from the one described by psychoanalytic theorists. In particular, the ability of the "new" unconscious is too limited to perform the types of processing required by psychoanalytic theory.

The debate over the nature of the unconscious will undoubtedly continue, but rapid and innovative advances in cognitive theory and methods hold some promise that many of the issues may be resolved and that the cognitive and psychoanalytic unconscious will eventually be integrated. Epstein (1991), for example, has recently proposed a theory of personality called cognitive-experiential self-theory that is based on two complementary modes of information processing: rational and experimental. The rational mode represents the cognitive unconscious. This mode involves basic cognitive processes, such as memory of whether or not an event occurred or associating features of the experimental situation with stimuli. The experiential mode has more of the characteristics of the psychoanalytic unconscious. It involves the active interpretation and transformation of material in memory so that events may be remembered as we wanted them to be rather than as they were. Epstein (1994) has marshalled an impressive array of evidence for the existence of these two modes and has demonstrated that his integration of cognitive and psychoanalytic traditions can account for a variety of observations.

## Defense Mechanisms

The mechanism used for ego defense is one of the primary variables in psychoanalytic theory. The use of different defensive strategies is one of the factors that makes individuals' personalities differ, and several hypotheses can be derived from psychoanalytic theory about the development and correlates of different patterns of defense. Thus, an important body of psychoanalytic research concerns the measurement of individuals' defensive strategies and the relations between those strategies and a variety of other variables.

In 1991a, Phebe Cramer provided a comprehensive summary of the theory, research, and assessment of defense mechanisms. In her review, "some 58 different measures of defense were encountered" (p. v.). These measures included scales derived from existing multi-item inventories such as the *Minnesota Multiphasic Personality Inventory* and the *California Psychological Inventory,* self-report scales written specifically to assess defense mechanisms such as the *Defense-Style Questionnaire* (Bond, Gardner, Christian, and Sigal, 1983) and the *Defense Mechanism Inventory* (Gleser and Ihilevich, 1969), measures derived by comparing self-descriptions with the subjects' description of others (e.g., Heilbrun,

1982), and projective techniques such as the *Defense Preference Inquiry* (Blum, 1950) which is based on the Blacky test (see Figure 4-1).

When using the *Defense Preference Inquiry* for studying psychoanalytic theories, subjects are presented with a picture such as the one in Figure 4-1 and are asked to tell a story about that picture. The story is then interpreted according to some specific criteria, such as omitting the mention of some details (such as the word "MAMA" on the collar) or misperception of the picture (such as describing the dog as calm). In general, the interpretive criteria are sufficiently specific to allow different interpreters to generally assign the same score to the same story. Cramer (1991a) provides a detailed scoring framework for measuring defenses from subject's responses to the *Thematic Apperception Test (TAT)* and the *Children's Apperception Test(CAT)*. Box 4-5 provides more discussion of projective techniques.

A large number of measures of defenses that represent all the major strategies (e.g., projective techniques, self-report, personality inventories) that have been used to assess personality are available. The advantage of these measures is that the assessment of defense mechanisms is no longer limited to a few individuals who have had intensive psychoanalytic training (Skodol and Perry, 1993). But do these measures actually indicate the tendency of individuals to use one or another defense mechanism? Recent reviews by Vaillant (1992) and Skodol and Perry (1993) have summarized the evidence for the reliability, validity, and utility of clinical interviews, self-report questionnaires, and projective techniques for assessing defenses. Personality scales and self-reports are the most efficient methods of assessing defenses. However, the evidence for the validity of these types of measures is not convincing. Indeed, the nature of defense mechanisms seems to make them inaccessible to self-report, and there is the possibility that a person would be defensive about reporting his or her defense mechanisms! Methods that use specific and reliable interpretative guidelines for scoring defenses from subjects' responses to projective stimuli or from clinical interviews are likely to yield the most valid measures. However, these methods have the disadvantage of generally requiring more time for administration and interpretation.

Cramer's research program is the best example of the use of experts to code and interpret subjects responses to study defense mechanisms. Cramer (1987) used the TAT and developed and validated a method of categorizing the stories produced by four age groups: preschool, elementary school, early adolescent, and late adolescent. She found that denial was used most frequently by preschool children and that they decreased their usage as they grew older. Identification was used very little by preschoolers but increased steadily through adolescence. The use of projection was most frequent in the two middle age groups (see Figure 4-4). These results are consistent with the hypothesized development of defenses in psychoanalytic theory.

In another study (Cramer, 1991b) anger was experimentally induced in college students who were then asked to tell stories about a set of TAT cards. The responses of the students were scored for the presence of different defenses according to Cramer's guidelines. The results indicated that the angered students

**Figure 4-1** ᏧᏩ A Blacky card.

exhibited more projection and identification than the nonangered students. Cramer also found that men used projection more than women.

## General Conclusion

Although they have a checkered history as targets for scientific research, psycho-analytic topics appear to be capturing the attention of contemporary personality investigators. Some of the results of that research are supportive, some are nega-tive, many are equivocal, but nearly all of them are provocative. What is clear from all this research is that there is a reasonable amount of support for several Freudian concepts such as repression, the unconscious, and defense mechanisms. However, much of this support is for versions of those concepts that are different from Freud's original conceptualizations. Thus, there is no unequivocal answer to the question "Was Freud right?" Such, of course, is the nature of science.

# Research on Jungian Concepts

Carlson and Levy (1973) contend that Jungian theory has been misunderstood and neglected by academic investigators. This is true in part because typologies have not been popular among personality psychologists. However, there has been some recent research on Jungian concepts. Jung argued that neurotics were

### BOX 4-5
## Projective Techniques and Assessment

To assess psychoanalytic constructs, psychologists have generally used projective techniques. The ambiguity of projective stimuli, the difficulty faced by respondents to present themselves in a favorable light or create the impression they wish, and the freedom of the subject to provide a multitude of responses make projectives ideally suited for psychoanalytic assessment. It is more likely that the person's responses will reflect unconscious processes that are the core determinants of personality. The ambiguity of the test material prevents the individual from relying on specific cues in the test for selecting a response. Instead, he or she must structure the stimulus material and in so doing reveals something of that inner core.

One of the most widely used projective instruments is the Thematic Apperception Test (TAT). The *TAT* was originally designed as a method of eliciting material analogous to that usually obtained through dreams and free associations (Morgan and Murray, 1935). The individual is asked to make up stories about a series of ambiguous pictures such as the one shown in Figure 4-2. The stories concern such information as what is happening, who the people in the picture are, what led up to the scene, and how it will turn out (Phares, 1988). A variety of interpretations are possible for any story. Traditionally, the interpretation was influenced by the nature of the client and the characteristics of the other stories, and it was not possible to read a story and then refer to a manual for the correct interpretation. Interpretation required training and experience and was best characterized as the generation and evaluation of hypotheses until a consistent interpretation emerged.

Perhaps the best known projective test is the **Rorschach Inkblots.** This technique is named after the Swiss psychiatrist who developed it to study the relation between personality and perception. The test consists of ten inkblots, such as the one shown in Figure 4-3. Subjects are asked to respond to the inkblots by indicating what the inkblot reminds them of and what it means to them. As with the TAT, traditional interpretation of the subject's responses was done by a well-trained, experienced clinician, who undertook the interpretation in the context of the subject's responses to other cards and any other information that was available.

For many years projective techniques were seldom used in research contexts because they did not meet even minimal standards as scientific measures. Specifically, two well-trained, experienced clinicians would often disagree about the interpretation of the same response, and the interpretations of the clinicians were seldom related to other characteristics of the subjects. Indeed, it appeared that the interpretation of a response to a projective technique provided more information about the person making the interpretation than the person who made the response! That is, the traditional approach to interpreting projective assessments lacked both reliability and validity.

*(continued)*

BOX 4-5 *(continued)*

Projective techniques have begun to reappear in personality research. The reason for this reemergence is the development of specific and systematic scoring systems for projective techniques. These scoring systems generally exhibit acceptable interjudge agreement, reliability, and validity (Parker, Hanson, and Hunsley, 1988). For the Rorschach Inkblots, the scoring system of John Exner (1974) has become the standard. For the TAT, several systems, each with a different purpose are available. One such system was developed by Cramer (1991a) for the assessment of defense mechanism. Thus, the often cited view of projective instruments as "unscientific" is unfair. The problem is not with the instruments but with how they were (and in some cases unfortunately still are) being used. With the development of more reliable and valid scoring systems, projective instruments can contribute meaningfully to personality research.

out of touch with their collective unconscious and hence developed numerous symptoms. To study this idea, Cann and Donderi (1986) used archetypal dreams. They predicted that subjects scoring high on a neuroticism scale would report relatively few archetypal dreams. More intuitively oriented subjects, being

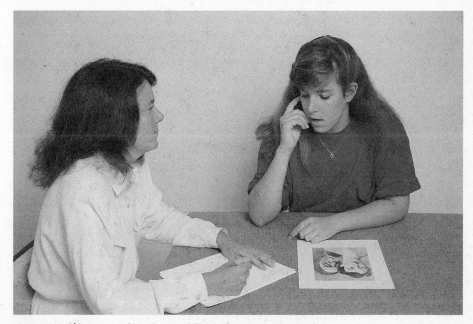

**Figure 4-2** Person taking the TAT (Thematic Apperception Test).

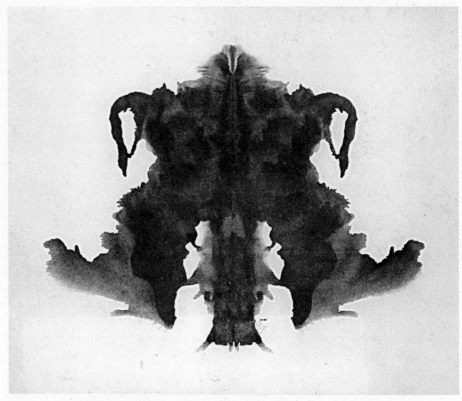

**Figure 4-3** A typical Rorshach inkblot.

in closer contact with their unconscious, would likely report more archetypal dreams. They obtained results that support these predictions.

## Research on Adlerian Concepts

Perhaps because it is easily and reliably measured, there have been many studies on the relation between birth order and a variety of psychological variables (Vockell, Felker, and Miley, 1973). For example, Falbo (1981) found that first-born and only children have higher levels of educational aspiration than later-born children. This may be because they receive more positive parental attention and are also the objects of higher parental expectations. Furthermore, last-born children show lower self-esteem than first-born children. Perhaps this is because last-born children have always had older and therefore more competent siblings against which to compare themselves.

Relative defense scores of primary, intermediate, early adolescent, and late adolescent groups.

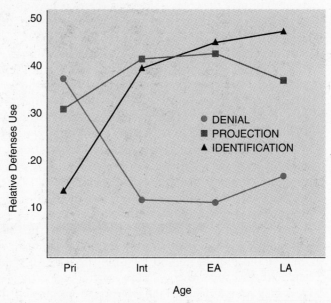

**Figure 4-4** Relative defense scores of primary, intermediate, early adolescent, and late adolescent groups.

From Phebe Cramer, "The Development of Defense Mechanisms." *Journal of Personality* 55:4, December 1987. Copyright © 1987 by Duke University Press.

Adler's concept of social interest has also been investigated. J. E. Crandall (1980) reviewed the meaning of the concept and developed of a scale to assess it. By use of this scale, a concern for others was found to be positively related to adjustment, although several variables, including sex, age, and stress, affect this relation. In addition, Crandall (1982) has investigated the connection between social interest and what Adler regarded as the tendency of neurotics to think in rigid dichotomies. He found that subjects low in social interest are more likely to make extreme judgments about themselves, others, and a variety of issues.

## Research on Ego Psychology

As with orthodox psychoanalysis, ego psychology has not been the subject of extensive experimental research. One exception, however, is the work of Wagner, Lorion, and Shipley (1983). They designed questionnaires to assess resolutions of the psychosocial crisis of ego integrity versus despair. In a sample of elderly subjects, they found that despair was related to insomnia. They interpreted this correlation as being consistent with the hypothesis that an ineffective resolution of the crisis of old age leads to a physiological symptom. With a college-age population they again found a greater incidence of insomnia in those students who had failed to resolve the crisis of identity versus role confusion.

Erikson argued that the ages of 35 to 45 were critical ones in adulthood. Levinson, Darrow, Klein, Levinson, and McKee (1978) studied a group of 40 male novelists, biologists, hourly industrial workers, and business executives who belonged to a variety of ethnic, racial, educational, and social class categories. Interviews, and in some cases later follow-up interviews, were conducted. Material on such variables as leisure-time activities, religious involvement, and reactions to the death of a spouse was collected. A research team then integrated all this information with Erikson's theoretical concepts. This procedure is not unlike what a psychoanalyst might do with a single case. However, in this instance there were multiple observers and 40 different subjects, so that comparisons and contrasts could be made. Analyses led Levinson and his colleagues to conclude that there are age-linked periods in adult development and that our lives can be viewed in terms of the choices we make and the coping strategies we employ. The major choices involved are concerned with occupation; marriage and family; friends; leisure; activities in the political, religious, and community spheres; and immediate and long-range goals. All these conclusions are consistent with Erikson's theory. However, a preexisting acceptance of Eriksonian ideas may have influenced the interpretations made by the investigators.

More recently, Van De Water and McAdams (1989) have suggested that to be generative in adulthood, people must have a fundamental "belief in the species" or a faith that human progress is possible and worth while. Using a variety of objective self-report questionnaires as well as less structured measures, they found some support for their hypothesis.

## Summary Evaluation

Psychoanalytic theory is not a unified and homogeneous set of propositions. It refers to early speculations by Freud during the Breuer era, but it also concerns his later views, such as changes in the nature of the role played by anxiety and the role of the death instincts. Furthermore, psychoanalytic theory is used to describe everyone from Jung to Erikson—from the orthodox Freudians to the neo-Freudians and the ego psychologists. As with most enduring theories, some of its features are real liabilities, but this does not mean that the theory as a whole should be discarded. Finally, there is a distinction between psychoanalysis as a theory and psychoanalysis as a form of treatment. Acceptance of the former does not automatically require that one accept all of the latter, or vice versa. Traditional psychoanalytic therapy procedures are not the only ones that can be deduced from psychoanalytic theory.

## Strengths

The following are some of the positive features of psychoanalytic theory.

Breadth. Psychoanalytic theory, especially the orthodox Freudian variety, is more comprehensive than other personality theories. It has been applied in almost all areas of human endeavor. Plays have been written with Freudian themes (e.g., those by Tennessee Williams and Lillian Hellman). The CIA has commissioned psychoanalytic studies of world leaders. Historical figures have been analyzed psychohistorically. Recently, the relevance of psychoanalysis for political theorists has been examined (Frosh, 1987). Even industrial firms buy advice about the unconscious reactions of potential consumers to their products. Regardless of how one evaluates the scientific legitimacy of the theory, there is no denying that Freud influenced the way we think about ourselves.

Systematic Organization. Psychoanalytic theory is complex yet systematic. It contains many concepts, more than in most theories. However, the concepts are all related. Knowing something about a person's ego very likely implies something about his or her tendencies to repress. Characterizing the nature of someone's Oedipus complex conveys information about the nature and extent of that person's adjustment status. The choice of defense mechanism is linked to psychosexual development. Freud wove an intricate theoretical pattern whose propositions are balanced and interlocked.

Of course, what is true in Freudian theory is not necessarily true for revisions of that theory. Both Adler's and Jung's theoretical constructs are few, and their theories are not as systematic as Freud's. In general, neither the neo-Freudians nor the ego analysts were the theory builders that Freud was. They generally used fewer concepts, and their work was often an extrapolation from Freudian ideas. Moreover, it is not always clear which aspects of Freudian theory they rejected and which they accepted. For example, Adler admitted to no formal concept of the unconscious, yet his theory requires this concept.

Psychic Determinism and Unconscious Motivation. Before the systematic observations of Freud, whole areas of human behavior seemed closed to rational analysis. People did weird things; therefore, they were weird. Or perhaps they were invaded by devils or influenced by forces not entirely of this world. However, with the introduction of unconscious motives and desires, irrational actions became open to rational analysis. The paralysis of an arm where no structural injury existed, the compulsive rush to destroy oneself by one stupid decision after another, the hatred of a surly son for a doting father—all these began to have meaning. Freud's brilliant insight led him to create a tool of unparalleled explanatory potential.

Role of Sexuality. The pervasive role of sexuality, from infancy to old age and from culture to culture, had not been recognized. With that recognition, much human behavior came into sharper focus. But when Freud saw sexual impulses in children, another major determinant of human behavior was discovered. The abuse heaped upon Freud is evidence that he had hit a social nerve. Many, including those neo-Freudians who broke with Freud, believed that he emphasized the role of sexuality much too much. However, although this emphasis may have served to blind him to the role of other important familial-cultural determinants, he had identified a pervasive factor in our lives.

**Freud the Observer.** Freud seems to have been an unusual and intrepid observer. Given the benefit of Freud's insights, it is no great feat to conclude that reaction formation may lurk behind the vehement outbursts of someone every time the topic of alcohol, for example, arises in conversation. But for Freud to derive the concept out of the rambling, incoherent mutterings of patients was a remarkable accomplishment. To formulate a general theory of infantile sexuality (especially in an era of Victorian repression) from the accounts of different patients is impressive. Thus, Freud was a keen observer and a creative scientist. That he was not always right does not detract from his overall achievements.

**Influence on Clinical Practice.** The general practice of psychoanalysis has been, and continues to be, a major therapeutic force. The psychoanalytic movement gave birth to techniques such as dream analysis, free association, and analysis of transference and resistance, all of which have become important both as assessment devices and as therapeutic instruments. And tests such as the TAT and other projective tests were influenced by psychoanalytic theory. Psychoanalytic treatment methods have percolated so far through the layers of clinical practice that we hardly notice their influence these days. But it is there. Whether as pure, orthodox psychoanalysis or as its less obtrusive descendants, the technique is influential and still widely practiced.

## Weaknesses

Psychoanalytic theory does have its share of problems that detract from its overall usefulness. Some of the more prominent of them are as follows.

**Problems of Measurement.** Perhaps nothing has created so many difficulties in establishing the utility of psychoanalytic theory and adding to our knowledge than the problems in measuring psychoanalytic concepts. For much of its history, the data upon which psychoanalytic theory was built and evaluated were not subjected to scientific evaluation. Moreover, not only did most psychoanalytically oriented psychologists have little interest in making their data scientifically acceptable, they actively resisted psychometric evaluations and improvements. They argued that the subjective impressions of experienced and well-trained psychoanalysts were the only meaningful data. The revival of interest in psychoanalytic concepts by research psychologists has resulted in substantial improvements in measurement. However, a cavalier disdain of measurement issues remains a legacy of psychoanalytic theory.

**Observational Bias.** The failure to evaluate the reliability and validity of observations increases the possibility of observer bias. From the very beginning, charges of bias were leveled at Freud's observations. Freud never checked his observations and inferences with other observers. Indeed, if anything, he became the standard against which others judged themselves. Recently, Mahony (1986) has examined Freud's process notes written while he was treating a patient referred to in his published writings as the "Rat Man." Mahony found marked discrepancies between those notes and the published case history.

**Limitations of the Single Case.** The single-case approach raises the question of sampling. How representative were Freud's cases—or, indeed, the cases of most psychoanalysts? Perhaps Freud was generalizing from the restricted perspective of one who saw too many hysterical, middle-class Viennese female patients. Likewise, how representative today are patients of psychoanalysts whose fees are rather large and who have exclusive offices in New York or Los Angeles? Thus, the cases from which analysts generalize may be so atypical that the concepts developed have little applicability to most patients. Moreover, many argue that psychoanalysis as both a theory and a method of treatment has no utility for those members of minority groups who must contend with issues of prejudice, poverty, and violence that may overshadow any unconscious defenses or unresolved Oedipal complexes.

Another problem with relying on single cases is the analyst's tendency to concentrate entirely on reports from patients. There is rarely any contact with relatives, spouses, friends, or employers. With no opportunity to check one's impressions of a patient against those of others, the way is opened for biases and self-serving errors.

**Picturesque Language.** Part of the problem in measuring psychoanalytic concepts results from facile descriptions couched in literary, picturesque language. To some extent, this reflects an implicit view that concepts such as the id, the ego, and the superego are real. However, they have no reality or specific location in the brain (where would you go in the brain to remove someone's ego?). They are simply constructs that have been developed to help explain our observations. Unfortunately, the ego too often conjures up such images as a person running about frantically plugging holes in the dike to ward off the waves of the id. And the id may be described as a region "down below" and the superego as "up there"—almost like heaven and hell. Although such vivid language and rich descriptions help make the theory attractive, extensive problems arise in restraining the language long enough to get independent observers to agree among themselves so that measurement can proceed.

Interpretational Excess.  Because of these measurement and language defects, there is a strong potential for interpretational excesses within the theory. For example, some analysts have been known to discuss the psychic life of a spermatozoon. Moreover, with concepts like reaction formation and the unconscious, it becomes nearly impossible to disprove a hypothesis. Any strongly held opinion can become subject to a charge of reaction formation. If it is said that a patient is pessimistic, yet on the TAT reports happy stories, this may be taken as confirmatory evidence. After all, these must be the products of reaction formation.

As a result, psychoanalytic theory is excellent at explaining things after they occur but very poor in predicting events. Suppose someone commits suicide by jumping off a bridge. To say that Thanatos made the person do it may be correct, but being able to measure the death instinct in advance, and thus ascertain its growing strength, is certainly the preferable alternative. But the behavioral signals specified by the theory are difficult to identify with any certainty.

Overapplication.  For many years, critics have argued that Freud's notions about psychosexuality have not been supported. Not every culture is like Western society. The universality of the Oedipus complex has been questioned by crosscultural research. Nor is it clear that Freud was right about the implacable march of the child through the psychosexual stages, driven by the beat of the instincts. But, then, it is hard to know how literal we should be in our understanding of psychoanalytic pronouncements. Does every little boy literally fear that his penis will be cut off, or is this again just a case of picturesque language rife with symbolism? There is always as tendency, too, for those who adhere to Freud's theory to wring every ounce of meaning from his statements, whether that is justified or not.

Overemphasis on Childhood.  Scarcely anyone would deny the importance of childhood in establishing predispositions for adult behavior. Yet, the Freudians place such an emphasis on childhood determinants that they sometimes seem to ignore the role of current determinants or situational factors. The individual is construed as being driven by internal forces established in childhood, and every adult event then seems to represent merely a reinstatement of some childhood occurrence. This tendency to blame the past rather than the present reality for patients' distress can be found in the therapy session as well. Patients' criticisms of their therapists are generally interpreted as evidence of negative transference rather than as reflecting real weaknesses of the therapists themselves. There is no systematic way in psychoanalytic theory to incorporate the role of present situational variables in the explanation of human behavior. To some extent, however, this criticism is tempered by the cultural emphasis of the neo-Freudians and the work of the ego psychologists.

The Feminist Critique.  There has always been a question about the validity of certain aspects of psychoanalytic thought when applied to women. For years, it was common to hear the remark "We, of course, do not understand the Oedipal (Electra) conflict in women as well as we do in men." Because most analysts are men, this lack of understanding about women may not be surprising. As men they were handicapped by a lack of firsthand knowledge of the female experience, and probably also by their share of male myths and stereotypes. Regardless of the reason, psychoanalytic theory emphasizes psychological development from the male perspective and thus may not be relevant to 50 percent of the population.

Analysts also tend to view women in undesirable terms. Women are described as more vain, sensitive, and dependent than men. They have also been described as displaying a "natural" masochism, and these attributes are viewed as an inherent part of being female. Women have often objected that Freud was wrong about penis envy as a basic motivator of women. They have also taken exception to the psychoanalytic implications that anatomy is destiny, arguing that this is just another instance of Freud's failure to appreciate the role of learning and culture.

The Psychoanalytic Cult. For some, psychoanalysis is viewed as a kind of cult. Many psychoanalysts have emerged from a medical background, characterized by an "appeal to authority" approach to evidence. The usual modes of experimental inquiry are foreign to them. Indeed, the process of becoming a psychoanalyst contributes to this dogmatic, cultish climate. Before a person can become a psychoanalyst, he or she must undergo a training analysis. But at the same time, the analysis may serve as a powerful tool of indoctrination that will later alienate the individual from other modes of inquiry. As further evidence there has long been a very strong psychoanalytic in-group, it was necessary a few years ago for psychologists to file legal action to gain admission to psychoanalytic institutes so that they could undergo training in psychoanalysis.

## Summary

- The chief method of investigation in psychoanalysis has always been the study of single cases. The case of Little Hans was offered as an example of Freud's approach.
- Freud used internal consistency as the criterion for verifying his hypotheses about these cases. Evidence from numerous separate elements of one case, or from numerous separate cases, were examined before he considered a hypothesis confirmed.
- Specific methods that were typically used included free association, dream analysis, and evidence from the psychopathology of everyday life.
- Other psychoanalysts, such as Jung, Fromm, and Erikson, sought evidence from comparative-anthropological sources.
- Freud is credited with developing the technique of psychobiography. Although the flaws in Freud's psychobiographical methods are now well documented, the development of new methods has resulted in a reemergence of this method in contemporary personality research.

- A similar technique is the psychohistorical approach pioneered by Erikson, in which historical figures are analyzed from the perspective of both history and psychoanalysis.
- Experimental research has never been a principal method of investigation in psychoanalysis. However, several psychoanalytic concepts have received attention from research psychologists.
- Repression has been studied through both experimental and correlational methods. In correlational research, measures of a repressive coping style have been developed and have been found to relate to several characteristics consistent with psychoanalytic theory.
- The unconscious has been studied from both a psychoanalytic and a cognitive perspective. Cognitive research suggests that the unconscious does not have the capabilities required by psychoanalytic theory. However, the existence of the unconscious is no longer an issue, which could be viewed as a substantial victory for psychoanalytic theory.
- Different strategies have been used to assess defense mechanisms. The most successful attempts use specific and reliable scoring procedures with projective stimuli and clinical interviews.
- Projective tests have long been favored assessment devices. Examples are the TAT and Rorschach Inkblots. The advantage of these instruments is their ambiguous stimuli, which permit free and varied response from the subjects. However, interpreting such responses is difficult. Traditionally, such interpretation was subjective and therefore did not provide a good scientific foundation for testing psychoanalytic hypotheses. The development of more objective scoring procedures such as the Exner system for the Rorschach Inkblots has increased the scientific utility of these techniques.
- Any evaluation of psychoanalysis must acknowledge the tremendous impact this approach has had on how we view ourselves. It has indeed altered the texture of Western society.
- The specific strengths of psychoanalysis include: its breath of description and application, its stature as a systematic statement of a point of view, its emphasis on psychic determinism and the role of the unconscious, its recognition of the importance of human sexuality, and its clinical influence. Above all, psychoanalysis as both theory and practice reveals the remarkable observational power of Freud.
- All theories of personality have limitations, and psychoanalysis is no exception. The problems with psychoanalysis include difficulties in measuring psychoanalytic variables, the use of vague or picturesque language, the potential for interpretational excesses, an overemphasis on psychosexual development, the potential for observational bias, the feminist critique, and the cultishness of the movement.

# Chapter 5
# Biological Influences: Behavior Genetics, Evolution, and Physiology

The Influence of Appearance and Body Type
    Sheldon's Constitutional Theory
    Critique of Constitutional Psychology
The Genetic Basis of Personality: A History
    Gregor Mendel: Linking Characteristics
      to Genes
    Chromosomes and DNA
    Francis Galton: Heredity and Individual
      Differences
Behavior Genetics
    Basic Models
    Methods of Behavior Genetics
Mechanisms of Influence on Personality
    Biochemistry and Neuroscience
    Evolutionary Theory
Uses and Limitations of Biology in Personality
Summary

The journal *Science* contains articles from all fields of scientific study, including the natural sciences such as physics, chemistry, geology, and biology; the social sciences such as economics, psychology, and anthropology; and mathematics and computer science. However, there is a clear bias: the vast majority of the articles published in this journal concern biology. This observation is best interpreted not as prejudice on the part of the editors but as the result of the rapid and extraordinary advances that are occurring in biological science. From the mapping of the human genome, to the technology of recombinant DNA, to the complexity of the world ecology, we live in the golden age of biology.

Many of our characteristics and much of our behavior as a species are related to biological functions, which include eating, surviving, reproducing, and dying. It would not be surprising if some of our differences and similarities in personality had, at least in part, a biological basis as well. For example, attraction between men and women is influenced by personality, and this attraction undoubtedly has some influence on reproductive behavior. The rapid and numerous developments in biological science and technology have aided our ability to formulate and test biological theories of personality (D. Buss, 1990). In this chapter, we will describe biological models that can be used to understand human behavior and personality. Fundamental to biological models of behavior is **genetic theory**. Genetic theory concerns the biological mechanisms of evolution, development, and differentiation. However, the influence of genes on behavior and personality is not direct, and genetics represents only one of several possible levels of biological analysis. Genes influence hormones, physical characteristics, brain structures, and sexual differentiation and are themselves influenced by the environment.

## The Influence of Appearance and Body Type

The easiest way to appreciate how biology can influence personality is by considering an individual's physical appearance. Height, weight, musculature, hair color, facial features, and other factors that contribute to appearance are all primarily biological characteristics. An individual's appearance (including, for example, whether he or she is taller than the average person, is overweight, or is physically attractive or unattractive), in turn, affects how that person acts toward others, the person's self-image, and how others act toward the person. Interpersonal behavior, self-concept, self-esteem, and the reactions an individual elicits from others are all important components of his or her personality.

The impact of physical attractiveness on the reactions of others and self-concept is a widely studied topic. Children adopt societal definition of attractiveness early in life (Lerner, 1982), and attractiveness has a powerful impact on friendship preferences, self-acceptance, teacher evaluations, and adjustment in adolescence (e.g., Lerner & Lerner, 1976). Weight, musculature, and body build are important components of attractiveness. From early childhood, both males and females report negative attitudes toward overweight children and adults, characterizing them as lazy, undisciplined, ugly, stupid, and nervous. It seems likely that such experiences have an impact on an individual's personality.

## Sheldon's Constitutional Theory

Sheldon (Sheldon, Stevens, & Tucker, 1940; Sheldon & Stevens, 1942) noted a tendency for people of similar body types to have similar personality characteristics and developed a method for classifying an individual's physique on each of three dimensions: (1) *endomorphy* (highly developed and massive visceral structure), (2) *mesomorphy* (predominance of musculature), and (3) *ectomorphy* (delicate, fragile, poorly muscled type). On the basis of nude photographs, Sheldon rated each of his subjects on a seven-point scale on each dimension. For example, a score of 7–3–1 would mean that an individual was highly endomorphic, somewhat mesomorphic, and not at all ectomorphic. The individual was labled by the dimension with the highest score; a 7–3–1 individual would be an "endomorph."

This method of classification was expanded into a theory of the relation between body build and personality called **constitutional psychology**. The key assumption of Sheldon's theory was that the genetic factor that causes the person's body build also causes the person to develop and display a particular type of temperament or personality. Thus, Sheldon did not view the person's body type as influencing temperament through the reactions it elicited from the self and others; rather, the body type was itself a diagnostic sign or correlate of temperament. According to Sheldon, the same genetic factors that resulted in a particular body type also produced particular personalities. Thus, endomorphs were *viscerotonic* (relaxed, comfort loving, sociable), mesomorphs were *somatotonic* (active, assertive, vigorous), and ectomorphs were typically *cerebrotonic* (restrained, inhibited, somewhat withdrawn).

## Critique of Constitutional Psychology

Although Sheldon's views have never had a major impact on psychological theory, they appear from time to time and are sometimes uncritically accepted in the popular press. Humphreys (1957) cogently attacked Sheldon's typology on both statistical and methodological grounds, pointing out that in Sheldon's studies the same person made the ratings of both body type and temperament, which might have biased the judgments to support the theory. Since Sheldon's initial work, few investigators have found any meaningful relations between social behavior and body type. Most important, even if such relations were found, their origin need not reside in constitutional and genetic factors. The more plausible hypothesis is that body types result in different interpersonal experiences that may influence personality. For instance, the strongly built individual may learn early that assertiveness and dominance are easily employed to gain his or her ends. The obese person may discover that humor and sociability are ready defenses against a fear of rejection. Or the ectomorph may soon realize that solitary pursuits are

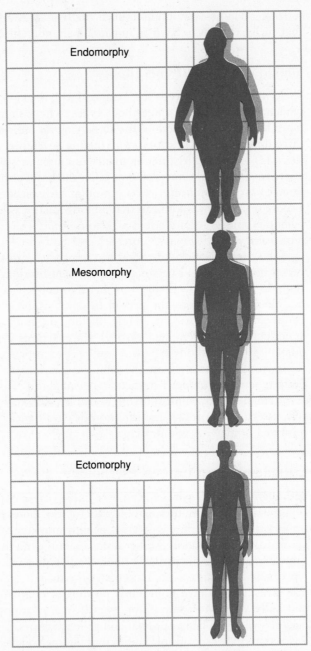

Subjects from Sheldon's research on body types and temperament. The illustration shows, from top to bottom, endomorphy, mesomorphy, and ectomorphy.

more likely to become a source of enjoyment than unsuccessful physical encounters with athletic peers. Finally, the empirical evidence for a relation between physical appearance and personality characteristics is not impressive (e.g., Rowe, 1994). Correlations between rated physical attractiveness and scores on personality scales are typically small. Thus, the long-term impact of appearance on personality (Hoffman, 1991) may be less than our intuitions suggest.

An interesting and scandalous account of Sheldon's research appeared in the *New York Times Magazine* (Rosenbaum, 1995) following the discovery of thousands of nude photographs of students from Wellesley College and Yale University, among others, who were subjects in Sheldon's research. This discovery, coupled with reports from former students at those institutions, indicates that Sheldon used deception and coercion to obtain his data. Being photographed in the nude was part of freshman orientation at these elite universities!

## The Genetic Basis of Personality: A History

Sheldon's theory was based on his perception of a relation between body type and personality. However, he did not directly address the biological mechanisms that result in variation in appearance or personality. Today, scientists believe that variation in personality can be linked to genetic variation. The work of Gregor Mendel and of Francis Galton, coupled with the profound observations of Charles Darwin, provided important clues for the biological origins, maintenance, and transfer of individual differences.

Darwin's theory of evolution through **natural selection** requires individual variation *within* a species. Natural selection operates through the advantages bestowed on some members of a species at the expense of other members of a species. Thus, without differences (variation) among individuals of the same species, natural selection would have no basis for functioning. The greatest initial problem for Darwin's theory was his inability to explain how *intra*-**species variation**—differences between two members of the same species (e.g., a collie and a dachshund) as opposed to differences between two members of different species (e.g., a dog and a cat)—originated and was maintained. Ironically, earlier work by Gregor Mendel, which was unknown to Darwin and most of the scientific community at that time, provided some important clues for the origin, maintenance, and transfer of individual differences.

### Gregor Mendel: Linking Characteristics to Genes

Like Sheldon's work, Mendel's work began with his observations of a relation among characteristics. However, the characteristics Mendel observed were of pea plants rather than of people. On the basis of his observations, Mendel established the two important principles that led to the science of genetics: **genetic seg-**

**regation** and **genetic independence**. Box 5-1 describes and illustrates these two principles.

Quantitative Characteristics and the Multiple Factor Hypothesis.   Mendel's observations of peas laid the foundation for genetic theory. However, the color and shape of pea pods are **qualitative characteristics**—features that differ in an all-or-none fashion. Most of the constructs studied by personality psychologists, such as extraversion, depression, or intelligence, as well as some physical characteristics such as height, are **quantitative characteristics**—those that vary smoothly along a continuum. The smooth variation of quantitative characteristics seems to contradict Mendel's theory that characteristics are inherited as a result of discrete factors or genes. The resolution of this inconsistency was a crucial step in applying genetic theory to personality.

## BOX 5-1
## The Principles of Segregation and Independence

Prior to Mendel, all theories of heredity were based on the principle of blending. For example, crossing a yellow pea with green pea would produce a yellowish-green pea. Mendel, however, did not observe blending in his pea plants. A yellow pea crossed with a green pea always resulted in a yellow pea. To complicate matters, in subsequent generations green peas would result from crosses of the yellow peas in a roughly 3 : 1 ratio of yellow to green. Mendel explained this surprising result with a theory that each color was the result of "factors" that remained **segregated** from each other. These factors were the forerunners of the present construct of a **gene**. The offspring received a duplicate set of factors, one from each parent. Thus, both a green factor and a yellow factor were present in the progeny, but the yellow factor was **dominant** in its expression, so that rather than blending with the green factor it eliminated its effect. In subsequent generations an offspring would have a 25 percent chance of receiving the **recessive** green factor from both parents, accounting for the 3 : 1 ratio. The principle of segregation provides an explanation for how a favorable variation in a species is maintained through subsequent generations rather than obliterated through blending—a problem that Darwin had been unable to solve. Figure 5-1 illustrates these phenomena.

The principle of **independence** was based on Mendel's discovery that characteristics in his pea plants such as color or shape occurred in all combinations and that the presence of one characteristic did not influence the likelihood of the presence or absence of another. If a pea was green, it might be round or wrinkled; if wrinkled, it might be green or yellow.

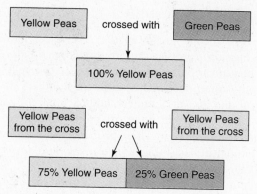

**Figure 5-1** An illustration of Mendel's observations that led to the principle of segregation.

Interestingly, Mendel had anticipated that some characteristics might be the result of several individual genes rather then one. This **multiple-factor hypothesis** (Nilsson-Ehle, 1908) is that characteristics such as height that appear continuous result instead from the transmission of a large number of discrete genes. Each individual gene will have the same discrete pattern of transmission hypothesized by Mendel, but when combined together across many discrete genes, the number of possible combinations becomes large and will give the appearance of continuity. For example, if height were the result of a single gene with two possible states (tall [T] or short [S]), people would be either tall or short. However, if height were the result of three genes, each with a T or S state, the possible combinations would range along a continuum.

**Phenotypes and Genotypes.** It is important to remember that Mendel developed his genetic theory by first observing the characteristics of peas. His accounting for the patterns of those characteristics required that he hypothesize unobserved genes. Thus, it is crucial to distinguish between the **phenotype,** the physical appearance of a characteristic of interest, from the **genotype,** the underlying genetic code that contributes to the phenotype. Although we often identify genotypes through their corresponding phenotypes, genotypes and phenotypes are not the same. In particular, phenotypes generally are influenced by factors other than genes, so the correspondence between the two is not perfect. The classic example is a genetic disorder called **phenylketonuria (PKU).** This disorder is the result of a rare recessive gene that affects children's metabolism. The result of this metabolic deficiency is severe mental retardation and behavioral problems. However, early diagnosis of this genetic disorder can allow physicians to change the diet of children with PKU, which greatly reduces or eliminates the retardation and behavioral problems. The children *still* have the PKU *genotype* and can pass the disease on to their offspring, but they no longer exhibit the associated *phenotype.*

## Chromosomes and DNA

Mendel's theory suggested that biological material was the basis for genetic transmission. Another important step in the development of genetic theory was the identification of **chromosomes** in the cells of humans and other species. Chromosomes occurred in different numbers in different species, they typically were found in even numbers, and each parent contributed half of the offspring's chromosomes, so that the offspring always had the same number of chromosomes as each parent. These properties of chromosomes suggested that they were the biological basis of genetic transmission.

Cells reproduce by splitting into two cells. **Somatic cells** (normal cells in the body) divide to form two cells in a process called **mitosis**. In this process, each of the 23 pairs (a total of 46) of chromosomes in normal humans duplicates itself, and then each pair of duplicates splits off into one of the 2 new cells. Thus, each new cell contains the same number (46) of chromosomes, and has the same genetic makeup as the original cell. However, **germ cells** (the sperm or egg cells involved in reproduction) are formed by a different process, called **meiosis**. In this process, the chromosomes do not duplicate but divide, so that only one chromosome from each of the 23 pairs goes into the sperm or egg. Thus, each parent contributes 23 chromosomes to the fertilized egg, which thus ends up with the usual 23 pairs or 46 chromosomes. However, this new cell will not have the same genetic makeup as either of the parent cells. As it grows, the egg undergoes the normal process of mitosis, so that each new cell has 46 chromosomes. The process of meiosis is illustrated in Figure 5-2.

Of the 23 pairs of chromosomes in the normal human, 22 are called **autosomes** and are the same in men and women. The remaining pair consists of the **sex chromosomes**. If the individual is female, this pair consists of two **X chromosomes** that are alike in size and shape. If the person is male, one of the chromosomes is an X chromosome, whereas the other is a **Y chromosome**. The Y chromosome is smaller and differently shaped than the X chromosome. The 23 chromosomes in a normal male and a normal female are shown in Figure 5-3.

The final step in linking Mendel's observations with biological processes was the discovery of **DNA (deoxyribonucleic acid)**, physical material that actually contains the genetic information on the chromosomes. The structure of DNA and the mechanisms through which it operates may be the most profound scientific discovery of the twentieth century. DNA molecules consist of two strands that wrap around each other in a manner that resembles a spiral staircase, called a **double helix**. Each strand contains four proteins: **adenine, thymine, guanine, and cytosine**. These proteins are paired across the strains in a specific fashion: adenine with thymine and guanine with cytosine. It is the sequence of these **base pairs** on DNA that provides the specific genetic code for everything from the color of peas to the personality of an individual. A partial picture of a DNA molecule with the pairing of the proteins in the production of new DNA is shown in Figure 5-4.

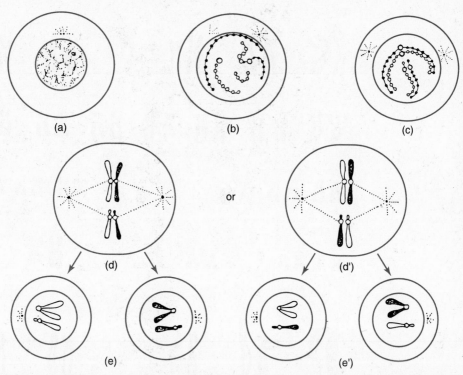

**Figure 5-2** ⊗ The process of meiosis, simplified, for a cell containing two chromosomes. The dark chromosomes came from the father, whereas the light chromosomes are from the mother. (a) Nucleus of the premeiotic germ cell. (b) and (c) Pairing of chromosomes. (d) and (d′) two possible arrangements of the chromosome pairs with the maternal and maternal chromosomes on the same (d) or on different (d′) sides. (e) and (e′) Four different patterns of sperm or egg cells (gametes) with a reduced (halved) set of chromosomes.

From G. E. McClearn and J. C. DeFries, *Introduction to Behavioral Genetics*, San Francisco: W. H. Freeman & Co., 1973, p. 40.

One of the most exciting areas of modern genetic research is the **human genome project** (Nowack, 1995). A major goal of this project is **gene mapping,** or physically locating genes on the human chromosomes. The progress of this project has been more rapid than anticipated, and the implications of this work are significant. Once specific genes are mapped on to a chromosome, the next step is to **sequence** that chromosome. Sequencing involves the identification of genes with specific sequences of the base pairs of DNA so that the precise location of the gene and its biochemical basis can be known. This in turn allows investigators to identify specific genes and to possibly correct those that may be harmful. Moreover, there is the possibility of **genetic engineering,** through which genetic

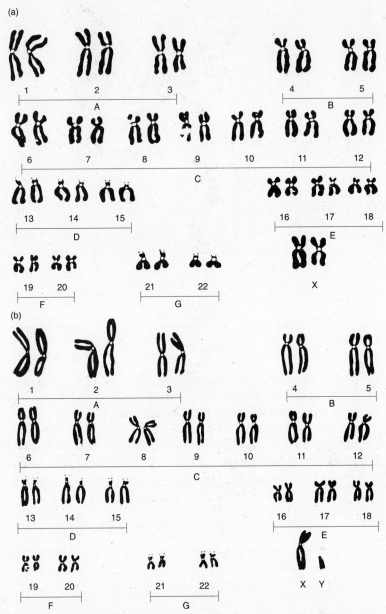

**Figure 5-3** &#8694; A normal female's (a) and a normal male's (b) set of 23 pairs of chromosomes. Human chromosomes are arranged by sixs into seven groups (A–G) and identified by a unique number. The X chromosome is a member of group C, whereas the Y chromosome is a member of group G.

From V. A. McKusick, *Human Genetics*, Englewood Cliffs, NJ: Prentice-Hall, 1964.

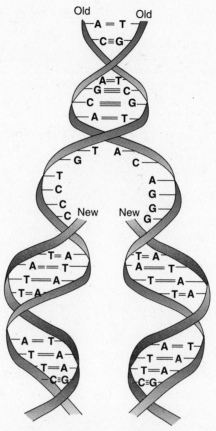

**Figure 5-4** ☙ Schematic diagram of the structure of DNA showing the pairing of the proteins during replication. A=adenine, T=thymine, C=cytosine, G=guanine.

From Louise Levine, *Biology of the Gene*, Third Ed., St. Louis: C. V. Mosby Company.

codes for specific types of characteristics may be inserted into the individual organism. The philosophic, ethical, and scientific implications of this are profound.

## Francis Galton: Heredity and Individual Differences

Genetic influence on individual differences in behavior and personality is an important and interesting possibility. However, it is essential to have accurate measures of those differences before we can consider the role genetics may play in their development. Individual differences in both physical characteristics such as height and body build, and psychological characteristics such as temperament

A
BRIEF
BIOGRAPHY
OF

# Francis Galton

Sir Francis Galton was born in Birmingham, England on February 16, 1822. He was the youngest of seven children born to Samuel Galton, a successful banker. Galton's mother, Frances Anne Violetta, was the daughter, by a second marriage, of Erasmus Darwin, whose first marriage had produced Charles Darwin, making Galton and Darwin half cousins. It was intended that Galton pursue a career in medicine, and he served several apprenticeships to medical men and studied medicine for a year at King's College in London. Later he enrolled at Trinity College in Cambridge, but illness prevented him from completing his coursework. In 1844 his father died, and this left Galton with a sufficient inheritance to allow him to abandon his proposed medical career.

Galton became an adventurer and sportsman, who made two significant journeys, one up the Nile to Khartoum and the other to Damaraland in southwest equatorial Africa. His published accounts of these travels made Galton well known as an explorer, and he played an active role in the Royal Geographical Society. After his return from Africa he traveled extensively in Europe, but he undertook no further trips of exploration because his health had suffered from the hardships of his previous journeys. Galton was active in the administration of science in Great Britain and did considerable research in meteorology. In 1863 he published *Meteorographica, or Methods of Mapping the Weather*, which formed the basis for weather forecasting for many decades.

Upon the publication in 1859 of the *Origin of the Species*, by his cousin Charles Darwin, Galton became a convert to the views expressed in that work and began to reflect on the influence of heredity on the human race. By 1865 he was already occupied with the research for which he is best known: the laws of heredity and their implications for the evolution of the human race. Galton was dissatisfied with the available data on human characteristics and so established an anthropometric laboratory in connection with the International Health Exhibition of 1884–1885 to systematically collect information from many individuals. This laboratory was the forerunner of the biometric laboratory at University College in London.

and ability, have been recognized for centuries. However, the precise measurement and statistical analysis of those differences is a relatively recent advance that can be attributed to Francis Galton.

## Heredity and Studies of Eminence.

Galton's primary interest was the cause of individual differences, which he attributed primarily to heredity. Much of his research was devoted to evaluating the relations between different family members

Galton was impressed with the observation that eminence or genius of various types seems to run in families. He therefore made several statistical inquiries designed to prove the heritability of genius. These investigations extended over 40 years and resulted in Galton's best-known publications: *Hereditary Genius* (1869), *English Men of Science* (1874), *Human Faculty* (1883), *Natural Inheritance* (1889), and *Noteworthy Families* (1906). An important auxiliary contribution of this work was the development, with the assistance of Karl Pearson and others, of the basic statistical methods and indices for assessing relations among variables.

Galton's research on heredity led him to conclude that the human race might gain considerably by increasing the offspring from the best individuals and restricting the breeding of the worst individuals. He gave the study of such selective breeding the label *eugenics*. He spent considerable energy developing eugenics societies to educate people about the importance of following hereditarian principles to better the human race. Unfortunately, Galton was under the influence of the racist and nationalist values of his era, and these values resulted in numerous prejudiced "applications" of eugenic principles that had no scientific basis. Galton's considerable scientific contributions will always be somewhat tainted by his association with the eugenics movement.

Galton received many scientific honors and in 1906 was knighted. Galton was married in 1853 but had no children. When he died in 1911, after several years of poor health, he left a considerable estate for the foundation of a chair in eugenics at the University of London, for which he wanted Karl Pearson to be the first professor. Galton's academic legacy includes, in addition to Karl Pearson, Charles Spearman, who was chair of psychology at the University of London. Spearman was succeeded by Sir Cyril Burt, whose two most famous students, Hans Eysenck and Raymond Cattell, have had a profound influence on personality psychology.

on measures of individual differences, particularly those involving mental abilities, or "genius" Francis Galton investigated the hereditary basis of individual differences in genius by studying a variety of family biographies and other descriptive accounts of **eminent persons.** His definition of eminence was strict; a single act of notoriety or the mere achievement of a prominent position in society was not sufficient. Instead, eminence was "the reputation of a leader of opinion, of an originator, of a man to whom the world deliberately acknowledges itself indebted" (Galton, 1869, p. 37). According to his definition only 1 in 4,000 individuals were regarded as eminent.

The general argument presented in his major work, *Hereditary Genius: An Inquiry into Its Laws and Consequences* (Galton, 1869), is that individuals endowed with high mental ability have a greater number of relatives of similar ability than would be expected by chance. Intelligence tests had not yet been developed, so Galton relied on reputation to identify people of eminence. His book includes the histories of 300 families that contained more than 1000 eminent individuals. Finding 1000 eminent individuals in 300 families is far greater than would be predicted by the 1 in 4000 ratio for people in general. Moreover, Galton found that individuals who were more closely related to the most eminent man in each family were more likely to be eminent than those more distantly related. Thus, he concluded that eminence was a familial trait, and he argued that heredity was the best explanation for this result. An example of Galton's analysis for the eminent painter Titian is shown in Figure 5-5.

Galton's finding that eminence "runs in families" is undoubtedly true and accords with everyday experience, which tells us that brightness and achievement run in families—not always, but often enough to make many of us believers in the effects of a person's family on his or her accomplishments. However, the *in-*

Vecelli, Tiziano da Cadore (Titian), (1477–1576); the great founder of the true principles of colouring. Showed considerable ability at the age of 18, and he painted until his death, by the plague, at 99.

There are eight or nine good painters in this remarkable family: Bryan mentions six of them in his Dictionary, but it seems that he is not quite accurate as to their relationships. The annexed genealogical tree is compiled from Northcote's descriptions. All those whose names appear in the diagram are painters. The connecting links indicated by crosses are, singularly enough, every one of them lawyers.

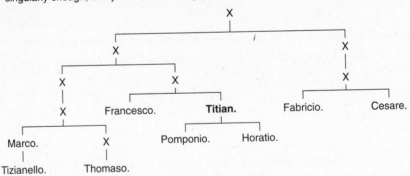

B. and 2 S. Titian's brother, Francesco, and two sons, Pomponio and Horatio, had all of them great abilities. The brother was chiefly engaged in military duties, and was never able to make a profession of painting. The sons wanted the stimulus of poverty, but there is no doubt of their large natural capacities for art.

**Figure 5-5** ⚬⚬ Galton's analysis of the family of the painter Titian.

From F. Galton, *Hereditary genius: An inquiry into its laws and consequences*. London: MacMillan and Company, 1869, p. 255.

*terpretation* of this finding as evidence that eminence is the result of inherited genes is far less certain. The flaw in Galton's reasoning is that it presumes that the *phenotype* of eminence is the result of a *genotype* for eminence. The undoubted environmental effects on the *phenotype* of eminence are ignored. Eminent people usually provide "eminent" environments for their children that generally include, social, educational, and financial advantages as well as role models of how to achieve and handle eminence. Thus, although Galton's results are consistent with a hereditarian position, they are also consistent with an environmental one. This example captures the essence of the nature–nurture debate in psychology. Unlike pea plants, human beings live in situations where the effects of genes and environments are not easily separated. As a result, how we choose to explain observations of family resemblance will generally reflect our values and politics rather than our dispassionate interpretation of the facts.

Certainly, Galton's decision to interpret the data as evidence of heredity is consistent with his values and political agenda. Galton was aware of the influence of environment on the phenotype of eminence. In Figure 5-5, Galton notes that the sons of the painter Titian did not achieve the same level of artistic eminence as their father because they "wanted the stimulus of poverty." However, he dismissed this environmental factor by then stating, "but there is no doubt of their large natural capacities for art."

Although Galton chose to emphasize heredity over environment to account for familial similarities, he did consider some environmental variables in his work. In 1874 he published the results of surveys showing that having a devoted, high-minded mother and being the first child born in a family were related to the development of genius. However, Galton's concern with environmental factors was primarily devoted to arguing against them. His arguments included the observations that (1) many men had attained a high rank in society despite a humble family background, (2) despite greater educational opportunities for people of the middle and lower classes in the United States, the United States had not produced more eminent people than Great Britain, and (3) adopted kinsmen of Roman Catholic popes who enjoyed great social advantage did not attain eminence at a higher rate than people in general.

**The Normal Distribution of Measures of Individual Differences.** Francis Galton is typically credited with founding the modern study of individual differences. Galton's interest in individual differences was motivated by his interest and respect for his half-cousin Charles Darwin's theory of evolution (see the Brief Biography, on page 154). Galton was also influenced by the work of Adolphe Quételet, who had found that human attributes were nearly always distributed in a **normal curve** around an average value. The normal curve is often described as "bell-shaped"; it is a symmetrical distribution that reaches its highest point at the average value and tapers off on either side. Galton referred to the observation that many human characteristics are normally distributed as "the very curious theoretical law of deviation from the average." Galton (e.g., 1879, 1887, 1894) developed apparatus and procedures for assessing a wide range of mental and psychological characteristics, including auditory thresholds, visual acuity, touch, smell, color vision, judgments of length, reaction times, and memory span. He also used questionnaires to assess imagery, temperament, and word associations. To obtain data from a large number of individuals he set up an anthropometric laboratory at an international health exhibition. He obtained data from over 9000 individuals who *paid* Galton for the privilege of being assessed!

Galton's contributions to the assessment and statistical description of individual differences, and his demonstration of the power of the normal curve for describing the variation of those characteristics in large samples of individuals, represent a crucial development in personality psychology. Indeed, Galton has been described as the founder of modern personality research (Rushton, 1990).

Eugenics. Galton's conclusions about the crucial role of heredity in the development and transmission of genius in families led him to consider how genetic principles could be used to improve the human race. He founded the study of **eugenics**, which is the promotion of breeding and reproduction by individuals with desirable traits (**positive eugenics**) and the prevention of reproduction by those with undesirable traits (**negative eugenics**). Galton is, perhaps unfortunately, best known for the concept of eugenics, as he devoted much of his later life to promoting eugenics principles and founding eugenics societies.

The idea of selective breeding was not new to Galton. It had been used with plants and animals almost since recorded history, and the Oneida Community, founded in 1848 in the United States by John Noyes (Holbrook, 1957), was a deliberate attempt to incorporate selective breeding into human society. However, Galton provided an extensive research foundation to justify the practice, and he gave it a scientific label.

The application of eugenics has a long and sordid history in the United States and abroad (Kamin, 1974). Eugenics was part of the "scientific" justification used in Nazi Germany for the programmed breeding of men and women to create a "pure" Aryan race (positive eugenics) and for the Holocaust (negative eugenics). In the United States the focus was primarily on eliminating undesirable characteristics through negative eugenics. Relying on the science of eugenics, vivid descriptions of "degenerate" families such as the "Jukes" (Dugdale, 1877) and the "Kallikaks" (Goddard, 1912) (see Box 5-2), and beliefs about the inherent undesirability and inferiority of various ethnic groups (Brigham, 1923; Lombroso, 1911), the United States adopted restrictive immigration quotas, instituted sweeping sterilization practices, and justified educational, economic, social, and political discrimination (Gould, 1981). Although of less apparent influence than they were in the early part of this century, ideas and proposals about eugenics still appear, usually amid much controversy, in both the popular (e.g., Herrnstein & Murray, 1994) and scientific (e.g., Rushton, 1988) literature.

Eugenics has always been an attractive solution to societal problems. It is appealing because it is thought to provide a permanent solution; if crime, poverty, and ignorance are entirely the result of heredity, then eliminating the "bad"

## BOX 5-2
# The Jukes and the Kallikaks

Whereas Galton emphasized positive characteristics in his studies of eminent families, other investigators applied Galton's methods to the study of degenerate families. Two such families were the Jukes, and the Kallikaks.

### The Jukes

In 1877 Dugdale, as a member of the executive committee of the Prison Association of New York, went on an inspection tour of the county jails. In one county he was impressed that six of the prisoners were related. He undertook an extensive survey of the family, which he traced back to six sisters whom he nicknamed the "Jukes." One sister had left the country and could not be traced. In 1916 Estabrook followed up on Dugdales observations. He wrote

> For the past 130 years they have increased from 5 sisters to a family which numbers 2,094 people of whom 1,258 were living in 1915. One half of the Jukes were and are feeble-minded, mentally incapable of responding normally to the expectations of society, brought up under faulty environmental conditions which they consider normal, satisfied with the fulfillment of natural passions and desires, and with no ambitions or ideals in life. . . . Heredity, whether good or bad, has its complemental factor in the environment. The two determine the behavior of the individual. (1916, p. 85)

Dugdale's statement was modest and assigned importance to both heredity and the environment, but the study was used primarily by hereditarians to bolster their position and came to be regarded as proof of "morbid inheritance." As with Galton's view of the cause of eminence, the possibility that the Jukes' degeneracy was a result of the impoverished and "faulty" environment in which they lived and in which they had been born and raised was not seriously considered.

### The Kallikaks

In 1912 H. H. Goddard published a book on a family that he nicknamed the "Kallikaks" (from the Greek for "bad and good"). In a manner similar to that of Dugdale, Goddard discovered this family through the large number of individuals it had contributed to the Vineland School for the mentally retarded. The important feature of this family was that it had two branches that both began with "Martin Kallikak." While a soldier in the Revolutionary War, Martin Kallikak had an affair with a feeble-minded girl whom he met in a tavern. When the girl gave birth to a son she named him "Martin Kallikak, Jr." After the war, Martin, Sr., returned home, married a girl of good family, and began the other branch of the family. Goddard wrote,

> The Kallikak family presents a natural experiment in heredity. A young man of good family becomes through two different women the ancestor of two lines

(continued)

**BOX 5-2** (*continued*)

of descendants—the one characterized by thoroughly good, respectable, normal citizenship, with almost no exceptions; the other being equally characterized by mental defect in every generation. . . . We find on the good side of the family prominent people in all walks of life and nearly all of the 496 descendants owners of land or proprietors. On the bad side we find paupers, criminals, prostitutes, drunkards, and examples of all forms of the social pest with which modern society is burdened. From this we conclude that feeblemindedness is largely responsible for these social sores. (p. 116)

A **pedigree** showing three generations of the Kallikak branches is in Figure 5–6.

The problems with Goddard's research are numerous and include the difficulty of assessing feeblemindedness and other defects from incomplete and retrospective reports, the possible bias of the single fieldworker who did all the interviewing and made the diagnoses, and the issue of whether Martin Kallikak was indeed the father of Martin Kallikak, Jr. However, the fundamental problem is again Goddard's failure to seriously consider the possibility that the undoubted differences in the environment between the two branches might have contributed to their disparity. Like Galton, Goddard construed his results as supporting a hereditarian view and was unwilling to acknowledge that his results were equally supportive of an environmental interpretation (Scheinfeld, 1944).

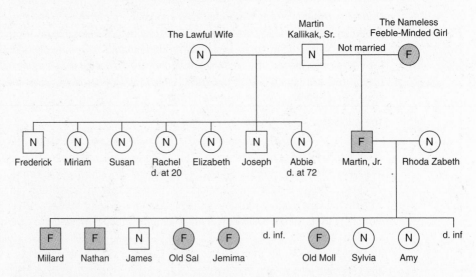

**Figure 5-6** ⌘ Three generations of the Kallikak family. N=normal; F=feeble-minded; d.=died; d. inf. = died in infancy.

Adapted from H. H. Goddard, *The Kallikak Family,* New York: Macmillan, 1912.

genes from the human gene pool rids society of those problems forever. It is also appealing because it locates the cause of society's problems on something other than its members or institutions. This means that *we* do not have to change, nor do *we* have to feel guilty. As Darwin observed, "If the misery of our poor is caused not by the laws of nature, but by our institutions, great is our sin" (1930, p. 526). More recently, Peter Breggin noted, "It is another way for a violent, racist society to say people's problems are their own fault, because they carry bad genes" (Mann, 1994, p. 1686). Despite its appeal, eugenics as a scientific discipline suffers from two fatal flaws. First, the decision of what is a desirable or undesirable phenotype is a value judgment, not a scientific one, and it is one that will change from situation to situation, society to society, individual to individual, and decade to decade. Second, eugenics is based on the *assumption* that heredity is the only important cause of whatever phenotypes we decide are desirable or not. Modern research in behavior genetics has shown this assumption to be false. "Research into heritability is the best demonstration I know of the importance of the environment" (Robert Plomin, quoted in Mann, 1994, p. 1689).

## Behavior Genetics

The field of eugenics is viewed by many as the forerunner of the contemporary field of **behavior genetics,** and Galton, therefore, is sometimes credited with founding the field. However, the likening of behavior genetics to eugenics is wrong. There is a crucial difference between eugenics and behavior genetics. Eugenics *assumes* that any familial resemblance is evidence of heredity, whereas the field of behavior genetics explicitly entertains the equally plausible hypothesis that environmental factors contribute to the similarity. Specifically, the goal of **behavior genetics** is to understand how both genetic and environmental factors contribute to the variations we observe in the characteristics of human and other species. The honor of founding behavior genetics is probably best reserved for John L. Fuller and W. Robert Thompson, whose monograph, *Behavior Genetics,* published in 1960, defined the field. Behavior genetics is an interdisciplinary blend of genetics and the behavioral sciences, particularly the psychology of individual differences.

### Basic Models

The fundamental, though greatly oversimplified, equation of behavior genetics is

$$P = G + E$$

where P is the phenotype, G is genetic factors, and E is all nongenetic factors, which include the environment and any error in the measurement of the phenotype. Although it is a useful starting point, this model, or theory of individual differences, is too simple to be of much use. One problem is that it concerns an *in-*

*dividual* phenotypic value, so does not concern individual *differences*. A study of individual differences requires that the phenotypes of a number of individuals be measured and an index of how much people differ on those measures be obtained. The standard index of how much people differ on a measure is a statistic called the **variance,** and behavior genetic analysis is concerned with how the variance on a phenotype can be assigned to differences (variance) in genotypes (G) and differences (variances) in environmental experiences and other nongenetic factors (E). Thus, the model is generalized to

$$V_P = V_G + V_E$$

where V stands for variance across a group of individuals. Box 5-3 provides an example of calculating phenotypic variances and applying this basic model to scores from a hypothetical study of friendliness using a measure of smiling behavior.

As the field of behavior genetics has developed, the theories and resulting equations have become more complicated. For example, it is likely that for some characteristics, genes and environments may not simply add independently to the phenotype, but influence each other as well. For example, friendly parents not only provide genes that may influence an offspring's friendliness but provide a friendly environment and serve as friendly role models as well. Alternatively, for some characteristics genes and environments may not only add together to influence the phenotype but combine in more complicated ways. Such a gene by environment **interaction** means that genes and environments together produce a different phenotype then would be expected by either alone.

For example, Meehl (1962) has proposed a diathesis-stress model of schizophrenia. According to this theory, some people inherit a genotype that produces a neural defect that might lead to schizophrenia. However, if these people grow up in nonstressful environments, they will not become psychotic. This view regards psychosis as an interaction between heredity and environment. Figure 5-7 is a simplified illustration of the operation of the gene by environment interaction described by Meehl's theory.

The division of the factors that contribute to phenotypic variance into a single general genetic and a single general environmental (technically "nongenetic") component is also an oversimplification. Several more specific types of genetic, environmental, and other factors can be considered. Considering all these specific factors and their interactions can result in a very complicated, but very powerful, theory of how various genetic and environmental influences combine to influence human characteristics and behavior. Often these theories are expressed in path diagrams (Wright, 1921) such as the one described in Box 5-4.

## Methods of Behavior Genetics

It is one thing to propose theories such as the one illustrated in Box 5-4; it is another matter to obtain data that can be used to test those theories. Before complex relations among observed phenotypes and unobserved genetic and environ-

BOX 5-3
## Calculation of Phenotypic Variance of the Percentage of Time a Subject Smiled in a Group Discussion and an Illustration of the Basic Behavior Genetics Model

In a study of friendliness 10 subjects were observed during a group discussion. For each subject, an observer used a stopwatch to record whenever the subject smiled during the discussion. The total time on the stopwatch (in seconds) was the subjects time smiling score (TS). The score of the 10 subjects are listed below.

| Subject | TS | −500.05 = | Squared |
|---|---|---|---|
| 1 | 450 | −50.5 | 2550.25 |
| 2 | 500 | −.5 | .25 |
| 3 | 535 | 34.5 | 1190.25 |
| 4 | 465 | −35.5 | 1260.25 |
| 5 | 570 | 69.5 | 4830.25 |
| 6 | 425 | −75.5 | 5700.25 |
| 7 | 580 | 79.5 | 6320.25 |
| 8 | 445 | −55.5 | 3080.25 |
| 9 | 525 | 24.5 | 600.25 |
| 10 | 510 | 9.5 | 90.25 |
| **Sum** | **5005** | **0** | **25,622.5** |
| **Average** | **500.50** | **0** | **2,562.25** |

The average TS is 500.5, but here the focus is on the differences among the subjects. For example, subject 6 smiled the least amount of time, subject 7 smiled the most, and subject 2 smiled an average amount. The goal of behavior genetics analysis is to understand how both genetic and nongenetic factors contribute to these observed individual differences in TS. To accomplish this, an index of how much people differ on the average in TS, called the **variance**, is calculated. To calculate the variance, the mean TS is subtracted from each person's score, as is shown in the third column above. The values in the third column indicate how much above (positive values) or below (negative values) each person is from the mean. These **deviation scores** are one reasonable way of showing how much, and in what direction, each person differs from the others. The direction (positive or negative) of the difference is not relevant to the issue of how much people differ, so the negative signs are removed by the operation of squaring, as is shown in the next column. To calculate the variance, the squared values are averaged;

(continued)

BOX 5-3 *(continued)*

that is, their sum (in this case 25,622.5) is divided by 10. Thus, the variance of these 10 TSs is 2,562.25. It is literally the **average** of the **squared deviations** of each person's score from the **mean**.

The variance is not a meaningful *description* of the differences among people's scores, but it is a useful statistical index in behavior genetics analyses. Specifically, by use of methods described in the text, the phenotypic variance of 2,562.25 is divided into genetic variance and nongenetic variance. For example,

$$V_P = V_G + V_E$$

2562.25 = 500 + 2062.5 (Most of the variance is due to nongenetic factors.)

or

2562.25 = 2000 + 562.5 (Most of the variance is due to genetic factors.)

mental variables can be evaluated, it is necessary to design studies that allow the investigator to separate the various types of genetic influence from the various types of environmental influence.

Scientists who study genetic and environmental influences on the behavior of nonhuman organisms have more flexibility in designing such studies because they can exercise considerable control over both the breeding and the environments of their subjects. The study of human behavior genetics is more difficult and less precise because we can control neither human mating patterns nor nat-

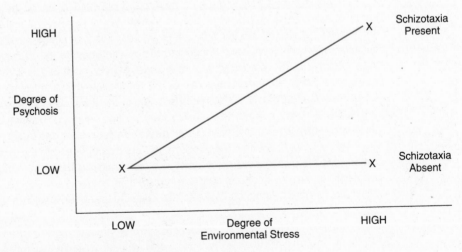

**Figure 5-7** ∞ Gene x environment interaction.

## BOX 5-4
## A Path Diagram Showing Hypothesized Genetic and Environmental Influences on Extraversion as Assessed by the Eysenck Personality Questionnaire

The **path diagram** shown in Figure 5.8 is an expression of a theory of genetic and environmental transmission of the trait of extraversion in the families of monozygotic twins. The diagram should appear symmetric, but it has been simplified (!) by omitting the spouse and the second child of one of the twins. Some of the symbols in the diagram are familiar:

**P** is the phenotype, in this case scores on the extraversion scale of the Eysenck Personality Questionnaire.

**G** is the underlying genotype.

**E** is the environment.

This is a complicated theory about the effects of genes and environments on extraversion. However, there are still many effects that have not been included in the model, and estimates of the values associated with the various paths via structural equation modeling techniques require more simplifying assumptions. The purpose of this presentation is to illustrate the level of sophistication achieved by behavior genetic theories. The question is not just one of genes versus environments any more.

ural human environments. Thus, the methods of human behavior genetics must rely on our knowledge of the degree of genetic relatedness among different types of relatives, "natural" experiments provided by social institutions such as adoption, and several simplifying assumptions. As a consequence, human behavior geneticists must be disciplined and cautious in the interpretation of their results.

Genetic and Environmental Relatedness. The design of behavior genetic studies begins with knowledge, based on our understanding of meiosis, about the degree to which different types of family members share genes. For example, siblings are expected, on the average, to have 50 percent of their genes in common, as is each parent and child. Grandparents and grandchildren, as well as aunts/uncles, nieces/nephews, and half-siblings, will have 25 pecent of their genes in common. First cousins will share 12.5 percent of their genes. Of particular interest to behavior geneticists are—as Galton first recognized—twins. Galton noted that twins were of two types; those alike at birth, which we now call **monozygotic (MZ) or "identical" twins,** and those unlike at birth, now called **dizygotic (DZ) or "fraternal" twins.** **MZ twins** are critical to behavior genetics studies because

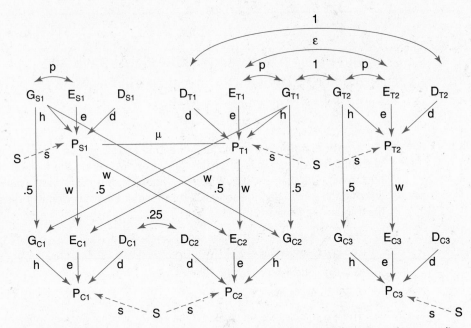

**Figure 5-8** ✆ Path diagram of a theory of genetic and environmental influences on the personality trait of extraversion.

From K. Tambs, J. M. Sundet, L. Eaves, M. H. Solaas, and K. Berg., Pedigree analysis of Eysenck Personality Questionnaire (EPQ) scores in monozygotic (MZ) twin families. *Behavior Genetics,* 1991, *Vol* 21, No. 4, 369–382.

they are, literally, genetic clones—they have 100 percent of their genes in common. **DZ twins,** on the other hand, have the same degree of genetic relatedness, 50 percent, as siblings born at different times.

It is important to realize that with the exception of MZ twins, for which the degree of genetic relatedness is fixed, the above percentages of genetic relatedness among relatives are estimates based on the simplifying assumption that mating in human populations is genetically random. For many characteristics, this assumption is known to be false. For example, there is a positive correlation between the measured intelligence of husbands and wives: more intelligent women tend to marry more intelligent men, and less intelligent women tend to marry less intelligent men (Spuhler, 1967). A relation between spouses on a genetic characteristic is called **assortative mating,** and this phenomenon is a further complication in behavior genetic models.

An even greater complication for human behavior genetic theory is the confounding between environmental and genetic relatedness. For example, parents and their children generally live in the same house and in the same town, and they generally spend more time together than an aunt and her nephew. Thus, the greater genetic similarity of parents and children relative to aunts and nephews is confounded by the greater environmental similarity experienced by parents and children. Likewise, MZ twins were born at the same time, have the same physical appearance, and therefore may be treated more similarly than any other types of relatives. Thus, their genetic identity may be confounded with a near environmental identity.

The task of separating environmental and genetic factors is made difficult for two reasons. First, there is no clear process such as meiosis that can serve as a starting point for estimating the degree of environmental relatedness among individuals. Moreover, we do not even know which particular types of environmental variables and experiences are important for the development of most characteristics. Thus, many simplifying assumptions about the degree and importance of different types of environmental similarity must be made. The legitimacy of these assumptions is often unknown. Second, even if we knew which environmental variables were important and had an acceptable method for estimating degree of environmental relatedness on those variables, we would be unable to exercise control over those variables to unconfound genetic and environmental relatedness. The result of these problems is that behavior geneticists must make "reasonable" simplifying assumptions in their theories and must rely on natural experiments to test them.

Twin and Adoption Studies.   Although it is possible to derive estimates of the genetic and environmental contributions to human characteristics from all types of relatives, the most powerful designs (i.e., the ones that require the fewest and most reasonable simplifying assumptions) are those that use twins, adopted children, and, most powerfully, adopted twins.

Galton's (1883) most important contribution to the study of the relative influence of genetic and environmental factors on human characteristics was the **twin study method.** To Galton, the essential question was the extent to which twins alike at birth became more dissimilar as they grow older, presumably as a result of different environmental experiences, and conversely the extent to which twins unlike at birth become more similar. When he made a qualitative assessment of questionnaires and biographical and autobiographical material, Galton found that the 35 pairs of twins who were alike at birth remained alike, whereas the 20 pairs of twins who were dissimilar at birth had not become more alike. "There is no escape from the conclusion that nature prevails enormously over nurture when the differences of nurture do not exceed what is commonly to be found among persons of the same rank of society and in the same country. My fear is that my evidence may seem to prove too much, and be discredited on that account, as it appears contrary to all experience that nurture should go for so little" (Galton, 1883, p. 241).

Since Galton's time the twin study has been widely used in behavior genetics research, and quantitative methods have been developed to analyze the observed differences between twins to calculate the **heritability** of a characteristic. Heritability is a statistic that estimates the proportion of phenotypic variance that can be attributed to genetic factors. Box 5-5 illustrates the calculation of heritabilities based on data from a twin study.

Another "natural" experiment for separating genetic and environmental effects is the **adoption study.** DeFries and Plomin (1978) have argued that the

---

## BOX 5-5
## Illustration of Calculations of Heritabilities from Twin Study Data

The simplest method involves the comparison of the degree of relation between a group of MZ twins using an **intraclass correlation** with the degree of relation between a group of DZ twins. Three assumptions are made: (1) DZ twins share half as many genes in common as MZ twins, (2) the genes act additively, that is, no there is dominance or epistatic variance, and (3) MZ and DZ twins experience the same shared environmental influences. From these assumptions, an estimate of the proportion of variance in a characteristic that is due to genetic variation is obtained by doubling the difference between the correlation for MZ and DZ twins. For example, if the correlation between MZ twins for height is close to .90 and the correlation between DZ twins for height is .50, the heritability of height is

$$2 \times (.90 - .5) = 2 \times .4 = .80$$

or about 80% of the variance in height is due to genes. Or if the correlation between MZ twins for the characteristic of *sociability* is .56 and the correlation for DZ twins is .33, then the heritability of sociability

$$2 \times (.55 - .33) = 2 \times .22 = .44$$

MZ and DZ correlations can also be used, under the same assumptions, to estimate the contribution of shared environmental factors to the observed differences in a characteristic. This estimate is twice the DZ correlation, minus the MZ correlation. For height, this is **(2 x .50) − .90 = 1.0 − .90 = .10.** For sociability, this is **(2 x .33) − .55 = .66 − .55 = .11.** Thus, environmental factors account for about 10 percent of the variation in height and for about 11 percent of the differences among people in how sociable they are. For sociability, 44 percent of the variance is genetic and 11% is shared environment.

The simple model evaluated by these twin study data accounts for only a little over half of the differences among people in sociability. The remaining 45 percent is a combination of unique environmental experience, nonadditive genetic influences, and errors in the measurement of sociability. Assessing the specific influence of these other factors would require a more complex experimental design and a more complex theory with additional and/or different assumptions.

adoption study overcomes many of the limitations of the twin study and is the most powerful design for disentangling genetic and environmental effects on the variability of human characteristics.

The focus is on children who are adopted at birth for whom information is available about their biological parents. Measures on the characteristic of interest are obtained from the child, the biological parents, and the adoptive parents. The correlation between the child and the biological parent (BC) is taken as an index of genetic relatedness because the biological parent has no impact on the environment of the child. The correlation between the adoptive parent and the child (AC) is taken as an index of environmental influence because the adoptive parent has no genetic relation to the child. Most studies employing this design have found that the BC correlation is larger than the AC correlations for most psychological characteristics; moreover, the BC correlation tends to increase as the child develops, whereas the AC correlation remains low and about the same. This pattern of results is interpreted as demonstrating genetic influence on the characteristic.

Although the logic of adoption studies is simple and persuasive, there are several difficulties with the design. Among them are the difficulty of obtaining measures on all individuals involved, particularly the biological parents and most particularly the biological fathers. Often the result is incomplete data or noncomparable measures. Most important, however, is the general failure of adoption studies to adequately assess the environment (DeFries & Plomin, 1978), which means that the absence of possible environmental effects on the BC correlation are assumed from the design rather than assessed in the study.

A combination of the twin study and adoption study occurs in those rare instances when MZ twins are raised in separate environments. Studies of **identical twins reared apart** can provide estimates of a variety of genetic and environmental influences on the variation of human characteristics (Bouchard & McGue, 1990; Bouchard, Lykken, McGue, Segal, & Tellegen, 1990).

## Mechanisms of Influence on Personality

When heritability estimates are reported for personality characteristics, such as the example of a heritability of .44 for sociability, it is easy to imagine the biological existence of a "sociability gene." However, a moment's thought should reveal that the effect of genes on personality and behavior can not be so direct. As biological constructs, genes cannot directly produce psychological constructs. There is no purely biological path from genetic material to sociability (or intelligence, or depression, or any other personality construct). Instead, genes are codes for the production of different proteins (**enzymes**), which, under the influence of the environment, result in the development of biological structures such as hormones and neurotransmitters, brain structures, neurological pathways, and patterns of cellular organization. These biological structures may place certain constraints on an individual's personality or make certain patterns of behavior—again in conjunction with environmental factors—more likely. Thus, genetic influences on behavior and personality operate through the effect of genes on other biological characteristics.

## Biochemistry and Neuroscience

There is substantial evidence that biochemical and hormonal factors influence behavior. For example, thyroid secretions can directly affect sleeping and level of arousal. Disturbed insulin secretions from the pancreas can result in mental confusion. There is some evidence that the adrenal glands play a role in such emotional reactions as anger. Unfortunately, the strongest evidence for a relation between hormones and behavior comes from animal research, and it is questionable how directly this research applies to humans, whose behavior is also influenced by cognitive and environmental factors. Because of the impact of cognitive and environmental variables on human behavior, the demonstration of a relation between hormone functioning and behavior can be difficult (Beach, 1975). Furthermore, when connections between personality functioning and biochemical factors are made, they often concern to extreme behavior disorders rather than normal personality functioning.

One of the most exciting new disciplines to emerge from the rapid developments of biological science is **neuroscience**. Neuroscience is an interdisciplinary field whose goal is to understand the relations between the biological structure and the functions of the brain and psychological experience of thoughts, feelings, and behavior. The areas of neuroscience are listed and defined in Table 5-1. As with the study of biochemistry and behavior, most of the work in neuroscience has been done with animals or concerns mental illness and brain abnormalities.

## Table 5-1
The Subdisciplines of Neuroscience

| | |
|---|---|
| **Neuroanatomy** | The study of brain structure |
| **Neurochemistry** | The study of the chemical processes that determine brain function |
| **Neuroendocrinology** | The study of the relation between glandular functions and brain functions |
| **Neuropathology** | The study of disease caused by disorders in the brain |
| **Neuropharmacology** | The study of the effect of drugs on the brain |
| **Neuropsychology** | The study of the relation between psychological experience and cognitive functions and brain structure |

However, as the discipline develops we expect that some of its models and methods will be applied to the study of normal human behavior.

Neuroscientists have shown that behavior and cognition result from the integration of networks of nerve cells. The activities of the nervous system are extraordinarily complex, and understanding them requires identifying the relevant structures, tracing the neurological connections, and recognizing the chemical factors involved in neural transmission. The relation of particular neural activities to the complex phenomena of human personality is a long way from being realized, and some suggest that for philosophical reasons it never will be. However, the tremendous advances that have occurred in neuroscience in the past decade suggest that this field may be able to contribute to the understanding of human personality, and that it may do so sooner than we might expect.

## Evolutionary Theory

The strong evidence for, and increasing acceptance of, genetic influences on personality and behavior has been one important factor in the increased interest in evolutionary theories of personality (Buss, 1991; Tooby & Cosmides, 1990). Once a genetic influence has been accepted, the question of where the genetic material originated and how it developed into its modern form becomes important. As Buss (1991) has noted, three theories only have been offered to explain the origin and development of present-day human genetic material. Two of these theories, the divine intervention of **creationism**, and the extraterrestrial intervention of **seeding theory**, although interesting, are scientifically untestable. Only **evolutionary theory** is consistent with current scientific thought and observation. The primary mechanism of evolution is genetic **mutation**, which is briefly described in Box 5-6.

Evolutionary theories of personality reflect the belief that evolutionary processes have had an important influence on contemporary human personality. In particular, it concerns the biological origins of human nature and human variability (Symons, 1990; Tooby & Cosmides, 1990). Evolutionary theory can be a difficult and scientifically treacherous area of study. The phenomena that are the targets of evolutionary explanations are the behaviors and personality of people today. Yet, evolutionary theory concerns events that occurred in the distant past. In addition, evolution is an exceedingly slow process. It operates not on the day-to-day or even decade-or-decade or century-to-century fluctuations in human behavior but on the gradual variation and change that have occurred across millennia. Because of this time scale, evolutionary experiments on human behavior are not possible. Evolutionary theory applies to an entire species. The characteristics and behavior of individuals or cultures are largely irrelevant to evolution; indeed, as we will see in the case of altruism, the behavior of individuals may be paradoxical. Yet, personality concerns individuals and the variation among individuals. Finally, evolution concerns genetic material, not the phenotypes such as personality constructs that might be associated with that genetic material. Indeed,

BOX 5-6
## Mutation and Evolution

Mendel's phenotypic observations, the behavior of chromosomes during reproduction, and the structure of DNA and the manner in which it replicates provide a basis for the maintenance and transmission of characteristics that are influenced by natural selection. But a crucial issue remains: where does genetic variation originate? This is a difficult question whose answers remain controversial. However, at the genetic level the variation or differences result from **mutations** in the genetic material. A mutation is a change in genetic material that occurs between generations.

The standard view is that mutations result from accidental errors that occur in the replication of DNA or in the pairing of chromosomes during meiosis. DNA replication is a chemical process, and no chemical process is absolutely repeatable. So, for example, sometimes an adenine appears opposite a guanine instead of the complimentary cytosine in a replicating strand of DNA. This mismatch puts a strain on the DNA molecule, and the cell contains repair machinery that detects such mismatches, cuts them out, and replaces them with the appropriate base. However, which strand is corrected to match the other is a matter of chance and results in a different phenotype. The different phenotype is acted on by natural selection so that if, in the unlikely event the new phenotype conveys an advantage, and/or if the organism with the new phenotype is simply lucky and survives to reproduce (Raup, 1991), the new genotype may continue into future generations.

The view that mutations and the resulting natural selection are entirely accidental is now largely discredited among evolutionary scientists (Ho, 1988). The problem is that there is evidence of far too many positive or adaptive changes than could plausibly be attributed to chance mutations. Thus some systematic (nonrandom) forces to guide mutations to be adaptive are being sought. The nature of these forces, which could include the chaotic process of complexity and self-organization (Kauffman, 1993), directed evolution (Ho, 1988), the inheritance of acquired characteristics (Lamarckianism), or even divine intervention are topics of intense study and debate among evolutionary biologists.

personality constructs have no biological or physical existence, so the relevance of evolutionary theory to contemporary personality theory is not always clear.

Testing evolutionary theory requires a willingness to speculate, make assumptions, and tolerate ambiguity. For these reasons, evolutionary theories of personality will generally be controversial. However, evolutionary theory is also exciting, intriguing, and almost certainly an important contributor to understanding human personality. Two areas of human behavior have received considerable attention from evolutionary theorists: altruism and sex.

### Altruism and Genetic Similarity Theory.

In 1975 E. O. Wilson published a book entitled *Sociobiology: The New Synthesis*. In this book, **sociobiology** was broadly defined as the study of the biological basis of all social behavior. The fundamental assumption of this approach is that all of the important ways in which organisms interact are the products of evolution. That is, at some point in the past, if not in the present, the patterns of social interaction that we now observe conferred an evolutionary advantage that, through natural selection, became a part of social behavior. The majority of Wilson's book was based on the organisms that had been the focus of his life's work—insects—and his conclusions regarding the interaction patterns of social insects such as ants and bees seemed reasonable. His book, however, generated much controversy, primarily because of the final chapter, in which he speculated that the social interaction patterns of humans similarly could be explained by sociobiological theory.

In particular, many facets of altruistic behavior have been explained by sociobiologists as the result of genetics and evolution. **Altruism** is generally defined as the tendency to help others without gaining any advantage to the self. This definition of altruism is broad, and most acts of kindness may vary in the extent to which they are altruistic. Pervin (1978) regards assisting others as increasingly noble or altruistic the more it is given without the expectation of external rewards and the more costly it is to the helper. From the perspective of the individual, altruism is *disadvantageous*. Helping someone by sacrificing oneself even to the point of giving one's life is not adaptive. From an evolutionary perspective, we would expect altruistic behavior to disappear from the gene pool because, by sacrificing themselves, altruistic individuals are less likely to reproduce. Yet, extreme altruistic acts happen rather frequently: individuals dive into flood-swollen rivers to save others, a person steps in to stop a fight between strangers, retreating soldiers go back into battle to save a comrade. Moreover, much of Wilson's (1975) book was devoted to documenting altruistic acts among insects, birds, and other members of the animal kingdom. For example, a bird may sacrifice itself to a predator and thereby lure that predator away from the nest. The result is that the individual bird dies but several other birds in the nest survive. Likewise, when an anthill is overturned, individual ants swarm out in response with no regard for their individual safety. Thus, altruism can not be explained by appealing to higher motives that are distinctly and essentially human.

From an evolutionary perspective it seems difficult to explain altruism. However, this difficulty is based on the error of applying evolutionary explanations to individual members of a species. Evolution is not about an individual's survival. Rather, it is about the survival of a **gene pool,** which is distributed across a species. If a group of individuals in a species survives, and specifically *reproduces* at a higher rate, that group's genes will be carried on into the future at a higher rate than the genes of other groups. It is the survival of the genes, not of the individual, that is the basis of natural selection. Thus, it is not necessary for the individual to reproduce; it is only necessary for genetically similar individuals to reproduce to obtain an evolutionary advantage. By committing an altruistic act and placing themselves at an *individual* disadvantage, the ants, the birds, and the soldiers may give their genetic material an evolutionary advantage. This phenomenon is called **inclusive fitness** (Hamilton, 1964), and it provides an evolutionary explanation of altruism. Because altruism more often occurs among relatives, it is sometimes cited as an example of **kin selection**, which is a special case of the more general phenomenon of **group selection** (Wilson & Sober, 1994).

Rushton and his colleagues have extended the concepts of kin selection and inclusive fitness in their **genetic similarity theory** (e.g., Rushton, 1989; 1990; Rushton, Russell, and Wells, 1984). This theory is designed to provide a biological explanation of not only altruism but human friendship, attraction, and support. The essence of genetic similarity theory is that it is evolutionarily advantageous for a gene to benefit any organism in which copies of itself are located (Rushton, 1990). This extends the rationale of kin selection beyond family members to socially unrelated individuals or even members of different species who have some genes in common. Genetic similarity theory predicts that more genetically similar individuals will show beneficial preference such as friendship, support, and altruistic acts toward each other relative to less genetically similar individuals. A requirement of genetic similarity theory is that individuals be able to detect genetic similarity.

Rushton and his colleagues have argued that there is evidence consistent with the ability of individuals to detect genetic similarity, although the mechanisms through which detection occurs remain to be specified. The phenomenon of assortative mating, in which people show a preference to marry and reproduce with individuals who are similar to themselves in values, abilities, and behaviors, is one example. Most intriguing, when genetic similarity is assessed among friends and mating partners by use of blood tests and differential heritability analyses, such individuals are found to be more genetically similar than are persons selected at random. Littlefield and Rushton (1986) found evidence for genetic similarity theory *within* families. Some children resemble one parent more than another, and Littlefield and Rushton found that following the death of a child, parents grieved most for the child perceived as resembling their side of the family. Perceived similarity among siblings was also found to be related to genetic similarity as determined by blood tests.

If people can detect genetic similarity and do change their behavior toward others as a function of that similarity, the implications are profound. It suggests that who we are friends with, who we fall in love with, and who we marry are, at least in part, driven by the efforts of our "selfish" genes (Dawkins, 1976) to survive. Rushton has also argued that genetic similarity theory can explain ethnocentrism because individuals of the same ethnic background are presumably genetically more similar than are individuals of different backgrounds. Indeed, if a pet dog and a pet fish are caught in a house fire, genetic similarity theory would predict that faced with a choice, we would save the dog.

Genetic similarity theory has an intuitive appeal. However, it is crucial to realize that it cannot be subjected to strong scientific evaluation. At best, evidence for genetic similarity theory is circumstantial. The strongest possible evidence one could hope for would be to identify phenomena that cannot be explained by any plausible theory other than genetic similarity, and no such phenomena have been identified. Assortative mating, friendship, and attraction may be consistent with genetic similarity theory, but they are also consistent with people of like values, abilities, and life circumstances having more in common and being more likely to meet. Saving the dog from the fire is consistent with genetic similarity theory, but it can also be explained by economic theory (the dog is more expensive than the fish) or by common sense (carrying a fish tank out of a burning building is more difficult than leading a dog). The problem is that we know so little about the environmental and cognitive factors that influence attraction and friendship that we cannot rule them out as alternative explanations to genetic similarity theory.

Sex and Reproduction. Interest in sex and reproduction is neither new nor restricted to scholars and scientists. However, the application of evolutionary theory to understand human sexual behavior and reproduction is a relatively new and intense area of study. As Kenrick and Keefe (1992) have noted, "evolutionary theory may be particularly pertinent to reproductive behavior, which is arguably the first line of evolutionary pressure. Differential reproductive success is, after all, at the heart of natural selection" (p. 75).

One of the most well-documented phenomenon regarding sex is the differences between men and women in their preferences for mates and the strategies they use to compete for desirable mates. Men are typically attracted to younger women and physically attractive women, whereas women are typically attracted to older and more resourceful men. Kenrick and Keefe (1992) have evaluated age preferences for mates across the human life span. In a series of studies using marriage records and "singles" advertisements from several cultures and time periods, they found that men's preferences for younger women was minimal during adolescence and increased as they aged. Young women, on the other hand, preferred older men, and women did not show as dramatic a change in age preference as they grew older.

Buss (1988) examined the strategies men and women use to compete for mates. College men reported displaying their physical attributes, showing off expensive possessions, and describing their future earning potential. College women, on the other hand, enhanced their physical appearance by using make-up, dressing up, and styling their hair. They also reported playing "hard to get." Buss (1989) subsequently found that the attraction of women to resources and status and the attraction of men to signs of sexuality and reproductive capacity was generally characteristic of men and women in 37 different cultures around the world.

Both Kenrick and Keefe, and Buss, have attempted to explain these observations using evolutionary theory. Building on earlier arguments by Trivers (1972), differences in mate preferences and selection strategies have been linked to the different biological roles men and women play in reproduction. Women make a greater investment in reproduction then do men. They carry the offspring for nine months, go through the process of giving birth, and subsequently have a greater responsibility for caring for the infant during nursing. The role of men in the process is brief, simple, and relatively effortless. From an evolutionary perspective, this suggests that women would adopt the strategy of delaying reproduction until the best available mate has been located and that the ability of that mate to provide resources for the offspring would be a crucial consideration. Men, on the other hand, should be less discriminating and attempt to copulate as frequently as possible with women who show signs of being most likely to conceive and bear children.

The observed differences between men and women in mate preference and strategies of sexual behavior are consistent with this evolutionary analysis. However, as was the case with the sociobiological analysis of altruism, the consistency between evolutionary theory and these observations does not provide proof, or even necessarily strong evidence, that human sexual behavior is driven entirely by evolutionary principles (Wallen, 1992). The evolutionary analysis is persuasive and may have some merit, but contrary to these evolutionary predictions, some women are promiscuous and many men are monogamous. Of course, additional evolutionary arguments can be developed to explain these exceptions (e.g., Gangestad and Simpson, 1990), but as additional assumptions, reasoning, and hypothesis are invoked the strength of evolutionary theory as an explanation of human behavior and personality is reduced.

## Uses and Limitations of Biology in Personality

Although humans are fundamentally biological, biological approaches to personality have been controversial, and the majority of personality research is conducted without reference to biological theories. David Buss (1990) notes that misunderstandings about the biological study of personality have contributed to the controversy and neglect. One misunderstanding is that biological theory is a single and unified approach. Instead, biological theories can be applied to human personality at several levels, including evolution, genetics, hormones, brain structure, sex differences, and physical appearance. Each level requires its own assumptions and methods. Moreover, within any level there are typically competing theories to explain the same data.

Another misunderstanding is that biological explanations are rigidly deterministic and do not allow for human adaptation and choice. Feminists, for example, "have been troubled by the definition of biology as an essential, innate, universal structure, that in principle can not be changed and that has been ideologically used to justify the inequality between the sexes" (Wright, 1992, p. 24). However, although biological factors are generally regarded as placing certain constraints on behavior and personality, contemporary biological theory is concerned with adaptation and change. "The whole reason for phenotypes having evolved is that they provide flexibility in meeting environmental contingencies" (Alexander, 1979, p. 14).

A final related misunderstanding is that biological models *compete* with environmental, cognitive, or social models of behavior. As Buss notes, the relation among these approaches is complementary; biological models supplement, and are supplemented by, these other models.

> But biology will not cannibalize personality psychology. Nor will it supplant the many approaches that have characterized the field since its inception. . . . Traditional personality research paradigms have generated basic findings that biological perspectives must confront and account for. It no longer makes sense, however, for the field to ignore the biological foundations of its central phenomena. (Buss, 1990, p. 15)

## Summary

- Darwin's theory of natural selection requires variation within a species, and Mendel's research on peas provided the basis for the maintenance and transfer of that variation.
- Mendel's principles of segregation and independence of "factors" provided the foundation of modern genetic theory, which includes the concepts of dominance, quantitative characteristics, and mutation.
- Phenotypes are observed characteristics, whereas genotypes are the unobserved underlying genetic material that *may* influence the phenotype.
- Genetic material is located on the chromosomes. The division of chromosomes during the reproductive process of meiosis is consistent with patterns of human inheritance.
- Genes are coded in four bases—adenine, thymine, guanine, and cytosine—on strands of DNA.
- Francis Galton's study of heredity was based on the study of eminent families. Unfortunately, Galton chose to largely ignore or discount environmental influences on behavior. This led him to found the field of eugenics, which in turn has been used by many to support prejudice, racism, and discrimination.
- Galton is credited with founding the measurement and study of individual differences, which he determined to be generally normally distributed.
- Unlike eugenics, the modern field of behavior genetics considers the complex actions of both genes and environments on human behavior and personality. In addition to their additive effects, the correlation between genes and environments, and their interaction to influence personality, are considered.

- Path diagrams are often used to express complicated behavior genetic theories. A statistic called the variance is fundamental to the analysis of data to test these theories.
- The methods of modern behavior genetic analysis include the twin study, the adoption study, and the study of identical twins reared apart. The confounding of environmental and genetic influences is a basic problem for behavior genetic data. However, when certain simplifying assumptions are made, it is possible to derive estimates of heritabilities from patterns of the correlations between individuals of different degrees of average genetic relation.
- Genes do not code directly for personality characteristics and behavior. The influence of genes on personality is through their influence of other biological structures, including body build, biochemistry, and neural structures, transmitters, and pathways.
- Evolutionary theory is designed to explain the origin of human nature and human variability. It is difficult to test evolutionary explanations of human behavior because evolutionary experiments are not possible. Instead, evolutionary theorists seek phenomena that are difficult to explain using nonevolutionary theories and that are consistent with the evolutionary explanations.
- Altruism and sex are two aspects of human behavior that have been explained with evolutionary models, including genetic similarity theory and theories of differential mate preferences between men and women.
- Although humans are biological, most theories and research on human personality do not explicitly consider biological mechanisms. This may be due to the mistaken belief by many personality psychologists that biological mechanisms are rigidly deterministic or that biological explanations compete with cognitive and environmental ones. Instead, biological theories complement other personality theories to provide a more complete understanding of human behavior.

# Chapter 6
# Biological Influences: Research and Summary Evaluation

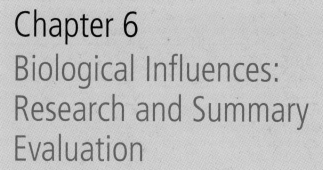

Behavior Genetics and Personality
    Twin Studies
    Family Resemblance and Adoption Studies
    Reconciling Twin and Adoption Study
      Results
    Environmental Influences
Biological Influences on Personality
    Physique and Personality
    Biochemistry and Personality
    Brain Structure and Personality
Evolution and Personality Psychology
    Human Nature and Individual Variation
    Evolution and Personality Structure
    Animal Personality
    The Continuity Between Animal Behavior
      and Human Personality
Summary Evaluation
    Strengths
    Weaknesses
Summary

Recent developments in our knowledge of biological structures and processes have resulted in stronger tests of more precise biological theories of human personality. Behavior genetics is a rapidly developing field that is characterized by advanced statistical techniques for disentangling genetic and environmental influences on behavior and sophisticated biological assay methods for identifying the location and nature of the genetic material that is related to personality characteristics. Advances in neuroscience have allowed behavioral scientists to establish the brain structures and functions that are associated with psychological processes, particularly those related to psychological dysfunction. And the introduction of evolutionary theory to the field of personality has provided an alternative perspective on many basic human behaviors. Our ability to relate mental processes to observable biological attributes has given us the capability to think more deeply and precisely about the interplay of biological and psychological factors in human behavior.

On the other hand, although psychological characteristics and processes can be related to biological ones, it is crucial to recognize that personality constructs are not, and can never be, fundamentally biological. Constructs such as "intelligence," "sociability," "repression," and the "id" have no biological reality. Ultimately, they exist in the minds of psychologists, not in the chemicals and brain structures of their subjects. Biology may influence the characteristics associated with these constructs, but so do environmental, phenomenological, dynamic, and cognitive processes. Efforts to reduce psychological phenomena to biological ones either trivialize the phenomena or are doomed to fail.

## Behavior Genetics and Personality

It has long been believed that family members resemble each other on a variety of personality, temperament, and cognitive dimensions. The temptation among hereditarians such as Galton has been to accept this similarity as evidence of genetic influences on personality. However, environmental factors such as the inclination of children to imitate their parents, and the tendency of parents of a certain disposition to create childhood experiences that foster those dispositions, have always been plausible counter-explanations to genetic ones. Moreover, it is possible that family resemblance is more apparent than real because of our expectation that family members should be alike. That is, the generally positive correlations observed among family members on personality measures may reflect biases among the raters and scales rather than their actual similarity on personality dimensions (e.g., Neale & Stevenson, 1989; Simonoff et al., 1995). Indeed, one problem with applying behavior genetic methods to disentangling these possible influences on personality as opposed to intelligence has been the difficulty of obtaining adequate measures of personality. However, as methods of personality assessment have become more sophisticated, more persuasive evaluations of behavior genetic models of personality have become possible.

## Twin Studies

Early behavior genetic research on personality suffered from other limitations. It relied almost exclusively on twin studies with small sample sizes, the particular personality dimensions varied from study to study, the measures of personality were generally not psychometrically sound, and the estimate of heritability was based on the oversimplified model of twice the difference between the MZ and DZ twin correlations (Goldsmith, 1983; Loehlin, Willerman & Horn, 1988). The results of this research suggested that approximately 50 percent of the variability in personality traits could be attributed to genetic factors. (Bouchard, 1994). However, the limitations of this research, particularly the simplified model on which the heritability estimates were based, led most personality psychologists to reject this finding. Specifically, the model included the assumption that MZ and DZ twins experience the same degree of shared environmental experience, and this was viewed as implausible.

Loehlin and Nichols. In 1976, Loehlin and Nichols published the results from a study of 850 twin pairs using the California Psychological Inventory (CPI), a well-established measure of a variety of personality characteristics. This study marks the beginning of modern behavior genetic studies of personality that use large samples, well-established personality measures, and more complex analytic models. The basic results of the Loehlin and Nichols study, shown as intraclass correlations computed separately for MZ and DZ twins, are shown in Table 6-1.

One of the more puzzling, and problematic, findings from this study is that all of the personality characteristics exhibit about the same degree of genetic influence: about 40 percent of the variance in personality can be attributed to genetic factors. Most behavior geneticists expect personality characteristics to be **differentially heritable;** that is, some characteristics will be more strongly influenced by genetic factors than others. For example, Gottesman (1966) and Vandenberg (1967) both suggested that those aspects of personality that concern interpersonal relations should be under substantial genetic control, whereas those concerning attitudes and intellectual interests would exhibit minimal genetic influence.

The failure of the Loehlin and Nichols study as well as other studies (e.g., Dworkin, Burke, Maher, and Gottesman, 1976) to find differential heritability raised the possibility that the heritability estimates were based on incorrect assumptions or on artifacts in the sample, design, or measures. One possibility, explored by Horn, Plomin, and Rosenman (1976), is that the scales on the CPI have overlapping items. When these investigators removed the overlapping items in a study of 99 adult male twins, they found evidence of differential heritability consistent with the predictions of Gottesman and Vandenberg.

Later Studies. Several large scale twin studies of personality have now been reported (Loehlin, 1992). They include an investigation of 7,144 twin pairs in

&#x6393; Table 6-1

Intraclass Correlations for the California Psychological Inventory Scales
for Male and Female MZ and DZ Twin Pairs

| | MZ Twins | | DZ Twins | |
|---|---|---|---|---|
| | Males | Females | Males | Females |
| Number of pairs | 199 | 288 | 124 | 193 |
| **Scale** | | | | |
| Tolerance | .60 | .47 | .30 | .28 |
| Achievement via independence | .58 | .50 | .39 | .41 |
| Responsibility | .58 | .43 | .30 | .40 |
| Dominance | .57 | .49 | .12 | .36 |
| Intellectual efficiency | .57 | .48 | .29 | .38 |
| Self-control | .56 | .57 | .27 | .36 |
| Capacity for status | .55 | .61 | .35 | .54 |
| Well-being | .54 | .45 | .32 | .26 |
| Social presence | .53 | .54 | .14 | .31 |
| Sociability | .52 | .54 | .23 | .33 |
| Socialization | .52 | .55 | .16 | .48 |
| Good impression | .48 | .46 | .30 | .28 |
| Psychological mindedness | .48 | .37 | .28 | .18 |
| Achievement via conformance | .47 | .44 | .06 | .27 |
| Flexibility | .45 | .51 | .24 | .18 |
| Self-acceptance | .42 | .55 | .12 | .37 |
| Femininity | .41 | .31 | .26 | .14 |
| Communality | .31 | .43 | .28 | .11 |

From Loehlin, J. C. and Nichols, R. C. (1976). *Heredity, environment, and personality: A study of 850 sets of twins.* Austin: University of Texas Press.

Finland using the Eysenck Personality Questionnaire (EPQ) (Rose, Koskenvuo, Kaprio, Sarna, and Langinvainio, 1988), an investigation of 12,777 twin pairs in Sweden that used a short version of the EPQ (Floderus-Myrhed, Pedersen, and Rasmuson, (1980), and a study of 2,901 pairs in Australia that again used the EPQ (Martin & Jardine, 1986). The large samples and comparable measures have allowed behavior geneticists to use sophisticated models to precisely estimate the contributions of various types of genetic and environmental influence on personality. These studies have found evidence of differential heritability, with the characteristic of extraversion more strongly influenced by genetic factors than the characteristic of neuroticism. However, summaries of the role of genetics in personality still often report an average heritability for personality in general. One estimate, based on these larger and more sophisticated studies, is that about 40 percent of the observed variance in personality is due to genetic factors, with some dimensions exhibiting somewhat greater genetic influence and others exhibiting somewhat less (Bouchard, 1994).

## Family Resemblance and Adoption Studies

Another advance in behavior genetics research on personality has been the use of data from designs other than the twin study. For example, the Hawaii Family Study of Cognition reported family resemblances between parents and children, husbands and wives, and among siblings on 54 personality dimensions (Ahren, Johnson, Wilson, McClearn, and Vandenberg, 1982). This research also suggests that individual differences in personality are influenced by genetics. However, the estimates of genetic influence derived from family resemblance were generally smaller than those obtained with the twin studies. Estimates of heritability are also smaller when they are based on data from adoption studies (Plomin, Chipuer, and Loehlin, 1990). Indeed, several adoption studies, such as the Colorado Adoption Project (Plomin, Coon, Carey, DeFries, and Fulker, 1989) and the Texas Adoption Project (Loehlin, Horn, and Willerman, 1981), have found that a comparison of the correlations between biological mothers and the child and adoptive parents and the child shows no evidence for genetic influence on personality.

## Reconciling Twin and Adoption Study Results

Behavior geneticists are concerned about this failure of family resemblance studies and adoption studies to replicate the heritability estimates from twin studies. The analysis of the family resemblance data and the adoption study data is based on different models and assumptions. When results differ so consistently, it suggests that at least one set of assumptions is wrong—but the problem is to decide which one. If the twin study assumptions are wrong, then the influence of heredity on personality may be much less than is currently believed.

One resolution to these different results has been to consider the role of more complicated patterns of genetic influence on personality (Plomin, Chipuer, and Loehlin, 1990). For example, genetic effects can combine multiplicatively rather than simply add together to influence a phenotype. Such **nonadditive genetic effects** are automatically included in twin-study heritability estimates because the similarity of identical twins will be the result of all possible genetic influences. However, heritability estimates based on family resemblance or adoption study models reflect only the simpler **additive genetic effects**. Another possibility is that the assumption that MZ and DZ twins experience equal environments is wrong.

Studies of Twins Reared Apart. The most powerful design for disentangling these possibilities is the study of twins who were reared apart and, therefore, presumably in different environments. The largest of these studies is the Swedish Adoption/Twin Study on Aging (Pedersen, Friberg, Floderus-Myrhed, McClearn, and Plomin, 1984) with personality data on 99 MZ and 229 DZ twins reared apart and 160 MZ and 212 DZ twins reared together. The average age of these twins was 59 at the time the personality data were collected. Another such study in the United States is the Minnesota Study of Twins Reared Apart (Tellegen, Lykken, Bouchard, Wilcox, Segal, and Rich, 1988). Table 6-2 presents correlations between MZ and DZ twins reared apart and reared together for several personality measures.

The pattern of these correlations suggests that the classic twin studies violate the **equal-environments assumption**. Specifically, the differences between the correlations for MZ and DZ twins raised together (e.g., .54 −.06 = .48 for extraversion in Table 6-2) are greater than those differences when the twins were raised separately (.30 − .04 = .26 for extraversion in Table 6-2). The most straightforward explanation for this is that the MZ twins reared together are more similar than those reared apart (.54 versus .30) because they are treated more similarly. The pattern of correlations also suggests that the violation of the equal-environments assumption in twin studies results from the MZ twins being treated more similarly than DZ twins (*assimilation*) rather than the DZ twins being treated more differently (*contrast*) (Loehlin & Nichols, 1976). Specifically, there is little difference between the correlations for DZ twins raised apart (e.g., .04) or together (e.g., .06). Moreover, there is little evidence in these results for nonaddi-

&#x0296;&#x0295;  Table 6-2

Summary of Some Personality Correlations Based on Data from the Swedish Adoption/ Twin Study on Aging

| Personality Characteristic | MZ Twins | | DZ Twins | |
|---|---|---|---|---|
| | Apart | Together | Apart | Together |
| Extraversion | .30 | .54 | .04 | .06 |
| Neuroticism | .25 | .41 | .28 | .24 |
| Openness | .43 | .51 | .23 | .14 |
| Conscientiousness | .15 | .41 | −.03 | .23 |
| Agreeableness | .19 | .47 | .10 | .11 |
| Sociability | .20 | .35 | .19 | .19 |
| Activity level | .27 | .38 | .00 | .18 |
| Hostility | .21 | .33 | .21 | .40 |
| Assertiveness | .16 | .32 | −.08 | .20 |
| Ambitious | .40 | .30 | .08 | .11 |
| Responsibility | .36 | .30 | .30 | .18 |

Adapted from Table 9-2 in R. Plomin, H. M. Chipuer, and J. C. Loehlin (1990). Behavior genetics and personality. In L. A. Pervin (Ed.) *Handbook of personality theory and research* (pp. 225–243). New York: Guilford.

tive genetic factors contributing to the greater heritability estimates of the twin studies.

Conclusion. The violation of the equal-environment assumption suggests that twin studies have *overestimated* the influence of genetics on personality, and Plomin, Chipuer, and Loehlin (1990) conclude that genetics accounts for about 20 percent (rather than 40 percent) of the variance in personality. However, the pattern of results shown in Table 6-2 was not replicated in the Minnesota twin study, and the Minnesota investigators have continued to propose a heritability estimate of .40 for personality (Bouchard, 1994). Obviously, much more research is needed to reconcile these results. A crucial advance will be the development of measures and methods to directly and accurately assess the environmental factors that contribute to personality development. Until such measures are available, we can only indirectly estimate environmental influence and will continue to debate and speculate about the extent to which violations of the equal-environments assumption in twin studies has affected heritability estimates. In the meantime, the safest conclusions are general ones: that genetics influences, at least to some extent, most personality characteristics; that some characteristics may be more influenced by genetics than others; and that twin studies probably overestimate the influence of genetic factors on the variance of personality characteristics.

## Environmental Influences

In contrast to the early research by hereditarians, modern behavior genetics research also focuses on the role of the environment on individual differences in personality. Indeed, behavior genetics provides some of the most compelling evidence of the importance of nongenetic factors on personality development. As Plomin noted,

> If you were an identical twin and your co-twin was schizophrenic, your risk for schizophrenia would be incredibly high—45 percent, as compared to the base rate in the population of 1 percent. Although this suggests genetic influence, it's important to remember that 45 percent is a long way from 100 percent. A genetic clone of a schizophrenic has only a 45 percent risk of schizophrenia—that's the best evidence we have for the importance of nongenetic factors in schizophrenia! (Plomin, 1987, p. 9)

Shared and Nonshared Environmental Experience. One of the most controversial findings from modern behavior genetics research concerns the environment. Typically, environmental influence is divided into shared and nonshared environmental experience. **Shared environmental experience** is defined as environmental experiences that are the same for all children in a family. These include common parental child rearing practices, common interactions with family friends and relatives, and common cultural experiences related to ethnic or religious background. **Nonshared environmental experience** is the unique experiences of each child. Some examples are birth order, different teachers at school, and any idiosyncratic experiences such as winning a music award or breaking an arm.

It has long been believed that child rearing practices, common cultural experiences, and other shared factors have a powerful effect on a child's development. However, the evidence from a large number of studies (e.g., Loehlin and Nichols, 1976; Plomin and Daniels, 1987; Rowe, 1994; Scarr, Webber, Weinberg, and Wittig, 1981) is that siblings exhibit little similarity on personality dimensions. The conclusion of many behavior geneticists is that although the environment has a substantial impact on personality, it is nonshared rather than common environmental factors that are responsible for the influence.

> Thus, a consistent—though perplexing—pattern is emerging from our data . . . . Environment carries substantial weight in determining personality—it appears to account for at least half the variance—but that environment is one in which twin pairs are correlated close to zero. . . . In short, in the personality domain we seem to see environmental effects that operate almost randomly with respect to the sorts of variables that psychologists (and other people) have traditionally deemed important in personality development. (Loehlin and Nichols, 1976, p. 92)

Only two exceptions have been found to this general conclusion: the political attitudes of *liberalism-conservatism* and *juvenile delinquency,* which show patterns of relations in twin studies consistent with a strong influence of common experience.

Implications.    The implications of this result for research on personality development are profound, as they suggest that development cannot be studied family by family but must be studied individual by individual. These results also suggest that the widely held belief that the consistent and common approaches that parents take to raising their children have an important impact on personality may be mistaken. Rather, the idiosyncratic and differential treatment of siblings is most important. Future research should focus on how variations *within* the family—as a function of such factors as birth order, accidents, illnesses, relocation, and gender—influence personality development. The generally accepted view among behavior geneticists about the role of genes and environment in personality is that the *similarity* among relatives on personality traits is due to shared genes. The *differences* among relatives on personality traits is due to environmental factors (Bouchard, 1994).

Dissent.    This conclusion has not gone without challenge (Hoffman, 1991), and the results of one large-scale twin study (Rose et al., 1988) are inconsistent with this interpretation Rose et al. studied 7144 pairs of twins in Finland. They assessed the personality of these twins using the *Eysenck Personality Question-*

*naire,* which provided measures of extraversion and neuroticism. In addition, the investigators obtained measures of the amount of social contact that occurred between the members of twin pairs, including the age at which the twins began to live apart, the frequency with which they contacted each other, and the nature (e.g., phone conversation and face-to-face interaction) of that contact. The assumption in this research is that the more social contact between the twins, the greater their shared environmental experience. The investigators were thus able to consider both the influence of genetic similarity (MZ versus DZ twins) as well as the amount of social contact on the twins' similarity on the characteristics of extraversion (E) and neuroticism (N).

Consistently with most other studies, Rose et al. found evidence of genetic influence on both characteristics, even after controlling for the amount of social contact, which was greater for the MZ twins. However, in contrast with previous research, they also found evidence that more social contact (shared environment) contributed to the twins' similarity after the effects of genetic similarity had been controlled. Rose et al. have recognized the limitations of their study, particularly their imprecise and indirect assessment of shared experience. "First, we urge readers to avoid the temptation to weigh genetic and social effects against each other via the proportions of variance for which they account in our analyses. The crudity with which we have assessed variations in social interactions of twins is no match for the accuracy with which we can distinguish differences in their genetic similarities" (p. 169). Resolving the controversy surrounding the role of shared experience on sibling personality, and generally advancing our understanding of the role of the environment in personality development, will be aided by more detailed theories about environmental variables and specific measures of them.

## Biological Influences on Personality

Behavior genetics research has provided compelling evidence that many personality characteristics are influenced by genetic factors. However, behavior genetics research typically does not specify the biological mechanism or process that carries that influence. In this section, some of the research linking biology to personality will be considered.

### Physique and Personality

Sheldon's constitutional theory of personality, which concerned the relation between Sheldon's body type indices and personality, suffered from poor methodology and an exaggerated interpretation of his results (see Chapter 5). However, over the years a few relations between different measures of physique and personality have been reported. For example, a review of the literature led Eysenck (1970) to conclude that extraversion and neuroticism are correlated about .40 with body type. Specifically, ectomorphs tend to be more neurotic and introverted than people with other body types. A problem with Eysenck's findings, and studies of Sheldon's body types in general, is that there is no theory to explain the observed results (Eysenck, 1990). In contrast, Schlegel (1983) has proposed and successfully evaluated one of the few theories concerning a link between physique and personality. Schlegel's theory is discussed in Box 6-1.

Another intriguing, although still immature, area of research concerns the relations between blood types and personality (Eysenck, 1990). As with Schlegel's theory, blood types are not viewed as directly causing personality. Rather, they are viewed as markers of biological processes that may be associated with both blood type and personality. Cattell, Young, and Hundelby (1964) first proposed a possible relation between blood type and personality. Significant differences have been reported in the frequency of blood groups for introverts and extroverts. Likewise, individuals with blood type B are found to be more emotional than individuals with blood type A. Jogawar (1983) assessed the personalities of

## BOX 6-1
## Schlegel's Theory About Personality and the Size of the Pelvic Outlet

The hormone testosterone acts on some portions of the brain during a child's development prior to birth. Testosterone is a masculinizing hormone, as it tends to produce physiological and psychological characteristics associated with males. However, both males and females are influenced by testosterone. Although the extent to which an individual is affected by antenatal exposure to testosterone is hypothesized to be related to personality characteristics related to social and sexual behavior, testing these hypotheses was difficult because no index of exposure to testosterone was available.

In 1983 Schlegel proposed that the diameter of the pelvic opening, which is largely determined by the amount of antenatal exposure to testosterone, could be used as the index. On the basis of this theory, Schlegel hypothesized that the physical characteristic of size of pelvic opening would be related to a variety of personality variables. Note that Schlegel did *not* propose that the size of a person's pelvic opening *caused* the personality characteristics, but rather that testosterone exposure caused both pelvic development and certain personality characteristics, and that is the basis for the relations. This theory is diagrammed in Figure 6-1. Consistently with his theory, Schlegel found in a sample of 200 male subjects that size of pelvic opening correlated −.43 with leadership, −.77 with preference for younger sexual partners, and −.90 with preference for an active sexual role. It also correlated +.35 with emotional reactivity, +.38 with need for social contact, and +.31 with suggestibility. These correlations are sensible on the basis of Schlegel's theory: the greater the exposure to testosterone, the smaller the pelvic opening, and the smaller the pelvic opening, the more the individual tends to show more masculine social and sexual behaviors.

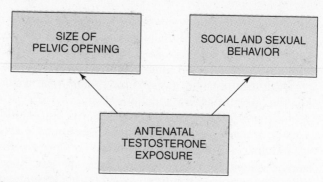

**Figure 6-1** ⊗ Diagram illustrating Schlegel's explanation for why size of pelvic opening is related to personality.

590 students using Cattell's Sixteen Personality Factors and determined their blood type. He found that students with Type A blood were more emotionally stable than Type B students. Likewise, the Type B students were more tense than the Type A students, and the Type A students were more self-sufficient than the Type B students.

It is important to note that this research has several limitations. First, many findings relating personality characteristics to blood types have not been replicated on new samples. Second, the size of the relations is typically small. Knowing a person's blood type is not a good basis for predicting what that person's personality will be. Finally, unlike Schlegel's research, there has generally been no theory offered for why blood types should be related to personality.

## Biochemistry and Personality

**Influence of Drugs.** Recreational drug users, smokers, and coffee and alcohol drinkers have long been personally, although anecdotally, aware of the impact of chemicals on behavior and mood. Much of the initial scientific evidence that hormones and biochemicals influence behavior and personality came from the successful use of pharmaceutical drugs in the treatment of psychological disorders, particularly schizophrenia. Until the 1950s, psychosis was an untreatable and devastating form of mental illness. Psychotic individuals were essentially incarcerated in the crowded back wards of mental institutions and ignored. In the 1950s, the drug chlorpromazine, an antihistamine, was synthesized in France for the treatment of hay fever. Two French psychiatrists, Delay and Deneker, tried the drug on their psychotic patients with remarkable results. The patients became calm and their contact with reality increased. Chlorpromazine was soon being used at all major mental hospitals, and it generally worked; even patients who had been held in back wards for years could be discharged. The success of **antipsychotics**, drugs that reduce the number and intensity of psychotic symptoms, was powerful evidence that biochemicals could impact behavior. Soon **psychopharmacology**—the use of drugs to influence psychological variables such as thoughts, feelings, and behavior—became the treatment of choice for many psychological disorders. Subsequently drugs were discovered that relieved depression (e.g., monoamine oxidase [MAO] inhibitors, tricyclics), manic depression (lithium), and anxiety (Valium, Miltown, and Librium).

Although research supports the general effectiveness of these drugs, the reason they work is generally unknown, and they do not work for all patients. The usefulness of these drugs as antipsychotics and antidepressants is often discovered by accident. In addition to being scientifically dissatisfying, this lack of understanding about why and how the drugs operate often results in unanticipated and unwanted side effects. For example, in about 30 percent of patients, antipsychotic drugs cause a condition called tardive dyskinesia by destroying something that is still unknown in the area of the brain that controls movement. The condition is irreversible (Gualtieri, 1991). One practical consequence of these side effects is that patients, once released from hospitals, often stop taking the drugs to avoid the side effects, with the result that the psychosis, depression, or anxiety returns.

The newest, and already the most widely prescribed, drug for altering personality and behavior is an antidepressant (fluoxetine) that works by inhibiting the reuptake of serotonin by nerve cells. This drug is best known by its brand name, Prozac. As an antidepressant Prozac is about as effective as others, but it appears to have fewer and milder side effects. However, Prozac's effects on personality and the self appear to be profound, and it often results in extraordinary personality transformations (Kramer, 1994—see Box 6-2). For this reason, Prozac is regarded in some circles as a quick and easy means to become a happier, more productive, and more satisfied individual. Some negative effects can occur with Prozac (e.g., Beaumont, 1990), and concerns about Prozac's already widespread use have been voiced (Breggin, 1994). Also, the effects of Prozac on personality do not appear to be permanent; individuals must continue to take the drug to maintain the "new personality." Thus, Prozac does not alter an individual's basic personality but instead results in temporary changes.

Influence of Enzymes and Hormones. The study of the role of biochemicals and hormones on normal human personality has not been as extensive as the research on the treatment of psychological disorders, but this research also strongly suggests that some personality characteristics have some biochemical basis (Zuckerman, Ballinger, and Post, 1984).

One of the most reliable relations is between monoamine oxidase (MAO) and sensation seeking (Zuckerman, 1984), described in Box 6-3. The relation between MAO and sensation seeking is consistent with the use of MAO inhibitors in the treatment of depression. MAO operates by degrading norepinephrine, dopamine, and serotonin, which generally act as arousing hormones. Thus, the more these hormones are reduced (degraded) by MAO, the less arousal occurs, which in turn may reduce sensation seeking. However, the operation of hormones is often more complex than this simple explanation implies. Also, the findings described in Box 6-3 are based on correlations, so it is not clear whether

## BOX 6-2
# Excerpts from Listening to Prozac by Peter D. Kramer (1994), and Commentary

Kramer's book *Listening to Prozac* is a popularized summary of his experiences and observations from prescribing Prozac to treat depression. One of the early observations that impressed Kramer was that patients who were treated with Prozac "became better than well." That is, Prozac not only alleviated the symptoms of depression but seemed to reshape the entire personality of some of his clients.

> Prozac seemed to give social confidence to the habitually timid, to make the sensitive brash, to lend the introvert the social skills of the salesman. (p. xv)
>
> Then I wrote about patients who became "better than well," patients who acquired extra energy and became socially attractive. My mnemonic for this effect was "cosmetic psychopharmacology." (p. xvi)
>
> And I asked just how far we—doctors, patients, society at large—were likely to go in the direction of permitting drug responses to shape our understanding of the authentic self. (p. 20)
>
> . . . we have found a medication that can affect personality, perhaps even in the absence of illness. . . . Either way, we are edging toward what might be called the "medicalization of personality." . . . If seriousness is subject to chemical influence, we can imagine a large collection of pairs of opposed traits that will be as well: contemplative/action oriented, rigid/flexible, cautious/impulsive, risk-averse/risk-prone, masochistic/assertive, by-the-book/by-the-seat-of-the-pants, deferential/demanding, and many others. The first element in any of these pairs might be equally associated with depressive or obsessional leanings and might equally be a candidate for drug treatment. (p. 37)

In essence, the effect of Prozac is to move people from being contemplative, introverted, and cautious to being impulsive, extraverted, and action oriented. Not all individuals like these changes, and in some the change can be too extreme, resulting in violence and suicide.

> It was not possible to keep Lucy on Prozac. She reported an increase in her sense of undirected urgency. Overcome with cravings, she did not know what she craved. She had to do something, but she did not know what. (p. 102)
>
> Altogether, Sam became less bristling, had fewer rough edges. He experienced this change as a loss. The style he had nurtured and defended for years now seemed not a part of him, but an illness. (p. x)
>
> In the final analysis, the uproar about Prozac and violence represents further testimony to our focus on biologically determined feelings and behaviors. The scare about violence contains a backhanded tribute to Prozac, an acknowledgement, albeit in nightmare form, that Prozac can transform the self. (p. 313)

BOX 6-3
## A Relation Between Sensation Seeking and Enzymes

Sensation seeking, the general tendency to seek stimulation, has been measured by a 40-item scale (Zuckerman, 1978). This scale contains four classes of items: (1) those related to physical risk taking (parachuting, skiing, etc.), (2) those reflecting an interest in new experiences through the mind and senses (music, art, certain drugs, traveling, etc.), (3) those that describe a hedonistic pursuit of pleasure (social drinking, sex, gambling, etc.), and (4) those involving an aversion toward routine activities, dull people, and the like. This is a reliable scale with behavioral correlates in sexual activity, drug use, volunteering for unusual activities, engaging in dangerous pursuits, and gambling. There are also predictable gender differences in sensation seeking, with males generally scoring higher than females.

An enzyme, monoamine oxidase (MAO), is present in the brain and most other tissues. When drugs that inhibit MAO action are administered, behavior changes often occur, among them euphoria, aggression, irritability, and hallucinations. In short, MAO appears to serve some dampening or regulatory role. Several studies (e.g., Zuckerman, Buchsbaum, and Murphy, 1980) have shown negative correlations between MAO and sensation-seeking scores. That is, high sensation seekers tend to have low MAO levels, which may account for the greater activity levels, sociability, and so on, normally found in such individuals. Likewise, women exhibit higher levels of MAO than males at all ages between 18 and 60 (Murphy et al., 1976), which is consistent with the lower scores of women on sensation seeking.

(1) lower levels of MAO cause sensation seeking, (2) higher levels of sensation seeking reduce the amount of MAO present in the blood, or (3) some third factor influences both.

**The Role of the Situation.** An illustration of the complexity of the relations between hormones and behavior is the classic study by Schachter and Singer (1962). These investigators injected subjects with epinephrine, a hormone that produces sweating, flushing, and rapid heart rate. Some of the subjects were told how epinephrine works; others were not. After being injected, one group of subjects was confronted by a confederate of the experimenter who acted to produce euphoria in the subjects. Other subjects were left with a confederate who engaged in a routine likely to make them angry. The results of the study showed that subjects who knew the effects of epinephrine attributed their increased sweating and heart rate to the hormone, whereas subjects who did not know described their physiological responses as either euphoria or anger, depending on the experimental condition in which they had been placed. Although not everyone has been able to replicate these results (Leventhal and Tomarken, 1986), this study suggests that humans do not respond as simple physiological machines. Instead, the nature of emotional reactions is a complex interaction between biochemical events, situational factors, and people's beliefs and interpretations.

An example of research that has explicitly recognized, and derived predictions from, the complex interaction of personality, situational factors, and biochemistry has been offered by Revelle, Humphreys, Simon, and Gilliland (1980). According to Eysenck's theory of extraversion, caffeine (a chemical stimulant), and introversion-extraversion (a personality variable) should interact to affect performance on a cognitive task. Specifically, the performance of people high on impulsiveness (a component of extraversion) should be helped by the arousing effect of caffeine, whereas the opposite pattern would characterize the performance of low-impulsive (more introverted) people. These predictions were derived from the hypothesis that extroverts are chronically underaroused, whereas introverts are chronically overaroused. Thus, caffeine would increase the arousal level of extraverts to an optimal level for good performance, whereas caffeine would increase the arousal level of introverts over the optimal level and thus hurt performance.

However, previous research (Revelle, Amaral, and Turriff, 1976) had indicated that these effects differed as a function of time of day (morning versus afternoon). Specifically, the results were as predicted from Eysenck's theory during the morning but were *reversed* in the afternoon. Revelle et al. (1980) suggested that if these results were replicated, Eysenck's theory would need to be modified, as the difference in arousal level between introverts and extroverts is not stable, but varies as a function of diurnal rhythms. The results of the replication studies by Revelle et al. (1980) are shown in Figure 6-2. As indicated in Figure 6-2, and consistent with the prediction by Revelle et al., caffeine does enhance the performance of high-impulsive people and impair the performance of low impulsive people, but only in the morning. In the afternoon, the effect of caffeine on performance is not so strong, but that effect is reversed for high- and low-impulsive individuals. This research accentuates the theoretical intricacy that results when biological variables are included in personality research.

## Brain Structure and Personality

Advances in neuroscience have just begun to allow scientists to relate specific structures and neural systems in the brain to behavior. Although a neuroscience of personality will not be realized for some time, contemporary neuroscience research has produced a few intriguing findings that are relevant to personality. One of the earliest suggestions that personality is under the influence of different parts of the brain comes from the bizarre accident that befell Phineas Gage. His story is summarized in the Case Study on page 195. Damasio, Grabowski, Frank, Gal-

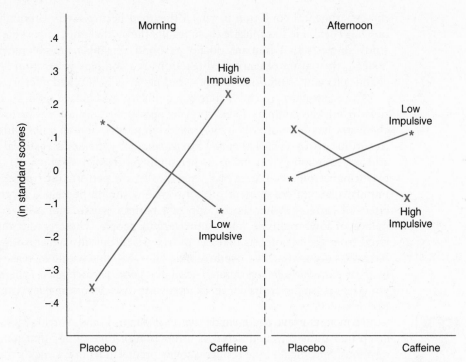

**Figure 6-2** GO The relation between impulsiveness, caffeine, and time of day and cognitive performance.

Adapted from Figure 1 in W. Revelle, M. S. Humphreys, L. Simon, and K. Gilliland (1980). The interactive effect of personality, time of day, and caffeine: A test of the arousal model. *Journal of Experimental Psychology: General, 109,* 1–31.

aburda, and Damasio (1994) used modern neuroimaging techniques on Gage's skull to determine precisely the location of the damaged areas (lesions) in Gage's brain. Figure 6-3 shows some of the images generated by this technique. Damasio et al. (1994) located the damage in the left and right prefrontal cortices in a pattern that, according to modern theory, is consistent with deficits in rational decision making and emotional behavior. Of course, the transformations in Gage's personality are also understandable as those of a man who has just survived, against all odds, a frightening accident. Such a man might well become cynical about society's arbitrary conventions, engage in more profanity, and show less commitment to work and other responsibilities as a result of the experience rather than the damage of the accident. His changes might also become magnified as his friends and families react to the contrast between his old and new behavior. The work of Damasio et al. and the consistency of Gage's injuries with those of others who have shown similar personality change is intriguing and makes a good story. However, separating organic, biological explanations for Gage's behavior from phenomenological ones will require going beyond the post hoc description of a single case to more controlled investigation on larger samples of individuals.

# CASE STUDY

## The Story of Phineas Gage

On September 13, 1848, Phineas P. Gage was 25 years old and working as a construction foreman for a New England railroad. Gage was in charge of some blasting so that new rails could be laid across Vermont. On that day Gage became distracted and began tamping gun powder with an iron rod before his assistant had covered it with sand. The result was an explosion that sent a pointed, 3-centimeter thick, 109-centimeter long iron rod through his face, skull, and brain. The rod went completely through his head and landed several yards away. Gage was stunned, but he regained consciousness and was able to talk and even walk with the help of his men. He survived until 1861, 13 years after the accident.

Gage's survival was an extraordinary event, but the significance of his case is that he survived a *different* man. Prior to the accident, Gage was described as a responsible, intelligent, and socially competent individual who was well liked by his family and friends and respected and trusted by his employers. The first signs of personality change appeared during his convalescence. As time went on, however, the changes became more dramatic and more difficult to understand. In some ways Gage recovered fully. He was physically and intellectually unaffected. He showed no impairment in movement or in speech, he could learn new material, and his memory was intact. However, Gage's personality underwent a profound change. He became irreverent, impulsive, and eccentric. His respect for social conventions vanished, and his abundant profanity was offensive. He became irresponsible and could not be trusted to honor his commitments. Gage began a new life of wandering that ended in San Francisco. He never returned to a fully independent existence and never held a job that was comparable in level to his position as a foreman.

When Gage died no autopsy was ever performed, although his physician, John Harlow, did argue that Gage's behavior and personality changes resulted from the damage to the frontal region of the brain. Harlow persuaded Gage's family to exhume Gage's body five years after his death so that the skull could be kept as a medical record. The skull and the tamping iron, which had been buried with Gage, are now at the Warren Anatomical Medical Museum at Harvard University.

Adapted from Damasio, Grabowski, Frank, Galaburda, and Damasio (1994). The return of Phineas Gage: Clues about the brain from the skull of a famous patient. *Science, 264*, 1102–1105.

Although the techniques and theories of neuroscience have advanced far beyond those available during the time of Phineas Gage's experience, the study of the relation between brain and neural structure and personality still relies primarily on animal research and case studies based on accidents. For obvious reasons, the brains of normal humans cannot be subjected to systematic lesions so that

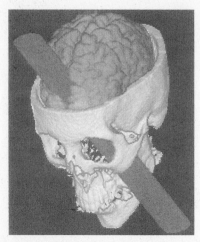

**Figure 6-3** ᏆᏩᏌ Neuroimages of the injuries to Phineas Gage.
From the cover of *Science, 264,* (May, 1994). Digital image by Hannah Damasio, Department of Neurology and Image Analysis, University of Iowa College of Medicine.

damage in specific areas can be related to changes in personality and behavior. However, despite this limitation, evidence continues to accumulate that certain specific brain structures have specific impacts on personality relevant variables. For example, animal studies suggest that the *amygdala* (see Figure 6-4 for the location of the major brain structures) is an important part of the brain for processing emotional information. Also, studies of nonhuman primates suggest that the *hippocampus* is an important brain structure for processing and learning factual information. However, the specificity of these structures to processing emotional and factual information in humans has been difficult to establish because it is rare for humans to suffer damage that is restricted to one of these areas. Bechara, Tranel, Damasio, Adolphs, Rockland, and Damasio (1995) managed to locate three patients who had experienced brain damage that was restricted to one or another of these areas. Using a conditioning paradigm, the authors found that the patient with specific damage to the amygdala could not process emotional information but could process factual information. On the other hand, the patient with damage specific to the hippocampus could process emotional information but not factual information. Finally, a patient with damage to both areas could not process either type of information. Of course, these results are based on single subjects whose unfortunate life experiences are, fortunately, rare. However, the specificity of the deficits as a function of the area of brain damage, and the consistency of the findings with animal research, provide compelling evidence of the location of emotional and factual information processing in the human brain.

   One advancement that promises to greatly enhance our ability to test hypotheses about the relation of brain structures to individual differences in behavior and personality is the development of brain scanning techniques such as

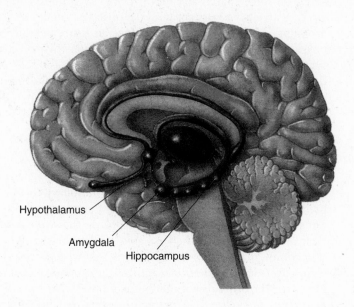

Hypothalamus

Amygdala

Hippocampus

**Figure 6-4** ❦ Diagram of the brain and limbic system.
From Zimbardo, *Psychology and Life, Thirteenth Edition,* New York HarperCollins.

**positron emission tomography (PET scan)** and **computerized axial tomography (CAT scan).** These scans produce three-dimensional images of the brain that highlight areas of higher metabolic activity (PET scans) or greater neural density (CAT scans). The areas of density can then be related to a variety of individual differences and/or to the performance of different tasks (Posner and Raichle, 1994). The advantage of this technology is that it does not damage the brain, so it can be used with more representative samples of normal individuals. Thus, many of the confounds that result from studying brain-damaged individuals or from generalizing from animal research are eliminated. For example, Gur, Mozley, Mozley, Resnick, Karp, Alavi, Arnold, and Gur (1995) used PET scans to evaluate gender differences in the metabolic activity of the brain during the processing of different types of information. A plot of the metabolic rates for men and women in different areas of the brain is shown in Figure 6-5. As indicated in Figure 6-5, overall the brain activity for men and women is similar. However, some points the level of activity differs (see arrow in Figure 6-5). Specifically, Gur et al. found that men had somewhat higher metabolic activity in the **temporal limbic** regions and the **cerebellum,** whereas women had somewhat higher metabolic activity in the **cingulate** regions. These findings are consistent with the observed differences between men and women in the processing of cognitive information; women perform better on some verbal tasks, whereas men perform better on some spatial and motor tasks. Even more compelling is that these differences are also consistent with the observed gender differences in emotional responding. Men tend to express emotion instrumentally through, for example, physical aggression and material help, whereas women tend to express emotion symbolically through, for example, verbal expression. Women have a higher incidence of depression and do better than men at discriminating among different emotions. These differences are consistent with known differences between the brain structures of men and women and with the PET scan results of Gur et al.

## Evolution and Personality Psychology

Personality research that is based on evolutionary theory is difficult and cannot use traditional designs. Any evolutionary adaptations that exist today were solutions to survival and reproductive problems that were faced by early humans and their ancestor species. The vast amount of time that has passed prevents direct observation of evolutionary processes. Likewise, as noted in Chapter 5, the millennia over which evolutionary forces operate make experimentation impossible. However, the difficulty of obtaining data relevant to evolutionary theory cannot be used as an excuse to ignore evolutionary explanations for what we observe in present-day human personality. As David Buss, a major contributor to evolutionary personality theory, has warned, "There is no reason to believe that we are somehow exempt from the organizing forces of evolution by natural selection. Personality theories inconsistent with evolutionary theory stand little chance of being correct" (1991, p. 461). The two major tactics in personality research based on evolutionary theory have been (1) to reconcile present-day observations

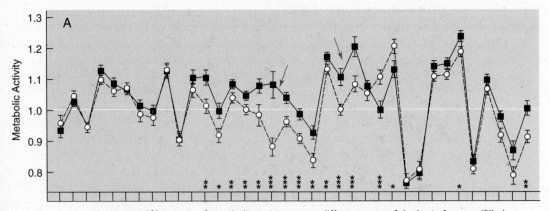

**Figure 6-5** &#x2109; Pattern of metabolic activity across different areas of the brain for men (filled squares) and women (open squares). Arrows indicate areas of difference.

From Figure 2 in Gur et al. (1995). "Sex differences in regional cerebral glucose metabolism during a resting state." *Science*, 267, 528–531.

with evolutionary principles and (2) to seek continuities between animal adaptations and human personality.

## Human Nature and Individual Variation

Two goals of personality psychology are (1) the identification of universal tendencies in human behavior that are part of "human nature" and (2) the description of individual variations of characteristics that allow us to recognize each individual as unique. Tooby and Cosmides (1990) have used evolutionary theory to reconcile the seeming contradiction between human commonalities and individual variation. In particular, the existence of substantial human genetic variation of personality characteristics is a major challenge for evolutionary theory. The forces of natural selection tend to reduce and eliminate genetic variability by favoring those particular characteristics that result in survival and, most importantly, subsequent reproductive success. The result, ultimately, is the elimination of those genetic combinations that are less successful. But then, if hard-working individuals are more likely to survive, and dominant, aggressive individuals are more likely to reproduce, why is it that we all know people who are lazy and/or submissive?

Tooby and Cosmides (1990) note that evolutionary forces result in adaptations that are specifically linked to reproductive success. There are three outcomes to this process: (1) adaptations that can be identified by a coordination between the phenotype and the environment that promotes reproductive success, (2) correlates of adaptations that are not plausibly relevant to reproductive success, and (3) random effects that are indicated by variability and an inconsistency between the phenotype and the environment. Human variation can result from any of these outcomes. The correlates of adaptations, and random effects that are reproductively neutral, would be maintained because they would not be influenced by natural selection. Tooby and Cosmides (1990) argue that these types of "genetic noise" are the best explanations of human genetic variability. Indeed, they suggest that the types of evidence needed to support the hypothesis that variation in personality reflects genetically different adaptations may not be available.

However, differential adaptations could occur in several ways. The complexity of the environments faced by our human ancestors may have resulted in different adaptations. The adaptations are universal in the sense that they address the same functional problems, but they vary because different specific environments make different adaptations functional. In addition, selection may be **frequency-dependent**. As one particular adaption becomes more frequent (universal), other adaptations that are rarer may become more adaptive. For example the initial advantage of aggressiveness for obtaining mates and reproducing may diminish as more and more individuals become aggressive. Less aggressive individuals may find that their access to mates increases as the more aggressive individuals fight among themselves. This would serve to maintain genetic variability in aggressiveness. Finally, different adaptations may have different benefits that result in the same level of reproductive success.

For example, Gangestad and Simpson (1990) have considered variation in women's sexual behavior. Women differ in the extent to which they engage in casual sex. No doubt the reasons for this variation are complex and include many factors other than biological ones. However, Gangestad and Simpson suggest that this variation could reflect two equally adaptive evolutionary strategies. Females who are less casual require more time, attachment, and commitment from their sexual partners, with the benefit of greater investment of paternal resources into the offspring that would enhance the offspring's chance of survival. More casual females require relatively less time, attachment, and commitment from their partners. The benefit here is that the offspring would inherit genes from these reproductively more successful males—that is, males who are able to mate with more women. This analysis leads to the striking prediction that more casual females would have more sons than daughters; that is, more casual women would violate the 50:50 ratio of sons to daughters predicted by standard genetic theory. The basis for this prediction is that the sons would benefit most from the genes of their reproductively successful fathers. Gangestad and Simpson found evidence, in three separate studies, that women with personality characteristics such as extraversion, and lack of inhibition, that are associated with more casual sexual behavior had, *contrary to standard genetic theory,* a higher ratio of sons to daughters than less casual women!

## Evolution and Personality Structure

The identification of the most important individual differences and their organization or structure are widely studied issues in personality. Evolutionary theory can provide important external criteria for identifying and structuring the most important individual differences. Specifically, individual differences that are related to survival and reproduction, the components of natural selection, would be viewed as "most important" from an evolutionary perspective. The personality characteristics identified by Gangestad and Simpson (1990) in their study of female sociosexuality are an example. Similarly, Kenrick, Sadalla, Groth, and Trost (1990) found that characteristics such as dominance, intelligence, kindness, and emotional stability had a strong influence on people's self-reported preferences for mates.

Perhaps the most compelling form of evolutionary analysis concerns gender differences on personality traits (Buss, 1994; Buss and Schmitt, 1993; Kenrick et al., 1990; MacDonald, 1995). Women make a more substantial investment in offspring than men do, but the limited commitment of men to the reproductive process makes it relatively easy for women to find a mate who will agree to engage in reproductive behavior. Men, on the other hand, may make a much smaller investment in offspring, but competition for mates is more intense because it is harder to persuade a female to make the more substantial commitment. These differences suggest gender differences in personality. Because competition for mates is a more high-risk activity for men, they are expected to be more impulsive, risk-taking, and sensation-seeking than women. Likewise, they are expected to be less cautious and fearful (Buss, 1994). Women have greater access to mates and are therefore expected to be less aggressive and more romantically involved. Consistent with their greater investment in offspring, women are also expected to be more nurturant. Analyses of gender differences in personality are generally consistent with these expectations.

## Animal Personality

Perhaps the most persuasive evidence of an evolutionary basis for at least some human personality traits is the manifestation of these traits in nonhuman species. The observation of these characteristics in animals other than ourselves often clarifies the roles of these characteristics in survival and reproduction. It is also difficult to explain these traits as solely the result of nonbiological factors such as socialization and higher-order cognitive functioning when they are observed in animals with relatively simple forms of socialization and cognition.

Of course, there is some question about the legitimacy of ascribing personality to animals. Observation of animal behavior and its subsequent translation into personality characteristics relies solely on the relation of the observed behavior to the characteristic. The contribution of internal feelings, motives, and thoughts to the behavior can not be assessed in animals. For example, one cannot ask a bird why it pecks at another animal. It is possible that the pecking is a behavioral sign of aggressiveness or dominance, but it could also be a sign of nervousness or hyperactivity. Because we cannot assess the animal's motives or the animal's subjective experience of events that led to the pecking behavior, personality attributions to animals are based on less information than personality attributions to humans and may therefore be less accurate or appropriate.

The study of personality and emotions in animals, however, has a long history. On the basis of his observations, Darwin (1872) argued that humans and other animals share many basic emotions. In 1962 Plutchik proposed a psychoevolutionary theory of emotions based on the premise that emotions were basic adaptations that helped species to effectively interact with their environment. Thus, emotions could be attributed equally to human and nonhuman species. Plutchik (1965) proposed eight basic emotions that are arranged in four pairs: protection-destruction, incorporation-rejection, reproduction-deprivation, and exploration-orientation. The Emotions Profile Index (EPI) is a personality test developed by Plutchik and Kellerman (1974) to assess these eight emotions. The EPI has been used to study emotions in humans, dolphins, and a variety of nonhuman primate species. The classic monograph by Van Lawick-Goodall (1968) that documented her extensive observations of chimpanzee behavior used a variety of personality terms to describe that behavior. Another major inventory to assess animal personality was developed by Stevenson-Hinde and Zunz (1978).

On the basis of an animal's behavior, observer's make subjective ratings of the animal's personality on characteristics such as aggressive, confident, popular, tense, curious, playful, and sociable.

Figueredo, Cox, and Rhine (1995) directly addressed the issues of the reliability and validity of subjective personality assessments of animals. They considered these issues in the context of assessing the personality of stumptail macaques (a type of monkey) and zebra finches (a type of bird). After analyzing data based on extensive observations of these animals over several years, the authors concluded, "Both Stumptail macaques and Zebra finches manifest measurable personality factors that are highly valid across multiple items, stable across multiple years, and reliable across multiple raters" (p. 167). The authors also note that consistently with the evolutionary view that the structure of animal personality should be consistent across species, the same personality model fit the pattern of the personality ratings for both of these diverse species. Further evidence of the stability of animal personality comes from observations of cowardly lions (Heinsohn and Packer, 1995) described in Box 6-4.

## The Continuity Between Animal Behavior and Human Personality

Evolutionary theories of personality such as Plutchik's (1962) emphasize the similarity of certain patterns of animal behavior and human personality characteristics. In 1988 Arnold Buss published a monograph entitled *Personality: Evolutionary Heritage and Human Distinctiveness,* in which he summarized the evidence for a continuity between the behaviors of nonhuman animals, particularly primates, and humans that seemed to indicate common personality characteristics. Specifically, Buss suggested that humans share seven personality characteristics with nonhuman primates. These characteristics and a summary of their associated behaviors and purposes are listed in Table 6-3. One of the continuities in these traits among the primates, including humans, is in gender differences. In humans, men tend to be more active, aggressive, and dominant, whereas women are more fearful, sociable, and nurturant. There do not appear to be gender differences in impulsivity. These gender differences are precisely consistent with differences in the observed behavior of male and female nonhuman primates (Buss, 1988). A second continuity is in the sequence of the development of these characteristics. In humans, fear, activity, and sociability generally appear during the first year of life. Impulsiveness and aggressiveness appear in the second year; dominance in the third year, and nurturance in the fifth year. This sequence of development is the same in nonhuman primates.

Although the continuities among primates imply some biological influence on these personality characteristics, Buss (1988) also notes evidence that the influence of biology on human personality is weaker than its influence on nonhuman personality. For example, relative to nonhuman primates, humans generally exhibit smaller gender differences with greater overlap between men and women on these characteristics. Likewise, humans exhibit slower development and less

BOX 6-4
## Cowardly Lions

When female lions are called upon to defend their territory, it is usual to observe some lions taking the lead in charging the invading lions, whereas other lions tend to charge more slowly. These slower "cowardly" lions wait for the "lionhearted" lions to make the initial, most dangerous, contact with the intruders, and they enter the fight only after it has been won by the brave lions. It is difficult to reconcile these behaviors with evolutionary theory. The brave lions take considerably more risk than the cowardly lions and are killed more often. Thus, the cowardly lions should have a long-run evolutionary advantage.

The most widely accepted explanation of these observations comes from the social theory of cooperation. Specifically, it is hypothesized that the lions alternate in their willingness to take the lead in repelling intruders. Lions that lag behind on one attack will take the lead on a subsequent one, with the result that across attacks, the risk is shared equally among the lions. This is referred to as a **tit for tat strategy,** in which cooperation by one individual in a situation elicits cooperation by that individual's partner in the next situation. Likewise, a failure to cooperate by one individual results in a lack of cooperation by the other individual the next time. This pattern would result in the stable pattern of mutual cooperation that has been used to explain the behavior of the lions. Moreover, it suggests that the lion's behavior does not indicate a stable personality trait of bravery or cowardice. Instead, the behavior of the lions changes from situation to situation.

In 1995 Heinsohn and Packer reported the results of an observational study of lions in Tanzania. In this study, a recording of the roar of a strange lion was played within the territory of a pride of lions. The lions nearly always moved to attack the strange lion that they believed was intruding into their territory. The most important, and unexpected, finding of this study was that the lions did not appear to attack the intruder according to the mutually cooperative, tit-for-tat strategy. Instead, the same lions consistently led the attack, whereas other lions consistently lagged behind. These observations support a personality interpretation that some lions are generally cowardly and others are consistently brave. It contradicts the social theory that bravery and cowardice depend on the situation. These observations also refute the accepted view of lion behavior and leave behavioral ecologists searching for another explanation that is consistent with evolutionary principles.

Adapted from a summary by Morell of research by Heinsohn & Packer (1995) in *Science, 269,* 1216–1217.

**Table 6-3**

The Seven Personality Characteristics Humans Share with Nonhuman Primates

**Activity**
   Level of total energy output as expressed by vigor and tempo.
**Fearfulness**
   The tendency to be wary, run away, or cower, as well as the accompanying arousal.
**Impulsivity**
   The tendency to act on the spur of the moment without pause or reflection; at the opposite pole is the tendency to inhibit action.
**Sociability**
   A preference for being with others rather than remaining alone.
**Nurturance**
   The tendency to help others, especially those who need it. It includes altruism.
**Aggressiveness**
   Attacking or threatening others.
**Dominance**
   Seeking and maintaining superior status over others; the opposite is submissiveness.

From A. H Buss (1988). *Personality: Evolutionary heritage and human distinctiveness* (p. 10). Hillsdale, NJ: Lawrence Erlbaum.

stability on these characteristics than nonhuman primates, and there are often substantial differences between different human cultures on these characteristics. The conclusion from these findings is that the biological influence on personality is generally weakened as cognitive development and socialization practices become more complex and advanced in a species.

## Summary Evaluation

 ### Strengths

**Humans Are Biological.** People are biological entities. We share biological processes and structures with many other animals. Thus, theories about human behavior and personality that incorporate biological principles will be more complete characterizations of people. It is not that all of human experience and personality can be reduced to biological structures and processes; they cannot be. However, explanations of human behavior that are inconsistent with known biological principles are, as David Buss has cautioned, likely to be incorrect. Our knowledge of genetics, evolution, brain structure, and biochemistry places important limitations on how we explain and understand human personality. To the extent that these limitations allow us to reject some models of human behavior, biological knowledge will have made an important contribution to personality psychology.

**This Is the Era of Biology.** Whereas psychology is in the midst of a period of emphasis on cognitive theory and research, the natural sciences are in the era of biology. Genetics, genetic engineering, the mapping of the human genome, neuroscience, biochemistry, behavioral ecology, and evolution are just some the areas of major advances in biological knowledge that are relevant to personality psychology. These advances have given personality psychologists a variety of methods, techniques, technology, and ideas that have the potential to be of great use. In addition, by linking some of their research to biology, personality psychologists can enjoy some of the excitement and credibility that the field of biology is currently experiencing.

**Biological Treatments of Psychological Problems.** Psychopharmacology has provided a variety of effective chemical treatments of psychological problems. The extraordinary effectiveness of antipsychotics in the treatment of schizophrenia ushered in an era that has seen an expanding use of drugs to reduce psychological distress. Some of these drugs, such as Prozac, seem to result in at least temporary personality change. In addition, advances in neuroscience have resulted in better diagnostic techniques for identifying abnormalities in brain structure that may cause psychological problems. In some cases, surgical intervention to alter brain structure may have a positive impact on maladaptive cognitive and personality processes.

**A Comprehensive Model of Individual Differences.** The work of Frances Galton ushered in the modern study of individual differences. Galton's inspiration for his research was his belief in the importance of inheritance for understanding human variability on nearly all characteristics. Although personality psychology is not restricted to the study of individual differences, its emphasis is on how the characteristics of persons influence behavior. Biological theories, particularly behavior genetics models, provide one of the most consistent and comprehensive accounts of individual differences. Behavior genetics models incorporate a variety of both environmental and personal (genetic) factors into their explanations of human behavior. Moreover, the interaction of these factors can also be evaluated.

**Advances in Statistical Techniques.** The observations of Frances Galton led directly to the statistical techniques of correlation and regression. Most forms of data analysis, particularly those in personality psychology are based on the correlation coefficient. More recently, the complexity of the models proposed by behavior geneticists has forced them to develop and refine several advanced statistical modeling and estimation procedures. Many of these models have applications that go beyond evaluating behavior genetic hypotheses.

## Weaknesses

Biology Is Not Destiny.  Most personality psychologists who work from a biological perspective explicitly recognize that biological processes are but one of many factors that influence personality. However, biological approaches have a legacy of emphasizing biological causes to the exclusion of others. The implications are often that an individual's abilities, behavior, and success are fixed by his or genetic endowment. Galton's eugenics movement is a clear example of this thinking, which had real and devastating consequences for people at the beginning of this century. Presumably unchangeable biological factors are often used to justify the unfair treatment of women and minority groups in a variety of situations. Perhaps because they have some physical reality, biological processes are often viewed as more powerful and less modifiable than other processes. Although one might hope that, at least, the modern scientific community now recognizes the inappropriateness of these beliefs, there continue to be examples of the view that biology is destiny (e.g., Whitney, 1995).

Personality Constructs Have No Biological Reality.  When biological models such as genes, brain structures, or hormones are invoked to help define personality constructs, there is a tendency to equate the constructs with the biological variables. However, personality constructs have no reality, biological or otherwise. Friendliness, depression, dominance, and conscientiousness exist in people's minds, not in their bodies. There is no such thing as a friendliness gene, a dominance hormone, or a conscientiousness neuron. Genetics, hormones, and brain structures may influence the behaviors that we associate with these constructs, but they are not the same as the constructs. This limits the degree to which biological models can account for human personality

Reductionism.  Because people are biological entities, there has been a persistent notion that explanations of human behavior and personality can be reduced to biological structures and processes. It is viewed as a matter of time and sufficient technological advance before we can perfectly predict behavior and explain personality using only biological variables. Within the field of neuroscience, this has been characterized as the "bottom-up" approach. "It counsels that if brains are, after all, just assemblies of cells, then once we truly understand every facet of cell function the principles of brain function will be evident, by and large" (Churchland and Sejnowski, 1992). To extend this logic further, once one understands every facet of brain function, the outputs of those functions such as cognition, emotion, and behavior will be understood. However, this reductionistic logic does not seem to work, even for the simplest systems such as the stomatogastric ganglion of the spiny lobster. Although a complete catalogue of the basic electrophysiological and anatomical features of the neurons in this ganglion is available (Selverston, 1988), that knowledge has not allowed scientists to perfectly predict or explain the higher-order functions of this system (Churchland and Sejnowski, 1992).

**Indirect and Atheoretical Research.** Many of the biological discoveries of the association of areas of the brain with psychological functioning or the effectiveness of biochemicals for altering personality have been accidental, and the reasons for the association or the effect remain unknown. Tests of evolutionary theories are necessarily indirect and therefore, individually, uncompelling. Several facts about the association between various biological processes and behavior have proved effective for the treatment of a variety of cognitive and behavioral problems. However, our continued lack of understanding about the mechanisms that underlie the effectiveness is scientifically unsatisfying. In addition, the lack of understanding often makes the side effects of these treatments difficult to predict and control.

## Summary

- Our knowledge of biological processes, and the technology available to study them, have increased rapidly over the past decade. Thus, stronger and more precise tests of biological hypotheses about human personality are possible.

- Twin studies compare the correlations across pairs of DZ twins with correlations across pairs of MZ twins to estimate the heritability of personality traits.

- Early twin studies of personality suffered from small sample sizes, personality measures of questionable reliability and validity, and analyses that required overly simplified assumptions about environmental influences. Thus, the results of these studies were often discounted by personality psychologists.

- Contemporary twin studies have overcome these limitations, and it appears that about 40 percent of the variability in personality can be attributed to genetic factors. More generally, it is no longer an issue that human personality is influenced by genes.

- A persistent and puzzling finding from twin research is that personality characteristics are not differentially heritable; that is, genetic influences are at about the same level for all personality traits.

- Adoption studies, family resemblance studies, and studies of twins reared apart provide alternative assessments, based on different assumptions, of the role of heredity and environmental factors on personality. These studies generally provide smaller estimates of the influence of genetics on personality.

- Another surprising result of behavior genetic studies is that the important environmental influences are not shared among family members. Thus, common experiences among family members due to similar child rearing practices, common culture, or socioeconomic status have a smaller impact on personality than the unique experiences of individual family members.

- Most of the results of behavior genetics research, particularly the specific estimates of the strength of different types of genetic and environmental effects, remain controversial. The resolution of many of these controversies will require advances in our understanding and assessment of how specific environmental factors influence personality.
- The hypothesis that body type influences personality and temperament has not received consistent support. Other physical characteristics, such as size of pelvic opening and blood type, have been found to be related to personality; however, these relations did not appear to be causal ones.
- Evidence of the influence of hormones and biochemicals on personality comes primarily from psychopharmacological treatment of psychological disorders. The relatively new drug Prozac appears to have a pronounced impact on the personality of some individuals.
- The relation between biochemicals and personality is complex and not always well understood. The most compelling results come from those few studies that have made specific predictions about how biochemical, personality, and situational factors interact to influence behavior.
- Locating cognitive, temperament, and personality processes in specific areas of the brain is an exciting recent development. The development of noninvasive scanning techniques (e.g., CAT scans and PET scans) holds great promise for advancing this area of research.
- Evolutionary theories of personality are difficult to test but impossible to ignore. Evolutionary analysis has been used to reconcile human nature and individual uniqueness and to identify the most important dimensions of personality. In particular, evolutionary theory provides some fascinating, although controversial, predictions about gender differences in personality.
- The study of personality in animals provides further evidence of the role of evolution in human personality. There is substantial evidence that animals show consistent and stable patterns of behavior that are consistent with measurable personality traits.
- Humans share many basic characteristics with non human primates. However, humans exhibit smaller gender differences, less stability, and slower development on these characteristics, which suggests the importance of non-biological factors in human personality.
- Biological theories have several strengths, including the recognition that humans are biological, a link to the rapid developments in biological science, a comprehensive model of individual differences, and some effective treatments of psychological problems.
- Biological theories have limitations as well, including a tendency to view biological influences as all-powerful and fixed, a reductionistic approach to understanding human personality that is inappropriate, and, on occasion, an atheoretical approach to research.

# Chapter 7
# Phenomenology and Social Cognition: The Self and Personal Constructs

The Nature of Phenomenology
The Self
    Components
    Development
    Function of the Self
Rogers: A Person-Centered Approach
    Basic Theory and Concepts
    Development of Personality
    The Nature of Adjustment
    Implications for Behavior Change
    The Humanistic/Existential/
       Phenomenological Approach
Maslow and Humanism
    Hierarchy of Needs
    Self-Actualization and Being
Existentialism
Kelly: A Personal Constructs Approach
    Basic Theory and Concepts
    Development of Personality
    The Nature of Adjustment
    Implications for Behavior Change
Social Cognition
    The Computer Metaphor as a Beginning
    Human Cognition in Its Social Context

    Some Basic Concepts
    Social Cognitive Theories of Personality
Summary

Biological and psychodynamic theories of personality emphasize the influence of internal forces on personality. Moreover, these forces, whether the result of genes, hormones, instincts, archetypes, or the id, are viewed as urges beyond our awareness, and largely beyond our control, that impel us to action. However, the experience of being human includes thoughts, feelings, beliefs, and ideas of which we are aware and, to some extent, can control. We know, at least partially, who we are and what we are like; we have a sense of self. We have ideas about how we developed, what we would like to be in the future, and where we belong in our social surroundings.

Historically, **phenomenological** and **humanistic** theories of personality addressed how our conscious experience of our selves and our social world influence our development, feelings, thoughts, and social behavior. To this tradition, contemporary social and personality psychology has contributed **social cognition**, which uses the theories and techniques of cognitive psychology to study how people think about their social worlds.

## The Nature of Phenomenology

The basic assumption of phenomenological theories is that our behavior is influenced by how we perceive and understand events. External events do not directly or unilaterally cause behavior. Before it influences our actions, an event must be perceived and interpreted. Thus, as a causal agent an external event is, at best, the starting point in a causal chain that may eventually result in some action.

A central concept of phenomenological theories is the **phenomenal field**. The phenomenal field is everything experienced by the person at a given moment. To predict and perhaps understand behavior, we must assess the individual's subjective phenomenal field as well as the objective events and biological characteristics that influence that person. In the novel *To Kill a Mockingbird* (Lee, 1960) the central character, Atticus, tries to explain the behavior of a strange neighbor to his daughter by saying, "you never really know a man until you stand in his shoes and walk around in them" (p. 294). This view is the essence of phenomenological theories of personality.

The reliance of phenomenological theories on subjective human experience can make them scientifically treacherous. When these theories are invoked to help explain behavior, it is important to avoid circular reasoning—for instance, saying that a person acted anxiously because that person perceived the situation as anxiety-arousing. Likewise, phenomenological theories can be difficult to disconfirm because it is tempting to explain away any behavior that is not consistent with a theory by arguing that the behavior is the result of an individual's idiosyncratic phenomenal field. However, it is cowardly to ignore the impact that a person has on his or her own personality and behavior simply because studying that impact is scientifically challenging.

The phenomenological movement is complex and diverse. The focus in this chapter will be on the three theorists who have historically been most influential on phenomenological theories of personality: Carl Rogers, Abraham Maslow, and George Kelly. In addition, the shift in emphasis in American psychology from behavior to cognition has created a more accepting climate for the study of how human cognition can affect behavior. Some of the ideas from the field of social cognition, which is the contemporary form of phenomenological theories (Abelson, 1994), will also be introduced.

# The Self

The central character in human experience is the self. The ability to conceptualize and to imagine ourselves separate from our daily experiences is a necessary component of most phenomenological, existential, humanistic, and social cognitive theories. However, although the self is a crucial element in phenomenological theories, there is little consistency or agreement about the nature of that self (Epstein, 1980; Baumeister, 1987). Indeed, the concept of self in psychology is over a century old, it has been studied with a wide range of methods and measures, and it has been reexplained and redescribed with whatever terms were popular at each point in its long history (Linville and Carlston, 1994).

The most succinct definition of the **self** is the "I" or the "me." This definition is inherently phenomenological because it presumes that the reader has an implicit experience of "I" or "me" that conveys a shared understanding about the concept. William James (1890) introduced the concept of the self to psychological study. He defined the self as the "total of all he can call his, not only his body and his psychic powers, but his clothes and his house, his spouse and his children, his ancestors and friends, reputation and works, and his land and horses, and yacht and bank account" (p. 291). Although this quotation is strikingly old fashioned—few of us have to account for a yacht when we think of our selves, and a self can be either a she or a he—it does capture the breadth of the concept. Of course, questions such as "Who am I?" are far older than the field of psychology. Understanding who we are has been a goal of human culture from its inception.

## Components

In most modern theories the self is described as a complex system of many separate components or **identities** that is constantly changing over time and situations (Markus and Wurf, 1987). Moreover, many of these identities may never have existed outside our imagination, and they may conflict with each other (Markus and Nurius, 1986). Ruth Wylie (1984) has had a substantial impact on psychological theories of the self and has proposed an organization of the self that has three major components.

**Personal Self-Concept.** One component is the **personal self-concept,** which refers to that part of the self that includes the physical, behavioral, and psychological characteristics that help establish one's uniqueness. For example, my eyes are green, my favorite color is purple, and I am an inveterate jogger. It includes racial or ethnic identity as well as age and gender. Although the personal self is generally stable over time, this stability reflects an average around which some variation occurs rather than a rigid constancy (e.g., though generally calm, John sometimes becomes anxious before an examination).

**Social Self-Concept.** The **social self-concept** refers to how the individual believes he or she is seen by others. Social self-concepts generally change to match the person or group with which the individual is interacting. For example, when Sally is with her mother she knows that her mother views her as selfish and materialistic. Yet, when Sally is with her friends she knows that they regard her as generous. Personal self-concepts may not always be consistent with social self-concepts.

**Self-Ideals.** Idealized images of what a person would like to be are termed **self-ideals.** Few people ever attain their ideal self, and often there is a conflict between ideal self and personal self (Higgins, 1987).

## Development

Cooley (1902) is generally credited with the influential idea that our concept of ourselves develops from the reactions, both real and anticipated, we elicit from others. He argued that our attitudes about ourselves are not objective self-appraisals but the result of worry over how others feel about us (see Box 7-1). Likewise, George Herbert Mead (1934) proposed that individuals attend to their own reactions and develop self-concept to improve their ability to predict and influence the reactions of others. Mead regarded the self as an object whose character was shaped by our beliefs about how others view us.

Whereas Cooley and Mead emphasized general social influences on the development of the self, Harry Stack Sullivan (1953) focused on the extensive role played by family members in shaping the child's self. The mother, father, and significant others influence the self of the child by their overt and subtle reactions. As a result of their interpersonal relationships, the child develops a three-component self-system: the **good-me,** the **bad-me,** and the **not-me** (Sullivan, 1953). The "good-me" is based on the positive reactions the child receives from the mother and others. High self-esteem results when the appraisals of significant others are generally favorable. The "bad-me" develops from negative evaluations and helps the child build a conscience. The "not-me" component arises from strong disapproval from others—a disapproval so strong that anxiety is the result. To avoid the anxiety, dissociation of the self from certain thoughts, feelings, or actions

## BOX 7-1
## The Looking-Glass Self

Cooley (1902) described his concept of the looking-glass self as follows: The kind of self-feeling one has is determined by the attitude . . . attributed to that other [person's] mind. A social self of this sort might be called the reflected or looking-glass self:

> Each to each a looking glass
> Reflects the other that doth pass

As we see our face, figure, and dress in the glass, and are interested in them because they are ours, and pleased or otherwise with them according as they do or do not answer to what we should like them to be; so in imagination we perceive in another's mind some thought of our appearance, manners, aims, deeds, character, friends, and so on, and are variously affected by it.

A self-idea of this sort seems to have three principal elements: the imagination of our appearance to the other person; the imagination of his judgment of that appearance; and some sort of self-feeling such as pride or mortification. The comparison with a looking-glass hardly suggests the second element, the imagined judgment, which is quite essential. The thing that moves us to pride or shame is not the mere mechanical reflection of ourselves, but an imputed sentiment, the imagined effect of this reflection upon another's mind. This is evident from the fact that the character and weight of the other, in whose mind we see ourselves, makes all the difference with our feelings. We are ashamed to seem evasive in the presence of a straightforward man, cowardly in the presence of a brave one, gross in the eyes of a refined one, and so on. We always imagine, and in imagining share, the judgments of the other mind. A man will boast to one person of an action—say some sharp transaction in trade—which he would be ashamed to own to another. (pp. 152–153)

(these are not me) may occur. The development of some types of psychopathology results from these "not-me" dissociations.

## Function of the Self

Lecky (1969) proposed that a major function of self-systems is their organization of experience. An individual's experienced personality provides an integrated, consistent scheme that helps make sense of the world. Without this organization, experiences and reactions become a chaotic collage of unconnected elements.

Therefore, individuals will protect the consistency and coherence of their self-systems. Experiences will be assimilated into the self-system only if they do not threaten the stability of that system. If the system becomes too rigid to allow the incorporation of new experiences, the individual may become maladjusted. Likewise, experiences that overwhelm the system can precipitate psychopathology.

The self has been a focus of thought and research throughout the history of psychology. It is also the central concept in the humanistic and existential movement in psychology. As with psychodynamic theories, traditional humanistic and phenomenological thinking has had as much impact on disciplines such as literature, philosophy, art, and education as it has had on psychological theory and research. Only in the last 15 years, following the translation of phenomenological concepts into the language of social cognition, have phenomenological concepts become the target of empirical research.

## Rogers: A Person-Centered Approach

 The phenomenological theory of Carl Rogers developed from his observations of troubled people during psychotherapy. Roger's person-centered theory evolved as he tried to explain the interactions and changes that occur during the course of therapy. Thus, the person-centered orientation is generally presented in the language of the therapist and is best appreciated by those who have some understanding of what transpires during psychotherapy.

We can best appreciate the significance and daring of Rogers' contribution by considering the character of personality theory and psychotherapy in the late 1930s. Psychoanalytic theory and practice were the dominant approaches. There were debates in academic circles about Allport's ideas, and the contributions of Lewin and others were receiving some attention. Also, the American behaviorist tradition was rapidly developing. However, those theories associated with specific forms of therapy were the most influential, and they were primarily psychoanalytic. Prominent Jewish psychoanalysts were forced to emigrate from Western Europe to escape Nazi oppression. Many of them came to the United States—most often to New York City. The effect of all this was to increase the visibility of psychoanalysis.

At this time, Rogers was an obscure clinical psychologist, attempting to solve the problems of disturbed children in Rochester, New York. Like most therapists at that time, Rogers was familiar with psychoanalytic thought. But in the pragmatic environment of a busy clinic grappling with real problems, Rogers was willing to consider any ideas and techniques that might make his work more effective. In this context, Rogers learned of the will therapy of Otto Rank and the relationship therapy of Jessie Taft. According to Rank, patients should be given the opportunity to exert their wills. Taft, a social worker, had brought Rank's ideas to the United States and emphasized the relationship between therapist and patient.

Although he was not as strictly fundamental as his parents, Rogers continued to be influenced by his religious upbringing. He found the ideas of Rank and Taft particularly congenial because they were consistent with his religious beliefs and his democratic convictions about the nature of human relationships in society. The belief that no one has the right to control another person's life found subsequent expression in his therapeutic practices of permissiveness, acceptance, and unwillingness to give advice. Later, as he sought to build a theoretical structure to account for his therapeutic techniques, he found the theoretical and philosophical ideas of phenomenology to be the most consistent with his approach.

## Basic Theory and Concepts

The basic elements of Rogers' theory of personality are presented as a series of propositions in what is still generally regarded as his major work, *Client-centered Therapy: Its Current Practice Implications, and Theory,* published in 1951. A shorter revised version appeared in 1959.

World of the Person. A person's world is experienced as a continually changing pattern of perceptions, feelings, thoughts, and events, with that person at the center. For Rogers, this experience is the phenomenal field, which in turn is the entire contents of the person's consciousness at a given moment. Although some unconscious elements may be included in the **phenomenal field,** Rogers' definition of the unconscious is most similar to the preconscious in psychodynamic theory. It is the phenomenal field that determines behavior. Consequently, the most valid sources of information about personality are the statements people make about themselves, that is, self-report data.

For the individual, the phenomenal field cannot be distinguished from reality. All reactions of that individual, then, are based on the phenomenal field as it is experienced and perceived. To understand and predict someone's behavior requires that we know how that person is experiencing the stimuli associated with that behavior. It is not enough to know stimuli X, Y, and Z are present; it is the person's interpretation of those stimuli that is crucial:

> The only reality I can possibly know is the world as I perceive and experience it at the moment. The only reality you can possibly know is the world as *you* perceive and experience it at this moment. And the only certainty is that those perceived realities are different. There are as many "real worlds" as there are people! (Rogers, 1980, p. 102).

Rogers' emphasis on the phenomenal field led him to focus on the present. Events are explained as products of one's current perceptions and not as outcomes resulting from the past. Although Rogers recognized that there is a past sequence of events associated with any behavior, he argued that it is not necessary

A
BRIEF
BIOGRAPHY
OF

# Carl Rogers

Carl Ransom Rogers was born in Oak Park, Illinois, in 1902. The fourth of six children, he grew up in a financially secure family. His father, a civil engineer and contractor, moved the family to a farm outside Chicago when Rogers was 12. The family was devoutly, almost dogmatically, religious. The parents' strict beliefs may have been responsible for the family's inward focus. As a result, Rogers had few friends and spent most of his time alone, much of it reading. Although an outstanding student in high school, he was not active socially.

In 1919 he began college at the University of Wisconsin, majoring in agriculture. For the first two years, he was active in his church. During this period, he attended the World Student Christian Federation Conference in Beijing, China. For the first time, he became aware of cultural and religious diversity. This prompted him to discard his traditional familial and religious views and adopt a less fundamentalist approach to God and family. In 1924 he received a degree in history.

Following graduation, he married Helen Elliott, with whom he had two children. They moved to New York City, where Rogers attended Union Theological Seminary for two years. A growing skepticism of religious doctrine coupled with a desire to help others prompted him to pursue a degree in clinical psychology at Teachers College, Columbia University. He received his Ph.D. in 1931.

His first position was as a staff psychologist in a child guidance clinic in Rochester, New York. During this period he encountered the ideas of Otto Rank, which had a profound effect on his developing views of therapy. He remained at the clinic for ten years and in 1939 published a successful book, *Clinical Treatment of the Problem Child.* Partly as a result of this suc-

to study the past to understand the present. If we understand the current perceptions of the conforming person, we will also understand why that person conforms: it is a response by the person to the world as it is perceived in the present.

The Basic Human Striving. Although basic motives such as hunger, sex, security, and achievement can be described, for Rogers all of these motives were simply different aspects of the single ultimate motive of **personal growth**. Striving for personal growth is an inherent quality that serves to move all living things forward; it is embedded in our very genetic fiber. We observe this striving everywhere—in the plant growing toward the sun as well as in the child learning to walk, in the adjusted, achieving person as well as in the regressed psychotic. Within each person there is a potential for growth that constantly seeks expression. Of course, many people have lived lives so barren, so fraught with fear and

cess, he was invited to become a member of the psychology department at Ohio State University. This appointment gave Rogers added recognition and also provided him the opportunity to refine his theoretical ideas through critical discussions with graduate students and faculty colleagues.

In 1945 he moved to the University of Chicago as professor of psychology and director of the counseling center. There his work began to have a major influence on humanistic psychotherapy and theory. In 1957 he took a position at the University of Wisconsin, where he attempted to extend his ideas to the understanding and treatment of schizophrenia. Unfortunately, his approach did not prove useful or successful with this form of psychopathology. Moreover, he did not find the critical and demanding academic-research establishment receptive to his accepting and unconditionally positive views about graduate students and their education.

As a result, Rogers moved to California, where he became a fellow in residence at the Western Behavioral Sciences Institute in La Jolla. In 1968 he left that position to join the Center for Studies of the Person, also in La Jolla. In his later years he worked toward the application of his person-centered approaches to school systems, industrial organizations, and the encounter movement. Rogers died in February 1987.

Rogers was the author of numerous books. His autobiography, written in 1967, is included in *A History of Psychology in Autobiography* (Vol. 5). He also published a paper in 1974 entitled "In Retrospect: Forty-Six Years," which appeared in the *American Psychologist*. *A Way of Being* was published in 1980 and provides some insight into the changes in his thinking over the years. A particularly sensitive and revealing portrait of Rogers—both psychologist and person—has been provided by Gendlin (1988).

threat, that they cannot readily perceive the choices open to them. But even in these cases, that inner potential is seeking release and awaits only the proper conditions to express itself.

Rogers (1980) described this actualizing tendency with a boyhood memory:

> I remember that in my boyhood, the bin in which we stored our winter's supply of potatoes was in the basement, several feet below a small window. The conditions were unfavorable, but the potatoes would begin to sprout—pale white sprouts, so unlike the healthy green shoots they sent up when planted in the soil in the spring. But these sad, spindly sprouts would grow 2 or 3 feet in length as they reached toward the distant light of the window. These sprouts were, in their bizarre, futile growth, a sort of desperate expression of the directional tendency I have been describing. They would never become

Every human endeavor, even dangerous ones such as firefighting, is an expression of the striving for personal growth.

plants, never mature, never fulfil their real potential. But under the most adverse circumstances, they were striving to become. Life would not give up, even if it could not flourish. (p. 118)

**The Self.** Rogers came to accept the necessity for the concept of the self when he realized the extent to which his therapy clients were committed to the concept. These clients typically expressed their problems in self-like terms. They spoke of their "real" selves and seemed always to include the self as a vital part of their experience. Or they sought relief from debilitating anxieties but did not want their real selves altered, demonstrating through their fear the vital reality and importance of the self. This self (or self-concept) has another feature. It contains the **ideal-self,** that is, what the person would like to feel, be, or experience. In that way, the ideal-self is similar to Freud's concept of the superego.

Rogers readily incorporated a focus on the self into his theory as a result of the preoccupation with the self that he observed in his clients. Some critics of Rogers have argued that the strong emphasis on the self in Rogers' and many other psychological theories has contributed to the selfishness, or **selfism,** that seems to characterize contemporary society (see Box 7-2).

## BOX 7-2
## The Self Versus Selfism

Contemporary society has been characterized by a focus on the self and self-indulgence. In the 1970s we often heard about the "me generation," and cultural observers such as Peter Marin (1975) and Christopher Lasch (1979) suggested that the search for self-identity and self-fulfillment had crossed over into self-indulgence. In the 1990s we have the "lost generation," or "generation X," which has emphasized the self by its absence—that is, a lack of identity and individuality.

The roots of self-focus, self-indulgence, or selfism are undoubtedly complex. But some observers contend that psychology has contributed to this development (Wallach and Wallach, 1983). Certainly, the Freudian movement has preached that neurosis results from insufficient satisfaction of instinctual drives (sexual and aggressive). Psychoanalytic therapy sometimes involves an emphasis on weakening the superego so that instinctual gratification can be more easily pursued.

In particular, Carl Rogers and Abraham Maslow are often cited to support the freeing of individuals from the restraints and demands of others, thereby permitting greater spontaneity. Both Rogers and Maslow seemed to encourage people to act in accord with their true feelings. The goal became the achievement of some inner potential (often tantalizingly elusive) or the self-actualization of one's life, even if this meant going rudely against the norms of society at times. They believed that only by being good to yourself could you be good to others.

But all this can become an invitation to selfishness. As the Wallachs (1983) put it, "Far as it was from [Maslow's and Rogers's] intention, these psychologists inevitably promote selfishness by asking us to realize ourselves, to love ourselves, to view the environment as a means for our own self-actualizing ends, and to consider whether something will contribute to our own development as the only real criterion for what we should do" (p. 196).

# Development of Personality

In contrast to psychoanalytic theory, Rogers did not believe that personality developed through a discrete series of stages. Rather, he construed development as a continuous process that depends upon the way a person is evaluated by others.

Positive Regard. The development of the self-concept depends on several factors associated with the person's interactions with the social environment. First, there is the powerful need for **positive regard,** which results from the approval of others. The child will do almost anything to satisfy this need. The child also develops a need for **positive self-regard,** which allows the child to obtain the same type of appreciation from the self that he or she needs from others.

The need for positive regard is an insistent, encompassing urge for love, acceptance, warmth, and respect from significant other people. Indeed, the child, and later the adult, may reach the point where the positive regard of others is so important that a person may violate his or her values and act against his or her beliefs to obtain it. Peer pressure during adolescence, which may compel teenagers, against their better judgment, to drink or smoke, is an example of the power of this need. Psychological maturity results only when the conflicts between the need for positive regard and the integrity of the self are resolved. Independence and maturity require the person to have developed positive self-regard to balance the need for the positive regard of others.

Conditions of Worth. The child depends upon others for positive regard. But positive regard requires that the child fulfil certain conditions. In one family, the child receives positive regard by receiving a grade of A in English; in another family, positive regard results from hitting a home run. The child learns these different **conditions of worth** as requirements for approval, attention, and rewards. When these conditions are met, his or her self-esteem will likely be enhanced.

These conditions of worth serve the important function of providing the structure for socialization. However they can also limit a person's experience and in some cases lead to maladaptive behavior. For the child, conditions of worth are defined by the significant others in the child's life. Some important segments of experience may not be valued by these significant others, and the child will forego those experiences. The potential for growth and actualization will be reduced accordingly.

Unconditional Positive Regard. Rogers believed that everyone should be loved and valued regardless of the conditions of worth defined by the others in a person's life. When parents say (or imply by word or deed) that their love is conditional on the child acting in certain ways, or on developing a particular set of skills, then the child cannot attain complete actualization. What is required is **unconditional positive regard,** which is complete and genuine love and respect for the individual, regardless of that individual's interests and actions. Rogers did not intend for this concept to imply that parents must allow their children to act in any way they like. Nor did he intend it to mean that standards and discipline cannot be maintained. Instead, he introduced the concept to convey the attitude or philosophy that an individual's worth and respect as a human being must be maintained even if that individual's beliefs are distasteful and his or her actions unacceptable.

**Consistency and Threat.** After a person has developed a sense of his or her phenomenal self, it is important that new experiences be generally consistent with that self. Although some inconsistency can lead to further growth and development, too much inconsistency can destroy the experienced self and leave the individual without a sense of identity through which further experiences can be processed and understood. Thus, a person generally strives to maintain consistency between the phenomenal self and experience, and incorporates experiences that are consistent with the structure of the self into that structure. Some experiences are ignored because there is no perceived relation to the self. But experiences that are inconsistent with the self, or with conditions of worth, pose a threat.

To counter the threat, the individual will often refuse to accept them into the self or else distort their meaning. For example, a person who perceives himself or herself as intelligent may refuse to admit a grade of D in a psychology class to his or her self-structure. Instead, the meaning of the grade is distorted through claims that the test was unfair or that the instructor was a terrible teacher. These distortions may occur without awareness. The danger, however, is that distortion and denial may prevent the person from obtaining new self-knowledge.

For Rogers the self is conservative and self-protective. It affects our perceptions and filters our experiences and memories. This screening function of the self explains why personality change is so difficult. Change involves threat, and this threat can be resolved by screening out that which is threatening. Thus, the need for change dissolves. Many conditions of worth will likewise lead to a narrow, constricted self-concept, and such narrowness ensures that many experiences, perceptions, and memories inconsistent with the self will not be permitted into our conscious thoughts and imagery.

## The Nature of Adjustment

To the extent that an individual's experience does not fit with his or her self-concept, there will be less than perfect adjustment. Also, the greater the inconsistency, the greater the tendency to deny and distort. Relatively moderate incongruence would likely lead to neurotic behavior. Extreme incongruence would end in psychosis. In the latter situation, the person's defenses disintegrate, and behavior becomes irrational. Often, this means that the psychotic person's behavior is consistent with those aspects of experience that have been denied rather than with the self-concept. The psychotic who reports wild fantasies of destroying the world may have once been an overcontrolled person who could not admit to feelings of hostility toward others. The essence of maladjustment is a denial of experience into the self-structure (Rogers, 1951).

In his 1961 book, Rogers describes the **fully functioning person.** Fully functioning persons live up to their potential, use their talents and capacities completely, and have phenomenal selves that are consistent with their experience. Such people are open to experience, are able to live every moment to its fullest, can rely on the self rather than on others, feel a sense of freedom to live any way they choose, and can respond to problems with creative solutions. "It involves the stretching and growing of becoming more and more of one's potentialities. It involves the courage to be. It means launching oneself into the stream of life" (Rogers, 1961, p. 196). Whether many people ever achieve this ideal level of existence is questionable. However, the process of striving to attain it may be its own reward.

The epitome of adjustment is the ability to use fully one's talents and capabilities.

## Implications for Behavior Change

The popularity of Rogers' theory of personality has been enhanced because of its association with a form of therapy. Over the years, the name of his therapy has changed from **nondirective** to **client-centered** and now to **person-centered** (Rogers, 1977). However, Rogers' approach to therapy remains unchanged. A proposition from Rogers' 1951 book clearly presents this rationale for client-centered approaches. "Under certain conditions, involving primarily complete absence of any threat to the self-structure, experiences which are inconsistent with it may be perceived, and examined, and the structure of self revised to assimilate and include such experiences" (p. 517).

Client-centered approaches are distinguished more by what the therapist does *not* do than by what the therapist does. Neither advice nor information is given, and reassurance and persuasion are considered inappropriate. Asking questions, making interpretations, and offering criticisms are likewise avoided. The major activities of the therapist are recognizing and clarifying clients' feelings so that the clients can discover the distorted self-images with which they have been shackled. For Rogers (1959), psychotherapy involved the "releasing of an already existing capacity in a potentially competent individual, not the expert manipulation of a more or less passive personality" (p. 221). Thus, therapy is not a set of techniques. If anything, the essence of therapy resides in the core of values and attitudes of the therapist.

A sense of what Rogers was trying to do is contained in the following description.

> Rogers eliminated all interpretation. Instead, he checked his understanding out loud, trying to grasp exactly what the patient wished to convey. When he did that, he discovered something: The patient would usually correct the first attempt. The second would be closer, but even so, the patient might refine it. Rogers would take in each correction until the patient indicated, "Yes, that's how it is. That's what I feel." Then there would be a characteristic silence. During such a silence, after something is fully received, the next thing comes in the client. Very often it is—*something deeper*. (Gendlin, 1988, p. 127).

In Box 7-3 some of Rogers' therapy techniques are further illustrated.

The Client–Therapist Relationship.  In later years, Rogers focused on the nature of the relationship between therapist and client as the essential ingredient for successful therapy. It is this relationship that can remove threat from the therapy situation. When threat is absent, clients will feel free to examine the experiences they have been denying or distorting. The way is then open for the person's growth potential to move toward self-actualization.

Three therapist characteristics are critical in this relationship: (1) accurate emphatic understanding, (2) unconditional positive regard, and (3) genuineness (also called congruence). When these three elements are present in the therapeutic situation, the client can achieve a feeling of personal worth and growth. The

## BOX 7-3
## Therapy, Rogerian Style

The following is a brief set of excerpts from the therapy sessions of a depressed young woman. It illustrates several typical Rogerian tactics.

*Client:* I cannot be the kind of person I want to be. I guess maybe I haven't the guts—or the strength—to kill myself—and if someone else would relieve me of the responsibility—or I would be in an accident—I—I—just don't want to live.

*Therapist:* At the present time, things look so black to you that you can't see much point in living.

*Client:* Yes—I wish I'd never started this therapy. I was happy when I was living in my dream world. There I could be the kind of person I wanted to be—But now there is such a wide, wide gap—between my ideal—and what I am.

*Therapist:* It's really a tough struggle—digging into this like you are—and at times the shelter of your dream world looks more attractive and comfortable.

*Client:* My dream world or suicide. So I don't see why I should waste your time—coming in twice a week—I'm not worth it. What do you think?

*Therapist:* It's up to you. It isn't wasting my time—I'd be glad to see you whenever you come—but it's how you feel about it—if you don't want to come twice a week—or if you do want to come twice a week—once a week?—it's up to you.

*Client:* You're not going to suggest that I come in often? You're not alarmed and think I ought to come in—every day—until I get out of this?

*Therapist:* I believe you are able to make your own decision. I'll see you whenever you want to come.

*Client:* (*note of awe in her voice*) I don't believe you are alarmed about—I see—I may be afraid for myself—but you aren't afraid for me.

*Therapist:* You say you may be afraid of yourself—and are wondering why I don't seem to be afraid for you?

*Client:* You have more confidence in me than I have. I'll see you next week—maybe. (Rogers, 1951, pp. 46–47)

From *Client-Centered Therapy: Its Current Practice, Implications and Theory* by Carl R. Rogers. Copyright 1951 by Carl R. Rogers. Reprinted by permission of Houghton Mifflin Company.

empathic therapist is one who can communicate to the client the feeling of being understood and can demonstrate sensitivity to the client's needs, feelings, and situation. Finally, genuineness allows the therapist to move beyond mere technique and participate in the client's problems in an emotional and involved fashion. A therapist who can convey all this will provide a climate in therapy that will enable the client to change.

It must be emphasized that this is an idealized description of an effective therapist. As Truax (1966) has tried to show, not even Rogers himself could, in every instance, respond in uniformly empathic ways throughout a therapy session. Just as clients continually strive to overcome their problems and become self-actualized, so therapists continually strive to become more effective in their therapeutic technique. Neither a client nor a therapist can be expected to achieve perfection.

**Other Applications.** The person-centered approach is a popular form of therapy. It is not technique-centered and thus appears easy to learn. It is not based on extensive knowledge of personality theory or diagnosis. Furthermore, it promises improvement in a shorter time than more traditional, psychoanalytically derived techniques. Its main requirement is the development of an attitude of genuine acceptance. As a result, the person-centered approach is applied in many human relations activities. Counseling and therapy remain its chief applications, but it has become a part of the education of those who work in crisis centers, paraprofessionals involved in counseling relationships, and volunteers in charitable organizations. The approach has been adopted in small therapy groups, often called **encounter groups.** Such groups are designed to help individuals experience and develop their feelings through encounters with other people in a supportive atmosphere. The person-centered approach is often used in institutional settings where one of the major goals is to foster improved human relations (e.g., in churches, businesses, and schools, or to solve racial confrontations).

## The Humanistic/Existential/Phenomenological Approach

The theory of Carl Rogers can be described as phenomenological because it emphasizes the importance of subjective experience for understanding behavior. However, it has also been referred to as an existential theory because it implies that people exercise control over their current actions and future development. Rogers' theory might also be called humanistic because it expresses optimism about individuals and the human condition, emphasizing people's creativity and assets rather than their failings. Although it is not logically necessary for these three philosophies to overlap, it is typical to find such similarity among phenomenological, existential, and humanistic theories.

## Maslow and Humanism

Maslow, unlike Rogers, was not a therapist. He studied people who were normal and healthy. Perhaps because of this, Maslow's view of personality is more optimistic than Rogers's. Abraham Maslow was an advocate of **humanism.** To him, this meant a focus on people's positive characteristics. Although he acknowledged the potential negative characteristics of human nature, he believed that the way to prevent psychopathology was by studying the good side. By understanding their capacity for **self-actualization**—the potential to be all that a person can become—people can eventually realize their potential. We will not grasp the meaning of the human experience by concentrating on our baser instincts, as do the psychoanalysts. Nor do we find the way to enlightened understanding by conceptualizing ourselves as mechanical robots activated by conditioned stimuli or reinforcers—the view of behaviorists. What Maslow advocated has come to be described as the **third force** in psychology, the first force being psychoanalysis and the second force behaviorism (see Chapter 9). The key concepts in this force are experience, choice, creativity, and self-actualization. The key goals are the dignity and enhancement of people.

## Hierarchy of Needs

According to Maslow (1970, 1987), humans are motivated by a group of innate needs that lend meaning and satisfaction to life. However, these needs recur and therefore require repeated satisfaction. Thus, the individual is always in a state of need deficit. Just as one need is satisfied, another demands gratification. The principle is best illustrated by physiological needs. It is not sufficient to eat only once to satisfy hunger; the need to eat recurs throughout the lifetime.

These needs are arranged in a hierarchy, as shown in Figure 7-1. Those needs lowest in the hierarchy are physiological (hunger, thirst, etc.) and must be satisfied before the next layer of needs, involving safety (pain avoidance, security, etc.), can be pursued. For example, the members of a primitive society cannot be concerned about their needs for self-actualization because they are constantly preoccupied with their physiological and safety needs. But in a more technologically developed society where the time and effort that must be devoted to physiological and security needs is reduced, needs for love, esteem, and actualization can become significant motives.

Below is a description of each of Maslow's six categories of needs.

- *Physiological Needs.* These include needs for food, water, sex, sleep, and elimination. Humans share these needs with most other animals. These needs must generally be satisfied before we can be influenced by the next level of needs. Although people can occasionally be preoccupied with higher-order needs while they are, for example, hungry or thirsty, persistent nonsatisfaction of physiological needs will inhibit the pursuit of needs at the next higher level.
- *Safety Needs.* These include needs for structure, security, order, avoidance of pain, and protection. The importance of these needs is especially apparent in children and in neurotics who constantly sense impending danger. These needs are also found in many animals.
- *Belongingness and Love Needs.* Once physiological and safety needs have been secured, needs for affiliation and affection receive attention. These are powerful motives. Maslow believed that certain characteristics of modern

## A BRIEF BIOGRAPHY OF

# Abraham Maslow

Abraham Maslow was born in Brooklyn, New York, in 1908. He was the son of Jewish parents who had emigrated from Russia. He described his childhood as terrible. Because he was the only Jewish boy in the neighborhood, he had few friends and was alone most of the time.

His parents insisted that he study law, but after only two weeks he quit. He first went to Cornell but later transferred to the University of Wisconsin, where he received the B.A. in 1930, the M.A. in 1931, and the Ph.D. in psychology in 1934. At the age of 20, he married Bertha Goodman; they had two children.

Initially, Maslow was attracted to behaviorism. However, after the birth of his first child, he found that behaviorism was unable to account for the miracle of a baby's experience. Also, the atrocities of World War II had a strong and persistent influence on his thinking. These factors convinced him to study factors that would improve the human experience.

After receiving his Ph.D., Maslow accepted a position as a Carnegie Fellow at Columbia University. He moved on to Brooklyn College, where he remained until 1951. That year, he went to Brandeis University as chairman of the psychology department. In 1961, he stepped down from that position but remained as professor of psychology. He became a resident fellow of the Laughlin Foundation in Menlo Park, California, in 1969. He died in June 1970.

Maslow is the author of several books. Three of the most influential are *Toward a Psychology of Being* (1962), *Religions, Values, and Peak Experiences* (1964), and *Motivation and Personality* (1970). His wife helped compile a posthumous volume, *Abraham H. Maslow: A Memorial Volume,* which was published in 1972. A summary of his theory is contained in Hjelle and Ziegler (1981). An interesting biography of Maslow has appeared recently (Hoffman, 1988). A review of that same book also contains some poignant insights into Maslow as a person (Bugental, 1989).

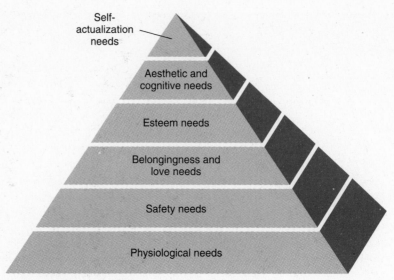

**Figure 7-1** ∽ Maslow's need hierarchy represented as a pyramid.

society such as urbanization, bureaucracy, and the decline of family ties led to widespread failures in their satisfaction. The result has been alienation, which, among other things, has led to the popularity of encounter groups and psychotherapy.

- *Esteem Needs*. These are the needs of self-respect and esteem from others. People need to feel personally competent and worthy, and they require that others recognize their value and competence. Failure to be accepted by the self or others leads to feelings of inferiority and discouragement.
- *Aesthetic and Cognitive Needs*. These are growth needs, whose satisfaction moves a person closer to the ultimate goal of self-actualization. They involve an awareness of knowledge, understanding, goodness, justice, beauty, order, and symmetry.
- *Self-Actualization Needs*. That unusual person who has generally satisfied all the previous needs is in a position to seek self-actualization. This person can pursue the attainment of his or her full potential. The goal is to become all that the person can become.

## Self-Actualization and Being

To those rare individuals who are generally able to satisfy the five types of lower-order needs comes the opportunity for self-actualization. Self-actualizers are qualitatively different from nonactualizers. The latter are motivated primarily by deficiencies such as lack of food, lack of love, or lack of esteem, whereas the former are guided by **being values**, or **metamotives**. Being values are growth motives whose purpose is to extend our experience and enrich our lives. This type of mo-

## Table 7-1
Some Characteristics of Self-Actualizers

- Perceive reality accurately and fully.
- Show greater acceptance of themselves, others, and things generally.
- Are spontaneous and natural.
- Tend to focus on problems rather than on themselves.
- Prefer detachment and privacy.
- Are autonomous and thus tend to be independent of the physical and social environment.
- Have a fresh outlook; appreciate much of life.
- Have mystical or peak experiences.
- Enjoy a spirit of identify and unity with all people.
- Have deep interpersonal relations with only a few people, who are also usually self-actualizers.
- Possess a character structure that emphasizes democratic ideals.
- Are ethical.
- Are creative.
- Have an excellent sense of humor that is philosophical rather than hostile.
- Resist enculturation; are not easily seduced by society.

tivation is not to compensate for deficits; rather, it is to open us to new experiences. Some of the characteristics of self-actualizers are shown in Table 7-1.

Self-actualizers are not perfect. They show human vanities and foibles. They can, at times, be victims of temper outbursts and be ruthless, boring, or stubborn. They are strong individuals, and this strength sometimes leads them to behave in a cold, detached manner.

Although Maslow claimed that the need for self-actualization is an innate quality that exists in all people, most people are not self-actualizers. The reason most people do not experience the motive to self-actualize is provided in Figure 7-1. The need for self-actualization is at the top of the pyramid. It occupies the least amount of space, which symbolizes that it is the weakest of all the human motives and thus can be dominated by other motives and environmental forces. In addition, pursuing self-actualization is a difficult undertaking that requires honest self-knowledge and a willingness to act against societal norms when those norms conflict with the person's beliefs. As Freud argued, most people find self-knowledge threatening and therefore resist it. Also, many people do not have the courage to confront and violate societal norms in the service of their personal growth.

Despite these difficulties, self-actualization is possible—but only in an environment that has satisfied all our other needs. In addition, that environment must have afforded the opportunity for free speech, freedom of action (assuming those actions do not harm others), freedom of inquiry, and freedom to defend oneself. The qualities of fairness, justice, and honesty must also be present. For all these personal, environmental, and societal reasons, most people are only able to work *toward* the top of the pyramid. The journey is all that most can experience, but for those select few who make it to the top, the feeling is profound (Jourard and Landsman, 1980).

# Existentialism

Because it emphasizes the present, existentialism is also often associated with humanism and phenomenology. Existentialism is a philosophy that has influenced many disciplines, of which psychology is but one. The work of Rogers and Maslow has some existential aspects, but their theories are best viewed as influenced by the existential movement in philosophy rather than as existential theories.

In **existentialism,** the present has no connection to the past; nor does it determine the future. The individual exhibits freedom of choice, and any stability and predictability to personality occurs only because the person's choices make his or her personality appear that way. Existentialists look upon Kierkegaard, the troubled Danish writer, as the founder of the movement. But the writings of Heidegger and Sartre are also representative of this philosophy. Inherent in the works of all three writers are six themes (Rychlak, 1981). First, there is **alienation.** Alienated people are those who have become separated or detached from their experience. They describe themselves or explain their actions in outdated and stereotyped terms.

Another prominent theme is **authenticity.** People who are not authentic allow others—such as their culture, church, or family—to define who they are and what they feel. Alienation arises out of the inability to be oneself, and it ends in failure to achieve one's potential. Three more themes are **anxiety** and **dread,** and **despair.** These are the emotions that sweep over those who cannot define their being. They are clues to the basic emptiness of the alienated individual. The last theme is **absurdity,** which refers to the essential nonsense or inanity of human beliefs, behavior, and life. Being born only to die is absurd. Teaching children to develop to be similar to ourselves is absurd. Perhaps the idea that one can learn by reading markings on a printed page is absurd! Because many of our beliefs are absurd, their very absurdity seems to lend credence to them.

Two prominent existentialists are Ludwig Binswanger (1963) and Medard Boss (1963, 1977). They reject traditional notions of causality in favor of *Dasein,* a German word translated as "being there." Their approach is **Daseinsanalysis,** that is, the analysis of immediate experience. They see motivation not in terms of past events but in the sense of Dasein offering future possibilities that draw us to them. For example, students work hard not because their parents have influenced them to learn and be successful, but because a part of their Dasein contains a potential for achievement toward which they strive.

The neurotic person is unauthentic and dominated by the wishes and plans of others. In extreme cases such as psychosis, they experience delusions and hallucinations, which reveal a new form of Dasein that is threatening to the individual.

Boss and Binswanger were trained in psychoanalysis. Consequently, their therapy has a distinct psychoanalytic flavor. Their interpretations, however, differ from Freudian ones. They emphasize clarifying the person's phenomenal world and taking charge of one's life and exercising free choice. Thus, as with psychoanalysis, the goal of existential therapy is insight—but an existential insight.

## Kelly: A Personal Constructs Approach

The theories of Rogers and Maslow emphasize the phenomenology of a person's feelings and experiences. As a result, they have a humanistic and existential value orientation. In contrast, the personality theory of George Kelly emphasizes the individual's thoughts, observations, and knowledge. Kelly's approach is more consistent with the contemporary views of cognitive psychology and is less strongly associated with humanistic values and existential philosophy. Although all of these theorists endorse the importance of the phenomenal world for predicting and understanding a person's behavior, their theories focus on different aspects of that phenomenal world.

Homeless individuals are examples of people who are physically and psychologically alienated.

The fundamental assumption of Kelly's theory is that people approach the world as informal scientists. In their work, scientists form hypotheses and make predictions. To test these hypotheses, the scientist makes observations and performs experiments. Kelly argued that this approach to knowledge is not restricted to formal science; it is how all people attempt to make sense of their lives and experiences.

> It is customary to say that the *scientist's ultimate aim is to predict and control*. . . . Yet curiously enough, psychologists rarely credit the human subjects in their experiments with having similar aspirations. It is as though the psychologist were saying to himself, "I, being a *psychologist,* and therefore a *scientist,* am performing this experiment in order to improve the prediction and control of certain human phenomena; but my subject, being merely a human organism, is obviously propelled by inexorable drives welling up within him, or else he is in gluttonous pursuit of sustenance and shelter." (Kelly, 1955, p. 5)

Thus, according to Kelly, all of us attempt to *construe* our world. We interpret, try to understand, and explain. To do this, people employ **personal constructs**. These represent individuals' conclusions, interpretations, and deductions from their everyday observations and experiences. They are the ideas and perspectives that individuals find personally useful and important for organizing their subjective experience (Sechrest, 1977).

## Basic Theory and Concepts

Kelly's theory is formally stated in a fundamental postulate and 11 corollary assumptions. The fundamental postulate states: "A person's processes are psychologically channelized by the ways in which he anticipates events" (Kelly, 1955, p. 46). This postulate indicates that the focus of the theory is psychological. The theory does not apply to biochemical events, nor does it address issues in sociology or economics. The postulate implies that human thought and action are designed to predict (anticipate) events. People strive to better understand the world. To do this, they make predictions. Some are correct, whereas others are wrong. But right or wrong, making and evaluating predictions is how people learn about their world.

People base their predictions on the similarities and differences of the events they observe. By learning these similarities and differences, they improve their ability to predict. However, because no one experiences the world in exactly the same way as anyone else, people will differ in what they construe as similar or different in their subsequent predictions. Therefore, constructions of events and observations are not the same as the reality of the event. Sechrest (1977) recounts Kelly's fondness for illustrating this point by telling an audience that the shoes of someone sitting in the front row are "neurotic." Everyone strains to look at those neurotic shoes to see what makes shoes neurotic. Kelly would then admonish his listeners for looking at the shoes rather than at him (Kelly). After all, it was he who construed them as neurotic!

**The Nature of Constructs.** People also develop personalized **systems of constructs**. These systems reflect how constructs are related to each other and how they combine to describe and explain events in the world. One important feature of a construct is its generality or range of application. For example, the construct *beautiful-ugly* may apply to nearly everything in the world, whereas the construct *intelligent-stupid* may apply only to humans. In addition, constructs may have hierarchical relations to each other so that one construct contains the other. Again, each person may have different hierarchies of constructs. Box 7-4 illustrates a construct hierarchy.

In Kelly's theory, constructs are conceptualized as **dichotomous**, that is, as consisting of a pair of concepts that are related in an either-or fashion. Because people develop constructs out of their perceptions of similarity and difference, people define constructs as contrasts. For example, a construal of Tom as "short" implies a contrast with something that Tom is not. The only way to develop such a construct is by observing contrasting events. To have abstracted the idea of shortness for Tom, one must have seen several "short" people who were similar to Tom, but also at least one person who differed from those short ones. Most likely, the "not-short" person was "tall." However, Kelly emphasized that people's personal constructs do not necessarily reflect such natural contrasts. It is possible that the person who was perceived as differing from Tom and the other short people was a woman or was unhappy—in which case the personal construct of short versus female or short versus unhappy could have developed.

The personal meaning of a description depends crucially on the contrast. For example, the construct "sweet" typically contrasts with "sour" or "bitter." If we use "sweet" to describe a person, the contrast is typically with "unkind" or "nasty." However, when presenting Kelly's theory to a class in the southeastern United States, one of the authors of this book discovered that the meaning of "sweet" differs in that part of the country. The students in that class indicated that the contrasting construct for sweet was "intelligent." With this insight, statements such as "Well, isn't he sweet," in response to a report that a person has just backed out of his garage without bothering to open the garage door, become sensible.

Although constructs are dichotomous, their application often reflects an appreciation for the underlying continuity of the dimension. Thus, at one moment in time my construct is tall versus short. At another time I may observe several people, some of whom are well above 6 feet, others about 5 feet 10 inches, and still others only 5 feet 5 inches. If I am choosing people for a basketball team, I may regard those well above 6 feet as tall and everyone else as short (a dichotomous construct). If I am choosing them for a baseball team, I may regard those

A
BRIEF
BIOGRAPHY
OF

# George Kelly

George Alexander Kelly was born in 1905 in Kansas. His parents were religious; his father, at one time a Presbyterian minister, turned to farming for reasons of health. At the age of 13, Kelly was sent away to school; he never really lived at home after that. He attended Friends University, a Quaker school in Wichita, and received his B.A. in physics and mathematics from Park College in 1926. Deciding against a career in engineering, he became interested in education and sociology and received his M.A. in 1928 from the University of Kansas. At this time, he began a series of teaching jobs, including positions at a junior college (where he met his wife), at a labor college, and as a speech instructor for the American Bankers Association. A scholarship enabled him to study under Sir Godfrey Thomson at the University of Edinburgh. In 1930 he returned from Scotland with an education degree and an interest in psychology. In 1931 he received a Ph.D. from the State University of Iowa; his dissertation dealt with common factors in speech and reading disabilities.

There then began a formative period in Kelly's life. With the onset of the Great Depression, he returned to Kansas to teach at Fort Hays State College, where he remained until the beginning of World War II. Here he developed a traveling clinic. Kelly and his students covered nearly the whole state, providing consultation services to help teachers better deal with problems with their students. This immersion in the world of psychological problems and how to deal with them influenced Kelly's thinking. His pioneer efforts are still remembered in Kansas.

well above 6 feet as giants and those below as of reasonable height (again, a dichotomous construct). At each moment of decision, I make a dichotomous judgment. But over a series of judgments, my awareness of gradations in height becomes apparent.

People can revise their constructs with experience. In particular, after several predictions based on one's construct system turn out to be wrong, the individual may decide to construe the world differently to avoid making errors. However, change is possible only for **permeable constructs** within the system. A permeable construct is one that can be applied to events not yet incorporated into the system. For example, a person may have the construct *sexual relationship–platonic relationship*. For a monogamous person, this construct is impermeable because it can be applied only to the one individual with whom the person has a romantic, sexual relationship. People other than that individual are not considered for the

Kelly left Kansas to serve in the Navy when World War II began. He became an aviation psychologist. During this time, he also came into contact with many other psychologists as the role of psychology in the armed forces was being defined. These contacts helped him secure a position at the University of Maryland in 1945. A year later, he moved to Ohio State University, where he established a training program in clinical psychology. This program, with the cooperation of Julian Rotter, developed into an outstanding model of the scientist-practitioner approach to Ph.D. training in clinical psychology.

At Ohio State, Kelly published his major work, *The Psychology of Personal Constructs: A Theory of Personality* (1955). With the acclaim that followed this publication, Kelly traveled extensively, receiving invitations to lecture all over the United States, as well as in Europe, the Soviet Union, South America, the Caribbean, and Asia. In 1965, he accepted an endowed chair at Brandeis University. He died in March 1967.

Kelly was not a prolific writer. Aside from his two-volume work, he wrote very little. Maher (1969) has collected some of his more important papers. Sechrest (1977) has an excellent chapter on Kelly's theory. Interestingly, since the 1960s, Kelly's work has attracted much attention in England, as is indicated in several recent books (e.g., Adams-Webber, 1979; Bannister, 1985; Button, 1985).

"sexual relationship" category. Such an impermeable construct closes off a portion of the construct system from change.

Some constructs may also be preemptive. A **preemptive construct** does not permit its elements to belong to any other category. For example, religious fanatics may label all who do not share their religious beliefs as evil. These nonbelievers cannot also be considered intelligent, dependent, skilled, or tall. Their evilness is the only relevant aspect of their description; it preempts considering them as anything else.

It is easiest to describe constructs with labels such as handsome or unattractive, intelligent or stupid. However, labels are not always attached to constructs, nor are constructs always verbal. In addition, although two individuals may use the same label for a construct, this does not imply that their constructs are identical.

# BOX 7-4
## Construct Hierarchy

Bannister (1970) illustrates the hierarchical relationships of constructs to one another:

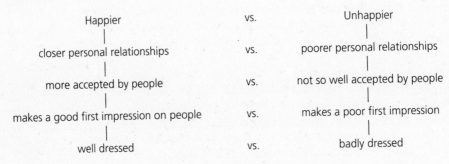

| Happier | vs. | Unhappier |
| closer personal relationships | vs. | poorer personal relationships |
| more accepted by people | vs. | not so well accepted by people |
| makes a good first impression on people | vs. | makes a poor first impression |
| well dressed | vs. | badly dressed |

The person was asked whether he would prefer to see himself as *well dressed* or *badly dressed* and replied that he would like to see himself as *well dressed*. He was asked "why" and he replied that it was to make a *good first impression on people*. . . . When asked "why" he said that once you have made a good first impression on people then you are *more accepted by them* and in response to "why" he said that in that way you could go on to form *better personal relationships with them*. When asked "why" he wanted to form better personal relationships he said that in that way he would be *happier*. When asked why he wanted to be *happier* he gave no direct answer but argued that it wasn't in aid of anything—it was what life was about. Thus he appeared to have reached his personal ceiling for this particular hierarchy—the overarching principle which, for the time being, was at the top of this particular ladder and which had no verbally accessible 'why' to it. (p. 56)

**Responses to Construct Inconsistency.** Construct change occurs throughout the lifetime as a result of inconsistency between constructs and experience. It is a natural and normal part of development that occurs as we learn. Changes can be minor and of little consequence. For example, discovering that a favorite writer has recently written a bad book might lead one to reconstrue the conception of him as the all-time greatest writer of science fiction. Other changes, however, can have a more serious impact. An individual may construe himself or herself as the leading scientist in a particular discipline. However, after several years of failed research programs, an inability to publish papers, and the rejection of several grant applications, the person may be compelled to reconstrue this aspect of himself or herself. This degree of change produces **threat**, which is an awareness of an imminent major change in a construct system. Thus, Kelly, like Rogers, considered consistency between constructs and reality to be an important component of mental health.

Kelly considered the feeling of **guilt** to result from a conflict between a person's actions and constructs. Certain aspects of a construct system concern predictions of our interactions with other persons or groups. Suppose, for example, that an employee construes herself as prompt, responsible, and hard-working. Yet, she finds that recently she has been coming to work late, leaving early, and not finishing all her work. She may respond by experiencing guilt.

Kelly viewed **anxiety** as an awareness that perceived events cannot be construed within one's construct system. A student who cannot learn how to write a term paper often experiences anxiety. This suggests that the individual cannot, with the constructs at hand, construe how to go about the task. When important events in life repeatedly fall outside the range of the person's construct system, an anxiety reaction will result. Another response that can occur when constructs are not working is **aggression**. Kelly used the term to refer to taking the initiative rather than as an attack. Aggression involves actively working to extend or elaborate the perceptual field and thereby incorporate a greater range of events into the system.

Kelly also considered **hostility**, which he described as a person's attempt to extort, either through positive or negative actions, validating evidence for a prediction that is failing (or has failed). Rather than change constructs, the person uses hostility to try to change the characteristics of what he or she is predicting. For example, a mother may insist on construing her little daughter as a budding homebody who loves to "help Mommy." But her little girl repeatedly forsakes helping for the lure of outdoor games. The hostile mother does not change her view of the girl. Instead, she starts offering her daughter money to help with the dishes and housework. Some mothers would simply have altered their constructs relating to their daughters. The hostile mother alters her daughter and thereby validates her constructs. In Kelly's view, hostility does not necessarily imply mean or negative actions; it simply designates any actions to change the person rather than the construct.

## Development of Personality

Kelly's theory is oriented toward the future. People attempt to anticipate, predict, and extend the range of their constructs. To understand people, we must understand their constructs *now*—not yesterday, not last year, and certainly not when they were 3 years old. The explanation for behavior lies in today's constructs and the likelihood of their changing in the future. Kelly's approach, like Rogers', is ahistorical; it is not necessary to consider the past to explain the present. Thus, Kelly wrote little about the development of the person.

## The Nature of Adjustment

According to Hjelle and Ziegler (1981), Kelly's perspective contains four characteristics associated with the healthy personality. Psychologically adjusted individuals exhibit these qualities:

- a willingness to evaluate their constructs and test the validity of their perceptions of others,
- the ability to discard constructs and alter their core systems when they appear to be invalid,
- a wish to extend the range or coverage of their construct systems, and
- a well-developed repertoire of roles.

## Implications for Behavior Change

Kelly was trained as a clinical psychologist. Consistently with his theory, he viewed his clients as rational "scientists" whose construct systems were not allowing them to predict events accurately. Thus, the goal of therapy was to assist these clients to revise and change their construct systems so that they would construe the world more usefully. He used a variety of therapeutic devices to induce change in his clients' construct systems.

Kelly described the therapy room as a laboratory in which the client could safely carry out experiments in cognitive change that would be risky in a real-life setting. Kelly advocated permissiveness because this encouraged the clients' experimentation. New ideas, plans, or behaviors could be contemplated without embarrassment or fear. Kelly would respond (by gesture, facial expression, and comment) to his clients experiments, which is how the clients could learn of the effects of their new actions. Kelly also emphasized the need to create novel situations for clients, in therapy and elsewhere in their lives. He saw this as a creative activity that promoted a change in the client's constructs by showing the client how ineffectual those constructs had been. For example, Kelly might encourage a client to date a woman the client thought he did not like just to prove to him that his ways of construing her were faulty. Another technique Kelly used was to encourage the client to make specific predictions. He thought that many clients would be unable to resist trying an experiment if they had actually made a prediction about its outcome.

Because it is consistent with his theory, Kelly advocated **fixed-role therapy**. Kelly would provide clients with a role, or *prescription,* which they would be asked to play in a variety of situations and for various lengths of time. A particular role was selected to provide contrasts with the client's customary behavior. This procedure was not meant to imply that the client should permanently take on the characteristics of the role. Rather, it was a technique used to alter constructs by showing the client that his or her predictions about what would happen to the person in the role were not necessarily correct.

## Social Cognition

Kelly's theory of personal constructs, with its emphasis on the phenomenological observations, knowledge, and thoughts of individuals, anticipated and contributed to a dramatic change that has occurred in American psychology. For the past several decades, the study of psychology has slowly shifted from an emphasis on behavior to an emphasis on cognition. Predicting and understanding behavior is still an important goal of psychology, but the focus is now on a thinking organism rather than a behaving one.

Initially the study of human cognition was confined to learning and memory of controlled stimuli in artificial laboratory settings. More recently the target of this research has expanded to how people process meaningful and personally relevant information in more naturalistic social settings. The term *social cognition* broadly describes research that uses the basic models and technology of cognitive psychology in the context of socially relevant information. The emphasis of this research may be primarily cognitive—evaluating the generality of cognitive models for describing human thought that were developed in the laboratory in more naturalistic social situations. Alternatively, the emphasis may be on social and personality issues, with the goal of using established cognitive models to understand important social phenomena such as stereotyping, the self-concept, or person perception.

### The Computer Metaphor as a Beginning

The study of human information processing concerns how people attend to information, store it, think about it, and retrieve it. All of these activities are also performed, more or less, by a computer, so the language of computers has provided a useful metaphor for describing human information processing. As with the computer, people *encode* information, then *recode* it by actively processing the information, and then *decode* its meaning by comparing it with, and combining it with, other stored information. The completion of all this activity results in some sort of *output* in the form of an action or a solution to a problem (Siegler, 1983). There are many obvious differences between computers and people, but the computer has provided a useful framework for describing and explaining how people think. Indeed, it has been possible to test some hypotheses about human cognition by programming computers to "think" as people are hypothesized to think and seeing whether outputs are consistent with the hypotheses. A classic model of basic human information processing is shown in Figure 7-2.

## Human Cognition in Its Social Context

One of the limitations of computers as models of human cognition is that computers process information without regard to its content or the context in which it is presented. In contrast, the content and context of the information people process is of crucial importance, and this is particularly true of social information. Early research on cognition was based on relatively simple models such as the one shown in Figure 7-2, and studies to test predictions derived from these models often used meaningless stimuli, such as nonsense syllables, that were presented in a minimal context. This strategy permitted psychologists to test hypotheses about basic cognitive processes without having to consider the complexities that result when the stimuli have personal meaning and relevance to the subject or when that meaning is qualified by the context in which the information occurs. Theories of social cognition, however, must account for the content and context of information, as well as the purposive and sometimes inconsistent

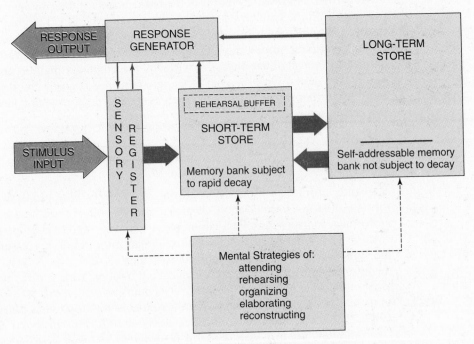

**Figure 7-2** ⟨⟩ Flow chart illustrating a model of information processing.

manner in which people think about themselves and others in their social environments.

The consequence of these additional considerations is that social cognitive theories are far more complex than the model shown in Figure 7-2. For example, Wyer and Srull (1986) have proposed a comprehensive theory of social cognition. In formulating their theory they assumed that the human cognitive system operates in a social context just as it does in any other context. The uniqueness of social cognition comes from internal input variables such as prior knowledge, expectations, stereotypes, and goals that are not considered by most general cognitive models. On the output side, social cognition results in impressions of people, social judgments, emotional reactions, and social behaviors that are also not typically part of general cognitive theories. Whereas the model in Figure 7–2 has 5 boxes and 10 arrows, a *partial* diagram of Wyer's and Srull's model has over 40 boxes of various shapes and over 60 arrows.

## Some Basic Concepts

Social cognition has three major premises. First, individuals organize their experiences according to the repetitive themes of those experiences. Second, this organization involves **schemas**, which are structures of knowledge that reside in memory. Third, these schemas can be used later to recognize and comprehend new stimuli and events.

Memory is critical in all cognitive models. Memory involving information about concepts and meaning is called **semantic memory**, whereas memory for events is referred to as **episodic memory**. In addition, information about behavior is also stored in our memories. Some of this information describes simple acts. But there are also **scripts**, which are organized representations of familiar daily activities. They can be used to perceive, understand, and influence events such as paying a bill, buying gasoline, or doing the wash (Schank and Abelson, 1977). Tomkins (1987) presented a script theory of personality that emphasized how a person's typical and consistent reactions to emotionally significant events are based on scripts about those events that have been developed from previous experiences.

Once behavioral information is stored in memory, the process of **self-regulation** becomes possible. Self-regulation is a continuous and conscious evaluation and monitoring of progress toward a goal, and the redirection of behaviors that do not contribute to that progress. Self-regulation occurs through a process called **feedback control** and is analogous to the operation of a thermostat (Powers, 1973). If monitoring fails to show any discrepancy between what a person intends and what the person is doing, the behavior will continue. Thus, if the thermostat fails to sense a difference between actual room temperature and that for which it is set, then the thermostat will not signal the furnace to come on. This view suggests that behavior is purposive and that a person's life can be understood as a set of goals and intentions. Current behavior can be understood in terms of feedback and adjustment so that acceptable progress toward the goals occurs (Carver and Scheier, 1981).

## Social Cognitive Theories of Personality

As with most relatively new areas of scientific study, social cognition has been characterized by a flurry of research activity. This research has been guided by a variety of goals and is based on several different techniques. Not surprisingly, the results of this research are open to various interpretations, and the field of social cognition is still somewhat fragmented and disorganized. However, two areas, social intelligence and self-schemata, have emerged to provide some focus to the field.

Social Intelligence.  The work of Wyer and Srull (1986) emphasizes the information processing tradition. Their model concerns how information processing models must be modified and expanded to handle the complexity and uniqueness of social cognition. However, their focus is on the *process* of social cognition. In contrast, Cantor and Kihlstrom's (1985, 1987, 1989) theory of **social intelligence** focuses on the implications of social cognition for personality. The emphasis is on the *content* of a person's social cognitive knowledge and how differences in content result in differences in personality.

The theory of social intelligence was developed to address questions of how individuals function in their social worlds. In particular, Cantor and Kihlstrom were impressed with the contemporary views of human intelligence that emphasize its role in problem solving. Social intelligence refers to the cognitive strategies that people use to solve problems that they face as they perform their **life tasks**. Life tasks are those goals, "current concerns" (Klinger, 1977), or "personal strivings" (Emmons, 1986) that motivate the individual and that command a substantial portion of the person's attention and resources. Life tasks are defined by the individual, and they change over time. However, for college students most life tasks fall into one of six categories: making friends, being independent of parents and family, developing an identity, making good grades, choosing a career, and managing time (Cantor, Norem, Niedenthal, Langston, and Brower, 1987).

Individuals employ a wide range of strategies in the pursuit of life tasks. These strategies develop out of a person's social observations and experiences and represent general styles or approaches that a person uses to solve a life task problem. One common adaptive strategy is **optimism**, which is a confident attitude that one can effectively cope with problems and handle life tasks. A related strategy is **hope** (Snyder, 1995), which consists of a sense of **agency**, which is the motivation to move toward one's goals, and **pathways,** which is knowledge of the plans or means for achieving the goals. The sense of optimism or hope is based on successful past experiences and on the desire to approach a problem with the appearance (to the self and other) of competence. To maintain optimism, individuals must select tasks that are manageable, and they must also have available additional strategies to cope with failure. For example, individuals can adopt a strategy of **defensive pessimism** (Norem & Cantor, 1986), in which they construe the task as one at which they expect to fail, or they can employ a **self-handicapping** strategy (Jones & Berglas, 1978), in which they set up conditions that provide a nonthreatening excuse if failure occurs. For example, a student who stays up all night studying can explain poor performance on a test the next day as due to exhaustion rather than to lack of ability. Although these strategies appear self-defeating, defensive pessimism can motivate increased effort (Norem and Illingworth, 1993), and self-handicapping increases self-esteem when success occurs (Rhodewalt, 1995; Tice and Baumeister, 1990).

Although people have preferred strategies, Cantor and Kihlstrom emphasize that people are flexible in strategy choice. A person may self-handicap in one life task domain but be confidently optimistic in another. To understand an individual's personality, it is necessary to know that person's current life tasks, social concepts (personal constructs), and cognitive strategies and styles. That is, we must heed the advice of Atticus and "walk around in that person's shoes."

### The Self and Self-Schemata.

Until recently, the self had been resistant to empirical study. The self was regarded as a broad, stable, but undifferentiated structure. Contemporary social cognitive theories of the self emphasize its role in the organization of knowledge (Kihlstrom and Cantor, 1984). In addition, social cognition has differentiated the self-concept into a collection of images, schemas, conceptions, and prototypes (Markus and Wurf, 1987). This differentiated view of the self into a set of cognitive structures that organize the knowledge gained from our experiences has made it possible to develop and test scientific hypotheses about the role of the self in social cognition (Greenwald & Pratkanis, 1984).

The self has been found to be a powerful cue for information retrieval (Rogers, Kuiper, and Kirker, 1977). In addition, people process self-relevant information more efficiently and with greater confidence (Markus, 1977) and selectively attend to self-relevant information (Bargh, 1982). **Self-schemata** also have a substantial impact on how we perceive and process information about others in our social environment (Markus and Sentis, 1982). However, although the self is powerful, it does not appear to be an extraordinary cognitive structure (Greenwald and Banaji, 1989). The substantial impact of self-knowledge on social cognitive processes appears to result from the large quantity and high level of organization of information we have about the self, not its unique character.

The conceptual and empirical work of Hazel Markus on **self-schemas** has provided the foundation for contemporary research on the self. Like all phenomenologists, Markus views people as constructive processors of information. Among other information, people must organize, summarize, and account for information about themselves. This results in the formation of cognitive structures about the self, or what are referred to as **self schemata,** or **self schemas.** These are "cognitive generalizations about the self, derived from past experience, that organize and guide the processing of self-related information contained in the individual's social experiences" (Markus, 1977, p. 64).

The self-schemata become cognitive representations based on specific life events. For example, "That test I took yesterday was tough, but I would have done better if I had been less nervous." But the representations may also become generalizations constructed out of repeated categorizations and evaluations both by the individual and by those with whom the person interacts in some way. Thus, "I am generous; after all, I just gave a hundred dollars to that charity." Or, "I am clumsy; my father always told me I couldn't walk and chew gum at the same time."

These schemata are derived from information the individual processes, and they influence input and output of information relative to the self. Self-schemata are, of course, stored in memory, but they are more than mere repositories of the cognitive representations of past experience that passively reside in our memories. They can become selective mechanisms that determine whether information is attended to, how important it is thought to be, and what happens to it later. Once they are established, and once repeated experiences have accumulated that are relevant to them, self-schemata become increasingly resistant to change, even in the face of inconsistent information.

As with Kelly's (1955) personal constructs, self-schemata develop from experience. Like personal constructs, they are helpful in understanding events and in guiding our behavior. They even allow us to look beyond present information and make educated guesses about the future. These self-schemata affect the manner in which information is processed. For example, Markus and Wurf (1987) have identified several consequences or effects: (1) heightened sensitivity to self-relevant stimuli; (2) more efficient processing of self-congruent stimuli; (3) enhanced recall and recognition of self-relevant stimuli; (4) more confident behavioral predictions, attributions, and inferences in areas relevant to the self; and (5) resistance to the acceptance of information that is not congruent with one's self-structure.

After reviewing their own research on self-schemata as well as other recent work on the self, Markus and her colleagues have described what they refer to as the **dynamic self-concept** (Markus and Wurf, 1987). It is an active, forceful, and changing structure. In this sense, it replaces older views of the self-concept as a passive reflection of ongoing behavior. It now becomes an active regulator of our behavior.

## Summary

- The emphasis in phenomenology is on the experiencing organism. This implies a focus on cognition, subjective experience, freedom of choice, and human values.
- In phenomenology, behavior is seen as an outgrowth of the phenomenal field, which is everything experienced by the person at a given moment.

- The self (the "I" or "me") is a prominent construct in most phenomenological approaches. The self is portrayed by Cooley and Mead as developing from, and reflecting on, the perceptions of others.
- An important function of the self is the organization of experience. Thus, maintaining a consistent self-concept is important.
- Carl Rogers developed one of the most influential phenomenological theories of personality. He stressed the importance of knowledge of the subjective world of the person as a prerequisite for understanding and prediction. He also believed the basic human striving to be the quest for self-actualization.
- In Rogers's theory, the growth of the self and the realization of one's potential are achieved when several conditions are present: the experiencing of positive regard, the presence of factors that lead to a feeling of worth, the presence of unconditional positive regard from significant others, and the absence of threat to the phenomenal self.
- According to Rogers, perceived threat leads to maladjustment. The ideal state of adjustment is the fully functioning person: the individual who lives up to his or her potential and who experiences every moment fully.
- One of Rogers's major accomplishments was the introduction of client-centered therapy. This clinical approach is characterized by complete acceptance of the person by the therapist and by an emphasis on the client–therapist relationship. The client-centered approach has now been widely applied in many nontherapeutic domains, including encounter groups, personal growth groups, industry, and education.
- Related to phenomenology is a set of approaches referred to as humanistic. Abraham Maslow, like all humanists, focused on the positive aspects of human experience (e.g., creativity and self-actualization).
- Maslow is best known for his concept of a hierarchy of needs. These needs range from physiological needs to self-actualization needs. A person cannot move on to the satisfaction of a higher need until the lower ones have generally been satisfied.
- Existentialism is also a form of phenomenology. It emphasizes freedom of choice as an inherent human quality.
- George Kelly represents a contrasting approach to phenomenology. His theory is based on the premise that all of us attempt to anticipate and predict our world much as scientists do.
- Kelly argued that we develop construct systems to enable us to anticipate events. These individual constructs are dichotomous (e.g., tall-short), and some are more pervasive than others. Still others are permeable; that is, they can be applied readily to new events. Others are preemptive in that they will permit an event to be described in only one fashion.
- As examples of the dynamics of Kelly's system, concepts of threat, guilt, anxiety, aggression, and hostility were described.
- Kelly paid little attention to how constructs develop, and in that sense, his is an ahistorical system.

- In Kelly's terms, adjustment may be said to exist when the person is willing to evaluate his or her constructs and alter them when they seem to be failing in prediction. Adjusted individuals try to extend their construct systems and to develop reasonably extensive repertoires of roles.
- Social cognition is the contemporary form of phenomenology. It is based on cognitive information processing models.
- The emergence of social cognition is consistent with the cognitive revolution that has occurred over the past several decades in American psychology. This revolution has changed the focus of attention, which is less on a behaving organism and more on a thinking one.
- An information processing approach relies on schemata, memory, and scripts and also involves self-regulation.
- Wyer and Srull have presented a comprehensive theory of human cognition in a social context. Their theory is the elaboration of general cognitive models to handle the processing of social information.
- The added complexity of social cognitive models occurs because they must incorporate prior knowledge—including goals, expectations, and stereotypes—into their models. Likewise, the output of social cognitive processing is typically a complex personal impression or emotional reaction.
- The theory of social intelligence of Cantor and Kihlstrom is designed to explain how people cope with their social world. Human behavior is viewed as motivated by life tasks that the individual approaches through various cognitive strategies. Personality is based on an individual's unique choice of life tasks and preferred strategies.
- The study of the self has been aided by the social cognitive view of the self as an organization of knowledge. The work of Hazel Markus on self-schemata has influenced the contemporary study of the self.

# Chapter 8
# Phenomenology and Social Cognition: Research, Assessment, and Summary Evaluation

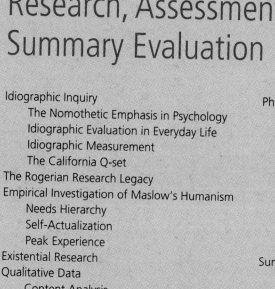

Idiographic Inquiry
    The Nomothetic Emphasis in Psychology
    Idiographic Evaluation in Everyday Life
    Idiographic Measurement
    The California Q-set
The Rogerian Research Legacy
Empirical Investigation of Maslow's Humanism
    Needs Hierarchy
    Self-Actualization
    Peak Experience
Existential Research
Qualitative Data
    Content Analysis
Research on Personal Constructs
    The Rep Test
    Change in Personal Constructs
    Complexity of Personal Construct Systems
Self-Schemata Research
Implicit Personality Theory
    Features of Implicit Personality Theory
    Validity of Implicit Personality Theory
    Implicit and Formal Theories of Personality

Phenomenology and Personality Assessment
    The Classic Semantic Differential Rating
      Scale
    Types of Personality Data
    Problems with Phenomenological Self-
      and Other-Reports
    Formal Versus Implicit Theories and
      Assessment
    Accuracy of Global Ratings
    Rating Agreement
Summary Evaluation
    Strengths
    Weaknesses
Summary

The classic phenomenological theories of personality and their contemporary evolution to social cognitive research have resulted in a broad assortment of approaches to research and assessment. At one extreme of the humanistic movement are those who view empirical research as antithetical to the values of humanism. The very act of studying another person is viewed as demeaning to that individual. However, most psychologists who work within the phenomenological tradition have attempted to present their theories in ways that result in scientifically testable hypotheses, and to develop methods that are appropriate for studying the subjective world of the individual person.

Phenomenological research methods form an eclectic collection that includes experimental and correlational techniques, as well as case studies and introspection. Humanistic philosophy is generally more compatible with idiographic research, that is, research that focuses on an individual person. However, there has always also been an interest in nomothetic principles and explanations; that is, those that can be applied to people in general. Despite this diversity, the techniques, data, and hypotheses have the common focus on the way people perceive events and themselves: **subjective experience**. Historically, this research focused on the self and the emotional experiences of actualization, enhancement, consistency, or esteem. However, the shift in emphasis to subjective knowledge and cognition in personal construct theory, and the extension of information processing models to the study of social cognition, have moved contemporary phenomenological research in the direction of experimental methods and nomothetic hypotheses.

## Idiographic Inquiry

### The Nomothetic Emphasis in Psychology

A fundamental characteristic of humanistic research is its focus on the individual. In general, psychological research is nomothetic; that is, it is based on aggregations of observations across a group of subjects, and the goal is to develop and test hypotheses that concern people in general. Likewise, the interpretation of scores of individuals on psychological tests is typically done by comparing the scores of an individual with **norms**, which are average responses of people who represent the comparison group of interest, such as people of the same age or gender. Finally, most data analysis begins with the computation of means or correlations, which indicate the average level of a group of subjects on a measure, or the average degree of relation between two variables. Such statistics communicate little about any particular individual, although we often forget that there are individual exceptions to the general conclusions we reach (Lamiell, 1981).

In contrast, humanistic research tends to be idiographic. That is, it focuses on the real individual instead of a hypothetical average person. Likewise, the meaning of an individual's experience is not based on other people's experiences. Rather, the meaning of an experience is regarded as personal and unique, and it is based on the individual's idiosyncratic past experiences and imagination. The field of psychology, and in many circumstances people as well, are strongly influenced by comparison with other people (Festinger, 1954). Thus, it is sometimes difficult to imagine using standards other than a normative one. Box 8-1 illustrates the difference between the typical normative standard and the two idiographic standards of ipsative and imaginary comparison and shows how these other standards might result in a different experience than the normative one.

## Idiographic Evaluation in Everyday Life

The idiographic evaluation of experience is philosophically consistent with humanistic theory. However, an interesting set of scientific questions concerns the type of standard people actually use to evaluate their experience (Lamiell, Foss, Larsen, and Hempel, 1983). For example, do people differ in their preferred standard, with some emphasizing normative comparisons and others idiographic ones (Chaplin and Buckner, 1988; Goolsby and Chaplin, 1988)? Do some types of experiences tend to lead to normative evaluations and others to idiographic ones (Wilson, Chaplin, Foster, and White, 1996)? Perhaps most important, is it more adaptive or psychologically healthy to use one type of standard rather than another ( Higgins, 1987; Higgins, Strauman, and Klein, 1986)?

One of the difficulties of scientifically evaluating how people evaluate their subjective experiences is that normative and idiographic standards are typically correlated (Block, 1957). That is, if a person evaluates an experience as positive using a normative standard, the experience will tend to be idiographically positive as well. For example, if a person receives the highest score in the class, it is likely that the score will be one of the highest the person has ever received, and one of the highest the person could imagine receiving.

Goolsby and Chaplin (1988) developed a paradigm to separate the effects of the different standards on subjects' evaluations. Subjects were presented with all possible combinations of positive and negative normative and idiographic standards for an academic performance. For example, in one combination, subjects were told that they had received the lowest score in the class, but that this was the best they had ever done on a test. Subjects were then asked to rate how they would feel about that experience. In the case of academic performance, the normative standard had the largest impact. Students were more concerned with their performance relative to the other students in the class than with their performance relative to themselves. Subsequently, Wilson, Chaplin, Foster, and White (1996) have shown, using the same paradigm with other experiences such as physical fitness, charitable contributions, and pain, that idiographic standards may have a larger impact on subjects' feelings about their experiences in nonacademic domains.

BOX 8-1

# Normative, Ipsative, and Imaginary Standards for Evaluating Experience

Experience:   You receive a score on a test in school.
    Normative Standard:     This is the highest score in the class.
    Ipsative Standard:     This is the highest you have ever scored on a test.
    Imaginary Standard:     This the highest you could have imagined scoring on this test.

Experience:   You jogged for 30 minutes.
    Normative Standard:     You covered more distance than the other people you were jogging with.
    Ipsative Standard:     You covered more distance than you have ever covered before.
    Imaginary Standard:     You covered more distance than you could imagine covering.

An **ipsative** comparison gives meaning to an experience by considering that experience in the context of what the individual person has done in the past, or in other situations, or with other experiences. Thus, a person might feel good about a jogging experience if he or she had covered more distance in 30 minutes than ever before, even if that distance was less than what other people on the track were covering. Likewise, doing better on a math test than ever before might be cause for celebration, even if the score is below the average of the class.

An **imaginary** standard is based on what a person can imagine doing or perhaps would like to do, even if he or she has never done so in the past (Higgins, 1987). Thus, a person might have left an examination imagining that he or she had done very poorly. If the score on the examination is higher than was imagined, the person might feel good about the experience even if the score is still low compared with the scores of other students or even to the person's past performance.

Adapted from Goolsby and Chaplin (1988) and Wilson, Chaplin, Foster, and White (1996).

Although it is possible to empirically compare people's use of idiographic and normative standards, the issue of whether research should idiographically focus on individuals or nomothetically focus on groups and averages is not an empirical question. That decision depends on the values of the experimenter and the goals of the research. However, the research reviewed in this section illustrates how subjective, phenomenological standards that people use to evaluate their experiences can be empirically and objectively investigated.

## Idiographic Measurement

Measures in psychology are also typically interpreted normatively by comparing an individual rating with the ratings of other people. Moreover, it is generally assumed that the ratings are based on a normative comparison. Thus, if a person is rated 6 or 7 on the friendliness scale, the presumption is that that person is generally more friendly than other people. Block (1978) described this as the **variable centered approach** to personality assessment because the analysis and interpretation of rating scale data are based on the means and correlations of variables rather than on the responses of individual people.

The Q-sort Technique. The normative interpretation of rating scale data is inconsistent with the idiographic or person-centered approach of humanistic psychology. In 1953, Stephenson described an approach to assessment that he called the **Q-technique.** Unlike rating scales, the Q-technique is an explicitly idiographic method of assessment in that its focus is on a pattern of characteristics *within* an individual rather than on differences in characteristics *between* people. Rogers and his colleagues developed a Q-sort adaptation of Stephenson's technique to assess and test hypotheses about the self-concept.

The **Q-sort** is a procedure in which the subject is asked to sort, into a series of piles, several statements about the self (e.g., "I am generally a happy person"; "I usually think of myself first"; "I am upset much of the time"; "I concentrate well"). Normally, the statements are printed on cards. The subject is instructed to read each statement and then place it along a continuum ranging from "Very characteristic of me" to "Not at all characteristic of me." The subject is also asked to place the cards along the continuum according to a prearranged scheme—usually a bell-shaped distribution that approximates the normal curve. Specifically, the largest number of cards must be placed at the middle of the distribution, the fewest at each extreme.

This forced distribution is what makes the Q-sort idiographic. Because the subjects are forced to place a specified number of characteristics in the highest and lowest categories, it is not possible to conclude that the subject is high on a characteristic relative to other subjects. Instead, one can only conclude that that characteristic is more like the subject than the other characteristics placed in lower categories. For example, consider the three characteristics of "unfriendly," "unreliable," and "unintelligent." Using a Q-sort procedure, the subject might be required to place one of these characteristics in the "most like me" category and another in the "least like me" category. If the subject places "unfriendly" in the "most like me" category that does not mean that the subject views him or her self as unfriendly *relative to other people;* the subject is instead indicating that he or she is more unfriendly than he or she is unreliable or unintelligent. Normative conclusions are not warranted from Q-sort data. Figure 8-1 illustrates the Q-sort technique.

The most common use of Q-sorts in humanistic research has been to assess the person's self-concept. In particular, it has been used to assess the discrepancy

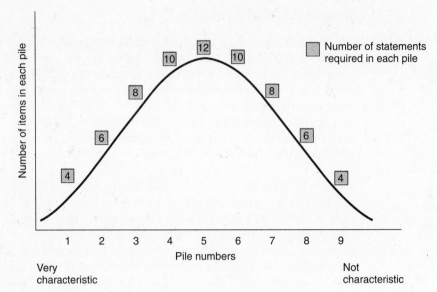

**Figure 8-1** ᐸᕽᐳ Illustration of self-statements in a forced-distribution Q-sort.

between the self and the ideal self. For example, on the basis of Rogerian theory, Butler and Haigh (1954) hypothesized that clients would be relatively dissatisfied with themselves prior to therapy but that following successful therapy this level of dissatisfaction would decline. They selected 24 clients in therapy and a control group of 16 demographically similar adults. The experimental group did Q-sorts prior to therapy, at the conclusion of therapy, and again at a point between six months and a year after therapy had been concluded. Control subjects, who were not in therapy, did the sorts at comparable points in time. At each point, subjects sorted 100 statements such as "I am an impulsive person" or "I am likable."

Subjects made two sorts on each occasion. The first was a self-sort (how they saw themselves at that time) and the second an ideal-sort (how they would most like themselves to be). Thus, each characteristic had two numbers: one was the pile number for the self-sort and the other the pile number for the ideal-sort. These numbers were then correlated across the 100 characteristics for each subject. Note that the correlation refers to a person, not to a variable. A high positive correlation would indicate a close relation between the ideal-sort and self-sort for a subject; a low correlation would indicate little relation.

The main results of this research are shown in Table 8-1. The members of the control group failed to show any change in their self–ideal-self correlation, whereas the mean correlations for the therapy group showed a significant change toward a greater relation between self and idea-self. The improved relationship was maintained during the follow-up period. As expected, the control group showed a higher level of initial correlation, and that level did not change over time.

## Table 8-1
Mean Self–Ideal Self Correlations for Therapy and Control Groups

| Group | Before Therapy | After Therapy | Follow-up |
|---|---|---|---|
| Therapy | .01 | .34 | .31 |
| Control | .58 | Not reported | .59 |

After "Changes in the Relation between Self-Concepts and Ideal Concepts Consequent upon Client-centered Counseling" by J. M. Butler and G. V. Haigh, in *Psychotherapy and Personality Change: Coordinated Studies in the Client-Centered Approach* by C. R. Rogers and R. F. Dymond (eds.). Copyright 1954 by University of Chicago Press. Adapted by permission.

## The California Q-Set

Although the Q-sort procedure can be used with any set of characteristics that are of interest to the investigator, the results of a Q-sort will be limited to only the characteristics selected for sorting. It is therefore important that the items be representative of the area under investigation. Beginning in 1952, Jack Block (1978) began developing the California Q-set to "permit the comprehensive description . . . of an individual's personality in a form suitable for quantitative comparison and analysis" (Block, 1978, p. 3).

After a number of revisions, the modern version of the California Q-set evolved as a set of 100 items that together form a comprehensive representative and standardized description of human personality. The 100 items are sorted into a forced distribution consisting of 9 categories, ranging from 1 = most undescriptive of the target to 9 = most descriptive of the target; the middle category is 5 = neither descriptive nor undescriptive of the target. The most extreme categories, (1) and (9), must contain 5 items each, categories 2 and 8 must contain 8 items each, categories 3 and 7 contain 12 items, categories 4 and 6 contain 16 items, and the middle category (5) must contain 18 items. Sample items from the California Q-set are shown in Table 8-2.

Prototypes. One of Block's concerns that led him to develop the California Q-set was the difficulty of using the phenomenological impressions of clinical psychologists in research. He wished to remove some of the ambiguity from clinical descriptions and provide an assessment of clinical impressions that would permit a rigorous evaluation of their reliability and validity. Block used the California Q-set to define **prototypes**, which are idealized descriptions of individuals who represent a clinical type. Some examples are "optimally adjusted person," "female hysteric," and "male paranoid." These prototypes were obtained by asking expert judges to sort the 100 Q-set items to describe the personality of a hypothetical person who would represent the clearest example of the prototype. The

**Table 8-2**

California Q-set Items from the Male Paranoid Prototype

**Items that are characteristic (positively defining) of the male paranoid**

Is basically distrustful of people in general; questions their motivations.
Tends to project his own feelings and motivations onto others.
Has hostility toward others.
Is basically anxious.
Is moralistic (regardless of the particular nature of the moral code).

**Items that are uncharacteristic (negatively defining) of the male paranoid**

Has insight into own motives and behavior.
Arouses nurturant feelings in others.
*Genuinely* submissive; accepts domination comfortably.
Emphasizes being with others; gregarious.
Enjoys sensuous experiences (including touch, taste, smell, physical contact).

From Block, J. (1978). The Q-sort method in personality assessment and psychiatric research. Palo Alto, CA: Consulting Psychologists Press.

sorts of the judges were then averaged to obtain the prototype. The prototypes can then be used to convey, in the rich descriptive language of the Q-set items, the nature of each type of person. In addition, the Q-sorts of real individuals can be compared with the prototypes for diagnosis or classification. A portion of the Male Paranoid Prototype is shown in Table 8-2.

Research with the California Q-set. The California Q-set has been routinely employed as part of the intensive personality assessment projects at the Institute for Personality Assessment and Research (IPAR) in Berkeley California since the 1950s. One example is from research on creativity in women mathematicians conducted by Ravenna Helson (Block, 1978). A highly selective sample of 40 women mathematicians were brought to IPAR and comprehensively assessed over several days. The assessment including a set of standard psychological tests; observations in interpersonal situations, including playing charades and participating in group discussions; experimental tests of perceptual motor skills; and an assessment of the women's mathematical creativity by a panel of mathematicians. At the end of the assessment the staff psychologist completed a Q-sort for each of the mathematicians. Of interest was the relation between some of the personality characteristics on the California Q-set and the level of mathematical

## ᘓᘔ Table 8-3

## California Q-set Items That Were Significantly Correlated with Ratings of the Creativity of Women Mathematicians

**Positively Correlated Items**

| r | Item |
|---|------|
| .64 | Thinks and associates ideas in unusual ways; has unconventional thought processes. |
| .55 | Is an interesting, arresting person. |
| .51 | Tends to be rebellious and nonconforming. |
| .41 | Is self-dramatizing, histrionic. |
| .36 | Expresses hostile feelings directly. |

**Negatively Correlated Items**

| r | Item |
|---|------|
| -.62 | Judges self and others in conventional terms like "popularity." |
| -.45 | Is a genuinely dependable and responsible person. |
| -.43 | Behaves in a sympathetic or considerate manner. |
| -.37 | Prides self on being "objective," rational. |
| -.35 | Is protective of those close to her. |

From Block, J. (1978). The Q-sort method in personality assessment and psychiatric research. Palo Alto, CA: Consulting Psychologists Press.

creativity judged by the panel of mathematicians. Table 8-3 shows some of the personality items that were significantly correlated with mathematical creativity.

Note that the idiographic nature of the Q-sorts does *not* allow us to conclude from these correlations that creative women mathematicians are more rebellious and nonconforming *than people in general or even than other less creative female mathematicians.* These results indicate that "rebellious" and "nonconforming" are better descriptions of creative women mathematicians than most of the other items on Q-sort. The focus is on the organization of personality within the individual, not with how an individual's personality characteristics compare with the personality characteristics of other people. It is possible, although perhaps unlikely, that relative to other people, none of the Q-set items are characteristic of the creative women mathematicians, but the nature of the Q-sort forced the judges to pick certain items as extremely characteristic. To determine whether creative women mathematicians are more rebellious and creative than people in general, we would need to obtain ratings on a scale that allowed the raters to make normative rather than idiographic judgments about the mathematicians.

## The Rogerian Research Legacy

Carl Rogers is generally perceived as a humanist who accepted people as individuals and who developed techniques such as encounter groups and client-centered therapy for helping people develop into whatever they wanted to become. Rogers is not generally considered an example of a scientist; indeed, he is often characterized as opposed to scientific values as a result of his famous exchanges with B. F. Skinner, which are summarized in Box 8-2 (Rogers and Skinner, 1956).

However, Rogers developed a variety of research methods, and he emphasized research in developing his major theoretical statement (Rogers, 1951). He also undertook the first sustained program of psychotherapy research. It was he who introduced the use of recordings of therapy sessions to study both process and effectiveness. Recorded therapy sessions are now common in clinical research and training, but prior to Rogers, the therapy room was considered the private domain of the therapist and client, and its sanctity was carefully guarded. Rogers made therapy and the personality processes within it objects of study rather than subjects of mystery. He also made available recordings and transcripts of therapy sessions in his work. Box 8-3 illustrates a therapy transcript.

## Empirical Investigation of Maslow's Humanism

Maslow's humanistic theory is often viewed as inconsistent with empirical scientific research. Research is a *critical* activity, whereas the emphasis of humanistic theory is on *acceptance* (Neher, 1991). However, Maslow understood experimental research and did not believe that experimental investigation should be abandoned. He did argue that the sterile methods of controlled laboratory experiment need to be replaced, or at least supplemented, with methods that highlight the meaningfulness, vitality, and significance of human existence (Aronoff, 1985).

### Needs Hierarchy

Maslow's theory of motivation is based on his hierarchy of needs. Specifically, lower needs on the hierarchy are viewed as stronger motivants than higher needs. Only when lower-order needs are met will the individual be motivated by the higher-order needs. In general, this prediction has been supported for physiological and safety needs. Research on the other needs, however, has not supported Maslow's hierarchical theory. For example, Leith (1972) placed subjects under stress that constituted a threat to their needs at the lower levels of the hierarchy. They were administered several tests of creativity immediately afterward. Contrary to Maslow's prediction, subjects *increased* both the number and originality of their responses in the face of threat to their basic needs. Likewise, Graham and Balloun (1973) predicted that when any two needs in Maslow's hierarchy are

## BOX 8-2
## The Exchange Between Rogers and Skinner About Science and Human Behavior

On September 4, 1956, Carl Rogers and B. F. Skinner agreed to participate in a symposium at the annual meeting of the American Psychological Association held in Chicago, Illinois. The purpose of this symposium was to allow the leaders of the rival humanistic and behavioristic movements in psychology to meet and discuss their points of agreements and disagreements. Skinner presented his views on the scientific control of human behavior, Rogers responded, and Skinner was then given an opportunity to rebut Rogers' remarks. The exchange was later published in an article in *Science* (Volume 124, 1956, pp. 1057–1066) entitled, "Some issues concerning the control of human behavior."

Skinner emphasized that the control of human behavior based on the application of rigorous scientific principles was both possible and necessary to promote the values of society.

> It is the experimental study of behavior which carries us beyond awkward or inaccessible 'principles,' 'factors,' and so on, to variables which can be directly manipulated. . . . It is the conception of human behavior emerging from an experimental analysis which most directly challenges traditional views. . . . Until only recently it was customary to deny the possibility of a rigorous science of human behavior by arguing, either that a lawful science was impossible because man was a free agent, or that merely statistical predictions would always leave room for personal freedoms. But those who used to take this line have become most vociferous in expressing their alarm at the way these obstacles are being surmounted.

In his response, Rogers did not dispute that experimental methods had advanced our ability to influence behavior.

> I believe we agree that the behavioral sciences are making and will continue to make increasingly rapid progress in the understanding of behavior, and that as a consequence the capacity to predict and control behavior is developing with equal rapidity. . . . Consequently Skinner and I are in agreement that the whole question of the scientific control of human behavior is a matter with which psychologists and the general public should concern themselves.

However, Rogers emphasized that there were several issues on which he and Skinner disagreed. In particular, Rogers argued that science was inherently influenced by subjective values and that these values would always remain outside the realm of science.

*(continued)*

BOX 8-2 (*continued*)

With these several points of basic and important agreement, are there any issues that remain on which there are any differences? I believe there are. They can be stated very briefly: Who will be controlled? Who will exercise control? What type of control will be exercised? Most important of all, toward what end or what purpose, or in pursuit of what value, will control be exercised? . . . . the major flaw I see in this review of what is involved in the scientific control of human behavior is the denial, misunderstanding, or gross underestimation of the place of ends, goals or values in their relationship to science. . . . In any scientific endeavor—whether "pure" or "applied" science—there is a prior subjective choice of the purpose or value which the scientific work is perceived as serving. This subjective value choice which brings the scientific endeavor into being must always lie outside of that endeavor and can never become part of the science involved in that endeavor.

Rogers' statement that science is influenced by subjective values is not particularly controversial today. However, in the 1950s, the position that there was any subjectivity in the scientific process was treated as heresy by much of the scientific establishment.

From Carl Rogers and B.F. Skinner (1956). "Some issues concerning the control of human behavior," *Science* *124:* 1056–1066.

paired, the one at the lower level will show greater evidence of having been satisfied. Interviews were used to classify need strength and satisfaction. The results were not clearly consistent with this prediction.

## Self-Actualization

At the top of Maslow's hierarchy is the *need for self-actualization*. Individuals who meet this need and become self-actualized are psychologically healthy; moreover, according to Maslow, self-actualization is necessary for psychological health. Maslow's (1970) well-known research on self-actualized individuals used the case study approach. He began by identifying psychologically healthy individuals, who, according to his theory, must be self-actualized. In one case he used psychological tests and interviews to select the most well-adjusted 1 percent of a large group of college students. Another defining feature of self-actualizing individuals is that they perform at their highest level of ability in their chosen field. Thus, Maslow also selected successful athletes, musicians, authors, artists, and politicians for his study. Using psychological tests and historical and archival data, Maslow identified the characteristics that were common to self-actualized individuals.

This research suffers from several flaws. First, it does not offer a test of Maslow's theory because it is not clear what observations would lead one to re-

BOX 8-3

## Excerpt from a Therapy Session Reported by Rogers (1951)

*Client:* It all comes pretty vague. But you know I keep, keep having the thought occur to me that this whole process for me is kind of like examining pieces of a jigsaw puzzle. It seems to me I, I'm in the process now of examining the individual pieces which really don't have too much meaning. Probably handling them, not even beginning to think of a pattern. That keeps coming to me. And it's interesting to me because I, I really don't like jigsaw puzzles. They've always irritated me. But that's my feeling. And I mean I pick up little pieces *(she gestures throughout this conversation to illustrate her statements)* with absolutely no meaning except, I mean, the, the feeling that you get from simply handling them without seeing them as a pattern, but just from the touch, I probably feel, well, it is going to fit someplace here.

*Therapist:* And that at the moment that that's the process, just getting the feel and the shape and the configuration of the different pieces with a little bit of background feeling of, yeah, they'll probably fit somewhere, but most of the attention's focused right on, "What does this feel like? And what's its texture?"

*Client:* That's right. There's almost something physical in it. A, a . . .

*Therapist:* You can't quite describe it without using your hands. A real, almost a sensuous sense in . . .

*Client:* That's right. Again it's, it's a feeling of being very objective, and yet I've never been quite so close to myself.

*Therapist:* Almost at one and the same time standing off and looking at yourself and yet somehow being closer to yourself that way than . . .

*Client:* Um-hum. And yet for the first time in months I am not thinking about my problems. I'm not actually, I'm not working on them.

*Therapist:* I get the impression you don't sort of sit down to work on "my problems." It isn't that feeling at all.

*Client:* That's right. That's right. I suppose what I, I mean actually is that I'm not sitting down to put this puzzle together as, as something I've got to see the picture. It, it may be that, it may be that I am actually enjoying this feeling process. Or I'm certainly learning something.

*Therapist:* At least there's a sense of the immediate goal of getting that feel as being the thing, not that you're doing this in order to see a picture, but that it's a, a satisfaction of really getting acquainted with each piece. Is that . . .

*Client:* That's it. That's it. And it still becomes that sort of sensuousness, that touching. It's quite interesting. Sometimes not entirely pleasant, I'm sure, but . . .

*Therapist:* A rather different sort of experience.

*Client:* Yes. Quite. (p. 505)

ject his view of self-actualization. Instead, Maslow's goal was to describe self-actualized individuals with the goal of discovering those characteristics that they had in common. Second, the selection of subjects for study and the interpretation of the historical and archival data are influenced by Maslow's biases and beliefs. Finally, although Maslow believed that *self-actualization* was the critical common characteristic of the people he selected, others (Mittleman, 1991) have reinterpreted his results to suggest that other characteristics, such as openness to experience, are the common feature of the individuals he studied. Despite its flaws, Maslow's study is widely cited as an example of research in the humanistic tradition.

## Peak Experience

**Peak experience** refers to the intense joy associated with an event, and such experiences are the highest level of human experience (Privette, 1983). Maslow (1962), in searching for the meaning of peak experiences, asked a group of 190 college students for their written responses to the following instructions:

> I would like you to think of the most wonderful experiences of your life; happiest moments, ecstatic moments, moments of rapture, perhaps from being in love, or from listening to music or suddenly "being hit" by a book or a painting, or from some great creative moment. First, list these. And then try to tell me how you feel in such acute moments, how you feel *differently* from the way you feel at other times, how you are at the moment a different person in some ways. (p. 67)

From these responses, Maslow was able to describe 19 characteristics of the "peak-experience cognition." An example is this: "The emotional reaction in the peak experience has a special flavor of wonder, of awe, of reverence, of humility and surrender before the experience as before something great" (p. 82).

## Existential Research

As with humanistic research, existential research emphasizes phenomenological description rather than experimental tests of hypotheses. The goal is to describe immediate experience through the analysis of verbal reports and behavior. One does not start with theories or psychological laws and then deduce hypotheses that will later be tested in the laboratory. W. F. Fischer (1978) illustrates this version of research from the existential perspective when he says: "I understand being empirical to mean that the researcher is open to all perceivable dimensions and profiles of the phenomenon that is being researched. Hence, the experiences of the subjects, as well as those of the researcher, are immediately acknowledged as potentially informative" (p. 168).

For example, van Kaam (1966) was interested in the experience of "being understood." High school and college students were asked to recall situations in which they experienced "being understood" and also how they felt in those situations. The descriptions were collected and the investigator analyzed them by asking these questions:

1. "Does this concrete, colorful formulation by the subject contain a moment of experience that might be a necessary and sufficient constituent of the experience of really feeling understood?"

2. "If so, is it possible to abstract this moment of experience and to label the abstraction briefly and precisely without violating the formulation presented by the subject?" (van Kaam, 1966, p. 323).

Descriptions not meeting these criteria were eliminated. By this procedure, the nine constituents listed in Table 8-4 were identified as elements of the experience of really feeling understood.

This research relies on the phenomenological reports of the subjects and the phenomenological impressions of the investigator. From a critical scientific perspective it is easy to dismiss these findings because of the biases and idiosyncratic opinions that likely influence such subjective evaluations. However, if the research is conducted so that the biases can be assessed and their effect on the data

## Table 8-4

Constituents of Being Understood

| Constituent | Percentage of Subjects Expressing Constituent |
|---|---|
| 1. Perceiving signs of understanding from a person. | 87 |
| 2. Perceiving that a person coexperiences what things mean to the subject. | 91 |
| 3. Perceiving that the person accepts the subject. | 86 |
| 4. Feeling satisfaction. | 99 |
| 5. Initially feeling relief. | 93 |
| 6. Initially feeling relief from experiential loneliness. | 89 |
| 7. Feeling safe in the relationship with the person understanding. | 91 |
| 8. Feeling safe experiential communion with the person understanding. | 86 |
| 9. Feeling safe experiential communion with that which the person understanding is perceived to represent. | 64 |

Source: *Existential Foundations of Psychology* by A. van Kaam (Pittsburgh, Pa.: Duquesne University Press), 1966. Copyright 1966 by Duquesne University Press. Reprinted by permission.

minimized, then phenomenological reports can provide unique, important, and scientifically legitimate insights into human experience, Unfortunately, traditional humanistic and existential research, with its emphasis on acceptance rather than criticism of personal reports of experience, has not generally been responsive to these scientific concerns.

## Qualitative Data

Phenomenologists such as Rogers, humanists such as Maslow, and existentialists such as Binswanger emphasize the subjective emotional experience of their subjects. One characteristic of research in this tradition is the qualitative data that it generates. These data results from listening to subjects and accepting the subjects' reports of their experiences. The transcript of the therapy session in Box 8-3 is an example of qualitative data. There are no numbers in that transcript. There is no quantification of the content or degree of the client's feelings. Although it appears that the client is gaining some insight into her problems, there is no measure of that insight. Also, the words used by the client and therapist, such as "the feeling that you get from handling [the pieces of her problem]" or "almost a sensuous sense," are vague and concern emotional experiences that would be difficult to quantify.

Qualitative data can be frustrating. The information from this transcript is difficult to verify, and it is not clear how this information might be used to test ideas or make predictions about the client or the course of therapy. However, the information in that transcript communicates a sense of the therapeutic process, and we are left with the impression that the client is making some progress toward self-understanding. Moreover, this transcript describes the reactions and feelings of the client and therapist more completely and naturalistically than a rating scale or a count of the number of times the client smiled during the session.

### Content Analysis

Before qualitative data can be used to test scientific hypotheses, they must be processed, interpreted, and transformed. It is important that the interpretation and transformation be based on a clearly specified set of standardized procedures that yield data that are consistent and that can be replicated by other investigators. The transformation of qualitative data into quantitative data that can be verified and subjected to statistical analysis is called **content analysis**.

A good example of early content analysis is a study by Raimy (1948). Raimy was interested in the way references to self change over the course of therapy. He selected six self-reference categories (positive or approving self-references, negative or disapproving ones, ambivalent ones, etc.) to study 14 clients who had undergone from 2 to 21 interviews. Transcriptions of each session were examined, and each client's self-references were sorted into the six content categories. Raimy discovered that clients generally made negative or ambivalent self-references at the beginning of therapy. By the end of therapy, clients whom judges determined to be improved were generally making positive references to themselves. Those who had showed no improvement were still making ambivalent and disapproving self-references.

One of the most efficient methods of content analysis is to have a set of judges rate qualitative data such as transcripts, diaries, or videotapes on a set of rating scales. This approach relies on the skills of the judges to interpret and transform the data to a set of numerical ratings. However, the assessment of the reliability and validity of the ratings is relatively straightforward.

An example is a validation study of the Process Scale by Tomlinson and Hart (1962). The Process Scale is used to rate therapy interviews and is based on seven categories:

- Feelings and personal meanings
- Experiencing
- Incongruence
- Communications of self
- Construing of experience
- Relationship to problems
- Manner of relating

Raters are trained to consider each category and then to make a global rating from 1 to 7 of the client's process level, based on the information that is made available to them. Tomlinson and Hart had two experienced coders rate nine 2-minute excerpts from each of 10 therapy cases. For each case, there was an interview late in the therapy series, and an early one as well. Each judge rated a total of 20 tapes.

Several results were obtained. First, interjudge reliability was satisfactory. The correlation between the ratings of the two judges across the 20 tapes was .60). Second, the Process Scale distinguished between more successful and less successful cases and indicated that the more successful ones begin and end at a higher level of process. Third, there was some indication of a greater process change in the more successful cases.

Another example of subjective ratings in content analysis is a study by Stoler (1963). Stoler's interest was in client likability and its relation to success in psychotherapy. He provided 10 raters with 20 2-minute taped segments of client–therapist interactions drawn from ten recorded cases. Five of the cases had been determined to be relatively successful, five unsuccessful. The judges rated each segment on a scale of liking to disliking the client. The results suggested that client likability is related to successful outcomes in therapy and that ratings of client likability can be reliably made from content segments of therapy exchanges.

## Research on Personal Constructs

Kelly's personal construct theory is linked to the instrument that Kelly developed to assess personal constructs, the **Role Construct Repertory Test (Rep Test)**. In his two-volume presentation of personal construct theory, Kelly (1955) carefully related his theoretical propositions to the methods that could be used to assess and test them. Kelly's work is an excellent and elegant example of how research and measurement should be derived from theory.

### The Rep Test

The Rep Test is based on the premise that the constructs that are important to an individual (personal constructs) are the ones that will be used by that individual to evaluate events. Thus, personal constructs can be identified from the similarities and contrasts people use to compare events, people, and ideas. Typically, a subject is asked to list a series of people or events he or she regards as important, such as relatives, teachers, and friends; or graduation, marriage, and purchase of a house. Once a list is generated, the individual items in the list are presented to the subject in groups of three, called triads. For each triad, the subject must indicate how two of the members of that group are alike and yet different from the third. By repeatedly presenting the subject with triads that consist of different combinations of items from the list, the subject's construct system is elicited.

The following example from a hypothetical counseling session with a male college student illustrates the technique.

| | |
|---|---|
| *Counselor:* | List three people you most admire. |
| *Client:* | My brother, my uncle, and my girlfriend. |
| *Counselor:* | How are any two of these alike and yet different from the third? |
| *Client:* | My brother and my uncle are calm. They don't get flustered, and they are usually very patient. My girlfriend flies off the handle—never stops to think. |
| *Counselor:* | How are your reactions to two of these individuals alike but different from your reactions to the third? |
| *Client:* | I suppose I respect my brother and my uncle but I react to my girlfriend as if she's not as bright as me. |

The Rep Test is flexible and can be adapted to almost any assessment situation in both research and counseling contexts. Computerized versions of the Rep Test that facilitate the elicitation and interpretation of personal constructs are available (Shaw, 1981) Variations of the Rep Test have been used in educational, industrial, and clinical settings; it has been adapted for use with children, and it has been used to assess political attitudes and responses to music and poetry (Fransella and Thomas, 1988). Unlike the semantic differential and the Q-sort,

## BOX 8-4
## Role Construct Repertory Test

Sechrest (1977) has provided the following example of Rep Test instructions and analysis for Sue B.

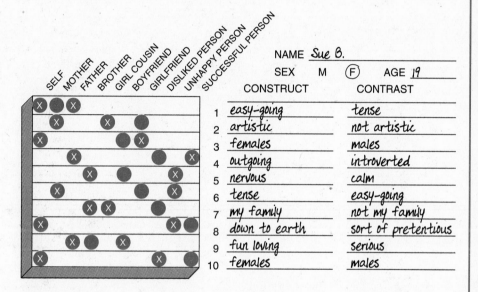

| | SELF | MOTHER | FATHER | BROTHER | GIRL COUSIN | BOYFRIEND | GIRLFRIEND | DISLIKED PERSON | UNHAPPY PERSON | SUCCESSFUL PERSON | | CONSTRUCT | CONTRAST |
|---|---|---|---|---|---|---|---|---|---|---|---|---|---|

NAME Sue B.

SEX  M  Ⓕ  AGE 19

| | CONSTRUCT | CONTRAST |
|---|---|---|
| 1 | easy-going | tense |
| 2 | artistic | not artistic |
| 3 | females | males |
| 4 | outgoing | introverted |
| 5 | nervous | calm |
| 6 | tense | easy-going |
| 7 | my family | not my family |
| 8 | down to earth | sort of pretentious |
| 9 | fun loving | serious |
| 10 | females | males |

### Instructions

**Step 1.** The three persons to be compared on each line have a circle under them. For example, on the first line, think of an important word that describes two of the persons (*self, mother, father*). Write that word on Row 1 under *construct* and also place an *X* in those two circles under the two people to whom the word applies. On Row 1 under *contrast,* write the opposite of that word. (For Sue B., *X*'s in the circles under *self* and *father* mean that she sees herself and her father as easy going in contrast to her mother, who is seen as tense.)

**Step 2.** Follow this same procedure for each of the succeeding nine lines.

### Analysis of Rep Test protocol for Sue B

**The first construct elicited** (*easy going–tense,* in this case) tends to represent a fundamental dichotomy for the subject. Sue B. chooses to view people in her life space in terms of how they approach the world. Some terms in her thinking are "loose,"

(continued)

BOX 8-4 *(continued)*

"relaxed," "free flowing," and some are "up tight," "constricted," or "wound up." Further evidence of the importance of easygoing versus tense for Sue B. is that it was elicited from the comparison of the *self, mother,* and *father,* three individuals who are typically of special significance. Finally, in Row 6 *(tense–easygoing)* this construct is repeated, and in Row 5 *(nervous–calm)* the construct is a synonym for tense–easygoing. For Sue this construct of tension versus calm in people is important. Everyone categorized as easygoing on Row 1 is calm on Row 5, and those tense on Row 1 are nervous on Row 5. Row 9 *(fun-loving–serious)* also appears to be a relabeling of *easygoing–tense.*

We can infer with some confidence that for Sue B. there are easygoing, calm, fun-loving people and nervous, tense, serious people. Note that a person can be down to earth without being easygoing, and one need not be tense to be artistic.

Most of Sue B.'s constructs are abstract and refer to psychological characteristics, but for some comparisons such as self-boyfriend-girlfriend and self-brother-cousin, she uses concrete and evaluatively neutral constructs such as *female–male* and *my family–not my family.*

From "Personal Constructs Theory" by Lee Sechrest. In R. J. Corsini, *Current Personality Theories,* copyright © 1977, pp. 224–225.

the Rep Test does not force the experimenter's constructs onto the subject, although the experimenter can select the people and events that are used to elicit the subject's constructs. Box 8-4 presents a more complete example of the Rep Test and its interpretation.

## Change in Personal Constructs

Several studies indicate that the constructs elicited by the Rep Test are stable over time (Bonarius, 1965; Landfield, Stern, and Fjeld, 1961; Pederson, 1958). However, under some conditions, constructs are predicted to change. In general, these changes have been found to be consistent with personal construct theory. For example, Poch (1952) asked subjects to make predictions about friends based on subjects' personal constructs. The predictions were experimentally manipulated to be accurate or inaccurate. **Validated constructs** (those that led to correct predictions) did not change during an intervening period, whereas invalidated ones did show some change. Moreover, invalidated constructs were less frequently used for a second set of predictions. In a related study, Levy (1954) observed that strongly invalidated constructs precipitated more changes in the construct system than weakly invalidated ones. Furthermore, **constellatory constructs** (constructs with many connections throughout the construct system) were especially potent in leading to changes. Similarly, Hinkle (1965) found that **superordinate con-**

structs—(broad constructs that contain several more specific constructs) that underwent change led to widespread changes in other constructs.

## Complexity of Personal Construct Systems

An individual's construct system provides a personal and idiographic description of how that individual views the world. Knowing an individual's personal constructs can give the scientist and the clinician important insights into a person's reactions to events and significant people in their lives. However, personal construct systems can also be used for nomothetic research by deriving general variables from the individualized content of the personal construct system. One aspect of personal construct systems that has been intensively studied is their complexity.

Complexity refers to the degree to which a construct system contains many constructs that are each applied to a limited number of individuals. Complexity was first studied by Bieri (1955), who indexed complexity as the number of constructs that were differentially applied to the self and other people. A **cognitively complex** individual employs a large number of constructs and uses them to characterize the differences among important people in his or her life. A **cognitively simple** person uses a smaller number of constructs and, therefore, emphasizes the similarities among people. Since Bieri's work with the Rep Test, cognitive complexity has been assessed using a variety of methods (e.g., Crockett, 1965; Rosenberg & Sedlak, 1972; Rosenberg and Gara, 1985; Linville, 1985, 1987).

In a recent study that bridges personal construct theory and self theory, Woolfolk, Novalany, Gara, Allen, and Polino (1995) demonstrated that cognitive complexity may vary across different domains. Specifically, they found that individuals differ in the complexity of both their positive and their negative self-concepts. Interestingly, people with more complex negative self-concepts were more likely to be depressed and were less likely to recover from depression. The study did not allow the authors to determine whether a more complex negative self-concept *caused* depression, perhaps by focusing the individual's attention on a variety of undesirable characteristics, or was an *effect* of the depression, perhaps from the elaboration of the undesirable qualities that results from negative rumination about the self.

## Self-Schemata Research

Much contemporary social cognitive research on the self has been targeted on self-schema theory and how it can be used to predict how people process self-relevant information (Markus, 1983). For example based on self-schema theory, Bruch, Kaflowitz, and Berger (1988) argued that individuals who were "schematic" for a particular construct would have more developed memory structures for that construct than subjects who were "aschematic." Therefore, they predicted that schematics would recall more words related to the construct than aschematics. Based on their self-ratings of the descriptiveness and importance to their self-concept of a set of adjectives related to assertiveness, a group of undergraduate subjects were classified as "schematics" and "aschematics" for assertiveness. Schematics were defined as those who described themselves as highly assertive or highly nonassertive, whereas aschematics were those who rated themselves in the middle of the scale for these adjectives. Few subjects described themselves as nonassertive, so only assertive schematics were included. Then, in another experimental session, subjects were presented with another rating task that contained some adjectives related to assertiveness. After completing the ratings, subjects were unexpectedly asked to recall as many words from the ratings. Consistent with having better developed memory structures for assertiveness, schematic subjects recalled more "assertive" adjectives during the recall period than did the aschematic subjects.

In a second study, schematics and aschematics were asked to determine, in a conflict situation, the reasonableness of another person's requests. It had been established in advance by the investigators that these requests were of high, low, or moderate legitimacy. Results indicated that in the high and low legitimacy conditions, schematics and aschematics did not differ in their judgments of reasonableness. But in the case of requests of moderate legitimacy, the assertive schematics judged the requests as less reasonable than did the aschematics. In relatively ambiguous (moderate) circumstances, one's assertive self-schemata will operate. In situations where the reasonableness of the requests are clear, individual differences in the assertiveness schema will be overridden by the situation. These results are shown in Figure 8-2.

One of the earliest and most influential studies based on self-schema theory was by Derry and Kuiper (1981). They had clinically depressed and nondepressed subjects provide a series of ratings of a list of depressed and nondepressed content adjectives. They hypothesized that the negative self-schemata of depressed subjects would lead them to recall the self-referent depressed adjectives more readily than nondepressed subjects. This hypothesis was supported when subjects were unexpectedly asked later to recall all the adjectives that they had rated earlier. A similar result was reported by Moser and Dyck (1989) using subjects with hostile self-schemata. They hypothesized that subjects with a hostile self-schema, after being exposed to uncontrollable failure, would show better recall for hostile adjectives than a comparable group of subjects who lacked such hostile schemata. The hypothesis was confirmed.

Finally, Klotz and Alicke (1989) investigated the effectiveness of a person-schema as an information processing structure when the schema is either appropriate or inappropriate. Subjects were asked to evaluate another person (either a liked or a disliked individual) while comparing that person either with themselves, with someone they liked, or with someone they disliked. It was predicted

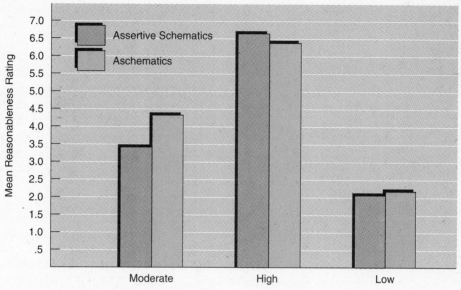

**Figure 8-2** ⚭ Degree of legitimacy and ratings of reasonableness.

Adapted from "Self-Schema for Assertiveness: Extending the Validity of the Self-Schema Construct" by Monroe A. Bruch et al. from *The Journal of Research in Personality*, vol. 22, no. 4, December 1988.

that the self and the liked-other would be appropriate schemas for the liked person, whereas the disliked-other would be appropriate for the disliked person. Subsequent recall of target information about the liked and disliked persons supported the hypothesis. These results support the hypothesis that individuals' schemata affect the ways in which information is received, stored, and retrieved.

## Implicit Personality Theory

Phenomenological approaches to personality emphasize the importance of the individual's perceptions and beliefs for understanding that person's behavior and personality. However, some (e.g., Hampson, 1988; Kelley, 1992; Sternberg, 1985b) have argued that phenomenology can be extended to be the basis for theories *about* personality and psychology. That is, the everyday knowledge and beliefs that people have about themselves and others not only affects those people's behavior but also can be a useful and valid source of information for constructing theories of personality. In 1954, Bruner and Tagiuri coined the term **implicit personality theory** to refer people's informal, unstated, everyday beliefs about personalty. Since that time, implicit personality theory has been the focus of intense scientific investigation.

## Features of Implicit Personality Theory

Hampson (1988) provides a summary of the conceptual and empirical status of implicit personality theory. She notes that implicit personality theories can refer to individual personality constructs such as "friendliness." In this case, implicit personality theories concern people's beliefs about what behaviors, thoughts, and feelings are associated with the construct. In addition, implicit personality theories can concern personality as a whole. In this case, the focus is on how personality is organized, including what constructs are associated with what other constructs.

Hampson (1988) argues that people use their implicit personality theories in two ways. First, people routinely include personality in their descriptions of people. When a friend asks another friend what a person is like, descriptions such as "He is kind and helpful, although sometimes he gets anxious with other people" are typical. Characteristics such as "kind," "helpful," and "anxious" are abstractions based on the behaviors, statements, and expressions that have been observed. It is implicit personality theory that is used to translate observations into personality descriptions. Second, implicit theories about how personality is organized allow people to form expectations of what a person is like based on a few descriptive terms. For example, if a person is described as reliable, we expect that person to be hard-working, punctual, and perhaps intelligent rather than lazy, late, and stupid.

## Validity of Implicit Personality Theory

There is no question that people have implicit personality theories and that they use them to describe and guide their interactions with other people. However, research on implicit personality theory indicates several aspects of people's implicit personality theories that call into question their validity.

Forming Impressions. In 1946 Asch conducted a classic study on how people form impressions of people. He presented subjects with a description of a target person as intelligent, skillful, industrious, determined, practical, and cautious. For half of the subjects, the target was also described as warm, whereas for the other half the target was described as cold. The subjects then wrote a short essay about the person and rated the person on a set of adjectives. Two important results were obtained. First, the subjects who heard the target described as cold showed a high degree of agreement in their subsequent descriptions of the target, as did the subjects who heard the target described as warm. Most important, however, the two groups of subjects provided remarkably *different* characterizations of the person, even though the initial list of descriptors was identical but for one word. This suggests that a subject's implicit personality theories may be unduly influenced by small differences in descriptors, particularly descriptors that differ strongly in evaluation.

### Systematic Distortion Hypothesis.

In 1982, Shweder summarized a substantial body of research conducted primarily by himself and D'Andrade that suggested that an individual's personality descriptions reflect the semantic similarity of the words more than actual behavioral observations and co-occurrence. Shweder (1982) proposed the **systematic distortion hypothesis** as a strong criticism of the validity of implicit personality theory. This hypothesis is that people will systematically distort their personality descriptions to maintain consistency with their preconceived beliefs about the structure of personality rather than to reflect their actual observations of behavior. The systematic distortion hypothesis has been strongly criticized on both conceptual and empirical grounds (e.g., Block, Weiss, and Thorne (1979); Romer and Revelle, 1984; Weiss and Mendelsohn, 1986), and as the primary explanation for people's personality descriptions, it is now largely discredited.

### Inconsistent Descriptions.

The logical consistency of subject's implicit personality theories is questioned by several recent studies showing that subjects have little difficulty with inconsistent personality information. In 1984 Asch and Zukier presented subjects with brief descriptions of a person that contained inconsistent information. For example, the target person might be described as both sociable and lonely, or as both foolish and brilliant. The subjects were asked to describe these targets and to explain how these inconsistent characteristics were related. The subjects could easily handle the inconsistencies. For example, a person was described as outwardly social but inwardly lonely. Or a person was described as brilliant in school but foolish in common sense. Similar results were obtained by Gergen, Hepburn, and Comer Fisher (1986).

One of the key elements of a scientific theory is its logical consistency, so subjects' ability and willingness to explain inconsistent personality descriptions questions the validity of implicit personality theories as inconsistent and difficult to disconfirm. However, Hampson (Casseldon and Hampson, 1990; Hampson, 1990, 1995) has argued that the results obtained by Asch and Zukier (1984) and by Gergen et al. (1986) demonstrate only that "when asked nicely, individuals are able to make sense of inconsistent information" (Casseldon and Hampson, 1990, p. 354). The studies do *not* demonstrate that subjects spontaneously incorporate inconsistent information into their implicit theories, neither did the studies assess how easily subjects could resolve the inconsistencies. Subjects in psychological experiments are well known for their willingness to do whatever the experimenter asks to the best of their ability. However, this does not mean that what subjects attempt to do in experiments is what they would do naturally. In later studies, Casseldon and Hampson (1990) supported the hypothesis that although subjects are able to reconcile inconsistent information within their implicit personality theories, they do so only with considerable difficulty.

## Implicit and Formal Theories of Personality

Hampson (1988) argues that the distinction between implicit and formal, or explicit, theories of personality is one of degree rather than kind. Formal theories of personality, such as those of Freud, Eysenck, Rogers, and Maslow, concern the content, structure, and development of personality. They are based on careful and systematic observations of human behavior by experienced and highly educated individuals. These theories are generally clearly and completely stated in the writings of the theorists. Implicit theories are people's everyday beliefs about personality that result from their more haphazard interactions with people in the course of their daily activities. Implicit theories "reside in people's minds and are waiting to be discovered" (Hampson, 1988, p. 102).

However, personality theorists started out as naive psychologists. Undoubtedly, their formal theories of personality were influenced by their implicit personality theories. Moreover, although formal theorists generally devoted much of their life to observing behavior and developing and revising their theories, this is what everyone does in interacting with people. The difference is that formal theorists may be more motivated and careful, and are often paid for their work. But the goals of the formal theorists and people in their everyday interactions are the same: the prediction, control, and perhaps explanation of people's behavior (Chaplin, John, and Goldberg, 1988).

The social constructivist movement in psychology (Gergen, 1985) emphasizes the importance of using both implicit and explicit theories. The social constructivist approach to personality *requires* that people's everyday interpretations and theories of personality be incorporated into formal theories because personality is a social construction. Personality does not exist outside people's heads (Hampson, 1984), so it can not be meaningfully described or studied without knowledge of people's interpretations.

In contrast to this position is the argument that implicit personality theory is at best irrelevant to formal personality theory, and at worst, deceptive and misleading. Although people have implicit theories, there is enough evidence that they are potentially invalid to suggest that using them is scientifically risky. The undue influence of evaluative descriptions, the possibility of some systematic distortion, and the inconsistencies in impression are all reasons for treating implicit theories with skepticism. Another argument against implicit theories is based on an analogy with the physical sciences. For example, people apparently have a well-developed and reasonably accurate implicit theory of gravity because they can move around, carry objects to desired locations, and place those objects with some precision. However, if a physicist were to stand on a street corner and ask people to describe and explain gravity, it is unlikely that the responses would be of much use for developing a formal theory of gravity. Likewise, simply because people have had experience and success interacting with other people, there is no reason to expect that this experience will be useful for the formal study of personality. This issue is far from resolved, but it has become the target of much discussion and research in personality psychology.

# Phenomenology and Personality Assessment

Phenomenology plays a central role in personality assessment. Indeed, the most common use of rating scales in personality psychology is for obtaining a quantitative assessment on the rating scale of a person's subjective impression of themselves or others on the rating dimension. For example, if the investigator is interested in a person's friendliness, it is common to use the subjective impressions of that person, or people who know that person well to assess the person's friendliness with a rating scale—for example, ranging from 1 = not at all friendly to 7 = extremely friendly. Rating scales can be used to obtain judges' interpretations of qualitative data on almost any dimension of interest. Moreover, rating scales can be constructed in a variety of ways (Nunnally, 1978). For example, the ratings can be obtained on 2, 5, 7, 9, 100, or whatever point scales, and the labels of the scales can be from negative to positive, or from none to many, or from agree to disagree. What is important is that the scales be constructed so that they are consistent with the dimension or category of interest, and that the ratings of the judges exhibit acceptable reliability and validity.

## The Classic Semantic Differential Rating Scale

One type of rating scale that has been widely used in phenomenological research and that has served as a model for many rating scales is the semantic differential (Osgood, Suci, and Tannenbaum, 1957). The semantic differential was originally developed to assess and test hypotheses about the phenomenological meaning people attach to events. Using the semantic differential, a subject rates a concept such as ideal-self, father, or narcissism on a series of seven-point scales. Each scale is defined by polar adjectives, such as *strong-weak, hard-soft, active-passive, and good-bad.* The subject's rating of the concept on a given scale is interpreted as the degree to which that descriptive dimension is applicable to the concept in question. Thus, the semantic differential is a way of measuring the personal meanings the individual attaches to concepts, events, or objects. It combines phenomenological experience with an objective approach to measurement. Table 8-5 illustrates how a semantic differential approach could be used to assess subjects' impressions of a woman described as victimized by a drinking, abusive husband.

Table 8-5

Example of the Semantic Differential

Below is a series of adjectives that might be used to describe someone. Use these adjectives to describe how you personally perceive the person we have just been talking about.

Example: If you perceive this person as slightly positive you would place your checkmark like this:

POSITIVE:—:—:—:X:—:—:—:NEGATIVE

SINCERE:—:—:—:—:—:—:INSINCERE
INTELLIGENT:—:—:—:—:—:—:UNINTELLIGENT
ALTRUISTIC:—:—:—:—:—:—:OPPORTUNISTIC
WORTHY:—:—:—:—:—:—:UNWORTHY
HONEST:—:—:—:—:—:—:DISHONEST
AMBITIOUS:—:—:—:—:—:—:UNAMBITIOUS

Source: *An Investigation into the Construct Validity of the Selfism Scale* by N. J. Erskine, 1981, Unpublished master's thesis, Kansas State University.

## Types of Personality Data

Cattell (1957) proposed a classification into three types of the data that can be used to study personality. **Self-report data** are obtained from the individual whose personality is being assessed. **Other-report data** are obtained from another person, often one who knows the subject well, and is based on his or her observations of the person in everyday life situations. Finally, **behavioral data** are derived from observing and recording the subject's behavior in standardized situations.

Historically, behavioral data were viewed as the best source of information about people because of its apparent objectivity—behaviors are viewed by coders who are trained to approach a 100 percent level of agreement in recording what they see. However, behavioral data must still be interpreted, typically by the experimenter, and these interpretations are necessarily subjective. Moreover, consistent with the social constructivist position, the valid interpretation of a person's behavior without input from the person or those who know the person well will generally be impossible (Block, 1977; Golding, 1978).

For example, consider the question "How often do you date?" Three different subjects answer the question by saying "Fifteen times a month." It is unlikely that this identical objective report of behavior for the three subjects has an identical implication for the three subjects' personality. One subject may date frequently to escape the monotony of classes or avoid studying; the second may have doubts about his personal acceptability and is seeking reassurance; the third may be extraverted and outgoing, and thus find himself frequently in the company of women. It is not possible to know which interpretation is correct without input from the subject or from people who know the subject well. Thus, self-reports and other-reports, both of which require at least some acceptance of phenomenological impressions as legitimate sources of scientific information, are essential for meaningful personality assessment. However, self- and other-reports vary substantially in the degree to which they reflect the informal phenomenology of the respondent rather than the formal theories of the investigator.

## Problems with Phenomenological Self- and Other-Reports

Self-reports and other-reports are often characterized as questionable sources of information about an individual's personality. There are several plausible potential problems with these sources of data. People are not always able to provide accurate insights about the meaning of their behavior, thoughts, and feelings (Janis, 1958; Nisbett and Wilson, 1977). In addition, phenomenological reports can be influenced by the assessment situation (Kanfer and Phillips, 1970), including how the question is phrased (Slovic, 1995), or by general tendencies to respond in certain ways regardless of the content of the question (Jackson and Messick, 1958). These tendencies are referred to as **response styles** (Rorer, 1965) and include **response carelessness** (a tendency to be inattentive or indifferent to the questions), **acquiescence** (a tendency to agree with or say "yes" to questions regardless of their content), **response extremeness** (a general tendency to use the extremes or the midvalues of a rating scale), and **social desirability** (a general tendency to give the desirable or socially acceptable response).

Most of the work in personality assessment has been devoted to assessing the impact of these problems on the validity of self- and other-reports for assessing personality (Wiggins, 1973). The evidence suggests that well-developed, multi-item, **objective personality inventories**—that is, inventories whose interpretation is so standardized that they can be scored by a computer—can overcome, or at least can detect, most of these problems (Jackson, 1971). On the other hand, **response sets**, which are deliberate faking on the part of individuals to create a certain impression (Rorer, 1965) are not so easily handled.

## Formal Versus Implicit Theories and Assessment

Formal Approaches and Their Problems. Objective personality assessment is based on formal definitions of personality constructs. The developer of a personality scale to assess, say, friendliness, begins by specifying a formal theory of friendliness that includes the types of specific behaviors, thoughts, and beliefs as well as the situations in which they occur. Items that reflect this theory are written and evaluated and refined. The process of item generation, evaluation, and refinement is often a long and difficult process that is, in essence, a test of the scientist's formal *theory* of friendliness (Jackson, 1971; Wiggins, 1973). It is this careful and rigorous process of scale development that overcomes many of the problems associated with self and other report data.

However, although objective personality scales rely on reports of the respondents, they ultimately reflect the formal theories of the investigator about the construct rather than the beliefs of the respondent. Thus, a formal theory of friendliness may emphasize aspects of friendliness such as extraversion and sociability and include items such as "I enjoy going to parties" and "I always strike up a conversation with people while waiting in line." An individual (or another theory) may instead emphasize the kindness and warmth of friendliness and include items such as "I help children cross the street" and "I try to see the good side of everyone." It follows, then, that if the investigator's formal theory for the scale does not match the phenomenological meaning of "friendliness" for the subject, the results will be inaccurate (Chaplin and Panter, 1993; Dunning and McElwee, 1995).

Implicit Approaches and Their Problems. The method of assessment that is most faithful to a subject's phenomenology is the **free description approach** (Fiske and Cox, 1979). In its most extreme form, an individual is presented with a blank piece of paper and is asked to write a description of himself or herself or another person. This approach will place the fewest constraints on the subject's impressions and will introduce the least amount of experimenter bias.

On the other hand, free descriptions have several problems. Subjects' responses will vary considerably in number and type. Subjects may write sentences or single words; some subjects will list specific behaviors, others will concentrate on physical characteristics, still others will report attitudes, and others may report person descriptive adjectives. This response variability makes the analysis of free descriptions difficult. Typically, experimenters resort to content coding the free descriptions, which means that the experimenter still provides the categories of interest and interprets the subject's responses. Thus, the extent to which the free descriptions reflect the subject's, rather than the experimenter's, phenomenology is reduced. Another problem is that subjects will not be as interested in the task as the experimenter, so they may not be sufficiently motivated to think deeply about the target. Thus, they may not think of important elements of their impressions of the target and fail to report them. The best example of this is subjects' tendency to overlook undesirable characteristics in their free descriptions, even though they acknowledge the existence of undesirable characteristics in themselves and their friends when explicitly asked about them (Markus and Wurf, 1987).

The Global Rating Compromise. A compromise between objective personality scales and free descriptions is the use of **global personality ratings**. Global ratings typically consist of one or more personality constructs, such as "friendly," "reliable," or "anxious." Subjects are asked to rate themselves or another target person on a scale reflecting how characteristic or descriptive each construct is of the target. Because the experimenter selects the terms, these ratings will not fully reflect the phenomenology of the subjects. "Self-descriptiveness ratings do not distinguish between personally relevant and irrelevant traits. When asked, subjects can usually rate the self-descriptiveness of most traits even if they have never thought about themselves in those terms" (Hampson, 1988, p. 177). However, in contrast to objective personality scales, global ratings allow the subjects to use their own phenomenological impressions, information, and definitions for making the ratings. Global self-ratings have become a widely used method for personality assessment, and the factors that affect subject's agreement and accuracy with global ratings have become a focus of intense theoretical and empirical research in contemporary personality psychology (Chaplin, 1991; Funder, 1987; Kenny, 1991).

## Accuracy of Global Ratings

During the early days of personality assessment, interest in the accuracy of global personality ratings was keen (Taft, 1955). For example, Vernon (1933) studied the ability of subjects to predict the scores of themselves and others on a variety of objective ability and personality scales. Dymond (1950) assessed the accuracy of ratings by determining how well subjects agreed with each other. These two studies reflect the two criteria that have generally been used to assess accuracy: predictive validity and interjudge agreement.

In 1955 Cronbach published a critique of studies on the accuracy of personality judgments that brought research on this important issue to an almost complete halt (Funder, 1987). The essence of Cronbach's critique was that ratings of personality were influenced by stereotypes, response extremeness, and other response tendencies that had nothing to do with the target's personality. In the absence of a well-established criterion measure of the target's "true" position on the personality rating scale, the influence of these response tendencies on measures of accuracy or agreement could be neither estimated nor controlled.

Errors and Mistakes.  Since that time, research on social judgments such as personality ratings has concentrated on demonstrating the flaws in subjects' judgments rather than directly addressing the accuracy of those judgments (e.g., Kahneman, Slovic, and Tversky, 1982; Nisbett and Ross, 1980). This research has clearly demonstrated that subjects are prone to a wide variety of errors in social judgment, and the general conclusion is that the existence of these errors means that social judgments are generally inaccurate. Yet, in 1987, Funder looked more deeply into the problem of assessing the accuracy of global personality ratings and concluded that there is a distinction between an **error** of social judgment and a **mistake**. Errors of judgment are evaluated in a laboratory using artificial and often simplified information that has a known correct answer. For example, subjects can be asked to judge the comparative length of two lines. An error occurs when the subject's judgment departs from the correct judgment.

Although errors are useful for studying the processes through which subjects make personality judgments, Funder argues that the artificial information on which they are based makes them largely irrelevant for conclusions about mistakes, which are error that occur in real-world situations and that have consequences for the individual. For example, the Asch (1946) experiment on implicit personality theory suggests that subjects generally make an *error* in forming an impression of a person by overweighting a single item of information. However, that research did not demonstrate that subjects would make similar *mistakes* when rating persons they know well. On the basis of this distinction, Funder noted that nearly all conclusions that subjects' personality ratings and other judgments are inaccurate is based on research on errors rather than mistakes. Thus, the widespread belief in the inaccuracy of social judgments was not justified. Funder's (1987) review has resulted in a renewal of interest in studying the accuracy of personality ratings, but it did not solve all the problems.

**The Criterion Problem.**  The lack of an acceptable criterion measure remains a major difficulty for research on accuracy. "If a subject claims that someone is 'friendly' or 'competent' on the basis of his or her acquaintance with that person, on what grounds can we assess whether the subject is right or wrong?" (Funder, 1987, pp. 76–77). Mischel (1972) and Scott and Johnson (1972) reviewed several studies and concluded that global self-reports about aggression, hostility, achievement, opinions of others' reactions to subjects, and personal feelings of distress often result in more accurate predictions than objective tests based on formal theories. However, the superiority of the predictive validity of global reports over objective measures is not universal and depends on the specific criteria that are to be predicted. Most important, although predictive validity is often viewed as evidence for the accuracy of a measure, it is, at best, an incomplete assessment of accuracy.

For example, a rating of friendliness might be evaluated by seeing whether it predicts whether or not a person smiles at another person whom he or she passes on the street. But there are many reasons a person may or may not smile that have little to do with friendliness, such as the location of the street (e.g., Tuscaloosa, Alabama, versus New York City) or the motives of the subject (e.g., genuine friendliness versus a manipulative desire to appear friendly). Prediction implies that a measure is related to a criterion, but not that it is the same as a criterion.

## Rating Agreement

**Agreement and Accuracy.**  The other major approach to evaluating subjective ratings is the degree of agreement between different raters about a subject's rating on a personality dimension. Funder (1987) notes that rating agreement does not necessarily imply accuracy. Raters may agree because they are both inaccurate, or they may agree for reasons, listed by Cronbach (1955), that have nothing to do with the subject's personality. However, Funder argues that in everyday personality description, agreement is often viewed evidence for accuracy. If two people report that another person is reliable we are likely to believe that assessment, whereas we are less likely to expect the person to be reliable, if one person describes the individual as reliable and the other describe the person as unreliable. More important, Funder contends that if two raters disagree in their assessment of a target, then at least one of them must be wrong. However, this argument is at odds with the social constructivist position that personality is constructed from the interactions between two individuals (Swann, 1984). If two individuals have two different interactions with the target person, then it is possible for them to disagree in their ratings, yet be accurate in the sense that each rating will predict how the target will act toward each individual (Casseldon and Hampson, 1990). Whether or not agreement, or lack of agreement, between the personality ratings of two individuals has any implications for the accuracy of those ratings, Funder's (1987) paper has contributed to the widespread interest in, and intense study of, rating agreement and the factors that may affect it.

Degree of Agreement. Reviews of studies of global ratings of personality (e.g., Taft, 1955; Shrauger and Schoneman, 1979) have reported a wide range of rating agreement. However, the general impression left by these reviews is that people show poor levels of agreement, and the dismal conclusion drawn from this finding is that global ratings are not useful for assessing personality. Funder (1987) has disagreed with this conclusion by noting that the vast majority of studies that found poor agreement among global ratings of personality used ratings from people who did not know the target. When ratings are obtained from individuals who know the target well, the level of agreement is often substantial (e.g., Norman and Goldberg, 1963), with the average correlations among raters ranging as high as .60. Nonetheless, the degree to which two raters will agree about a target's personality will vary, with some raters exhibiting substantial agreement and others showing little agreement or even disagreement.

A Theory of Rating Agreement. In 1991, David Kenny proposed a model of rating agreement that combines the major variables that contemporary personality psychologists believe influence the extent to which raters will agree about a target individual's personality. The variables in Kenny's model are listed and defined in Table 8-6. Kenny's model, as with most pervious models of interpersonal percep-

⊗⊗ Table 8-6

The Major Parameters in Kenny's (1991) Model of Agreement for Global Personality Ratings

| 1. **Acquaintance** | The amount of information the raters have about the target person. |
|---|---|
| 2. **Overlap** | The extent to which the raters have viewed the same set of target behaviors. |
| 3. **Shared Meaning** | The degree of agreement among the raters about the meaning of the target behaviors they have observed for the characteristic they are rating. |
| 4. **Consistency** | The similarity of the target's behavior across time and situations. |
| 5. **Communication** | The extent to which the raters share their impressions of the target with each other. |
| 6. **Unique Influences** | Factors unrelated to the target's actual behavior that may influence a rater's ratings. |

tion (e.g., Jones and Davis, 1965; Reeder and Brewer, 1979), have adopted Kelly's (1955) view that people approach their social world as scientists. The model begins with observed data such as behaviors, appearance, or statements that are treated as objective facts (in the sense that they would not be disputed by anyone with the opportunity to observe them.) Three of the variables in Kenny's model, **acquaintance, overlap,** and **consistency,** concern the quality and similarity of the data available to the raters. Subsequently, these data are interpreted by the raters into personality descriptions. These interpretations, as with all scientific interpretations of empirical phenomena, are not themselves empirical or objective. The third variable in Kenny's model, **shared meaning,** concerns how similarities and differences in raters' interpretations of the same data (observations) influence agreement. The remaining two variables, **communication** and **unique influences,** are not easily categorized into the observation or interpretation stages of the process. Communication can apply to both stages because it allows raters to share data and to persuade each other about the interpretation of the data. Unique influences are the extent to which the rater-as-scientist models of interpersonal perception are inadequate. Kenny's model has helped to organize research and theory about the complicated process of interpersonal perception and rater agreement. It has also generated new research on the topic (e.g., Chaplin and Panter, 1993; Kanfer and Tanaka, 1993).

## Summary Evaluation

 ### Strengths

Phenomenology and Human Experience. Phenomenological approaches emphasize that biological, behavioral, and psychodynamic models do not fully capture the human experience. People are not merely bundles of instincts, urges, or habits. Likewise, they do not passively and mindlessly respond to drives or external stimuli. Humans interpret their experience, make choices, set goals, and change themselves. In phenomenological research, the essential human qualities of inner experience and self-awareness are not ignored because their study is scientifically challenging. Instead, the importance of assessing subjective experience and incorporating its influence into models of human thought and action is recognized, and the development of rigorous methods for doing so is the central concern, particularly of the contemporary form of phenomenology called social cognition.

Emphasis on the Positive. Theorists such as Maslow and Rogers focus on people's capacity for positive growth and desirable behavior. In much of psychoanalysis and psychology, the emphasis is on psychopathology, sickness, and behavior deficits. Often these approaches ignore the reality of mental health and well-being. However, phenomenological approaches as incorporated into humanistic and existential theories include phenomena such as love, creativity, health, competence, and the actualizing potential. The assessment of human competencies as well as deficits is now viewed as important (Sundberg, Snowden, and Reynolds, 1978). Likewise, the goals of psychotherapy have expanded from the simple reduction of pathology and distress to the expansion of awareness and the enhancement of feeling and freedom. Therapy is no longer only for neurotics and psychotics but a place where anyone can grow, actualize, and encounter the self.

**Emphasis on the Present and Future.**  Most psychological theories are deterministic: they emphasize past events as the cause of human behavior. Phenomenological theories are more present- and future-oriented. People's actions are influenced not only by childhood conflicts, previous conditioning, and genetic legacy but also by how they think about those events in the present. Phenomenologists emphasize free will. The future goals we *choose* and the present interpretations we *select* are as important in causing our behavior as the past. The debate over free will versus determinism is ancient and unresolved. However, it is clear that deterministic models of behavior have not answered all of the questions of the psychology of personality. Phenomenological approaches serve an important function by introducing a self-guided, free-will component into personality theory.

**Idiographic Focus.**  Although personality psychology is often characterized as the study of individuals and their uniqueness, most personality theories and research have little to do with individuals (Lamiell, 1981). Rather, the emphasis is on constructs and individual differences so that research papers may report that, say, the construct depression is related to the construct anxiety, but not indicate anything about a specific individual's experience or level of depression and anxiety. Phenomenological theories and research have helped to correct this imbalance by complementing psychology's traditional nomothetic emphasis with an idiographic one.

**Contribution to Personality Assessment.**  Two of the major sources of data used to study personality, self-reports and the reports of others, rely to a greater or lesser extent on phenomenology. Phenomenological theory and research contribute to our ability to interpret such reports meaningfully in a scientifically valid manner. By clarifying the cognitive processes that influence interpersonal perception, and understanding the factors that contribute to the accuracy and agreement among self-reports and other-reports, phenomenological approaches play a crucial role in the study of personality.

**Rogers: Some Specific Strengths.**  Rogers is one of the best-known psychologists, both within and outside the field. His theory has generated much research and has had a substantial applied impact in many fields. Much of the research based on Rogers' theory concerns processes in psychotherapy and, at a minimum, demonstrates that investigating the therapeutic process is possible. Rogers developed a comprehensive and systematic theory of personality, which he stated in a propositional form that enhanced its clarity. Rogers will be best remembered for his introduction of client-centered therapy—the first major alternative to psycho-analysis. His emphasis on the therapy relationship and his de-emphasis of the necessity for an elaborate reconstruction of the past produced a set of therapy procedures that both shortened the process and required less training on the part of the therapist. This, in turn, has led to the development of encounter groups and self-help groups, making available to more people the possibility for personal growth and enhancement.

**Kelly: Some Specific Strengths.** Kelly's theory is also stated formally as a set of propositions and postulates. It is likewise a comprehensive and systematic formulation. With its emphasis on how people construe events, it has provided the foundation for the application of cognitive theory and research to the study of personality. Personal construct theory, with its use of the scientist metaphor to characterize how people come to know their social world, is an important precursor of attribution theory, implicit personality theory, and social cognition. Kelly's introduction of the Rep Test was an equally important contribution. Similarly, fixed-role therapy, a method logically derived from Kelly's theory, is a significant addition to therapeutic practice.

**The Emergence of Social Cognition.** The introduction of cognitive theory and research to the processing of social information is one of the most significant developments in personality psychology. The unquestioning acceptance or automatic rejection of phenomenological data has been replaced by research methods and conceptual advances that allow the formulation and testing of specific hypotheses about how people process social information. Research on the self-concept, social judgments, and even the unconscious has become scientifically acceptable to a larger number of psychologists than ever before.

## Weaknesses

**Subjective Experience and Scientific Research.** That subjective experience can have an important impact on behavior and also provide important information about personality may be an obvious truth. Determining how to assess subjective experience and incorporate it into scientific theory is less obvious. How can we see the world through the eyes of another person? More important, how can we know when we have done so? As people, scientists have their own idiosyncratic biases and phenomenal fields. How can we separate those biases from our assessment of another person's beliefs? These are serious problems, whose ultimate resolution may lie in philosophy rather than in empirical research. In any case, it is likely that phenomenological theories and research will always be plagued by these issues and doubts. For some scientists, these problems necessarily make phenomenological data scientifically unacceptable.

**Unquestioned Acceptance of Another's Reports.** The search for the understanding of the meaning of another's experience requires an almost exclusive reliance on the reports of the subjects about themselves, others, and their experiences. Self-reports and other-reports have been used by psychologists to study many phenomena, but these reports are typically subjected to carefully evaluation for reliability and validity. However, phenomenologists, particularly those who have adopted humanistic values, sometimes accept the reports of their subjects and clients without question. Indeed, to question another's statements is at odds with the principle of unconditional acceptance that is characteristic of humanistic philosophy. The possibility that both conscious response sets and unconscious response styles might reduce the validity of those reports is overlooked. So, too, is the possibility that some people may not be motivated and/or able to report extensively on their feelings and experiences.

**Limited Generality.** Both Kelly and Rogers worked primarily with college students and based their theories on research with them. Indeed, the client-centered movement developed on college campuses. As a group, college students are brighter and more verbal than the average population. They are also likely to have more resources for coping with their problems. Thus, college students are the ideal group for eliciting personal constructs or for probing verbalizations to understand phenomenal fields. Likewise, they are more likely to have met life's basic needs and so be able to develop self-awareness and seek self-actualization. When one moves off-campus to a less verbal and less resourceful population, the application of phenomenology to understanding and helping individuals may be reduced (as Rogers discovered with a schizophrenic population). This does not make phenomenological theory and methods wrong. The alienated, constricted person searching for the meaning of life may benefit greatly from an existential approach. However, the generality, or range of convenience, of phenomenological approaches may be limited.

**Disregard of Development.** The present and future focus of phenomenological approaches such as self-theory, personal construct theory, and existentialism has resulted in a disregard of development. This ahistorical position, although theoretically consistent, is a serious omission. To know a person, we may need only to know the person's phenomenal field today, but that field did not suddenly spring into existence. Child-rearing practices, behavior change, and a fuller description of an individual's phenomenology might be better understood through study of how individuals have acquired their construct system or their particular phenomenal field.

**Potential for Circularity.** Because the phenomenal field of another can never be observed, it must be inferred from a person's behavior and verbalizations. It is easy for this process to become circular, which makes phenomenological explanations scientifically untestable because they can not be disproved. For example, suppose a subject appears anxious and uncomfortable following a question about his relationship with his father. On the basis of this observation, I make the inference that the question is threatening. I then explain his discomfort as being due to the threat. This really amounts to little more than saying he acted in a threatened manner because he acted in a threatened manner. I inferred the explanation from the very behavior I was trying to explain. If, instead, the subject had acted calm when questioned about his father, I might have concluded that he was not threatened by his relationship with his father, and I would be using the same kind of circular reasoning. Because any reaction can be "explained" phenomenologically, it is crucial that some external criterion be adopted for evaluating phenomenological hypotheses. Selecting that criterion, and sticking with it if one's theory is disconfirmed, is a major challenge for phenomenological research.

**Vagueness of Language.** Phenomenological theory relies on everyday language, which is often vague and difficult to specify. Definitions of the self as the "I" or "me" are simply restatements. Measures such as the California Q-sort and the semantic differential were designed to bring more specificity into phenomenological descriptions, as was Kelly's Rep Test, which required respondents to clarify the meaning of their constructs by providing antonyms. However, the imprecision of language increases the difficulty of measurement and of achieving reliability among observers. In existentialism, the problem is particularly pronounced. There is an intentional undisciplined quality to the writing that ensures that independent observers will draw different inferences from the same data. Terms such as *internal silence, from here-to-there rhythmic awareness exercises, peak experience, Dasein, authenticity, being-in-the-world, sick point,* or *whatness* do not facilitate scientific communication. Every theoretical framework in psychology has its own jargon, but the humanistic-existential approach particularly seems to disguise its concepts in vague terminology.

**Limitations of Cognitive Theory.** The cognitive revolution has had a substantial impact of personality psychology. In particular, the computer metaphor, with observations labeled as "inputs" and responses labeled as "outputs," has resulted in a "boxes and arrows" approach to social cognitive theory. However, although human cognitive activity is similar in some ways to computers, processes, they are far from identical, and the ease with which boxes and arrows can be drawn should not persuade us that they exist in our heads.

Others have commented about the "homunculus" problem. For example, the self has sometimes been regarded as a little executive "in the mind" who issues orders or processes information. Such views beg the question, however, of how the mind works. As Epstein (1980) has said, "It is then no easier to account for the behavior of the little person than to account for the behavior of the big one" (p. 88). The same point applies to the computer issue. Computers function because they are programmed. So, who has programmed the computers in our heads?

Also, some argue that the view of people as naive scientists has put too much emphasis on thinking and not enough on the affective aspects of human beings. In essence, personality psychologists have allowed their own phenomenology of being scientists to have too much influence on their theories. Carver and Scheier (1988), however, contend that emotions are, indeed, included as an important part of the information processing perspective.

## Summary

- The basic content of phenomenological research is subjective experience. Consequently, phenomenological research is often qualitative and idiographic, although it can be experimental and nomothetic.
- The distinction between idiographic and nomothetic research is in the types of standards, such as normative, ipsative, and idiographic ones, that are used to evaluate and assess observations. In addition to the scientific implications, the types of standards people employ to evaluate everyday experience has become a focus of empirical study.
- Phenomenological research owes much to Carl Rogers, the person who pioneered the use of tapes, recordings, and transcripts in his extensive program of research into therapy processes and outcomes.
- As an example of humanistic research, work by Maslow on self-actualization and the hierarchy of needs was noted.
- Several principles characterizing the existential research approach were briefly described.
- Content analysis is used to evaluate phenomenological data. Typically, this involves having trained judges classify phenomenological reports, such as interview content, into categories (e.g., positive versus negative self-references). A similar approach involves the use of rating scales such as the semantic differential, to assign values to phenomenological data on dimensions that are of interest to the investigator.
- Rogers and his colleagues made extensive use of the Q-sort method. In this technique, subjects are asked to sort statements about the self or other targets into various piles according to whether the statements are characteristic or uncharacteristic of the self or the target.
- The California Q-set has been widely used in phenomenological research. Expert judges have developed several descriptions of idealized targets, such as a "well-adjusted person" or a "male paranoid." These descriptions can then be used for interpreting an individual's sorts.
- Kelly's personal construct theory is most commonly investigated using the Rep Test, an instrument devised by Kelly as a method of eliciting the personal constructs used by the individual.

- Examples of nomothetic research using personal constructs are studies of the complexity of the self-concept and how complexity relates to a number of variables such as depression and self-esteem.
- Self-schema theory has been a fruitful source of contemporary research on the self. In particular, self-theory has benefited from developments in social cognition.
- Implicit personality theory concerns a person's beliefs about the behaviors that are related to specific traits and to the organization of personality. Implicit personality theory has been a focus psychological research since the 1950s. A controversial use of implicit personality theory is the development of formal, or explicit, personality theories from the collective everyday wisdom embodied in people's implicit theories.
- Some criticisms of implicit theory are the systematic distortion hypothesis, people's ability to explain away inconsistent personality information, and the impact of evaluative characteristics on people's impressions of others' personalities.
- Phenomenology is the basis for two of the three main sources of information used to study personality: self-reports and other-reports. The extent to which self- and other-reports rely on phenomenology depends on how much formal theory is imposed on the reports. Objective personality scales contain the most formal theory and the least phenomenology; free descriptions are the most phenomenological. Global personality ratings are somewhere in between.
- The accuracy of global ratings was widely studied in the first half of this century. However, a methodological critique of the study of accuracy by Cronbach brought research on accuracy to an abrupt halt.
- Interest in accuracy has been rejuvenated by Funder's review, which distinguishes between errors and mistakes in people's personality judgments.
- One criterion for accuracy is interjudge agreement, although social constructivists contend that agreement has little to do with accuracy because individuals experience one another differently.
- Regardless of its relevance for accuracy, rating agreement has become the focus of intense study in personality psychology. Kenny has proposed a model of agreement that incorporates most of the variables that personality psychologists view as important for understanding rating agreement.
- In a summary evaluation, several positive features of phenomenology were described. Phenomenology holds that humans are not mindless—they interpret their experience, make choices, set goals, and change themselves. This approach encourages a positive view of human beings and does not focus exclusively on pathology or incompetencies. There is recognition that the past is less important than our awareness of the present and our anticipation of the future. This approach also brings an idiographic emphasis to per-

sonality research, and it is crucial for evaluating two-thirds of the types of data used for personality assessment.

- Several specific strengths associated with Rogers, Kelly, and social cognition were mentioned.
- There are also some weaknesses of phenomenology. We can never be certain whether one person can understand another's phenomenology. The unquestioned acceptance of another's reports is scientifically unacceptable. Phenomenological theories, with their heavy reliance on college students as subjects, may be of limited generalizability. Other criticisms include a lack of interest in developmental issues, the potential for circularity in phenomenological explanations, and the excessive use of imprecise language.
- Some specific weaknesses of cognitive models were also mentioned, including limitations of the computer metaphor, the homunculus problem, and the overemphasis on the rational, thinking aspect of phenomenology.

# Chapter 9
# The Behavioral Tradition

The Beginnings of Learning Theory
    Classical Conditioning
    Watson's Behaviorism
    Thorndike and Hull and the Era of
        Behaviorism
Skinner's Operant Conditioning
    Basic Skinnerian Concepts
    Structure of Personality
    The Idiographic Method
    Development of Personality
    Nature of Adjustment
The Reinforcement Theory of Dollard and
    Miller
    From Animal Behavior to Human
        Personality
    Basic Concepts of Reinforcement Theory
    Structure of Personality
    Development of Personality
    Nature of Adjustment
Summary

For many people, the study of personality is defined by a focus on the identification and study of the internal characteristics that guide human behavior. Indeed, up to this point in the book the focus has been mainly on what goes on inside people. Whether it be the instincts and mental apparatus described by Freud, the genes and hormones of biological models, or the growth potential postulated by Rogers, the emphasis of these approaches is within the person. Of course, people such as Adler discussed family organization, Rogers enumerated some of the conditions under which self-esteem arises, and genes interact with the environment to produce phenotypes. Yet, these external factors are often viewed as limiting conditions or modifiers of the internal factors in these theories, not as the primary source of personality.

However, our understanding of personality would be limited if we failed to recognize the powerful influence that situational and environmental variables have on an individual's behavior. Of course, when we do look closely at behavior, we cannot fail to find evidence for its stability over both time and situations. But equally impressive is the way it can change and grow over time and the manner in which it can vary across situations. Moreover, if people did not respond to, and learn from, their environment, it is doubtful that the human species would exist. To appreciate and understand the powerful influence of the environment on behavior and personality, we need to consider the principles of learning theory. These principles concern the conditions that influence how people learn to respond to environmental stimuli. If we arrange conditions so that a child learns to be anxious, we can, by applying the same principles, rearrange conditions so that they will promote relaxation instead. What has happened here is that our interest begins to shift from the internal elements of personality that mark each person as different to the processes by which learning occurs. And the principles by which these basic processes operate are the same for everyone.

The implications of this shift in focus are profound. In the present chapter, some of these behavioral learning developments will be traced and their implications for a psychology of personality elaborated.

## The Beginnings of Learning Theory

The work of Ivan Pavlov is generally viewed as the beginning of **learning theory**, which concerns how the responses of people (and other organisms) to events are influenced by those people's past environmental experiences. Pavlov, a Russian physiologist, was studying the digestive process in dogs when he observed, almost casually, that the dogs would begin to salivate even before food was placed in their mouths. Table 9-1 defines the basic concepts of **stimulus**, the event to which an organism reacts, and **response**, the reaction of the organism to a stimulus, that Pavlov used to characterize his observations. It is noteworthy that in

## &#x2767; Table 9-1
### Basic Types of Stimuli and Responses

**Unconditioned stimulus:** An event that elicits a reflexive or automatic response in the absence of learning. For example, a mild electric shock will cause a person to jerk back even if the person has never been exposed to a shock before.

**Unconditioned response:** A reflexive or automatic response to a stimulus in the absence of learning, for example, perspiring in response to being outside on a hot day.

**Neutral stimulus:** A stimulus that does not elicit any response in the absence of learning. For example, a crack in a concrete driveway does not generally elicit even a passing glance.

**Conditioned stimulus:** An initially neutral stimulus that elicits a response because of its association with an unconditioned stimulus. For example, if a person receives a shock while stepping on a crack in the driveway, the next crack sighted might cause him or her to jerk the foot back and step over the crack.

**Conditioned response:** A learned response that is elicited by a conditioned stimulus, for example, responding to a crack in the driveway by deliberately stepping over it.

contrast to most personality research, Pavlov's work on learning not only occurred in a controlled laboratory setting but also used nonhuman animals as subjects.

## Classical Conditioning

Pavlov's observations led eventually to the concept of classical conditioning. **Classical conditioning** is the process whereby a previously neutral stimulus (e.g., a bell) becomes conditioned or associated with an unconditioned stimulus (one that naturally evokes a response such as salivation, e.g., food). Of course, the conditioned stimulus (bell, in this case) must be associated repeatedly with the unconditioned stimulus (food), and the interval between pairings of the stimuli must not be long. If, in the example used here, the bell fails over a series of trials to be followed by the food, the association may be broken, and salivation in response to the bell will cease.

Recently, however, Rescorla (1988) has argued that such descriptions of conditioning are inadequate. Instead, he says, classical conditioning should refer to the information one stimulus conveys about another. According to Rescorla, simply associating a conditioned stimulus with an unconditioned one will not produce learning. Instead, the neutral stimulus must reliably predict the unconditioned stimulus.

Ivan Pavlov, a pioneer in the study of learning, investigated classical conditioning in dogs.

## Watson's Behaviorism

A second major figure in the rise of learning theory was John B. Watson. Watson is usually regarded as the founder of **behaviorism**, which is the view that the only appropriate subject for psychology is behavior, because behavior, unlike events transpiring in the head, is readily observable. Thoughts, wishes, or expectancies are private; they can only be inferred from behavior. Therefore, if we are going to build a science of psychology, we must commit ourselves to the study of behavior rather than inferred states of consciousness (Watson, 1919). Watson argued that personality was best viewed as a collection of learned habits. His view is illustrated in Figure 9-1.

In contrast to biological, psychoanalytic, and phenomenological theories, Watson and his fellow behaviorists viewed behavior as function of the environment. This is consistent with behaviorism's emphasis on direct observation. Environmental stimuli, because they are outside the organism, can be more readily observed than internal thoughts, wishes, or brain structures. Our behavior, he asserted, is determined by the associations we learn to make between stimuli and outcomes. To emphasize this point, he made the following oft-quoted and rather exuberant remarks: "Give me a dozen healthy infants, well-formed, and my own specified world to bring them up in, and I'll guarantee to take any one at random and train him to become any type of specialist I might select—doctor, lawyer, artist, merchant-chief, and, yes, even beggar-man and thief, regardless of his talents, penchants, tendencies, activities, vocations, and race of his ancestors"

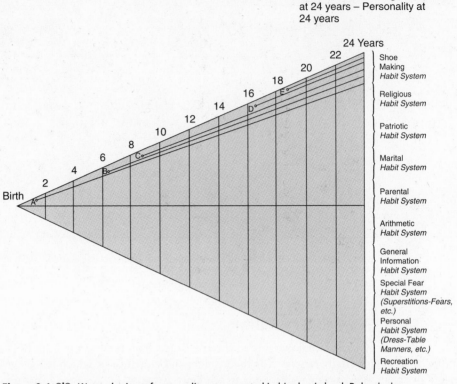

**Figure 9-1** &#x6969; Watson's view of personality as presented in his classic book <u>Behaviorism</u>.

(Watson, 1930, p. 104). To be fair, it should be noted that Watson himself viewed this position as an exaggeration to make a point. The quotation continues, "I am going beyond my facts and I admit it, but so have the advocates of the contrary and they have been doing it for thousands of years" (p. 104).

Perhaps the best-known study conducted by Watson is the laboratory research on Little Albert and the white rat (Watson and Rayner, 1920). The study was an illustration of the conditioning of an emotional reaction, and it purported to demonstrate how a neurosis can develop in a child. In the Pavlovian tradition of conditioning, Little Albert was given a white rat to play with. But each time the rat was present, a loud noise was simultaneously introduced. After several such trials, the white rat (previously a neutral stimulus) brought forth in Albert a very strong fear response that generalized to similar furry objects. Upon closer examination, this experiment is not as convincing as it might first appear (Harris, 1979). But it has become to be the classic example of the behaviorist position rather than a tentative conclusion based on a pilot study, as it should be (Samelson, 1980).

Mary Cover Jones (1924) demonstrated that learned fears such as Little Albert's can be removed. Peter, a 3-year-old boy, was afraid of rabbits, rats, and other similar animals. To erase the fear, Jones moved a caged rabbit closer and closer as Peter was eating. The previously feared object thus became associated with the pleasant experiences of eating, and after a few months Peter's fear of rabbits disappeared. Of course, one must make sure that conditioning does not flow in the opposite direction. That is, if Peter's fear of the rabbit had been very intense, he might have developed negative responses to the food. In any event, Jones's work was an early precursor of systematic desensitization, a widely used therapeutic technique.

## Thorndike and Hull and the Era of Behaviorism

Another important early learning theorist was Edward L. Thorndike. Thorndike's main contribution was his **law of effect** (Thorndike, 1905). This law states that when a specific stimulus precedes a specific response and that response is, in turn, followed by a positive outcome, the bond between that stimulus and that response will be strengthened. When the response is followed by a negative outcome, the bond will be weakened. For example, if I eat coffee ice cream while studying for an examination and I do well on the examination, I will be more likely to eat coffee ice cream while studying for the next examination. However, if I do poorly I may switch to chocolate ice cream, or not eat ice cream at all, while studying for the next examination. This is a simple concept but one that had important consequences for psychological theory. Essentially, this law provided the justification for psychologists to restrict their explanation of behavior to observable stimuli and observable responses. There was no need to consider unobserved properties of the organism such as its thoughts, feelings, or perceptions in the explanation of its behavior. Thorndike's work solidified the status of learning in psychology and increased the emphasis on behavior and the environment. Rewards and punishments and the internal states they produce are defined solely in terms of the operations that produce them. For example, a satisfying goal is one that induces movement in the organism toward it; an unpleasant goal is one that causes movement away from it. The prediction of behavior is possible through an understanding of the laws of learning, and the role of internal factors is superfluous.

The final figure in this brief historical sketch is that of Clark L. Hull. His approach is now mainly of historical interest. But beginning in 1930 and for the next 30 years or so, his learning theory was a major force in psychology—perhaps the most important one. His *Principles of Behavior,* published in 1943, stated what became the foremost example of a mathematical-deductive theory in psychology. It was a rigorous, systematic presentation of the conditions leading to the formation of habits. **Habits** are stimulus–response associations that occur as the result of rewards. This was an **instrumental conditioning** theory, which means that the events (rewards and punishments) following a response were the critical elements affecting the subsequent likelihood of the response occurring again. His was a grand theory—an elegant conceptual presentation that captured the imagination of many theorists and elevated the role of learning to a commanding position in American psychology. Eventually, the theory faded as psychology began to be absorbed with other topics. But its influence had been felt even by those who had definite sympathy for the psychoanalytic perspective.

## Skinner's Operant Conditioning

The purest and most extreme version of behaviorism is the work of B. F. Skinner and his followers, the **radical behaviorists**. Skinner's operant philosophy is that behavior is maintained by its consequences, that is, by rewards and punishments. We do not control our behavior through choice or free will, nor does the control reside in any mind entities or traits. Rather, our behavior is determined by events in the environment. When these environmental events are identified, we have the key to the understanding and control of human behavior. The system of rewards that keeps a troupe of trained dogs performing to the delight of audiences is no different in principle from that which impels the performance of a troupe of Shakespearean actors.

Moreover, Skinner and his followers would reject personality theory; indeed, they rejected all theory as the basis for scientific understanding. Instead, they regard their work as guided entirely by the results of empirical research. This atheoretical approach to science, in which the discovery and accumulation of facts is the basis for knowledge, is not widely endorsed by modern scientists. Indeed, it has been argued that decisions about which "facts" to discover and how to accumulate them require some form of theory. Operant psychology does contain concepts and has implications for personality, but the radical behaviorists would argue that these concepts and implications have been discovered from empirical research rather than formulated in their heads.

Skinner believed that all behavior is determined by a lawful and systematic set of principles. No behavior is impulsive, and nothing arises out of free will. This view implies the corollary belief that behavior can be controlled. This promise of control can be achieved through the **functional analysis of behavior**, which refers to the analysis of how responses follow stimuli, as well as the specific conditions in which the pairings occur, to discover the cause-and-effect relations between stimuli and responses.

Skinner was not interested in variables inside the organism that might be said to mediate these relationships. Some have even said that Skinner regarded the human organism as an "empty box." A more precise way of saying this is that he saw no necessity for opening the box. A stimulus impinges on the box, and a response emerges from that box. For Skinner, this was the essence of a science of psychology: the discovery of the lawful relationship between inputs and outputs.

For example, in this class you may read every assigned article on the course syllabus and follow every casual suggestion by the instructor to read books that are mentioned in class. Perhaps you have a thirst for knowledge. Perhaps you want a good grade. Perhaps you just do what you are told by authority figures. Skinner would say that none of this matters; there is no way of knowing which of these reasons for your behavior is correct. Moreover, he would argue that there is no need to know why you study so much. What is clear is the systematic relation between stimulus (syllabus or suggestion) and response (reading). And we can control the response by manipulating the stimulus. If all this sounds simple, it is—in a way. But it is not necessarily very easy. The functional analysis of complex behaviors can be very difficult, time-consuming, and intricate.

Skinner was not unaware of genetics. He did admit that we are evolutionary products and that we have certain species-specific capabilities and characteristics. Our individual repertoires of responses do give us identities that have arisen out of the learning situations to which we have been exposed over the course of our lives. What I do today says something about the stimuli that control my behavior. But that I have been able to acquire this repertoire of behavior through conditioning reflects my genetic endowment as well. Behaviorally, however, Skinner was less interested in genetics than in conditioning processes.

## Basic Skinnerian Concepts

The concepts that Skinner employed are founded in learning theory and were discovered in the research laboratory, often with nonhuman subjects such as pigeons and rats.

The presence of this policeman should have been a cue for the driver to slow down.

## A BRIEF BIOGRAPHY OF

# B. F. Skinner

Born in 1904 in Susquehanna, Pennsylvania, B. F. Skinner grew up uneventfully in a home marked by stability and warmth. His father was a lawyer, and his mother has been described as ensuring that he learned the difference between right and wrong. During his childhood he was constantly building things, from wagons and slingshots to gliders and kites. He even tried his hand at creating a perpetual motion machine. Interestingly, in his subsequent professional career he often made use of novel laboratory equipment. The continuity between childhood and adulthood seems clear.

He attended Hamilton College as an English major and hoped to become a writer. He even sent several short stories to Robert Frost, from whom he received encouragement. Trying his hand full-time at writing, he lived for a while at home and then in Europe, and he even spent six months or so in Greenwich Village. Finally, he concluded that a writing career was not likely to bear fruit. Even though Skinner had no background in psychology, he began to read about the work of Pavlov and Watson. He applied to and was accepted for graduate work in psychology at Harvard. During this period his interest in animal behavior developed. Receiving his Ph.D., he moved to the University of Minnesota in 1936 to assume his first academic post. He remained at Minnesota for nine years. After a brief stint at Indiana University, he went back to Harvard in 1948 and remained there until his death in 1990.

If his work at Minnesota established him as an experimental psychologist of national repute, his later years at Harvard witnessed his becoming a major scientist with a worldwide constituency. Many regarded B. F. Skinner

**Respondents.** Skinner referred to classical conditioning as **respondent behavior**—behavior that is a response to some identifiable stimulus. A low-flying aircraft causes us to duck; an instructor asks you a question in class and you become nervous; someone compliments you and you smile shyly.

**Operants.** Respondent behavior is important, and its conditioning has been used to account for the acquisition of a wide array of behavior, including fears and attractions. Skinner, however, was always more interested in what he termed **operant behavior**. This refers to behavior acquired on the basis of instrumental conditioning. Behavior is *emitted*, and the frequency of its occurrence depends upon the effects it has on the environment or the consequences that follow from it. Operant conditioning does not apply strictly to laboratory settings, nor does it involve only the behaviors of pigeons pecking at colored disks to receive a pellet of food or of rats doing strange things to obtain a treasured drop of water.

as the world's foremost psychologist. Certainly he received many honors, including the Distinguished Scientific Award of the American Psychological Association, membership in the National Academy of Sciences, the position of William James Lecturer at Harvard, and the President's Medal of Science.

Although Skinner may have failed in his early literacy aspirations, he continued to write for general audiences. In 1948 he published *Walden Two*, a novel depicting an experimental society built on a foundation of psychological principles. His single most important scientific work is probably *The Behavior of Organisms*, which appeared in 1938. Many other significant works followed, including *Science and Human Behavior* (1953), *Verbal Behavior* (1957), and *About Behaviorism* (1974). A brief autobiography has appeared in Boring and Lindzey's *A History of Psychology in Autobiography* (Vol. 5)(1967). Skinner also completed the first volume of a two-volume autobiography, *Particulars of My Life*, which appeared in 1976. His most controversial book, however, was his 1971 national bestseller, *Beyond Freedom and Dignity*. In it, he argued that concepts such as freedom and dignity should be set aside and that we should look to the manipulation of environmental conditions and rewards in building a better society. This prescription touched off a firestorm of criticism, shock, and outrage. But Skinner was not one to be dissuaded easily from his beliefs. His behaviorism remains a potent forces.

His final book, *Upon Further Reflection*, published in 1987, is a collection of essays covering many topics from international relations to self-management.

People continue to flip light switches because doing so results in a consequence: the light comes on. If you are friendly to another person but get only an icy stare, you stop being friendly.

Discriminative Stimuli.  Some stimuli serve a discriminative function. They act as cues or signals that a given response is likely to be rewarded and are called **discriminative stimuli**. A mother's frown becomes a signal that one kind of response rather than another is more likely to win her approval. A highway patrol car is a cue that I had better reduce my speed or risk a citation. This does not mean that a discriminative stimulus completely controls our behavior. There is still the outcome itself—such as receiving a $50 fine. But a discriminative stimulus does suggest to us which behavior should be selected so as to achieve a desirable (or less undesirable) consequence. It is through discriminative stimuli that our world is rendered more predictable and therefore more manageable.

## BOX 9-1
## The Reinforcement of New Behavior

Allen, Hart, Buell, Harris, and Wolf (1964) described the case of a four-year old girl, Ann, who was enrolled in a preschool class. Before long Ann started paying less and less attention to the other children and increasingly wanted to be near the teachers. She began to just stand about, stare, pick her lower lip, pull on her hair, or rub her cheek. All her behavior seemed geared toward obtaining attention from adult teachers. At the same time, this behavior directly interfered with her playing with the other children.

A program was initiated so that Ann was rewarded by attention from a teacher whenever she played with another child. This was done so it did not interrupt her play with that other child. When she was alone, no attention was provided. There was an immediate and obvious increase in her play with other children and a corresponding drop in her behavior directed toward adults, as can be seen in Figure 9-2.

But can we be sure it was the teachers' reinforcement that was responsible for the change in Ann's behavior? After five days, the teachers reversed their reinforcement patterns. They went back to reinforcing Ann for her withdrawn, shy behavior. As the figure shows, her behavior quickly returned to its original "baseline" level. After five more days, Ann was once more reinforced only for playing with other children, and her behavior changed again. Toward the end of this latter period, the teachers began reinforcing her intermittently to build up her resistance to extinction. After 25 days, no particular effort was made to sustain Ann's new behavior. But postexperimental checks coming on Days 31, 38, 40, and 51 indicated that her interaction with other children was continuing. Ann now seemed to be receiving reinforcements from her play with the other children so that the interaction was maintained.

**Reinforcers.** Any event or stimulus that follows a response and is found to have increased the likelihood that that response will occur again is called a **reinforcer.** This concept is nontheoretical. That is, the reinforcer is discovered empirically by its effects on the behavior in question. In principle, the determination of a reinforcer for the response we wish to produce in a particular person is based on trial and error. Sometimes we may have clues about where to begin searching for a reinforcer from the general culture in which we are working. In our culture, money or approval will probably work. In a rat's culture, food pellets are likely to work better. But in dealing with one specific individual we must sometimes go beyond the culture and examine the individual's life history for clues about what will be reinforcing. Once we find a reinforcer, we can begin to exert the control necessary to regulate the individual's behavior. An example of how this works is presented in Box 9-1.

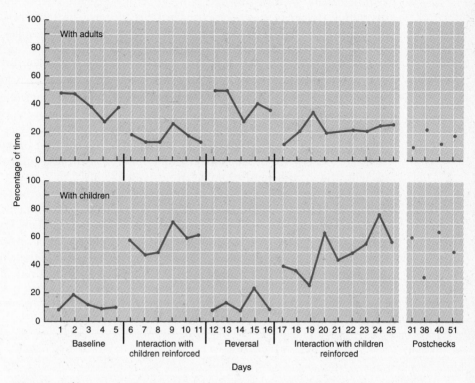

**Figure 9-2**   A graphic representation of Ann's behavior. The percent of time Ann spent interacting with adults is shown in the upper panel; the lower panel depicts her interaction with other children.

Schedules of Reinforcement. The world is not organized so that every response is reinforced. This is true in everyday life when, for example, children seek approval from their parents for picking up their room and the parents are too busy to notice. It is also true in research settings when a delivery system jams and rats are not given pellets on schedule. Skinner began to think about **schedules of reinforcement** when he decided that he would rather reinforce his rats less frequently for the desired response than spend all day manufacturing food pellets. This initiated a series of studies that culminated in a book on schedules of reinforcement (Ferster and Skinner, 1957).

The effects of various schedules or patterns of reinforcement on behavior is one of the most intensely studied issues in operant psychology. At one extreme is **continuous reinforcement,** which occurs when every response is reinforced, that is, when reinforcement occurs 100 percent of the time. At the other extreme is no reinforcement, when a response is never reinforced. In between these extremes are various forms of intermittent or **partial reinforcement**. It might seem that the effectiveness of reinforcement would range from none under conditions of no reinforcement to greatest under conditions of continuous reinforcement. However, it was discovered that partial reinforcement schedules of learning are more effective than continuous schedules at maintaining a response even after a fairly lengthy period of nonreinforcement. For example, if I learn that smiling at people on the street is frequently but not always followed by a smile in return (partial reinforcement), I will continue to smile at strangers for a long time, even after I move to another part of the country where smiles hardly ever bring a response. In Table 9-2, several of the more common reinforcement schedules are described and illustrated with some examples from everyday life.

Schedules of reinforcement are most easily identified and studied under controlled laboratory conditions. However, these schedules are thought to apply to nearly all of our activities, including behaviors that indicate personality characteristics. The father who will not attend to his child during a televised football game is placing the child on a fixed-interval schedule. But if the child is active, demanding, and persistent, then a ratio schedule of some sort may develop. The

〄 **Table 9-2**

Schedules of Partial Reinforcement

| Schedule | Description | Ilustration |
|---|---|---|
| Fixed-interval | Reinforcement is given for responses after a specified time interval has passed. | Paid once a week, the worker continues working throughout the work week. However, the pace of the work usually accelerates on payday and then decreases thereafter. |
| Fixed-ratio | Reinforcement is given after a specified number of responses are made. | In industry, workers are paid on a piecework basis. Theoretically, the workers will produce numerous pieces to increase their wages. |
| Variable-interval | Interval between reinforced responses varies, but on the average, reinforcement occurs after a specified interval (e.g., every 2 minutes). | On a fishing boat, the crew is rewarded, on the average, with a catch every 45 minutes. But sometimes the interval is 5 minutes and at other times 2 days. |
| Variable-ratio | Reinforcement is given, on the average, after some specified number of responses. | The slot machine pays off, on the average, every tenth play. But sometimes it may take only 5 plays and at other times 15 plays. |

Source: After *Abnormal Psychology* by M. Duke and S. Nowicki, Jr. Copyright 1979 by Wadsworth Publishing Company, Inc. Reprinted by permission of the publisher, Brooks/Cole Publishing Company, Monterey, California.

child may learn that emitting enough demanding behavior will be rewarded with the father's attention. In any case, stable patterns of behavior that might result in the characterization of the child as "demanding" are established by a schedule of reward.

**Secondary Reinforcement.** **Primary reinforcers** are necessities such as food or water. Neutral stimuli consistently paired with a primary reinforcer will become reinforcers in their own right. **Secondary reinforcers** eventually may have as much or more influence on human behavior as primary reinforcers. A host of secondary reinforcers can develop and can include smiles, compliments, money, awards, grades, and recognition.

Some secondary reinforcers are associated with more than one kind of primary reinforcement. For example, a mother's presence may become associated with the satisfaction of hunger, reduction in physical discomfort, and other pleasant experiences. This is an example of a **generalized reinforcer**—a reinforcer that does not depend solely on one drive state. Money is another example because it is associated with nearly all primary reinforcers such as physical comfort, food, and drink.

Secondary reinforcers can also be **chained**. That is, secondary reinforcers can produce additional secondary reinforcers through pairing. Mother is associated with hunger reduction, then perhaps mother also becomes associated with music, and so music is now a secondary reinforcer. Music, in turn, becomes associated with a group of friends, which takes on reinforcing properties—and on and on. The process of chaining accounts for the complex system of reinforcers in every person's life.

**Shaping.** Before reinforcement can act on behavior, that behavior must be emitted. So, how do we learn complicated behavior that consists of many separate responses and actions and thus, in total, has never occurred before? In addressing this issue, Skinner discovered what every good animal trainer knows: you **shape** the behavior— that is, behavior is gradually molded into the desired form. This is done by reinforcing some responses and not others and by **successive approximation**—reinforcing those responses that progressively bring the animal closer and closer to the desired behavior.

Suppose you wish to train a rat to dance—hardly a normal behavior for the rat. You might begin by pairing food and a "click" so that the latter becomes a secondary reinforcer. Clicks are easier to administer than food as the rat moves about. Now, when the rat looks up, you reward it with the clicking noise. Next, you reward it with the click only when it really stretches its head upward and, eventually, only when it rears up on its hind legs. Then, you reward it for taking steps to the right; then to the left. When you are done, you have a dancing rat!

The same principle works for humans, and it is how we learn complex skills and behaviors. Sometimes it happens haphazardly and inefficiently. But when the technology of shaping is carefully harnessed, it can become a potent method for producing desired behaviors. Hergenhahn (1972) provided an illustration of how reading can be shaped in a young child:

1. Have many children's books available and leave them where the child is likely to see them.
2. If a child avoids books, reward activities related to reading such as noticing signs or naming and/or labeling objects.
3. As the activities in 2 are rewarded, the child will tend to do them more often, and when the child does, one must become more rigorous in what is expected before giving additional rewards, for example, reading longer signs and attending to more detailed labels.
4. A next step could be to ask the child to get you certain books, such as the red one, the one with the duck on the cover, the one with the ABCs on it. When the child does, a reward is given.
5. The next step involves getting the child still more involved with the book, for example, asking the child to find certain pictures. Again, the child is rewarded in some way for doing this.
6. The above process is continued and refined until the child is reading without your prompts.
7. To maintain this interest in reading once it has been brought about through these procedures, it is important to continue rewarding the child even after the child has begun reading, at least to begin with. Eventually, the content of the stories will begin to be enough of a reward to maintain the child's interest in reading. (pp. 40–41)

## Structure of Personality

Skinner was not concerned with describing the structure of personality; he considered personality to be at best an unnecessary concept, and at worst to serve only to obstruct and confuse the one legitimate concern of psychologists: the modification of behavior. Skinner's interest was mainly in modifiable behavior and the environmental events that control it. His contention was that ego, trait, and mind are unnecessary concepts and that he could, with his operant methods alone, do an acceptable job of prediction and control.

## The Idiographic Method

For Skinner, personality was a collection of behavior patterns that are distinctive and allow us to easily recognize one person from another. The approach to studying personality was the intensive idiographic analysis of the individual's history of reinforcement. Personality, then, is the distinct pattern of relations between an individual's behavior and its reinforcement consequences. The pattern will be different for each person, even though the principles of learning by which the pattern was acquired apply to everyone. These patterns are revealed not by projective tests and the like but by an intensive behavioral analysis. An individual's unique genetic background combines with an equally distinctive set of environmental conditions to produce a personality or pattern of behavior.

## Development of Personality

Skinner believed that the principles of learning were the basis of the development of personality and social behavior in humans. He saw no need to treat these behaviors as any different from the behaviors of a pigeon in a laboratory. Of course, it may be more difficult to identify exactly what the social stimuli are in a given situation or even what may be serving as secondary reinforcers. It is easier with rats—we can use food pellets or clicks that have been linked with food. Moreover, because we have done the training ourselves, we know exactly what the chain of learning events has been. But though all of this is more difficult and complicated with humans, the process is the same.

**Development of Cooperation.** To illustrate how the development of behaviors normally thought of as belonging to the domain of personality can be explained, let us consider an experiment by Azrin and Lindsley (1956). They took 20 children (ages 7 to 12) and divided them into 10 teams. The 2 children in each team were, in turn, seated on opposite sides of a table. Confronting each child was an apparatus containing three holes and a pencil-like rod that would fit into the holes. If both children placed their rods in the holes directly opposite each other (cooperative response), a red light flashed and a single jelly bean was delivered to the table. When they put their rods in holes not directly opposite (uncooperative response), no reward was forthcoming. All 10 teams learned very quickly to be cooperative, and, almost as quickly, 8 of the teams divided the candy. In the other two cases, one child took all the candy until the other child refused to cooperate. At that point, they came to an understanding and began to divide the candy. This simple laboratory example can provide insight into how a host of responses during childhood can be developed through conditioning.

**The Making of a Worrier.** Suppose a child's parents are anxious and worry about many issues. They worry about whether the doors are locked, the food is possibly tainted, their feet will get wet in the rain, their bowel movements are regular, and on and on. The child notices this. But even more important, that child is probably reinforced for worrying about the same things. The child's request for guidance about wearing galoshes brings approval from the mother. Returning to see whether the garage door is locked prompts a nod of approval from the father. Over time and instances, the child has become a worrier through operant principles. Later, of course, when the child is less supervised by the parents, reinforcement will not be so consistent. Rather, it will be intermittent, and this will retard the extinction of worrying. Perhaps another child with a similar reinforcement history has developed the ability to discriminate among cues. Such a child may be free from worry when outside the home only to become a worrier once more when interacting with the parents at home.

## Nature of Adjustment

For the behaviorist, maladjusted behavior is not the product of an underlying disease, nor is it a bizarre outgrowth of warfare among the id, the ego, and the superego. Maladjusted behavior is simply a failure to make appropriate responses (Ullmann and Krasner, 1975). Inappropriate responses are learned in the same manner as appropriate ones. Maladjustment is not a set of symptoms brought about by some underlying disease process. Instead, certain individuals either learn to make responses that are inappropriate in specific situations or never learn to make the appropriate response. Thus, they develop a faulty conditioning history. Sometimes this history is only mildly faulty, resulting in neurotic behavior. In other cases there have been gross distortions in learning, resulting in psychosis.

According to Davison and Neale (1990), the behavioral perspective has several important implications on adjustment. First, the influence of physiological factors on maladjustment is seen as minimal. The focus is on what and how the individual has learned. Second, the gap between normal and abnormal behavior is narrow because both develop by the same process. Third, adjustment becomes a relative concept. What is normal depends on the cultural milieu and its values. Shoplifting on the part of a wealthy executive is maladjusted; that same shoplifting by a 15-year-old gang member is probably reflective of the learned values shared by the gang.

A good example of the behavioral approach to maladjustment is an explanation of school phobias. A child, for a variety of reasons, may not want to go to school. Perhaps the child fears other children at school; perhaps a younger sibling at home is seen as a rival for the mother's attention. For operant theorists, however, the causes mediating such fears are largely irrelevant. What happens, they assert, is that certain behaviors such as reporting an upset stomach or a headache, or expressing anxiety over a long bus ride, bring about certain outcomes. The parents reward such responses by allowing the child to remain at home, and a learned connection is formed. The phobic reactions occur because of the rewarding consequences of their expression.

In general, the operant approach emphasizes several factors in the production of maladjusted behavior. There can be **behavioral deficits** brought about by poor reinforcement histories. This often translates into inadequate socialization, which then prevents the individual from coping adequately with environmental demands. In other cases, it seems that the schedule of reinforcement is the problem, as in the case of some depressions. The person possesses the correct or desirable responses, but the environment does not reinforce them properly. In still other instances, there seems to be a failure in the **discrimination of cues;** that is, individuals do not pay attention to the environment is the same way as most people. Perhaps this is because the proper cues have become associated with punishment, while the improper ones lead to reward. This is sometimes said to occur with schizophrenics and other psychotics. For example, a schizophrenic may have learned long ago that paying attention to people leads to rejection and heartache. But paying attention to inanimate objects avoids this pain of rejection and is, therefore, rewarding. What appears to be bizarre behavior would become clear if only we understood the person's complete reinforcement history. Finally, some individuals have acquired an **inappropriate set of responses,** that is, responses that are unproductive or idiosyncratic. The neurotic who compulsively counts heartbeats does so because the act is rewarded by preventing unpleasant thoughts. One cannot count and think of other things at the same time. Thus, absorption in counting is reinforcing even though it may appear bizarre.

## The Reinforcement Theory of Dollard and Miller

Behaviorism and psychoanalysis are often viewed as antagonistic theoretical systems. For behaviorally oriented psychologists, psychoanalysis contains two fatal flaws. First, it is presented in such vague language that it is not possible to design meaningful measures of many of its constructs. Second, unambiguous predictions of behavior are difficult to derive from the theory. John Dollard and Neal Miller (see Brief Biography on pages 306–307) understood psychoanalysis and knew that for all its flaws, it was based on a rich store of astute observations of human behavior. They attempted to summarize and present these observations within a framework that was acceptable to behavioral psychologists. The framework they chose was the learning theory of Clark Hull.

Drawing upon Hullian learning theory, psychoanalytic theory, and social anthropology, Dollard and Miller developed a theory about the ways habits develop in human beings. These **habits** are stable connections between stimulus and response, and Dollard and Miller used them to account for and describe unconscious processes, motives, conflicts, and defenses. They blended the findings from laboratory research on animals with the skilled clinical observations of Freud. Some have dismissed their work as a mere translation of Freudian concepts into more palatable learning terms. But from this "translation" emerged a bridge from the psychodynamics of Freud to learning theory and, ultimately, to social learning theory, which has become a powerful influence on contemporary personality research.

### From Animal Behavior to Human Personality

The research from which many of Dollard and Miller's ideas were derived was carried out with animals. Relative to humans, rats are simple organisms. Therefore, it is possible to observe features of their behavior that are difficult to disentangle from the greater complexity of human behavior. Rats are easier to manipulate and study because they can be placed in more controlled environments for longer periods of time than human subjects. They also can be selectively bred to

## BRIEF BIOGRAPHIES OF

# John Dollard and Neal Miller

Because of their collaborative work on learning and imitation, John Dollard and Neal Miller are often linked. Dollard was born in 1900 in Menasha, Wisconsin, and died in 1980. His undergraduate work was done at the University of Wisconsin, and he received his Ph.D. in sociology from the University of Chicago in 1931. Neal Miller was born in 1909 in Milwaukee, Wisconsin. He attended the University of Washington and was awarded the Ph.D. in psychology in 1935 from Yale University.

Dollard became an assistant professor of anthropology at Yale University in 1931. A year later he joined the Institute of Human Relations at Yale as an assistant professor of sociology. He maintained his affiliation with Yale and the Institute until his retirement in 1969. Miller was appointed to the same Institute at Yale in 1936. During World War II, Miller directed an Army Air Force research project. He rejoined Yale in 1946 and in 1952 became the James Rowland Angell Professor of Psychology. In 1966 he moved from Yale to Rockefeller University as professor of psychology and head of the Laboratory of Physiological Psychology. Neal Miller has received numerous honors for his work. For example, he was elected to the National Academy of Sciences (a prestigious honor), served as president of the American Psychological Association, was a recipient of the Warren Medal from the Society of Experimental Psychologists, and was awarded the President's Medal of Science.

While at Yale, Dollard and Miller began their collaboration, which has so influenced psychology. Dollard brought to this joint effort an anthropo-

control for individual differences that are influenced by genetics. Although the implications of the results of animal research for human personality are limited and must be generalized cautiously, animal research can be a useful tool for evaluating some hypotheses whose validity can later be checked with humans.

Consider the following classic experiment on learning in the rat. A rat is placed in a white compartment whose floor contains an electrified grid that allows us to deliver a painful shock to the rat (Miller, 1948). Adjacent to the white compartment is a black one. The compartments are separated by an open door. Placed in the white compartment, our rat shows no fear. But now we begin to shock it. Very quickly it learns to flee through the door and escape into the black compartment. In a short time, it learns to escape from the white area as soon as it is placed in it. Later, we note that the rat will show all the signs of fear when placed in the white compartment even though we have stopped administering shock. Despite the lack of shock, our rat continues to run to the black area.

logical-sociological perspective. Miller contributed an approach from experimental psychology. Beyond that, they shared a psychoanalytic viewpoint. Dollard had been trained in psychoanalysis at the Berlin Psychoanalytic Institute, and Miller underwent a training analysis at the Vienna Institute of Psychoanalysis. So it was that in the stimulating environment of the Institute of Human Relations, they were able to fuse their interests in psychoanalysis, Hullian learning theory, and social interactions into a provocative new theory of personality development.

Although both Dollard and Miller published numerous writings separately, they are best known for their collaborative efforts. They, along with several other members of the Institute of Human Relations, published a 1939 monograph called *Frustration and Aggression*. In 1941, Miller and Dollard's *Social Learning and Imitation* appeared, and in 1950, Dollard and Miller's *Personality and Psychotherapy*.

Interestingly, an observer who was unaware of the events that led to the development of the rat's habit would find it difficult to explain the animal's behavior and would probably label it as "irrational." Why should the rat run from an innocuous compartment? Had that observer been present from the beginning, however, the behavior would have appeared perfectly reasonable—a logical outcome of the rat's experience. There is a parallel with those who find a neurotic's behavior to be silly or unreasonable. You have to be there from the beginning to appreciate the full meaning of what appears to be unreasonable behavior. An example of this at the human level is shown in Box 9-2.

## Basic Concepts of Reinforcement Theory

The Four Fundamentals.  Dollard and Miller (1950) argued that the simple experiment with the rat illustrates the **four fundamentals of learning**, which apply as

## BOX 9-2
## A Pilot's Phobia

Phobias are learned, just like any other behaviors. During Desert Storm, a pilot flew a dangerous mission. While on the way to attack a key airfield near Baghdad, the pilot and his squadron came under heavy enemy antiaircraft fire. In addition, he had to fly at rooftop level toward the targets. Some oil tanks exploded, and several planes disappeared in the wall of flame. Managing to get through all this, the pilot had to return at reduced speed because of aircraft damage. He was subjected to repeated enemy fighter attacks and eventually had to ditch the plane in the Mediterranean. After drifting in an open life raft, he was eventually rescued. Prior to this mission, the pilot had shown no evidence of any fear of airplanes. Yet shortly after returning to his base, he began to exhibit all the classic signs of a phobia. He was now frightened to death of airplanes. Why?

Dollard and Miller's reinforcement theory can provide an explanation of the pilot's fear. During the mission, the pilot was exposed to terrifying and fear-provoking stimuli such as explosions, fire, and the death of comrades. Cues present in the situation at the time became associated with the intense fear. The plane, the sound of engines, and even images of or thoughts about the plane and the mission came to evoke fear. A drive of intense fear, then, had been learned in response to these cues. But unfortunately, such a fear does not remain confined to one specific set of cues. It generalizes to other, similar cues and situations. So it was with the pilot. Being near other planes, thinking of planes, being asked about flying were all cues that served to stimulate fear and panic.

But we learn that as we move away from a feared event, the fear tends to diminish. Therefore, our pilot quickly discovered that he felt better when he avoided planes. When he talked about flying, the old anxiety returned; when he changed the topic of conversation, the anxiety lessened. These and other avoidance responses became learned as habits. Whatever reduced his fear became a learned avoidance response.

This analysis illustrates how learning can shape personality functions. However, some might argue that something is still missing in this case of the pilot. Why, for instance, did not every pilot react to such experiences with a phobia? Were there ingredients in the specific flight experiences that were different for those who became phobic, compared with those who did not? Or are we back with the familiar personality theme? That is, can we ignore preexisting personality differences in our learning explanations?

Based on Dollard and Miller, *Personality and Psychotherapy* (New York: McGraw-Hill, 1950).

much to human behavior as they do to the rat's behavior. Miller and Dollard (1941) proposed that "to learn one must want something, notice something, do something, and get something" (p. 2). This progression becomes clear as we contemplate our rat's behavior. It *wanted* something: escape from the pain it was experiencing. Among other things, it *noticed* the adjoining black compartment. It *did* something when it ran through the open door and into the black compartment. By doing this, it *got* something, namely, relief from a painful shock. This demonstration illustrates four basic aspects of learning: drive, cue, response, and reward.

**Drives** are strong internal stimuli that impel the organism to action. They may be innate (primary drives, e.g., hunger, thirst, pain) or they may be learned (secondary drives, e.g., fear, guilt, need for approval). But whether a **drive** is primary or secondary, it has the same effect—it energizes the organism.

**Cues** are stimuli that determine what response the organism will make, when it will be made, and where it will be made. **Cues** may be external events or stimuli, or they may be internal stimuli. Drives not only energize but can also serve as cues. Any stimulus, either internal or external, that the organism can distinguish from another stimulus is capable of acting as a cue.

For a **response** to be reinforced, it must first occur. But if learning can take place only if a response is reinforced, how is it that responses occur initially? It must be that certain responses will occur prior to any reinforcement. Dollard and Miller suggest that an organism's responses can be ranked into an **initial hierarchy**. This hierarchy reflects how innate responses vary in their probability of occurrence. What learning does is alter the rank order of response hierarchies. For example, a response rather weak in its initial potential for occurrence may become more likely to occur after learning has taken place.

**Reward** is the fourth basic factor of learning and is defined as anything that increases the probability of a given response to a particular stimulus or cue. Responses that reduce the strength of a drive will gain in their potential for occurrence the next time that the cue or circumstances are similar.

**Liberalization of Stimulus–Response.** Applying Dollard and Miller's concepts of drive, cue, response, and reward to the rat is straightforward. But as we move to the pilot's case the analysis becomes less objective and precise. Stimuli are not just observed explosions; they are also internal thoughts about planes and memories of a distant terror. Likewise, responses are not merely avoiding airplanes; they also refer to subtly changing a conversation or changing one's unobserved thoughts. By broadening the definition of what constitutes a stimulus and a response, Dollard and Miller transformed learning theory from a set of concepts that seemed to explain only the trivial behaviors of simple organisms to one that has meaning and application to human personality. Naturally, the fundamentalists claimed that the loss in the precision and direct observability of the definitions of stimulus and response put learning theory in the same predicament as psychoanalytic theory—it became imprecise and more difficult to evaluate. However, it also broadened the scope of traditional learning theory so that it could be applied to more complex and interesting human behaviors.

**Extinction: When Reinforcement Fails.** If a certain behavior is going to occur, it must continue to be reinforced when it is expressed. **Extinction** is the reduction and eventual disappearance of a response that results from the continued absence of reinforcement. For example, when you were a child your parents may have stopped paying attention to you when you were showing off. Eventually you got bored and stopped. But assuming that attention from others is a strong drive, you as a child were faced with a problem: how to satisfy the attention drive. It is out of such problems that new learning arises. You may have eventually tried a new response that again got your parents' attention. Of course, it may have been a desirable form of new learning (e.g., studying and doing well in school) or an undesirable one (e.g., whacking your younger brother until someone paid attention and made you stop). In any event, changes in behavior occur in the face of our failures to achieve drive reduction by using an old response.

Sometimes a behavior is resistant to extinction. Many conditions may account for such a strong habit, including the strength of the drive, how often the response has been rewarded in the past, how satisfying the rewards have been, and the availability of alternative responses. Also important is the schedule of reinforcement. As Skinner found, many behaviors are difficult to extinguish because they are partially reinforced.

**Importance of Learned Drives.** Another important contribution of Dollard and Miller was showing how learned drives (secondary drives) develop. In complex societies, behavior is not strongly regulated by primary reinforcements such as food and water, except under dire circumstances. Our lives are shaped through the pursuit of such goals as prestige, happiness, and wealth. How this comes about is, in principle, no different from the experience of the rat in the shock compartment. In the rat's case, fear was learned as a response to a previously neutral set of cues, and escape from these cues was a learned response calculated to lead to a reduction in fear. The fundamental argument that Dollard and Miller made is that the acquisition of our most civilized and sophisticated drives arises out of the early satisfaction of primary drives.

How is it, for example, that children come to love their mothers, seek approval from them, or strive to be near them? Dollard and Miller would claim that any stimulus or cue associated frequently with the satisfaction of a primary drive will eventually itself become a secondary reinforcement. For a child, the sight, feel, smell, and touch of the mother are discernible cues that occur repeatedly in direct connection with the satisfaction of hunger and the relief from various physical discomforts. The association is learned. And once learned, the sight of the mother and her presence will become powerful reinforcements to be sought independently of their connection to food and comfort. According to this analysis, then, there is no reason why other learned drives or motives such as status, money, or dependency cannot be traced to an early association with primary-drive reduction. Of course, the chain of events and associations is a complex one that offers challenging problems for those who would trace the origins of secondary drives. But in principle tracing those origins is possible.

There are two interesting facets of secondary drives. First, when secondary drives repeatedly fail to be reinforced, they become weaker. This is in contrast to primary drives. For example, frequent nonreinforcement of the thirst drive would likely increase our efforts to find water. But repeatedly finding that our achievements fail to impress our parents will often teach us to decrease our efforts in this direction. However, some behaviors in pursuit of secondary reinforcements are sometimes persistent and do not weaken quickly.

This brings us to the second point, which is an observation about the strength of certain secondary drives. It is paradoxical that some secondary drives, even though they developed from an early association with the satisfaction of hunger, thirst, and need for physical comfort, may later persist even in the face of the threat of starvation or excruciating pain. For example, the value of truth and integrity may become so strong that even the prospect of death will not deter some individuals from maintaining them. Fragile learned associations can become more powerful than some primary drives.

**Stimulus Generalization.** Long before Dollard and Miller, psychologists recognized that responses learned in connection with one stimulus will also occur in relation to other, physically similar stimuli. This is called **stimulus generalization**. In addition, the more the second stimulus is like the first one, the more probable it is that generalization will take place. So it is that behaviors, emotions, thoughts, or attitudes learned in one situation will occur in other situations that are similar.

Another kind of generalization is particularly important to humans. It is called **mediated stimulus generalization** and refers to those instances in which a response learned in one setting generalizes to another setting because the latter is classified or labeled as similar to the first. The similarity is not, however, always obvious. Consider a person who is taught that all Russians are untrustworthy. Upon meeting someone who is introduced as Russian, the person immediately responds with distrust. Generalization here is not based upon any physical similarity among Russians. Rather, the generalization is mediated by the label *Russian*.

Language, then, produces cues that can facilitate generalization across physically dissimilar situations. Such **cue-producing responses** can also facilitate discrimination among situations that may otherwise seem similar. This cue-producing role of language is also important in arousing drives. Thus, a male may become more easily sexually aroused in the presence of a female labeled as "responsive" than by one who is physically similar but thought to be "cold." Language can likewise influence our behavior in the present by allowing us to think of its future consequences. I can decide that the drudgery of studying is worthwhile because it will pay off three years in the future and that the joy of reading novels every night is unwise because it may have negative consequences for projected goals.

Labeling, imagining, planning, and reasoning are all important cue-producing responses that enable us to think our way through life rather than having to deal with every problem on a separate trial-and-error basis. Such cue-producing responses are also what separate the human from the beast. The less able we are to employ these mediating processes, the more likely it is that we will have adjustment problems, suffer disappointments, or become the captives of events rather than their masters. By introducing these ideas, Miller and Dollard were trying to reconcile learning theory with human cognitive behavior. Many had previously thought that learning theory was helpful in explaining the viscerally dominated behavior of laboratory animals but almost irrelevant to the complex behavior of humans, who depend so much on higher mental processes. Miller and Dollard attempted to alter this conception.

## Structure of Personality

Dollard and Miller never had any intention of trying to describe personality structure, identify traits, or otherwise catalog enduring personality characteristics. Rather, they were concerned with the *process* of learning. They described the processes through which human behavior is acquired and changed. The closest they came to a basic structural element was habit, and their view of personality was similar to Watson's diagram, shown in Figure 9-1. The conditions that facilitate the acquisition of these associations or that subsequently extinguish them are the focus of Dollard and Miller's theory.

## Development of Personality

The Basic Characteristics of the Infant.  First, each infant is endowed with a set of **specific reflexes** that make it responsive to a very narrow range of stimuli in any given situation. Second, there are **innate response hierarchies.** On an innate basis, certain responses are more likely to occur in a specific situation than are other responses. Third, there is the usual set of **primary drives.** The infant with these three rather limited features moves from an initial primitive state to a complex adult through learning. Through the ever-present mechanism of drive reduction, existing responses become attached to new stimuli, new responses are reinforced, secondary motives arise out of primary ones, and higher mental processes flourish through mediated stimulus generalization. It is through these processes multiplied by a million occasions that the human organism becomes an adult.

But any learning process occurs in a context. Without knowing the cultural environment and the family milieu, one cannot predict the outcome or content of a person's learning. Whether a child learns to be aggressive or passive is not inherent in the learning process but rather is determined by what reinforcements the environment provides. Germans, Australians, and Japanese each learn different responses. My child's learning is different from that of any other child. However, everyone learns according to the same rules.

Four Critical Training Situations.  Not unlike Freud, Dollard and Miller discuss four sets of early social situations important for the learning that shapes adult personality. The child is helpless in these situations. Children are at the mercy of adults, so what the child learns depends heavily upon the training situations provided by those adults.

First, there is the **feeding situation,** where much initial learning occurs. For example, if children are not fed when they cry but are left to "cry themselves out," the foundation may be laid for the creation of apathy or apprehensiveness. On the other hand, a pleasant feeding situation can be the basis for subsequent feelings of sociability and love. At the same time, an infant who is fed when not hungry may never truly learn to appreciate the full value of food rewards, and thus little association between gratification and the presence of the mother will develop. This may retard the growth of social feeling. The child who often experiences hunger while alone will learn to fear being alone and may come to desire obsessively the presence of others. Weaning can also be fraught with difficulties and pain. The nature of these initial learning experiences helps determine the degree of conflicts that may arise later. This is what Dollard and Miller call the "secret learning of the early years."

Next, there is **cleanliness training**. Learning to control the processes of urination and defecation is a complex and difficult task. But this learning is important to many parents. When the child has accidents and is punished, he or she may develop a learned association between parents and punishment. Avoiding the parents can then become an anxiety-reducing response. In other cases, children may get the feeling that they are pursued by all-seeing parents who can literally read their minds. In the face of such superior odds, the child may become excessively conforming. All of this is an example of how Dollard and Miller reworked the observations of Freud into a learning framework.

**Early sex training** is another potential source of conflicts. Taboos on masturbation can result in the parents inculcating in the child severe anxiety over sexuality. Sex-typing begins at an early age and provides a context in which to learn the taboo on homosexuality.

Another set of conditions can provoke **anger-anxiety conflicts.** Parents often become upset when their child exhibits angry behavior. They punish such behavior in various ways, and the child may, as a consequence, learn to suppress anger. As Dollard and Miller (1950) put it, "Robbing a person of his anger completely may be a dangerous thing since some capacity for anger seems to be needed in the affirmative personality" (p. 149).

## Nature of Adjustment

Types of Conflict. Dollard and Miller share with psychoanalytic theory the view that conflict is an essential feature of maladjusted behavior. On the basis of animal research, Dollard and Miller identified three types of conflict situations. When two positive motives are in conflict (e.g., watch an exciting TV program or go to an equally exciting movie), they classified it as an **approach-approach conflict. Avoidance-avoidance conflicts** confront the person with two equally negative possibilities (e.g., mow the grass or wash the car). A third situation is the **approach-avoidance conflict** (e.g., a student is angry over receiving a D on a term paper; should that anger be expressed [approached], thereby satisfying a motive, or will doing so result in retaliation from the instructor [something to be avoided because it might prevent the satisfaction of another motive—getting a decent grade for the course?]). Dollard and Miller proposed five principles for predicting the outcome of these conflict situations:

> One's tendency to approach a positive goal becomes stronger the closer one is to that goal.
>
> One's tendency to avoid a negative goal becomes stronger the closer one is to that goal.
>
> The tendency to avoid a negative goal is stronger than the corresponding tendency to approach a positive goal.
>
> An increase in drive strength will increase the tendency to approach or avoid a particular goal.
>
> Whenever there are two competing responses, the stronger will win out.

Figure 9-3 is a representation of an approach-avoidance conflict.

**The Unconscious.** Neurotic behavior entails the individual's search for ways to resolve or minimize conflict. But much of that conflict is not consciously recognized. For example, an individual does not know that an obsessive preoccupa-

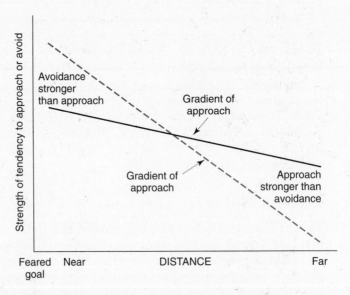

**Figure 9-3** ⬡ Representation of an approach-avoidance conflict.

tion about orderliness is an unconscious way of masking hostile thoughts that would provoke considerable anxiety were they conscious. For Dollard and Miller, the unconscious can also be understood using learning theory. As Levy (1970) puts it, "They conceive of the unconscious as the equivalent of the unlabeled" (p. 400). Labels are cue-producing responses, and an absence of labels cuts down the degree to which our own thought processes can monitor and control unconscious events. This is one reason why neurotics are so often unable to understand the nature of their own behavior—why it fails to make sense to them. Similarly, Dollard and Miller regard **repression** as "stopping thinking," even though most of us are not accustomed to regard "not thinking" as a response. But it can be viewed that way. When it is, repression becomes a learned inhibition about thinking of events that stimulate strong anxiety or guilt. The "not thinking" response is reinforced because it leads to anxiety reduction. In Box 9-3 some behavioral analyses of other defense mechanisms are presented.

**How a Neurosis Is Learned: A Case Example.** Dollard and Miller (1950) argued that neuroses are learned, and they described a case to illustrate how this learning occurs. That case also shows how directly removing a symptom without attacking its cause will increase drive which, in turn, produces a dilemma for the patient. Current behavior therapists might, however, disagree. They tend to argue that the symptom is the problem, and its removal will not necessitate resolving some presumed unconscious conflict. In any event, the case in question involved Mrs. C and her fear of sex. Mrs. C had not really wanted to marry but did so only to escape her mother. After marriage her aversion to sexual intercourse became extreme, and she hated being "touched" by her husband. Eventually, she developed a paralysis of the legs. In the words of Dollard and Miller (1950):

> [S]he was shortly brought to the hospital with her legs in an acute spastic condition. She was unable to flex her knees, to walk, or to stand. According to our analysis, this symptom must have been reinforced by the reduction in anxiety that the condition produced by making intercourse impossible. At the time she was brought in, her anxiety level was low; she accepted the symptom and displayed that *belle indifférence* of which Charcot spoke.
>
> The doctors proved that the symptom was not organic. The signs of organic paralysis were not present, and the limbs were freely movable when the patient was under the influence of pentothal. The patient, however, was highly resistant to any explanation of her symptom on the basis of emotional factors. She said it is something "organic, inwardly, not emotional." The fact that the symptom had been producing the kind of reduction in anxiety and conflict that would be expected is demonstrated by the increase in drive that occurred after its removal. Mrs. C was angry at her doctors and suffered an attack of rage at one of the nurses on the very night that she was first convinced she could walk.

BOX 9-3
Dollard and Miller on Defense Mechanisms

### The Explanation for Rationalizations

According to our analysis a rationalization involves the following steps: Social training of the type described [previously] produces a need to have a logical explanation for obvious features of one's behavior and plans; the person tends to feel uneasy in the presence of any behavior that is illogical or unexplained. In some instances, however, the true explanation would provoke anxiety, guilt, or some other drive. Thus the person is motivated to find *some* explanation but to avoid the true one. When he happens to hit upon a rationalization that meets cultural standards of sensibleness, it is reinforced by a reduction in anxiety about unexplained behavior. Furthermore, if some of the sentences that would constitute a true explanation have been tending to come into the subject's mind and elicit anxiety or guilt, the alternative sentences in the rationalization tend to block them out and hence remove the anxiety or guilt that they elicit. When this occurs, it serves as an additional reinforcement. (1950, pp. 177–178)

### An Example of Projection

The subject was homosexually excited by this particular associate. The incipient homosexual responses and thoughts aroused intense anxiety and were repressed. Because of the conflict, the subject felt miserable whenever he was in the presence of the other man and better whenever he avoided him. He reacted to this state of affairs with thoughts such as "I don't know why but I don't like him!" But as long as there was no rational explanation for this behavior, he felt uneasy. In previous situations the dislike had often been mutual and involved aggressive and discriminatory acts on the part of the other person. The thought that the other person disliked him and was persecuting him occurred and was reinforced by the reduction in anxiety it produced through providing a logical explanation. (1950, p. 183)

### An Example of Reaction Formation

For example, as a little girl Mrs. A. hated her mother but was severely punished whenever she expressed her anger in any way. When she apologized by saying that she really loved her mother and by acting like it, the punishment was terminated. In this way, she learned to substitute statements of love for statements of hate. Years later, when she started to hate her mother-in-law, this aroused intense anxiety that could only be reduced by protestations of love. The mechanism was discovered through the fact that Mrs. A. most protested her love just at the time her mother-in-law was treating her in a very nasty way. (1950, p. 184)

The increase in drive motivated the kind of trial and error that almost certainly had occurred and failed to solve her problem before the symptom was learned. When she was released from the hospital and returned to her home, she tried a series of new escape responses. She first considered divorce, but this measure threatened to produce still new conflicts—moral scruples and fears of loss of financial support for herself and children. She went to live with her sister, using the rationalization that she was not yet strong enough to run her own house. This means of escape kept her out of contact with her husband but created problems with her sister's husband and family, so she eventually had to come home. After she came home, Mrs. C refused intercourse with her husband and avoided all occasions when it might occur. Of course, this created problems with him but not sufficiently severe ones to make her willing to risk sex relations. Finally she sought and received contraceptive advice but then did not actually make use of it. Evidently her fears were attached to the sex act as well as to pregnancy, since she was not willing to use contraception to avoid pregnancy while accepting sex relations.

In this case the motivation for the symptom is clear. The fact that it allowed the patient to escape an anxiety-provoking dilemma is clear, but the details of the reinforcement and learning were not observed. After the symptom was removed, it is clear that the patient was put back into a high state of motivation and a severe learning dilemma. (passages excerpted from pp. 169–170)

## Summary

- The origins of the behavioral tradition in personality can be traced to the early conditioning research of Pavlov. However, the founder of behaviorism is generally regarded to be John Watson. Other important learning theorists were Edward Thorndike and his formulation of the law of effect, and Clark Hull, who developed an elegant mathematical-deductive theory.
- B. F. Skinner developed the most extreme form of behaviorism, sometimes refereed to as radical behaviorism. His operant approach made him one of the best-known psychologists of this century. Through a functional analysis of the manner in which responses follow stimuli, he believed we can understand and control all human behavior.
- Skinner's focus was always on operants, that is, behaviors whose frequency of occurrence depends upon their effects on the environment. Other major concepts are discriminative stimuli (stimuli that signal that a given response will likely be rewarded) and reinforcers (events that follow a response and increase the likelihood that the response will occur again).

- Schedules of reinforcement received much attention from Skinner, and his work on intermittent versus continuous reinforcement helped considerably in accounting for how a variety of everyday human behaviors are maintained.
- Skinner described a chaining process whereby secondary reinforcements arise out of associations with primary reinforcements, ultimately creating networks of reinforcers.
- Skinner used the idea of shaping to explain how complex acts are built out of a series of simpler ones. Through reinforcement for successive approximations of the desired behavior, the organism learns complicated skills.
- Although Skinner disdained the personality structures that so many theorists have discussed, he did employ an idiographic method involving the intensive analysis of the reinforcement history of the individual. Personality for the individual thus is the distinct pattern of relations between behavior and its reinforcement consequences.
- Skinner did not discuss personality development because he viewed it as no different from the development of any other pattern of behavior. For example, the development of cooperative behavior is the result of rewards that follow from cooperation.
- In the Skinnerian system, maladjustment is regarded as a failure of the individual to make appropriate responses in a given situation. This may mean either that appropriate responses have not been learned or that inappropriate ones have been reinforced. The focus is on behavior and not on a hypothetical set of underlying symptoms.
- Although Skinner clearly rejected the mediating concepts and personality structures that fascinate so many personologists, his work has had a major impact on the field.
- John Dollard and Neal Miller translated the insights of Freudian theory into a Hullian learning framework and thereby stimulated a whole new generation of personality psychologists.
- For Dollard and Miller, the four fundamentals of the learning situation were drive, cue, response, and reward. These elements can be used to account for the simple behavior of a rat as well as for complex human behavior.
- Through the work of Dollard and Miller, definitions of what constitutes a stimulus and a response were liberalized to encompass complex human behavior. Basic learning concepts such as extinction and partial reinforcement were also expanded to apply to the personality domain.
- Dollard and Miller explained the growth of secondary drives, such as those that result in the pursuit of happiness or wealth, through early associations with primary drives.
- Dollard and Miller used principles such as mediated stimulus generalization and the concept of cue-producing responses to account for such behaviors as thinking, reasoning, and planning.

- Because Dollard and Miller were mainly concerned with the process of learning, they focused little on personality structures except for habit, the learned association between stimulus and response.
- Dollard and Miller did discuss four critical training situations in their analysis of how personality develops. They are the feeding situation, cleanliness training, early sex training, and situations involving anger-anxiety conflicts. Although these are similar to the Freudian developmental stages, their analysis is based on learning theory.
- Dollard and Miller's analysis of conflict relates to the individual's attempts to cope with three types of conflict situations: approach-approach, avoidance-avoidance, and approach-avoidance.
- Another interesting idea of Dollard and Miller was their description of repression as a form of "stopping thinking."
- The discussion of Dollard and Miller's theory ended with a presentation of a case illustrating how a neurosis is learned.

# Chapter 10
# Behaviorism: Therapy, Assessment, and Summary Evaluation

Behavior Therapy
    Counterconditioning
    Systematic Desensitization
    Aversion Therapy
    The Operant Approach
The Engineered Society
Cognition as Behavior
    Cognitive Restructuring
    Stress Inoculation
    The Hidden Goal of Understanding
Behavioral Assessment
    Sign Versus Sample
    SORC Model
    Interviews
    Inventories and Checklists
    Direct Observation
    Controlled Settings
    Role Playing
    Self-Monitoring
Summary Evaluation
    Strengths
    Weaknesses
Summary

One method for testing theories and models of personality is to evaluate the success with which therapeutic techniques derived from these theories are successful at changing behavior. This type of evidence gives impressive support for behavioristic theories. Of course, demonstrating that behavioral techniques influence behavior is not proof that the behavioral theories are either necessary or sufficient for explaining human behavior. But, such evidence is consistent with behavioral theory and suggests that it has some utility.

Many approaches to therapy emphasize verbal transactions between therapist and client. In contrast, the behavioral tradition, with its emphasis on external, environmental factors as the basis for predicting, influencing, and presumably understanding behavior, results in a different approach to therapy and behavior change. This approach deemphasizes internal, person-oriented variables and focuses directly on the undesirable behavior: behavior that, in turn becomes the target of a variety of methods of conditioning and relearning.

## Behavior Therapy

Dollard and Miller are credited with providing the foundation for behavior therapy. For Dollard and Miller, ridding neurotics of their problems is straightforward. If neurotic behavior is learned, it can be unlearned according to the same principles by which it was acquired. Just as bad tennis habits can be broken by a good coach, they argue, so too can bad mental or emotional habits be corrected by a good therapist.

The contribution of these two men lies not in any therapeutic innovations but in their use of learning theory to explain traditional psychotherapy. For example, the sympathetic, understanding therapist becomes a source of reinforcement, and the patient behaves, at least verbally, in ways that elicit the rewarding approval of the therapist. Because the therapist does not reward the expression of neurotic anxiety, emotions, and guilt in the therapy room, these neurotic symptoms will often eventually be extinguished. Although Dollard and Miller did not develop any new therapeutic techniques, their reconceptualization of psychotherapy as implicit learning led others to develop therapeutic techniques that explicitly used classical conditioning and general stimulus-response theory.

### Counterconditioning

A distressed mother once remarked: "I don't understand it. Most kids see a puppy and they want to pick him up. But my son only wants to run away!" In the language of learning, what the mother wants is that her son make a different response to a particular stimulus. The technique of **counterconditioning** was developed to accomplish this goal. It is the conditioning of a desirable response, incompatible with the undesirable one, that now occurs to a given stimulus. This mother must get her son to approach rather than avoid puppies. If she can get him to approach a puppy, the problem is solved because approach and avoidance are incompatible responses; the son cannot run toward and away from the puppy at the same time

Mary Cover Jones has been called the "mother of behavior therapy" (Mussen and Eichorn, 1988). In 1924 she provided an excellent clinical example of counterconditioning. A three-year-old boy, Peter, was afraid of rats, rabbits, and related objects. To eliminate the fear, Jones began bringing a caged rabbit closer and closer to the boy as he was eating. The feared rabbit thus became associated with food, and after a few months Peter's fear of the rabbit disappeared. Of course, Jones recognized that counterconditioning can work in reverse and warned that fear of the rabbit must not be so intense that the child develops an aversion to food.

## Systematic Desensitization

Some years later, Joseph Wolpe (1958) used a similar technique with phobic patients. The idea is that an individual cannot be simultaneously anxious and relaxed. Therefore, if we can get the individual to relax in the face of a previously anxiety-producing stimulus, we will have solved the phobic problem. In effect, the person is **systematically desensitized** to the fearful stimulus by virtue of having experienced or confronted it in a relaxed state.

To employ systematic desensitization, the clinician first examines the patient's complaints and background data to identify the problem. Next, the nature of the problem, how it developed, and how it can be changed are all carefully laid out in learning terms that the patient can understand. The actual desensitization procedures are illustrated in Box 10-1.

## Aversion Therapy

In **aversion therapy,** negative feelings or reactions are induced to a stimulus that is regarded as attractive by the individual but is viewed as undesirable by society. As Wolpe (1973) says, "Aversion therapy consists, operationally, of administering an aversive stimulus to inhibit an unwanted emotional response, thereby diminishing its habit strength" (p. 216). Over the years, many forms of aversion therapy have been used. For example, to reduce the attractiveness of alcohol, patients are given a drug that produces nausea or vomiting. Then they are given a drink. Soon these patients become quite ill. The combination of drug and alcohol is given for seven to ten days, and eventually the sight or smell of alcohol is enough to induce vomiting or nausea—a simple example of classical conditioning.

Aversion therapy is controversial. First, there are issues of human dignity and whether people can ethically be punished for what amounts to undesirable behavior as defined by someone else. Second, there is evidence that the improvements brought about by aversion techniques do not produce lasting behavioral

BOX 10-1
## Systematic Desensitization Procedures

The following case example of systematic desensitization procedures was provided by Davison and Neale (1990):

The thirty-five-year-old substitute mail carrier who consulted us had dropped out of college sixteen years ago because of crippling fears of being criticized. Earlier, his disability had taken the form of extreme tension when faced with tests and speaking up in class. When we saw him, he was debilitated by fears of criticism in general and by evaluation of his mail-sorting performance in particular. As a consequence, his everyday activities were severely constricted and, though highly intelligent, he had apparently settled for an occupation that did not promise self-fulfillment.

After agreeing that a reduction in his unrealistic fears would be beneficial, the client was taught over several sessions to relax all the muscles of his body while in a reclining chair. A list of anxiety-provoking scenes was also drawn up in consultation with the client.

You are saying "Good morning" to your boss.

You are standing in front of your sorting bin in the post office, and your supervisor asks why you are so slow.

You are only halfway through your route, and it is already 2:00 P.M.

As you are delivering Mrs. McKenzie's mail, she opens her screen door and complains how late you are.

Your wife criticizes you for bringing home the wrong kind of bread.

The officer at the bridge toll gate appears impatient as you fumble in your pocket for the correct change.

These and other scenes were arranged in an anxiety hierarchy, from least to most fear-evoking. Desensitization proper began by instructing the client to relax deeply as he had been taught. Then he was to imagine the easiest item, remaining as relaxed as possible. When he had learned to confront this image without becoming anxious, he went on to the next scene, and so on. After ten sessions the man was able to imagine the most distressing scene in the hierarchy without feeling anxious, and gradually his tension in real life was reduced. (pp. 48–49)

changes outside the therapeutic context. For example, most alcoholics are smart enough to realize that if they stop the ingestion of the nausea-producing drug, nausea will not follow drinking. Human beings are thinking organisms; they are not automatically at the mercy of simple classical conditioning procedures.

## The Operant Approach

Skinner's contribution to behavior therapy is based on his operant theory of behavior. The fundamental principle of operant approaches to therapy is that the goal of therapy is not to remove some inner turmoil. There are no "cures" for behavioral "diseases"; there is only the modification of behavior. According to the ideas of Skinner, the therapist is an engineer of behavior—one who carefully examines the undesirable behavior, analyzes the reinforcements inherent in the situation, and then develops a plan to produce the desired behavior.

Conditioning in the Cafeteria.  In institutions for the severely disturbed, some patients often fail to pick up the proper eating utensils before entering the cafeteria line. As a result, they eat with their fingers, perhaps use only a knife, or do not eat. Many of these patients are so withdrawn that they do not react to verbal or written instructions. To study and solve this problem, Ayllon and Azrin (1964) selected a group of patients who behaved as described here. Their behavioral plan was to reward patients who picked up all three utensils by giving them immediate access to the food line. Likewise, patients who failed to pick up all three would be negatively reinforced by being forced to return to the end of the line (or, if already last, to wait five minutes). To test their plan, Ayllon and Azrin introduced their plan in a series of steps. For the first ten meals, no instructions were provided to the patients, nor were consequences introduced (baseline period). During the next ten meals, instructions to take all three utensils were given, but again, no consequences ensued for either following or not following the instructions. For the next ten meals, the instructions continued to be given, and the planned consequences resulted. Doing as instructed led to immediate access to the food counter; not following instructions meant going to the end of the line.

In the initial period, there was rarely an instance of the correct behavior. The addition of instructions in the second period resulted in 40 percent of the patients selecting the proper utensils, but the behavior was not consistent from day to day. In the third phase, during which proper selections led to immediate entry to the cafeteria counter and improper selection meant the end of the line, correct responses increased to 80 percent over the first four meals. For the fifth meal, the rate was up to 90 percent.

Thus, a simple system of reinforcement led to dramatic improvement of behavior in the cafeteria. The evidence also suggests that placing consequences on the behavior, not simply knowledge of the desired behavior, was the most important component of treatment. It is now common to find operant programs in institutional settings, as they have been shown to facilitate institutional management.

Time-Out.  Another classic example of an operant intervention was reported by Wolf, Risley, and Mees (1964). They describe a case study of an autistic child.

Some common characteristics of **autism** are being absorbed in the self, communicating poorly, showing little interest in others, and the appearance of mental retardation. In addition, this child had severe temper tantrums, and the investigators hypothesized that the tantrums continued because they were rewarded by attention from others. To test this hypothesis, they isolated the child for brief intervals whenever a tantrum began. It took very little time for the behavior to be eliminated. This procedure is called **time-out** because the individual is removed from situations where positive reinforcement from the unwanted behavior is possible. Note that the child continued to be diagnosed as autistic; the behavioral intervention did not change that. However, the goal of the intervention was not to cure autism but to stop the tantrums, and that was accomplished.

**Token Economies.** One of the most successful examples of the operant philosophy is the **token economy**. A token economy is a system of exchange based on plastic "coins" that can be used to buy privileges and desired items in an institutional setting. It is widely used to improve the quality of life of long-term patients in mental hospitals. The most thorough research on the implementation and effectiveness of token economies is the work of Ayllon and Azrin (1968), whose experiments were based on earlier research by Staats and Staats (1963).

The purpose of token economies is to provide explicit rewards whenever patients behave in desirable ways as determined by the staff. For example, behaviors such as making one's bed, washing, and dressing are reinforced. Undesirable behavior—for example, screaming, being uncooperative, and fighting—is not reinforced. Typically, plastic tokens are awarded whenever the desired behavior occurs. These tokens can be exchanged later for a variety of special privileges, such as going to a movie or visiting the canteen. The program is organized carefully so that it is a focal point in patients' lives. The token economy is carefully explained to the patients so that they understand the rules. There is little doubt that the token economy can have a marked effect on behavior (e.g., Brondolo, Baruch, Conway, and Marsh, 1994; Swiezy, Matson, and Box, 1992). It is important to emphasize that such operant programs have not "cured" patients, and often the results do not generalize beyond the treatment setting (Corrigan, 1991). Token economies have, however, made institutions more livable and the patients more responsive to rehabilitative programs.

There are critics of the token-economy approach. Some argue that what people learn in the system is that everything has a price. How much is a smile worth? What will I get if I learn to read faster? If everything in life is reduced to tokens, it might lead to a cheapening of relationships and make it more difficult for patients to learn that some behaviors have value beyond the tokens. Gagnon and Davison (1976) also suggest that what token economies teach is that the right behavior is inevitably followed by a reward. But in real life, reinforcement is not so predictable. The art of successful living, so some argue, is learning to accept that sometimes life is not only unpredictable but also unfair.

Biofeedback. **Biofeedback** occurs when a person is given information about his or her muscle activity, skin temperature, heart rate, blood pressure, or even brain waves. Normally, individuals are not aware of these activities. But by using electronic monitors, people can receive nearly instantaneous feedback about their biological activities. Clinical use has involved the treatment of essential hypertension, headache, epilepsy, and many other conditions.

Many regard biofeedback as an example of operant conditioning. Thus, for example, a reduction in heart rate is followed by a signal from the apparatus that a specific degree of change has occurred. This information is construed as a secondary reinforcer that will enhance the strength of this response. However, there are other interpretations. For example, the signal does not have to be viewed as a reward. It may be that the signal provides increased information, and the response of lowered heart rate is the result of what the person has learned rather than a function of some secondary reward. In any event, biofeedback techniques are controversial. The harsh judgment is that "there is absolutely no convincing evidence that biofeedback is an essential or specific technique for the treatment of any condition" (Roberts, 1985, p. 940).

## The Engineered Society

From Watson to Skinner, learning theorists have focused on the conditions in the environment that can be manipulated to produce a desired outcome. Watson's exaggerated claim about his ability to mold, through the strict application of learning, a child into any type of individual Watson wanted that child to become is threatening. The perceived power of learning for shaping people and society is reflected in contemporary concerns over the possibilities of brainwashing or the programming of minds attributed to religious cults.

To some, the effort to identify the conditions that can shape people and their minds has the potential to make us forget our individuality. It is true that individuality is a relatively unimportant concept for learning theorists. Indeed, for behaviorists, whatever individuality we possess comes from the application of the same general principles that influence any behavior. In this sense, individuality is an accident of different learning histories rather than a fundamental feature of our humanity.

Over the years, Skinner's writings contributed to these concerns. If you can manipulate a rat's environment so as to make the rat dance, who is to say that by manipulating the human environment you cannot make us all dance? In *Walden Two*, his 1948 novel, Skinner described how a society could be built and could function on the principles of reinforcement. And in 1971 he published *Beyond Freedom and Dignity*, in which he explicitly stated how reinforcement contingencies could be applied to religion, politics, government, business, and indeed every corner of modern society.

Central to Skinner's prescriptions for an engineered society is a good behavioral technology. According to Skinner, however, we can never accomplish this if we continue to hold our beliefs about autonomy and free will. All of our behavior is determined by genetic predispositions and chains of environmental influences. The environment acts, and the person reacts.

Depending on your interpretation, all this is a prescription for horror or a design for a utopian existence. Images of dictator-like technocrats compete with dreams of the Good Life. As Skinner (1948) put it:

> The one fact that I would cry from every housetop is this: the Good Life is waiting for us . . . . It does not depend on a change in government or on the machinations of world politics. It does not wait upon an improvement in human nature. At this very moment we have the necessary techniques, both material and psychological, to create a full and satisfying life for everyone. (p. 193)

## Cognition as Behavior

The behavioral tradition as represented by the work of Dollard and Miller, Skinner, Wolpe, and others has had an important impact on the practice of psychotherapy. A variety of behavior therapy approaches have been developed, ranging from systematic desensitization to token economies. But in recent years there has been a growing cognitive emphasis in the field of behaviorism. That is, the role of the mind of the organism in perceiving, interpreting, and responding to environmental stimuli is being considered in some behavioral theories and therapies.

For the radical behaviorists, cognitive concepts remain unacceptable on ideological grounds. The introduction of such terms represents, at best, an unnecessary addendum to the study of human behavior and, at worst, a harmful addition to the efficient modification of behavior. For the less radical behaviorists, however, the introduction of these concepts has expanded the types of behavior and human problems that can be changed using behavioral techniques. To address people's thoughts, feelings, and beliefs, it is necessary to expand the definition of behavior to include the covert, internal events that occur in people's heads. If a thought is a behavior, then it should be modifiable using the same principles that are used to modify overt acts (Meichenbaum, 1992).

As behavior therapists started to consider a wider range of human problems, they began to realize that there was more out there than just phobias and simple behavioral deficits. Some patients were alienated; others felt inferior; some just seemed unfulfilled. To develop a credible approach that would apply to the entire range of human problems, cognitions had to be conceptualized as behaviors (Meichenbaum, 1993).

## Cognitive Restructuring

On the basis of work by Albert Ellis (1962), Goldfried and Davison (1976) suggest that much human misery results from inappropriate ways of construing the world. Methods must, therefore, be found to get these maladjusted people to label situations more adaptively. Patients need to be taught that when they begin to feel upset in a given situation, they must pause and reflect on what it is they are telling themselves about the situation. **Cognitive restructuring** is a set of techniques designed to manipulate patients' thoughts, just as formerly, in the strict behavioral tradition, certain stimuli were introduced to manipulate overt behavior. This approach is compatible with the ideas of Dollard and Miller because it is an attempt to induce the client to label situations more rationally and thereby perceive environmental cues more appropriately. Box 10-2 illustrates how cognitive restructuring might occur in a therapy session.

By reconceptualizing cognitions as behaviors, principles of behavior modification can be applied to thoughts, beliefs, and perceptions just as they are applied to overt behaviors.

## BOX 10-2
## A Brief Example of Cognitive Restructuring

The following dialogue is an example of cognitive restructuring with a student who was about to graduate from college and was experiencing episodes of anxiety and depression.

> *Student:* I feel so anxious about my future; I am sure I won't get a job.
>
> *Therapist:* It is interesting that uncertainty in the future can make some people feel anxious and makes others feel excited and challenged. Why do you see it as anxiety-provoking?
>
> *Student:* I don't know. I am always anxious when I feel uncertain.
>
> *Therapist:* How would it feel to be excited about the future?
>
> *Student:* I don't know; good I guess.
>
> *Therapist:* Let's think of some good things that could come out of your graduation, and see how that makes you feel.
>
> *Student:* Well, if I was to get a good job and show my parents I could take care of myself, I would feel really good.
>
> *Therapist:* Then why don't we spend some time thinking of strategies for getting a good job?

The session continues with the student giving further examples of anxieties over the future and the therapist offering alternative ways of thinking about the future.

## Stress Inoculation

The term *inoculation* is used to emphasize that this technique is analogous to medical inoculation against biological diseases such as polio or smallpox. That is, patients are given psychological resources to prevent them (inoculate them) from distress when they are exposed to a stressful situation. Meichenbaum (1985) has described **stress inoculation,** and Novaco (1977) has provided an example of its application to the anger of depressed patients. With this technique, patients are cognitively prepared and then taught to acquire, rehearse, and practice the skills necessary to deal with their problem. For example, they are given instructional manuals that describe the nature of anger and how it functions. Illustrations of situations in which anger can be a problem are provided, along with examples of what causes anger and how it can be regulated. Patients are taught how to view provocative situations in alternative ways and how to consider the perspective of the person who is causing their anger. Methods of relaxation are also taught, as are methods of seeing the humor (a response incompatible with anger) in anger-provoking situations. Finally, anger-producing situations are induced by imagination and role playing. Hierarchies of anger situations are generated. By gradually working up the hierarchy (first by imagination and then by role playing), patients learn anger-management skills.

## The Hidden Goal of Understanding

Behavior therapists emphasize that their goal is behavioral change rather than the patient's achievement of understanding or insight. But people often want to understand a problem—to know why it occurred and how it was fixed. If we are depressed, we go to a therapist to become happy, or at least to have our depression lifted. Some of us, however, are not content with just this outcome. We also want to know *why* we became depressed. As patients, we have not only behavioral goals but cognitive ones as well. This cognitive need for understanding is found in behaviorists as well. Arnold Lazarus (1971) describes his discovery that twenty-three clinical psychologists who described themselves as "behavior therapists" were undergoing psychoanalysis or a related form of nonbehavioral psychotherapy.

Behavior therapists publicly criticize such mentalistic phenomena as insight, transference, and resistance when dealing with their own patients. They prefer to change behaviors or build up behavior repertoires. Why would behavioral therapists seek the very thing they condemn as superfluous? In Lazarus's (1971) own words:

> From what I know of the behavioral clinicians who have elected to undergo nonbehavioral therapies themselves, they are all relatively assertive individuals without debilitating phobias, compulsions, or sexual aberrations, who wish to be in better touch with their own feelings and who desire a better appreciation and understanding of the antecedents of their current actions. (p. 350)

Lazarus is suggesting that behavioral therapies are suitable when the problem is a specific behavioral deficit but that more cognitively oriented therapies are preferable when the goal is the nonspecific one of understanding or determining the meaning of one's life.

## Behavioral Assessment

Psychological assessment is typically viewed as focusing on characteristics of the person such as abilities, attitudes, traits, and feelings. Most people are familiar with intelligence tests or personality inventories, and many have completed such measures at some point in their lives. Not surprisingly, the emphasis of behavioral assessment is different. Table 10-1 summarizes the major differences between traditional personality assessment approaches and the behavioral approach.

## Sign Versus Sample

The major distinction between traditional and behavioral personality assessment is how a subject's response is interpreted (Goodenough, 1949). The traditional approach to personality assessment views test data as **signs** or indicants of some underlying construct. Unhappy TAT stories are signs of an underlying depression. Macho talk may be interpreted as indicating insecurity. Within behavioral assessment, responses are viewed as **samples** of a larger pool of possible observations that could be made in other situations. These responses are not interpreted as indicants of some underlying personality construct, because the focus of treatment and understanding is the response, not what it might represent. When a patient is untalkative, appears tired, and does not respond to humor, this would be seen by the behavior therapist as a sample of the patient's demeanor outside the consulting room. Avoiding the threatening portions of a Rorschach card would be viewed not as a symptom of some malignant underlying problem but as a sample of avoidant behavior that may appear and cause problems in other, more critical situations.

## SORC Model

Behaviorally oriented clinical psychologists are interested in four types of variables that are represented by the acronym **SORC**, which stands for stimuli-organism-response-consequences. First, there is $S$: the stimuli or environmental settings that appear to cause the behavior of interest. Second, there is $O$: the physiological and psychological state of the organism when the behavior occurs. For example, an individual's depressed outlook might be related to the use of certain drugs or perhaps to negative internal self-statements. For radical behaviorists, psychological O variables are not of much interest. The third variable, $R$, is the overt, observable responses that represent the problem. The identification and modification of $R$ variables is the goal of behavior therapy. The fourth variable, $C$, signifies the consequences of the individual's behavior. These are the reinforcements that presumably maintain the behavior (R) that is to be modified. For example, does a child's disruptive classroom behavior *(R)* lead to the positive consequences *(C)* of attention from the teacher? A variety of behavioral assessment techniques can be used to assess these four classes of variables.

## Interviews

The interview is as important a source of information for the behavioral clinicians it is for the psychodynamically or phenomenologically oriented one. The difference is in the types of questions asked in the interview. Goldfried and

## ❦ Table 10-1
### Differences Between Behavioral and Traditional Approaches to Assessment

| | Behavioral | Traditional |
|---|---|---|
| **I. Assumptions** | | |
| 1. Conception of personality | Personality constructs mainly employed to summarize specific behavior patterns, if at all | Personality as a reflection of enduring underlying characteristics |
| 2. Causes of behavior | Maintaining conditions sought in current environment | Intrapsychic or within the individual |
| **II. Implications** | | |
| 1. Role of behavior | Important as a sample of person's repertoire in specific situation | Behavior assumes importance only insofar as it indexes underlying causes |
| 2. Role of history | Relatively unimportant, except, for example, to provide a retrospective baseline | Crucial in that present conditions are seen as a product of the past |
| 3. Consistency of behavior | Behavior thought to be specific to the situation | Behavior expected to be consistent across time and settings |
| **III. Uses of data** | To describe target behaviors and maintaining conditions | To describe personality functioning and etiology |
| | To select the appropriate treatment | To diagnose or classify |
| | To evaluate and revise treatment | To make prognosis; to predict |
| **IV. Other characteristics** | | |
| 1. Level of inferences | Low | Medium to high |
| 2. Comparisons | More emphasis on intraindividual or idiographic | More emphasis on interindividual or nomothetic |
| 3. Methods of assessment | More emphasis on direct methods (e.g., observations of behavior in natural environment) | More emphasis on indirect methods (e.g., interviews, and self-report) |
| 4. Timing of assessment | More ongoing; prior, during, and after treatment | Pre- and perhaps posttreatment or strictly to diagnose |
| 5. Scope of assessment | Specific measures and of more variables (e.g., target behaviors in various situations, of side effects, context, strengths as well as deficiencies) | More global measures (e.g., of cure or improvement but only of the individual) |

Adapted from "Some Relationships Between Behavioral and Traditional Assessment" by D. P. Hartmann, B. I. Roper, and D. C. Bradford, *Journal of Behavioral Assessment, 1*, 4, 1979. Reprinted by permission of Plenum Publishing Corporation and Donald P. Hartmann.

Davison (1976) have offered a pragmatic description of interview procedures calculated to elicit behavioral information. Establishing rapport with the individual is important so that he or she will be willing to provide accurate and honest information. The questions are designed to elicit the information described in the SORC model. The interviewer needs to know about the stimuli that are associated with the problem behavior, any factors within the person that are involved, the nature of the problem behavior itself, and events following the behavior that may be maintaining it. Relevant case history data are obtained, and the client's current strengths and past attempts to cope with the problem are assessed. Many clinicians also find it important to solicit the individual's expectations regarding therapy.

## Inventories and Checklists

A variety of paper-and-pencil, self-report instruments have been used to identify behaviors, emotional reactions, and perceptions of the environment. A good example is the *Fear Survey Schedule* (Geer, 1965). This instrument describes fifty-one potentially fear-arousing situations and asks the individual to rate the degree of fear or the extent of unpleasant reactions produced by each. Examples of these situations include anticipating having an operation, being in a high place, hearing thunder, and speaking before an audience. Insel and Moos (1974) have developed an inventory that assesses the person's perception of several aspects of different social environments, such as home, school, or work.

Another approach is to adapt traditional personality measures to assess individuals' feelings and reactions in a specific situation. An example of this is the state form of the *State-Trait Anxiety Inventory (STAI)* (Spielberger, Gorsuch, and Lushene, 1970). The state form measures anxiety not as a chronically experienced personal characteristic but as a transitory-state reaction to specific situations. What distinguishes these approaches from traditional personality assessment is that they focus on specific behaviors and reactions to specific situations.

## Direct Observation

The direct observation and recording of behavior is a distinctive and prominent method of behavioral assessment. At the extreme of this approach are naturalistic observations that involve meticulous recordings of a person's every move. An example is the research of Barker and Wright (1951), in which the detailed activities of a seven-year-old were minutely noted over an entire day. In most instances, however, such extensive observations are impractical and, fortunately, also unnecessary for answering most questions of interest to behavioral psychologists. More common are the limited observations of a subject in a more confined environment. For example, Ayllon and Michael (1959) had nurses systematically observe and record the behavior of patients in an institutional setting. In this case, a given patient was watched for one to three minutes every thirty minutes. Another example is provided by O'Leary and Becker (1967), who developed an objective method for observing the presence, duration, and frequency of behaviors such as raising one's hand or pushing. Their interest was in assessing the effectiveness of a token reinforcement program in a class of disruptive children. Patterson (1977) and his colleagues have used the *Behavioral Coding System (BCS)* to record observations in the homes of predelinquent boys exhibiting problems in aggressiveness and noncompliance (see Figure 10-1).

## Controlled Settings

Naturalistic observations are not always possible or practical. Also, observing people without their knowledge or permission raises some ethical issues. These issues become more complex when the behavior of friends and associates of the

Blank Sample Coding Sheet for the BCS

Family number ____________

ID number ____________

BEHAVIOR CODING SHEET

Phase ____________

Subject ________ Observer ______ Date _____ No. _____

| | | | | | |
|---|---|---|---|---|---|
| AP | Approval | HU | Humiliate | PP | Positive physical contact |
| AT | Attention | IG | Ignore | RC | Receive |
| CM | Command | LA | Laugh | SS | Self-stimulation |
| CN | Command (negative) | NC | Noncompliance | TA | Talk |
| CO | Compliance | NE | Negativism | TE | Tease |
| CR | Cry | NO | Normative | TH | Touching, handling |
| DI | Disapproval | NR | No response | WH | Whine |
| DP | Dependency | PL | Play | WK | Work |
| DS | Destructiveness | PN | Negative physical contact | YE | Yell |
| HR | High rate | | | | |

| | | | | | |
|---|---|---|---|---|---|
| 1 | | | | | |
| 2 | | | | | |
| •<br>•<br>• | | | | | |
| 10 | | | | | |

Description ____________________

**Figure 10-1** A blank sample coding sheet from the Behavioral Coding System (BCS).

person being observed is also recorded. But, as soon as individuals are informed of the observation so that their permission can be obtained, the naturalness of their behavior is compromised. Beyond these important problems, however, naturalistic observation can be inefficient because the observer is dependent on the complexity and changes in life events to yield the behaviors, situations, and responses of interest. A lot of time may pass before the combination of events of interest occurs, if it occurs at all.

For all these reasons, controlled observations are often used to evaluate scientific hypotheses. Controlled observations enable the observer to make specific observations of the behaviors of interest without depending on natural events to provide the opportunity. One must be careful about generalizing from observations made under controlled and artificial conditions to natural events. But if the hypotheses tested concern the artificial setting, the results may have scientific validity.

An example of controlling the setting to increase the opportunity to observe the behaviors of interest is a case described by Arnold Lazarus (1961). He observed and assessed a patient's claustrophobic behavior by placing him in a closed room made progressively smaller by moving a screen closer and closer to him. The direct observation of his fear reactions by the clinician produced information unfiltered by the subjective reports of the patient or his friends. Such assessment procedures are also illustrated by the following example from the Bandura, Adams, and Beyer (1977) study of chronic snake phobias:

> *Behavioral Avoidance.* The test of avoidance behavior consisted of a series of 29 performance tasks requiring increasingly more threatening interactions with a red-tailed boa constrictor. Subjects were instructed to approach a glass cage containing the snake, to look down at it, to touch and hold the snake with gloved and then bare hands, to let it loose in the room and then return it to the cage, to hold it within 12 cm of their faces, and finally to tolerate the snake crawling in their laps while they held their hands passively at their sides . . . Those who could not enter the room containing the snake received a score of 0; subjects who did enter were asked to perform the various tasks in the graded series. To control for any possible influence of expressive cues from the tester, she stood behind the subject and read aloud the tasks to be performed. . . .
>
> The avoidance score was the number of snake-interaction tasks the subject performed successfully.
>
> *Fear arousal accompanying approach responses.* In addition to the measurement of performance capabilities, the degree of fear aroused by each approach response was assessed. During the behavioral test, subjects rated orally, on a 10-interval scale, the intensity of fear they experienced when each snake approach task was described to them and again while they were performing the corresponding behavior. (pp. 127–128)

## Role Playing

Rotter and Wickens (1948) first suggested **role playing** as a technique of behavioral assessment. Many situations and problem behaviors can not be systematically observed. Role playing is acting out a problem or situation with the resulting opportunity to observe how the patient reacts. Although by definition role playing is not natural, it is a practical compromise in many instances (Goldfried, 1976).

## Self-Monitoring

Another solution to the cost, difficulty, and ethical issues associated with using observers to record the behavior of subjects is to ask the subjects to record their own behavior and the details of the situations in which the behavior occurs (Wolpe and Lazarus, 1966). This procedure of **self-monitoring** is one in which individuals maintain their own diaries or records according to the behavioral psychologist's instructions. Self-monitoring has often been used with specific target behaviors such as smoking or eating. One of the limitations of this approach is the uncertain reliability and validity of self-recorded behavior, particularly when the behavior is undesirable. In addition, although behaviorists have long argued that behavioral recording is objective, there is generally some subjective interpretation involved in deciding whether, and under what conditions, a behavior occurred. Thus, self-monitoring requires training individuals in exactly how to observe and record their own behavior.

An interesting result of self-monitoring is that people may respond to their own observations by reducing the frequency of the problem behavior. Thus, self-monitoring has the potential to be a **reactive** form of measurement; that is, the act of measuring a behavior changes the behavior. Although this is a problem for self-monitoring as an assessment technique, it makes self-monitoring a potential means for therapeutic behavior change. For example, consider the study of smoking behavior reported by Lipinski, Black, Nelson, and Ciminero (1975). In this study, two groups of college students were the subjects. One group was solicited through advertisements for "individuals who want to stop smoking." The other group responded to an advertisement which asked only for "individuals who are cigarette smokers." Initial instructions were provided in separate meetings for each group. The instructions required all subjects to keep a daily count of the number of cigarettes they smoked. All subjects were told that the self-monitoring might tend to reduce their smoking. Each subject was then given a card on which to record the daily cigarette consumption for one week. Subjects turned in their weekly records for a four-week period. The results, shown in Figure 10-2, indicate that motivated subjects reduced their smoking during the course of the experiment. At least with motivated subjects, then, the very act of self-monitoring can produce behavior change.

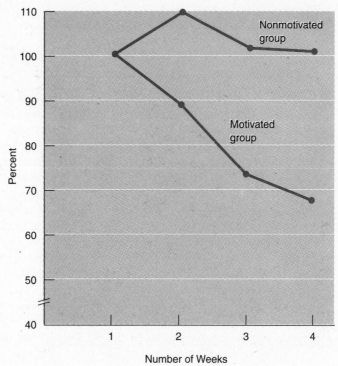

**Figure 10-2** ∞  Motivation and the reactive effects of self-monitoring.

## Summary Evaluation

Learning theory is primarily a product of American psychology, and research strategies that emphasize the quantification and careful control of variables have generally appealed to psychologists in the United States. It is not surprising that the forms of behavior therapy that developed from the theories of Dollard and Miller, Watson, and Skinner are widely employed by therapists in this country. Academic clinical psychologists have generally avoided the psychodynamic theory as the basis for their research. Indeed, there has traditionally been animosity between the psychoanalytically oriented and behaviorally oriented psychologists. For example, Wogan and Norcross (1982) comment that the psychodynamic school typically regards behavior therapists as "naive, unanalyzed symptom treaters who are acting out their impulses to control" (p. 100). Wolpe (1981) represents the behaviorist when he says, "In actuality, not a single one of the [psychoanalytic] theory's main propositions has ever been supported" (p. 160).

The increased recognition of the importance of cognition for understanding and changing behavior has provided a basis for combining these approaches in some instances, but the tension between these groups has not disappeared. The comments and debates between these groups help to clarify the strengths and weaknesses of the behavioral learning point of view.

## Strengths

Synthesis of Laboratory and Clinic.  Until the work of Dollard and Miller, little was shared between the animal learning laboratory and the therapeutic consulting room. Dollard and Miller's translation of psychodynamic processes into the language of learning provided the basis for linking the two. Their translation was based on a liberalization of the definition of both *stimulus* and *response*. They also added sociocultural variables, and they drew on the data of cultural anthropology to create a theory that has had a powerful impact on the study of personality. Although their work is now not often cited in the research journals, their analyses of the acquisition and function of neurotic behavior remain compelling. Dollard and Miller provided extensive descriptions of how learning influences personality. Not all learning theorists accept their approach. Eysenck, Wolpe, Skinner, and Bandura have all argued that Dollard and Miller accept too much of psychoanalytic theory.

Skinner's work is also the basis for many therapeutic techniques. Although Skinner never expressed interest in clinical applications, his followers have been especially active and ingenious in their search for the therapeutic application of operant principles. Dollard and Miller relied primarily on the traditional verbal psychotherapy model and translated it into learning terms. But the Skinnerians created new methods that have found application everywhere, from prisons and institutions for the retarded to day-care centers and family therapy.

An Empirical Approach.  Dollard and Miller were among the first to show that personality could be studied empirically. They did this by carefully defining their concepts so that they could be measured and manipulated. Their approach had been polished in the laboratory, and they did not find it necessary to appeal to either intuition or authority. Hall and Lindzey (1978) describe their perspective as both rigorous and empirical.

Dollard and Miller insured that their concepts could be empirically studied and made it clear that their concepts did not have a physical or biological existence. Concepts were not defined by metaphors but in terms of the operations used to measure them. Freudian concepts appeared to have some reality; the id was a seething cauldron of impulses internally driving behavior. The concept of an avoidance gradient does not have this vividness. This concept is defined by how it is measured—by the direction and speed of movement with respect to an object or event. Dollard and Miller understood that a theory is a set of concepts that aids us in making predictions rather than a map of reality.

Skinner resisted the label of theorist. Indeed, he argued that theory was both unnecessary and pretentious. He based his conclusions on the results of meticulously controlled and replicated laboratory experiments rather than on argument. Each finding was systematically followed by new experiments designed to extend and clarify it. By this process he was able to identify many important components of the learning process. Skinner was an innovative experimenter, who developed many novel techniques and apparatus to study behavior. Had this been his only contribution, he still would have had a significant impact on experimental psychology.

**Broad Application.** Because they are based on basic and simple principles, learning applications have a broad range of application. The work of Dollard and Miller and of Skinner was initially generalized to clinical settings. However Skinner's operant methods can now be found in many settings. Educational institutions now use self-paced instructional procedures that rely on operant principles. Programmed learning and teaching machines are also common. And, of course, Skinner promoted the ultimate application: a society run on operant principles. By creating a society where one's acts are carefully regulated by the consequences they engender, he hoped that a more nearly perfect life would result for all of us. A society engineered and directed by operant principles is certainly a remarkable aspiration and a testimonial to Skinner's confidence in his own research. Whether it provides a blueprint for the future or a threat for everyone is still uncertain. What *is* certain is that Skinnerian principles have been successfully employed in a variety of settings, including animal training, education, therapy, and sales and advertising.

**An Idiographic Approach.** One of the appealing features of Skinner's work is its idiographic emphasis. The focus of operant research has always been on individual organisms, whether they be pigeons or persons. Psychological research is typically characterized by the formulation of general principles from data averaged over many subjects. The applicability of results from the hypothetical average person to specific individuals is always a concern. In contrast, Skinner averaged data over trials for each separate individual. As a result, there emerged a psychology of the individual. Skinner combined laboratory precision, control, and rigor with a focus on the single person.

**Schedules of Reinforcement.** One of the most influential, robust, and useful concepts of learning theory is schedules of reinforcement. On the basis of extensive research, the acquisition and extinction of discrete responses in both animals and humans can be predicted with great accuracy. The basis of these predictions is the pattern or schedule of the reinforcement influencing the behavior (Ferster and Skinner, 1957).

**Behavioral Assessment.** Learning theory emphasizes the assessment of specific behaviors in specific situations. Behavioral assessment is based on a diverse set of techniques, including interviewing, inventories, observation, role playing, and self-monitoring. However, the common focus of these techniques is what the person or organism *does*. The specificity and focus of behavioral assessment is an important contribution to the goal of understanding personality. Although there is more to a person than what he or she does, knowing how a person acts and when he or she can be expected to act in those ways is undeniably important for understanding the person. In addition, that information is useful for helping the person, or society, change undesired behaviors.

**Behavior Therapy.** The major contribution of behavioral theories of personality to psychology has been the introduction of methods of behavior change such as systematic desensitization, aversion techniques, and token economies. These methods have been useful for influencing behaviors that had been resistant to the more traditional insight-oriented therapies. These newer, more direct, and short-term techniques have also made therapy available to more individuals. Traditional approaches to therapy were often available only to the affluent, the very intelligent, or the middle and upper classes—those persons who have the money, time, and "psychological-mindedness" for traditional therapy. Behavior therapy works for these people, but it also is useful for individual with more modest verbal skills. And because less time is required, the methods are more available to those of limited financial resources. Even the poorly endowed retardate or the regressed schizophrenic can profit to some extent from these techniques.

Most important for the field of personality and clinical psychology, the success of these behavioral methods has challenged many of the assumptions and beliefs we have made about people and how they change and develop. It has forced a reexamination of our theories and models that, although sometimes threatening, has had a constructive impact on those theories.

## Weaknesses

**The Wrong Emphasis.** Many have argued that any approach based on animal research will have limited applicability to people. Rats scurrying into safe compartments are less an analog of the human condition than they are a travesty of it. To build a science of human behavior out of the data from Skinner's pigeons pecking at colored disks is worse than a bad joke. The behavior studied is so molecular and superficial that it can relate only to the most simplistic of human actions. The emphasis on primary drives denies the possibility that humans are guided less by their physical needs than they are by their aspirations, feelings, goals, and beliefs. To see people as animals is to deny the existence of complex cognition and the choice and free will it makes possible.

**Too Much Environment and Too Little Cognition.** The behavioral tradition depicts the human being as a creature at the mercy of environmental forces. In its extreme form, Skinnerian doctrine portrays us as "empty boxes." There is environmental input by the way of stimulation, and there is output by way of our responses. But what transpires within the box? Surely we do not all respond to the same stimulus in the same fashion. It is not clear that different reinforcement histories can account for all the individual differences we observe. People are constantly placed in new situations and are able to cope effectively in those situations. Likewise, how can we explain behaviors, such as suicide, that happen only once? By their nature, these behaviors cannot be learned through repeated patterns of exposure and reinforcement.

The inability and unwillingness of behavioral theories to consider any mediating cognitive variables, or to infer any personality characteristics, limits the range of applicability of those theories. A large portion of a pigeon's behavior in a simplified laboratory setting can be predicted and controlled through schedules of reinforcement and without reference to the pigeon's personality. The complexity of human behavior in social situations has proved more difficult to control and predict. And, if the goal is explanation and understanding, individual differences in personality and cognition are likely to be crucial concepts.

The philosophic foundation of behaviorism requires that scientific study be restricted to phenomena that can be objectively observed. But, this so restricts the types of human activities that can be studied that most interesting and important aspects of our humanity must be ignored or labeled "unscientific." So much of human behavior is covert that methods for studying it must be developed. Although one can admire the discipline exercised by behaviorists in limiting what they will study, one must also be concerned about the severe limitations that this discipline places on what we can learn. As Hall and Lindzey (1978) put it, restricting our attention to overt behavior is the same as studying a "decorticate" organism.

### Definition of Stimuli, Reinforcements, and Responses.
The effectiveness of behavioral techniques to change responses requires that the behavior analyst and the subject show some agreement about the response that is the target of change. Indeed, in his earliest writings, Skinner (1938) argued that stimuli, reinforcers, and responses must all be defined functionally and interdependently. In practice, however, the definition of these terms has been haphazard. People or organisms are exposed to bells and whistles, buttons and keys, and food and water in the hope that the stimuli, responses, and reinforcers that make up the operant situation will be discovered. As Kileen (1994) recently noted, "Modern behavior analysis succeeds to the extent that our definitions and instrumentation of these key terms have themselves been selected to respect animals' definitions as best as we can intuit them" (p. 105).

The problem of defining the operant situation for animal subjects is exacerbated when we use behavioral techniques to change and predict the behavior of humans in less controlled naturalistic situations. What is a stimulus for the experimenter may not be a stimulus for the subject. Dollard and Miller have often been criticized (sometimes by behaviorists) for their inability to identify specifically what is a stimulus for a given person. As they broadened the definition of a stimulus and moved outside the laboratory, the rigor and definitional clarity of the learning approach were reduced. Thus, their liberalization of what can constitute a stimulus has had some negative consequences.

## THE FAR SIDE                    By GARY LARSON

"Stimulus, response! Stimulus, response!
Don't you ever *think*?"

Likewise, learning theorists often have difficulty in identifying in advance what will turn out to be reinforcing for a person in a given situation. If an event has been reinforcing in the past, it will likely be so again. But there is a circularity to this definition of a reinforcement. A reinforcement is whatever exerts an effect on behavior. Sometimes it is difficult to specify a reinforcer in advance, particularly in the case of maladjusted people who do not view either stimuli or rewards in the same way as we do. For example, some individuals actually regard pain as positively reinforcing and make every effort to subject themselves to it. Although a behavioral analysis of masochism is possible (Brown, 1965), such an example does illustrate the problems these learning approaches can have in defining reinforcements before the fact.

Lack of Theory. Whereas Dollard and Miller showed an appreciation for the role of theory in science, Skinner has tried to maintain an explicitly atheoretical approach. He argues that neither he nor anyone else is sufficiently insightful or knowledgeable to propose a theory of behavior until the results of many carefully controlled experiments are available. Moreover, Skinner (1969) argues that if one can control and predict behavior, than understanding and explaining it are not of much importance. Skinner's atheoretical approach is consistent with his research. He does not attempt to define the operant situation; rather, he discovers—or allows the subject to discover—the crucial stimuli and responses. A reinforcement is defined as whatever strengthens responses, and responses are defined as whatever is strengthened.

Although this approach seems atheoretical and objective, many argue that this is an illusion. In the view of many scientists, no one can approach a field of study without some assumptions and presuppositions. It is hard to believe that any research is simply the result of random manipulations and measures. One has to decide what or who to study, what to observe or measure, and what to manipulate. Once a program of research is begun, these decisions can be based on previous work, but the program has to start somewhere. Also, some thought must guide the changes in the design of the new studies. All that Skinner has done, the critics argue, is to make these decisions implicit and therefore more difficult to discuss and evaluate. It is better to make the assumptions and beliefs that motivated the research and the design of studies explicit (that is, present a theory) to provide a context for interpreting the results and to allow alternative interpretations to be considered.

Behavioral Assessment.  Behaviorally oriented diagnosticians emphasize the rigor and objectivity of their approach to measurement. However, the apparent objectivity of recording observed behaviors has generally led behaviorists to presume that their techniques are valid and reliable rather than to scientifically demonstrate that the techniques have those properties (Johnson and Bolstadt, 1973). In fact, behavioral assessment is a heterogeneous collection of techniques that are often neither rigorous, objective, nor psychometrically adequate. Within behavioral assessment, the possibility that subjects or patients are responding to characteristics of the assessment situation that differ from those in the mind of the assessor is rarely considered. We know considerably less about the psychometric properties of behavioral assessment than we do about any other form of psychological measurement.

Moreover, there is reason to believe that behavioral measures are psychometrically treacherous. The reliability of a single behavior in a single situation as a representation of a person's typical behavior is likely to be low (Epstein, 1979a). So many factors influence a single act that predicting it is nearly impossible, and how a person acts from situation to situation often changes dramatically (Mischel, 1968). Likewise, the interpretation of a specific behavior is difficult. The objectivity of behavioral recording has led many to assume that the interpretation (validity) of that recording is also objective. This is a false assumption (Golding, 1978). Consider a study of assertiveness training in which the amount of time a person talks in a group discussion about a controversial issue is used to assess the effectiveness of assertiveness training. In general, this appears to be a straightforward "objective" measure of assertiveness: more assertive people talk more. However, consider the student who participated in the study of assertiveness training as a course requirement and who resents having to participate in psychology experiments to pass the course. The student comes to all the sessions and the final group discussion to obtain credit but resolves not to talk or otherwise participate any more than absolutely necessary. This student would receive a score on talkativeness that would be interpreted as a lack of assertiveness; yet, the student is asserting his or her resentment by not talking. The same behavior can, and often does, have different meanings for different people. Recording behavior may be objective; interpreting it generally is not. One should not assume that any technique described as "behavioral" is automatically objective and psychometrically sound. Indeed, the evidence suggests that the opposite is closer to the truth.

**Behavior Therapy.** Lazarus and Wilson (1976) remarked that behavior therapy has

> no universally accepted definition, no consensus as to goals, concepts or underlying philosophy, no agreement as to its purview, no monolithic point of view, no overriding strategy or core techniques, no single founding father, no general agreement about matters of training, and there is no single profession to which primary allegiance is declared. (p. 153)

Despite the frequent claims that behavior therapy is steeped in an experimental-learning tradition, others have observed that it has no more claim to scientific respectability than other forms of therapy (Breger and McGaugh, 1965). Locke (1971) has even argued that many methods of behavior therapy contradict every major premise of behaviorism. What, for example, is objective or observable about an image conjured up by a patient in the middle of an anxiety hierarchy?

Regardless of the coherence or philosophical consistency of behavior therapy, the most important pragmatic issue is its effectiveness. Some have suggested that although behavioral techniques do relieve anxiety or lessen symptoms, they are not useful for promoting inner growth, providing us with insight, or helping us reach our potential. However, these alternate goals of therapy represent per-

# Calvin and Hobbes                                    by Bill Watterson

spectives that are outside the range of behavioral theory and application. Thus, they are easily dismissed by those who have adopted a behavioral philosophy.

Of more relevance is the ability of behavioral techniques to resolve problems that are manifested in thoughts and feelings rather than overt behavior. Specific fear of snakes or elevators is different from feelings of depression, an enveloping sense of life's basic meaninglessness, or a moral dilemma. Behavioral approaches seem to be limited to the correction of specific behavioral deficits or the reduction of specific anxieties. However, as the definition of *behavior* has expanded to include the covert behavior of thoughts and feelings, the effectiveness of behavior therapy for these problems may increase.

Another issue is whether the effects of behavior therapy generalize to novel situations. This issue is relevant to all forms of therapy, but the inherent specificity of behavior therapy has made this issue particularly compelling. For example, token economies are often effective in sheltered institutions where it is easy to exert control over a person. But when that person leaves the controlled setting, the positive effects of the therapy frequently do not generalize to the new environment. Whether such behavior modification techniques are useful in natural, uncontrolled settings is still an issue. Such problems have led some to characterize these methods as superficial, simplistic techniques that produce little of lasting value. Furthermore, Condrey (1977) has observed that when we use external incentives to induce behavioral changes, we are undermining any intrinsic motivation to change that the person may have. Indeed, once the external incentives are removed, learning theory predicts that the desired behavior will disappear unless other sources of reinforcement are found.

A moral issue has been whether behavior therapies are improper attempts to control and manipulate people. Are they really insidious efforts to undermine the person's capacity to make decisions, assume responsibility, or maintain dignity? It is not hard to see behavior therapy in that light when we think about electric shocks, drugs to make a person ill when drinking, or tokens to induce a person to behave in a manner desired by institutional authorities. However, as Goldfried and Davison (1976) assert, such criticisms are less relevant when the techniques are used with adults who voluntarily seek such treatment. But in the case of children, incompetent adults, prisoners, and others who do not have control over their lives, such questions are difficult. Also, critics of behavior therapy sometimes make contradictory arguments. If behavioral techniques are superficial and simplistic, then it is hard to describe them as powerfully insidious and mind-altering.

Finally, behavioral techniques are often a blend of several theoretical traditions, including operant conditioning, classical conditioning, and, more recently, cognitive psychology. This theoretical or atheoretical chaos makes it difficult to understand and explain how behavior therapy works and why it is effective. For this reason, evaluating the effectiveness of behavior therapy is not a complete or definitive test of learning theories of personality. Behaviorists must eventually provide a theoretical framework for their approach so that explanations can be tested in addition to techniques.

# Summary

- The primary method used to evaluate learning theories of personality has been to show that techniques derived from these theories can influence behavior. These methods have provided some impressive support for learning theory.
- The major contribution of Dollard and Miller to the practice of psychotherapy lies in their translation of traditional methods into learning terms.
- Counterconditioning methods of behavior change arose out of the classical conditioning paradigm. The individual is conditioned to make responses incompatible with the undesirable ones (e.g., relaxation rather than anxiety). Wolpe's method of systematic desensitization is a popular example of this general approach.
- A variety of aversion techniques have also been developed. In aversion therapy, the habit strength of an undesirable response is reduced by associating the response with an unpleasant stimulus.
- Skinnerian approaches are based on operant principles, wherein behavior is modified by making the achievement of reinforcements contingent on the person's emitting the desired behavior. The time-out procedure briefly removes the individual from the situation in which positive reinforcement for an undesirable behavior occurs until more desirable responses begin.
- Token economies are examples of the operant technology. Tokens are given to the individual whenever the desirable behavior occurs. These tokens can be exchanged at a later time for reinforcements of value to the individual.
- Biofeedback is giving the individual information (feedback) about his or her biological responses, such as skin temperature or heart rate. Presumably, such information serves as a secondary reinforcer that can enhance the strength of the response (e.g., lowered heart rate). The technique has been used to treat a variety of conditions ranging from headache to hypertension. However, the effectiveness of biofeedback is controversial.
- Skinner proposed that operant conditioning can and should be used to create a better society. Skinner's prescriptions have been hotly debated. Some describe them as the way to a utopian society; others see them as the road to tyranny.
- In recent years, the behavioral tradition has begun to incorporate cognition. The focus remains on behavior, but now a variety of covert behaviors are included. For example, the cognitive restructuring technique teaches individuals to reflect on how they construe certain situations in ways that are upsetting. With stress inoculation, patients are cognitively prepared to cope with threatening situations.
- In behavioral assessment, the major goals are the identification of the specific behavior that requires change, the most practical means of changing that behavior, and the determination of the factors in the environment that maintain it and have led to its acquisition. Such assessment is oriented not toward discovering underlying pathology (signs) but toward eliciting representative samples of behavior.

- Four types of data are obtained in behavioral assessment: the stimuli that elicit the undesirable behavior, the associated organismic factors, the responses that ensue, and the consequences that result from these responses.
- A variety of techniques are used for behavioral assessment, including interviews, inventories and checklists, direct observation, the use of controlled settings, role playing, and self-monitoring.
- The behavioral approach has several strengths. They include its ability to integrate data from the laboratory with clinical information and practice; its basis in scientific methodology; its broad set of applications with relevance for therapeutic, educational, and even social and institutional practices; its idiographic focus; and its concern with precise methods of administering reinforcement.
- Behavioral assessment techniques have provided personality psychologists with methods for observing what people do and when they do it. This type of information is an important addition to more traditional measures of personality.
- Behavior therapy methods have turned us away from the exclusive reliance on insight as the way to mental health and have taught us to look at the individual's specific complaints rather than underlying pathology. As a result, therapy has now become available to more people and has been applied to a greater range of problems.
- The behavioral movement also has some weaknesses. They include an emphasis on superficial behavior derived from a laboratory model of animal behavior; a disregard of cognitions, the most human of all data (although the gathering cognitive emphasis is beginning to blunt this criticism); a narrow focus on environmental contributors to behavior at the expense of the ways in which we process information about that environment; the failure to consider predispositions such as genetic endowment; problems in defining exactly what constitutes a stimulus or a response; and the lack of a general, explicitly stated theory of behavior.
- Behavioral assessment is a heterogeneous set of techniques that often fail to meet standardization criteria and whose reliability and validity are frequently a problem.
- Behavior therapy, too, is a loosely defined set of methods. Behavior therapy is most effective with specific anxieties or behavioral deficits. More global complaints involving thoughts and feelings are less amenable to behavioral treatment. The ability or willingness of patients to generalize what they have learned in controlled settings to natural situations is another potential limitation. Ethical questions have sometimes been raised, especially regarding aversion therapies, and behavioral methods have been characterized by some as dehumanizing.
- There is no integrating theoretical framework for explaining how and why behavior therapy works. Thus, the ability of these techniques to influence behavior provides only modest support for the learning theories that they represent.

# Chapter 11
## Social Learning Theory

Rotter's Social Learning Theory
    Assumptions and Basic Principles
    Theory and Concepts
    Development of Personality
    Nature of Adjustment
    Implications for Behavior Change
Bandura's Social Cognitive Theory
    Two Theoretical Principles
    Reciprocal Determinism
    Observational Learning
    Vicarious Reinforcement and
      Conditioning
    Self-Regulation
    Self-Efficacy
    Development of Personality
    Nature of Adjustment
    Implications for Behavior Change
Mischel: A Cognitive Social Learning
  Reconceptualization of Personality
    Competencies
    Encoding Strategies
    Expectancies

    Subjective Values
    Self-Regulatory Systems and Plans
Summary

S ituational and environmental variables have a powerful influence on how people act, and learning theory has provided a clear and consistent basis for understanding how the environment influences behavior. The theories and research of Watson, Skinner, Dollard and Miller, and contemporary behaviorists have provided important insights into why people react to situations differently on the basis of their individual learning histories. It is these different reactions that are the basis for characterizing individual's personalities. One of the most compelling features of learning theory is its range of applicability. The principles of learning apply not only to all people but to all behaving organisms. Thus, from a general set of principles many individual differences can be understood.

However, the generality of learning theory is also a liability. We recognize that people differ from other organisms. The nature of this difference is sometimes difficult to specify, but, in general, the basis for the differences is cognition. The cognitive revolution in psychology provided a framework for considering how uniquely human cognitive processes may contribute to human behavior. We think, we plan, we believe, and we imagine: these are the abilities that differentiate us from the lonely pigeon in the operant box and that limit learning theory as a basis for explaining all of human behavior. Reinforcement does not just occur; it is interpreted and evaluated (Kileen, 1994). Moreover, we actively select and influence our environments just as they influence us.

Out of an appreciation of the importance of cognition to understanding people's actions arose what is probably the most influential and widely applied theoretical framework for understanding behavior and personality today. It is generally referred to as **social learning theory**, or cognitive social learning theory. The essence of social learning theory is the combination of cognitive theory with behavioral principles. Social learning theory does not overlook or deny the important role of the environment on behavior; rather, it recognizes that the effect of the environment is often not as direct as learning theory would imply. Stimuli are perceived and processed by people on their way to producing a response. Thus, social learning theory is a powerful blend of two of the major sources of influence on personality. People differ not only because they have had different experiences but because they have interpreted and evaluated similar experiences differently.

Although the origins of social learning theory and the disputes over who deserves to be called a social learning theorist are not easily resolved (Woodward, 1982), John Dollard and Neal Miller were among the first to use the term *social learning*. Julian Rotter (1954) is usually credited with the development of the first social learning theory. The major theorists are usually considered to be Julian Rotter, Albert Bandura, and Walter Mischel.

## Rotter's Social Learning Theory

The development of Rotter's social learning theory began in the late 1940s and early 1950s. Rotter's personal association with Alfred Adler helped shape his theory, as did ideas from Clark Hull, Edward Thorndike, Sigmund Freud, and B. F. Skinner. Rotter's theory thus reflects a heterogeneous intellectual heritage that ranged from the importance of family relationships, environmental influences, and the self-concept to conditioning, repression, and cognitions. Such variety is appropriate for Rotter's goal: to construct a learning theory that would be broad yet systematic, and of use to the practicing clinician as well as to the research-oriented personality psychologist.

## Assumptions and Basic Principles

As Rotter proceeded with the construction of his theory he made several important assumptions and decisions (Rotter, 1954). He has stated them formally in a series of seven postulates and twelve corollaries, which can be summarized by five ideas.

A Construct Point of View.  Rotter consciously tried to build a theory that would help us predict and understand human behavior in a social setting. He believed that focusing exclusively on the facts of the situation would be inadequate for such a theory. Instead, he recognized that our interpretation of facts is crucial. In this sense there is no one "true" reality but only our personal construction of it. The similarity of this view to George Kelly's theory of personal constructs, discussed in Chapter 7, is not a coincidence; the two worked together at Ohio State while developing their theories.

A Specific Language of Description.  At the time Rotter began to formulate his theory, the most prominent personality theories were either psychoanalytic or phenomenological. Both of these approaches contained terms and concepts that were broad and that were difficult to translate into precise measures. Therefore, Rotter resolved to provide objective definitions of his concepts so that different observers using his concepts would agree among themselves in their judgments of that event. He also tried to avoid using different terms to describe the same phenomenon.

A Social Learning Perspective.  The label *social learning* that Rotter applied to his theory is designed to communicate the importance of the social context for human learning. In Rotter's words, "It is a *social* learning theory because it stresses the fact that the major or basic modes of behaving are learned in social situations and are inextricably fused with needs requiring for their satisfaction the mediation of other persons" (1954, p. 84).

Motives and Cognitions.  One of the most distinctive assumptions that Rotter makes is that human behavior is determined not simply by the rewards that follow it but by our expectations that the actions we choose will bring about reinforcement. Although he realized that human beings, like the animals in experimental research, are motivated by needs, he also believed that an essential human quality is our pervasive tendency to think and to anticipate. We are not mechanical beings that respond passively and automatically to reinforcement. The relation between expectancy and behavior has a long history in psychology (Zuroff and Rotter, 1985). Rotter was able to combine expectancy and reinforcement within the same theory.

**Performance Versus Learning.** Rotter's theory concerns why people choose to behave one way rather than another. He accepts basic learning and conditioning as the means through which the individual develops a large repertoire of behaviors. His focus is on predicting and understanding which of the many acquired behaviors will occur in a specific situation. Thus, his theory might be better characterized as concerning choices and performance rather than learning and capabilities.

## Theory and Concepts

Rotter's theory can be introduced by an example. At some point you will be a college senior planning your future. Let's say you schedule an appointment at the university placement center and manage to locate two job opportunities that match your training and interests. The first job pays $18,000 per year; the second, $25,000. Based on monetary reward, the second job is more reinforcing, and we might expect you to apply for it rather than the $18,000 job.

However, for Rotter, two factors would influence your decision about which job to seek. First, there is the reinforcement value of the goal toward which the behavior is directed. Undoubtedly, you would prefer to make $25,000 rather than $18,000, and so we could be confident that the former is more reinforcing than the latter. The second factor represents the focus of Rotter's theory—the role of expectancy. You might not apply for the higher-paying job if your expectancy of being offered that job is lower than your expectancy of being offered the lower paying one. Rotter's contention is simply that in predicting human behavior in complex social situations, we must consider both the value of the goal of the behavior and the person's expectancy that the behavior will achieve that goal.

**Behavior Potential.** In any particular situation, individuals have at their disposal many possible behaviors with which to attempt to achieve their goals. For example, when I meet a person for the first time and want to make a good impression, how should I act? Shall I remark about all the good things I have heard about the person? Shall I tell a joke? Or should I work into the conversation a reference to my latest personal accomplishment? I am capable of doing any of these and

A
BRIEF
BIOGRAPHY
OF

# Julian Rotter

Julian B. Rotter was born in 1916 in Brooklyn, New York. He was the third son of immigrant parents. His father emigrated from Austria at the age of thirteen, and his mother from Lithuania when she was a one-year-old. Rotter remarked once how rough it was growing up in Brooklyn and how quickly one learned the world of the streets. As a student, his academic marks were generally good, and better than his grades for conduct. He often checked books out of the public library; those by Adler, Freud, and Menninger seem to have sparked his interest in psychology. Nevertheless, he majored in chemistry at Brooklyn College.

In the 1930s Rotter was aware of, and protested against, social injustice, and this probably increased his desire to help others. Perhaps because of this, he decided to pursue a career in clinical psychology.

He attended graduate school at both the University of Iowa and Indiana University, receiving his Ph.D. in 1941 from the latter institution. He then entered Officer Candidate School in the U.S. Army and served his tour of duty doing work that involved military psychology and officer candidate selection.

In 1946 he joined the faculty of Ohio State University, where, in collaboration with George Kelly, he helped build a clinical psychology training program of national renown—one that became a model of the scientist-practitioner tradition. It was here that he completed his major theoretical work. In 1963 Rotter moved to the University of Connecticut,

more. In Rotter's conceptual framework, **behavior potential (BP)** is the potential for a behavior to occur in a specific situation as a means for achieving a particular goal. Any possible behavior has a potential. The higher the potential, the more likely it is that the behavior will occur. Obviously, the potential for a behavior to occur may be strong in one setting and weak in another. Telling jokes may be high in potential at a party but low at a funeral.

Rotter conceptualizes behavior broadly. Anything that a person does in response to a stimulus is included, assuming it can be detected and measured by some objective method. Observable actions such as writing a letter, flipping a coin, and tying shoelaces all qualify. But, thoughts and feelings that are less directly observable, such as having an erotic fantasy, feeling guilty, or being uneasy, are included as well. Behavior, "may thus consist of actual motor acts, cog-

where he continued to teach, supervise students, and contribute to national professional committees. Although best known for his prolific scientific career, Rotter has always maintained his identity as a practicing clinician. In 1987 Rotter retired from his post at the University of Connecticut. However, he continues to teach and supervise the research of graduate students.

Rotter has been the author of numerous papers, chapters, monographs, books, and test manuals published over the years. His best-known work, *Social Learning and Clinical Psychology,* was published in 1954 and is the major statement of his theory. In 1972, with the collaboration of June Chance and Jerry Phares, he published *Applications of a Social Learning Theory of Personality.* A monograph on the topic of internal versus external control of reinforcement was published in 1966, and it has had a major influence on the study of this personality dimension. In recent years, Rotter has turned his attention to the study of interpersonal trust. A chapter providing an overview of social learning theory and its background, concepts, research, and implications may be found in Phares (1980). A collection of Rotter's important papers has appeared more recently (Rotter, 1982).

In 1989 Rotter was the recipient of the American Psychological Association's Distinguished Scientist Award for his pioneering efforts in establishing a social learning framework that transformed behavioral approaches to personality and clinical psychology.

nitions, verbal behavior, nonverbal expressive behavior, emotional reactions, and so on" (Rotter and Hochreich, 1975, p. 96).

Expectancy. The central focus of Rotter's theory is **expectancy** (E). Expectancy refers to a person's subjective probability that a certain reinforcement will occur if a specific behavior is selected in the situation in question. In one situation, my expectancy that hard work will pay off may be high; in another situation, my expectancy regarding the utility of hard work may be low. Behavior potential is determined not just by how badly we want a certain goal but also by the extent to which we believe that a specific behavior will help us reach it.

A person's expectancies do not always correspond to reality. Some people are often overconfident or have unrealistically high expectancies for their success in a given situation. In other cases, individuals consistently underestimate the

According to social learning theory, behavior is determined by expectancy and reinforcement value. How hard this person studies depends on how well he thinks he will do, and how much value he places on doing well on an exam.

likelihood of their own success. But if we are to predict a person's behavior we must consider the subjective probabilities of that person and not those that are based on empirical study or the opinion of experts.

Rotter distinguishes between expectancies that are specific to one situation—**specific expectancies (E')**—and **generalized expectancies (GE)**, those that are more general and apply to several situations. A good example of this distinction is the case of a student who has a low specific expectancy for doing well in an algebra class but has a rather high generalized expectancy for academic success in other classes. A generalized expectancy reflects experiences accumulated over a variety of related situations (in this example, academic ones). A specific expectancy, in contrast, is based upon experience in one particular situation (an algebra class, for example).

This distinction helps account, in part, for the difference between a person's subjectively held probability for the success of a given behavior and what others feel should be a realistic expectancy. The individual may know of similarities between a certain situation and other previously encountered ones and generalize accordingly. Observers may not know of this similarity and fail to make the generalization. Consider a basketball team that has won ten games in a row and tonight is playing a team that has won only one game. Going by this information, we are puzzled to learn that the star player of the team expects the game to be close and is not confident of victory. What we do not know is that the star player's parents will be attending the game. He knows from past experience that he rarely plays well in front of them, and he is generalizing his low expectancy for victory from that specific experience rather than from the previous ten games and tonight's weak opponent.

Another point illustrated by the basketball example is that expectancy for success is influenced by both specific and generalized expectancies. The star player's expectancy resulted from the combination of his expectancies based upon prior experience with his opponents and those generalized from what he knew about his performance in front of his parents. Of course, when we face a situation for the first time, expectancies generalized from past related situations will have a strong influence on our expectancies in the new situation. As we gain more experience in the situation, specific expectancies for that situation will develop. For example, when students first enroll in a class, their expectancies for passing the course will be based almost entirely on their overall experience generalized from related classes. However, after they are two-thirds through the term and have taken four examinations, their expectancies will then be determined almost exclusively by their specific experience on the four examinations rather than their generalized expectancies.

**Reinforcement Value.** Suppose you could have a new wardrobe, an A in this class, or a new friend? Which would you choose? This illustrates the essence of **reinforcement value (RV)**, which is the degree to which an individual prefers one outcome over another. This is the motivational component of Rotter's theory that combines with his cognitive variable of expectancy. Just as people differ among themselves regarding their expectancies, they also differ in the value they place on various reinforcements. I prefer steak over seafood; you do not. You order salad; I order soup.

Reinforcement value is a relative term. The reinforcement value of an outcome can be determined only by comparing that outcome to other possible outcomes. Thus, if you ask someone to go to a movie and he or she agrees, you know little about the reinforcement value of movies for that person (other than that the person would rather go to the movies than do nothing). If you ask the person if he or she would like to go to a movie, or to dinner, or to a concert and the person chooses a movie, then you can infer that the reinforcement value of a movie is greater than dinner or a concert—at least in this situation. Thus, the reinforcement value of a given event has no absolute value, only value relative to other available events.

What determines the value of a reinforcement? This is a difficult question, one that is not fully answered by Rotter's theory. For Rotter, the value of a particular reinforcement is determined by the expectancy that the reinforcement will lead to other reinforcements of value. For example, money has value not in and of itself but because it buys things of value such as food, clothes, and prestige. But then the value of food, clothes, and prestige must be determined. What Rotter is implying is that no reinforcement has value in and of itself. It achieves value only through the individual's expectancy that it will, in turn, lead to something else. Thus, it is not possible to provide an ultimate answer to the question of what determines reinforcement value. Rotter's theory provides a means for measuring reinforcement value, but it does not fully explain it.

**The Psychological Situation.** Rotter emphasizes the explicit role of the **psychological situation** as a determinant of behavior. By using the term *psychological* situation, Rotter emphasizes the person's interpretation of a situation rather than its physical characteristics. Also, he recognizes that the same physical situation may be psychologically different for different people. For example, you may love this course and your roommate may hate it. This makes sitting in this classroom psychologically different for you and your roommate even though you are in the same physical situation. Although Rotter recognizes the influence of enduring predispositions, he argues that for too long, personality psychologists ignored the role of situational contexts and their effects on human behavior (Rotter, 1981). His contention is that in every case, we must calculate the value of a reinforcement or the magnitude of an expectancy in relation to a specific situation. We learn through experience that a goal is more attainable in one situation than in another. We also learn that attainment of a goal in one setting is more valuable than it is in another. For example, a child may learn that a kiss from mother is reinforcing at home but that in the park it may lead to mocking taunts from other children that considerably reduce its value.

**The Predictive Formulas.** The manner in which behavior potential, reinforcement value, expectancy, and the psychological situation combine to influence goal-directed behavior is described by the following formula:

$$BP_{x, s1, Ra} = f(E_{x, Ra, s1} \text{ and } RV_{a,s1})$$

That is, the potential for behavior $x$ to occur in situation 1 ($s1$) in relation to reinforcement $a$ ($Ra$) is a function of the expectancy of the occurrence of reinforcement $a$ following behavior $x$ in situation 1 and the value of reinforcement $a$ in situation 1 (Rotter, 1967b, p. 490).

This equation provides a summary of Rotter's theory, but it is not a precise equation. For example the function that combines expectancy and reinforcement value is not defined. Likewise, what constitutes a situation and the determination of reinforcement value and expectancy are also not specified. Thus, this equation could not be used to make precise predictions about a person's behavior. Instead, its value is **heuristic**; that is, it provides a general framework for considering how the elements of Rotter's theory combine to influence a person's behavioral choices. For example, imagine being faced with a choice between going to a football game on Saturday afternoon or going to the library to work on a term paper. The behavior with the higher potential is the one you will choose. If we knew the value of the reinforcements associated with each behavior and the corresponding expectancies that each behavior would lead to the reinforcements involved, I could readily predict which of the two options you would choose.

There is another limitation in this formula. It concerns specific behaviors in specific situations in relation to single, specific reinforcements. Thus, it is not useful for describing a person's general tendencies to act in certain ways across a range of situations. For example, an academic counselor is usually not interested in the occurrence of the specific behavior of a student's cutting a chemistry class on one particular day. More likely, the counselor is concerned with that student's general tendency to avoid academic responsibilities in all classes by engaging in a variety of behaviors such as skipping class, being late with assignments, and failing to study. Understanding general tendencies or dispositions requires the consideration of multiple behaviors, expectancies, and reinforcement values.

Rotter (1954) proposed the following heuristic formula to characterize how this might be accomplished in the context of social learning theory:

$$NP = f(FM \text{ and } NV)$$

This equation indicates that the potential for the occurrence of a set of behaviors (**need potential [NP]**) that leads to the satisfaction of a certain general need is a function of (1) the expectancies (**freedom of movement [FM]**) that these behaviors will satisfy that need and (2) the value of that need (**need value [NV]**).

To continue the previous example, the academic counselor wonders why the student's need potential for academic recognition is low. The counselor discovers that the student assigns a high value to reinforcements that together represent the need value for academic recognition (e.g., A's in class, praise from teachers, and recognition from peers). However, the student has a low expectancy that studying will help performance, is not confident that teachers will show respect for a good performance, and doubts that peers will care much about academic achievements. Thus, the student's overall expectancy (freedom of movement) that academically oriented behaviors will bring academic recognition is low. From a social learning perspective, this is why the student fails to study, cuts class, daydreams, and so on. The contrast between the *BP* and *NP* formulas is shown in Table 11-1.

### Generalized Expectancies for Solving Problems.

Every situation presents individuals with different "problems" that must be solved to obtain reinforcement. In their pursuit of goals, people develop generalized expectancies or attitudes as to how best to approach or construe situations to obtain reinforcement. Individuals differ in their general expectations for problem solving on the basis of their unique prior experiences. One important generalized expectancy is **interpersonal trust**: the extent to which one can rely on others for solving problems and obtaining reinforcement (Rotter, 1971). We know from research that a person high

## ◑ Table 11-1

## Specific Versus General Prediction

| BP | | E | | RV |
|---|---|---|---|---|
| 1. Potential for: Attending chemistry class | is determined by | Expectancy that attending class will lead to a passing grade | and | Value of achieving a passing grade in chemistry |
| **NP** | | **FM** | | **NV** |
| 2. Potential for the following set of behaviors: studying, reading assignments, attending class, writing optional papers | is determined by | Average expectancy that the set of behaviors will satisfy the need for academic recognition | and | Average value of the following goals that together constitute the need for academic recognition: good grades, making the honor roll, praise from teachers and peers |

in interpersonal trust is likely to trust others when confronted with a problem situation involving statements by other people.

Another important generalized expectancy is **internal versus external control of reinforcement (I-E),** or, as some refer to it, **locus of control.** Locus of control refers to a person's belief about what generally controls the reinforcements he or she receives. This expectancy is one of the most intensively studied personality constructs (Phares, 1976; Rotter, 1966). People who are internally oriented tend to attribute the outcomes of their behavior to their own efforts or to personal characteristics. More externally oriented persons are likely to view outcomes as the result of luck, fate, and other powerful forces. This distinction is illustrated by the ways different people may approach a problem. When "internals" are faced with a problem, they tend to confront it actively because they expect that their efforts can make a difference. On the other hand, "externals" are more likely to respond passively because they believe that outcomes are the result of forces that they can not influence.

Although the expectancies of interpersonal trust and locus of control are used to describe individuals' general or typical approach to situations, these attitudes may differ in the same individual across domains. For example, an individual may be trusting of health professionals but not of salespersons. Likewise, an individual may have an internal locus of control in academic situations but be an external in social settings.

## Development of Personality

Rotter's theory does not explicitly address personality development, although this does not mean that social learning has no implications for personality development. Indeed, social learning theory has generated a variety of empirical studies in areas such as children's behavior, parental attitudes, and the development of achievement motivation (e.g., Grusec, 1992).

Following Dollard and Miller as well as Maslow, Rotter believes that psychological needs arise out of the satisfaction of physiological ones. Rotter (1954) has described six broad categories of needs that are the motivation for human behavior.

- *Recognition-Status:* Need to excel, to be viewed as competent, good, or better than others in domains such as school, occupation, athletics, social standing, and appearance.
- *Dominance:* Need to control others; exercise power and influence over others.
- *Independence:* Need to make own decisions, rely on oneself, achieve goals without help from others.
- *Protection-Dependency:* Need to have others prevent frustrations, provide protection and security, and help one achieve valued goals.
- *Love and Affection:* Need to be accepted and liked by others, to have the devoted interest, concern, and affection of others.
- *Physical Comfort:* Need to enjoy physical satisfactions associated with security and a feeling of well-being, to avoid pain, to experience bodily pleasures.

## Nature of Adjustment

According to social learning theory, the question of maladjustment is an ethical one, and the definition of maladjusted behavior resides in cultural norms or in personal attitudes. Consequently, there are no social learning principles that apply to maladjustment separate from behavior generally. However, social learning has some definite implications for the nature of maladjustment (Katkovsky, 1976; Phares, 1972).

Low Freedom of Movement—High Need Value. In general, maladjustment results when the individual places a high value on the satisfaction of a particular need but has very low freedom of movement (expectancies) for the success of behaviors that could lead to the satisfaction of that need. For example, consider a socially awkward man who wants love and affection from women but does not believe he possesses the behaviors likely to achieve those goals. His low expectation will result in a low need potential (NP) for those behaviors that might help him to obtain love and affection. He will have a tendency to avoid women, fail to show up for a blind date, or engage in excessive fantasy behavior. Of course, if this individual were gay, or did not otherwise value heterosexual love and affection, his low expectancies would not be a problem.

Most neurotic symptoms represent a set of avoidant behaviors calculated to handle the discrepancy between need value and freedom of movement. These maladaptive behaviors are used because the person hopes to avoid the punishment or discomfort of trying to satisfy valued needs and failing. Thus, for the man in our example, repeatedly missing parties avoids the punishment that would occur if the women at the party ignored him.

**Conflict.** In some cases, the individual places a high value on needs that are incompatible. This generally results in a conflict that is not easily resolved, and also leads to maladaptive avoidant behaviors. For example, a homosexual who wants acceptance from his traditional parents will find it difficult to maintain his sexual orientation and satisfy his need for parental acceptance. Thus, he may hide his sexual orientation from his parents, or he may avoid spending time at home.

**Lack of Competency.** Repeatedly avoiding certain situations prevents the individual from learning the behaviors that would result in competency. Not attending parties precludes the development of both dancing and conversational skills. Indeed, it may be the absence of certain skills that is the basis for low expectations of success. For example, a child with a chronic, severe physical ailment may not have been able to interact with other children to develop good social skills. Subsequently, the lack of those skills may lead to a variety of adjustment problems.

**Minimal Goal Level.** In social learning theory, **minimal goal level** refers to the lowest goal in a hierarchy of reinforcements that is perceived by the individual as reinforcing. Thus, for some students a grade point average of C is viewed as reinforcing—their minimal goals are low in the academic need area. For other students only A's are reinforcing. In the absence of competency, high minimal goal levels will increase the possibilities of experiencing failure and disappointment. In other instances, people have low minimal goals and thus appear so unmotivated that others in the culture may regard them as deviant individuals with many problems.

**Failure to Discriminate.** Sometimes the value of a need may become so high that it dominates the person's life. This may result in a variety of distortions of reality or in a failure to discriminate among situations. For example, an individual may have such a strong need to be liked that he or she indiscriminately gives expensive gifts to casual acquaintances. Very likely, such behavior will come to be regarded as rather bizarre by others. The case study, on pages 361–362, deals with a social learning theory analysis of anxiety reactions in an executive and illustrates several of these causes of maladjustment.

**Enhancement Behaviors.** Rotter (1982) has also discussed enhancement behaviors. Such behaviors may allow the person to behave in a way that allows the effects of positive reinforcement to be prolonged or the effects of punishment or

# CASE STUDY

## A Social Learning Theory Case Study

A thirty-five-year-old insurance executive reports that for the past two months he has been experiencing intermittent panic reactions, nausea, insomnia, and a variety of other physical complaints. A complete medical workup fails to reveal any medical problems. The patient himself is alarmed and, despite the negative medical report, feels that he has some dread and yet subtle disease. He can provide no psychological explanation and reports that everything in his life is going well. With reluctance, he accepts his physician's recommendation and visits a psychiatrist. With the material elicited during his therapy contacts it was possible to characterize his problem using the principles of social learning theory.

For many years the patient had been motivated by strong needs for achievement and recognition. His father had been prominent in the community, and his mother had made it clear in abundant ways during his childhood that great things were expected of him.

However, he had doubts about his capabilities. Thus, his expectancies for the achievement of success and recognition were not commensurate with the strength of these needs. In most instances, however, during childhood, high school, and college he operated in fairly structured situations and was able to perform quite well. Prior to examinations in both high school and college he would become anxious. The examination situations were so overwhelming that the discrepancy between expectancy for success and the strength of his recognition needs generated distress. Through diligent preparation, however, he was able to overcome the effects of the anxiety and perform well. Indeed, at the time this anxiety did not alarm him, because he "explained" it to himself as purely situationally determined and something that everybody experienced.

After college he joined the insurance firm and through hard work, loyalty, and good performance, he was steadily promoted. During this period he married, had two children, and acquired all the usual responsibilities of a middle-class American. It was only after his promotion to the executive position that the anxiety reactions occurred. Suddenly he was placed in an unstructured position—he was no longer following orders, he had to establish policy, develop original ideas, and give orders to others. His expectancies were low that he could achieve success in such a situation. Through generalization, he construed the present situation, wherein both his employers and family expected great things from him, as similar to those situations early in life wherein his parents expected him to achieve in the image of his father. Now he was expected to achieve in the image of an executive.

Placed in this situation, he expected to fail. Adding to his distress about failure was the disruption that failure would cause to the lives of his wife and children. From

(continued)

Case Study (*continued*)

a social learning perspective, the goal of therapy would be to reduce the conflict be-tween the high need to succeed as an executive and the low expectation for success. Several strategies could be employed. He could resign his position and return to the job at which he felt confident. Alternatively, if he wanted to keep his promotion but lacked the competence to develop plans and give orders, some training to improve these skills would be appropriate. However, simply acquiring these skills might not be sufficient. Some form of cognitive restructuring to help the executive believe that he could do the job might also be necessary. (Phares, 1972, pp. 458–459)

discomfort to be diminished. For example, some people are generally happy, content, optimistic, or in a good mood most of the time. But their objective life circumstances may not differ from those of others who are typically unhappy, discontented, pessimistic, or depressed. Perhaps there are specific cognitive be-haviors that some people use to maintain a good feeling. These behaviors might include imaginative rehearsal of good outcomes, conscious resistance to raising one's minimal goals, or a tendency to focus on positive features of situations rather than their negative aspects. Although some would generally regard such cognitions as distortions of reality that are unhealthy, Rotter thinks otherwise. He believes that these cognitions may help prevent or reduce the effects of stress.

## Implications for Behavior Change

Rotter's social learning equations make it clear that behavior change will result from changes in the values of various needs, the expectancies the individual has about satisfying those needs, or both. Therefore, if behavior is to change, free-dom of movement or need value must first be altered. As a therapist, Rotter em-phasized the need to work directly on values and expectancies to change behav-ior and to examine the role of situational or environmental contributors to the patient's problems.

Rotter's social learning theory is useful for analyzing patients' problems and aiding in the setting of therapeutic goals. For example, when the theory is used as a framework, the patient's needs can be identified along with the corresponding expectations for their fulfillment. Once this is done, therapeutic goals often be-come apparent. A patient expressing severe anxiety might turn out to have very strong needs for dependency. Yet, his wife is not very supportive, with the result that his expectations for satisfying these needs have declined to the point where a variety of symptoms have arisen. Likewise, social learning theory provides a framework for disentangling, clarifying, and targeting the cause of the patient's problem. For one patient, the problem is a behavioral deficit. For another, it is low expectancies for success or perhaps needs that are too high. In still another case, the individual's minimal goals may be too high (or too low).

Social learning theory has a variety of other implications for therapeutic practice (Rotter, 1970), a few of which are listed here:

- Therapy is a learning process through which the therapist helps the patient achieve planned changes in behavior and thinking.
- A patient's difficulties are best viewed as efforts to solve problems.
- Very often the therapist guides the learning process so that inappropriate behaviors and attitudes are weakened and more appropriate ones are strengthened.
- Particular attention should be devoted to the manner in which inappropriate behavior and expectancies arise and also to the ways in which patients overgeneralize from their previous experience.
- New experiences in real life are often effective in bringing about behavior changes and are at least as important for change as what transpires during the therapy session.
- Therapy can be viewed as a form of social interaction.

The foregoing implications specifically suggest flexibility of techniques from one patient to another, the desirability of enhancing patients' problem-solving skills, an active role for the therapist ranging from interpretations to direct reinforcement, the importance of guiding patients into real-life settings that will help promote change, and the idea that those principles that apply to behavior generally also apply to the therapy process. Moreover, they emphasize the importance of cognition in conjunction with environmental factors for understanding and influencing a person's actions. This blend of cognition and learning theory is what has made social learning theory one of the most compelling models of human personality.

## Bandura's Social Cognitive Theory

Albert Bandura's approach to social learning (or what he has recently been referring to as **social cognitive theory**) is complementary to that of Rotter. Bandura's theory concerns how people develop or learn the behaviors that they choose, whereas Rotter's theory is an explanation of how people choose between different possible actions. For Rotter the emphasis is on choice; for Bandura it is on acquisition.

Bandura has been successful at integrating ideas from older theories with newer perspectives and developments. For example, like Rotter, he believes that behavior is determined by both reinforcement and expectancies. Unlike many earlier learning theorists, however, he contends that behavior can be learned in the absence of reinforcement. Specifically, Bandura emphasizes the importance of **observational learning**, which is the ability to perform many behaviors by observing and copying others. But whether or not we then exhibit those behaviors depends on our expectations for reinforcement. More recently, Bandura has developed the concept of **self-efficacy**, the belief that one can successfully perform a given behavior as a central component for predicting human behavior. He regards one's personal sense of self-efficacy to be a powerful influence on thought patterns, behavior, and emotional arousal (Bandura, 1982).

Bandura's work is also characterized by a commitment, by both word and deed, to the role of empirical research in personality study. He has produced a large volume of research that has establish the credibility of his theoretical ideas both within and without the laboratory.

## Two Theoretical Principles

Bandura has proposed a number of influential theoretical concepts, including reciprocal determinism, observational learning, vicarious reinforcement, and self-efficacy. All of these concepts are based on an expanded view of the concept of reinforcement and on the importance of cognition for human behavior.

### Beyond Direct Reinforcement.
Direct reinforcement is inadequate as an explanation of the acquisition of all human behavior. If every single response unit in complicated social acts had to occur separately and then be reinforced, it would take forever to learn anything. Although Bandura recognizes the importance of reinforcement, he does not regard it as the only way behaviors are acquired. People can learn merely by observing others and can then repeat what they have seen.

The customary reinforcements on which classical and operant conditioning depend are not always necessary. For example, children born in the United States have grown up in an automobile-oriented country. Most have ridden in cars for longer than they can recall. Therefore, when they finally begin to learn to drive, they have already acquired many of the needed techniques by observation. In contrast, young adults who come to the United States from Third World countries sometimes have great difficulty with driving, largely because they have had much less opportunity to observe this activity as youngsters.

However, Bandura does not claim that reinforcement is irrelevant for the performance of complex behavior. Once a behavior is learned, reinforcement is important in determining whether that behavior will occur. Therefore, although I may learn much about driving by observing others, whether I climb behind the wheel and turn the ignition switch depends on the goals toward which the behavior is directed.

### Cognition.
Behavior is determined not just by actual reinforcement but also by anticipated reinforcement. This suggests the importance Bandura attaches to cognition. Traditional learning theorists were often hampered by their inability (or unwillingness) to come to grips with cognitive processes. Bandura sees the human organism not merely as a machine guided by the judicious application of reinforcements by others. He views us as thinking, knowing creatures who use images, thoughts, and plans. We plan for the future, we regulate our behavior through internal standards, and we foresee the consequences of our behavior.

## A BRIEF BIOGRAPHY OF

# Albert Bandura

Albert Bandura was born in 1925 in a small town in Alberta, Canada. He received a B.A. degree in 1949 from the University of British Columbia. His M.A. (1951) and Ph.D. (1952) degrees were from the University of Iowa. During that time, psychology at Iowa was strongly influenced by the presence and scholarship of Kenneth Spence. The emphasis was on Hullian learning theory and vigorous conceptual analysis and experimental rigor. After a clinical internship at the Wichita Guidance Center, Bandura accepted a faculty position at Stanford University, where he remains today.

His career at Stanford has been prolific. In his early years, his research was focused on psychotherapy processes and the role of family patterns in producing aggression in children. Since then, his interests have included behavior modification, modeling, observational learning, self-regulatory processes, and self-efficacy.

Bandura has received many professional honors. In 1980 he received the Distinguished Scientist Award from the American Psychological Association for being a leader in the application of the social, symbolic, and self-regulatory determinants of meaningful learning and behavior change. Following that he was elected president of the American Psychological Association. At Stanford he continues teaching both undergraduate and graduate courses.

Because Bandura has been such a prolific contributor to the literature over the years, it is difficult to single out just a few works. Two early well-known books, *Adolescent Aggression* (1959) and *Social Learning and Personality Development* (1963), were written in collaboration with the late Richard Walters. *Principles of Behavior Modification* appeared in 1969, followed by *Aggression: A Social Learning Analysis* in 1973. In *Social Learning Theory,* published in 1977, he integrates theoretical and experimental work in the field of social learning. His most recent book, *Social Foundations of Thought and Action: A Social Cognitive Theory,* appeared in 1986. He is also the author of many articles and chapters.

This view goes beyond the animal model of behavior that developed out of the experimental laboratories.

## Reciprocal Determinism

For Bandura, behavior is the result of both personal and environmental variables. In personality, three views of these variables combine to influence behavior. First, persons and situations can be treated as independent variables that, when brought together, produce behavior. Thus, to explain why someone gets involved in a fight in a bar, you would consider his characteristic trait of aggression and the situational fact that there was an especially obnoxious person standing next to him.

A second view is that the combination of personal and environmental factors is not accidental or random. Instead, an individual's personal characteristics may lead that individual to seek out or create situations in which those characteristics can be exhibited. A person with aggressive needs may seek out situations that present opportunities that stimulate those very same needs. So it is that an aggressive person repeatedly patronizes a bar that caters to the kind of people who pick fights with other customers.

Bandura has emphasized a third possibility, which he has labeled **reciprocal determinism**. This view emphasizes how all three variables—behavior, person, and situation—mutually influence each other. Getting into the fight stimulates aggressive needs, which in turn impel the person to seek out the bar again, which will provide the opportunity to satisfy the aggressive needs. Behavior influences needs, which influence behavior, which influences needs, which influence the environment, which . . . These three views are illustrated schematically in Figure 11-1.

For Bandura (1986), people are neither autonomous nor mechanical responders to environmental influence. They are, instead, active contributors to their own motivation and action. Behavior, thought, emotion, other personal factors, and environmental events all combine to determine behavior.

## Observational Learning

**Observational learning** is learning through observing the behavior of others. This is a simple concept and one that we can all illustrate by a thousand examples from our own experience. Children learn how to smoke by watching their parents. Young teenagers learn the newest slang by listening to their older peers. First-time parents learn about child rearing from watching and consulting parents who have brought up several children.

Bandura recognized that this simple concept was in need of elaboration if it were to provide a compelling basis for learning. We do not just imitate the actions of others by rote. We pick and choose from different models and instances and combine them into novel behavioral products (Bandura, 1974). Again, we are not mere parrots but thinking consumers of the examples of others.

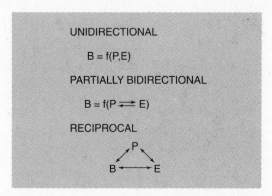

UNIDIRECTIONAL

$B = f(P, E)$

PARTIALLY BIDIRECTIONAL

$B = f(P \rightleftharpoons E)$

RECIPROCAL

P

B ← → E

**Figure 11-1**    Diagram of interactional patterns. B=behavior, P=person, E=environment.

For example, the struggling young singer may begin by imitating the style of her idol. But gradually she takes a bit from this singer, copies a little of the style of another, and imitates some of the gestures of still another. She processes, codes, and stores this information in memory so that it will be available on subsequent occasions should the need arise. Ultimately, this mixture is fashioned into a single, unique style scarcely recognizable as an imitation. Thus, she has learned without being reinforced.

Observation provides us with information. But what are the processes that occur in observational learning? For Bandura (1977), observational learning is a four-stage process.

**Attentional Processes.** The first stage comprises **attentional processes**. We learn through observation only if we attend to the model's behavior, recognize its important aspects, and differentiate among its distinctive features. Thus, for observational learning to occur, there must be the opportunity for observation. The child who never sees anyone at home read a newspaper has little opportunity to observe such behavior. Likewise, we are not likely to attend to people who are viewed by others as unimportant or lacking in value. People who are interpersonally attractive, glamorous, or magnetic are more likely to influence us as models. Then, too, able, competent people more frequently get our attention.

**Retention Processes.** Often we see a model only infrequently. Therefore, to reproduce the model's behavior, we must remember it. Our capacity to recall the critical elements of the model's behavior is crucial. Bandura proposes that our **retention processes** (second stage) are facilitated in two principal ways. We form mental images that provide us with long-lasting and readily retrievable sources of information about the model. We also verbally code the model's actions. For example, I may say to myself, "The pitcher steps on the mound, looks at the runner on first, takes a deep breath, and looks to the catcher for the sign." These verbal cues provide me with a helpful code that I can invoke later when it's my turn to go to bat.

**Motor Reproduction Processes.** In the third stage, the previously coded mental images and verbal cues are translated into **motor reproduction**—I do what those images and cues tell me that my model did previously. This translation may take time, effort, and practice, depending upon the level of complexity and skill involved. Although executing a dance step may appear simple, I will likely be less than graceful on my first few attempts, no matter how well I have attended to and retained the actions of my dancer-model.

**Motivational Processes.** Observational learning can occur in the absence of reinforcement. But **motivational processes** (fourth stage) are still important. The manner in which we attend to models has already been identified as being influenced by motivation. Whether we do what we have observed is also affected by motivation. Without motivation, the processes of attention, retention, and reproduction may not occur. But in combination with motivation, these processes are powerful determinants of the acquisition and performance of complex social behaviors. Together with conditioning, they explain much of human social behavior.

## Vicarious Reinforcement and Conditioning

By observing models, we learn how to act in ways we have not acted before. But in some instances, we have already learned the behavior, and the effect of the model is to teach us when we should or should not exhibit that behavior. The concepts of vicarious reinforcement and vicarious conditioning were introduced to explain how this occurs.

**Vicarious reinforcement** occurs when watching a model receive reinforcement for acting in a certain way also reinforces, albeit less intensely, the observer. If I watch someone tip a headwaiter and then be rewarded with an excellent table, I can vicariously experience the reward. The result is that I am more likely to tip (assuming I have the money and wish to have a good table). The same principle applies to punishment. Observing a police officer writing a ticket for a speeder leads me to reduce my speed because I vicariously experience the other driver's punishment. Naturally, I will imitate only those behaviors leading to outcomes that are, for me, reinforcing and avoid those behaviors resulting in consequences that are, to me, negative.

**Vicarious conditioning** also occurs. Through classical conditioning a person can be taught to react fearfully to a buzzer if it is consistently followed by a painful electric shock. What is also interesting, however, is that someone merely observing this model will often become vicariously conditioned and likewise react to the buzzer with fear (Bandura and Rosenthal, 1966). This suggests that a variety of human fears are learned not through direct personal experience but by watching the experience of others.

## Self-Regulation

The extreme view of reinforcement proposed by radical behaviorists (e.g., that of Skinner) would seem to portray us as being at the mercy of whatever external rewards and punishments we have experienced. They would suggest that we constantly look to the environment to check the consequences of our latest behavior. If the behavior is rewarded, we will do it again; if not, we try something else. This is not Bandura's view. His is a more complex perspective that takes into account the possibility of self-reinforcement. In addition to being governed by external rewards and punishments, our behavior is also governed by **internal standards,** which are the reinforcements we dispense to ourselves: I feel pride when my performance exceeds my expectations; I push myself to greater effort when I fail to achieve the goal I have set for myself. People constantly monitor their own behavior. Consequently, our actions are regulated not just by environmental rewards and punishments but by self-regulated standards. This gives a consistency and coherence to our behavior and cognitions that would not exist if we were completely at the mercy of external events.

We learn our standards through the rewards and punishments administered by significant others in response to our behavior. When a child brings home a C in arithmetic, her mother may frown and demand that she work harder. Another mother might have been pleased with a C, in which case the daughter would have learned to be satisfied with such a grade. These standards acquired from others form the basis of one's self-regulatory system. This concept is similar to Rotter's minimal goal levels. There is also evidence to suggest that these standards can be acquired from others vicariously. For example, children who observe the behavior of a model with low standards may impose lower standards for their own behavior (Bandura and Kupers, 1964).

## Self-Efficacy

Bandura (1982) has increasingly emphasized the role of self-efficacy. **Self-efficacy** is the belief that one can successfully execute a given behavior. The belief that one can do something has a powerful effect on behavior, emotions, and motives (Bandura, 1989). We act on the basis of an assessment of our capabilities; our judgments determine not only whether we will act but also how long we will persist and how much punishment we will absorb in carrying out the action.

Our beliefs about self-efficacy also determine how extensively we will prepare ourselves for tasks and which ones we will select. Beyond that, self-efficacy influences our thought patterns and emotions. A person lacking in confidence often dwells on personal inadequacies and typically judges tasks as more difficult than they really are. This increases the likelihood of failure through misplaced concentration.

Kirsch (1985) has observed that Bandura's concept of self-efficacy is similar to Rotter's expectancy concept. Indeed, the assessment of self-efficacy and expectancy is virtually identical. Moreover, whenever an attempt is made to disentangle these two concepts through different measures, the two measures are correlated and predict behavior about equally well (Maddux, Norton, and Stoltenberg, 1986).

## Development of Personality

Bandura emphasizes the differences among individuals of a similar age and sees in them proof of the role of biological, socioeconomic, ethnic, and cultural factors. He does not regard people as passing through well-defined stages of development and, indeed, asserts that stage theorists rarely agree among themselves about the characteristics of the stages or even their number (Bandura and Walters, 1963). For Bandura, issues of development center on changes in individuals' goals, plans, self-efficacy, and other cognitive factors that influence how they respond to the environment. These changes may be understood through the principles of observational learning, vicarious reinforcement, self-regulation, and reciprocal determinism.

## Nature of Adjustment

Bandura's social cognitive theory is similar to behavioral theories in its characterization of adjustment and maladjustment. As with these theories, social cognitive theory focuses on environmental factors that currently serve to maintain undesirable behavior, and it views maladjustment as a set of overt behaviors rather than as the product of underlying pathology. Maladjustment arises out of the learning process either as the result of direct experience or through vicarious learning. Once acquired, deviant behavior is also maintained by direct and vicarious reinforcement.

However, with his emphasis, Bandura goes beyond the simplicity of Skinnerian notions of maladjustment. Expectancies, self-regulation, and observational learning can modify and contribute to the environmental contingencies. Expecting that certain behaviors or situations will lead to negative reinforcement often causes the person to use a variety of defensive behaviors. Note that for Bandura defenses are conscious acts to avoid an unpleasant experience. This differs from the Freudian concept of defense as an unconscious mental operation to keep disturbing thoughts from the conscious mind. For example, if the individual expects to be rejected by others or is low in perceived self-efficacy for obtaining social reinforcement, the result may be to avoid people. This, in turn, may lead others to regard the person as someone to avoid. Ultimately, then, the environment reinforces those maladaptive expectancies and beliefs. Similarly, if the person imposes exceptionally high standards on himself or herself, the result may be frequent failure, which may force the individual to resort to a variety of defenses.

Although defensive behaviors protect the person from feeling bad, they generally have negative consequences. They tend to remove the individual from situations in which new learning is possible. If a person never ventures into new settings, the old maladaptive expectancies and beliefs about self continue. Furthermore, the individual does not get the opportunity to come into contact with new models. For example, suppose your parents have consistently told you that you are unimportant or stupid. They repeatedly play on your negative self-image. These, then, are your models. Because they have taught you to be unsure and to lack confidence, you become fearful of meeting new people, engaging new ideas, or trying new behaviors. As a result, you avoid the very things that might rescue you from inadequate parental models and provide you with the opportunity for changing your expectancies and beliefs about self-efficacy.

## Implications for Behavior Change

Bandura's research on approaches to changing behavior generally involves specific behavior problems such as phobias. Whether the results of this work will apply to the entire panorama of human complaints such as psychoses, alienation, or identity crises has not yet been demonstrated.

Guided Participation. The basis of most of Bandura's treatment is observational learning through the technique of **guided participation**. In guided participation, the patient or subject is led by assistants through a series of steps that ultimately end in the performance of the desired behavior. The best illustration of this procedure comes from a widely cited study by Bandura, Blanchard, and Ritter (1969). These researchers were interested in the relative efficacy of several methods of treating snake phobias in adults. Their subjects, all intensely afraid of snakes, answered a newspaper advertisement that promised help for their fears. The subjects were randomly divided into four groups. The first of the three experimental groups received Wolpe's behavioral systematic desensitization treatment (described in Chapter 10); the second, a form of symbolic modeling via watching a film; and the third, access to a live model with guided participation. The fourth group consisted of control subjects who received no treatment.

Subjects in the symbolic modeling condition viewed a film depicting children, adolescents, and adults who gradually became involved in more and more "frightening" contact with a snake. This contact ranged from handling plastic snakes to allowing a large and very real snake to crawl all over them (Figure 11-2). These subjects also learned how to relax during the course of the film, and they could stop the film when they felt anxious or rewind it to an earlier, less threatening segment. This procedure is similar to the use of anxiety hierarchies in systematic desensitization. Subjects in the live modeling group observed a model (behind a window) handling a snake in a relaxed manner. Then the model came

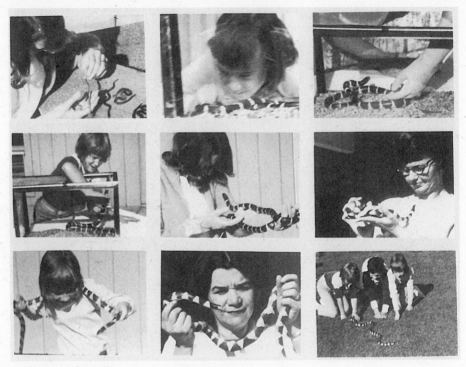

**Figure 11-2** &#x6208;&#x6208; Models handling snakes in Bandura's research.

out from behind the window and continued handling the snake in the presence of the subject. Gradually, the model induced the subject to participate by touching, rubbing, and eventually holding the snake. At first the subject used gloves, then bare hands. The whole procedure was self-paced and was based on the subject's level of anxiety at each stage.

The results indicated several things. First, control subjects showed no changes in their fear of snakes over the course of the study. Second, subjects in both the systematic desensitization and symbolic modeling groups showed significant reductions in fear. However, the live modeling–guided participation group demonstrated the greatest reduction in fear. The improvement of subjects in the live modeling group was so great that all of them eventually could sit for thirty seconds with a live snake crawling about their laps. These results are shown in Figure 11-3.

**Self-Efficacy as an Explanation.** A behavioral explanation of these results would use the concepts of counterconditioning and extinction. Bandura's social cognitive theory, however, uses the concept of self-efficacy. The perception of oneself as competent and in control can have a substantial effect on one's anxieties, defensive symptoms, and behavior. Through the methods of observation and guided participation, an expectancy of self-efficacy arises from four principal

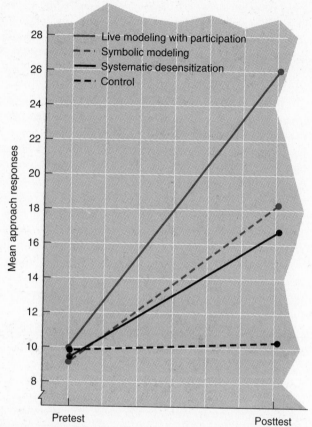

**Figure 11-3** ∞ Mean number of approach responses performed by subjects before and after receiving their respective treatments.

sources. The most influential source is **enactive attainment,** which is one's own performance in the dreaded situation. But self-efficacy can also result from the **vicarious experience** of watching the performance of others, verbal persuasion from others, and one's own physiological state.

## Mischel: A Cognitive Social Learning Reconceptualization of Personality

Mischel's social learning ideas have been influenced by Rotter's theory and by his close contact with Bandura at Stanford. Initially, Mischel's view of personality had a behavioral emphasis that stressed the importance of situational variables for understanding behavior. He is generally regarded as the most influential and vocal opponent of the role of personal characteristics in influencing behavior. In

1968 he published *Personality and Assessment,* a book that criticized the utility of internal person variables, such as traits and psychodynamic concepts, for predicting behavior. This book had a devastating effect on the field of personality from which it is just now recovering (Funder, 1994). This attack was, in effect, an argument for the role of situational variables and was in tune with the behavioral orientation of the day.

In later years, however, Mischel has become increasingly involved in the cognitive movement within social learning theory (Mischel, 1973). He has tempered his earlier strong situationist position by proposing that we must also consider person-focused variables such as individual differences that influence the meanings attached by the person to stimuli and reinforcements. These meanings are usually called strategies or styles, and they develop through the individual's previous experience with both situations and rewards. It appears that Mischel's (1979) emphasis on these cognitive person variables marks a change from his previous situationist position to a more explicitly interactionist approach wherein the influence of both personal and situational factors is stressed.

The person-focused variables that Mischel endorses are not the traditional traits or psychodynamic concepts. They are cognitive variables that are of five types: competencies, encoding strategies, expectancies, subjective values, and plans.

## Competencies

**Competencies** refer to what a person knows and can do. They are not simply static accumulations but abilities to generate, transform, and use information to create thought and to solve problems. They refer to competency, intelligence, ego development, social and intellectual achievements and skills, and social and cognitive maturity.

## Encoding Strategies

**Encoding strategies** concern how people represent and symbolize information. We categorize, code, and select information, thereby giving it a meaning beyond its raw stimulation properties. The information "We are going to have a test next week" is coded by some students as an opportunity to demonstrate their abilities and by others as a source of anxiety. People, then, differ in the way they process the same information. Encoding strategies are similar to Kelly's personal constructs (Chapter 7).

## Expectancies

**Expectancies** are the same as Rotter's concept, although Mischel's classification of expectancies differs from Rotter's classification. For Mischel, three types of expectancies are important. First, there are expectancies for the outcomes of the behavior we select. For example, if I believe that there is little likelihood that I have the skills to pass a calculus course, I will probably not enroll in that course. Second, there are expectancies for stimulus outcomes. A smile leads me to expect friendliness from another person. A haze around the moon may mean to me that it is going to rain tomorrow. Finally, there are self-efficacy expectations. These reflect a person's confidence in being able to perform an act successfully. I can find a job or I can impress other people. Although similar to behavior-outcomes expectancies, these expectancies refer to a generalized self-confidence or belief about one's competency.

## Subjective Values

Another important determinant of behavior is the value attached to the outcomes of that behavior. Money is important to me but less so to you. I like candy; you prefer ice cream. Values refer to our preferences and aversions, our likes and dislikes.

The subjective values that people place on specific activities will play a major role in what they choose to do. Depending on how much a person values jogging as a competitive sport, he or she may or may not run in a marathon.

## Self-Regulatory Systems and Plans

These refer to the ways we regulate our own behavior by self-imposed goals and standards. They also refer to self-produced consequences like self-criticism or self-praise. We also adopt plans or rules that will guide our behavior even in the absence of environmental restraints or pressures.

## Summary

- Contemporary social learning theory developed because of what many perceived to be inadequacies of traditional learning theory: underemphasis of cognitive variables, a model based on animal experimentation, failure to recognize the importance of social and interpersonal factors, and a view of the human being as a passive recipient of environmental stimulation.
- Rotter developed what might be called the first comprehensive social learning theory designed to be useful to clinician and personality psychologist alike.
- Rotter's theory is characterized by several features. It emphasizes a construct point of view and uses a careful, concise language of description. It adopts a social perspective that stresses the importance of both cognitive and motivational variables. Finally, it explains why individuals select one behavior instead of another. It does not address the issue of how the behavior is acquired.
- Rotter's theory includes four major variables: behavior potential, expectancy, reinforcement value, and the psychological situation. Behavior potential in a given situation is determined by the strength of one's expectancy for the success of the behavior in question and the value of the goal toward which that behavior is directed.
- Rotter argues that expectancies in a given situation are determined by specific experience in that situation and by experience generalized from related situations. Reinforcement value is determined by the value of the reinforcements to which the reinforcement in question leads. Value, then, is not absolute but relative to the subsequent reinforcements involved.
- Often we wish to predict not a specific behavior but a class of related behaviors, all oriented to achieve similar goals. In such instances, the constructs of need potential, freedom of movement, and need value are employed. These are broader analogs of Rotter's basic constructs.
- More recently, Rotter has emphasized the importance of problem-solving generalized expectancies. These represent beliefs about how best to construe situations so as to solve the problems they present. Two prominent generalized problem-solving expectancies are interpersonal trust and internal versus external control of reinforcement.
- Rotter has little to say regarding formal stages of development. However, he does accept the ideas of Dollard and Miller that psychological needs develop

out of the satisfaction of physiological needs. He has described six psychological needs: recognition-status, dominance, independence, protection-dependency, love and affection, and physical comfort.

- The maladjusted person in Rotter's system has low expectancies (freedom of movement) for the satisfaction of important needs. Conflict, lack of competency, deviant minimal goal levels, and inability to discriminate among situations that do or do not offer the possibility of need satisfaction are also often involved in maladjustment. In contrast, enhancement behaviors may facilitate adjustment.

- Although Rotter has never developed any distinctive methods of therapy, his theory does have several therapeutic implications. These include flexibility in techniques, the enhancement of patients' problem-solving skills, an active role for the therapist, and an emphasis on behavior.

- The second major social learning theorist to be discussed was Bandura. Like Rotter, Bandura has emphasized the role of both cognitive and motivational factors. He also contends that although reinforcement may be necessary for the performance of a behavior, it is not necessary for the acquisition of behavior. More recently, he has emphasized the role of self-efficacy in both learning and behavior.

- In addition, Bandura uses the concept of reciprocal determinism. This means that all three critical variables—the behavior, the person, and the situation—affect one another.

- Bandura contends that people can learn not just by experiencing reinforcement themselves but also by the process of vicarious reinforcement, that is, by observing others being reinforced. This emphasizes Bandura's commitment to cognitive variables. Indeed, he believes that our behavior is guided not just by reinforcement but by our expectations of being reinforced.

- Much learning occurs through our observation of models who are attended to on a selective basis. Bandura describes a four-stage process of observational learning that involves attention, retention, motor reproduction, and motivation.

- According to Bandura, by observing models we learn to do things we have not done before. Observation often involves both vicarious reinforcement and vicarious conditioning.

- Bandura also argues that much of our behavior is self-regulated through internal standards acquired through the rewards and punishments administered to us by significant others early in life.

- Self-efficacy, the belief that we can successfully execute a given behavior, is also a potent determinant of behavior in Bandura's theoretical framework.

- Like Rotter, Bandura does not describe stages of development. Development is change in goals, plans, self-efficacy, and expectations.

- Bandura invokes no special processes to account for deviant behavior. Maladjusted behavior is learned in the same manner as adjusted behavior. One especially malignant feature of defensive behavior, however, is that it often removes the individual from settings in which more adjusted behavior could be learned.

- In discussing behavior change and therapy, Bandura focuses on observational learning. For example, phobias have been shown to yield to techniques that enable the person to watch others who are not fearful. Phobic individuals can be guided into previously feared situations by models who demonstrate the desired behavior. Bandura suggests that successfully performing the previously feared behavior enhances the person's feelings of self-efficacy.

- The third major contributor to social learning theory has been Mischel. Blending concepts from Rotter, Bandura, and Kelly, he has fashioned a cognitive social learning reconceptualization.

- Mischel is probably best known for his critique of those approaches to personality that involved internal personal variables. In that critique, Mischel promoted the importance of situational variables for predicting behavior.

- Interestingly, Mischel's reconceptualization incorporates several personal variables that emphasize individual differences in cognitive styles. These variables are competencies, encoding strategies and personal constructs, expectancies, subjective values, and self-regulatory systems and plans.

# Chapter 12

# Social Learning: Research, Assessment, and Summary Evaluation

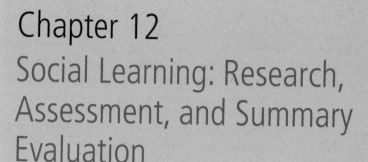

Research on Rotter's Concepts
    Early Research Supporting Social Learning
        Theory
    Extensions of Social Learning Theory:
        Response Expectancy
    Generalized Response Expectancies
    Applications of Social Learning Theory
Research on Bandura's Cognitive Social
   Learning Theory
    Observational Learning
    Self-Efficacy
    Goal Setting and the Immediacy of
       Reward
Mischel and the Delay of Gratification
    Role of Expectancy
    Effects on Reward Value
    Imitating Delay Behavior
    Personality Correlates
Social Learning Theory and Assessment
    Measuring Expectancies
    Assessing Reinforcement Value
    Projective Techniques

    Incomplete Sentences
    Measurement of Internal-External Locus
       of Control (I-E)
Summary Evaluation
    Strengths
    Weaknesses
Summary

S ocial learning theory is a hybrid of two of the most influential schools in psychology. The work of Rotter, Bandura, and Mischel has clear links to the powerful behavioral tradition in American psychology. Equally clear, however, is the influence of classic phenomenological theories and their modern social cognitive counterparts. The blending, within social learning theory, of an appreciation of the power of the environment for influencing and constraining behavior with the recognition that people actively perceive, process, interpret, and influence the environment has made social learning theory broadly applicable and has enhanced our understanding of much of human behavior.

In addition, social learning theory has, from its inception, emphasized the scientific evaluation of its propositions. Social learning research is characterized by the application of rigorous empirical research methods to a subject matter that has often been viewed as too vague for empirical study. In so doing, it has convinced many skeptics that the study of human personality need not be restricted to the nonempirical methods of literature, philosophy, and the fine arts.

## Research on Rotter's Concepts

Social learning, as an approach to understanding personality, began in 1954 with the publication of Rotter's theory. Rotter's focus was on a theory whose basic concepts had a solid empirical foundation, and research provided early support for many of Rotter's basic concepts. Moreover, this research was generally able to demonstrate some crucial differences between *social* learning theory and *behavioral* learning theory.

### Early Research Supporting Social Learning Theory

Generalization of Expectancies. People's expectations for reinforcement are a fundamental component of Rotter's social learning theory. However, Rotter treated expectancy as a cognitive variable that could influence behavior in ways that could not be explained by traditional learning theory. As an internal cognitive variable, expectancy for reinforcement had to generalize beyond the physical similarities of the operant situation. Otherwise, expectancy could not be distinguished from the behavioral learning principle of stimulus generalization.

Chance (1959) studied the extent to which expectancies will generalize from one situation to a physically different one when both situations concern similar needs. She used two personality tests with her undergraduate participants. One group was told that both tests measured the same characteristic (similar needs), whereas the other group was told that the tests measured different characteristics (different needs). All participants indicated what scores they expected to receive on both tests prior to taking either. After the first test, participants received scores that were either 7 or 14 points higher than their stated expectancy. Before taking the second test, participants again estimated their probable score for that test. Expectancy generalization was measured by taking the difference between the first and second estimates for the second test. Participants who generalized were those who were influenced by their scores on the first test and thus raised their estimates for the second task over what they had initially stated. Crucial to the interpretation that greater generalization would occur as a function of the similarity of needs was the finding that there was more generalization when the tests were described as measuring the same characteristic, even though they were physically different tests.

V. J. Crandall (1955) approached the question of generalization differently. He developed two equivalent sets of nine pictures each so that he could measure freedom of movement in three need areas. There were three pictures for each area. The need areas were recognition for physical skill, recognition for academic skill, and love and affection. One group of male participants made up stories to the physical skills pictures. Participants were then asked to perform difficult co-ordination tasks at which they all failed. To measure any changes in freedom of movement in the three need areas, the equivalent set of pictures was administered following the participants' experiences of failure and frustration. Judges rated all stories for freedom of movement on a scale of zero to ten. A control group of male participants was administered both sets of pictures, but instead of the inter-vening failure, they spent the same amount of time in a neutral activity. The results of the study are shown in Figure 12-1, which depicts the degree of lowering of freedom of movement in the three need areas for the frustrated participants compared with the control group. Failure had the effect of disproportionately re-ducing participants' expectancies for success (freedom of movement) in the physical skills need area. Crandall's study shows how failure can influence freedom of movement through the process of generalization and also how the amount of generalization is related to the degree of similarity among need areas.

### Reinforcement Value.

One of the most difficult concepts in social learning theory is reinforcement value. The idea that reinforcers vary in how much they are valued in different situations or by different individuals is indisputable. However, it has proved difficult to establish how reinforcers come to take on different values. One of the early studies that successfully manipulated a reinforcer's value was carried out in 1953 by Dunlap. Dunlap predicted that the relative value of a rein-forcer could be influenced by that reinforcer's association with other reinforce-ments. Dunlap investigated this prediction by studying the preferences for toys of 8- to 10-year-old boys. In the experiment, a group of boys ranked a set of nine toys in terms of preference. This ranking was a measure of the (relative) rein-forcement value of the nine toys. The crucial toy was a plastic brick set. Any par-ticipant who failed to rank the bricks fourth to seventh was discarded because this toy had to be free to move either up or down in value (ranking).

Participants were assigned to one of four conditions: (1) play with the bricks did not bring any comments from the experimenter (control group); (2) play was followed by mild criticism; (3) play was followed by strong praise; (4) play was

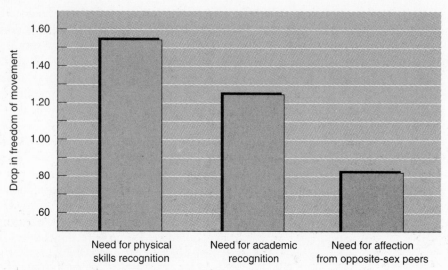

**Figure 12-1**&#x6103; Effects of failure on reductions in freedom of movement.

From data reported by Vaughn J. Crandall, "An Investigation of the Specificity of Reinforcement of Induced Frustration," *Journal of Social Psychology, 41* [1955]: 311–18, in Julian B. Rotter, *Clinical Psychology*, 2nd Ed., 1971b, p. 91. Reprinted by permission of Prentice-Hall, Inc., and The Journal Press.

followed by strong praise along with the direct suggestion that people other than the experimenter would also approve.

Following this experimental manipulation, participants were asked to rank the nine toys again. Dunlap found that the changes in rankings were consistent with the prediction that the reinforcement value of the bricks would be influenced by the subsequent reinforcement that resulted from that toy. The greatest increase in value occurred for the group that was praised and also given the suggestion of approval from others. The next greatest increase was for the simple praise group, followed by the control group, which showed a slight increase. A small decrement in the ranking of the plastic bricks occurred in the mild criticism group. Dunlap's work, then, suggests that the value ascribed to a reinforcement in a given situation is dependent on the subsequent reinforcements to which it is expected to lead. If playing with plastic bricks is expected to result in criticism, the value of such play will decline.

**The Psychological Situation.** That situations can, and generally do, influence behavior is not a controversial idea. An important contribution of social learning theory is the recognition that situations have psychological as well as physical components. These psychological components are reflected in changes in people's perceptions, beliefs, and values from situation to situation. An early demonstration of the psychological components of situations is a study by Phares and Rotter (1956). They devised a list of 18 reinforcements. Of these, 6 were athletic reinforcements (e.g., win a wrestling match with a friend), 6 concerned manual skills (e.g., win a prize for building the best lamp in woodworking class), and 6 were academic (e.g., receive an A in English). All were designed for the junior high school age range, and each set of 6 had approximately the same mean reinforcement value. The 18 reinforcements were rank-ordered under three conditions by seventh- and eighth-grade male students. The three conditions were (1) a gym class, (2) an English class, and (3) a woodworking shop class. It was found that reinforcements changed their rank (value) depending on the class in which the ranking took place. For example, academic reinforcements moved up in value when they were ranked in the English class compared with the gym class. Thus, cues in each specific situation influenced the value of specific reinforcements occurring in that situation.

## Extensions of Social Learning Theory: Response Expectancy

More recently, research has expanded on earlier social learning theory, particularly the concept of expectancy. For example, Kirsch's (1985a) work on response expectancy has provided a social learning explanation for placebo effects and hypnosis.

The concept of expectancy in Rotter's social learning theory refers to outcomes. That is, a response is expected to produce a certain outcome, or an event is associated with a certain outcome. Moreover, the impact of an **outcome expectancy** is limited to **voluntary behavior**, that is, behavior that requires effort and is under the control of the individual. In 1985a, Kirsch expanded on the concept of expectancy by introducing a hypothesis about **response expectancy**. Response expectancy refers to the subject's belief that certain **nonvoluntary responses** will occur as a result of other responses or in the presence of other stimuli. A nonvoluntary response is one that occurs automatically and without effort. Some examples are emotional responses such as fear, sadness, sexual arousal, and pain. Like outcome expectancies, response expectancies can influence a subject's voluntary behavior. For example, people who are afraid of flying may choose not to fly because of their expectation that they will experience the unpleasant responses of fear and anxiety if they get on a plane. In addition, it appears that expectancies of their occurrence can elicit or enhance involuntary responses (Kirsch, 1985a).

Placebo Effects.   One area of research that has documented the power of response expectancy is placebo effects. **Placebos** are substances that do not have any known effects on behavior or physiological responses but are administered under the pretense of having such effects. A **placebo effect** occurs when a person is administered a placebo and experiences the described effect, such as a reduction in pain, an increase in pulse rate, or whatever response the person has been led to expect. Placebo effects have traditionally been explained as the result of classical conditioning (e.g., Siegel, 1983). However, in some instances, placebo effects are stronger than would be predicted by a conditioning model (e.g., Ross and Buckalew, 1983) or occur in a direction opposite from that predicted by a conditioning hypothesis (e.g., Bridell, Rimm, Caddy, Krawitz, Sholis, and Wunderlin,

1978). These results are more easily explained by a response expectancy interpretation than by a conditioning theory of placebo effects (Kirsch, 1993). In reviewing placebo effects in the treatment of pain, Turner, Deyo, Loeser, and Von Korff (1994) concluded that a patient's expectations that his or her pain will be reduced by a placebo is an important component of the treatment process.

**Hypnosis.** Research on the phenomenon of hypnosis is another area that has supported expectancy effects. As noted in Chapters 3 and 4, hypnosis has been used in psychoanalytic research as a means of obtaining unconscious material from participants. However, the nature of hypnosis as an altered state of consciousness has always been a source of controversy. Response expectancies have been used to explain many hypnotic phenomena (Council, Kirsch, and Grant 1996; Kirsch and Council, 1992). Specifically, the response expectancy hypothesis predicts that the extent to which subjects expect (1) the situation to be hypnotic and (2) themselves to be good hypnotic subjects should explain the strength of their hypnotic response. This relation has generally been found (e.g., Spanos, Burgess, Dubreuil, and Liddy, 1995), although the effect of response expectancy on hypnotic response is moderated by other cognitive and situational variables (Spanos, Burnley and Cross, 1993).

## Generalized Response Expectancies

Rotter's social learning theory is best known to contemporary personality psychologists through its concept of generalized expectancy. In particular, an individual's generalized expectancy about the locus of reinforcement has proved to be a powerful construct for explaining a wide variety of behavior (Rotter, 1990; 1992). Interpersonal trust and selfism are two other generalized expectancies that have been the target of research.

**Internal-External Locus of Control.** In 1966, Rotter published his monograph on internal versus external generalized problem-solving expectancies. This monograph is the basis for one of the most widely studied constructs in psychology, **locus of control.** As its name implies, this construct concerns the site where individuals believe that control over reinforcement is located. Specifically, individuals may believe that they have personal or **internal control** over reinforcements, or they may believe that reinforcement is beyond or **external** to their personal efforts and abilities. Within social learning theory, locus of control is a generalized expectancy. Thus, it will have an important impact on the behaviors an individual will select in meeting the problems posed by both the social and the physical environments.

Locus of control is conceptualized as a stable individual difference. Individuals differ in the strength with which they hold these expectancies, and individuals are relatively stable in the extent to which they have an internal or external locus of control. However, this stability may be specific to different domains. That is, the same individual may have a more external locus of control for academic reinforcement but a more internal locus of control for social reinforcement (Strickland, 1977). Knowledge of a person's locus of control should be useful for predicting that individual's behavior, and differences in locus of control may, in part, account for why different persons select different behaviors in response to situations that are objectively similar.

There is a vast amount of research demonstrating the relation between locus of control and behavior in many situations (e.g., Burger, 1985; Findley and Cooper, 1983; Phares, 1976; Lefcourt, 1981, 1982, 1984, Rotter, 1990; Strickland, 1979, 1989). Locus of control is related to social influence, information seeking, achievement, health, coping with stress, creativity, and many other variables. Indeed, the generality of this construct is so great that the challenge is to find variables to which it is *not* related.

An example of research on this construct is reported in Ritchie and Phares (1969). These investigators hypothesized that students with an external locus of control would be more influenced by the opinions of prestigious individuals than by the opinions of unimportant individuals. People with an external locus of control need, or at least believe that they need, to be sensitive and responsive to the opinions of important others because it is these powerful others who control reinforcement. The opinions of less powerful individuals can be more safely ignored. People who believe that reinforcement is more under their own internal control have less reason to be concerned about the prestige of the source of an opinion because they believe that they are less dependent on others for reinforcement. To test these hypotheses, college students' general locus of control was assessed using the I-E scale (Rotter, 1966), and they were asked to complete a survey about their attitudes toward the national budget. Two weeks later the students completed the survey a second time. During the two-week interval, half the students had heard arguments about the budget that were attributed to a famous economist. The other half heard the same arguments but were told that they were those of an unknown graduate student at a small college. The two groups were matched on their initial opinions.

The results of this study are shown in Figure 12-2. As expected, those students with an external locus of control changed their attitudes more in response to a high-prestige other than to a low-prestige other. Externals also changed more than internals when both received a high-prestige communication. In contrast, there was little difference between the degree of attitude change shown by internals in response to a high- or low-prestige source.

Interpersonal Trust. Each of us must constantly make decisions about whether, and how much, to trust other people and institutions. Should I trust the filling station attendant who gives me directions? Do I believe a student who tells me a term paper is late because of an illness? Can I believe the president when I am told military action was necessary because of a "clear and present danger" to national security? How trusting I am will influence how I act in each of these situations.

Rotter (1967a) developed a questionnaire to assess people's generalized trust expectancies. This questionnaire is the basis for his program of research on both

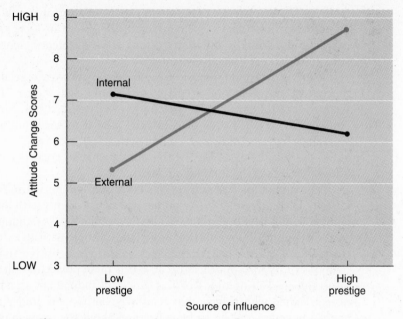

**Figure 12-2** ᏸ Attitude change as a function of locus of control and the prestige of the source of influence.

(Adapted from Ritchie and Phares, 1969)

unwarranted distrust and the personal costs of being too trusting (Rotter, 1971, 1980). In general, people who are more trusting are less likely to lie and probably less likely to cheat or steal. They are prone to give other people a second chance and to respect the rights of others. Also, they are less likely to be unhappy, conflicted, or maladjusted. They tend to be sought as friends more often than are distrustful persons. Interestingly, however, more trusting individuals are not typically characterized as gullible or naive.

People low in interpersonal trust are likely to be suspicious of strangers. Wright, Maggied, and Palmer (1975) were interested in how this suspiciousness would be exhibited. They reported a study in which they compared the behavior toward strangers of college students who differed in interpersonal trust. A group of students completed the Interpersonal Trust Scale and gave the experimenters their telephone numbers so they could be contacted later to participate in additional experiments. Later, groups of high and low trusters were called to take part in a study, and the questions the subjects asked about the study were recorded. Participants high in interpersonal trust asked fewer questions indicating suspicion (e.g., "How did you get my name?" "What is the experiment about?" "Why me?"). They also asked fewer questions in general (e.g., "Where is the experiment?" "Could you repeat the instructions?" "Could I participate at a different time?").

Another characteristic of low-trusting individuals is a sensitivity to stimuli suggesting the negative aspects of trustworthiness. In their desire to see the world as they believe it to be, low-trusting persons are on the alert for evidence that is consistent with their beliefs. Gurtman and Lion (1982), using a tachistoscope that flashed words on a white background at rapid exposure rates, asked participants to identify the exposed words. Words were either trusting (e.g., *loyal, sincere, truthful*), neutral (e.g., *healthy, slender, barefoot*), or distrusting (e.g., *reckless, deceitful, malicious*). As hypothesized, participants low on interpersonal trust showed better recognition of the distrustful words than they did of the trustful or neutral ones. Participants high in interpersonal trust showed no differences in recognition across the three categories of words.

Selfism. The concept of narcissism, love of self, or self-interest has long been a focus of psychological inquiry (e.g., Emmons, 1987; Kohut, 1977; Rhodewalt and Morf, 1995). The concept of narcissism developed out of psychoanalytic theory, where it was viewed as a disorder involving an excessive emphasis on the self and an inability or unwillingness to consider the needs and perspectives of any but the self. From a social learning perspective, narcissism or **selfism** can be viewed as a generalized problem-solving strategy. When faced with problems, some people may have developed the generalized expectancy that they will be most successful at solving them if they think of themselves first.

Phares and Erskine (1984) developed a scale to assess this generalized expectancy, which they called the Selfism Scale. The correlation between the Selfism Scale and a more traditional measure of narcissism is .45 (Emmons, 1987). To further test the validity of the Selfism Scale, Erskine (1981) hypothesized that participants who scored high on the Selfism Scale would interpret altruistic behaviors as cynical or opportunistic acts. In addition, participants high on selfism would see altruistic people as less sincere, intelligent, and worthy than would participants low in selfism. These predictions were based on the assumption that participants whose generalized expectancies were self-oriented would project those attitudes onto others.

Erskine tested her hypotheses by first selecting groups of high and low scorers on the Selfism Scale. Each participant was then given a series of brief descriptions of a variety of situations in which the main character was depicted as helping another person. Following each description was a series of potential explanations for the main character's behavior. Three explanations were self-serving ones, and the fourth was altruistic in nature. Consistent with the hypotheses, people who scored high on the Selfism Scale endorsed the self-serving motives more strongly than did low scorers.

## Applications of Social Learning Theory

One of Rotter's goals was to develop a theory of personality that could be usefully applied to important real-world problems. An example of the application of social learning theory is the role of expectancy in alcohol abuse and in the psychotherapeutic process.

Low expectancies for success can sometimes lead to a reliance on alcohol as a compensation.

**Expectancies and Drinking Patterns.** Drinking alcohol in excess is a major national problem that undoubtedly has many causes. From a social learning perspective, one explanation for excessive drinking is that the drinker perceives drinking as a way of attaining goals that are otherwise unattainable. To test this possibility, Jessor, Carman, and Grossman (1968) studied a group of undergraduates. Questionnaires measuring needs for achievement and affection as well as expectancies for meeting these needs (freedom of movement) were given to 38 men and 50 women. In addition, a questionnaire about frequency of drinking, amount consumed, and frequency of drunkenness was administered. Correlations computed among the scales indicated that lower expectations of achieving need satisfaction in the two areas were related to increased drinking. The relations were stronger for women than for men. Other results were also consistent with the hypothesis that drinking served as an escape or relief from problems or as a way of achieving goals that could not otherwise be reached. Again, these relations were stronger for women than for men.

The reason for the gender difference is unclear. It may be that women provided more valid data because of their tendency to be more truthful in answering questionnaires. It may also be that drinking by men is determined more by social norms and expectations, whereas for women it is more directly linked to personality factors. Despite this unexpected but intriguing gender difference, the overall results are consistent with the social learning hypothesis.

**Quitting Therapy.** Entering psychotherapy is a serious decision made by many people at one or another time in their lives. The evidence is clear that in general, psychotherapy has beneficial effects in reducing human misery and increasing life satisfaction and productivity (Smith, Glass, and Miller 1980). Despite these benefits, patients sometimes terminate their therapy prematurely. There are surely many reasons for termination, but social learning provides one set of explanations, based on the concepts of expectancy and reinforcement value, that may be useful for reducing the number of dropouts.

Piper, Wogan, and Getter (1972) studied 97 male and female patients at a campus mental health clinic. Participants were administered a questionnaire listing a variety of problems and were asked to check those that were of concern to them. Also, for each item checked, they indicated on a five-point scale whether they expected therapy to make the problem better or worse. They also rated each problem, this time on a four-point scale, on its importance to them. These two ratings served as measures of expectancies and reinforcement value, respectively. *Terminators* were defined as patients who completed three or fewer sessions and then left therapy. As predicted, terminators had lower combined scores of expectancy and reinforcement value than did patients who remained in therapy.

This result is not surprising; it is consistent with the common-sense view that people stay in psychotherapy if they think it is helpful and quit psychotherapy if they do not. The importance of this study is that it provides an explicit definition of "think it is helpful" using the concepts *expectancies* and *reinforcement value*. Once having identified the role of specific expectancies and reinforcement values in individual clients, therapists can work to increase patients' expectancies that therapy will help them and can enhance the value of that help to the patients. Thus, the social learning conceptualization, although "just common sense," provides an explicit and useful set of procedures to act on the vague suggestion to make clients "think that therapy is helpful."

# Research on Bandura's Cognitive Social Learning Theory

Bandura's cognitive social learning theory is the basis for a substantial body of research in personality psychology. Part of the reason for this has been Bandura's commitment to providing clear definitions of his constructs that allow them to be measured and tested. Another reason is the wide range of phenomena to which his concepts can be applied. Observational learning, self-efficacy, and goal setting are three areas that have received substantial research attention.

## Observational Learning

One of Bandura's main contributions to social learning theory has been his explanation for how people learn or acquire the behaviors that they subsequently may choose to perform. The concept of observational learning is central to Bandura's theory about how people acquire behaviors. The distinction between acquisition and performance is well illustrated in a classic study of aggression.

To demonstrate the acquisition of aggressive responses, Bandura (1965) used 33 boys and 33 girls who were enrolled in the Stanford University Nursery School. Two men served as models, and a female experimenter conducted the study.

> The children were shown a five-minute film in which the model walked up to an adult-size plastic Bobo doll and ordered the doll to move. After glaring for a moment at the doll the model exhibited four novel aggressive responses, each accompanied by a distinct verbalization.
>
> First, the model laid the Bobo doll on its side, sat on it, and punched it in the nose while remarking, "Pow, right in the nose, boom, boom." The model then raised the doll and pummelled it on the head with a mallet. Each response was accompanied by the verbalization, "Sockeroo stay down." Following the mallet aggression, the model kicked the doll about the room, and these responses were interspersed with the comment, "Fly away." Finally, the model threw rubber balls at the Bobo doll, each strike punctuated with "Bang." This sequence of physically and verbally aggressive behavior was repeated twice. (pp. 590–591)

But what happened to the model after he aggressed against the Bobo doll? Was he rewarded or punished? Bandura hypothesized that the outcomes of aggression would affect the child's tendency to imitate and acquire the model's behavior. To determine this, one group of children observed the film without seeing any consequences following the model's behavior (the control condition). A second group—the model-rewarded condition—observed the following scene, which was appended to the previous film.

> A second adult appeared with an abundant supply of candies and soft drinks. He informed the model that he was a "strong champion" and that his superb aggressive performance clearly deserved a generous treat. He then poured him a large glass of 7-Up, and readily supplied additional energy-building nourishment including chocolate bars, Cracker Jack popcorn, and an assortment of candies. While the model was rapidly consuming the delectable treats, his admirer symbolically reinstated the modeled aggressive responses and engaged in considerable positive social reinforcement." (p. 591)

The third group of children—the model-punished condition—observed the earlier five-minute film plus the following final scene:

The reinforcing agent appeared on the scene shaking his finger menacingly and commenting reprovingly, "Hey there, you bully. You quit picking on that clown. I won't tolerate it." As the model drew back he tripped and fell, the other adult sat on the model and spanked him with a rolled-up magazine while reminding him of his aggressive behavior. As the model ran off cowering, the agent forewarned him, "If I catch you doing that again, you big bully, I'll give you a hard spanking. You quit acting that way." (p. 591)

To determine the extent to which the aggression would be spontaneously performed, each child was taken to a room after viewing the film. The room contained numerous toys (balls, mallet, dollhouse, plastic animals, Bobo doll, etc.) Behind a one-way mirror, observers recorded the extent of spontaneous play, both aggressive and nonaggressive. After this phase, the experimenter entered the room and offered rewards of fruit juice and sticker pictures for every response of the model's the child could imitate. These two procedures, then, constituted the measures of performance and acquisition, respectively.

In Figure 12-3, it is clear that acquisition and performance are not the same thing. In particular, children *acquire* (learn) more responses than they actually *perform* in a free-play situation. Not only that, watching a model who is punished versus one who is rewarded leads to greater differences in performance than acquisition.

The recent introduction of the "V-chip," which will allow parents to have some control over what their children watch on television, illustrates the extent of society's concern over the power the media has for observational learning.

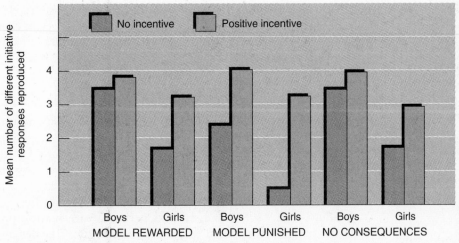

**Figure 12-3** Imitative responses under reward and free-play conditions as influenced by three modeling experiences.

After "Influence of Models' Reinforcement Contingencies on the Acquisition of Imitative Responses," by A. Bandura, *Journal of Personality and Social Psychology*, 1965, *1*, 589–595. Copyright 1965 by the American Psychological Association. Used with permission.

Box 12-1 summarizes some of the issues regarding the extent to which children learn aggressive and violent behavior through observing it on television and in the movies.

## Self-Efficacy

Another key concept in Bandura's social learning theory is **self-efficacy**. Bandura argues that we need to know "how people judge their capabilities and how, through their self-percepts of efficacy, they affect their motivation" (Bandura, 1982, p. 122). Self-efficacy is perhaps the most widely studied and applied concept in contemporary personality research.

**Self-Efficacy and Clinical Treatment.** Bandura, Adams, Hardy, and Howells (1980) studied several agoraphobics (individuals who show unreasoning fears of leaving their homes). After these participants were trained in a variety of coping skills (e.g., relaxation techniques), therapists accompanied them into community settings involving such activities as shopping, walking alone, climbing high stairs, and entering restaurants. All of these situations had been previously feared by the participants. As their ability to function in these settings improved, their expressed feelings of self-efficacy also increased.

The relation between participants' confidence in their ability to overcome problem behaviors (self-efficacy) and their observed ability to overcome those problems is now well documented. For example, Baer, Holt, and Lichtenstein (1986) studied participants who were in a program to help them quit smoking. Those participants who, at the end of the program, were confident that they could resist smoking for at least six months were indeed better able to do so than participants who had been less confident. Likewise, overweight clients of Weight Watchers who reported relatively low self-efficacy were more likely to drop out of the program than were clients with stronger feelings of efficacy (Mitchell and Stuart, 1984).

**Self-Efficacy and Aversive Experiences.** Pain and stress are complex experiences that are affected by numerous factors, including the intensity of stimuli, the focus of the participant's attention, and how the subject evaluates the experience (Wilson, Chaplin, and Thorn, 1995). Two studies (Bandura, Cioffi, Taylor, and Brouillard, 1988; Bandura, O'Leary, Taylor, Gauthier, and Gossard, 1987) suggest that self-efficacy is an important factor in understanding how people experience and cope with aversive experiences such as stress and pain.

Bandura et al. (1988) had students perform mathematical problems under conditions in which they could exercise full control over the demands of the task (self-efficacy) or in which the demands of the task exceeded their capabilities (inefficacy). The self-efficacious participants showed little stress, whereas the inefficacious participants experienced both stress and high levels of autonomic arousal. Figure 12-5 shows the differential stress experienced by participants

BOX 12-1
## Learning Violence and Aggression Through Television

What do children see on TV and in the movies these days? They see blood spurting everywhere. They see eyes being gouged out. They see cars engulfed in flames. They see limbs being severed. This is not the "gentle" aggressions of Daffy Duck that so many adults seem to remember.

Children spend a large amount of time viewing TV each day (Liebert and Sprafkin, 1988). What is more, the amount of TV-viewing is a stable behavioral pattern that persists over substantial periods of time (Tangney and Feshbach, 1988). For many people, the point of all this is simple—children imitate what they see (as do many adults). This means that children will learn new ways of behaving violently. And maybe it also means that children will learn that people often get away with violence; they are not always caught and punished.

There is considerable evidence from laboratory studies that connects the observation of violence on film with the expression of aggression by its viewers. For example, Josephson (1987) studied boys in grades two and three. They watched violent or nonviolent TV in groups of six. Half of these groups were later exposed to a cue associated with the violent TV program. Either before or after viewing TV, they were frustrated. The children were observed and ratings of aggression were made while the boys played floor hockey. It was discovered that violent television did increase aggressive behavior, but mainly among groups who had been earlier rated as disposed toward aggressiveness. The same boys were also more likely to become aggressive when the violence-related cue was present than when they were exposed to the violent content only.

Research outside the laboratory has also produced results implicating the role of observing filmed violence in aggressive behavior. For example, Eron and Huesmann (1984) have reported a strong relation between TV viewing at an early age and subsequent crime, as is shown in Figure 12-4. Also, Eron (1982) has described the results of two large-scale longitudinal studies. One involved 875 children 8 years old from a semi-rural upstate New York county, and the other 750 children who were 8 to 10 years old and came from suburban and inner-city Chicago. In summarizing the research, Eron (1982) had this to say:

> One persistent and ubiquitous finding deserves special consideration, and that is the relation between the continued observation of television violence and aggressive behavior. It is now apparent that the relation does not just go in one direction. Although we have demonstrated that television violence is one cause of aggressive behavior, it is also probable that aggressive children prefer to watch more and more violent television. The process is very likely circular.

*(continued)*

BOX 12-1 (*continued*)

Aggressive children are unpopular, and because their relations with their peers tend to be unsatisfying, they spend more time watching television than their popular peers. The violence they see on television reassures them that their own behavior is appropriate while teaching them new coercive techniques that they then attempt to use in their interactions with others, which in turn makes them more unpopular and drives them back to television, and the circle continues. (p. 210)

along with the mental strain from time pressure and perceived stress-induced impairment in problem-solving.

### Self-Efficacy and Organizational Effectiveness.
Bandura and Wood (1989) contrived a simulated managerial situation. When participants who managed the organization believed that such organizations are not easily controlled, their feeling of self-efficacy was low even when organizational goals were easily attainable. In contrast, participants who had a strong sense of self-efficacy set increasingly

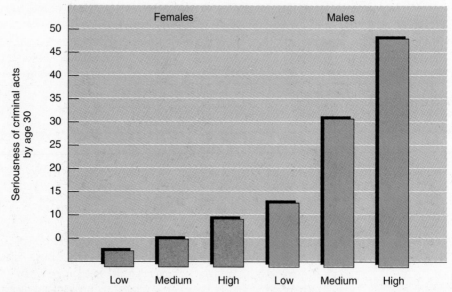

**Figure 12-4** ᏯᎦᏅ Relation of TV viewing frequency at age 8 to seriousness of crimes committed by age 30.

From R. J. Blanchard and D. C. Blanchard: The control of agressive behavior by changes in attitudes, values, and the conditions of learning. *Advances in the Study of Agression, 1,* 1984.

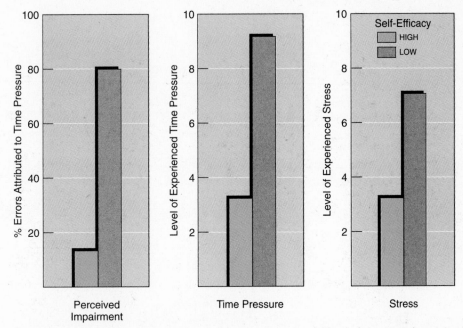

**Figure 12-5** ꙮ Performance, mental strain from time pressure, and level of experienced stress in high and low self-efficacy subjects.

Adapted from Albert Bandura, et al., "Perceived Self-Efficacy in Coping With Cognitive Stressors and Opioid Activation," *Journal of Personality and Social Psychology*, September 1988. Copyright 1988 by the American Psychological Association. Reprinted by permission of the author.

challenging goals and were effective in their analytic thinking. Likewise, the extent of subsequent attainments was directly linked to the level of one's self-efficacy. The pattern of these findings is illustrated in Figure 12-6.

## Goal Setting and the Immediacy of Reward

A basic finding from learning theory is that rewards are most effective if they occur shortly after the desired behavior has occurred. However, people will often perform difficult and immediately unrewarding behaviors, such as studying or practicing, to obtain rewards—such as a college degree, a record contract, or an Olympic medal—that will occur far in the future. One way of explaining this is that people attain smaller goals or rewards during the time they are working toward achieving major ones. In addition to their more immediate reward value, attaining these subgoals is also thought to increase people's sense of self-efficacy that they will be successful at achieving long-term rewards. The increase in self-efficacy then serves to further motivate behavior.

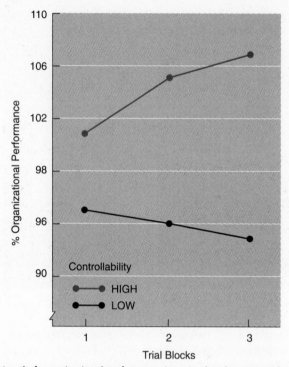

**Figure 12-6** ⮾ Level of organizational performance in a simulated managerial setting.

Adapted from Bandura and Wood, "Effect of Perceived Controllability and Performance Standards on Self-Regulation of Complex Decision Making," *Journal of Personality and Social Psychology*, May 1989. Copyright © 1989 by the American Psychological Association. Reprinted by permission of Albert Bandura.

These ideas gained some support from a study by Bandura and Schunk (1981). In this research, children of about 8 1/2 years who showed gross deficits and disinterest in mathematical tasks were selected as participants. They were put into one of two self-directed programs of learning. The first was a learning condition that used *proximal goals*. Here, the experimenter suggested that the children set for themselves the goal of completing at least six pages of instructional items each session. The entire set of items covered 42 pages. The second group was given a *distal goal* treatment, in which the experimenter suggested that they might set for themselves the goal of completing the entire 42 pages by the end of the seventh session. Self-efficacy was measured by very briefly showing the children sets of mathematical problems and then asking them to rate their ability to solve those types of problems.

The results indicated that with proximal subgoals, children progressed rapidly in their self-directed learning. They also substantially mastered the mathematical operations involved and developed a sense of self-efficacy. In contrast, the use of distal goals produced no demonstrable effects in any of these areas.

# Mischel and the Delay of Gratification

 Walter Mischel (1966) has developed a comprehensive program of research on the **delay of gratification**. Delay of gratification refers to the ability to refuse immediate, smaller rewards to obtain larger but delayed ones. The capacity to endure self-imposed delays has been described by some as willpower and by others as ego strength. Delay of gratification is a key component of what Goleman (1995) has called **emotional intelligence**, which concerns the ability to control impulses, exert self-discipline, and persist in difficult tasks. Social learning theory has been particularly useful for understanding this capacity. Much of Mischel's work has highlighted the critical role of expectancies in the ability to delay gratification.

## Role of Expectancy

In one of the first studies of this topic, Mahrer (1956) assumed that as they are growing up, children accumulate experiences with delayed and immediate gratifications. These experiences may demonstrate to the children that delaying gratification is, or is not, worthwhile. For example, when told that if they will stop playing and help clean up the yard, they can go to a movie next Saturday, some children are taken to the movie whereas for other children the promise is forgotten or ignored. Mahrer's contention is that our ability to tolerate self-imposed delay of reward is determined, in part, by our expectancies that the delayed reward will occur.

Mahrer used three groups of second- and third-grade boys. Each group was given a series of training trials in which they were promised that the experimenter would return the next day with a free balloon if only they would help him select some pictures. This was done for five consecutive days. With one group, the experimenter fulfilled his promise four out of the five days to create a high expectancy for delayed reinforcement. A second group was given the balloon on two of the promised days (moderate expectancy), and a third group was never given the balloon (low expectancy). Three days after this training sequence, the experimenter returned and offered to give each of the boys a small toy airplane immediately or a large toy flying saucer the next day. It had been determined that most boys valued the flying saucer more than the airplane. Also, to evaluate whether the experience with one experimenter would generalize to a different experimenter, half of the participants, were given their choice by the first examiner, who was a man, and the other half by a woman.

The results showed that boys who had been trained to expect delayed rewards more often chose the flying saucer (delayed reward) over the toy airplane (immediate reward). Their tendency to do this was significantly greater than it was for either the moderate- or low-expectancy groups. Furthermore, these effects were confined to participants offered choices by the male experimenter. In the case of the female experimenter, there were no differences among the three expectancy groups in their choice of delayed versus immediate gratification. Thus, whether generalization occurs from one set of experiences to another may depend on the similarity of the people involved in the two situations.

## Effects on Reward Value

Mischel has also suggested that the act of delaying may further enhance the perceived reinforcement value of the anticipated reward. Mischel and Masters (1966) showed sixth-grade boys and girls an exciting film. At the climax of the film (the launch of a spaceship), the projector broke. The children were told it was due to a damaged fuse. Under one condition, the children were told there was a 100 percent chance the film would resume. For two other groups, the probabilities were 50 percent and zero, respectively. A control group viewed the film without interruption. The children were asked to assign a value to the film both before and after the imposed delay. After the film ended, the children once more rated it for its attractiveness. The major finding was that participants who were led to believe there was no chance of the film being resumed increased their evaluation more than did participants in the other groups. In addition, this difference was maintained even after the entire film was shown. These results, shown in Figure 12-7, indicate that a blocked or delayed reward can rise in value simply by virtue of the expectancy that it is unlikely to occur. Controlled experimental research, then, is consistent with our folk wisdom that telling people they cannot have something only makes them want it more.

## Imitating Delay Behavior

Bandura and Mischel (1965) provide an illustration of how willingness to delay gratification can be influenced by observational learning. They chose to study fourth- and fifth-grade boys and girls who characteristically chose either a small immediate reward or a larger delayed one. There were three experimental conditions. In the first, children were exposed to live adult models whose choice behavior was the opposite of their own. For example, a child who characteristically chose immediate rewards observed a model who chose delayed rewards. The children not only observed these choices but also listened to accompanying comments from the models, such as "The wooden chess figures are of much better quality, more attractive, and will last longer. I'll wait two weeks for the better ones" (Bandura and Mischel, 1965, p. 701). In the second condition, the children did not observe live models but instead were exposed to a written record of the model's choices. This was called the symbolic condition. In the control condition, children were not exposed to any models. Children's own choices for immediate versus delayed rewards were tested immediately after they were exposed to the models. To determine whether the children's choice behavior was stable over time, the initial set of choices was readministered four to five weeks after the ex-

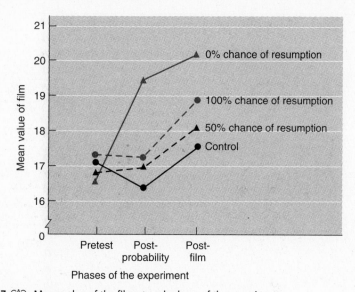

**Figure 12-7** ⧉  Mean value of the film at each phase of the experiment.

From Mischel, W. and Masters, J. C.,: Effects of probability of reward attainment on responses to frustration. *Journal of Personality and Social Psychology, 3*, 1966, 390–396.

periment. The results of this study showed clearly that children's subsequent choices were markedly affected by their experience with both live and symbolic models. Also, this effect persisted over time.

## Personality Correlates

How are the personalities of children who are able to delay gratification described? Funder, Block, and Block (1983) presented 4-year-old children with laboratory tasks measuring delay of gratification. Personality test data and descriptions by teachers and examiners were available on these children when they were at the ages of 3, 4, 7, and 11 years. Table 12-1 shows the personality characteristics that were associated with the ability to delay gratification in a laboratory setting.

Will children who were able to delay gratification when they were preschoolers show distinguishable personality characteristics a decade later? Mischel, Shoda, and Peake (1988) were able to secure personality ratings by parents for 95 children who ten years earlier had been studied for their delay abilities. Specifically, children of both sexes who had been able to wait longer at ages 4 or 5 grew into adolescents whose parents rated them as more academically and socially competent, verbally fluent, rational, attentive, playful, and resistant to stress and frustration.

**Table 12-1**
Personality Characteristics Associated with Delay of Gratification

| Children Who Delayed Gratification | Children Who Did Not Delay Gratification |
|---|---|
| **Boys** | |
| Deliberative | Irritable |
| Attentive | Restless and fidgety |
| Able to concentrate | Aggressive |
| Reasonable | Generally not self-controlled |
| Reserved | |
| Cooperative | |
| Able to modulate impulses | |
| **Girls** | |
| Intelligent | Go to pieces under stress |
| Resourceful | Victimized by other children |
| Competent | Easily offended |
| | Sulky |
| | Whiny |

Source: Adapted from "Delay of Gratification: Some Longitudinal Personality Correlates" by D. C. Funder, J. H. Block, and J. Block, 1983, *Journal of Personality and Social Psychology, 44,* pp. 1198–1213. Copyright 1982 by the American Psychological Association. Reprinted by permission.

These personality descriptions and the experimental studies on self-imposed delay of gratification reported here are based on normal, low-risk young children. Recent work suggests that the results of such studies also apply to older children (6 to 12 years) who show adjustment problems (Rodriguez, Mischel, and Shoda, 1989).

## Social Learning Theory and Assessment

Although it emphasizes the importance of cognition as an independent variable, observable behavior is the primary dependent variable in social learning theory. That is, the goal of social learning theory is the same as the goal of classic learning theory: the explanation and prediction of behavior. Thus, many of the behavioral assessment techniques described in Chapter 10 are used by social learning theorists. In his 1954 book, Rotter devoted considerable space to a description of what he called controlled behavioral tests. However, it has been Bandura's work that has helped elevate behavioral assessment to its current prominence.

Unlike classic learning theorists, social learning theorists have also had to develop a variety of techniques to measure their cognitive independent variables, such as expectancies and reinforcement values. These cognitive variables are often conceptualized as stable and consistent characteristics, such as internal-external locus of control, self-efficacy, and Mischel's person variables such as competencies and encoding strategies.

## Measuring Expectancies

Rotter (1954) defines an expectancy as a subjectively held probability that a particular behavior will lead to a particular reinforcement. This definition suggests that the easiest method for assessing expectancies would be to ask participants to rate how confident they are that their behavior will achieve a certain outcome. Unfortunately, such a direct or obvious approach may not provide an accurate assessment of what people expect. People may not always be aware of their expectations, as when a rating is influenced by wishful thinking. Or people may not be willing to report their true beliefs, as in cases where they feel the need to appear especially confident. Moreover, it is never clear that what one participant means by a rating of say, "very confident" is the same as what another participant or the experimenter means by such a rating. These problems are inherent in the assessment of psychological constructs and are the reason that psychological measurement is often based on multiple methods or items that have been extensively studied and developed rather than on single, direct questions.

For example, in addition to a direct rating, betting techniques can be used. In this approach, participants are asked to bet on their expectancies. A bet of two dollars is interpreted to reflect greater confidence than a bet of one dollar. Furthermore, if my expectancy statement (bet) does not match my subsequent task performance, I lose the money. This provides an incentive for the participant to be accurate and discourages both defensiveness and wishful thinking. Another method is to ask participants which score, in a series of possible scores, they are most confident of achieving.

Bandura (1982) has defined self-efficacy as self-confidence that one can accomplish what a given situation demands. This definition is similar to Rotter's definition of expectancy. Consequently, the measurement techniques are also similar. Often the method used requires participants to specify their degree of confidence that a given task can be successfully executed. The measure can be made as broad or narrow as one wishes (e.g., "How confident are you that you will solve this arithmetic problem on the next trial?" or "At a social gathering, how likely is it that you will make a good impression on the other guests?").

Ryckman, Robbins, Thornton, and Cantrell (1982) have developed a physical self-efficacy scale. This is a 22–item instrument in which subjects express the extent of their agreement or disagreement with each item. Three examples of these items are given here:

1. I have excellent reflexes.
11. I am not hesitant about disagreeing with people bigger than me.
20. I find I am not accident prone. (p. 893)

Because the scores are based on multiple items rather than on a single question such as "How effective are you at solving physical problems," we have greater confidence in the legitimacy of the score as a reflection of the person's self-efficacy beliefs. Also, the scale has been found to be correlated with measures of self-esteem and self-consciousness, it discriminates between participants who perform well or poorly on a physical skills task, and it predicts who will report an active involvement in sports activities. This type of evidence increases our confidence that this measure is a valid reflection of the inherently unobservable, but important, construct of self-efficacy.

## Assessing Reinforcement Value

Reinforcement value is defined as the degree of preference for a given reward to occur if its occurrence were certain (Rotter, Chance, and Phares, 1972). The typical measurement procedure is to provide subjects with a list of potential rewards and simply ask that they be rank ordered in terms of decreasing preference. Subjects would also be instructed to assume that they could, in fact, have any of the rewards involved.

## Projective Techniques

Rotter and his colleagues have made considerable use of the Thematic Apperception Test (TAT) to assess generalized expectancies and needs. Careful and explicit manuals have been constructed so that reliable inferences can be made from the stories. Interpretation of the meaning of stories is based on an explicit set of rules rather than on unspecified intuitions. For example, inferring the presence of low generalized expectancies for success would be based on the following types of responses across a set of pictures:

- Environment is described as threatening, hostile, or unpredictable
- Central character shows withdrawal, guilt, suspiciousness, denial, etc.
- Central character expresses feelings of self-doubt or inadequacy
- Stories show unrealistic endings

The following are responses about the central character that might be used to infer a strong need for academic recognition:

- Attends college despite family objections
- Reduces extracurricular activities to concentrate on studies
- Feels college is essential to get the right job
- Expresses unhappiness over an average grade

## Incomplete Sentences

The **Rotter Incomplete Sentences Blank (ISB)** (Rotter and Rafferty, 1950) is a widely used personality test that also allows subjects to freely react to a set of stimuli. The ISB consists of 40 sentence stems, for example, I like _____; What annoys me _____; I wish _____. The participant's task is to complete each stem. Each completion is scored from 1 to 7, based on the correspondence between the expressed need and the ability of the participant to meet that need (freedom of movement). Low scores (maladjustment) suggests low freedom of movement coupled with strong need value, whereas high scores (adjustment) implies a balance between the two.

## Measurement of Internal-External Locus of Control (I-E)

The concept of internal-external locus of control was first introduced by Phares (1957), who demonstrated that participants developed expectancies differently when they believed that success on a task was determined by skill rather than by chance. The essence of the results was that changes in expectancies following success or failure were greater under skill conditions than under chance conditions. A variety of other studies showed that the generalization and extinction of expectancies vary depending upon whether skill or chance situations are involved (see Phares, 1976). These experimental studies not only provided important clues about how perceptions of control influence the role of reinforcement, but also suggested that if specific skill (internal) and chance (external) experiences can produce detectably different outcomes in the laboratory, then the same expectations may explain differences in people's everyday behavior.

The I-E Scale (Rotter, 1966) is designed to assess stable individual differences in participants' natural expectancies about the control of reinforcement in their lives. The I-E Scale consists of 23 forced-choice items, along with 6 filler items added to help disguise the purposes of the test. Table 12-2 lists some sample items.

The Rotter I-E Scale is one of the most widely used in psychology. Although it originally treated I-E as a broad, generalized factor, over the years increasing evidence has accumulated that I-E is not a unidimensional concept but a multidimensional one consisting of several elements.

## Summary Evaluation

Rotter and Bandura have been responsible for the major theoretical advances in social learning theory, and their work has been complementary. For Bandura, the focus is on explaining how social behaviors not presently in the person's repertoire can be learned. For Rotter, the problem is accounting for the choices

Table 12-2

**Items Similar to Those on the I-E Scale; These Are Drawn from Unpublished Preliminary versions of the 1966 Scale**

I more strongly believe that (choose a or b for each question)

1. a. Many people can be described as victims of circumstance.
   b. What happens to other people is pretty much of their own making.
2. a. Much of what happens to me is probably a matter of luck.
   b. I control my own fate.
3. a. The world is so complicated that I just cannot figure things out.
   b. The world is really complicated, all right, but I can usually work things out by effort and persistence.
4. a. It is silly to think one can really change another's basic attitudes.
   b. When I am right I can convince others.
5. a. Most students would be amazed at how much grades are determined by capricious events.
   b. The marks I get in class are completely my own responsibility.

among behaviors that have already been learned and are available. The third theorist highlighted in these chapters, Walter Mischel, is best known for his critique of dispositional and psychodynamic personality theories and for his explicit social learning reconceptualization of person variables.

## Strengths

**Research Emphasis.** Social learning theorists have a tradition of answering questions or resolving controversies by marshaling evidence derived from carefully controlled experimental research. This tradition is especially notable in the work of Bandura, whose career is characterized by a substantial quantity of high-quality research on a wide variety of specific content areas.

**Influential Ideas.** Rotter, Bandura, and Mischel have each articulated ideas and issues that have captured the attention of those in the field and have influenced the course of research. Although in hindsight their ideas may seem simple or obvious, at the time they were presented they represented important new insights. First, there was Rotter's insistence that human behavior should be regarded as determined both by reinforcement and by expectancies. His ability to integrate two major themes in psychology—motivation and cognition—into one broad theoretical schema has had a substantial impact on personality psychology. Bandura's emphasis on the role of observational learning in humans was not a new idea. But his rigorous analysis of observational learning, supported by numerous compelling studies, gave it scientific credibility. In the process, he was able to illustrate that learning does occur in the absence of any apparent reinforcement. Mischel's critique of the role of traits as determinants of behavior served to correct some misconceptions and overstatements that had plagued some personality research and particularly personality assessment. In retrospect, his critique is also an overstatement, but it has served to revitalize the field and to broaden the scope of personality research to include situational as well as person variables.

### Human Issues.

The strong behavioral emphasis of American psychology had led many psychologists to limit their research to those behaviors that can be studied in animals in controlled laboratory settings. The power of learning theory is demonstrated by the extent to which human behavior can be predicted from models derived from simple animal behaviors in artificial settings. However, many of the most crucial problems and issues that people and society face can not be addressed by such simple models and experiments. Social learning theory is able to consider more complex and uniquely human behavior without relinquishing those aspects of learning theory that do apply to people.

### Open-Ended Theory.

Rotter's and Bandura's versions of social learning theory are dynamic. Bandura's focus has changed and evolved. Beginning with observational learning and aggression, the emphasis has shifted to cognitive processes, self-regulation, and self-efficacy. This evolution has been possible because Bandura operates from a loosely structured theory. Because of this ability to gradually shift emphasis, social learning has been able to address contemporary issues.

Although Rotter's theory is more structured, its concepts are open-ended and allow for the addition of variables. Rotter's theory is content-free in that it specifies certain types of variables (needs, expectancies, etc.) but does not fix their content. For example, although any expectancies will influence behavior in similar and predictable ways, the specific content of a person's expectancies are not limited by the theory.

### Cognitive Emphasis.

It is the addition of cognitive concepts to classic learning theory that has made social learning theory applicable to human behavior and issues. People are not mere accumulations of conditioned responses. Their capacity for thinking, planning, expecting, and reflecting is more completely represented by the current cognitively based social learning theories than by the older, more mechanistic, animal-based learning models. This cognitive emphasis is what has enabled social learning theory to engage matters of social concern—those that are typically human in character. Moreover, when cognitive theory became the central focus of psychology, social learning theory was easily incorporated into this perspective.

**Behavior Change.** Bandura's research on observational learning and modeling has many applied implications. His focus on the means by which behaviors are acquired and changed in the social context has helped to increase the use of various behavior therapy techniques.

**Role of the Situation.** Social learning theory has also emphasized the role of situational factors in the determination of human behavior. People do not make up the world in their heads; rather, they process and interpret a situational reality. Although personality psychologists have always recognized the general importance of situational factors in human behavior (Goldberg, 1972), Rotter, Bandura, and Mischel have explicitly and specifically studied the role of the situation. Rotter stresses the interaction between situational variables and more enduring personality characteristics. Bandura and Mischel were initially less attentive to individual difference variables, but their introduction of concepts such as self-efficacy and Mischel's outline of five cognitive social learning person variables indicates that individual differences will play an increasingly important role in their theories.

**Theoretical Structure.** Rotter's social learning theory is the most contemporary of the grand attempts to articulate a broad and formal theory of personality. His is a classical approach to theory construction, with its formal statement of assumptions, postulates, and corollaries. Since Rotter's work, personality psychology has been characterized by a microtheoretical approach in which the range of convenience of personality theories is limited to specific person characteristics and situations. Because of its formality and its broad incorporation of cognitive, motivational, behavioral, and situational variables, Rotter's theory has the potential to integrate many of the issues and phenomena studied by contemporary personality psychologists.

## Weaknesses

**Narrowness.** Although social learning theories recognize the importance of internal cognitive variables for understanding human behavior, the focus of most social learning analyses is predicting observable behavior. Internal outcomes such as emotions, beliefs, and attitudes are not generally addressed by social learning theories. Also, the development of personality is not addressed by this approach. Although many of Bandura's studies involve children, and Rotter's concepts have been applied to the development of achievement behavior in children (e.g., Crandall, Good, and Crandall, 1964), there is no description of stages of development. For many, this is a critical omission. There are biological, hormonal, and physical aspects of development that learning can not explain.

**Theoretical Integration.** Rotter's theory is both formal and systematic. However, the same cannot be said for Bandura's approach. It is neither systematic nor unified. Bandura's work is best characterized as a loose collection of concepts (e.g., observational learning, self-regulation, self-efficacy) that have been rigorously investigated. But there is no comprehensive framework for organizing these concepts. In Rotter's system, the relations among concepts are carefully stated, often through the use of heuristic formulas. By quantification of each variable in the formula, specific predictions can be made about the behavior of a given person in a specific situation. No such possibility is readily available in Bandura's scheme.

A similar lack of unification characterizes Mischel's presentation of the five person variables that constitute his reconceptualization of personality. Although intriguing and potentially of great utility, these variables are simply listed and briefly described. There are no statements about how they relate to each other.

**Observational Learning.** Fundamental to social learning is the ability of people to learn by observing. Bandura has carefully described observational learning, and his work has demonstrated that it occurs. However, social learning theorists have not provided an explanation of observational learning. We know what it is, but we do not know how or why it occurs. Although a person may be observed to learn without reinforcement, this does not exclude the possibility that somewhere in the past the person was rewarded for observation, thus leading to a generalized tendency to observe and learn in the presence of certain cues. If so, there is no "learning without reinforcement."

Another potential problem with observational learning as a theoretical concept is its breadth. Observational learning can include nearly all sources of information, from actual persons to written instructions and imagined models. This breadth makes hypotheses about observational learning difficult to specify and test because the source of observational learning may be unknown. That is, if a study fails to demonstrate observational learning, that result can be attributed to learning that has occurred from an unknown source.

**Nothing New.** Rotter's theory was based on the ideas of a diverse group of learning theorists such as Tolman, Skinner and Thorndike. Likewise, Bandura's work has been viewed as a recycled amalgam of Miller and Dollard's work on imitation, Rotter's cognitive concepts, Tolman's latent learning, and Staats's (1975) social behaviorism. Undoubtedly, Bandura has been influenced by all these sources. To some, the work of Rotter and Bandura is largely a relabeling of already established concepts, which limits the scope of their contributions. The alternative view is that the strength of Rotter's and Bandura's work is their capacity to integrate new and old ideas into a program of empirical research. The final product, although not unique, represents a new perspective that contributes to our understanding of personality processes.

Social learning theory does not represent any distinctive or special principles of learning. It refers not to a separate set of principles but to the social context in which one gathers data and makes decisions (Levy, 1970). The uniqueness of social learning resides not in its concepts but in its functional application to understanding and studying human behavior.

## Summary

- The chief research strategy used by social learning theorists has been an experimental one.
- Early research by Rotter and his colleagues focused on the goal of providing a solid scientific foundation for the basic concepts of expectancy, reinforcement value, and the psychological situation. Two studies were presented to illustrate how expectancies generalize across situations and need areas. Another study was described to show how the value of a reinforcement is affected by the value of subsequent reinforcements that are associated with it. Finally, it was shown how the situation can differentially affect the value of reinforcements.
- Research on Rotter's theory has also documented its applicability to important clinical issues. Experiments linking expectancies and reinforcement value to drinking patterns and to termination of psychotherapy were described.
- Research on problem-solving generalized expectancies has been prominent in recent years. Internal versus external control of reinforcement and interpersonal trust have been the focus of much of the attention. Internal-external locus of control is one of the most widely studied concepts in psychology. This variable is related to a wide variety of important human behavior, including conformity, attributions, achievement, and well-being.
- High interpersonal trust has been shown to correlate with a reduced tendency to lie, cheat, and steal. High trusters tend to be better adjusted, more sought after as friends, and not especially naive or gullible. Low trusters are more alert to negative stimuli and more suspicious of strangers. Evidence also suggests that distrust increased during the 1960s. More recently, work has begun to determine the correlates of selfism—another problem-solving generalized expectancy.
- In Bandura's work, observational learning has been the object of considerable investigation. In a now classic study of the modeling of aggression, Bandura was able to show that children can acquire more responses than they actually perform and that a punished model is responded to differently than one who is rewarded.
- Self-efficacy has been an increasing subject of research. Several studies indicate the importance of this concept. For example, modeling can enhance feelings of self-efficacy, which in turn are good predictors of mastery or

competency with specific tasks. Research indicates that as self-efficacy increases, so too does one's ability to cope with previously threatening stimuli or activities, deal effectively with pain, and better regulate one's behavior. The growth of self-efficacy feelings can be facilitated by ensuring that rewards for doing well occur soon after a successful performance.

- The ability to delay gratification is another concept based on social learning concepts. Early studies implicated the role of expectancies by showing that participants who expected a delayed reward of greater value to occur were more likely to choose it over an immediate but lesser reward.

- Mischel is a leading figure in the research on delay of gratification. He has, for example, shown that a delayed reward will increase in value because of the expectancy that it will not occur. He and Bandura have also been able to demonstrate that choices of delayed versus immediate rewards can be influenced through modeling. Finally, there are personality correlates of the ability to delay gratification, and these may well last at least through childhood.

- A variety of assessment techniques have been employed by social learning theorists. To measure expectancies, Rotter has used two chief methods: subjects' ratings of their confidence in being successful and betting techniques. Similarly, Bandura has used self-confidence ratings as indicators of self-efficacy.

- Reinforcement value has typically been measured by asking subjects to rank-order a list of reinforcements while assuming that they could, in fact, have any of the reinforcements listed.

- Broader concepts such as freedom of movement and need value have frequently been assessed via responses to projective stimuli. Typically, manuals are developed to enhance the reliability and validity of the interpretations of subjects' responses. Rotter has also used incomplete-sentences methods to measure the discrepancy between need value and freedom of movement, which is interpreted as maladjustment.

- Objective questionnaires have been developed to measure problem-solving generalized expectancies such as internal versus external control of reinforcement and interpersonal trust.

- Social learning theory has several strengths. First, there is its research emphasis. Also important has been the application of social learning theory to the study and understanding of important and uniquely human issues such as aggression, self-efficacy, modeling, interpersonal trust, delay of gratification, and control of reinforcement.

- Other strengths include the dynamic nature of social learning theoretical systems, their cognitive emphases, their effectiveness at changing behavior, and their explicit recognition of the role of the situation on influencing what people do.

- Also noteworthy is Rotter's achievement in constructing a systematic, integrated theoretical framework whose breadth contrasts sharply with the minitheoretical approach of contemporary personality psychology.

- Of course, social learning theory also has some weaknesses. For example, despite Rotter's attempt to construct a broad theory, there is an element of narrowness in both his and Bandura's approaches. Especially lacking is a systematic focus on internal outcome (dependent) variables and human development. The emphasis on learning theory results in a relative inattention to behavioral and personality features that are linked to biological and hereditary factors.
- Bandura's approach is not well integrated. Bandura does not have a formal theory. Similarly, Mischel's reconceptualization, which involves several person variables, does not provide a framework for integrating those variables.
- Some critics have also noted that Bandura's work on observational learning is descriptive rather than explanatory. The concept of observational learning is also so broad that it is difficult to evaluate specific hypotheses about its operation.
- Social learning theory has drawn ideas from many diverse sources. Some have argued that it represents a mere relabeling of already established concepts and models. Social learning theory has not developed any new principles of learning. Rather, it is a means of extending learning theory to human behavior.

# Chapter 13
# Trait Theory: Personality Dispositions and Personality Description

Personality Description and Personality Theory
    Trait Constructs
    Advantages of Trait Constructs
Traits: The Dispositional View
    Historical Beginnings of Dispositional
     Theory
    Traits and Types
Allport: A Trait Theory
    Basic Theory and Concepts
    Development of Personality
    Nature of Adjustment
    Implications for Behavior Change
Cattell: A Factor Theory of Traits
    Basic Theory and Concepts
    Development of Personality
    Nature of Adjustment
    Implications for Behavior Change
Eysenck: A Theory of Types
    A Hierarchical Personality Structure
    Basic Types
    Nature of Introversion-Extroversion
Murray: A System of Needs
    Traits as Needs and Motives
    Basic Concepts

Achievement Motivation
Need for Power
Need for Affiliation
The Trait–Situation Controversy
    Dispositional Traits and Situational
     Specificity
    Conclusion
Traits as Descriptions, Not Causes, of Behavior
    The Act-Frequency Theory of Traits
    The Big Five Model of Personality
     Description
Summary

The English language contains over 18,000 words that can be used to describe people. Knowing whether a person is reliable or untrustworthy, friendly or aloof, sophisticated or crude, nervous or relaxed, or assertive or submissive is important for planning our interactions with that person. Thus, it is not surprising that describing our own and others' personalities is a common and important everyday human activity. Personality description is also important for the scientific study of personality. Before we can meaningfully propose and evaluate theories about the causes and consequences of peoples' personality and behavior, we must systematically describe the phenomena we are studying. Description is generally regarded as a necessary initial step in scientific research. In this chapter we will consider some of the issues involved in personality **description** and discuss the major theories or systems of personality description.

## Personality Description and Personality Theory

The previous chapters have reviewed the major theories of personality. These theories have emphasized the role of biological, cognitive, and environmental forces in shaping personality. Most of these major personality theories have not emphasized the systematic description or classification of personality or behavior. Personality description is not a central goal of those theories; instead, their goal is to explain personality and behavior in terms of their underlying causes. The perspective taken in this chapter is that *after genes, biochemicals, learning, phenomenology, cognition, psychodynamic forces, and the environment, singly and in combination, have had their influences, we are left with an individual with a personality that needs to be described.*

The difference between the **descriptive theories** presented in this chapter and the **casual theories** described in earlier chapters is that descriptive theories are *not* designed to explain why people behave, think, and feel as they do. Instead, their focus is on useful, comprehensive, and compelling systems for organizing and summarizing the characteristics we observe in people, regardless of what forces have caused those characteristics to develop. For example, a *friendly* person is one who smiles, helps others, and is talkative and outgoing, regardless of the forces that caused him to be friendly. Likewise, a *conscientious* person is one who is neat, on time, and does reliable work, and it matters little for the description how she became that way.

### Trait Constructs

Different theories of personality will emphasize different types of constructs and levels of description, and require those different constructs and levels for their evaluation. However, the most comprehensive and systematic descriptive theories of personality have employed **trait constructs** at a relatively high level of abstraction. A trait construct is typically represented by a single adjective such as "reliable" or "gentle" that is used to describe people in everyday discourse. In addition, a trait description is generally viewed as predictive of how a person will act, think, and feel in the future. The prediction of future behavior may imply a causal link between the trait and behavior, or it may simply reflect the commonsense idea that past behavior is a good indication of future behavior. When prediction is based on a causal link, traits are viewed as **dispositions,** which are inclinations or tendencies that help direct and motivate behavior.

## Advantages of Trait Constructs

There are several advantages to the use of traits in personality description.

1. Traits are nonconditional and therefore indicate general trends and expectations (McAdams, 1995). A **nonconditional description** means that no qualifications are placed on the description, as in "she is dominant" or "he is talkative," whereas **conditional descriptions** place situational restrictions on the description. Thorne (1989) has provided examples of conditional personality description, "My dominance shows *when my competence is threatened;* I fall apart *when people try to comfort me;* I talk most *when I am nervous*" (p. 149). Conditional descriptions are undoubtedly more accurate than nonconditional descriptions because of their specificity. However, conditional descriptions are inefficient and, by their nature, difficult to generalize to future situations involving new conditions.

2. Traits are easily compared on quantitative dimensions. One person's degree of friendliness can be normatively compared with the friendliness of another; a student's level of conscientiousness can be ipsatively compared between freshman and senior years of college. The comparative nature of trait constructs permits the use of powerful statistical techniques such as factor analysis to develop and evaluate descriptive systems. It also makes it easy to obtain quantitative traits ratings from also anyone; scientist and nonscientist, laypersons and experts alike.

3. Trait constructs can be used **hierarchically;** that is, broader traits summarize more specific traits, which summarize even more specific traits, and so on. Not only are some traits more general than others (Hampson, John, and Goldberg, 1986) but traits provide general summaries of behaviors (e.g., Buss and Craik, 1983) as well as goals, expectations, genetic factors and other types of descriptions. Thus, descriptive systems based on traits can organize personality descriptions from a variety of other levels and domains.

4. Trait constructs provide a common language, not only among different types of formal personality theories but between formal theories and people's everyday informal personality descriptions. The universality of trait concepts is a powerful unifying force in the study of personality.

## Traits: The Dispositional View

Although the emphasis in this chapter is on the descriptive role of traits, traits have historically been conceptualized as more than descriptions. Specifically, traits were treated as causal dispositions, and trait theories were viewed as having the same explanatory goals as psychodynamic, biological, behavioral, cognitive, and phenomenological theories. "In its simplest form, dispositions and their behavioral expressions were assumed by definition to correspond directly: the more a person has a conscientious disposition, for example, the more conscientious the behavior will be" (Mischel and Shoda, 1995). That is, the description of the behavior and the dispositional cause of the behavior were inextricably intertwined.

### Historical Beginnings of Dispositional Theory

The early Greeks often used **characterology** to classify a variety of human types. In characterology, categories are constructed and then people are described as belonging to a particular category, or **type**. A type is considered to be well defined if it provides a description so vivid and concise that everyone immediately recognizes the type of person being depicted. For example, Aristotle is said to have described the "magnanimous man" and Theophrastus the "penurious man." It was Hippocrates who contended that there are four basic types of temperament and that each can be accounted for by a coexisting and predominant body fluid, or "humor," as shown in Table 13-1.

Another historically popular approach to personality characterization has been **physiognomy**. This is a method by which personality is inferred from appearance, especially from the shape and expression of the face. For example, Chaucer, in the *Canterbury Tales,* implied that the Wife of Bath was sexually promiscuous because of the gap in her teeth and that the Miller used impious language because his mouth was red like the fires of hell. Part of the humor in the Canterbury tales is based on the naivete of the pilgrim who narrates the story because he does not notice these cues that have obvious indications about the personality of the characters. There has never been much scientific support for the

❧ Table 13-1
The "Humoral Psychology" of Hippocrates

| Humor | Corresponding Temperament |
|---|---|
| Blood | Sanguine (optimistic) |
| Black bile | Melancholic (depressed) |
| Yellow bile | Choleric (irritable) |
| Phlegm | Phlegmatic (listless, calm) |

relation between physiognomy and personality Nevertheless, belief in the relation persists, and nearly everyone from time to time makes personality judgments on such a basis. The modern legacy of this approach is the search for correlations between physique and temperament (see Chapter 5).

## Traits and Types

In some instances, classification systems have dealt with types; in other cases, a classification of traits has been developed. The classical distinction between these two concepts is based on the differences between discrete categories and dimensions. A **typology** is most often viewed as a set of discrete categories into which people can be sorted. Thus, you are classified either as an introvert, an extravert, or an ambivert. In contrast, traits represent continuous dimensions. You can, for example, possess the trait of aggressiveness to a marked degree, moderately, or almost not at all. In illustrating this distinction, Allport (1937) remarked: "A man can be said to *have* a trait; but he cannot be said to *have* a type. Rather he *fits* a type" (p. 295).

In practice, the trait versus type distinction is often blurred. For example, Sheldon (Chapter 5) developed a typology of physique (with corresponding temperaments), but he allowed people to be classified on a seven-point scale. Similarly, as we shall see, Eysenck (1970) has tried to discover the basic personality types; yet, he views them not as discrete categories but as dimensions on which people differ. Also, typologies most often deal with a small number of concepts—usually from two to seven categories. But in the case of traits, their number can be large depending upon the methodological approach used by the investigator. As a result, typologies are vulnerable to the criticism that they attempt to explain behavior by recourse to a small number of simple variables.

## Allport: A Trait Theory

Gordon Allport's theory of traits was influenced by phenomenological and humanistic ideas. Phenomenologically, Allport attended to how people perceive themselves and others, as well as to factors that influenced everyday personality descriptions. Indeed, he was the first to systematically explore the natural (English) language for clues about the nature and structure of personality traits (Allport and Odbert, 1936). As a humanist, Allport appreciated the uniqueness of every individual and stressed an idiographic characterization of the person that emphasized the organization of traits within an individual. Allport's work indicates an eclectic theoretical stance, and his theory of personality reflects the influence of various disciplines, including literature, philosophy, sociology, religion, and psychology. The common element in Allport's work was the use of traits to communicate and structure his descriptions of people and to explain their behavior. For this reason, Allport is generally regarded as a trait theorist.

Perhaps because of his eclecticism, Allport's influence on psychology and personality has been broad and persistent. Although few psychologists describe themselves as "Allportian," it is common to see personality psychologists from a variety of schools of thought link their work to his name.

## Basic Theory and Concepts

Allport defined personality as "the dynamic organization within the individual of those psychophysical systems that determine his unique adjustments to his environment" (1937, p. 48). The word *dynamic* indicates that personality constantly changes and evolves; yet, there is a persistent *organization* that lends structure and coherence to personality. Thus, an individual's personality is characterized by stability in general organization and change in specific features. By *psychophysical*, Allport emphasized the role of both the mind and the body in personality. The personality is everything a person is—flesh as well as self. Finally, personality tendencies *determine* characteristic behavior and thought.

Nature of Traits.  Allport defined a trait as *a neuropsychic structure having the capacity to render many stimuli functionally equivalent, and to initiate and guide equivalent (meaningfully consistent) forms of adaptive and expressive behavior* (1961, p. 347). A trait is a readiness to think or act in a similar fashion in response to a variety of different stimuli or situations. As shown in Figure 13-1, a trait has the capacity to average the differences among situations and to prompt responses to them that are basically alike.

For Allport, aggressiveness, dishonesty, friendliness and all other traits are not hypothetical constructs that have some dispositional implications for our behavior. Instead, traits have a reality; they exist within the person. Traits also actively cause or impel behavior that will result in our being aggressive, dishonest,

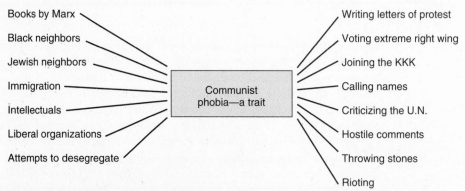

**Figure 13-1** &#10019; "The operation of a Communist phobia trait." A trait operates something like a filter by rendering a variety of stimuli more alike than they otherwise would be. The result is a set of behaviors which, although not identical, are still clearly related.

(Adapted from Allport, 1961).

A
BRIEF
BIOGRAPHY
OF

# Gordon Allport

Gordon W. Allport was born in 1897 in Indiana and grew up in Cleveland. He was the youngest of four brothers, one of whom, Floyd, became a renowned social psychologist. Allport's father was a doctor, who, because of inadequate local hospital facilities, often brought his patients home. He was also a believer in hard work. As a result, young Gordon learned very early about the world of work—from washing bottles to tending patients. His relationship with his father was also marked by trust and affection.

Allport was academically inclined almost from the beginning. After graduating second in his high school class, he followed his brother Floyd to Harvard. He majored in economics and philosophy, receiving his B.A. in 1919. During a brief teaching stint in Turkey, he was awarded a fellowship for graduate study in psychology at Harvard. On his way home, he arranged an interview with Freud in Vienna (Allport, 1968). When they met, Freud had little to say, and Allport grew increasingly uneasy over the lengthening silence. In desperation, Allport recounted an incident that occurred on a streetcar while he was en route to Freud's home. It involved a young boy who was quite fearful about getting dirty and the boy's mother, who appeared obsessed with cleanliness. To Allport's surprise and chagrin, Freud responded with only a slightly veiled suggestion that perhaps this incident had aroused some unconscious conflict in Allport. This encounter with Freud may have reinforced Allport's growing suspicion of theories such as psychoanalysis, which heavily emphasized unconscious motives at the expense of conscious ones.

In 1922, Allport was awarded the Ph.D. After some additional postdoctoral work and two years of teaching at Harvard, he accepted a teaching post at Dartmouth. In 1930, he returned to Harvard, where he remained on the faculty until his death in 1967.

Allport's best known book is his personality text published in 1937 and revised in 1961 as *Pattern and Growth in Personality*. Another widely read book is *Becoming: Basic Considerations for a Psychology of Personality*, published in 1955. His autobiography appears in the 1967 *A History of Psychology in Autobiography* (Vol. 5).

or friendly. However, some traits or dispositions (e.g., politeness) are stylistic rather than motivational. Stylistic traits influence behavior to manifest itself in certain forms rather than motivate or initiate it.

Allport also differentiated traits from other concepts such as habits. **Habits** are limited or narrow dispositions that are confined to specific situations. The executive who characteristically cleans off and arranges her desk carefully before leaving the office at the end of the day is manifesting a habit. That habit, however, may be part of a larger trait system such as "orderliness" that integrates several habits. However, this executive may have other habits that are not consistent with a trait of orderliness. Allport recognized such inconsistencies but did not view them as invalidating his concept of traits. The orderliness trait may not be well integrated or important for the executive. Alternatively, two traits that may occasionally conflict may be involved. The executive may have an orderliness trait related to her professional life but not to her private life, where behavior may be guided by a different trait, such as comfort. In still other instances, a behavior may be determined by a particularly compelling situational stimulus. In sum, Allport did not propose that traits would rigidly and consistently influence every aspect of a persons' behavior in all situations. Allport recognized that people had some behavioral flexibility and that both traits and situations combine to produce behavior (Zuroff, 1986).

**Classification of Traits.** Allport proposed three types of traits that differed in the pervasiveness of their influence on behavior. First, there are **cardinal traits**. These are powerful traits that act as master motives or ruling passions; they influence every segment of a person's life. A person possessing such a trait would exhibit obsessive, single-minded behavior consistent with that trait. Such a person would spend every waking hour seeking, for example, to become more attractive, make friends, keep his or her possessions organized, or make money, depending on the trait.

More typically, people are influenced by a relatively small number of **central traits,** which together influence much of their behavior. When someone writes a letter of recommendation and characterizes another person as reliable, punctual, self-starting, and trustworthy, these are descriptions of central traits. Central traits are relatively pervasive and are usually apparent to other people.

Beyond this intermediate level are the **secondary traits**. Such traits, although influential, are less consistent and generalized than cardinal or central traits. A preference for certain clothes or automobiles or a dislike of specific types of movies are examples of secondary traits. Being aware of a person's secondary traits requires substantial knowledge about that individual. So it is that many acquaintances might agree that Joe Smith is industrious, neat, and charming, whereas his wife knows that he is also slovenly when it comes to household repairs, never shaves on the weekend, and barks at the children when they interfere with Monday night football. These three classes of traits form a hierarchy of influence on behavior. Cardinal traits have the most pervasive influence, with central and secondary traits following, in that order.

Shakespeare's characters embody a complex interaction of traits. For example, in <u>Othello</u>, Iago would be characterized as up-front and trustworthy (central traits). However, his cardinal trait, or ruling passion, is to drive Othello mad—a pull so strong that Iago can hardly articulate why.

Allport also emphasized the uniqueness of each individual through his definition of another type of trait, **personal traits**. Personal traits are unique to each person and serve to explain why no two people are alike. In one sense, Allport believed that all traits were personal because they occurred in a different context and were manifested in different ways for each person. However, at another level Allport recognized **common traits,** which are those traits that concern people's similarities and permit comparisons across individuals. As a common trait, aggressiveness could be studied by comparing the scores subjects receive on an inventory designed to measure that trait. As a personal trait, my aggressiveness would result from different stimuli and be manifested in different ways than your aggressiveness, and therefore we could not compare our personal aggressiveness.

Intentions. Allport viewed behavior as influenced more by the anticipation of future events than by past experiences. Understanding behavior requires knowledge of **intentions**, that is, a person's hopes, plans, wishes, and aspirations. As with Adler's psychodynamic theory, Allport believed that individuals are not so much pushed by the past as pulled by their expectations about the future.

Functional Autonomy. Also indicative of Allport's rejection of the past as the source of behavior was his concept of **functional autonomy**, which is the theory that some behaviors will persist for no other reason than that the person likes the activity. For example, a child may have developed a passion for reading because it led to recognition by an esteemed teacher or a loving parent, but eventually reading may become valued as an end in itself. It is not that reading persists because it has become linked to some new set of motives; it is functionally autonomous from any external motives or goals. However, Allport did not believe that all adult behavior is functionally autonomous from its past influences.

Proprium.    Allport (1961) used the term **proprium** to describe the essential features of the self. The proprium is composed of everything important in the personality that a person regards as his or her own. It includes bodily sense, self-identity, self-esteem, self-extension, rational thinking, self-image, knowing, and propriate striving. This proprium develops as the person grows and experiences; it is not innate.

## Development of Personality

According to Allport, personality development does not begin immediately after birth. The early months of life are spent in the pursuit of pleasure and the avoidance of pain, and the only reality for the child is a biological one. The child's responses are largely instinctive and are motivated by primitive needs. Only in the second six months does the infant begin to show signs of some elemental emotional characteristics that appear to be distinctly human.

Allport relies on the principles of learning and conditioning, although he occasionally resorts to psychoanalytic defense mechanisms, to explain early development. However, Allport did outline a series of stages that correspond to the evolving sense of self. Specifically, he described seven aspects of selfhood, or the proprium (Allport, 1961):

- *Sense of Bodily Self*—The sense of bodily "me," which emerges at about the age of 15 months.
- *Sense of Self-Identity*—The recognition of oneself as separate and distinctive; language is vital in enhancing this identity, and one's own name further helps solidify this sense as it develops from the second year onward.
- *Sense of Self-Esteem*—Self-enhancement is important at about the age of two years. Often this appears as negativism. But by the age of 4 or 5, the desire to enhance the self turns negativism into competitiveness.
- *Extension of Self*—This is an egocentric period. It is also marked by extreme possessiveness. The focus is on things and events as they relate to "me." This period lasts from the age of about 4 to about 6.
- *The Self-Image*—Another aspect of the 4 to 6 period is the manner in which others evaluate the child. Starting school triggers an incorporation of the perceptions of others. These expectations of others are important.
- *The Self as Rational Coper*—From 6 to 12, the awareness of self as one who can cope, solve problems, and think rationally emerges. The capacity to

"think about thought" begins. This is also a period of close alliance with family, peer group, and social institutions—the age of conformity.

- *Propriate Striving*—This refers to the tendency to seek self-enhancement through the choosing of a life goal. The mature stage of propriate striving is realized when we have a well-conceived and well-articulated sense of purpose.

## Nature of Adjustment

Allport's view of the healthy personality and psychological adjustment has a clear humanistic emphasis. Unlike many personality theorists, Allport had little experience with psychotherapy or psychopathology. Many clinical psychologists and psychiatrists view neurotic or even psychotic behavior as being continuous with normal behavior. This means that the differences between the normal and abnormal person are not in kind but in degree. But Allport saw normal persons and neurotics or psychotics as qualitatively different from one another. He did not view psychopathology as an unhealthy exaggeration of normal traits. Nor

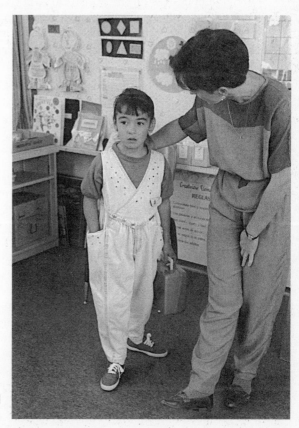

According to Allport, how a teacher encourages or discourages a child early on can influence how the child perceives herself.

did he view psychological health as simply the absence of neurotic problems. Instead, psychological health resulted from self-esteem and competence. Hjelle and Ziegler (1981) have summarized Allport's criteria for psychological maturity:

- An extended sense of self
- An ability to relate warmly to self and others
- Emotional security or self-acceptance
- Realistic perceptions, skills, and assignments
- Capacity for self-objectification and of insight in humor
- A unifying philosophy of life

## Implications for Behavior Change

Two themes in Allport's writings have important implications for behavioral change, although in one sense they are contradictory. The first theme is Allport's emphasis on dispositional traits. For Allport this implies substantial stability in both the desirable and undesirable aspects of personality throughout a person's life. The second theme is Allport's concept of functional autonomy. Here, the emphasis is on the transformation of motives over time. So within the same system, Allport describes significant opportunities for both stability and change. Unfortunately, there is little in the theory that allows us to predict when functional autonomy will prevail and when the enduring aspects of traits will dominate. This is a critical omission that makes it difficult to evaluate these two aspects of the theory. It also limits the application of the theory to psychotherapy and behavior change.

## Cattell: A Factor Theory of Traits

Although both are trait theorists, Raymond Cattell's theory differs substantially from Allport's, primarily because of the difference in their methods. Allport was a humanist who emphasized the unique, idiographic aspects of personality. In contrast, Cattell is a sophisticated mathematician who emphasizes the use of multivariate statistical analyses to identify the important traits of human personality.

Cattell is easily the most productive personality psychologist in the history of the field. His breadth of interests is astonishing; indeed, there is a feeling among personality psychologists that any "new" ideas, measures, or experimental techniques they develop will, at some point, have already been described and discussed by Cattell. Cattell's work relies on the statistical method of factor analysis. The general rationale for factor analysis is relatively straightforward (McArdle, 1996). However, the specifics of the technique can be complicated and controversial and often require substantial mathematical sophistication in their presentation. To students of personality put off by approaches that seem to focus more on statistical applications than on people, papers cluttered with formulas and equations do more to confuse than enlighten.

## Basic Theory and Concepts

Cattell has not proposed a general definition of personality. Instead, he defines personality empirically as whatever it is that allows us to predict what a person will do in a specific situation (Cattell, 1950). His definition of personality resides in his descriptions of the various types of traits he has identified. For Cattell, traits are the elements out of which the structure of personality is formed. More specifically, they are mental structures inferred from behavior, which predispose the individual to behave with consistency from one situation to another and from one time to another. Cattell describes several classes of traits.

Surface Versus Source Traits.   A **surface trait** is represented by a series of behaviors that all have some elements in common. Even the casual observer would identify a trait of friendliness by noting that behaviors such as saying hello on the street, smiling, and responding to a greeting all generally occur together and indeed belong together. A surface trait is not an explanatory concept; it is a description of an observation that a group of behaviors or characteristics tend to be correlated. On the other hand, **source traits** have an explanatory role. They are the basic, underlying structures that Cattell regards as constituting the core of personality. They are what cause behavior and, in that sense, determine the consistencies in each person's behavior. Because one source trait will influence several surface traits, it follows that source traits are fewer in number.

Cattell also believes that everyone possesses the same source traits, but not to the same degree. Thus, everybody has a source trait that we might call guilt. One individual may be predisposed by this trait of guilt to such an extent that he or she becomes very depressed, moody, or self-reproachful. Another person, at the opposite extreme, would be cheerful and self-confident. Most people occupy a place midway between these two extremes. In addition, a strong source trait will influence a wide variety of behavior, thoughts, and feelings, whereas a weak source trait will have correspondingly little influence.

Hereditary Versus Environmental Traits.   As noted in Chapter 5, the field of behavior genetics has established that behavior is generally the result of genetic and environmental factors. Cattell has explicitly acknowledged the role of both of these factors, arguing that surface traits are the product of such joint influences. However, in the case of the source traits, he contends that some are **constitutional traits**, which are of genetic origin, whereas others are **environmental-mold traits**, which develop out of experience and learning. Cattell believes the evidence suggests that a given source trait develops from *either* hereditary *or* environmental influences but not from both.

Ability Traits.   Some traits determine how effective we are in our pursuit of goals. These are **ability traits**. Perhaps the most important of these is intelligence. Cattell (1971) differentiates between crystallized and fluid intelligence. **Crystallized ability** is a broad, general intelligence that reflects experience in

## A BRIEF BIOGRAPHY OF

# Raymond Cattell

Raymond B. Cattell was born in England in 1905. He was 16 years old when he enrolled at the University of London. Majoring in chemistry, he received his B.Sc. degree in 1924. His growing awareness of social problems led him to an increasing interest in psychology. He finally decided to pursue graduate work in psychology and was granted the Ph.D. in 1929 from the University of London. During his graduate study, he worked closely with Charles Spearman, a noted psychologist and statistician, who pioneered the method of factor analysis. Cattell was impressed with this technique, and it has been central to his research throughout his career.

Following the award of the Ph.D., Cattell held what he regarded as a minor teaching post and subsequently a clinical position in Leicester, England. In 1937, the famous American psychologist Edward Thorndike invited him to become his research associate at Columbia University. The same year he was awarded a D.Sc. degree by the University of London for his outstanding contributions to personality.

Adjusting to the United States was difficult for Cattell. But he concentrated on his work and, as a result of the recognition it brought him, was offered the post of G. Stanley Hall Professor of Psychology at Clark University. He remained at Clark until 1941, when he moved to Harvard University.

school and in related activities in a given culture. **Fluid ability**, in contrast, represents a person's biological capacity and manifests itself regardless of exposure to any formal learning opportunities.

### Temperament Traits.

A **temperament trait** is a constitutional source trait that influences a person's level of emotionality of different types. Such a trait determines emotional reactivity, including the speed, energy, and intensity with which the person responds to environmental stimulation.

### Dynamic Traits.

**Dynamic traits** are those that motivate a person. Whereas temperament traits may determine the style of the individual's response, and ability traits the effectiveness of the response, dynamic traits set the response in motion. Cattell describes several types of dynamic traits. For example:

**Erg:** A dynamic constitutional source trait that motivates the individual. It is innate and determines several surface traits. Examples of ergs are pugnacity, self-assertion, and gregariousness.

**Sentiment:** An environmental-mold trait that arises out of experience with various sociocultural institutions and customs.

Cattell moved again in 1947 to the University of Illinois, where he remained for 30 years. He was Distinguished Research Professor of Psychology and Director of the Laboratory of Personality Assessment at Illinois until his retirement in 1973. Since then, he has been a visiting professor at the University of Hawaii and has also established an institute in Boulder, Colorado. In 1953, he was awarded the Wenner-Gren prize by the New York Academy of Science for his work on the psychology of the researcher.

Only a few examples of Cattell's most important works can be mentioned here. A series of three books provides an adequate representation of his views on personality: *Description and Measurement of Personality* (1946), *Personality: A Systematic, Theoretical, and Factual Study* (1950), and *Personality and Motivation Structure and Measurement* (1957). He wrote a less technical introduction to his ideas, *The Scientific Analysis of Personality*, which was published in 1965. A good summary of his work is presented in Hall and Lindzey (1978). A more recent book Personality and Learning Theory: Vol. 2. A Systems Theory of Motivation and Structural Learning (1980), deals with personality and learning theory.

**Attitudes:** Overt expressions of interest marked by a particular level of intensity (e.g., the fanatic golf fan or the old-movie junkie). There are virtually endless numbers of attitudes.

**The Dynamic Lattice.** Cattell believes that behaviors are related to one another because we engage in one behavior to allow us to engage in others. Specifically, dynamic traits are interrelated in a hierarchy in such a way that one is subsidiary to another. In general, ergs are superior to sentiments, which in turn are superior to attitudes. These relations represent the **dynamic lattice**. An example is illustrated in Figure 13-2. The right portion of the figure presents this individual's ergs—the basic innate motivational elements that direct his life. Closer to the middle of the figure are several sentiments toward wife, country, God, and so on. It can be seen that each of these sentiments is determined by, and subsidiary to, several ergs. Sentiment toward wife, for example, is connected to the ergs of sex, gregariousness, protection, and self-assertion. The left side of the figure depicts the individual's attitudes toward several specific issues, events, or behaviors. Each of these attitudes is subsidiary to several sentiments, and some are directly subsumed by an erg. Thus, traveling to New York is subsidiary to both bank account and

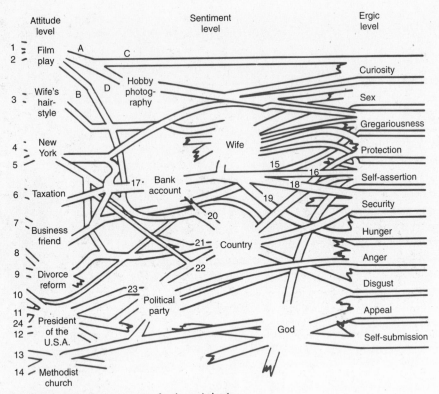

**Figure 13-2** &#x43B; One segment of a dynamic lattice.

country but also to gregariousness. Although trait theorists are sometimes accused of having a simplistic view of human motivation, the dynamic lattice demonstrates that Cattell's theory is complex.

**Unique Versus Common Traits.** Like Allport, Cattell believes that some traits apply, although in varying degrees, to all members of the same culture. These are **common traits**. In addition, an individual will have **unique traits**. Furthermore, the strength of both unique and common traits will vary over time within the same person.

**The Specification Equation.** Cattell's definition of personality is based on the prediction of behavior in a specific situation. Thus, the manner in which information about the various types of traits is combined to predict behavior in a specific situation is fundamental to Cattell's theory. The basis for making behavioral predictions is the **specification equation**. Cattell presents the equations as follows (1965, p. 265):

For Cattell, one behavior relates to another. Riding a roller coaster can be a way of achieving a more remote goal such as challenging ourselves or demonstrating our courage to others.

$$P_j = s_{jA}A \ldots + s_{jT}T \ldots + s_{jE}E \ldots + s_{jM}M$$
$$\ldots + s_{jR}R \ldots + s_{jA}S$$

where

$P_j$ = Performance in Situation j

$A$ = Ability source traits—how well the performance is executed

$T$ = Temperament traits—the style of behavior

$E$ = Ergic drives—the first class of dynamic traits

$M$ = Sentiments—the second class of dynamic traits

$R$ = Roles demanded by the situation

$S$ = Temporary moods and bodily states (e.g., anxiety, illness)

$s$ = Weighting factor to indicate the importance of Situation $j$

What this formula signifies is that the nature and quality of a person's response ($P$) in a given situation ($s_j$) can be predicted from that person's trait characteristics ($A$, $T$, $E$, $M$), and two transient variables ($R$, $S$), with each weighted by its relevance for the specific situation. The trait variables in this equation were all previously discussed. The transient variables are states and roles. **States** refer to temporary conditions such as fatigue, illness, or anxiety. **Roles** suggest that a person may act in different ways depending upon the role he or she is playing in the situation. For example, as a politician a person might respond to a personal question by refusing to answer, but as a close friend the person might respond by revealing something intimate about him or herself. The specification equation illustrates the complexity with which Cattell views human behavior.

## Development of Personality

Cattell considers both heredity and the environment as important determinant of personality. He has developed a theory for a complex set of statistical techniques to analyze data from personality measures to estimate the ratio of hereditary and environmental influences on each trait. Included in his model is the assertion that one's genetic background will indirectly affect personality development by influencing the reactions one receives from other people. For example, height is influenced by genetic factors, and tall men are often perceived as dominant. Thus, a tall man may become more dominant because he elicits reactions from others that place him in a dominant position in interpersonal situations.

Learning.  Cattell also emphasizes the basic learning principles of classical conditioning and instrumental conditioning to account for the influence of environmental experience and personality. As described in Chapter 9 in classical conditioning, a new stimulus becomes capable of eliciting a response previously produced by a different stimulus. In the case of instrumental conditioning, the person learns to perform a response to achieve a particular reward. Cattell considers classical conditioning to be particularly important because through it we come to respond emotionally to specific environmental stimuli. For example, I learn to become anxious at dinner because in the past this was followed by a fight between my parents. The sight of a dinner table becomes a signal that something bad is about to happen. Instrumental conditioning is the process through which we learn to satisfy our ergs via particular behaviors. In Figure 13-2 the man in question learns that going to New York will satisfy his gregarious urges or that joining a church will satisfy his needs for submission. This is a form of instrumental conditioning.

Cattell also considers **integration learning**. Integration learning occurs when we repress, suppress, or even sublimate some ergs while other ergs are being satisfied. This represents a level of maturity that is similar to the ability to delay gratification discussed in Chapter 11.

Syntality.  The personality development of individuals is also influenced by their culture, subcultures, and groups to which they belong. Therefore, a complete understanding of personality development and behavior in general requires consideration of the individual's church, family, school, and any other groups or institutions with which the individual is associated. In the same way that people may be said to have traits, groups also have traits. The dimensions along which groups can be described are called their **syntality**.

## Nature of Adjustment

Cattell views maladjustment as conflict. Ergs are often stimulated by a variety of events, but their satisfaction is sometimes thwarted. When this occurs there is a failure to achieve gratification, which leads to conflict, anxiety, and ultimately neurosis. Using his specification equation, Cattell has also attempted to express the degree of conflict inherent in a proposed behavior by assigning positive or negative weights to each entry in the equation. Negative weights, for example, are assigned to ergs, sentiments, or other traits that portend negative outcomes, whereas positive weights are attached to those that signal the potential for reward. The amount of conflict associated with a given course of action then becomes the ratio of the sum of negative weights to the sum of positive weights for those source traits involved. In analogous fashion, the degree of conflict throughout the entire personality could be computed by considering all the person's generalized traits.

## Implications for Behavior Change

Cattell recognizes that the complexity of the human personality, provides people with the capacity to change. However, the ability of his theory to explain personality and behavior change is limited by his emphasis on traits that by definition imply considerable stability over time and consistency across situations. Cattell views maturation as an important factor in the orderly change of traits across age levels. Also, Cattell distinguishes between **states** and **traits**. In contrast to traits, states are elements in an individual's personality that are expected to be unstable and to change from situation to situation. For example, Cattell and Scheier (1961) observe that in the case of anxiety, some individuals are chronically anxious, whereas others are acutely anxious some of the time and not anxious at other times. Chronic anxiety is a trait, whereas acute anxiety is a state. Both traits and states are important components of personality, but the focus of Cattell's theory is on traits and the stable structure of personality rather than on states and the processes and conditions under which they change.

## Eysenck: A Theory of Types

Like Cattell, Hans Eysenck is committed to factor analysis as a method of studying the basic dimensions of personality. However, factor analysis is not a single method but a collection of techniques that reflect different theoretical assumptions, perspectives, and interpretations. In addition, the results of a factor analysis depend on the nature and number of variables that are included in the analysis. The decisions about which form of factor analysis to use and which variables to factor analyze are therefore influenced by the theory of personality that is being described and evaluated. This is an example of the old saying that "there is no truth separate from the means of discovering it." A prime example of this is the work of Eysenck and Cattell. Factor analysis has led Cattell to compile a lengthy list of source traits, but Eysenck's analyses convince him that there are only three basic personality dimensions, which he calls types.

Eysenck's philosophy of the use of factor analysis also differs from that of Cattell. It is Cattell's belief that if many different measures are administered to large numbers of subjects and the responses undergo factor analysis, the basic dimensions of personality will be *discovered*. In contrast, Eysenck begins with hypotheses about how measures should be related, then *tests* those hypothesis with factor analysis. Eysenck calls this strategic use of factor analysis to test, rather discover, theories **criterion analysis** (Eysenck, 1950).

## A Hierarchical Personality Structure

A major feature of Eysenck's theory of personality is its **hierarchical structure** (Eysenck, 1947). At the top of the hierarchy are three personality types. However, Eysenck's concept of a type differs substantially from Allport's definition. For Eysenck, types are not qualitative categories into which people are classified. Instead, they are quantitative dimensions along which people differ. Thus Eysenck's "types" are more similar to Allport's concept of a trait. Eysenck uses the term "type" to distinguish the broad dimensions at the top of his hierarchy from the more specific traits at a lower level of his hierarchy.

Figure 13-3 illustrates Eysenck's hierarchical theory of personality structure for one of his major types, the introversion end of the **introversion-extroversion** dimension. The basic personality types exert a powerful general influence over behavior. Types are composed of **traits,** which in turn, are comprised of numerous **habitual responses**. Finally, there are a multitude of **specific responses**, which are the elements of habits.

## Basic Types

Eysenck's initial theory of personality was based on two principal types: *introversion-extroversion (E)* and *emotional stability-instability*. The latter dimension is generally referred to as *neuroticism (N)*, which emphasizes the unstable end of this dimension. These two types are viewed as having a strong biological and genetic basis that can be traced to the influence of different brain structures on personality. Eysenck's decision to relate his types to biological factors was influenced by his observation that writers and philosophers had, for centuries, consistently identified four basic human temperaments: sanguine, melancholic, choleric, and phlegmatic (see Table 13-1), and linked them with the four "humors" of the body (Kagan, 1994).

To test the central role of E and N in personality, Eysenck gathered data based on ratings of subjects and their responses to questionnaire items. Factor analyses of data from many measures and thousands of subjects convinced him that these two dimensions were the most fundamental and useful for structuring personality. Moreover, Eysenck believes that these dimensions have confirmed some of the wisdom of those ancient humoral conceptions of personality, as illustrated in Figure 13-4. In Figure 13-4, the older temperaments are shown in relation to the two major type dimensions. In addition, trait adjectives from a

## A BRIEF BIOGRAPHY OF

# Hans Eysenck

Hans J. Eysenck was born in 1916 in Berlin, Germany. When Hitler rose to power, Eysenck emigrated to England. At the age of 18 he began the study of psychology at the University of London. During that time, and throughout his career, Eysenck has been influenced by the statistical work of Spearman, by early typologists such as Jung and Kretschmer, and by Burt's work on the heritability of intelligence. He also was influenced by Hull's systematic learning theory.

During World War II, Eysenck worked at an emergency hospital in England where military patients suffering from stress reactions were treated. This led to his interest in the factors that predispose certain people to be more debilitated by stress than others. He approached the study of this issue with the tools of factor analysis, learning theory, typology, and heritability indices.

Eysenck has been a prolific author (over 30 books and 600 articles) and an investigator who is well known throughout Europe and in the United States. But he has been an outspoken and controversial figure as well. In part this has been due to his polemical attacks on psychoanalysis and the conventional methods of psychotherapy. Although his critiques have not always been well received, they have had the positive effect of inspiring psychotherapists to produce better arguments and more data to support their positions. More recently, Eysenck has been embroiled in another heated debate with Leon Kamin over the controversial topic of the heritability of intelligence.

Some of the more widely cited of Eysenck's many books include *Dimensions of Personality* (1947), *The Scientific Study of Personality* (1952), and *The Structure of Human Personality*, which was revised in 1970. *Sense and Nonsense in Psychology* appeared in 1957 and is an entertaining introduction to Eysenck's strongly held opinions about several controversial topics. He is coauthor with Kamin of *The Intelligence Controversy: H. J. Eysenck vs. Leon Kamin*, published in 1981. A more recent book, *Personality and Individual Differences: A Natural Science Approach*, was published in 1985 with his son as co-author.

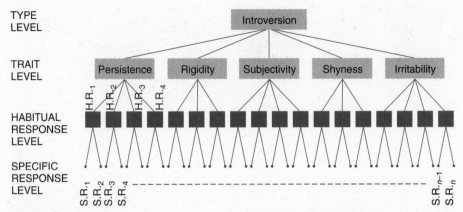

**Figure 13-3** &#x2709; Eysenck's structural model of the personality as illustrated by introversion.

lower level of the hierarchy that help clarify the characteristics associated with each type are presented.

In addition, Eysenck (1975) has proposed a third type, which he calls *psychoticism (P)*. Psychoticism refers to a dimension marked by emotional independence or psychopathy at one extreme and strong superego control and conventionality at the other. An individual at the psychotic extreme of this dimension would be solitary, without loyalties, uncaring of others, and insensitive. These descriptions are consistent with a clinical diagnosis of a psychotic individual or one with and psychopathic tendencies. Unlike E and N, psychoticism has not been linked to specific brain functions. However, Eysenck regards P as primarily genetic; it is also more common in men than in women.

Eysenck views these three types as essentially independent because they are based on biological systems that are independent. E concerns a biological **arousal system,** N concerns an **activating system,** and P concerns genetic tendencies toward **impulsivity versus control.** However, Eysenck recognizes that a strong link between biological systems and these dimensions of personality is not fully established (Eysenck, 1990). Indeed, Eysenck considers Gray's (1972, 1981) attempts to reinterpret the P, E, and N types to fit a general biological theory of personality as inconsistent with the data, although they are important and innovative. The most widely studied dimension in Eysenck's system is introversion-extroversion. The most persuasive evidence linking a type with a biological system is for the E dimension.

## Nature of Introversion-Extroversion

The introversion-extroversion concept was first identified by Carl Jung. Eysenck (1947) however, developed a psychometrically sound instrument, the Maudsley Personality Inventory, to measure the construct so that hypotheses about the construct could be rigorously and empirically tested. In general, introverts, com-

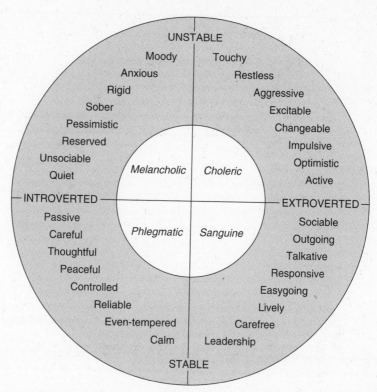

**Figure 13-4** ⊗ Eysenck's dimensions of personality and their relationship to Greek temperamental types.

pared with extroverts, are oriented toward internal stimuli—they are concerned with their own thoughts, reactions, and moods. As a result, they tend to be more shy, self-controlled, and preoccupied. They are introspective and reserved, and their behavior seems more inhibited. In contrast, extroverts are externally focused. They are more likely to be exuberant, sociable people who crave activity and like parties and excitement, to frequently seek new sensations and experiences, and to be disinhibited (Zuckerman and Como, 1983). To the question "Are you always ready for adventure?" the extravert would respond "yes" and the introvert "no". To the question "Are you put off by loud and rowdy parties?" the introvert would likely say "yes" and the extravert no.

The basis for these differences is thought to be differences in the brain functions related to cortical arousal of introverts and extroverts. For example, introverts and extroverts differ in their arousal level, as shown by electroencephalographic measures, with introverts showing greater levels of arousal. Thus, introverts may avoid stimulation from external sources because their arousal level is "naturally" high and increases substantially in response to stimulation.

---

### BOX 13-1
## The Lemon Juice Demonstration

A component of the theory of introversion-extroversion is that the same level of stimulation is more arousing for introverts than extroverts. If so, introverts should produce more saliva in their mouths in response to a saliva-producing stimulus than extroverts. Indeed, it has been reported that introverts produce more saliva than do extroverts (Corcoran, 1964). The following test has been used as a simple method of determining one's position on the introversion-extroversion dimension.

A length of thread is tied to the center of a double-tipped cotton swab. It should be tied so that when the swab is held by the thread, it hangs in a perfectly horizontal plane. Next, the person swallows three times and then immediately puts one end of the swab on the tongue, holding it there for thirty seconds. Then, four drops of lemon juice are placed on the tongue. After swallowing, the person places the other end of the swab on the same portion of the tongue. After the swab is held there for thirty seconds, it is removed and allowed to hang by the thread.

If all goes according to the hypothesis, the swab will remain virtually horizontal for extroverts. But for introverts the swab should hang down on the lemon juice end. This indicates that a relatively large amount of saliva has been produced in response to the lemon juice. The lemon juice was more arousing for introverts than for extroverts.

---

Extroverts constantly seek stimulation because their arousal level is "naturally" low and is less affected by stimulation (Geen, 1984). The famous lemon juice demonstration illustrates this arousal phenomenon (see Box 13-1).

## Murray: A System of Needs

 Henry Murray was perhaps the first psychologist to systematically study personality. Murray viewed traits as sources of motivation and an individual's personality as a function of the particular pattern of motivations that guide the individual's behavior.

### Traits as Needs and Motives

The dispositional view of traits implies that traits have a motivating effect on behavior. **Motivation** refers to the forces within us that activate our behavior and direct it toward one goal rather than another. The related concept, **motive**, is the goal or outcome that a given behavior seeks to attain. For example, a person's

Eysenck believes that introverts are more likely to be attracted to quiet, solitary pursuits. They tend to be preoccupied with their own thoughts and to be reserved.

motivation may be achievement, and the related motive toward which achievement motivation is directed may be to become a company vice-president, get a raise, or make good grades.

Innate Motives.  **Innate motives** are based in the physiology and neural structures of the body. All humans share them, and they relate directly to the survival of individuals and the species. We all need food and drink to live. And although an individual can survive without sex, the species cannot. For people in modern industrialized societies, the innate motives can be readily achieved. Food, water, and protection from the cold are all easily attained. Therefore, they do not become major motivators. But for the poor, the homeless, or many in deprived Third World countries, much energy is devoted to getting enough to eat and drink and to finding adequate shelter. As Maslow observed, however, once these motives can be satisfied, the learned or acquired motives become prominent in directing our lives.

Acquired Motives.  **Acquired motives** are learned both in the sense of the motive's value and in the behaviors necessary to satisfy it. Not everyone places the same value on a given motive, nor does everyone so motivated attempt to satisfy it in the same fashion. Acquired motives or needs can therefore be expected to differ from person to person. Thus, it is acquired motives that are particularly relevant to the study of personality.

## Basic Concepts

Needs. Murray based his theory of personality on the concept of **needs**. He construed needs as forces that organize and give direction to feelings, thoughts, and behavior so that an unsatisfying state of affairs can be remedied (1938). Needs help determine the ways in which a person responds to or seeks out environmental stimulation. Thus, needs, as motivations, are causal forces that can be used to explain human behavior.

There are the **primary** (viscerogenic) **needs,** which are physiological (e.g., needs for air, water, and food), and the **secondary** (psychogenic) **needs,** which arise out of primary needs but are not specifically connected with organic processes (e.g., achievement, affiliation, and nurturance). Most individual differences in human behavior are the result of secondary needs because the primary needs and the behaviors that meet them are generally the same for all individuals. Thus, primary needs are important for understanding the universal qualities of human nature, and secondary needs are important for understanding the aspects of personality that make each individual unique. Personality is a function of needs, and behavior results from the interaction of these needs with environmental forces that must be confronted and used to meet them. Although needs may be intense or weak, enduring or momentary, Murray viewed needs as relatively stable across time and consistent across situations. Thus, individuals with a need for affiliation will seek to satisfy that need across time and in different situations. Table 13-2 illustrates 20 of the more common secondary needs in Murray's system.

Sometimes, needs are inhibited or repressed because they are regarded as threatening or unacceptable. Needs may be broad and diffuse or specific and focused. The latter can be satisfied only by a narrow range of behaviors and outcomes. Needs often occur in combination; one need may become subordinate to another or may assist in the satisfaction of another need. Thus, satisfying a need for affiliation may also place the person in a position where a need for nurturance or a need for sex can be satisfied. However, needs may also conflict with each other, and this can result in distress. A need to dominate may conflict with a need for affiliation, with the result that behavior toward others is inconsistent and neither need may be met. These complex and potentially contradictory relations among needs can make it difficult to identify and organize the needs that characterize an individual.

Press. Needs are the internal determinants of behavior, and Murray also recognized the importance of external determinants. A **press** is a characteristic of the environment that either facilitates or interferes with the efforts of the individual to satisfy a need. Some examples of environmental presses are these:

lack of family support

absence of a parent

poverty

## Table 13-2
Examples from Murray's Taxonomy of Needs

| Need | Definition | Sample Test Item |
|------|-----------|------------------|
| Abasement | To submit, surrender, admit inferiority. | My friends think I am too humble. |
| Achievement | To accomplish tasks, surpass others. | I set difficult goals for myself which I attempt to reach. |
| Affiliation | To approach liked others, win their affection. | I become very attached to my friends. |
| Aggression | To fight opposition, attack, seek revenge. | I treat a domineering person as rudely as he treats me. |
| Autonomy | To seek freedom, independence, resist coercion. | I go my own way regardless of the opinions of others. |
| Counteraction | To overcome past failure, repress fear, master weakness. | To me a difficulty is just a spur to greater effort. |
| Defendance | To defend oneself against attack, criticism, blame. | I can usually find plenty of reasons to explain my failures. |
| Deference | To admire, praise, imitate, and support another person. | I often find myself imitating or agreeing with somebody I consider superior. |
| Dominance | To control others, to influence, persuade, command. | I usually influence others more than they influence me. |
| Exhibition | To impress, excite, amaze, fascinate, or shock others. | I am apt to show off in some way if I get a chance. |
| Harmavoidance | To avoid pain, injury, illness, danger, death. | I am afraid of physical pain. |
| Infavoidance | To avoid humiliation, embarrassment, failure. | I often shrink from a situation because of my sensitiveness to criticism and ridicule. |
| Nurturance | To give sympathy, support, and to console others. | I am easily moved by the misfortunes of other people. |
| Order | To put things in order, be neat, organized, clean. | I organize my daily activities so that there is little confusion. |
| Play | To seek fun, jokes, laughter. | I cultivate an easy-going, humorous attitude toward life. |
| Rejection | To avoid, exclude, snub disliked others. | I get annoyed when some fool takes up my time. |
| Sentience | To seek and enjoy sensuous experiences. | I search for sensations which shall at once be new and delightful. |
| Sex | To form erotic relationships, have sex. | I spend a great deal of time thinking about sexual matters. |
| Succorance | To have others give sympathy, support, and consolation. | I feel lonely and homesick when I am in a strange place. |
| Understanding | To seek answers, to enjoy analysis, theory, logic, reason. | I think that reason is the best guide in solving the problems of life. |

From *An Introduction to Personality*, 3rd edition, by Donn Byrne and Kathryn Kelley. Copyright 1981 by Prentice-Hall, Inc. Reprinted by permission.

inclement weather

fire

accident

religious training

physical inferiority

birth of a sibling

praise

prejudice

betrayal by a friend

Murray also noted that some environmental forces influence behavior only because a person perceives them to be significant. These he called **beta presses**. Other environmental characteristics affect the individual directly, regardless of how they are perceived. Murray referred to these as **alpha presses**.

Thema. The combination of a person's needs with particular environmental presses may result in a constellation of behaviors that Murray labeled a **thema**. For example, an experience of rejection might engage a person's need for abasement, which in turn leads to passive behavior or the wish to blame oneself. The concept of thema provides a way of organizing and understanding behavior that reflects the influence of both characteristics of the person and the situation.

Unconscious. Murray also viewed **unconscious processes** as important for understanding personality and behavior. His ideas reflect a neo-Freudian influence, and he even recommended that serious personologists undergo psychoanalysis so that they will better understand their own psyches. There are other aspects of Murray's system that involve the id, ego, and superego. Likewise, he discusses many aspects of development. However, his most extensive and influential contributions to contemporary personality theory and research are his concepts and taxonomies of needs, presses, and themas.

## Achievement Motivation

The most intensively studied of Murray's psychogenic needs (see Table 13-2) has been achievement (often referred to as *n* Achievement or *n*Ach for **need achievement**. The focus on achievement reflects the high value placed on achieving in Western society. In school and at home, children learn quickly that they will be rewarded for achieving and punished for failing. The competitive climate that the emphasis on achievement has fostered in Western society has been viewed as both a strength and a weakness, but the pervasiveness of an emphasis on achievement can not be denied.

The central figure in the study of *n*Ach is David McClelland. He and his colleagues (McClelland, Atkinson, Clark, and Lowell, 1953) published *The Achievement Motive* and thereby launched a tide of research that has made *n*

Achievement one of the most heavily studied variables in the history of personality. McClelland chose to study achievement largely because it was possible to arouse the need in laboratory situations and because a method, the TAT, existed to measure it.

The Nature of *n* Achievement. Not all of the research on *n* Achievement has produced consistent results, but some general features of this need have been identified (McClelland, 1985). The need is a stable disposition that is consistently manifested in many areas of an individual's life. People high in *n* Achievement tend to differ in several ways from those low in *n* Achievement. For example, they are more likely to be competitive, and they are also more likely to take responsibility for their own successes. What is more, they expect that if they exert the proper effort, they will succeed. They set challenging goals that are nevertheless realistic. As a result, they perform better in most situations than individuals low in *n* Achievement. They prefer tasks of intermediate difficulty wherein neither success nor failure is guaranteed. Low *n* Achievement individuals, in contrast, generally prefer easy tasks (wherein success is virtually inevitable) or else difficult tasks (wherein failure is sure and therefore no one can blame them for failing). High *n* Achievement people select tasks in which performance provides information about their ability. Tasks that are too difficult or too easy are similar in that they do not offer the opportunity to learn about one's abilities.

Other characteristics of those high in *n* Achievement include a tendency to go into sales or into a business that involves some risk but also that is within the range of their abilities. They avoid routine jobs. They take pride in their accomplishments and are able to delay gratification of smaller, immediate rewards in favor of later, larger rewards. They have a positive self-concept and in school they are likely to earn good grades when those grades are important for success in their subsequent careers.

Development of *n* Achievement. Three important factors appear to be related to the development of *n* Achievement. First, there is the degree of emphasis that a child's parents, subcultures, and cultures place on high achievement (McClelland, 1961). Second, children taught to be self-reliant and confident and urged to establish their own goals seem more likely to become high achievers (Rosen and D'Andrade, 1959). However, because the research here is not always consistent, McClelland (1961) has suggested an "optimal level" hypothesis: independence training instituted too early may actually inhibit the development of the achievement motive. Third, the father's or mother's occupation may play a role. More specifically, a father whose job involves decision making and initiative may lead the child toward the development of achievement motivation (Turner, 1970).

Achievement and Society. McClelland (1961) has extended his ideas about the influence of parents, culture, and social class on individual's *n* Achievement to economic growth at the societal level. He argues that as a society's children become more achievement oriented, the general level of productivity will rise in the decades to follow as those children become adults. For example, he argues that the *n* Achievement themes in children's readers in the second, third, and fourth grades from 1925 and 1950 for 23 countries were correlated with an index of economic growth rate and industrialization between 1929 and 1950 (see Figure 13-5).

**A Model for Achievement Behavior.** Atkinson (1957, 1964) has developed a theory or model of achievement behavior based on the conflict between approach and avoidance tendencies. When one succeeds, there is pride and a sense of satisfaction. When one fails, there is a feeling of shame and unhappiness. The relative strengths of these expected emotions determine when the person will approach or avoid a given set of achievement-oriented activities or tasks. When a person's need for achievement is strong, when that person expects that a given behavior will achieve the goal, and when there is "excitement" generated by the achievement-oriented behavior, the chances are good that achievement-oriented behavior will occur. In contrast, when those three variables are relatively low in strength, the person will likely avoid behavior that might result in achievement.

## Need for Power

The **need for power** (*n* Power) bears some similarities to *n* Achievement and has been investigated in much the same way. It is the desire to exert control over the events that affect our lives (McClelland, 1975). If anything characterizes the history of human beings, it is their incessant struggle for power. This motive has triggered wars, fueled political turmoil, and stimulated innumerable interpersonal conflicts.

Winter and Stewart (1978) have identified several features that characterize those who are high in *n* Power. For example, there is a tendency to select careers that allow one to control others through the application of rewards and punishments. Such careers might include public office, teaching, business, journalism, and religion.

Many who seek power are individuals who want to achieve recognition. They have the tendency to build loyal groups of supporters who will help them attain their desired goals. David Koresh, the leader of the religious cult called the Branch Davidians, who led his followers to perish in a fire rather than surrender to authorities in Texas, is an example of someone who is high in *n* Power.

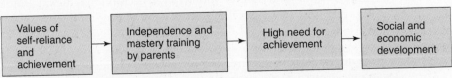

**Figure 13-5** &#x63a;&#x63a; Achievement motivation and economic growth. (After McClelland 1961.)

## Need for Affiliation

Another widely studied need has been affiliation. **Need for affiliation** (*n* Affiliation) is high in those who are motivated to seek out others, to value being with people, and to care about others. They have learned that others can offer aid and comfort or that others can provide information helpful in achieving goals. People high in *n* Affiliation are more likely than others to conform to the wishes of others. They need to be liked and accepted and to seek out the friendship of others. They tend to be more active socially. It often seems, too, that caring for others as well as being cared for by others can reduce the stress that results from a competitive and achievement-oriented lifestyle (McClelland, 1982).

# The Trait–Situation Controversy

The traditional view, taken in the theories of Allport, Cattell, Eysenck, Murray, and McClelland, of traits as dispositions, needs, and motives with a causal influence on behavior led, eventually, to formidable problems for personality psychology. The simplest way to appreciate the difficulty is to recognize the inherent circularity that results from using traits to both describe and explain behavior. The statement "Mary is friendly because she is friendly" is both trivial and unacceptable as a scientific prediction. Although the statement "Mary behaves in a friendly manner because she has the trait of friendliness, or because she has a need to be friendly" may sound less circular, it suffers from the same problem, particularly because the description of the behavior and the inference of the disposition generally rely on the same observations and data.

## Dispositional Traits and Situational Specificity

A key characteristic of dispositional traits is that they exhibit stability over time and consistency across situations. The intelligent woman acts intelligently not just today, but did so yesterday and will tomorrow. The hostile man is one who exhibits that hostility in response to many different stimuli in a variety of situations. At least, people's dispositions should systematically combine with features of situations so that one's predispositions combined with situational cues produce behaviors that are predictable. Thus, we do not expect a friendly person who acts warmly toward a person he or she meets at a party to exhibit the same warmth toward someone who has just bent his or her fender in a parking lot. But we might expect the person to be less hostile in the parking lot than a less friendly person might be.

As early as the 1920s (e.g., Hartshorne and May, 1928; Newcomb, 1929) some disconcerting evidence began to accumulate that people's behavior is relatively unstable and inconsistent. This evidence was viewed as disconfirming a fundamental component of dispositional trait theories. If traits are dispositions, then how can people's behavior be so variable across time and situations that it is unpredictable from trait measures or previous behavioral observations? Some (e.g., Mischel, 1968) have argued that a person's behavior is controlled not by stable traits but by the special characteristics of each situation in which he or she functions. Box 13-2 provides an illustration of the some of the issues in the person-situation debate.

The evidence on which this conclusion was based was the finding that the correlations, labeled **cross-situational coefficients**, between behavior in two different situations are typically low, although not zero. Also, the typical correlation between a trait measure of personality and its associated behaviors seldom exceeds .30 and is often substantially lower. Mischel labeled correlations of this magnitude **personality coefficients.** These correlations are now generally accepted as fact by personality psychologists, although the implications of these

---

BOX 13-2
## Who is Responsible: The Person or the Situation?

About two days before Christmas several years ago, a 14-year-old boy entered a large downtown department store in Chicago. At first he wandered around aimlessly. But he had a furtive look about him that attracted the attention of a store detective. The boy finally stopped at a perfume counter and began examining the various bottles. At the same time he surreptitiously glanced around to see whether anyone was watching him. Finally, with a casual yet swift movement, he dropped a very expensive bottle into his jacket pocket. As soon as he stepped outside the store, the store detective caught up with him and arrested him for shoplifting.

This is a common scenario today—one that is acted out over and over throughout the nation. But how do we explain this boy's act? Was he basically just a thief? Did an urge to give his mother a Christmas gift account for the behavior? Was this the inevitable response of someone with criminal tendencies? Or was the boy perhaps unstable, a victim of his own internal psychopathology? These are some of the possible *personality* explanations.

But then again, maybe he was simply caught up in the Christmas spirit reflected in thousands of stimuli around him. Perhaps such behavior is routine for his peer group. Or possibly he would never have stolen the perfume had it not been displayed so temptingly or openly. All of these explanations suggest that the boy's behavior was determined by the overall *situation* in which he found himself. Change the situation (e.g., make the merchandise less accessible), and you change the behavior.

Also possible is an interpretation that would explain his behavior as a complex *interaction* between *personality* (love for his mother, criminal tendencies) and the *situation* (Christmas season, accessible merchandise).

facts for the study of personality remain a matter of discussion (Epstein, 1979a; Mischel, 1984).

**The Moderator Hypothesis.** In one of the most widely cited reports in the personality literature, Bem and Allen (1974) proposed that there are individual differences in the stability and consistency of traits. For any given trait, such as friendliness, some people exhibit consistency, whereas others, perhaps the majority, would not. Thus, personality psychologists had erred by assuming that all traits applied to all people, and the situationists had erred by assuming that no traits applied to any people. The solution was to identify those individuals who had a particular trait and to expect consistency on that trait for only those individuals. The Bem and Allen report (1974) resulted in an enormous amount of research to identify **moderator variables** that would separate consistent from inconsistent people (e.g., Baumeister and Tice, 1988; Cheek, 1982; Kenrick and Stringfield, 1980, Lanning, 1988; Zuckerman, Bernieri, Koestner, & Rosenthal, 1989). Subsequently it has been recognized that the conceptual, statistical, and measurement issues involved in moderator research are far more complex than originally thought (Chaplin, 1991; in press), and the promising results reported by Bem and Allen and others have proved difficult to replicate (Chaplin and Goldberg, 1984). Although, ultimately, the moderator hypothesis that there are individual differences in trait consistency and stability did not serve to resolve the trait-situation debate, it led to a tremendous amount of useful research that has provided personality psychologists with many new insights.

**Interactionism.** A second proposal for reconciling the two sides in this debate was **interactionism** (Bowers, 1973). The interactionist position is an old one that has appeared in several forms (Brunswik, 1943; Kantor, 1924; Lewin, 1935; Murray, 1938; Rotter, 1954). The basic idea behind interactionism is the common-sense one that personality traits combine with situational factors to produce behavior. Behavior requires a person to exhibit it and a situation for it to be exhibited in.

From this perspective, the question of which is more important, the person or the situation, is a silly one because the answer is always that both are necessary to produce behavior. However, as Rotter (1981) points out, when presumed person-situation interactions were used in specific contexts to predict behavior, the results were often disappointing. To a large extent, this was due to difficulty in deciding how to assess the situation. Situations can be cataloged in many ways: They can be described by their physical characteristics (e.g., size of the room, temperature of the environment, number of people present), the behaviors they typically elicit (e.g., aggression, dependency, sexuality), or the needs they satisfy (e.g., love and affection, achievement). They can likewise be organized according to the way they are perceived by the person. All of these approaches have been employed, and the usefulness of any of these measures is dependent upon the goals of the research.

The prediction of complex human behavior in the social context must rely on more than mere physical descriptions of situations. One must know what the situation means to the individual. For example, what kinds of situations does the person see as threatening? The answer will lie less in the physical properties of situations than in the cues they offer. As Rotter (1981) describes it, these cues (subtle as well as obvious) will trigger in the individual expectancies that certain behaviors will be rewarded or that achievement of these rewards will lead, in turn, to still other rewards. Situations that contain similar cues (even though the situations are physically different) will be construed as similar or functionally equivalent. For example, if classroom settings, one-to-one conversations with women, and confrontations with college presidents all contain cues that I am going to appear foolish, I may well act the same (e.g., withdrawing to avoid negative outcomes) in all of them. All these situations, then, are similar because they contain cues that lead to expectancies for a particular outcome.

Also, to predict behavior in a given situation, one needs to know about the individual's general personality characteristics (e.g., fear of failure) and also about the subjective meaning of that situation for that person. Prediction will be superior when information from both situation and person is available. Unfortunately, determining the subjective meaning of situations for an individual is rarely easy. Nor is it easy to identify the situational cues that lead an individual to attach a particular meaning to a particular situation.

In general, a person's response to a vague, indeterminate stimulus will tell us more about that person than that person's response to an intense, unambiguous situation. For example, if a snarling lion is suddenly let into your personality class, nearly everybody is going to run. Likewise, a red traffic light will cause nearly everyone to stop, and a ringing telephone will prompt most people to answer it. On the other hand, when situational stimuli are weak or ambiguous, behavior is more likely to be predicted accurately from personality information. Indeed, the whole field of projective testing is predicted on the idea that ambiguous stimuli (e.g., inkblots) will produce interpretations influenced by personality characteristics.

### Reconceptualizing Person Variables.

In 1973 Mischel sought to reintroduce the study of the person to personality psychology. Specifically, he reconceptualized person variables as cognitive and phenomenological rather than as dispositional. His argument was that characteristics of people are important for understanding and predicting behavior, but that the focus on traits as the most important person variables was not useful. More recently Mischel and Shoda (1995) have proposed **cognitive-affective system theory,** which provides a reconciliation between the general analysis of personality at the level of traits with the more specific analysis of personality at the level of behavior and cognition. The benefit of Mischel's reconceptualization and reconciliation is that it has justified and motivated the study and description of personality at different levels.

### Reliability, Construct Validity, and Aggregation.

Probably the most widely accepted strategy for reconciling the study of traits with the observation of behavioral inconsistency relies on the application of the basic measurement concepts of reliability and validity. Specifically, the importance of situational influence on behavior is acknowledged, but the single behavior of the individual in any one situation is not accepted as a particularly valid or reliable indication of that person's personality. Here the **principle of aggregation** is useful. To obtain valid and reliable behavioral measures of a trait, the person is observed in multiple situations and his or her behavior is aggregated (averaged) over those situations. It is the average behavior that is accepted as a valid and reliable indication of the individual's personality. In 1979a, Epstein provided a powerful demonstration of the power of aggregation for reconciling behavioral inconsistency with stable traits. In his research Epstein correlated behavioral measures of various traits between Day 1 and Day 2 of his observations. The average correlation between these single behavioral observations was an unimpressive .06. However, when the behavioral measures taken on the odd days of the month were averaged, the behavioral measures taken across the even days were averaged, and these odd-even averages were correlated, the average correlations was a substantial .74! In a historical review of the person-situation debate, Epstein and O'Brien (1985) examined a variety of studies. In every instance they found that the aggregation approach provides strong evidence for the stability of behavior over time and the consistency of behavior across situations.

**Reliability** concerns chance errors of responding that undermine the fidelity with which an observed score represents the person's true score. On a personality scale to measure friendliness, a person might accidentally circle *false* to the item "I like to meet people" when that person meant *true*. If this were the only item used to measure friendliness, that person's score would be in error. However, if the scale contains 20 items concerning friendliness, the accidental response to 1 item will introduce a much smaller amount of error to the person's total score based on all 20 items. This problem is identical for behavioral observations. A friendly person passes an acquaintance in the hallway and fails to smile. This behavior is inconsistent with the person's friendliness. However, many accidental factors might affect whether the person smiles or not (e.g., the person just received a bad grade on a test, the person had something in his or her eye). The failure of the person to smile is an error, not a true indication of what the person typically does. If we observe the person on several occasions, the accidental factors will have less impact, and we will obtain a truer indication of their typical behavior.

Aggregation also increases a measure's construct validity. One of the most persuasive arguments in the person-situation debate was that the low correlations between single behavioral measures and trait measures indicated the invalidity of *behavioral* measures rather than the trait measures (Block, 1977; Golding, 1976). Multi-item scales are used not only to increase reliability but to increase validity. Consider a measure of mathematical ability that consists of the single question "What is the natural logarithm of .56?" A person could have substantial mathematical ability but not know how to find natural logarithms. In this case, the inability to answer the question is not an accident but a true reflection of lack of knowledge. However, mathematical ability is more than finding logarithms; it includes algebra, calculus, geometry, and basic arithmetic. If the only area of mathematics that the person does not know is logarithms, the single question is an invalid indication of the person's mathematical ability, although it may be a reliable measure of the person's knowledge of logarithms. A trait is generally indicated not by one specific type of behavior but by a variety of related behaviors.

## Conclusion

This brief summary of the person–situation debate does not do justice to the enormous amount of thought and research that was devoted to this issue. Nor does it convey the extraordinary bitterness that characterized much of this debate. Many explanations were offered by psychologists about why people (and misguided personality psychologists!) continued to "believe" in traits in the face of the overwhelming evidence of low cross-situational and personality coefficients. After extensive and careful research, we now know that *none* of the following statements are supported (Kenrick and Funder, 1988), although all of them were at one time (and in a few circles still are) generally accepted as true by non–personality psychologists.

- Personality traits are merely in the eye of the beholder; they are mainly the byproduct of faulty information processing.
- When people agree about a given person's traits, agreement is due to shared delusions based on common linguistic usage.
- Agreement among observers of trait behavior is an artifact of the base rates for the trait in the general population.
- Interrater agreements are often due to stereotypes based on obvious but erroneous cues (e.g., fat people are jolly).
- Agreement on traits and behaviors is due to discussions among observers.
- The reason behavior seems consistent over situations is that we see others in the same setting repeatedly (e.g., my student seems consistent in her behavior only because I never see her anywhere but in school).
- Relations between traits and behavior are too small to be of any importance.

## Traits as Descriptions, Not Causes, of Behavior

The application of psychometric principles led to the realization that low cross-situational and personality coefficients are not surprising, nor are they reasons to reject traits as scientific concepts. However, the use of psychometrics to rescue traits does have crucial implications for how traits are used and conceptualized. By accepting that traits are related to *aggregates* of behaviors, but seldom to *specific* ones, the dispositional status of traits as causes of behavior was no longer viable. Instead, traits became descriptive and, on the average, predictive of behavior. This new **descriptive-predictive** view is different from the **dispositional-explanatory** view of traits that was explicit in the traditional trait theories of Allport, Cattell, Murray, and to some extent Eysenck.

## The Act-Frequency Theory of Traits

In 1983 Buss and Craik offered the first explicit and comprehensive theory of traits as descriptions of, rather than as explanations for, behavior. In their **act-frequency theory** of traits, Buss and Craik contend that traits are labels intended to summarize the cumulative acts we observe a person perform. For example, the label *deference* might include the following behaviors: apologizing profusely, letting others talk first, asking your friend where she wants to eat, and waiting patiently for an acquaintance. The act-frequency approach begins with a catalogue of the acts or behaviors that are characteristic of a broad trait category and then assesses the relative frequency with which different individuals engage in those acts over a fixed period of time. An individual who engages in more of those acts than another individual would be described as having more of the associated trait. Thus, if person A exhibited 14 dominant acts over a one-week period and Person B exhibited only 4 such acts, the act-frequency approach would assess Person A as more dominant than Person B. The application of the term "dominant" to person A is a **summary description** of what we saw Person A do, not an explanation for what we saw.

Of course, the reason Person A engaged in so many dominant acts might be that the person has a disposition to be dominant. Indeed, the observation of so many dominant acts reflects a behavioral trend that almost implies such a disposition. The important point is that the act-frequency approach is neutral with respect to dispositional inferences. It does not deny dispositional tendencies, but neither does it require them. This descriptive use of traits to summarize observations is consistent with the principle of aggregation that rescued trait concepts from behavioral inconsistency. The descriptive use of traits does not imply that one can predict specific acts, although it does imply that one can predict **act trends**. All of these aspects of the act-frequency approach are consistent with the empirical evidence, whereas the dispositional view of traits is not. It also avoids the deadly circularity of explaining and describing personality with the same observations and data.

One other important feature of act-frequency theory is that it recognizes a hierarchical structure in personality description. At the most abstract or **superordinate level** is the general class of behavior such as "interpersonal style." At the more concrete or **subordinate level** are the specific acts that concern interpersonal style such as "taking charge at a meeting." In between these levels are the trait categories (in the above example, "dominance") that reflect a more specific aspect of interpersonal style, but a more abstract summary of specific behaviors. Buss and Craik (1983), following the seminal work of Rosch (1978) on categorization, refer to this level as the **basic level** of personality description. The basic

A
BRIEF
BIOGRAPHY
OF

# Lewis R. Goldberg

Lewis R. Goldberg was born on January 28, 1932 in Chicago, Illinois. He followed in his father's footsteps by attending Harvard College, where he majored in social relations. The first course he took in the department of social relations was personality taught by Gordon Allport. He took no courses in the famous department of psychology at Harvard, which was dominated by learning theorists such as Skinner. Indeed, he never heard of Skinner until after he left Harvard.

Goldberg completed an honors thesis at Harvard in which he studied people's reactions to the exciting new technology of tape recording. After graduating from Harvard he attended graduate school in clinical psychology at Michigan, primarily because he "could not think of anything better to do."

Goldberg's interest in personality assessment was sparked by a course on assessment methods taught by E. Lowell Kelly at Michigan. Kelly later became Goldberg's mentor and dissertation supervisor. During his fifth year at Michigan, one of his dissertation committee members left and was replaced by a new Ph.D. on the faculty, Warren Norman. It was Norman's early work on personality and language, and factor analysis, that introduced Goldberg to the problem of the language of personality description.

level of categorization appears to be the most efficient and useful level for describing and communicating information. There is also some evidence that it is the level people most often use when describing personality (Hampson, John, and Goldberg, 1986). The strong preference of both personality psychologists and lay persons to use trait terms for describing personality can be understood from the utility of the middle or basic level in category hierarchies.

## The Big Five Model of Personality Description

One of the most difficult problems faced by the field of personality has been the historical lack of consensus among investigators about how to describe personality. The lack of consensus is in part a result of the sheer number of words that are available to describe personality. In 1936, Allport and Odbert compiled a comprehensive list of all the words in the English language that can be used to describe people. There were over 18,000 words on that list. In 1967, Warren Norman updated the Allport and Odbert list. Norman eliminated from his list all but the most common trait descriptive adjectives, but this still left roughly 2,800 terms. A second factor that has contributed to the lack of consensus is the large number of different structural models of personality, each with their accompanying assessment inventory, that have been proposed. Among the more notable of these systems and inventories are Cattell's 16-Personality Factors; Eysenck's

Goldberg's first job was as an acting assistant professor at Stanford University where his closest colleagues were Jerry Wiggins and Albert Bandura. He left Stanford in 1960 to join the faculty at the University of Oregon and to join the newly founded Oregon Research Institute in Eugene, Oregon. He has been a Fulbright professor at the University of Nijmegan in The Netherlands and Istanbul University in Turkey, a fellow-in-residence at the Netherlands Institute for Advanced Study, and a visiting professor at the University of California at Berkeley. Otherwise, he has remained in Oregon.

Goldberg has served as a consultant to the U.S. Peace Corps as a Selection Officer and the Intelligence Division of the U.S. Secret Service. His contributions to the scientific literature include over 100 articles on topics such as clinical judgement and decision-making, the comparative validity of different strategies of test construction, the properties of personality questionnaire items, the impact of college instructional procedures and grading practices on student performance, and most recently, the development of taxonomies of personality descriptive terms.

three-factor P-E-N model; Murray's system of needs, which is the basis for Jackson's *Personality Research Form;* the interpersonal circumplex model (Wiggins and Pincus, 1992); and the empirically derived *California Psychological Inventory.* There are many other systems and related inventories.

Over the past decade, however, there has been an emerging consensus about a general framework, the **Big Five,** for organizing personality description (Goldberg, 1993). Although numerous individual's have contributed to the development of this framework, Lewis R. Goldberg has played a key role in promoting this model.

The Big Five is based on what has been called the **lexical hypothesis** (Saucier and Goldberg, 1996). This hypothesis is that "the most important individual differences in human transactions will come to be encoded as single terms in some or all of the world's languages" (Goldberg, 1993, p. 26). Thus, by analysis of the descriptions people make of their own and other's personalities on a representative sample of terms, the common dimensions and structure of personality can be empirically discovered. As early as 1938, Thurstone had factor analyzed the descriptions of 1,300 raters on 60 common personality adjectives and had found five independent common factors. Subsequently, Cattell employed the lexical hypothesis in his explorations of personality. Although Cattell's work suggested upwards of 12 factors, only 5 of those factors have proved to be consistently replicable (John, 1990).

The Big Five Factors have traditionally been numbered and labeled, although the labels have varied over the years, and from investigator to investigator. Table 13-3 lists the **Five Factors** with their numbers and common labels. The Big Five is explicitly recognized as part of a hierarchical structure of personality description in which the Five Factors are at the most abstract level of behavioral description, with hundreds of more specific descriptive terms located at lower levels in the hierarchy (John, Hampson, and Goldberg, 1991). Thus, the Big Five is intended not to reduce personality to five factors but rather to provide a broad framework for organizing the substantial number of individual differences that characterize people. This conception of the Big Five is well represented by Eysenck's model, which was shown in Figure 13-3. Table 13-3 also shows examples of more specific traits located within each of the Big Five Factors.

The Big Five has proved to be a remarkably robust structure for organizing personality. Roughly the same five factors have been discovered repeatedly over the decades by a variety of investigators with a variety of stimuli. The Big Five has been able to incorporate several other structural models of personality, including the interpersonal circumplex (Hofstee, de Raad, and Goldberg, 1992) and Eysenck's P-E-N model (Goldberg and Rosolack, 1994). The Big Five applies to both self-descriptions and other descriptions of personality (Goldberg, 1990), and it appears across a variety of specific measurement strategies and factor analytic techniques (Peabody and Goldberg, 1989). The Big Five is approach-

---

## ⟨⟩ Table 13-3
### The Big Five Model of Personality Description

Factor I (Extraversion or Surgency)
    talkativeness, assertiveness, and activity level *versus*
    silence, passivity, and reserve.
Factor II (Agreeableness or Pleasantness)
    kindness, trust, and warmth *versus*
    hostility, selfishness, and distrust.
Factor III (Conscientiousness or Dependability)
    organization, thoroughness, and dependability *versus*
    carelessness, negligence, and unreliability.
Factor IV (Emotional Stability *vs.* Neuroticism)
    nervousness, moodiness, and tempermentality *versus*
    relaxation, poise, and steadiness.
Factor V (Culture, Intellect or Openness to Experience)
    imagination, curiosity, and creativity *versus*
    shallowness, imperceptiveness, and stupidity.

Based on Goldberg, 1993.

ing the status of a paradigm for personality description that provides a common framework for selecting stimuli in experimental studies and organizing the results from naturalistic ones.

However, as Goldberg (1993) has noted, "An emerging consensus is not the same as universal agreement" (p. 31). Not surprisingly, neither Eysenck nor Cattell has accepted the five-factor model, with Cattell arguing that five factors are too few and Eysenck arguing that five is too many (Eysenck, 1992). In addition, Block (1995), McAdams (1992), and Westen (1995) have offered strong critiques emphasizing the limitations of the five-factor model. Zuckerman (1992) has offered an alternative five-factor model, and Hogan (1986) has suggested a six-factor variant of the Big Five. Finally, Waller and his colleagues (Almagor, Tellegen, and Waller, 1995; Benet and Waller, 1995) have proposed a seven-factor structure based on the argument that the Big Five is based on an overly restrictive selection of person-descriptive terms (Tellegen, 1993).

## Summary

- Trait psychology involves the development of comprehensive systems for classifying and describing the characteristic and enduring ways people differ from one another. Trait theories differ from the other theories reviewed in this text because they emphasize the comprehensive description of behavior.
- The description of personality is an important everyday human activity and is crucial for the scientific study of personality.
- Although personality can be described at a number of levels and with many different types of constructs, traits have a provided a common language for personality description that is general, quantitative, and easily communicated.
- Traits most often refer to the personality dimensions along which people differ, whereas types tend to represent discrete categories. However, not all theorists accept this distinction. In addition, types are usually thought to be few in number, whereas traits are potentially very numerous.
- For Gordon Allport, traits lead the person to respond to differing situations in a generally similar fashion, producing the consistency so characteristic of individuals. Traits are broad concepts, whereas habits are more narrow, situationally specific tendencies.
- According to Allport, there are cardinal traits, central traits, and secondary traits. These types of traits differ in the pervasiveness of their influence in guiding behavior.
- Allport also emphasized personal traits, which are unique to the individual, and common traits, which are relevant to everyone. Intentions also play an important role in shaping our lives by orienting us to the future rather than to the past.

- Allport claimed that some behavior loses its connections to the past and becomes self-motivating. This is called functional autonomy. He also described the proprium, a concept that refers to the self and integrates the various elements of the personality.
- Allport did not accord infantile or childhood experiences nearly so important a role as did Freud. Although his description of human development was a bit vague, he thought of development largely in terms of the self. Similarly, his concepts of psychological health involved the growth of self-esteem and competence. His views on behavior change were likewise not explicit.
- Raymond Cattell has his theoretical rationale strongly anchored in statistical-mathematical procedures.
- Cattell distinguishes between surface traits and source traits. Surface traits refer to behaviors that all relate to a common theme. Source traits are the basic elements that explain behavior. Source traits that develop out of experience or learning are called environmental-mold traits, whereas constitutional source traits reflect hereditary influences.
- Cattell also describes temperament traits, which involve emotionality and are constitutional, as well as ability traits, which can be the result of either hereditary influences (fluid ability) or experience (crystallized ability).
- Motivational traits are referred to by Cattell as dynamic source traits and are subdivided into ergs (constitutional) and sentiments (environmental-mold). Attitudes are the overt expressions of interest from which we infer ergs and sentiments. The interplay of all these concepts can be depicted by the dynamic lattice.
- Cattell believes that some traits are unique to the individual whereas others are common to all of us.
- The specification equation is the means by which Cattell combines a variety of trait information to predict behavior in a specific situation.
- Cattell views personality development as a function of both hereditary and environmental factors. For this reason, he regards classical conditioning and instrumental conditioning as important. He also discusses integration learning as it relates to ergs, as well as syntality, which refers to the influence exerted by groups and social institutions.
- For Cattell, adjustment is related to conflict, and although he recognizes the human potential for change and the importance of states, his emphasis is on the stability of personality.
- Hans Eysenck was another theorist discussed in this chapter. Using statistical methods, he focuses on types but regards them as dimensions rather than discrete categories. Eysenck's three principal personality dimensions are introversion-extroversion, stability-instability (neuroticism), and psychoticism.
- Other dispositional approaches emphasize needs and motives (both innate and acquired). An early example of such an approach is Murray's system. He developed a lengthy list of needs and suggested that behavior is an outcome of needs that combine with an environmental press.

- Other examples of needs that have been intensively investigated are achievement, affiliation, and power.
- The dispositional view of traits has been a source of major problems for personality psychology. The dispositional view results in an unsatisfying circularity between the description and explanation of behavior. Also, evidence summarized by Mischel in 1968 that there is little stability and consistency among individual behaviors is inconsistent with a strong causal model of traits.
- Several hypotheses were proposed to resolve the trait-situation controversy, including the moderator variables and interactionism. The most compelling resolution came from the application of psychometric principles to the measurement of individual behaviors. When behaviors are aggregated to increase the reliability and validity of their measurement as indicants of traits, the utility of traits becomes apparent.
- However, this resolution of traits changed their status from dispositional/explanatory constructs to descriptive/predictive ones.
- The act-frequency theory of traits was the first systematic and comprehensive treatment of traits as descriptive constructs. This approach used contemporary views of categorical structure in treating traits as summaries of acts.
- The Big Five is a comprehensive descriptive model of traits that organizes the vast number of terms that can describe people using five broad factors. The Big Five has proven to be a robust and replicable model that is emerging as a common basis for personality description.

# Chapter 14
## Traits: Assessment, Research, and Summary Evaluation

Allport: The Search for Individuality
    Letters from Jenny
    Expressive Behaviors
    Assessment of Values
Cattell's Psychometric Approach to Trait
  Research
    Bivariate-Multivariate-Clinical Axis
    Factor Analysis
    Hypothetical Example of Factor Analysis
    Sources of Data
    Empirical Identification of Traits
    Analysis of Heredity and Environment
    Measurement of Similarity and Change
Eysenck's Search for Types
    Criterion Analysis
    The Biological Basis of Eysenck's Factors
Murray's Research Legacy
    Intensive Study of Individuals
    The Diagnostic Council
    The TAT
    Enhancing Achievement Striving
Descriptive Models: Research and Critique
    Act-Frequency Research
    The Category View of Personality
      Description

Critique of the Act-Frequency Approach
Research Based on the Big Five
Summary Evaluation
    Allport's Strengths
    Allport's Weaknesses
    Cattell's and Eysenck's Strengths
    Cattell's and Eysenck's Weaknesses
    Murray's Strengths
    Murray's Weaknesses
    Descriptive Theories: Strengths
    Descriptive Theories: Weaknesses
Summary

Research based on the concept of traits has attempted to identify the most important characteristics for describing individuals and to establish how those traits might be most usefully organized. Trait-based research has relied heavily on personality assessment and has, in turn, been the basis for the development of numerous personality inventories and scales. Trait-based research is generally based on naturalistic observations and data from several sources. The primary statistic of trait research is the correlation coefficient, which is the basis for the technique of factor analysis.

## Allport: The Search for Individuality

 The focus of Allport's work is individuality. He emphasized idiographic methods and the intensive study of the individual to bring about an understanding of personality. Allport's approach to assessment emphasized self-report inventories, the best known of which was based on his study of values.

### Letters from Jenny

Allport advocated the use of personal documents such as diaries, letters, autobiographies, and interviews to aid the understanding of an individual personality. This is exemplified by his study of a collection of 301 letters written by Jenny Masterson (not her real name) over a period of 11 years. The result of this study was his famous *Letters from Jenny,* published in 1965. This research also illustrates Allport's belief that an understanding of personality is better obtained from the intensive (idiographic) study of an individual rather than a more superficial (nomothetic) study of large groups of people.

Jenny was widowed shortly before the birth of her son, Ross, in 1897. Jenny and Ross were very close until Ross left home to attend Princeton University. He later enlisted in the Army and served in France during World War I. He was a changed person when he returned, and he and his mother quarreled frequently. He was also beset by a series of personal failures. Jenny's letters were written to two of Ross's friends. The following are excerpts from those letters (Allport, 1965):

> Well, that's the way—there is nothing in this life worth living for except money, and one must find that while they are young. If one is so ridiculous as to slip into old age without money one must put up with being crowded into insanity, or "take arms against a sea of troubles, and by opposing, end them." (p. 133)
>
> You have all my best love. I am going out to the Sea now to blow the horror of Ross's women out of my brain and to try to believe that there is indeed a God somewhere. (p. 54)

Have you read "The Magnificent Ambersons" by Tarkington? If not get it, it's about an only son, and how his *mother* ruined him. (p. 99)

Allport asked 36 judges to read Jenny's letters. On the basis of their everyday experience describing people, the judges listed 198 trait terms to describe Jenny. Several of these trait terms overlapped in meaning, so Allport was able to reduce the list to eight traits that he believed were most descriptive of Jenny's personality. These traits are shown in Table 14-1. Subsequently, Baldwin (1942) analyzed Allport's data statistically and replicated the reduction of the descriptions of Jenny's personality to those eight central traits. Then, in 1966, Paige published a computer analysis of the letters. Using the statistical technique of factor analysis, he identified several trait factors that also replicated those in Allport's list. Indeed, the similarity of the results of these statistical analyses to Allport's intuitive one was so great as to lead Allport to conclude that although the statistical analysis was nice, it added little to his own work.

Although Allport was firmly committed to idiographic studies, he recognized their potentially limited generalizability. However, this limited generalizability was partially offset by the rich and revealing information they could provide. Knowledge of the unique experiences of a subject, and of the particular context in which the person's behavior and expressions occurred, formed a stronger basis for making inferences about individual personality and its structure. Allport's use of personal documents and other archival information in his study is also an unusual, and underused (Wrightsman, 1981), research strategy.

## ✂ Table 14-1
## Jenny's Central Traits as Revealed by Two Methods

| Commonsense Traits (Allport) | Factorial Traits (Paige) |
| --- | --- |
| 1 quarrelsome-suspicious; aggressive | 1 aggression |
| 2 self-centered (possessive) | 2 possessiveness |
| 3 sentimental | 3 need for affiliation; need for family acceptance |
| 4 independent-autonomous | 4 need for autonomy |
| 5 esthetic-artistic | 5 sentience |
| 6 self-centered (self-pitying) | 6 martyrdom |
| 7 (no parallel) | 7 sexuality |
| 8 cynical-morbid | 8 (no parallel) |
| 9 dramatic-intense | 9 ("overstate") |

Source: From "Traits Revisited" by G. W. Allport, *American Psychologist*, 1966, *21*, 1–10. Copyright 1966 by the American Psychological Association. Reprinted by permission.

## Expressive Behaviors

Allport regarded all behavior as having two components. There is an adaptive function, which is the effect of the behavior. But there is also an expressive element, which is the style that characterizes behavior, regardless of its function. For example, if a person cuts in front of me in line, I may ask the person to move in a hostile tone of voice, whereas you might use a more polite tone. The tone of voice is an example of **expressive behavior**. Allport was particularly interested in the expressive component of behavior. The functional aspect of behavior is generally influenced by situational factors and is guided by the end result the behavior is supposed to produce. The expressive aspect of behavior is more likely to reflect the individual's personality because it is less influenced by functional considerations. In this respect Allport was similar to Freud. Both men believed that even trivial behaviors can be diagnostic of the central, underlying features of personality. Whereas one's reasons for doing something may only reflect the fleeting demands of the moment, the style in which one does it is more basic.

Allport's best-known work on expressive behavior was with P. E. Vernon (Allport and Vernon, 1933). They tested 25 participants on three different occasions; all sessions were separated by an interval of about four weeks. The tests included estimation of weights, speed of walking, and strength of handshake. In other instances, raters observed the subjects' speech fluency, neatness, and voice intensity. Allport and Vernon found that both the consistency (reliability) of the various acts and the ratings of them over time were acceptably high. They also found that there was consistency in the same act performed by different muscle groups or, for example, by the left arm versus the right arm or by arms versus legs. This meant, Allport decided, that some central structure must mediate behavior, lending it a characteristic style regardless of which part of the body is involved. Additional evidence for this central mediation hypothesis was found by intercorrelating all 38 measures used. These correlations were predominantly positive and led to the impression that there were three general factors behind the separate measures. From their overall analysis, Allport and Vernon (1933) decided the following:

> From our results it appears that a man's gesture and handwriting both reflect an essentially stable and constant individual style. His expressive activities seem not to be dissociated and unrelated to one another, but rather to be organized and well-patterned. Furthermore, the evidence indicates that there is a congruence between expressive movement and the attitudes, traits, values, and other dispositions of the "inner" personality. (p. 248)

Although identifying the specific cues that enable people to infer personality from expressive movement has proved to be difficult, the ability to make consistent and stable inferences from whatever cues are used is well documented (Riggio, Lippa, and Salinas, 1990).

## Assessment of Values

Allport argued that normal individuals are motivated by conscious needs that they can easily describe, although neurotic individuals may be dominated by unconscious ones. Consequently, he argued that projective techniques are appropriate for disturbed individuals but are not necessary for normal persons. Therefore, Allport is most closely identified with self-report inventories.

Allport believed that people have a unifying philosophy of life or a system of values that directs and gives meaning to their lives. These basic values act as central dispositions that influence behavior in a variety of domains. The identification and assessment of values was the focus of Allport's contributions to personality assessment. The *Study of Values* was first published with Vernon in 1931; it is now in its third edition (Allport, Vernon, and Lindzey, 1960). The scale assesses the extent to which an individual emphasizes the following values in life:

*The Theoretical*—This person emphasizes the search for truth.

*The Economic*—Whatever is useful is valued. This is a pragmatic person.

*The Aesthetic*—Artistic experiences are sought. The value is on form and harmony.

*The Social*—Love of people characterizes this person. Warm human relationships are vital.

*The Political*—This person is motivated by the search for power and influence.

*The Religious*—An almost mystical belief in the essential unity in the universe describes this person.

The reliability of the scale has generally been found to be acceptable, and several construct-validity studies support it. For example, physicians scored high on the theoretical and social values, and men in business scored high on the economic and political values. These value measures were obtained while the respondents were still undergraduates (Huntley and Davis, 1983). The scale is a simple, straightforward instrument that in many ways reflects Allport's faith in the importance of conscious determinants. Some sample items from the scale are shown in Table 14-2.

# Cattell's Psychometric Approach to Trait Research

Factor analysis is fundamental to research and assessment based on trait concepts, and Cattell is the leading figure in the factor-analytic approach to trait theory. He has contributed to the mathematical and statistical development of factor analysis, and he has extensively applied factor analysis to a variety of different types, and treatments, of data. Cattell's approach to factor analysis is

## Table 14-2
### Sample Items from the Study of Values

**From Part I (30 questions)**

1. The main objective of scientific research should be the discovery of truth rather than its practical application.

(a) Yes     (b) No

4. Assuming that you have sufficient ability, would you prefer to be:

(a) a banker?

(b) a politician?

15. At an exposition, do you chiefly like to go to the buildings where you can see:

(a) new manufacturing products?

(b) scientific (e.g., chemical) apparatus?

Source: From *A Study of Values* by G. W. Allport, P. E. Vernon, and G. Lindzey (Boston: Houghton Mifflin), 1960. Copyright © 1960 by Houghton Mifflin Co. Reprinted by permission.

consistent with his philosophy of science and his views of the nature of psychological research.

## Bivariate-Multivariate-Clinical Axis

Cattell is critical of the **bivariate research** strategy. Bivariate research is based on a relatively simple methodology and is therefore used to introduce students to research methods. It is also characteristic of much of the early, and some of the contemporary, research in psychology. In bivariate research, only two variables are considered at one time. The **independent variable** is manipulated by the experimenter, who then observes its effects on the **dependent variable**. For example, success or failure on a task (independent variable) might be varied to learn what happens to the subject's anxiety level (dependent variable) following the experience. Thousands of bivariate experiments, each dealing with a different independent variable, would have to be conducted to bring about an understanding of anxiety. However, even after conducting all those studies, we would not have a good understanding of anxiety because we would not have any idea how the variables from these separate studies combine to influence anxiety. Moreover, by considering anxiety in isolation from other variables such as competency, adjustment, and confidence, we cannot know how the presence of these other variables affects anxiety or how they relate to any of the independent variables. Bivariate research is so simple that Cattell believes it can make almost no meaningful contributions to our knowledge of personality.

In contrast, Cattell endorses **multivariate research.** This approach is based on designs that employ multiple independent and dependent variables. Thus, one can evaluate the causes and effects of each variable on other variables, both singly and in combination in the context of several other variables. In much of Cattell's research, the variables are assessed naturalistically and are not manipulated to reduce the artificiality of the observations. By obtaining multiple measures and evaluating them in the context of one another, a more realistic, and more complicated, set of relations can be described.

A third strategy is the **clinical method**, which Cattell argues is similar to, though less rigorous than, multivariate research.

> In this respect, the emphasis on "wholeness" in the multivariate method is actually the same as in the clinical method, but it is quantitative and follows explicit calculations of laws and general conclusions. For the clinician appraises the total pattern "by eye," and tries to make generalizations from a good memory, whereas the multivariate experimenter actually *measures* all the variables and may then set an electronic computer to abstract the regularities which exist, instead of depending on human powers of memory and generalization. The clinical approach to personality is thus really that of a multivariate experimenter without benefit of apparatus–and has had the additional drawback that it produces its personality theories from data gathered from abnormal, diseased processes rather than normal ranges. (1965, pp. 21–22)

Fundamental to multivariate behavioral research is the set of statistical techniques called factor analysis.

## Factor Analysis

From the perspective of bivariate research, the existence of 2,800 words that describe relatively common personality traits (Norman, 1967) poses a nearly insurmountable problem for anyone who wishes to understand the general pattern and structure of personality description. Among 2,800 terms there are 3,918,600 different correlations that can be computed. Even if the set of 2,800 were reduced to the 100 most common and least redundant terms, this would still require examining and interpreting 4,950 correlations. The magnitude of evaluating this mass of relations has led some investigators to restrict their study to a single trait, such as authoritarianism, or narcissism, or self-monitoring, with the result that the study of personality is fragmented. Other investigators have adopted a clinical strategy and simply argue that in their experience, people fall into two or three categories or else are motivated by a few basic traits. There is no quantification or measurement, only an appeal to the authority of clinical experience, which makes the conclusions of these investigators untestable. The problem, then, is to develop methods that make it possible to identify the underlying factors that organize and explain the mass of observed correlations—methods that can be replicated and that do not rely solely on clinical judgment.

The problem which baffled psychologists for many years was to find a method which would tease out these functionally unitary influences in the chaotic jungle of human behavior. But let us ask how, in the literal tropical jungle, the hunter decides whether the dark blobs which he sees are two or three rotting logs or a single alligator? He watches for movement. If they move together—come and disappear together—he infers a single structure. (p. 56)

What Cattell is suggesting by his metaphor about moving alligators is that we use correlational methods to determine the degree of covariation among different measures. In essence, a correlation is a quantitative index of the degree of relation between *two* sets of scores. However, as we have seen, computing individual correlations among all possible pairs of variables is not helpful. The technique of **factor analysis** was developed to consider the *many* separate correlations and determine which *groups* of variables increase or decrease together and therefore can be considered functionally related. The technique of factor analysis is based on the principle that when variables (e.g., behaviors, test responses, emotional reactions) change together, they have some element in common that is responsible for their relation. By examining large arrays of correlations, one can, through factor analysis, determine the basic elements, dimensions, or factors of personality.

## Hypothetical Example of Factor Analysis

Problem.  An investigator is interested in the major dimensions of *interpersonal behavior*. People can exhibit a variety of characteristics in their interactions with other people. Determining the major underlying dimensions of such behavior would simplify the study of interpersonal behavior and more efficiently describe it. Such dimensions might also be useful for predicting which people will work together more effectively, or become friends.

Data Collection.  100 participants are asked to describe themselves on seven scales that concern how they act toward others. The scales are these:

  A = Warm
  B = Helpful
  C = Generous
  D = Caring
  E = Dominant
  F = Assertive
  G = Strong

The Correlation Matrix.  The next step is to correlate each of the scales with every other scale. These correlations can be arranged in a **correlation matrix**. An example of such a matrix with hypothetical correlations entered is shown in Table 14-3. Inspection of the correlation matrix reveals a clear pattern. Measures A, B, C, and D all show a strong positive relation (i.e., the correlation between any two measures in this group of four is between .70 and .80). Moreover, measures E, F,

## ♆ Table 14-3
### Hypothetical Correlation Matrix for Seven Interpersonal Scales

| Test | A | B | C | D | E | F | G |
|------|---|-----|-----|-----|-----|-----|-----|
| A |  | .70 | .80 | .75 | .15 | .20 | .10 |
| B |  |  | .75 | .70 | .12 | .10 | .10 |
| C |  |  |  | .70 | .18 | .15 | .11 |
| D |  |  |  |  | .12 | .14 | .12 |
| E |  |  |  |  |  | .80 | .85 |
| F |  |  |  |  |  |  | .75 |
| G |  |  |  |  |  |  |  |

and G also correlate highly with one another (i.e., from .75 to .85). However, there is virtually no relation between the group E, F, G and the group A, B, C, D (e.g., the correlation between A and E is .15; for B and F, $r = .10$; for D and G, $r = .12$). What these patterns suggest is that A, B, C, and D all indicate the same underlying construct, or are influenced by the same general characteristic. Likewise, E, F, and G form another construct that is different from the first.

This example is limited to seven variables with a clear and simplified pattern of correlations to illustrate how factors are identified. The interpretation of patterns of correlations becomes more difficult when, say, 100 or more measures are used. In these more complex cases, we depend on the technique of factor analysis and the computer to process the data. But the principle is the same; the reduction of data by means of factor analysis to a small number of dimensions, or **factors**. Factor-analytic formulas are complex, and the interpretation of the results of factor analyses requires a number of difficult and sometimes controversial decisions. A more detailed, but nonmathematical, discussion of factor analysis can be found in Goldberg and Digman (1994). Basically, factor analysis does statistically with large correlation matrices what we did by inspection of the 21 correlations in Table 14-3.

**Factor Loading.**  In the example, we decided that two factors characterize the relations among the seven variables. Factor "X" is the basis for the relations among A, B, C, and D. Factor "Y" accounts for the relations among E, F, and G. Together, these two factors account for all the relations in the matrix. A, B, C, and D, are said to "**load**" on Factor X, whereas E, F, and G load on Factor Y. Thus, the aspects of interpersonal behavior represented by the seven scales can be summarized or explained by two factors.

**Factor Names.**  Although the conclusion that two factors can summarize interpersonal traits is of some interest, generally it is also useful to determine what those factors represent. That is, calling one factor "X" and the other "Y" communicates that two dimensions characterize interpersonal behavior, but the content or meaning of those factors is not specified. *Factor naming* is an inherently subjective process that can result in disagreement and controversy. The name chosen for a given factor may imply meanings that were not intended by the factor analyst. For example, I may extract a factor that loads on measures of self-interest, selfishness, and greediness, and name the factor *narcissism*—a term with psychoanalytic implications. However, none of the measures contain psychoanalytic data. Therefore, choosing narcissism as a label may suggest something about the factor that goes far beyond the measures used. Because of the subjectivity and possible overinterpretation of factor names, some investigators restrict the labels of factors to numbers (e.g., I, II, III) and allow the meaning of the factors to be indirectly communicated by the variables that load on them. Cattell, to emphasize the theoretical difference between underlying **latent** factors and the observed **manifest** variables that serve to identify them, makes up factor names that do not have any obvious content. For example, Cattell has labeled one particular source trait *parmia versus threctia*. Again, to obtain some idea of what parmia or threctia represent, one has to examine the original measures and their loadings on the factor.

However, the use of numbers or "meaningless" words to label factors only postpones the problems of interpretation and places the burden of interpretation on the reader. Most factor analysts, therefore, offer some meaningful labels for their factors with the understanding that these labels do not constitute an objective summary of the factors content. In the present example, A, B, C, and D load on Factor X. According to the content of four variables, a reasonable name for this factor might be *interpersonal warmth* or *love*. Factor Y might be named *interpersonal power* or *dominance*.

## Sources of Data

Factor analysis is a powerful technique, but no matter how sophisticated the factor analyst may be, no amount of sophistication can overcome poor data. If data are drawn from stimuli or assessment procedures that are trivial, superficial, biased or confounded, no amount of statistical analysis is going to salvage the research. One of Cattell's most important methodological contributions is his systematic consideration of the sources of data used to study personality. Cattell has classified data as coming from three basic sources: life records, or L-data; self-rating questionnaires, or Q-data; and objective tests, or T-data.

**L-data.** **L-data** can consist of a wide range of sources, including school grades, medical records, court records, and other archival data. Most often, however, the L-data used by Cattell have come from ratings of the person on personality characteristics such as friendliness, emotionality, patience, or assertiveness. These are ratings are provided by individuals who are well acquainted with the person in different life domains.

Q-data. **Q-data** are self-report data that come from self-ratings or from the person's statements about his or her behavior, feelings, or thoughts. Such data reflect the individual's introspections and self-observations. The essential characteristics of L-data and Q-data sources are summarized in Table 14-4. On the basis of ratings by observers and responses by subjects themselves, Cattell has identified a source trait of *tender-mindedness—tough-mindedness.* The upper portion of Table 14-4 shows observer or L-data items, and the lower portion illustrates Q-data items that assess this trait.

T-data. Finally, there are **T-data,** which come from objective tests. *Objective* in this context means that independent judges will arrive at the same conclusions when the participant's responses are scored. Thus, T-data differ from Q and L

---

## ⟨⟩ Table 14-4
### Tender-Minded—Tough-Minded Source Traits as Identified Through L-data and Q-data

**L-Data (Observer Ratings)**

| Loads Positively | | Loads Negatively |
|---|---|---|
| Demanding, impatient | vs. | Emotionally mature |
| Dependent, immature | vs. | Independent-minded |
| Gentle, sentimental | vs. | Hard, realistic |
| Expresses fastidious feelings | vs. | Overrules feelings |
| Enjoys imaginative fancies | vs. | Not fanciful |
| Easily anxious | vs. | Does not show anxiety |
| Likes to be with people | vs. | Self-sufficient |

**Q-data (Subject's Questionnaire Responses)**

Are you brought to tears by discouraging circumstances?
(a) *yes*                                             (b) no

Would you rather be:
(a) *a bishop*                                        (b) a colonel

Do you have good physical endurance?
(a) yes                                               (b) *no*

Would you rather work:
(a) *as a guidance worker for young*                  (b) as a manager in a
*people seeking careers*                              technical manufacturing concern

Do your friends regard you as:
(a) practical                                         (b) *soft-hearted*

Note: Italicized response indicates tender-mindedness.
Source: From *The Scientific Analysis of Personality* by R. B. Cattell (Baltimore, Md.: Penguin), 1965. Copyright 1965 by R. B. Cattell. Reprinted by permission.

data in that Q and L data require the raters to *implicitly* integrate an *unspecified* set of *naturalistic* observations of themselves or others into an impression, whereas T-data *explicitly* prescribe how a fixed set of *controlled* observations are to be combined. T-data can come from a variety of situations: paper-and-pencil tasks as well as contrived laboratory behavioral settings. The defining characteristic, according to Cattell, is that participants are placed in situations without knowing what aspects of their behavior will be observed. Although the objectivity of T-data makes them appear more scientific, Block (1977) has argued, and provided evidence, that the contrived nature of T-data often makes them less valid than Q or L data for assessing personality. Figure 14-1 provides an example of a source of T-data. This item presumably measures one's capacity to integrate. Cattell has found that this type of task loads significantly on a source trait called *regression*, which is an aspect of neuroticism.

## Empirical Identification of Traits

To identify source traits, Cattell began with the list of traits produced by Allport and Odbert (1936). He selected the most common and least redundant trait terms, which resulted in a list of 171 terms. He selected a heterogeneous group of 100 adults and asked people who were well acquainted with them to rate them

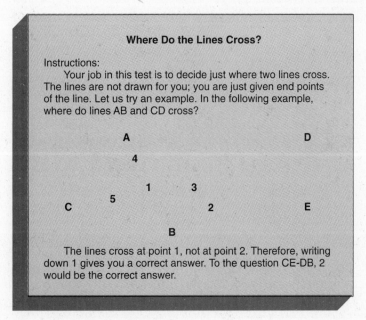

**Figure 14-1** ⊗  Spatial judgment: a T-data task.

From *The Scientific Analysis of Personality* by R. B. Cattell (Baltimore, MD: Penguin), 1965. Copyright © 1965 by R. B. Cattell.

on all 171 traits. Through factor analysis, these L data ratings were further reduced, and an additional group of over 200 men was rated on this shortened list
of trait variables. A few of the traits on which these subjects were rated were
*emotional, conscientious, tender,* and *self-effacing.*

Based on factor analyses of these ratings Cattell identified 16 factors from
which he and his colleagues developed a self-report (Q-data) personality questionnaire called the 16 *Personality Factor Questionnaire (16 P-F Questionnaire).*
The 16 factors are shown in Table 14-5. The first 12 are factors found in both
Q-data and L-data. The last 4 factors are from Q-data and were not found in the
L-data. Three sample items from the 16 P-F Questionnaire that load on Factor A,
which Cattell has named *sizothymia-affectothymia,* illustrate the format of the
test:

| | |
|---|---|
| I could stand being a hermit: | True or false |
| I trust strangers: | Sometimes or practically always |
| I would rather work as: | An engineer or a social science teacher |

## Table 14-5
The Sixteen Major Factors Represented on the 16 P-F Questionnaire

| Factor | High Score | vs. | Low Score |
|---|---|---|---|
| A | Reserved (Sizothymia) | | Outgoing (Affectothymia) |
| B | Less intelligent (Low $g$) | | More intelligent (High $g$) |
| C | Emotional (Low ego strength) | | Stable (High ego strength) |
| E | Humble (Submissiveness) | | Assertive (Dominance) |
| F | Sober (Desurgency) | | Happy-go-lucky (Surgency) |
| G | Expedient (Low super-ego) | | Conscientious (High super-ego) |
| H | Shy (Threctia) | | Venturesome (Parmia) |
| I | Tough-minded (Harria) | | Tender-minded (Premsia) |
| L | Trusting (Alaxia) | | Suspicious (Protension) |
| M | Practical (Praxemia) | | Imaginative (Autia) |
| N | Forthright (Artlessness) | | Shrewd (Shrewdness) |
| O | Placid (Assurance) | | Apprehensive (Guilt-proneness) |
| $Q_1$ | Conservative (Conservativism) | | Experimenting (Radicalism) |
| $Q_2$ | Group-tied (Group adherence) | | Self-sufficient (Self-sufficiency) |
| $Q_3$ | Casual (Low integration) | | Controlled (High self-concept) |
| $Q_4$ | Relaxed (Low ergic tension) | | Tense (Ergic tension) |

The 16-PF is one of the best known personality inventories. It is generally regarded as a research instrument, although it has been used in applied settings to characterize the personality of individuals. In applied settings, profiles of the individual's scores across the 16 scales are usually reported. These profiles can be used for occupational decisions, such as hiring and promotions; in counseling, and as a component of clinical assessment. Originally Cattell tried to incorporate T-data measures into the 16-PF, including an objectively scored intelligence test. However, the loadings of the T-data measures did not generally converge with the Q- and L-data factors, and the T-data measures were subsequently dropped.

## Analysis of Heredity and Environment

Cattell (1965) has said that "one can conclude that roughly four fifths of the differences we obtain on intelligence tests would disappear if people were all of identical heredity, whereas two thirds of the variance on extraversion-introversion would vanish if all people were brought up identically" (p. 33). Cattell bases this statement on the most comprehensive and complex behavior genetics model ever developed. Cattell has named this model, which is both a theory and a statistical technique, **multiple abstract variance analysis (MAVA)**. According to Cattell, this method is superior to conventional approaches to the study of heredity–environment differences, which rely primarily on comparisons between identical and fraternal twins.

In practice, several personality measures are administered to all the members of many different families. Data are also collected from twins and siblings raised together and those adopted by other families. The data are then analyzed via a series of simultaneous equations, and four types of influence are assessed: within-family environmental differences, between-family environmental differences, within-family hereditary differences, and between-family hereditary differences. The use of MAVA so far suggests that for intelligence, the contribution of heredity is 80 percent and the environmental contribution 20 percent. For the temperament trait of tough-mindedness—tender-mindedness, the hereditary contribution is about the same. However, for neuroticism, the hereditary component is only about 35 percent (Cattell, 1965). The complexity and sophisticated mathematics of MAVA make it a difficult model for many to comprehend and to comprehensively test. Thus, these estimates are not universally accepted.

## Measurement of Similarity and Change

The emphasis of trait theory is on the stable and consistent aspects of human personality. Cattell's research on the identification and structure of the major personality traits reflects this emphasis. However, unlike most trait theorists, Cattell has also devoted considerable effort to understanding those aspects of human personality that change over time and situations. Cattell's approach to the study of personality change is also based on factor analysis. The difference is that the techniques of factor analysis are applied to different types of correlation matrices.

R-technique.    The standard correlational matrix in psychology is based on what Cattell has termed **R-technique**. In R-technique, the correlations are computed between variables (e.g., tests, scales, ratings) across people. Thus, the correlations provide an index of the extent to which two variables are related by assessing the extent to which subjects are ordered similarly in their scores on the two variables. The factors derived from such a correlation matrix thus reflect the commonalities among the variables.

P-technique.    To study change, Cattell has used the **P-technique**. In this case, a single individual is measured on several variables at different times and situations. The correlations are computed between the different times or situations across the measures. The correlations thus index the extent to which different situations and times are related by assessing the extent to which a single subject's scores on a set of measures are ordered similarly in those situations. The factors thus derived identify the situations and times for which the individual exhibits personality consistency, and the situations and times in which the individual is inconsistent.

Differential R-technique.    Another approach to studying change is called **differential R-technique**. In this technique, measures are obtained from a group of participants on two occasions and the change in the magnitude and direction of participants scores are computed. These change scores between the pairs of measures are correlated across the participants. The resulting factors indicate which variables exhibit similar patterns of change. The P-technique and the differential R-technique are regarded by Cattell as crucial for studying transient and unstable states. He views states such as anxiety and depression as important characteristics of human behavior that can also be described and classified through factor analysis. The descriptive use of trait and state terms is discussed in Box 14-1.

Q-technique.    A final type of correlation matrix that Cattell has used in his factor analytic studies is based on **Q-technique**, which has no relation to Q-data. In Q-technique, the usual computation of correlations between variables across subjects is reversed. Thus, correlations are computed between individuals across variables. Factor analyses of such a matrix will produce factors of people rather than factors of variables. Cattell uses this method to identify different types of people. He has also used it to identifying roles such as father, business executive, banker, and scientist. Of course, the interpretation of Q-factors requires that additional information about the subjects, such as gender, occupation, attitudes, and whatever is of interest to the investigator, be available. Otherwise, the meaning of the factors or clusters of people cannot be interpreted.

### BOX 14-1
## The Description of Traits and States

The study of states has been a source of some controversy in personality description. Some theorists (e.g., Allen and Potkay, 1981) have argued that terms that describe states and traits are indistinguishable except in a particular context. For example, the statement "I am an anxious person" refers to trait anxiety, whereas the statement "I am anxious right now" refers to state anxiety. Thus, the term *anxiety* can refer to either a trait or a state, depending on the context (Spielberger, Gorsuch, and Lushene, 1970).

In 1988, Chaplin, John, and Goldberg studied participants' phenomenological impressions of a sample of 75 descriptive terms. They found that participants could reliably distinguish terms that typically implied states from terms that typically imply states independent of any context. The features that distinguish trait-descriptive terms from state-descriptive terms are these: trait terms describe behaviors that occur more frequently, are more stable, and are thought to result from internal person factors rather than external situational ones. Although acknowledging that context can change the trait-state implications of a term such as anxiety, Chaplin et al. argued that the general trait-state implications of terms are an important component of everyday personality description. Specifically, the state or trait implications of descriptive terms are important for anticipating and planning social interactions. State terms such as "infatuated" or "nervous" describe behaviors in another that we can plan to control or manipulate, whereas trait terms such as "gentle" or "dominant" describe behaviors that can be anticipated and predicted.

## Eysenck's Search for Types

Eysenck views the personality structure as hierarchical, and his research has focused on those types that are at the top of hierarchy. The breadth of Eysenck's types means that they likely subsume Cattell's source traits, which would appear at the next lower level in the hierarchy. Eysenck argues that the three broad types, introversion-extraversion, neuroticism, and psychoticism offer the greatest potential for prediction and understanding.

Like Cattell, Eysenck prefers large-scale research efforts to small, bivariate investigations of isolated traits. He also believes that factor-analytic studies too often emphasize self-ratings, questionnaires, and subjective data. He prefers to include behavioral observations whenever possible. Of greatest importance for Eysenck is that the study of personality not be restricted to a particular type of data.

## Criterion Analysis

Unlike Cattell's use of factor analysis to *discover* the major dimensions of traits, states, or roles, Eysenck uses factor analysis to *test* his theoretical hypotheses about the major dimensions of personality. Eysenck calls this use of factor analysis **criterion analysis**. Eysenck begins with a hypothesis about a basic trait or type and selects a series of measures that are theoretically indicative of this dimension. Next, he chooses two criterion groups known to differ along the dimension in question. Each measure is then correlated with criterion group membership. These correlations indicate the degree of association between such measures and the underlying dimension that defines the criterion groups.

As an illustration, consider the dimension of neuroticism. Eysenck (1952) and his colleagues selected two groups, each containing slightly more than 200 participants. The normal group included male soldiers of at least average intelligence who had served in the Army for at least six months. The neurotic group contained soldiers who were discharged because of psychiatric problems. Although otherwise well matched with the neurotic group on other variables, subjects in the normal group were somewhat more intelligent. The participants were administered a large number of personality measures over a two-day period. All measures were selected because they were hypothesized to be related to the underlying dimension of neuroticism. Twenty-eight of the measures were found to distinguish between the neurotic and normal groups. The correlations among these measures were computed, and the resulting correlation matrix was then factor analyzed. The factor analysis was used to confirm the general neuroticism factor that was common to all the measures and to identify more specific subcomponents of neuroticism that formed lower levels of the neuroticism hierarchy. From these and other results, Eysenck (1952) concluded that "in neuroticism we are dealing with a personality factor which can be measured as reliably and as validly as intelligence" (p. 155).

## The Biological Basis of Eysenck's Factors

Eysenck views the three major types as having a strong biological basis related to different brain structures that are associated with arousal and activation. Consistent with a biological theory of neuroticism, psychoticism, and extroversion is the evidence from behavior genetics (e.g., Pedersen, Plomin, McClearn, and Friberg, 1988) that these types have high heritabilities. In addition, the work of Revelle and his colleagues (e.g., Revelle, Anderson, and Humphreys, 1987) on arousal-based theories of personality, and Zuckerman's (1994) work on sensation-seeking and augmenting/reducing biological systems, provide further support for a biological basis for these types. However, Eysenck (1990) has cautioned that his theory is based primarily on patterns of correlations among *descriptive* measures. He has also argued that his biological theory is *weak*, in the sense that strong and unambiguous tests of it are not possible.

We are dealing with a *weak* theory (Eysenck, 1960) . . . In a weak theory we cannot make assumptions that K [e.g., the validity of our measures, representativeness of our subjects, unimportance of mediating concepts] is true, and consequently failure of the experiment may be due to wrong assumptions concerning K rather than to H's [our theory] being false. (Eysenck, 1990)

**Gray's Reinterpretation.** In contrast to Eysenck, Gray (1972, 1981) has proposed a strong biological theory of Eysenck's extroversion (E) and neuroticism (N) factors. As part of his theory, Gray has reinterpreted these factors as blends of Eysenck's original dimensions. Specifically, Gray has hypothesized one factor that combines neuroticism and introversion (N+, E–), which he calls *anxiety*. The other factor is a combination of neuroticism and extroversion (N+, E+), which Gray calls *impulsivity*. Gray argues that higher levels of anxiety reflect sensitivity to punishment and the absence of reward, whereas higher levels of impulsivity reflect sensitivity to reward and the absence of punishment. Thus, Gray has linked personality to patterns of behavior relevant to classic learning theory.

The biological basis of Gray's theory about anxiety is a **behavioral inhibition system (BIS)**. The BIS operates in the hippocampus and through the biochemical influences of monamine oxidase. Gray also postulates a biological structure for impulsivity called a **behavioral activation system (BAS)**, although the specifics of this structure are not yet well developed. Gray's work has inspired a variety of research that has attempted to relate personality to learning theory and to explain individual differences in conditioning (e.g., Avila, Molto, Segarra, and Torrubia, 1995; Newman, 1987; Zinbarg and Revelle, 1989). In addition Gray's theory has been used as a framework for conceptualizing personality disorders in clinical diagnosis (Farmer and Nelson-Gray, 1995). Specifically, Gray's dimension of anxiety was found to be related to the personality disorders of *dependent, avoidant,* and *obsessive-compulsive*. The impulsivity dimension was related to *histrionic, narcissistic, borderline*, and *antisocial* personality disorders. Although Gray's reinterpretation of the E and N factors has been influential, the strong biological basis for his interpretations has been evaluated almost exclusively with nonhuman animals. Generalizing these results to humans is a matter of conjecture. Also, Eysenck argues that the descriptive evidence is not consistent with Gray's interpretation of anxiety and impulsivity as a function of low and high levels of E, respectively, in the presence of high N. Specifically, measures of anxiety correlate with measures of N, not E, and measures of impulsivity correlate most strongly with measures of psychoticism (P), which is outside the domain of Gray's theory.

**Cloninger's System.** Cloninger (1987, 1991) has also proposed a three-dimensional theory of personality that has a biosocial basis, and he has developed a self-report questionnaire (Cloninger, Przybeck, and Svrakic, 1991) to describe subjects on those dimensions. Cloninger's dimensions are labeled *harm avoidance, novelty seeking*, and *reward dependence*. These dimensions have some similarity to Eysenck's dimensions and Gray's reinterpretation of those dimensions.

However, a recent behavior genetic analysis comparing the Cloninger system with Eysenck's system (Heath, Cloninger, and Martin, 1994) suggests that "the personality systems of Eysenck and Cloninger are not simply alternate descriptions of the same dimensions of personality, but rather each provide incomplete descriptions of the structure of heritable personality dimensions" (p. 762).

## Murray's Research Legacy

Research in personality is often based on small samples of participants' behavior obtained from a single experimental session or measured naturalistically at a single point in time. White (1981) has argued that such investigations ignore the complexity of personality. There are some notable exceptions, such as the Berkeley longitudinal personality studies of Jack Block and Ravenna Helson (Block, 1971; Helson, 1992; Helson and Moane, 1987; Helson and Roberts, 1994). Other examples are the intensive individual assessments associated with the Institute of Personality Assessment and Research (IPAR) at the University of California at Berkeley and the VA Selection Project of Clinical Psychologists (Kelly and Fiske, 1951). However, most personality research is neither longitudinal nor intensive. White (1981) referred to this as "studying personality without looking at it" (p. 15). More than any other personality psychologist, Murray emphasized methods that avoid the narrowness of experimental or correlational methods that take "snapshots" of people but fail to capture them as lives in progress (Phares and Lamiell, 1977).

### Intensive Study of Individuals

Murray promoted the intensive study of small numbers of normal participants—an approach that yields large amounts of data on those participants. Studies of large numbers of participants whose responses are tabulated and then averaged are of little use for understanding any individual. For example, knowing that 75 percent of our participants respond a given way does not tell us why the other 25 percent responded differently, nor is it of much help in predicting and understanding the behavior of any one participant. Lamiell's (1987) strong critique of personality research is based, in part, on this problem.

Of course, the intensive examination of individuals limits the number of participants that can be studied by a given investigator over time. The benefit is a more complex and therefore more realistic understanding of the individual's personality and the processes that led to its development. Such a strategy, however, is difficult for many to follow because they see their professional advancement as hinging on the production of a large number of publications—the so-called "publish or perish" syndrome.

Murray also contended that our emphasis should be on the intensive study of *normal* participants in natural settings. Because we ultimately wish to understand the behavior of individuals in real-life settings, Murray believed that it was illogical to focus our studies exclusively on contrived or laboratory situations. We should emphasize the systematic study of individuals in their "natural habitats."

Finally, Murray was a pioneer in assembling an **interdisciplinary** staff to study people. The staff at the Harvard Psychological Clinic, for example, included psychiatrists, psychologists, anthropologists, and sociologists (Hall and Lindzey, 1978). An illustration of Murray's approach to research and assessment is described in Box 14-2.

## The Diagnostic Council

Murray emphasized the importance of direct observation in the assessment of personality. Although tests and rating scales are important, Murray argued that they could not provide a complete assessment of personality. However, Murray also recognized that observers are imperfect. They are sometimes biased and at other times not sensitive. Thus, Murray was committed to improving the reliability, precision, and efficiency of human observations. One method he used was the **diagnostic council**. Having several observers study the same individual is a means of overcoming the limitations of any one observer. A council involves several observers who meet for a discussion of their separate views, interpretations, and conclusions about a given participant. The group considers all the interpretations and comes to a consensus about the final product or conclusion. This approach is similar to that used in clinical settings where group decisions are made about a patient's diagnosis or course of treatment. This approach also makes use of the principle of aggregation, which generally improves the reliability and validity of all types of measures.

## The TAT

The **Thematic Apperception Test (TAT)** is Murray's major contribution to personality assessment. This instrument is considered a projective test and was published by Christiana Morgan and Murray in 1935. The test was developed at the Harvard Psychological Clinic as part of a long-term study of 51 college-age men. It was used along with other tests, interviews, and autobiographies to formulate hypotheses about the participants' personalities. The TAT consists of a series of pictures about which participants are asked to make up stories. Murray (1951) interprets a participant's responses to the TAT in terms of his system of needs. He has described several propositions that should guide interpretations of the imaginative fantasies or stories produced by subjects in response to the TAT pictures. Siipola (1984) has summarized them as follows:

BOX 14-2
## Assessment in War

Murray was an integral part of one of the early intensive assessment projects in this country. The project was operated by the Office of Strategic Services (OSS), which was the World War II forerunner of the present CIA, in the early 1940s. The purpose of the assessment program was to evaluate candidates for espionage and intelligence missions overseas, often behind enemy lines.

The strategy was to put the candidates through an intensive, three-day series of activities. The goal was the identification of intelligent, resourceful individuals who could effectively cope with stressful situations and thereby successfully carry out a variety of dangerous missions. The candidates were from diverse backgrounds. Some were civilians; some were in the military (both officers and enlisted men). Their identities were kept secret. Everyone wore the same clothing without any external markings or insignia that could reveal a person's status or rank. Nor were any personal belongings permitted that might suggest something about the candidate (no letters, no pictures, no newspapers, etc.). All assessments were conducted on a large estate outside Washington, D.C.

Many traditional psychological tests (ability, intelligence, personality) were administered, along with many interviews. Life histories and medical dossiers were likewise available. The candidates were intensively observed in groups and individually. Although they were admonished not to reveal their true identities, OSS staff often attempted to trick or fool them into doing so. Sometimes confederates of the assessors acted as informants or were used to mislead the candidates. This was wartime, and it was vital that clever, stress-resistant personnel be discovered. A variety of situational tests were also employed to evaluate candidates' reactions to stressful demands, to gauge their spontaneous problem-solving aptitudes, and to observe their leadership potential. Here is Anastasi's (1976) description of one OSS task:

> [In] the Construction Test . . . a 5-foot cube had to be assembled from wooden poles, blocks, and pegs. The examinee was informed that, since it was impossible for one man to complete the task within the 10 minutes allotted for it, he would be given two helpers. Actually, the helpers were psychologists who played prearranged roles. One followed a policy of inertia and passive resistance; the other obstructed the work by making impractical suggestions, asking irrelevant and often embarrassing questions, and needling the candidate with ridicule and criticism. So well did the helpers succeed in frustrating the candidates that the construction was never completed in the history of the assessment program (p. 596)

Although the demands of war did not permit many good opportunities for the rigorous validation of the OSS assessment program, it did raise many issues and identify several problems associated with personality assessment (Wiggins, 1973). It also provided a paradigm of intensive, multidimensional personality assessment that has been the model for other such assessment projects. (OSS Assessment Staff, 1948).

The TAT reveals drives, emotions, complexes, and conflicts of the personality.

The participant will identify with the main character in the TAT story and project his or her own perceptions, motives, feelings, and thoughts onto that character.

In describing other figures in the stories, the participant may reveal attitudes toward significant others (e.g., parents, siblings, spouse).

Not all material produced is significant. However, significance tends to be suggested by the following elements:

Repetition

Uniqueness

Self-involvement

Symbolic significance

Interrelatedness (one theme relates to or is consistent with another)

Murray also recognized that although TAT stories may predict the participant's overt behavior on occasion, the TAT should not be viewed as primarily a means for predicting specific behaviors. The relation between TAT scores and behavior depends on the degree of conflict over the behavior. For example, sexual themes might not be indicative of the participant's actual behavior unless no conflict or guilt over sexuality is exhibited by that participant.

**Procedure.** The same basic procedures are used for measuring most needs with the TAT, although most of the research has been on *n* Achievement, followed by *n* Affiliation and *n* Power. Moreover, there has been little change in these procedures since research on needs began more than 40 years ago (McClelland et al., 1953).

Some four to six TAT pictures are administered (often in a group setting). Participants are given four minutes to write a story in response to each picture. They are instructed to answer the following questions in their stories: What is happening? What led up to this situation? What is being thought? What will happen? Each story is then judged for the presence of achievement imagery. For example, stories that describe unique accomplishments, the desire to be successful, competition with a standard of excellence, or the like would qualify (see Table 14-6). Consider, for example, the following story given in response to the TAT picture shown on page 477:

Here is a student preparing for an upcoming exam. He is studying hard because on the last exam he got a B but wants to do better this time. He is thinking about what questions will be on the exam. He looks like he will do well and eventually after graduation will get a good job somewhere.

All stories are scored according to a detailed scoring manual that contains a variety of subcategories such as affect ("He feels depressed"), instrumental activity

⊗ Table 14-6

Typical Stories Produced in Response to Achievement, Affiliation, and Power Cues

| Achievement Arousal | Affiliation Arousal | Power Arousal |
|---|---|---|
| George is an engineer who (need, + 1) wants to win a competition in which the man with (achievement imagery: standard of excellence, + 1) the most practicable drawing will be awarded the contract to build a bridge. He is taking a moment to think (goal anticipation, +1) how happy he will be if he wins. He has been (block, world,+ 1) baffled by how to make such a long span strong, but remembers to specify a new steel alloy of great strength, submits his entry, but does not win and (goal state, negative, +1) is very unhappy. **Thema +1. Total n Achievement score = +7.** | George is an engineer who is working late. He is (affiliation imagery +1) worried that his wife will be annoyed with him for neglecting her (block, world, +1) She has been objecting that he cares more about his work than his wife and family. (block, personal, + 1) He seems unable to satisfy both his boss and his wife. (need, + 1) but he loves her very much, and (instrumental act, +1) will do his best to finish up fast and get home to her. **Thema +1. Total n Achievement score = + 6.** | This is Georgiadis, a (prestige of actor + 1) famous architect, who (need, + 1) wants to win a competition which will establish who is (power imagery, +1) the best architect in the world. His chief rival, Bulakovsky, (block, world, +1) has stolen his best ideas, and he is dreadfully afraid of the (goal anticipation, negative, + 1) disgrace of losing. But he comes up with (instrumental act,+1) a great new idea, which absolutely (powerful effect, +1) bowls the judges over, and he wins! **Total n Power score = +7.** |

("He will study carefully"), and obstacles to achievement ("His father hasn't the money to send him to school"). With only modest training, judges can readily learn to produce reliable scores.

McClelland's Defense of the TAT. The major criticism of the TAT methods is that respondent's stories tend to be unstable across time (Entwisle, 1972). That is, respondents will often tell different stories in response to the same picture on two different occasions. McClelland (1980) counters with the argument that because projective measures encourage creativity they inevitably promote a degree of instability. He argues that self-reports, although stable, become so by sacrificing validity.

A typical picture for eliciting achievement themes.

More specifically, the central role of the TAT in research is based on McClelland's psychodynamic view of motives and needs. Although he acknowledges that questionnaires, ratings, and behavioral observations are often reliable, he contends that their validity as indices of underlying motives is not easily established. For example, more objective measures will likely be influenced by a variety of motives, such as acquiescence or the desire to make socially acceptable responses. The use of a projective measure whose stimuli (pictures) do not have obvious content is based on a psychodynamic tradition. This tradition views our unconscious, more pervasive motives as best able to find expression in response to ambiguous stimuli that arouse those unconscious motives but fail to alert our more consciously directed motives and purposes.

**Alternative Measures.** Despite the psychometric objections to the use of the TAT to assess *n* Achievement, few alternatives have been developed. However, Murray's theory of needs is also the basis for Jackson's (1985) *Personality Research Form (PRF)*, a widely used objective inventory of normal personality. Jackson's (1965) *PRF* has an achievement scale. Typical items on this scale are these:

I look more to the future than to the past or present (T or F)

I enjoy situations that allow me to use my skills (T or F)

Unfortunately, the objective self-report measures of achievement and the projective TAT measures are generally found to be uncorrelated. In the absence of any independent criteria of $n$ Achievement, it is not possible to decide which, if either, type of measure is correct. McClelland, Koestner, and Weinberger (1989) suggest that the two types of measures reflect different achievement processes. They hypothesize that the TAT measures indicate motives that have been built on early affective experiences, before the development of language. Self-report measures indicate motives that are developed later, after the concepts of self and other, as well as the values attached by society to different goals and behavior have been learned.

Validating the TAT Procedure.  In the absence of clear criteria for establishing the TAT as a valid measure of $n$ Achievement, a construct validation approach must be used. In this approach, theoretical predictions are made about how $n$ Achievement would be affected by experimental manipulation. If the TAT scores of $n$ Achievement show a pattern that is consistent with the theoretical analysis, then there is evidence that the $n$ Achievement scores reflect the underlying $n$ Achievement construct.

For example, McClelland, Clark, Roby, and Atkinson (1949) asked 200 male college students to write 5-minute stories in response to several slides. However, before writing the stories, the participants were administered preliminary tests under one of two conditions. The first was a relaxed condition in which the tests were described as in the development stage. There was no emphasis on achievement. The other condition involved failure—a manipulation designed to arouse achievement motivation. Here, the preliminary test was introduced as an IQ test, and the levels of performance required for success were set so high that all participants did poorly. Following these manipulations, the TAT measures of $n$ Achievement were administered.

An $n$ Achievement score was computed for each participant and a clear effect of motivation was evident. Thus, when $n$ Achievement was aroused through failure, the ensuing TAT performance yielded higher achievement scores than scores following the relaxed condition. Results from these and other studies support the construct validity of TAT stories to measure individual differences in $n$ Achievement.

## Enhancing Achievement Striving

Many relations between $n$ Achievement and behavior have been observed over the years (McClelland, 1985). Our society values and promotes such achievement and its related behaviors. A substantial amount of research effort has been devoted to enhancing achievement striving in people who are, relatively speaking, unmotivated. In addition, interventions to counteract the negative motivational and behavioral consequences of fear of failure have been developed and tested.

For example, Kolb (1965) was interested in raising the level of academic achievement in a group of underachieving high school boys. In a 6-week summer school session, boys with IQs above 120 but grades below C participated in a program designed to teach them the characteristics of people high in *n* Achievement. The training program included the use of positive role models, the development of positive expectancies about the outcome of participating in the program, learning and practicing the *n* Achievement scoring system, and participation in games that simulated achievement-related situations. The boys also received basic summer school classroom training. A matched control group, however, received only the classroom training without the achievement training.

The initial results indicated a rise in *n* Achievement scores for the experimental group, but not the control group, during the 6 weeks of training. The critical outcome, however, was subsequent grades. After 6 months there were no differences between the experimental and control groups in school grades. But after a year and a half, the grade point average of the experimental group had improved significantly over that of the control group.

A second example is work by Dweck (1975). She studied 12 students (ages 8 to 13) who had been identified by school officials as failure-oriented. The goal of this research was to determine whether alterations in the way the students interpreted failure would improve their reactions to failure in problem-solving situations. She taught them that failure in these situations was due to lack of effort. In contrast, the accepted method of treatment using principles of behavior modification entails simply providing students with success experiences. Therefore, a control group was included in this study—a group that experienced just the customary success that had been thought effective for teaching students not to expect failure. As Dweck hypothesized, teaching children to take responsibility for failure and to attribute it to poor effort resulted in smaller decrements in performance following failure (see Figure 14-2). Part of the "achievement syndrome" is taking responsibility for our behavior, and teaching people to do this enables them to better resist the effects of failure.

## Descriptive Models: Research and Critique

### Act-Frequency Research

The act-frequency approach (Buss and Craik, 1983) represents the first explicit theory of traits to emphasize their descriptive role. Indeed, Buss and Craik specifically argue that traits are not internal entities that cause behavior, but descriptive summaries of that behavior, however it was caused. Research on the act-frequency approach has followed the same basic paradigm as the one used by Buss and Craik (1980) in their initial studies. First, participants are asked to generate a set of acts or behaviors that are characteristic of a particular trait. Buss and Craik have labeled these lists **act nominations**. These nominated acts are then edited and consolidated and are presented to a second group of participants, who rate the **act prototypicality** of each act as a representative of the trait category.

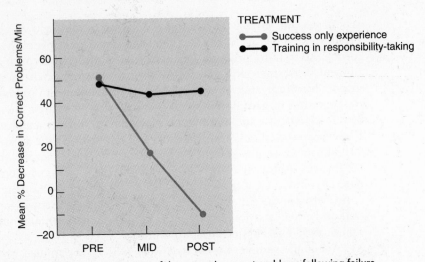

**Figure 14-2** ⊗ Mean percentage of decrement in correct problems following failure.

Adapted from "The Role of Expectation and Attribution in the Alleviation of Learned Helplessness" by Carol Dweck, *Journal of Personality and Social Psychology*, Vol. 31, No. 4, April 1975. Copyright © 1975 by the American Psychological Association.

The instructions for these ratings are based on the work of Rosch and her colleagues (e.g., Rosch and Mervis, 1975) in their study of human categorization. Specifically, subjects are asked to rate "how good an example" each act is of the trait concept. The higher the rating of the act as an example, the more central or prototypical the act is of the trait category. Some examples of the most prototypical dominant acts from Buss and Craik's (1980) study of the trait category of dominance are these:

He/she issued orders that got the group organized.

He/she decided which program they would watch on TV.

He/she demanded that he run an errand.

He/she took the lead in organizing a project.

He/she told her to get off the phone so that he/she could use it.

On the basis of the act nominations and prototypicality ratings, 100 acts that differed in their prototypicality for Dominance were assembled into an **Act Report**. A new set of participants were asked to indicate, for each of the 100 acts, whether they had ever performed that act during their lives. These participants also completed several traditional trait measures (e.g., the dominance scale from Jackson's *PRF*) of dominance.

From these data, Buss and Craik obtained several results that they interpreted as supporting the act-frequency theory of traits.

1. They found that, in the aggregate, judges exhibited a substantial degree of agreement about the relative prototypicality of the acts. This finding is consistent with the view of traits as summary categories of acts because subjects are consistent in how they structure acts within the category. In addition, participants found that deciding which acts were better examples of dominance, and which acts were worse, to be a sensible and meaningful task.

2. Consistent with psychometric principles, Buss and Craik found that aggregating the participants' dominant act reports across the 100 acts predicted their scores on the dominance scales better than any single act report. Thus, the treating traits as summaries of multiple acts increases the predictive validity of acts as indicants of traits.

3. Most interestingly, scores aggregated across the most prototypical acts predicted trait scale scores better than scores aggregated across the least prototypical acts. This finding supports the validity of organizing trait categories on the basis of the relative prototypicality of the acts they summarize.

Numerous other studies have replicated these findings on a variety of other traits, including *agreeableness, aloofness, gregariousness, quarrelsomeness, and submissiveness* (Buss and Craik, 1983). In addition, the act-frequency approach has been used to conceptualize the diagnosis of psychopathology (Buss and Craik, 1986) and personality disorders (Buss and Craik, 1987).

## The Category View of Personality Description

In addition to providing a direct procedure for assessing personality with act reports, the act-frequency approach has also been influential in fostering the application of the basic cognitive study of human categorization to personality. In 1975, Rosch provided empirical evidence supporting the view that many **natural categories** of objects and phenomena were "fuzzy" (Wittgenstein, 1953; Zadeh, 1975) with **graded membership** (for example, for the category BIRD, the instance *robin* is viewed as a better (more prototypical) example than the instance *penguin*), and **unclear boundaries** (for example, the instance *couch* falls somewhere in the murky boundary region between the categories BED and CHAIR). This view of categories differs from the **classic** view of categories, in which membership was clear and all-or-none rather than ambiguous and graded. For example, the categories EVEN NUMBER and ODD NUMBER are classical. Every even number (e.g., 2, 16, 258) is as good an example of an even number as another even number. And, a number is clearly even or odd. There is no ambiguity at the boundaries as there is for *couch*. This conceptualization of **natural categories** resulted in a tremendous amount of research and intriguing theoretical developments in cognitive psychology.

Over the years a more complex set of results began to emerge that required a variety of reconceptualizations of initial models of human categorization (e.g., Armstrong, Gleitman and Gleitman, 1983; Barsalou, 1985; 1987; Lakoff, 1987;

Smith and Medin, 1981.) However, the basic idea of natural categories has been a particularly useful and fruitful tool for studying person description. In addition to the act-frequency approach, natural category concepts have been used to study the distinction between trait and state concepts (Chaplin, John, and Goldberg, 1988), to understand the process of everyday trait description (Hampson, John, and Goldberg, 1986; John, Hampson, and Goldberg, 1991), to establish the meaning of individual trait terms (John, 1986) and to study basic human emotions (Fehr and Russell, 1984; Ortony, Clore, and Foss, 1987).

## Critique of the Act-Frequency Approach

The act-frequency approach has generally been well received by personality psychologists (Pervin, 1985), and it has generated and supported much research on personality description. However, the approach is not without its critics. In particular, Jack Block (1989) has been disenchanted with the act-frequency approach (AFA): "However, some psychologists, I among them, do not view the AFA as being especially helpful to the understanding of personality processes, personality development, and personality differences, or as offering technical or conceptual improvements in the necessary field of personality assessment" (Block, 1989, p. 234).

Block's critique is broad and concerns several features of the act-frequency approach. At a technical level, Block argues that the act-frequency approach offers little that is new to personality measurement. The acts used by Buss and Craik are indistinguishable from items that are typically used on most personality inventories. In addition, the aggregation of acts is identical to the scoring of items on traditional personality inventories; both are based on a psychometric principle that has been known for decades. Thus, according to Block, the only difference between the act-frequency approach and traditional personality assessment is the new label that Buss and Craik have applied to their procedures.

At a conceptual level, Block argues that the category view of traits offered by Buss and Craik is an oversimplification of the natural categories studied by cognitive psychologists. In addition, Block argues that the level of interjudge agreement in the prototypicality ratings of acts is unacceptably low; at the level of the individual judges, the correlations of the prototypicality ratings average about .20. It is only by aggregating the judges that the internal consistency of the ratings becomes high. Thus, for individual descriptions, trait categories based on act frequencies are too idiosyncratic to be scientifically useful. Most important, Block argues against the view of traits as purely descriptive constructs. By reducing traits to summaries of observed behavior, an understanding of that behavior is lost.

Thus, if I affirm the context-unspecifying statement, 'I demanded a backrub' (a dominance 'act' statement) the AFA is not interested in and cannot know the meaning of my yes response. Did I pay for a backrub at a massage parlor that I then did not receive? Did I in a jocular but loving vein 'demand' a backrub from my lover? Did I, at long last, having given hundreds of backrubs to others, finally 'demand' one for myself? . . . The conceptual position of AFA, by explicitly adopting the 'summary' or frequency concept of disposition view, excludes both the internal motivational context influencing the actor and the external situational context as it registers on the actor (p. 238).

Without knowledge of the motives, goals, and external constraints of a behavior, it is not possible to meaningfully assign it to a trait category. In the above example, the same behavior (demanding a backrub) has clearly different meanings for personality, depending on these other factors. On the other hand, if acts include more context (e.g., I demanded a backrub because I had paid for it and because I have been cheated by massage parlors before and I believe in standing up for my rights and not being taken advantage of), the efficiency and generality of acts will be lost. This issue is actually fundamental to any descriptive system. The more general and efficient the descriptive system, the less accurate will be the descriptions it produces. Indeed, the use of traits to describe people has been both criticized and praised for these same reasons. Block's critique of the act-frequency approach is an important caution against interpreting or applying it too broadly. However, the explicit descriptive emphasis of the approach has provided a useful counterpoint to the historical treatment of traits as causal dispositions.

## Research Based on the Big Five

The emerging consensus that five factors can adequately organize the myriad of personality characteristics is regarded by many as an important step in the development of personality as a science. Just as advances in chemistry occurred following the development of a common scheme (the periodic table) for organizing the basic elements of matter, so it is hoped that advances in personality will result from a similar organizing framework. The Big Five is already being widely used to summarize the results of research (as we saw in Chapter 5 for studies of the heritability of personality). It is also used to systematically select stimuli for personality research on other topics (e.g., Chaplin and Buckner, 1988). Finally, the Big Five is being used as a scheme for organizing clinical diagnoses, particularly the personality disorders (Widiger, 1993; Widiger and Trull, 1992)

Which Big Five? Although there have been some notable exceptions (e.g., Almagor, Tellegen, and Waller, 1995; Tellegen, 1993; Zuckerman, Kuhlman, and Camac, 1988), the robustness of five-factor solutions of personality ratings has been remarkable (Digman, 1990; John, 1990; Ozer and Reise, 1994). However, beneath this consensus there is still substantial disagreement about what the five dimensions represent (Briggs, 1992; John, 1990; Saucier, 1992).

Part of the reason for this disagreement is the difficulty and subjectivity of naming factors. Factor naming requires examining the variables that load highly on a factor and then deciding what those variables have in common. However, personality descriptive terms have multiple connotations. For example the word *stingy* means that a person is careful with money, but it also implies that this is an undesirable characteristic. *Thrifty,* on the other hand, also means that the person is careful with money, but now the implication is that this is a desirable quality (Peabody, 1967). Likewise, one person may interpret the term *friendly* to mean warm and empathic, whereas another may interpret it as talkative and outgoing. The first interpretation of *friendly* emphasizes its qualities of agreeableness (Factor II), whereas the second interpretation emphasizes its qualities of extroversion (Factor I). Many personality terms are such **blends** of the Big Five factors (Hofstee, de Raad, and Goldberg, 1992).

The other reason for alternative interpretations of factors is that the results of a factor analysis depend on the specific variables that were factored. If a particular type of characteristic is omitted from the analysis, then that characteristic cannot appear on any factor. Given the dependence of factor analysis on the variables in the analysis, the consistency of the Big Five solution across cultures and languages (e.g., Paunonen, Jackson, Trzebinski, and Forsterling, 1992) age groups (Donahue, 1994), and data sets (Costa and McCrae, 1988; McCrae and Costa, 1989; McCrae, Costa, and Busch, 1986; Peabody and Goldberg, 1989) is remarkable.

However, there have been exceptions to this consistency. For example, Tellegen and Waller (1987) argued that the Big Five is based on personality descriptors that deliberately exclude evaluative terms (e.g., excellent, ordinary, evil, decent) and state or mood descriptors (e.g., happy, anxious). When such terms are included in factor analyses, a "Big Seven" emerges. This Big Seven includes two evaluative factors and variants of the Big Five (Tellegan, 1993). Table 14-7 presents a sampling of the different interpretations of the Big Five Factors. The major points of controversy in interpreting the Big Five concern Factors I, II and III, and V. Factor I is typically called extroversion, but there are several aspects of extraversion that have been emphasized by different theorists (McCrae and Costa, 1987). For some, assertiveness is a key element, whereas for others, confidence and a self-assured happiness is the central component. Moreover, sociability, a quality normally associated with extroverts, is not generally represented by this factor (Watson, Clark, McIntyre, and Hamaker, 1992).

Factor III is typically called conscientiousness. This label is itself a problem because the term *conscientious* is itself a blend of Factor III and Factor II, agreeableness. In Eysenck's three-factor system, agreeableness and conscientiousness are represented by the psychoticism factor. Specifically, high scores on the psychoticism scale on the *Eysenck Personality Questionnaire* are associated with low scores on measures of agreeableness and conscientiousness. The combination of these two factors seems to define individuals who are well liked (warm and dependable) or strongly disliked (disagreeable and undependable).

Table 14-7

## Various Interpretations of the Big Five Factors

| Factor | I | II | III | IV | V |
|---|---|---|---|---|---|
| *Investigator(s)* | | | | | |
| Tupes & Christal (1961) | Surgency | Agreeableness | Dependability | Emotional stability | Culture |
| Norman (1963) | Surgency | Agreeableness | Conscientious-ness | Emotional stability | Culture |
| Digman & Takemoto-Chock (1981 | Extraversion | Friendly Compliance | Will to achieve | Ego strength (Anxiety) | Intellect |
| Goldberg (1989) | Surgency | Agreeableness | Conscientious-ness | Emotional Stability | Intellect |
| McCrae & Costa (1985) | Extraversion | Agreeableness | Conscientious-ness | Neuroticism | Openness to experience |
| Botwin & Buss (1989) | Extraverted | Agreeable-Stable | Conscientious | Dominant-Assured | Intellectance-Culture |
| Peabody & Goldberg (1989) | Power | Love | Work | Affect | Intellect |

Adapted From Table 3.1 in John (1990).

Factor V is the most controversial of the Big Five. When Cattell introduced T-data measures of intelligence into his personality inventory, this aspect of personality had a clear association with intellect. Subsequently, when Cattell stopped using measures of intelligence, he labeled the factor culture or cultural sophistication. As Peabody and Goldberg (1989) have noted, if measures of intelligence are included among the variables in the factor analysis, they load with the culture variables on a factor that again is best labeled intellect. This is a clear example of how the selection of variables for the analysis can have a substantial impact on the interpretation of the resulting factors. Costa and McCrae (1985) have offered another interpretation of this factor that emphasizes characteristics such as narrow-minded versus wide interests and simple versus curious. The have labeled this factor openness to experience.

The emergence of the Big Five holds considerable promise for the field of personality. However, the robustness of the model at a general level disguises substantial controversy and uncertainty at other levels. The breadth of application of the Big Five remains to be established, as does the meaning of its factors. Jack Block (1995) has again taken on the role of critic and has urged caution amid the clamor of enthusiasm over the Big Five.

## Summary Evaluation

More than any other set of approaches, trait theory is what comes to mind when people think of personality. Traits are common concepts in both psychology and everyday human interactions. The traditional view of traits as causal dispositions that can explain behavior has been tempered by the view of traits as primarily descriptive and predictive concepts that may or may not have any explanatory status. Whether descriptive or explanatory, trait theories represent a diverse set of approaches, each with some unique and some common strengths and weaknesses.

### Allport's Strengths

The Unique Organism. Allport's approach emphasizes the uniqueness and individuality of every person. For those who view personality as the study of the individual (e.g., Lamiell, 1987), Allport's theory provides a foundation and historical justification. Allport developed and advocated a variety of idiographic methods for studying people—methods that do not require comparing people with one another or reducing people to points under a normal curve. Allport's studies of expressive behavior demonstrated these methods on an important facet of human behavior. Likewise, his concept of functional autonomy emphasized accepting human behavior as it occurs and not demanding that it always be interpreted as a means to an end. Finally, the humanistic theme of his research emerged in his belief that human beings are oriented toward the future and that a deterministic analysis of their past is not sufficient for understanding them.

The Rational Person. Allport emphasized the importance of studying human personality in normal, as opposed to neurotic or distressed, individuals. He argued that normal individuals exhibit a level of rationality and self-awareness that allows them to directly provide information about themselves. There was no need to restrict the assessment of personality and behavior to techniques that disguise the goals of the research (e.g., projective techniques) or that rely on individuals (e.g., trained observers) other than the subject to provide information about the person. Indeed, the individual research participant is viewed as a collaborator in the search for understanding rather than as a subject of those efforts. Thus, Allport provided the foundation for the use of self-report questionnaires, personal letters and documents, and a subject's free descriptions to assess personality. His study of values is an influential self-report measure that is still in use.

### Allport's Weaknesses

Conceptual Ambiguity. The most obvious criticism that can be made about Allport is his conceptual imprecision and ambiguity. Examples are the "proprium," which is defined as including everything that could conceivably related to an individual's personality. The issue of what this includes is not addressed.

Another example is "functional autonomy." How and why it develops is not specified. Likewise, it is not clear whether all motives are functionally autonomous. If they are not, the criteria for deciding which are functionally autonomous, which are not, and why are not specified. One result of this ambiguity is the small amount of research that has been based on Allport's theory. At a general level, Allport's ideas are widely cited, but almost no research has been stimulated by his theory or has demonstrated its utility.

**The Nomothetic Critique.** Allport's emphasis on idiographic methods is regarded by many as his most important contribution. But idiographic methods have been criticized as failing the scientific requirement of replication. If a method is designed to yield unique and idiosyncratic results, those results can not be verified by replication. In addition, the study of unique individuals will not produce general principles for understanding behavior and personality. Allport's plea for the study of individuality can lead at best to pointless ruminations about individual cases that have no generalizability to others.

## Cattell's and Eysenck's Strengths

Although the theories and methods of Cattell and Eysenck differ in a variety of ways, the strengths and weaknesses of their approaches are similar.

**A Rigorous Empirical Approach.** Both Cattell and Eysenck have emphasized rigorous research with clearly defined concepts that are subject to strong empirical evaluation. Their theories are based on, and evaluated by, carefully collected objective data and replicated findings. Both investigators have written prolifically on a wide variety of topics in personality. The magnitude of Cattell's work is awe-inspiring. The hundreds of publications and thousands of separate factor analyses attest to his convictions. Eysenck is not far behind. The sheer amount of data collection and analysis, and the accompanying theoretical structure to support the results, are achievements of the first magnitude for both individuals.

**Factor Analysis.** For both Eysenck and Cattell, factor analysis is the centerpiece of their analytic strategies. Although this method remains controversial, its contribution to refining and summarizing the large number of correlations typical of personality research is important. Indeed, factor analysis is a widely used tool outside of personality psychology. As a method of multivariate analysis, it lends itself to the complex study of many simultaneously interacting variables. Thus, it has provided a means for psychologists to test more complex, and therefore more realistic, theories of human behavior. Cattell has been instrumental in developing and elaborating factor-analytic techniques for discovering underlying causal elements in a set of related variables. Eysenck has developed the use of factor analysis to test theories of relations.

A Focus on the Basic and Most Important Individual Differences.  Both Cattell and Eysenck have focused on a central issue of personality psychology: the comprehensive identification and classification of the stable, enduring traits of personality. They have identified and promoted different basic structures, but their basic goal has been the same. Their work has also provided a foundation for the strong interest in developing structural models of personality which has become a major focus of personality, research in the past decade.

## Cattell's and Eysenck's Weaknesses

Data Sources.  Cattell in particular has been criticized for the indiscriminate use of data from sources that are unrepresentative or tests that have questionable validity. It sometimes appears that Cattell employs numerous measures in the hope that he will discover meaningful factors. More often this "shotgun" approach will result in random patterns of correlations and the discovery of factors that are difficult to interpret. This may account for the large number of factors (16) in Cattell's system relative to Eysenck's system (3) or the Big Five. Eysenck, on the other hand, carefully selects tests on the basis of their hypothesized connection with a set of factors. However, both Eysenck and Cattell rely primarily on self-report questionnaires. The extent to which self-reports reflect subjects' biases or response styles rather than their true thoughts and behavior is an issue that Cattell and Eysenck often overlook.

Strong Opinions and Idiosyncratic Presentation.  Neither Cattell nor Eysenck has been shy about defending his theories and the structures that have resulted from these methods. Their demand for rigor and their critical skills have been applied most strongly to those who have proposed alternative structures or criticized their methods. This attitude has made Cattell and Eysenck and their students appear dogmatic. In addition, Cattell in particular has an idiosyncratic writing style that has made his complicated theories and their sophisticated mathematical formulations almost impossible to follow. Cattell's fondness for neologisms in naming his traits has made it difficult to compare his theory with other theories. This has not been of much concern for Cattell because of his belief that these other theories are incorrect! To be fair, for those who have expended the effort to understand Cattell, his ideas and methods can generally provide significant and interesting insights.

Factor Analysis.  Factor analysis is a powerful statistical tool, but many scientists have been strongly critical of it. Because factor analysis is a set of techniques that are based on mathematical formulas and computer analysis, its results are often viewed as objective and robust. However, factor analysis requires subjective decisions that can dramatically affect the results. These decisions include the number of factors to extract, the specific analytic method to use to identify factors, the criteria for determining the loadings of the variables on the factors (factor rotation), whether factors should be independent (orthogonal) or related (oblique), and the names to be assigned to factors. In addition, the results of a factor analysis depend crucially on the variables chosen for the analysis. There is widespread debate among factor theorists about how each of these decisions should be made. The differences in opinion account for the large number of different results in the analysis of personality data. Thus, factor analysis is not likely to produce a replicable structure, let alone identify a "true" one (Peterson, 1965).

## Murray's Strengths

**Intensive and Multidisciplinary Research.** Murray emphasized sustained contacts with subjects and an interdisciplinary approach to understanding personality. Thus, he explicitly recognized the limitations imposed by one-session studies with few measures for adequately characterizing an individual. He also recognized the importance of using multiple observers in his diagnostic council—observers that represented different disciplines and approaches.

**Situational Variables.** Murray was an advocate of needs as internal motivators of human behavior, and his work had a strong psychodynamic emphasis. However, Murray's concept of press explicitly recognized the importance of situational factors in human personality. His work was an early version of contemporary studies of person-×-situation interactions.

***n* Achievement.** The study of achievement and the factors that promote it has been a major focus of personality and social psychology. Under the influence of the work of McClelland and Atkinson a theory of achievement has emerged and has been widely examined. Innovative applications of achievement theory and measurement technology have occurred for such concerns as understanding economic growth and enhancing individual achievement and for studying the effect of attributions on achievement motivation.

## Murray's Weaknesses

**Conceptual Ambiguity.** The breadth of Murray's theory has resulted in some ambiguity. It is a difficult theory to empirically evaluate, and as a result, Murray's methods have been more widely adopted than his substantive views.

**Questionable Measures.** The reliance of Murray and McClelland on the projective TAT for much of their research limits the generalizability of their results and the efficiency of their studies. The TAT requires extensive administration time, and it is difficult to score. Moreover, there are serious doubts about the measure's reliability.

## Descriptive Theories: Strengths

A Uniform Language.   The development of compelling scientific explanations generally requires a clear, compelling, and consensual description of the phenomenon to be explained. In chemistry there is the periodic table; in biology there is the taxonomic classification of organisms by phyla, classes, families, species, and so on. Descriptive models of personality have begun to provide a similar taxonomic system for the complex language of personality. Although far from universally accepted, the Big Five is a robust descriptive model that is beginning to provide a common organizational framework for the first time since the ancient Greeks.

A Revival of Traits as Scientific Constructs.   The view of traits as descriptive and, in the aggregate, predictive of behavior, rather than as dispositional, causal, and explanatory, has removed many objections to traits as scientific concepts. This view avoids the deadly circularity of claiming to have explained behavior simply by describing it ("He is friendly because he is friendly"). It also reconciles the concept of traits, via the psychometric principle of aggregation, with the empirical finding that trait measures are not strongly related to individual instances of behavior in specific situations.

## Descriptive Theories: Weaknesses

Lack of Theory.   Descriptive models of personality, particularly the Big Five, are not the product of a theory. Instead, these models are empirically discovered from the pattern of correlations among large numbers of personality descriptive terms. The danger in this approach is that it makes it difficult to understand and explain results that are inconsistent with a descriptive model. It also leaves a gap in our knowledge because the question "Why Five (or Three, or Seven, or Sixteen)" has no compelling answer. It leaves personality psychologists in the same position as the frustrated parent who eventually resorts to "Just because" in response to a child's series of "Why" questions.

Static Individuals.   Once an individual has been described by a series of traits, there is a tendency to view those descriptions as rigidly stable. There is generally no indication in the description of how an individual's personality has developed or how we can expect it to change. No descriptive theory suggests that individuals never change or that behavior never varies from situation to situation. However, the approach does not address issues about development, change, and therapeutic intervention. Indeed, it is left to the other theories that have been reviewed in the earlier chapters of this text to address these issues.

# Summary

- The idiographic approach advocated by Allport is illustrated by his *Letters from Jenny*. The intuitive analysis of these letters allowed him to infer eight traits that described her personality.
- Another illustration of Allport's concern with uniqueness is shown by his studies of expressive behavior, which he saw as a basic to central dispositions. This was, however, a nomothetic series of studies.
- Allport's best-known personality measure is the Study of Values, which assesses value orientations along six dimensions.
- Cattell's research exemplifies the multivariate strategy, that is, obtaining and simultaneously evaluating many measures on the same person. He prefers this to the bivariate approach, which focuses on one variable at a time.
- The technique of factor analysis was illustrated on the issue of describing interpersonal behavior. On the basis of correlations among a set of measures of interpersonal behavior, common aspects of subsets of these measures are identified, their loadings on these common factors are calculated, and the factors are named on the basis of these factor loadings.
- Cattell uses three data sources: life records (L-data), self-rating questionnaires (Q-data), and objective tests (T-data).
- Cattell has empirically derived 16 source traits through factor analysis. The 16 P-F Questionnaire was devised to obtain self-ratings from subjects relevant to these 16 source traits.
- Cattell has developed a statistical tool, multiple abstract variance analysis, to assess the relative contributions of heredity and environment to a given trait.
- Cattell developed several analytic techniques to address change and instability in human behavior. The P-technique analyzes the stability and instability of one person's behavior over time. The differential R-technique is a method for factoring changes in measures over time. The Q-technique is a means of identifying people's roles in various situations.
- The research of another noted trait theorist, Eysenck, was described, and his method of criterion analysis was illustrated. This method dictates that we start with a hypothesis about the nature of personality structure. Measures are selected on the basis of this hypothesis.
- Eysenck's three-factor model has been reinterpreted by Gray on the basis of a strong biological theory involving behavioral activation and behavioral inhibition systems. Cloninger has offered another interpretation.
- Murray views traits as underlying "needs that motivate behavior." His legacy to personality theory is the intensive study of individuals, the use of a diagnostic council, and the development of the TAT method.
- Of Murray's needs, *n* Achievement has been most widely studied. McClelland developed a standardized TAT method for identifying *n* Achievement that has been validated in a variety of ways. Atkinson has developed a theory that has resulted in techniques for enhancing achievement strivings.

- Research on the act-frequency approach to personality description was summarized. The research relies on act nominations and prototypicality ratings. Block, however, has been critical of this approach.
- The category view of traits as summaries of behavior has been applied to several issues including the study of states, emotions, and everyday personality description.
- The Big Five is emerging as a consensual descriptive structure for personality. However, there is still substantial disagreement about the specific nature of the Big Five factors.
- Allport's particular strengths are his emphasis on the unique organism and his view of the individual as a rational being.
- There is a conceptual ambiguity in Allport's theory, and some view his idiographic methods as nonscientific.
- Cattell and Eysenck bring to personality theory and research a method that is rigorous, objective, and empirical. Their use and development of factor-analytic techniques to identify and describe trait structure are notable achievements.
- Cattell's and Eysenck's strong reliance on self-report data has the potential for limiting the structures they have identified. In addition, they both have strong opinions that has given their work dogmatic overtones.
- Although factor analysis is a powerful and sophisticated tool, there is substantial subjectivity in its application. The results of factor analyses can be difficult to replicate, and their interpretation can be controversial.
- Murray's influence comes more from his conduct of personality research than from his theory of needs.
- The *n* Achievement tradition benefited from Murray's work and provided a model projective method of measuring motives. It also has produced a theory of achievement along with a series of methods for increasing achievement striving.
- Descriptive models may provide a uniform language that can improve personality research. The descriptive/predictive rather than the dispositional/explanatory view of traits has also revitalized the field.
- Descriptive models are generally atheoretical and are best used in conjunction with the explanatory theories described in the earlier chapters of this text.

# Part 3

## Applications of Personality Theory and Research

In Part 1 the general field of personality was described and the major methods for studying and assessing personality were presented. Part 2 concerned the major perspectives and their associated theories of personality and personality description. At this point the student should have a relatively detailed knowledge of personality psychology but may be feeling the temptation to ask, "So what?" In this final section we attempt to provide some answers to this question by considering the application of personality to several different and important areas of human functioning.

Part 3 consists of four chapters. Chapter 15 concerns intellectual activities and abilities. The nature of intelligence, its relation to personality, and some important personality characteristics that have an impact on how people approach the task of understanding events in their lives are discussed. In Chapter 16 the relation of personality to mental and physical health is considered. It has become increasingly clear that personality variables have a crucial impact on how people react to and cope with stress, anxiety, and negative experiences. Chapter 17 concerns how personality may affect performance and satisfaction in the workplace. It is now commonplace for employers to consider personality variables in deciding who to hire and who to promote. Likewise the impact of personality on productivity, leadership, and employee relations is a target of increasing study and application. Chapter 18 concerns the role of personality in understanding the differences and similarities between men and women. Each of the major theories of personality can provide an explanation for the development of gender differences in personality. Thus, this chapter also provides a final review of each of the major approaches to studying personality.

# Chapter 15
# Personality and Intellect

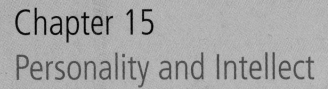

Personality and Intelligence
    Judgments Versus Sentiments
    Differences Between Measures of
       Intelligence and Personality
    Reconciling Intelligence with Personality
       Theory
Nature of Intelligence
    Definitions
    Prototype Approach
Formal Theories of Intelligence
    g Versus s factors
    Hierarchical Models
    The Structure of Intellect Model
    Cognitive Theories
    Triarchic Theory
Assessment of Intelligence
    The Stanford-Binet
    The Wechsler Scales
Major Correlates of IQ
    Correlation and Explanation
Heritability of Intelligence
    Role of Heredity
    Studies of Adopted Children
    Environments, Genes, and Innate
      Potential

Group Differences in Intelligence
    Ethnic Differences
    Social Policy Implications
    Test Bias
Intelligence: Summary and Conclusion
Creativity
Cognitive Style
Need for Cognition
Absorption
Openness to Experience
Summary

Intelligence is by far the most widely studied individual difference variable in psychology. It is hard to imagine any comprehensive account of human behavior without the inclusion of intelligence. Intelligence, ability, competence, or whatever term we choose is viewed as the single most crucial variable for predicting educational attainment, job performance, and general success in life. Most tendencies to think, act, or feel in characteristic ways are affected by intelligence. Indeed, intelligence is so broadly related to human thought and behavior that it is difficult to think of a characteristic that is *not* related to intelligence, or to improve upon measures of general intelligence for predicting most performance criteria. Concerns about intelligence in children launched the entire field of clinical psychology—a field that now boasts more members than any other single branch of psychology. For the general public, psychology is often considered synonymous with "mental testing."

Given the value placed on intelligence and its widespread influence on employment and educational decisions, it is not surprising that society has devoted considerable resources to measuring intelligence and trying to raise the level of individuals' intelligence. It is also not surprising that people view intelligence seriously, and that controversy has surrounded the concepts of intelligence and intelligence testing since their inception. Some of the most controversial issues concern possible differences among ethnic groups in intelligence, the genetic influence on intelligence, and the bias of intelligence tests against certain groups that may result in unfairness and discrimination. Consider these examples:

1. In 1986 Judge Robert Peckham upholds his judgment that California schools may not use IQ tests to assess black children for placement in special education classes.

2. In a 1977 editorial, a college newspaper proclaims, "The only fair IQ test is no test at all."

3. At the 1976 meetings of the American Psychological Association in Washington, D.C., Ralph Nader assails the influence of educational testing on the lives of students.

4. In 1994, following the publication of *The Bell Curve* (subtitled *Intelligence and Class Structure in American Life*) (Herrnstein and Murray, 1994), scholarly electronic mail networks come alive with a bitter exchange of comments pro and con. In a manner reminiscent of the Civil War, former friends and colleagues, and students and mentors, engage in heated and personal attacks over the book that end their friendships and professional collaboration.

5. In 1995, the president of the Behavior Genetics Association publicly discusses genetic differences among racial groups, as a possible cause of cognitive and behavioral differences among those groups. This results in widespread calls for his resignation and the resignation of many prominent members from the association.

This chapter concerns intelligence and its position in personality psychology. However, the title of this chapter is "Personality and *Intellect*" to emphasize that personality psychology has historically had an uneasy relation with intelligence and mental ability as a personality variable. Within personality, intellect refers to a broader array of behaviors, interests, and motives—such as cognitive style, curiosity, openness to experience, sophistication, and need for cognition—than the traditional **intelligence quotient**, or **IQ**.

## Personality and Intelligence

Personality traits are usually treated as **individual difference variables:** variables whose meaning derives from the inference that differences among individuals' scores on the variable reflect differences in the degree to which those individuals have the attribute indicated by the variable. Although alternatives have been suggested (e.g., Lamiell, 1987; Wilson, Chaplin, Foster, and White, 1996), personality psychology is dominated by the individual difference perspective. As a powerful and widely studied individual difference construct, intelligence might be expected to play a prominent role in personality psychology. However, intelligence is often curiously absent from personality texts and is generally not included in personality research.

### Judgments Versus Sentiments

Perhaps the most persuasive reason for separating the study of intelligence from the study of personality is that the construct of intelligence and its associated measures are qualitatively different from personality constructs and their associated measures. Intelligence is an ability, whereas personality constructs are characteristics. Thus, measures of intelligence are based on **judgment responses**, that is, responses that can be scored objectively as correct or incorrect. Personality measures are based on **sentiment responses** (Nunnally, 1978), that is, responses that do not have an objective right or wrong answer. The intelligence question "Is Canada north of the United States?" has an objective correct answer. Although a person's answer to the personality question "Do you enjoy chatting with friends?" may be correct or incorrect depending upon whether or not that person is telling the truth, there is no objective way of scoring the answer right or wrong.

### Differences Between Measures of Intelligence and Personality

This difference between personality constructs and intelligence has several important implications. First, the psychometric properties of measures of intelligence, such as their validity and reliability, tend to be higher and more easily established than those properties for measures of personality. In addition, measures of intelligence are **maximum performance tests**, that is, tests for which it is not possible for a person to score higher—except by chance—than their maximum level of performance allows. It is not generally possible for a person to fake a higher level of intelligence than he or she has. For personality measures it is possible for individuals to consciously or unconsciously answer in ways that make them appear to have more of the characteristic than they actually do. Individuals can appear more friendly than they really are, but they can not pretend to be smarter than they are. Finally, if I claim to be a friendly person but my friend claims that I am not, it is hard to know who is right. Discrepancies among measures of personality are not easily resolved. Thus, measures of intelligence are generally considered to be more objective and are viewed with less suspicion than are personality measures. Indeed, in his strong critique of personality, Mischel (1968) singled out intelligence and measures of abilities as exceptions to his general conclusion that measures of traits are poor predictors of behavior.

## Reconciling Intelligence with Personality Theory

Despite these differences, intelligence has appeared in some theories of personality. As noted in Chapter 13, Cattell initially included an objective intelligence test in his *Sixteen Personality Factors Questionnaire*. For a variety of reasons, including the difficulty of combining this measure with personality ratings, Cattell dropped the intelligence test from later versions of the questionnaire. This is viewed as the point in history when intelligence, the most powerful of individual difference variables, disappeared from the study of personality.

More recently, the debate among Big Five theorists about the meaning of Factor V reflects the controversy over the extent to which intelligence might be considered a personality variable. Costa and McCrae have labelled Factor V "openness to experience." Items that measure this factor include "I have a lot of intellectual curiosity" and "I am intrigued by the patterns I find in art and nature." Such items reflect behaviors, attitudes, and interests that might be associated with an intelligent person, but they do not refer directly to that person's ability. For example, a person could answer true to both questions, but be below average in intelligence. In contrast, Goldberg, John, and others have labeled Factor V "intellect." For these theorists, Factor V, in addition to the behaviors and attitudes of openness, also explicitly refers to intelligence and ability. For example, in his Big Five Inventory, John includes the items "is a clear thinker, intelligent" and "is ingenious, a deep thinker."

Whether intelligence should be included in the study of personality or treated as a separate domain will continue to be a matter of discussion. The inclusion of this chapter in this textbook reflects the authors' belief that the domain of intelligence is too important a human characteristic to be omitted from the study of personality. However, in viewing intelligence as a component of personality, we emphasize **intellect**, which includes the behaviors, motives, attitudes, and interests generally associated with intelligence, as well as the mental abilities.

# Nature of Intelligence

All cultures recognize individual differences in the general ability we call intelligence, but there is much less agreement about its specific components, causes, and consequences (Weinberg, 1989). Most often it is considered to be a stable trait that exhibits substantial cross-situational consistency. However, there are many views about intelligence, how it should be measured, and how it should be studied (Sternberg and Detterman, 1986).

## Definitions

There is no universally accepted definition of **intelligence**. However, most definitions emphasize one of the following broad perspectives: (1) the ability to adjust to the environment, adapt to new situations, or deal with a broad range of situations; (2) the ability to learn or the capacity for education (broadly defined); and (3) the ability to employ abstract concepts and to use a wide range of symbols and concepts.

## Prototype Approach

In response to the varied definitions of intelligence, some psychologists have adopted a **prototype** approach to defining and assessing intelligence. The essence of this approach is the recognition that there is no single defining characteristic of intelligence. Instead, intelligence is viewed as consisting of an imperfectly correlated "bundle" of features and aspects that together represent intelligence. As Neisser (1979) argues:

> Our confidence that a person deserves to be called "intelligent" depends on that person's overall similarity to an imagined prototype, just as our confidence that some object is to be called "chair" depends on its similarity to prototypical chairs. There are no definitive criteria of intelligence, just as there are none for chairness; it is a fuzzy-edged concept to which many features are relevant. Two people may both be quite intelligent and yet have very few traits in common—they resemble the prototype along different dimensions. Thus, there is no such thing as *chairness*—resemblance is an external fact and not an internal essence. There can be no process-based definition of intelligence, because it is not a unitary quality. It is a resemblance between two individuals, one real and the other prototypical. (p. 185)

This prototype approach was used by Sternberg and his colleagues to develop an understanding of people's informal theories of intelligence. For example, Sternberg, Conway, Ketron, and Bernstein (1981) carried out three experiments. First, they approached people studying in a college library, entering a supermarket, and waiting in a train station and asked them to list behaviors characteristic of either intelligence, academic intelligence, everyday intelligence, or "unintelligence." Second, experts and laypersons (including students) were asked to rate how important or characteristic of intelligence the behaviors listed in the first experiment really were. Third, laypersons were given written descriptions of behaviors characterizing fictitious people and asked to rate the intelligence of those people. The investigators found that people do have well-developed prototypes for intelligence and that these prototypes are similar for layperson and expert alike. Furthermore, intelligence seemed to be constituted of several behaviors, including problem solving, verbal facility, social competence, and possibly motivation.

## Formal Theories of Intelligence

A theory of intelligence needs to specify its components, origins, and influences. Many theories of intelligence have been proposed. Some have emphasized neurological and biological aspects; others have focused on learning and developmental features (Maloney and Ward, 1976). However, psychometric approaches based on factor analysis have had the greatest impact on education, assessment, and social policy (Brody and Brody, 1976).

### g Versus s factors

Charles Spearman (1927) decided on the basis of factor analyses of test scores that all intellectual activity was dependent on a broad, **general factor (g) of intelligence.** He also recognized that several **specific factors (s factors)** were important, and his theory was that the common element in tests could be represented by *g*, whereas those elements unique to a given test would be *s* factors. Nonetheless, his emphasis was on intelligence as a broad, generalized entity. As Sternberg (1995) has noted, "This idea was the theoretical basis for the notion that you could capture all that really matters about human abilities in a single number" (p. 1).

In contrast, Louis Thurstone's (1938) factor analyses persuaded him of the importance of **group factors of intelligence**—factors neither as broad as *g* nor as specific as *s* factors. He described seven group factors: number, word fluency, verbal meaning, perceptual speed, spatial judgment, reasoning, and memory. Yet another view was presented by Edward Thorndike and his colleagues (Thorndike, Bregman, Cobb, and Woodyard, 1926), who argued against a broad *g* factor and claimed instead that intelligence should be considered as numerous specific factors. More recently, Gardner (1983) has also proposed a theory of multiple intelligences, including linguistic, musical, logic-mathematical, spatial, bodily-kinesthetic, intrapersonal, and interpersonal. The disagreements among these theorists are similar to those discussed in Chapter 13 among Eysenck, Cattell, Goldberg, and others who have attempted to specify the structure of human personality. Because of the different methods of factor analysis used and the varieties of assumptions made by the various investigators, several interpretations of the same set of correlations are often possible.

### Hierarchical Models

One way to reconcile broad general factors with more specific ones is by combining them into a hierarchical model. Cattell (1963) and Horn (1968) have proposed their versions of a **hierarchical model of intelligence**, in which more specific abilities are combined into broader abilities. Their models emphasize the central role of a *g* factor. Subsumed under the *g* factor are somewhat narrower group factors, and at the lowest level are the specific factors. Moreover, Cattell has partitioned Spearman's *g* into two components: **fluid ability** (biological capacity) and **crystallized ability** (capacities attributable to culture-based learning). An example of a hierarchical model of intelligence is shown in Figure 15-1.

## The Structure of Intellect Model

The most detailed model of specific intellectual abilities is Guilford's (1967) **structure of intellect model**. In contrast to other theorists who inferred a model of intelligence from the results of their factor analyses, Guilford (1967) proposed a model and then developed measures based on his model to evaluate its validity. His model classifies intelligence along three dimensions: **operations** (what the subject does; for example, memory), **contents** (the material or information on which the operations are performed; for example, visual stimuli), and **products** (the form in which information is processed; for example, classifications). Guilford's model consisted of all possible combinations of five operations, five contents, and six products, which result in 150 separate intellectual abilities.

## Cognitive Theories

The cognitive revolution in psychology has also had an impact on theories of intelligence. In contrast to theories based on factor analyses of items that assess what people know, cognitive theories of intelligence focus on the processes a person uses in an attempt to solve a problem—from the moment a stimulus is recognized to the person's verbal or motor response. This is a dynamic view of intelligence compared with the older static theories of mental components. Investigators sometimes focus on speed of information processing and sometimes on strategies of processing. One of the crucial issues in this approach is whether there is a central processing mechanism (Gardner, 1983). Other important issues are whether processing elements change as the person develops and whether there are general problem-solving skills or only skills specific to certain ability areas.

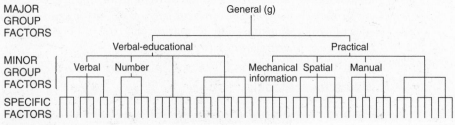

**Figure 15-1**  Hierarchical model of the organization of abilities.

From *The Structure of Human Abilities* by P. E. Vernon [London: Methuen], 1960. Copyright © 1960 by Methuen and Co.

## Triarchic Theory

Sternberg (1985a) has proposed a **triarchic theory of intelligence**. He argues that intelligence is influenced by three types of mental processes or components. The **metacomponents** are those processes that direct problem solving and include defining the problem, selecting the steps to solve the problem, and deciding when the problem is solved. The **performance components** are the processes that actually solve the problem and are specific to the type of problem the person is confronting. The might include inferring relations, classification, and transforming the problem. Finally, there are **knowledge-acquisition components** that concern how a person learns and stores knowledge that will be used to solve future problems.

The term *triarchic* is used to emphasize that intelligence impacts three aspects of our lives: dealing with our internal processing of information, dealing with experience, and dealing with the external world. The internal aspect of intelligence consists of processes involved in thinking, the experiential aspect of intelligence concerns how we profit from experience by making some processes automatic, and the external aspect of intelligence concerns how we adapt to and mold our environments. Sternberg emphasizes that the important aspect of intelligence is *how* we acquire and use knowledge rather than *what* the content of knowledge is.

Sternberg (1995) has criticized traditional theories and measures of intelligence as focusing too much on performance components that emphasize the individual's prior knowledge. He argues that knowledge-acquisition components and metacomponents need to be included in the assessment of a person's intelligence. Including those components would make the measure applicable to a broad array of life domains, such as social intelligence, everyday problem solving ("practical intelligence"), and emotional intelligence (Goleman, 1995). Current measures of intelligence are limited to the particular type of knowledge—academic and verbal intelligence—that the elite of our society values. Broadening the assessment of intelligence would make the measures more generally useful and reduce the influence of a particular value system on how society evaluates and treats people.

> Personally, I'm lucky. Our culture values writing, and I'm a decent writer. Not every culture even has analogous written forms of expression, however. Put me in a culture that highly values hunting skills, navigational finesse under the stars, or, for that matter physical prowess, and I will look stupid pretty fast. . . . There is nothing special about IQ over the range of space and time, even if we make it special in our current culture" (Sternberg, 1995, p. 7).

## Assessment of Intelligence

Sternberg and Wagner (1986) have developed measures based on Sternberg's triarchic theory of intelligence that show considerable promise for predicting aspects of work performance that are largely unrelated to traditional IQ measures. Historically, however, measures of intelligence were developed for making pragmatic predictions in educational and employment settings, without reference to any particular theory of intelligence That is, the goal of intelligence testing was *prediction*, not *explanation*. Indeed, the founder of intelligence testing, Alfred Binet, selected items to assess intelligence solely on the basis of their empirically discovered ability to distinguish older children from younger ones. He offered no other explanation for why the items were chosen, but then, the goal of the test did not seem to require one.

There are a vast number of measures of intelligence and ability in use. Some measures are designed for group administration; others are individually administered. Some measures are short and are designed to provide a quick assessment of general intellectual functioning, whereas other measures are long and provide a comprehensive assessment of a variety of abilities. Group tests are often used to make selection decisions in education, employment, and military settings. Some examples include the Scholastic Aptitude Test (SAT), Graduate Record Examination (GRE), Law School Admission Test (LSAT), and the Armed Services Vocational Aptitude Battery (ASVAB). The main advantage of group tests is that they can be efficiently administered to large groups of individuals and scored in a short amount of time. The disadvantage of such tests is that they do not permit as flexible or as precise an assessment of an individual's abilities as individually administered tests. Individually administered tests in which a single examiner assesses a single examinee are used primarily in clinical and educational settings where the comprehensive evaluation of an individual is required. The two best-known comprehensive individually administered intelligence tests are the Stanford-Binet and the Wechsler. These tests are the ones that most people think of as intelligence tests.

## The Stanford-Binet

The event that shaped modern methods of measuring intelligence occurred in 1905. This was the publication of the **Binet-Simon Scale**. Alfred Binet was commissioned by the Paris school system to develop a method of predicting which children would not profit from ordinary classroom instruction. The enlightened concern of the French school administrators was that teachers' subjective predictions of which children could learn in the classroom might be influenced by biases such as the child's family background or likability that were unrelated to the child's actual capacity to learn. Thus, an objective assessment of intellectual capacity was required. With the assistance of Théodore Simon, Binet assembled a scale containing items that seemed related to the types of knowledge and abilities most related to learning. Because learning was related to age, Binet reasoned that items on which older children performed better than younger children would be the most valid. Thus, the focus of intelligence testing on academic knowledge is at least partly an accident of the task that Binet was given.

During the first half of this century, the Binet test was the preeminent individual measure of intelligence. It underwent revisions in 1916, 1937, 1960, and 1972. The latest version of what has been called since 1937 the Revised **Stan-**

Alfred Binet

ford-Binet appeared in 1986 (Thorndike, Hagen, and Sattler, 1986). Until this latest revision, the Stanford-Binet had maintained its emphasis on age as the basis for defining intelligence. It was organized into 20 age levels, beginning at Year 2 and proceeding through Superior Adult Level III. There were six items at each age level. Each item passed was converted into one or two months of mental-age credit (depending on whether it was located before or after Year Level V). The number of mental-age units (MA) were summed, divided by the examinee's chronological age (CA), and multiplied by 100 (to avoid decimals). The resulting number was the **intelligence quotient (IQ)**. Thus, (MA/CA) x 100 = IQ.

The 1986 version of the Stanford-Binet is radically different from the older versions. First, it is based on a hierarchical model of intelligence. That is, a general reasoning factor *(g)* is at the top. There are two additional levels, as shown in Figure 15-2. Also shown are the specific types of items on the test and the abilities they are supposed to measure. There are, then, a series of subtests, each composed of items of the same general type but of varying levels of difficulty suitable for ages 2 through adulthood. Another difference from the older versions is the use of an adaptive testing procedure called **multistage testing**. This means that the examiner first gives the vocabulary subtest to determine the point on each remaining subtest at which testing should begin for a given person. With this adaptive format, not all examinees of the same age are necessarily given the same items. Moreover, age is no longer the basis for calculating IQ. Instead the proportion of items the examinee passes relative to his comparison group is the basis for assigning an IQ score.

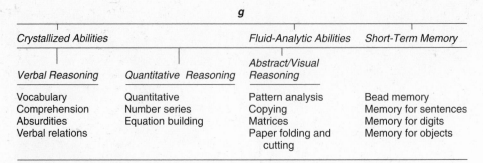

| | | *g* | |
|---|---|---|---|
| *Crystallized Abilities* | | *Fluid-Analytic Abilities* | *Short-Term Memory* |
| *Verbal Reasoning* | *Quantitative Reasoning* | *Abstract/Visual Reasoning* | |
| Vocabulary | Quantitative | Pattern analysis | Bead memory |
| Comprehension | Number series | Copying | Memory for sentences |
| Absurdities | Equation building | Matrices | Memory for digits |
| Verbal relations | | Paper folding and cutting | Memory for objects |

**Figure 15-2**  ⌘  Cognitive-abilities factors appraised in the Stanford-Binet: Fourth Edition.

## The Wechsler Scales

In 1939, David Wechsler published the **Wechsler-Bellevue Intelligence Scale.** This was an individual test specifically designed to correct some of the deficiencies of the Stanford-Binet. First, it was a test for adults, and its content was therefore more focused on adult-level knowledge. It was also less focused on classroom learning and was not as verbally oriented as the Stanford-Binet. Another difference was that all similar items were grouped together into one subtest, whereas the Stanford-Binet's diverse items were arranged in age levels. For example, in the Wechsler, all arithmetic items are grouped into one subtest and arranged in order of increasing difficulty. The entire test is divided into a Verbal Scale (six subtests) and a Performance Scale (five subtests), and, in addition to a Full Scale

David Wechsler

IQ, separate IQ scores can be calculated for each of the two scales. The deliberate inclusion of performance items was to rectify the Stanford-Binet's bias in favor of verbal items. Box 15-1 briefly describes the various Wechsler subtests. The first six subtests are verbal, whereas the last five are performance.

Since the publication of the original Wechsler-Bellevue, a series of related tests and revisions have appeared. The Wechsler Intelligence Scale for Children (WISC) was first published in 1949 and was revised in 1974 (WISC-R). The Wechsler Preschool and Primary Scale of Intelligence (WPPSI) first appeared in 1967 and was revised in 1989 (WPPSI-R). The Wechsler Adult Intelligence Scale (WAIS) was initially published in 1939 and revised in 1955. A further revision, the WAIS-R, was published in 1981.

## Major Correlates of IQ

The items on most intelligence tests have some face validity as indicants of knowledge and mental abilities associated with academic learning and classroom performance. However, the absence of a strong theory for guiding the selection of most items makes the interpretation of IQ scores difficult and controversial. Research to clarify the meaning of IQ scores relies heavily on identifying the correlates of these scores. IQs have been shown repeatedly to correlate highly with grades in school and with achievement tests that measure what has been learned in school. IQ and occupational status are also related, and this relation is found whether occupational status is defined by income or by social prestige. However, once one has entered a given occupation, degree of intelligence does not appear to separate the more eminent achievers from the less eminent ones (Matarazzo, 1972). One explanation for this is that obtaining a particular occupation requires some minimal level of ability, whereas the degree of subsequent success depends upon nonintellectual factors such as motivation, perseverance, and social skill. Because IQs are consistently found to be higher among people of higher occupational status, IQ is also related to socioeconomic status (SES) or social class. For example, the average IQ of people in the lowest 25 percent of SES is about 95, in the middle 50 percent about 101, and in the upper 25 percent about 110 (Broman, Nichols, and Kennedy, 1975).

### Correlation and Explanation

Unfortunately, the strategy of identifying the correlates of IQ to determine its meaning is inherently flawed. The problem is the well-known fact that correlation is not causation. Even after correlates of IQ scores have been identified, the reason for the correlation must be explained. Explaining why IQ is associated with academic performance, occupation, and social status is a source of tremendous controversy (e.g., Gould, 1994; Herrnstein and Murray, 1994; Sternberg,

BOX 15-1
# A Description of the 11 Wechsler Subtests

1. *Information*—29 items that assess the knowledge one acquires in the normal course of living (e.g., "What is the capital of Spain?").
2. *Comprehension*—16 items that ask the subject to explain certain procedures, interpret proverbs, or decide on a course of action (e.g., "What should you do if you find a child much younger than yourself wandering about lost?").
3. *Arithmetic*—14 items similar to ordinary arithmetic problems in elementary school texts.
4. *Similarities*—13 items, each of which names two things. The subject must identify their similarities (e.g., "How are a comb and a brush alike?").
5. *Digit Span*—Two lists of numbers that contain from three to nine digits. Each set of digits is read aloud to the subject. For the first list, the subject must repeat the digits in order. For the second list, the digits must be repeated in reverse order.
6. *Vocabulary*—35 words that the subject is asked to define.
7. *Digit Symbol*—A code-substitution task in which subjects are asked to draw its corresponding symbol in the box under each number. The test is timed, and the number of correct symbols drawn is the subject's score on the task. (see Figure below).

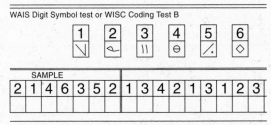

WAIS Digit Symbol test or WISC Coding Test B

**Courtesy of The Psychological Corporation.**

8. *Picture Completion*—20 cards, each with a part missing which the subject must identify (see Figure below at right).
9. *Block Design*—A series of designs printed on cards. The subject must assemble blocks to reproduce the design on each card.
10. *Picture Arrangement*—Several sets of cartoon drawings presented in a mixed-up sequence. The subject is to arrange each set so that it tells a logical, coherent story.
11. *Object Assembly*—Four puzzles or cut-out objects that the subject must put together correctly.

1995). One explanation is that IQ is determined principally by the genes. This being so, brighter individuals will rise to the top socioeconomically and pass their genes along to their offspring. Over many generations, this means that the upper classes and the higher occupations are going to be largely populated by genetically superior individuals. The reverse scenario applies to those less well endowed genetically. Such a theory has been propounded for a thousand years (Gould, 1994); its most recent manifestation appeared in *The Bell Curve* by Herrnstein and Murray (1994).

Others have argued just as forcefully that higher socioeconomic status confers on the child a greater opportunity for education, social graces, values, connections, and all the benefits likely to propel one ahead in life. For example, it is more likely that reading material will be available, along with the opportunity to take enriching vacations and so on. Moreover, Sternberg's (1995) point that most IQ tests assess a particular and limited type of ability (academic learning) that explicitly favors the upper class must be considered. IQ tests and their use in education and hiring decisions may be a "civilized" means through which the upper class maintains its favored position without resorting to force.

## Heritability of Intelligence

In any group of people, both genetic and environmental factors contribute to the variations in IQ among the members. As we saw in Chapter 5, geneticists have developed a measure called **heritability** to index the relative influence of genetic factors on the observed variation. Heritability is the proportion of variance of IQs in a given population that is the result of genetic variations among the individuals in the group.

It is important to understand that heritability applies to groups, not to individuals. If some expert claims that the heritability ratio for intelligence is .80, this does not mean that 80 percent of a person's intelligence is inherited and 20 percent is due to the environment. For the individual, environment is just as important in shaping intelligence as is heredity. But within the large group to which that individual belongs, the expert is asserting that 80 percent of the variation among members is due to genetic factors.

In addition, heritability is a *relative* index. As circumstances change, so will estimates of heritability. Thus, the assertion that 80 percent of the variation in IQ among members of a group is due to genetic factors is not an absolute truth or scientific law. Heritability is a statistic that applies only to a specific sample at a specific point in time. For example, when we report that the mean height of a sample of sixth-graders is five feet, we recognize that that estimate of height is not an absolute truth about the height of all people or even about that sample at a later point in time. As the sample develops, or as we measure new samples that

contain different age groups or different numbers of men and women, the estimate of mean height will change *relative* to those other factors. The statement
that the mean height of our sample is five feet is not a lie; it is just not true for all
time or for all samples.

With these limitations in mind, it is interesting that heritability estimates for
intelligence seem to vary with the dates of the research in question. Methodolo-
gies change and with them the resultant heritability estimates. For example, studies published before 1963 produced estimates as high as 80 percent. Those published after 1975 seemed to be closer to 50 percent. Now, the estimates are back
up to about 80 percent (Loehlin, Willerman, and Horn, 1988).

## Role of Heredity

In Chapter 5 it was observed that Galton's investigations of the hereditary basis of
genius were flawed because he could not separate the effects of environment from
those of heredity. Studies that compare fraternal and identical twins (e.g., Jensen,
1972) likewise have the problem that identical twins typically have environments
that are more alike in both subtle and overt ways than those of fraternal twins.

The study of twins reared apart (again, see Chapter 5) overcomes some of
these confounds. However, it is hard to locate such twins, we are not always sure
they really are identical, sometimes they are reared apart but only after having
spent considerable time together, and sometimes their separate environments were
actually rather similar. Although research based on such unusual individuals is
suggestive, it is not definitive in identifying the relative importance of heredity and
environment on intelligence. Although these limitations preclude a compelling explanation, there is little doubt that individuals who are more similar genetically
exhibit greater similarity in their measured intelligence. Table 15-1 provides a representative set of average correlations from a classic review of 52 studies by Erlenmeyer-Kimling and Jarvik (1963). More recent studies and surveys (e.g.,
Bouchard and McGue, 1981; Henderson, 1982) report similar correlations.

## Studies of Adopted Children

Adopted children provide another source of information about the role of heredity and environment on IQ. A common finding is that the IQs of adopted children more closely resemble the IQs of their biological parents than those of their
adoptive parents. For example, Horn (1983) found that the correlation between
adopted children's IQ and their biological parents' IQ was .28, whereas the correlation between the adopted children and the adoptive parent was only .15. This
finding was replicated by Horn, Loehlin, and Willerman (1979), who found correlations of .31 and .17 between adopted children and their biological and
adopted mothers, respectively.

On the other hand, Skodak and Skeels (1949) reported that adopted children
have IQs that clearly surpass those of their biological parents. This finding does

❧ Table 15-1

Median Correlations in IQ Scores from Individuals Who Differ in Their Degree of Relationship and Genetic Similarity

| Genetic Relationship | Developmental Status | Median Correlation |
|---|---|---|
| Unrelated persons | Reared apart | −.01 |
| Unrelated persons | Reared together | .23 |
| Foster-parent-child | Living together | .20 |
| Parent-child | Living together | .50 |
| Siblings | Reared apart | .40 |
| Siblings | Reared together | .49 |
| Dizygotic twins | Reared together | .53 |
| Monozygotic twins | Reared apart | .75 |
| Monozygotic twins | Reared together | .87 |

Adapted from "Genetics and Intelligence: A Review" by L. Erlenmeyer-Kimling and L. F. Jarvik, *Science*, December 1963, Vol. 142, p. 1478. Copyright 1963 by the American Association for the Advancement of Science. Reprinted by permission of the AAAS and Dr. L. Erlenmeyer-Kimling.

not contradict the correlational results, but it does indicate that the *level* of an adoptive child's IQ may increase if the adoptive parents provide superior environments that have beneficial effects. Likewise, Horn, Loehlin, and Willerman (1979) also identified families in which there were both an adopted child and a natural child of the same parents. The correlations between the mother's IQ and each of her two different types of children were virtually identical (.20 for mother and biological child, .22 for mother and adopted child).

Thus, we have results that are difficult to reconcile with either a strong genetic or a strong environmental position. The larger correlations between biological parents and adopted children imply some genetic influence, whereas the increase in the level of adopted children's IQs suggests an environmental impact. Moreover, these and other data are subject to a variety of interpretations. Not only is there disagreement, but the arguments can become heated, as is illustrated in the following exchange (Eysenck and Kamin, 1981). From these data, Kamin concludes:

> The data on heredity and IQ are, at best, ambiguous. Though some are consistent with the notion that IQ is heritable, others are not. The data consistent with a genetic interpretation seem equally consistent with an environmental interpretation. The plausible environmental interpretations have been ignored or soft-pedalled by behavior geneticists, which might, I have argued, reflect social and political as well as just plain professional bias. (p. 54)

But then Eysenck argues:

> Kamin is entirely wrong in thinking that there is no evidence to support the view that genetic factors play an important part in producing differences in cognitive ability between people. This notion runs counter to all the available evidence, is contradicted by every expert who has done work in the field, and leaves completely unexplained the quantitative agreement found between many different avenues of approach to the problem of estimating the heritability of intelligence. (p. 171)

## Environments, Genes, and Innate Potential

The bitterness of the controversy over genetic influences on intelligence reflects, in part, confusion about the nature of intelligence and the role of genetic and environmental factors on its development. The confusion results from a tendency to think of intelligence as a simple, unitary potential with which we are endowed at conception. Typically, this potential is viewed as determined by the genes and as basically unmodifiable. The role of the environment, according to this view, is that it can determine whether or not we achieve that innate potential. When our environment during the formative years is perfect we will come close to achieving that potential. But nothing can happen that will allow us to exceed it.

This, however, is too simplified a view. As Liverant (1960) has pointed out, we may indeed inherit an intellectual potential, but that potential will vary depending upon the environment we encounter during development. Thus, my potential IQ may be 110 if I am raised in a stimulating environment. But were I to be raised in another set of circumstances, that potential IQ might be only 87. And, as we saw in Chapters 5 and 6, our lack of knowledge about the crucial environmental influences on behavior and intelligence makes it impossible for us to adequately control for environmental effects in any behavior genetic study or to even know what constitutes a "stimulating" or "impoverished" environment.

In extreme cases we can gain some insight into the issue. For example, cretin children are born with a thyroid deficiency. Without early diagnosis and treatment, they will likely be doomed to function at a mentally defective level with an IQ scarcely above 55. But proper treatment with thyroid extract may permit them to escape this fate and function with an IQ in the normal range. What, then, is their true potential: an IQ of 55 or an IQ in the normal range? It may be that genes set the intellectual limits for a given person within a given environment. But those limits will change as the environment changes. Each person is born with multiple intellectual potentials, and for each possible environmental manipulation there is another set of limits. Therefore, it is just as fair to say that the environment sets limits as it is to say that the genes set limits. Figure 15-3 will help clarify this point.

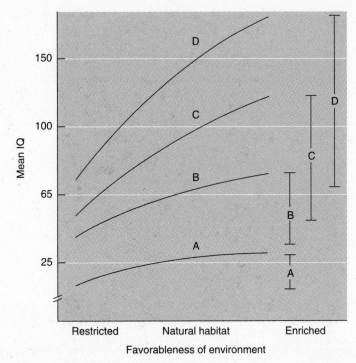

**Figure 15-3** The interaction between heredity and environment. Each curve represents an individual with a particular intellectual potential depending on the nature of the environment. The lines on the right indicate the range for each person.

## Group Differences in Intelligence

The debate over the role of genes and environments in the development of intelligence in the *individual* has been bitter and controversial. However, that debate appears mild compared with the debate over group differences in intelligence. In his critique of *The Bell Curve*, (Herrnstein and Murray, 1994), Sternberg notes that two initially unrelated developments have combined to form the basis for modern views of intelligence and its measurement. One event was Spearman's theoretical model of *g*, the hypothesis that all mental ability is influenced by a *single* broad factor. The other event was Binet's development of a test to identify an individual's level of ability to learn in school that indexed this ability with a *single* number (IQ). Spearman provided a theory but no measure of *g*, whereas Binet provided a measure with no theory.

In a sense, the contributions of Binet and Spearman were each innocuous in their own right. Together, the contributions had the potential to serve as a binary explosive. . . . All that was needed was for someone to combine the materials and light the fuse. The fuse was lit when, early in the century, psychologists such as Carl Brigham and Henry Goddard, and others, argued that the tests could be used not only to distinguish among individual's but among racial and ethnic as well as other groups. (Sternberg, 1995, p. 1)

Gould (1981) has discussed the problems with the views of these early psychologists and has documented the excesses that resulted from society's acceptance of these views. However, the fact that there are differences among socioeconomic, ethnic, and racial groups in measured IQ continues to be an explosive issue whose discussion usually ends in controversy and acrimony.

## Ethnic Differences

It is a fact that different ethnic groups differ in their average scores on measures of IQ. East Asians (e.g., Chinese and Japanese), whether they live in America or in Asia, score on the average higher than Caucasians on intelligence and achievement tests. This difference appears to be primarily on the nonverbal component of intelligence tests. Likewise, European Americans, on the average, score higher than African Americans on IQ tests. These differences occur at all levels of socioeconomic status (SES). For example, the average IQ score of whites in the lowest 25 percent on SES is 95.6, whereas for blacks the average score is 88.0. For the middle 50 percent on SES the average IQ is 101.2 for whites and 92 for blacks, and for the upper 25 percent on SES the averages are 110.9 for whites and 98.1 for blacks. Thus, the obvious difference in SES between African Americans and Caucasian Americans does not appear to explain the differences in IQ.

The fact of this difference has long been a source of discomfort and controversy, and its implications for social policy and educational practice have been hotly debated. The problem with this fact is that it is a correlational one. As noted in our discussion of the major correlates of IQ, correlational facts—in this case the relation between ethnic identity and IQ score—are not explanatory. Instead, correlational facts require an explanation, and the various explanations of this fact that have been proposed have often reflected more about our society's racial stereotypes and attitudes, or the personal inclinations of the investigator, than scientific analysis.

For example, in 1969, Arthur Jensen, an educational psychologist, wrote an article in which he asserted that the commonly observed finding that blacks, on the average, have IQs below those of whites is very likely attributable to hereditary factors. The ensuing controversy was both immediate and vehement, and it continues to this day. Although a genetic difference is one possible explanation, the fact that African Americans are at significant environmental disadvantages in our society hardly needs documentation. The discrimination and deprivation they have endured stretches so far back into American history as to be part of their cultural heritage. The reality of prejudice, discrimination, and the ensuing inequality of opportunities for blacks makes the hypothesis that they are genetically inferior to whites in intelligence untestable and unconvincing. Until racism ceases to exist and the environments of the two groups become the same, the question whether IQ differences are genetically determined is unanswerable.

Whatever hope there may be of closing the racial gap by environmental intervention will require educational, psychological, cultural, and economic programs targeted at both children and their parents. When such programs, coupled with cognitive training, begin early in life and continue through the formative years, change seems possible (Anghoff, 1988).

## Social Policy Implications

The social consequences of accepting a genetic or environmental explanation for the differences in the measured IQs of African and Caucasian Americans are not trivial. The genetic position, typified by Jensen, asserts that 80 percent of the variance in IQ scores is attributable to genetic influences. Because of this, it is argued that remedial and compensatory programs such as **Head Start** are doomed to failure. As a result of this heritability factor, the brighter individuals will move up in society and achieve better jobs, seek more education, and generally become socioeconomically advantaged (Herrnstein and Murray, 1994).

The environmental explanation of the difference has different implications. Many environmental factors can affect test performances and may place blacks in a poorer light. Samuda (1975) has reviewed several of these. For example, much of the early IQ data were gathered before the rise in black self-awareness and identity. When one has a poor self-concept or expects to do poorly, the effect on test performance can be disastrous. These problems are often compounded by schools that make little attempt to recognize the disadvantages under which a black child may labor in a system dominated by whites. The nature of IQ tests and the circumstances that surround their use clearly give white middle-class children an advantage. The amount of experience with verbal testing situations can affect the IQ obtained.

Another of Jensen's contentions was that supportive educational programs such as Head Start do not redress the IQ deficits in culturally deprived groups. But more recent evidence (e.g., McKey, 1985; Zigler and Valentine, 1979) suggests that providing disadvantaged young children with the opportunity to develop learning readiness skills prior to entering the formal school system has paid rich dividends in better academic performance and social responsibility. Other information also suggests that environmental factors rather than genetics are at work. Both Klineburg (1935) and Lee (1951) discovered that the IQs of southern black children increased when the children moved to northern cities such as New York and Philadelphia. Moreover, the extent of that increase was directly linked to the number of years they spent in northern schools. Jensen (1977) himself has reported that IQs of rural blacks in Georgia decline between the ages of 5 and 16, whereas the IQs of whites during the same years do not. Similarly, the differences in IQs between young blacks and young whites are minimal, but as the children grow older the differences become noticeable (Osborne, 1960). Finally,

Scarr and Weinberg (1976) have found that when black children are adopted by white families whose socioeconomic level is solid, these children show both IQ scores and school achievement as good as those of adopted white children.

## Test Bias

The one point of agreement between the proponents of genetic or environmental explanations is the acceptance of the differences among ethnic groups on measured intelligence as real and meaningful. An alternative perspective—one that many find more comfortable—is to dispute the difference directly. The argument is that the observed difference in scores between blacks and whites on intelligence tests is due to **test bias**. Intelligence tests were developed by and large by whites, and therefore the tests likely reflect the values, culture, knowledge and abilities of the Euro-American (white) culture. From this perspective, African Americans score lower on the tests because they are at an unfair disadvantage, not because they are less intelligent. In short, the differences in scores are not meaningful and would disappear if the tests were fair to both groups. Box 15-2 illustrates the nature of this bias.

Culture-fair Tests. The proposal that standard intelligence tests are unfair to minority group members is plausible. It is also a comforting proposition because it explains away racial differences that, regardless of their cause, raise difficult moral, educational, and social issues. Testing this proposition requires tests that are not linked to any particular cultural knowledge or values. The development and use of such **culture-fair tests** has been the target of intense scientific investigation.

Several so-called culture-fair tests have appeared. These are tests that attempt to rule out the effects of factors that distinguish one culture or subculture from another—that is, to neutralize the operation of any knowledge, strategies, and abilities that are specific to a particular culture. Ideally, the use of culture-fair tests should prevent individuals from being penalized by factors that reflect cultural background instead of innate capacity. Consider a factor as basic as language. Administering the Stanford-Binet to a child who does not speak English (or even one who comes from a family whose first language is not English) will likely produce results that reflect the language handicap. Speed of reaction is another important factor. Many tests require the person to answer items within a certain time limit or else award point bonuses for quick answers. But some cultures (and even subcultures) are not geared to quick responsiveness—they do not consider faster to be better.

In the United States, a multiracial and culturally diverse nation, questions have long been raised about the fairness of tests for those who are not from the dominant white middle or upper class. It seems unlikely that tests designed by one cultural group will be as valid for other cultural groups such as inner-city blacks, Hispanics, or rural populations. Indeed, the experiences of the white suburban child seem most relevant for a good performance on the tests. By the same token, little of a rural black child's experience seems relevant for the testing situation.

## BOX 15-2
## A Black Alternative

Many IQ tests contain items that measure, in effect, how much and what kind of information the individual has acquired as a normal part of living. Supposedly, these acquisitions reflect intellectual capacity. But what is "a normal part of living?" Some have vigorously contended that the type of information elicited by IQ tests depends primarily on the white middle-class experience. To illustrate this point, Williams (1972) described a Black Intelligence Test of Cultural Homogeneity (BITCH). A typical item is this:

Running a game means
 a. writing a bad check
 b. looking at something
 c. directing a test
 d. getting what one wants from another person or thing

The means score on this test for 100 black teenagers was 30 points higher than for 100 comparable whites.

Cronbach (1978) described the contributions of tests such as the BITCH to the issue of cultural fairness when he remarked:

To publicize BITCH as an "intelligence" test is a gesture of political propaganda. By not taking the word "intelligence" seriously, BITCH mocks and discredits established instruments and so strikes a blow to gain respect for persons who score low on them. By taking street slang seriously, BITCH dramatizes the concept of cultural pluralism. By showing educated whites an intellectual task on which they do poorly, BITCH challenges whites to defend the functional worth of other tests loaded with culture-specific tasks. (p. 250)

Situational variables in the testing interaction can also be important. For example, some studies have suggested that black children achieve lower IQ scores when the test is administered by a white examiner than when the examiner is black, although this conclusion has been questioned (Sattler and Gwynne, 1982). Whether all the differences between racial groups or between subcultures and the dominant group are simply attributable to the test or to examiner characteristics is still being debated (Lambert, 1981).

Typically, culture-fair tests adopt one of two strategies: items are employed with which everyone is thought to be equally familiar or else equally unfamiliar. A good example of a culture-fair test is the **Progressive Matrices** developed by Raven in 1938. The subject examines a series of geometric figures, tries to discover the element common in each, and then applies this knowledge to a specific problem involving those figures. Figure 15-4 presents a sample item from this test.

Another approach is through drawing a person. The **Goodenough-Harris Drawing Test** (D.B. Harris, 1963) requires children to draw pictures of a man, a woman, and of themselves. The assumption is that everyone is equally familiar with the persons being drawn, and thus the task is appropriate regardless of culture.

Although sound in theory, culture-fair tests have been difficult to develop. It appears that for some subjects, the whole idea of being tested is a foreign one, and the attempt to remove language barriers has not cancelled the subtle effects of cultural or familial background. In addition, the ambiguous content of such tests makes it difficult to determine which, if any, type of intelligence the test is assessing. Moreover, some have suggested that intelligence is culturally defined, so removing cultural knowledge and abilities from the test renders the test meaningless. Finally, minority subjects or those from other cultures continue to show deficiencies on these tests, although the differences are often not as pronounced (Kaufman, Kamphaus, and Kaufman, 1985).

**Evidence of Test Bias.** The hypothesis that intelligence tests are biased against African Americans and other minority groups seems so reasonable that it has been accepted by many without question. It has also been accepted because it is a comforting hypothesis that means that the social, educational, and economic implications of a *real* difference need not be considered. However, accepting test bias as the explanation for the differences in the performance of minority and majority group members on IQ tests is not as benign or enlightened as it may appear. In particular, the test bias hypothesis excuses us from having to confront the racism, prejudice, and economic, educational, and social inequalities that characterize our society. To the extent that these factors impact the development of intellectual ability, the differences in test performance between blacks and whites document real problems that must be solved. The test bias hypothesis allows us to avoid confronting issues that are uncomfortable and whose solution often seems impossible. Thus, before the test bias hypothesis is accepted, it is important that it be tested and evaluated. If the test bias hypothesis is not sup-

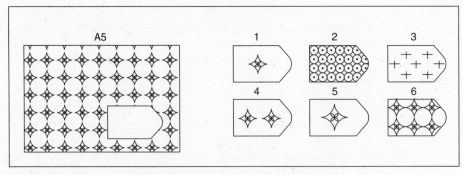

**Figure 15-4** &#x2298; Sample item from the Raven Progressive Matrices. Subjects must select from the alternatives to the right of the large box the one that fits the blank item.

From the *Raven Standard Progressive Matricies.*

ported, then we, as a society, have a great deal of work to do to eliminate those inequities.

In fact, there is little reason to believe that the differences in the average scores of blacks and whites on intelligence tests are the result of test bias. On tests designed to be culture fair, the same differences in the scores between blacks and whites are found as on traditional IQ tests. Most important, the correlations between IQ test scores and a variety of criteria are the same for blacks and whites. If the tests were biased, we would expect that blacks' scores would be less predictive of their performance on tasks requiring intellectual ability than the scores of whites. However, this difference in predictive accuracy has seldom been found, and when it has, it has proven difficult to replicate. A host of large sample studies using sophisticated psychometric techniques such as **item-response theory** have repeatedly found little evidence of bias on tests such as the Graduate Record Examination (GRE), Scholastic Aptitude Test (SAT), or any other widely used tests of intelligence and mental ability.

The clear conclusion is that test bias is not the explanation for the observed differences. As we have seen, a genetic explanation, although possible, is not testable until racism and the environmental inequalities between blacks and whites that it fosters are eliminated. Thus, at this point, we can not blame the tests, nor can we, with any scientific justification, blame genes and natural selection for the differences. We must blame society and ourselves for creating an unequal environment that disadvantages many in our nation. Fixing those inequities will be difficult and expensive, and it will require time and patience. However, that is our only reasonable and scientifically justified alternative, and it is time we got on with it.

## Intelligence: Summary and Conclusion

In this section we have provided a brief overview of the major theories of intelligence, its measurement, and its salient issues. As an ability rather than a characteristic, the inclusion of intelligence in a text on personality may seem out of place. However, to ignore intelligence would be to eliminate one of the most powerful individual difference variables from the study of human thought and action. Any discussion of personality without attention to intellectual processes must be considered incomplete. Intelligence is closely related to what Mischel (1973) refers to as competence variables. It reflects our ability to generate both cognitions and behaviors. How we act, how we interpret our experience, and how we develop our skills are all influenced by intelligence. The marked individual differences we observe in all these personal areas are affected by intellectual differences. In the remainder of this chapter, personality characteristics that are related to intelligence, but that concern values, motives, and dispositions rather than abilities, will be described.

## Creativity

One characteristic that combines intellectual ability and personality is **creativity**. Creativity is a valued characteristic that is easy to apply to specific products such as art, literature, and solutions to problems, but that has proved difficult to define in general. Some definitions of creativity include "seeing the world in new and different ways," "finding novel solutions to problems," and "generating useful ideas that combine old patterns and concepts in innovative ways." Most definitions of creativity emphasize the unusual and novel nature of creative thought but also require that the thoughts be useful and adaptive. That is, thoughts and behavior that are merely bizarre are not generally considered creative.

Although creativity is often associated with intelligence, the relation between measures of creativity and traditional intelligence tests is not strong (Horn, 1976). Indeed, Wallach (1971) argues that intelligence and creativity are separate abilities. Creativity does appear to require a minimum level of intelligence (Nicholls, 1972), but many intelligent people such as lawyers, doctors, business people, and professors never produce much of what is commonly thought of as creative. The crucial difference between creativity and intelligence is, according to many theorists (e.g., Guilford, 1959), **divergent thinking**. Divergent thinking involves generating many diverse ideas and solutions to problems. The goal of divergent thinking is to provide a range of alternatives by thinking as broadly and as freely as possible. The everyday concept of "brainstorming" refers to divergent thinking. In contrast, most measures of intelligence and most classroom learning emphasize **convergent thinking**. Thinking convergently involves narrowing a list of alternatives to converge on the correct solution. An example is a multiple-choice examination, in which the goal is to narrow the choices by eliminating options that are incorrect. Measures of creativity emphasize divergent thinking. Some examples of questions on a measure of creativity might be these: (1) List as many uses as you can for a *hammer*. (2) Imagine that people were as large as elephants, and list as many consequences of this as you can. (3) Write as many words that you can think of that begin with *M* and end with *T*.

Creativity seems to depend on several factors besides intelligence. Bloom (1985) and his colleagues at the University of Chicago developed detailed case histories of 120 exceptional individuals, such as concert pianists and artists, from a variety of fields. A crucial environmental factor in these individuals' success was high-quality training. Amabile (1983) has also written extensively on the situational factors that contribute to creativity. However, many personality characteristics are also related to creativity. In particular, a dogged determination and self-discipline to keep working were characteristic of nearly all the individuals in the University of Chicago study (Sloane and Sosniak, 1985). Likewise, research by Barron (1968) and MacKinnon (1965) suggests that creative individuals such as writers, artists, and architects are self-confident, highly motivated, and committed to their work. Roe (1953), in a study of eminent scientists, found them to be absorbed in their work, devoting enormous amounts of time to it over many years. In addition, the willingness to think divergently seems to be enhanced by the traits of independence and nonconformity (Barron and Harrington, 1981). Creative people also seem more able to tolerate ambiguity, complexity, and contradictions and to be more open to experiences. Thus, creativity seems to require not only some mental abilities such as divergent thinking, but the situational opportunities to develop those abilities and the personality characteristics to be willing to apply those abilities and take advantage of those opportunities.

## Cognitive Style

One of the most widely and intensively studied personality variables is **cognitive style**. Cognitive style refers to the characteristic manner in which an individual approaches cognitive tasks, and several styles have been identified. **Leveling versus sharpening** refers to a tendency to smooth over (level) unusual or novel aspects of a situation versus a tendency to overemphasize (sharpen) and focus on the exceptional details in a situation. **Reflectivity versus impulsivity** is based on the observation that in solving problems, some people reflect on the problem, analyze it, and think it through before acting, whereas others react to a problem quickly and impulsively on the basis of the first solution or action that comes to mind. **Field dependence versus independence** is conceptualized as a continuum that represents the extent to which an individual's perceptions and analysis depends upon (or is independent from) the context (field) in which the stimuli or problem occurs. Each of these styles is relatively independent of an individual's level of general intelligence, and each style may be adaptive or maladaptive depending on the problem and the situation.

Field dependence–independence, in particular, has exhibited stable and consistent individual differences across time and different situations. As a result, it has been widely investigated as an important aspect of personality and behavior. In 1954, Witkin and his associates (Witkin et al., 1954) discovered the ability of some individuals to resist the distraction of conflicting contextual cues. They studied this ability with the **rod-and-frame test,** in which a subject is asked to align a rod in a true vertical position when it is surrounded by a frame that was skewed from the true vertical. Individuals who can accurately place the rod at vertical regardless of the position of the surrounding frame are called field independent, whereas those whose placement of the rod is more consistent with the tilted frame are field dependent. The study of the trait of field dependence was initially based on studies of perception. However, the large and consistent individual differences on this trait moved the research into the domain of personality. Specifically, field dependence was viewed as the perceptual component of a broader personality dimension called global versus articulated cognitive style, or **psychological differentiation** (Witkin, Dyk, Faterson, Goodenough, and Karp, 1962).

One factor that contributed to the widespread study of psychological differentiation was the availability of a paper-and-pencil test, the Group Embedded

Figures Test, to assess the construct. Two demonstration items from this test are shown in Figure 15-5. Individuals who can correctly identify more embedded figures are considered more field independent. Among the many intriguing correlates of psychological differentiation is the finding that field-independent individuals use active, participant approaches to learning, whereas field-dependent persons learn from watching. Field-dependent persons appear to be better at interpersonal situations because they are more attentive to social cues, more responsive to other people, and more open emotionally. Women, on average, are more field dependent than men (Witkin et al., 1962).

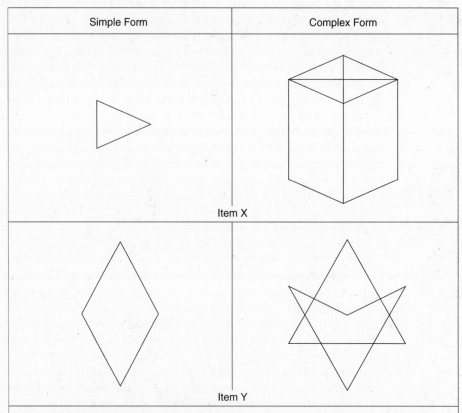

| Simple Form | Complex Form |
|---|---|
| | |

Item X

Item Y

Try to find the simple form in the complex figure and trace it in *pencil* directly over the lines of the complex figure. It is the SAME SIZE, in the SAME PROPORTIONS, and FACES IN THE SAME DIRECTION within the complex figure as when it appeared alone.

**Figure 15-5** ᏻᏸ Demonstration items from the Group Embedded Figures Test.

## Need for Cognition

A widely studied personality variable that concerns intellectual activity is **need for cognition**. Need for cognition refers to a general tendency "to engage in and enjoy thinking" (Caccioppo and Petty, 1982). That some individuals like to analyze events; organize, elaborate, and evaluate information; and exert cognitive effort, whereas other individuals do not enjoy such cognitive activity, was recognized early by several social and personality psychologists (e.g., Asch, 1952; Maslow, 1943; Murphy, 1947). In 1955, Cohen, Stotland, and Wolfe first characterized this individual difference as a "need for cognition," which they defined as "a need to structure relevant situations in meaningful, integrated ways. It is a need to understand and make reasonable the experiential world" (p. 291).

Modern research on the need for cognition began with the publication, by Caccioppo and Petty in 1982, of a 25-item paper-and-pencil self report scale to assess that construct. Although Caccioppo and Petty linked their scale to the earlier work of Cohen et al. (1955), an important difference between the two constructs is that Caccioppo and Petty emphasize the intrinsic enjoyment of cognitive activity. The earlier scale, on the other hand, concerns the reduction, via cognitive effort, of the unpleasant arousal brought on by complex and ambiguous stimuli. Although both views result in a need for cognition, the motive for that need is different (Thompson, Chaiken, and Hazelwood, 1993). Caccioppo and Petty conceptualized the need for cognition as a unitary construct. However, more sophisticated psychometric and factor analyses suggest that need for cognition may have three different components (Tanaka, Panter, and Winborne, 1988). These components are cognitive persistence, cognitive confidence, and cognitive complexity. Each of these components represents a different type of elaborative thinking that may have different implications and correlates.

Caccioppo and Petty (1982) developed the Need for Cognition (NC) scale for their research on persuasion and attitude change, and need for cognition has been found to be related to a variety of social information processing variables. For example, high NC individuals base their attitudes on issue-relevant information rather than peripheral information, whereas low NC individuals are more influenced by peripheral information (Caccioppo, Petty, and Morris, 1983). NC is also related to resisting primacy effects in impression formation (Ahering and Parker, 1989), attitude-behavior consistency (Caccioppo, Petty, Kao, and Rodriguez, 1986), and the persistence of attitude change (Haugtvedt and Petty, 1992). With respect to other personality variables, NC is positively related to self-esteem, masculine sex-role attitudes, absorption (see below), and private self-consciousness. NC is negatively related to social anxiety and public self-consciousness (Osberg, 1987) and positively related to measures of intelligence. However, NC is a characteristic rather than an ability. Although high NC individuals tend to be intelligent, a person can be intelligent and low in NC. Likewise, a high NC person need not have a high level of intellectual ability.

## Absorption

The phenomenon of hypnosis has been of long-standing interest to psychologists. One characteristic of hypnosis is that individuals exhibit substantial variability in their response to hypnotic procedures; some individuals are deeply and easily hypnotized, whereas others show little, if any response to hypnosis. The construct of **absorption** developed out of research to identify the personality and individual differences that were related to individuals' hypnotizability and could therefore predict it (deGroh, 1989). In 1974, Tellegen and Atkinson showed that hypnotizable individuals were open to experiences that could so fully engage their attention that their sense of reality seemed altered. In their research, Atkinson and Tellegen used the Tellegen Absorption Scale, which has been revised and included in Tellegen's (1982) Multidimensional Personality Questionnaire. The positive relation between openness to absorbing experiences (absorption) and hypnotizability is now well established (Roche and McConkey, 1990). More recently, Tellegen (1987) has broadened the definition of absorption as a "disposition to enter states characterized by marked cognitive restructuring" and a "readiness to depart from more everyday life cognitive maps and to restructure . . . one's representation of one's self and its boundaries."

## Openness to Experience

The construct of absorption has some clear similarities to the broader personality construct of **openness to experience** ("**openness**") that Costa and McCrae (1976) have used to label Factor V in their five-factor model of personality. The tendency to become absorbed in experiences would seem to require the more general inclination to be open to experiencing new and unusual ones. Indeed, in their initial work on the three-factor NEO (neuroticism, extroversion, and openness) model, Costa and McCrae (1985) explicitly acknowledged the influence of Tellegen and Atkinson's (1974) concept of absorption on their thinking. In particular, the relative independence of absorption from neuroticism and extraversion led Costa and McCrae to view openness as a separate and important aspect of personality.

A number of Big Five theorists (e.g., Digman, 1990; Goldberg, 1981; John, 1990) have viewed Factor V as, in part, an intellectual ability and cultural knowledge dimension. In contrast, McCrae and Costa (1990) have deemphasized intelligence and cultural sophistication and emphasized curiosity, fantasy, artistic sensitivity, liberal values, and self-awareness in their formulation. For Costa and McCrae, Openness represents the non-ability characteristics that may be associated with intelligence but that do not imply the possession of an ability. One does not need to be intelligent to be curious or to have a rich fantasy life or to be self-aware, although such characteristics all tend to be related. Openness is a broad factor that has various components or facets that represent behaviors, motives, and values in more specific experiential domains. These facets include fantasy, aesthetic sensitivity, awareness of feelings, need for variety in behaviors, openness to unusual ideas, intellectual curiosity, and liberal values. Interestingly, the subscales of openness that assess fantasy, aesthetic sensitivity, and awareness of feelings are related to measures of absorption and to hypnotizability, whereas the other subscales are not so related (Glisky, Tataryn, Tobias, Kihlstrom, and McConkey, 1991).

## Summary

- Intelligence is of such central importance to every facet of human activity that its measurement has become a matter of legislative and public policy debate.
- In contrast to personality characteristics, intelligence is an ability. Thus, intelligence is often not included in the domain of personality psychology. Instead, it is treated as a separate topic.
- Although it differs from personality characteristics, intelligence is such a powerful individual difference variable, influencing so many human activities, that failure to consider it and its related motivational, behavioral, and value aspects would leave a substantial gap in the study of personality.
- Numerous definitions of intelligence have been provided. However, there is some evidence that experts and laypersons agree that in some fashion intelligence comprises problem-solving ability, verbal facility, social competence, and possibly motivation.
- Theories of intelligence have ranged from Spearman's emphasis on a broad, general underlying factor coupled with specific factors to Thorndike's claim that intelligence can be reduced to numerous specific factors. Thurstone argued for a compromise view that entailed a small number of group factors intermediate between specific and general factors.
- Others have proposed hierarchical models in which a general factor subsumes group factors, which in turn subsume specific factors. Cattell has postulated that general intelligence can be partitioned into fluid ability (biological capacity) and crystallized ability (culture-based learning). Guilford has classified intelligence along three dimensions—operations, contents, and products—resulting in 150 separate abilities.
- More recent approaches have emphasized the role of cognitions or information processing. In particular, Sternberg's triarchic theory of intelligence has broadened the conceptualization of intelligence to make it more applicable to a variety of life domains other than those that emphasize academic learning.
- Binet, who in collaboration with Simon developed the Binet-Simon Scale, is generally regarded as the founder of the intelligence testing movement. Binet

regarded mental age as an index of mental performance. When each test item was assigned a given number of months' credit and then this credit was added up for all items passed, a person's mental age could be determined.

- Individual tests of intelligence (those administered to one subject at a time) are usually the preferred assessment devices because they permit clinical observations that aid in the interpretation of the IQ score. However, group tests of ability such as the GRE or SAT are more efficient and are more commonly used to make employment and educational decisions.

- The Stanford-Binet has been a widely used test for children and is a direct descendent of the Binet-Simon Scale. Several features of the newly standardized version of the Stanford-Binet were described. This test employed the IQ concept: ratio of mental age to chronological age multiplied by 100.

- Wechsler developed several intelligence tests that are widely employed. They include adult, child, and preschool versions.

- The meaning of intelligence test scores is generally based on its correlates. The major correlates are school success, occupational status, and socioeconomic status.

- Relying on correlations to decide the meaning of intelligence is inherently flawed because correlation does not imply causation. The finding that IQ correlates with, say, SES still requires an explanation. The different explanations that have been offered, genes or environments, are a primary source of controversy and acrimonious debate.

- The heritability of IQ is another source of controversy. Heritability is often estimated from the differences between correlations of individuals of different degrees of relatedness Although IQ correlations for identical twins are greater than they are for fraternal twins, the role of the environment cannot be adequately controlled.

- To control for common environmental influences, identical twins reared apart have been studied. Any differences in IQ should be attributable to the role of the environment. However, a variety of methodological problems in such research prevents us from fully ascertaining the heritability of intelligence.

- Relations between the IQs of adopted children and both their biological and adoptive parents have also failed to provide definitive answers for either the genetic or the environmental position.

- The contribution of genetic and environmental variables to the development of intelligence is complicated. Both types of variables may impose limitations on intellectual development, so neither can sensibly be considered independently of the other.

- The role of genes and environments on intellectual development becomes even more controversial when group (e.g., gender, race) differences in IQ are considered.

- White Americans, on the average, typically show higher mean IQs than black Americans. Explaining this difference has occupied investigators for many years. Unfortunately, many explanations are possible, and whether one accepts genetic and biological explanations or environmental ones seems to reflect stereotypes, the political climate of the times, or the personal inclinations of the investigator rather than clear scientific evidence and analysis.

- Because blacks as a group have been disadvantaged for so long in our society, any explanation of IQ differences must begin by considering the effects of growing up in a racist society and the unfairness that this causes.

- Test bias is often used to explain the difference between the scores of blacks and whites on IQ tests.

- To neutralize the effects of cultural bias on IQ scores, some have tried to develop culture-fair tests, such as Raven's Progressive Matrices and various drawing tests. These tests consist of items with which everyone is presumed to be equally familiar or equally unfamiliar. Although compelling, such tests are difficult to interpret, and they have not eliminated the differences in the scores between blacks and whites.

- The test bias explanation is comforting because it avoids the problem of facing the moral and practical dilemmas of a real difference. It is also saves society from the expense and effort of correcting injustices. In general, however, there is little evidence to support the test bias explanation. Thus, as a society we cannot avoid facing and correcting the substantial economic, educational, and cultural discrepancies between the races that have resulted from our racism.

- In addition to mental ability, a number of motivational, behavioral, and stylistic components of cognitive activity have been identified. Although these components are often associated with intellectual ability, they are conceptually and empirically distinct from measures of intelligence. Thus, these components represent the personality aspects of intellectual and cognitive behavior.

- Some of these components include creativity, cognitive style such as field dependence, need for cognition, and absorption.

- The construct of openness to experience has been proposed as the broad dimension or factor that represents the non-ability aspects of intellectual behavior and cognitive activity.

# Chapter 16
# Personality and Anxiety, Stress, and Health

Specific Versus General Psychological Causes
Anxiety
    Definitions of Anxiety
    Anxiety and Learning Theory
    Different Conceptions and Measures of
      Anxiety
Stress
    Definitions of Stress
    Phenomenological Appraisal
    Types of Stressful Events
    Responses to Stress
Type A Behavior Pattern
    The TABP Construct
    Measurement of TABP
    TABP and CHD
    Components of TABP
Personality Characteristics That Strengthen
    Optimism and Hardiness
    Self-Efficacy
    Ego Control and Ego Resiliency
    Motives
    Humor
    Personal Control

Critical Issues in Personality and Health
    Mechanisms
    Women and Minorities
    Outcome Measures
    Neuroticism and Negative Affectivity
Summary

The idea that psychological variables are related to, and perhaps have a causal influence on, physical health is an old one (Suls and Rittenhouse, 1987). The realization that nonphysiological factors are critical in disease outcomes can be traced back further than Aristotle, and as recently as the 19th century people believed that tuberculosis was caused by excessive feeling. During the early part of this century, **psychosomatic medicine,** which is the study of the contribution of psychological factors to physical complaints, emerged. Today, many physical complaints such as peptic ulcers, essential hypertension, and bronchial asthma are viewed as being psychologically caused (Alexander, 1950). In the past two decades, the importance of psychological factors for understanding and treating physical problems has been increasingly recognized, and the field of **health psychology/behavioral medicine,** which concerns the contribution of psychological factors to the etiology and treatment of problems of physical health is one of the most rapidly growing in psychology.

Several disciplines of psychology, particularly social and clinical psychology, have made contributions to health psychology. However, personality variables have long been considered important to the understanding of physical health. Historically, the individual difference variable of anxiety, often in conjunction with the environmental variable of stress, played a central role in psychological theories of illness. Other widely studied personality variables that are related to health include the **Type A construct, hostility, locus of control,** and **explanatory style.** More recently, variables that are important for promoting health such as **optimism, sense of humor,** and **hardiness** have been proposed.

## Specific Versus General Psychological Causes

During the early part of this century the psychodynamic construct of **neurotic anxiety,** which results from repressed sexual or aggressive urges, came to be viewed as the basis for a variety of physical problems. It was believed that each psychosomatic illness had a different, specific underlying unconscious conflict that predisposed a person to the disorder (Dunbar, 1947). For example, chronic repressed hostility supposedly helped to precipitate rheumatoid arthritis. However, the accumulated research demonstrated that specific psychogenic factors were not predictive of specific illnesses. As a result, a general, nonspecific relation between stress, conflict, and anxiety became the focus of research. For example, Engel (1968) proposed that events such as bereavement or personal loss could promote feelings of helplessness or hopelessness, which in turn led to physiological reactions involving the autonomic nervous system or the immune system. These reactions increased a person's susceptibility to illness. Table 16-1 summarizes the historic progression from specific to general or nonspecific explanatory factors and their role in precipitating disease.

## ⟨⟩ Table 16-1
### The Move from Specific to Nonspecific Explanatory Factors in the Precipitation of Disease

#### I. Psychosomatic medicine in the 1940s

There are *seven* psychosomatic diseases:
1. Peptic ulcer
2. Essential Hypertension
3. Bronchial asthma
4. Thyrotoxicosis
5. Rheumatoid arthritis
6. Ulcerative colitis
7. Neurodermatitis

There is a *specific* underlying unconscious conflict for each disease. For example, the chronic conflict over the wish to be fed or cared for leads to increased secretion of stomach acid, which leads to the development of ulcers.

#### II. Psychiatry in the 1960s

There are *nine psychophysiological* disorders:

1. Skin disorders (e.g., acne, eczema, psoriasis)
2. Musculoskeletal disorders (e.g., backache, tension headache)
3. Respiratory disorders (e.g., bronchial asthma, hyperventilation)
4. Cardiovascular disorders (e.g., essential hypertension, migraine headache, Raynaud's disease)
5. Hemic and lymphatic disorders
6. Gastrointestinal disorders (e.g., gastric ulcers, gastritis, mucous colitis)
7. Genitourinary disorders (e.g., dysmenorrhea, impotence, vaginismus)
8. Endocrine disorders (e.g., goiter, obesity)
9. Disorders of organs of special sense (e.g., Ménière's disease)
10. Other types

#### III. Present day psychiatry

There is *one broad* category (but *no specific* ones):

Psychological factors affecting physical condition.

> This category can be used for any physical condition to which psychological factors are judged to be contributory. It can be used to describe disorders that in the past have been referred to as either "psychosomatic" or "psychophysiological."

> Common examples of physical conditions for which this category may be appropriate include, but are not limited to: obesity, tension headache, migraine headache, angina pectoris, painful menstruation, sacroiliac pain, neurodermatitis, acne, rheumatoid arthritis, asthma, tachycardia, arrhythmia, gastric ulcer, duodenal ulcer, cardiospasm, pylorospasm, nausea and vomiting, regional enteritis, ulcerative colitis, and frequency of micturition. (American Psychiatric Association, 1980, p. 303)

# Anxiety

Dictionaries define **anxiety** as a state of apprehension or uneasiness. Anxiety often results from environmental **stress**, which is a situation or event that has, or at least is perceived as having, some elements that are upsetting. In practice, however, the terms *anxiety* and *stress* are often used interchangeably. It is difficult to objectively define an event as stressful without considering the level of anxiety of the individual who is experiencing that event. Nonetheless, this text's treatment of the two concepts will be based on Lazarus's (1969) distinction between anxiety as an individual difference variable and stress as an environmental variable.

## Definitions of Anxiety

Different personality theorists have defined anxiety in distinctive ways. For example:

*Freud:*    (Neurotic) anxiety stems from unconscious conflicts and serves as a signal that unconscious impulses may erupt into consciousness.

*Rogers:*    Anxiety is the outgrowth of a perceived threat to the self-concept.

*Kelly:*    Anxiety stems from a realization that one's construct system is not leading to valid predictions.

*Cattell:*    Anxiety is the sum total of our unfulfilled needs and the degree of our confidence in their being satisfied.

*Rotter:*    Anxiety reflects a discrepancy between needs that are strong and expectancies for their satisfaction that are relatively low.

The existence of so many different definitions of anxiety (Epstein, 1972) may hamper our ability to study this construct. Fortunately, there are some common themes in these and other definitions (Maher, 1966). First, anxiety refers to an aroused state of the nervous system that is manifested by cardiovascular, respiratory, and gastrointestinal symptoms (e.g., heart palpitations, breathlessness, nausea). Second, this state often occurs when the person perceives a stressful or threatening event, is unprepared to respond adequately, or both. Third, there is a disruption or breakdown in effective coping and problem solving. Fourth, this state may be labeled neurotic when it occurs in the face of no clearly perceived stimuli or of stimuli that objectively pose little or no danger.

## Anxiety and Learning Theory

Anxiety occurs naturally and, in its clinically relevant forms, is often manifested idiosyncratically in response to a particular set of circumstances that are unique to the individual. However, there is a long tradition of conceptualizing anxiety by applying the general principles of learning theory. Although a particular person's anxiety may be in response to a unique set of stimuli, general models of learning have been used to explain anxiety and to create it in the laboratory. For example, Pavlov (1927) was able to induce in animals what he regarded as an experimental neurosis. He accomplished this by first conditioning dogs to expect food whenever a circle was presented and to expect electric shock whenever an ellipse was presented. When he gradually made the ellipse and the circle more and more alike, the dogs eventually could not differentiate between the stimuli and lapsed into states of howling, barking, and struggling against their restraining harnesses.

Over 20 years of research and study convinced Mowrer (1960) that we learn to be anxious through classical conditioning but that we learn to reduce this anxiety through instrumental acts. Thus, as we saw earlier with Watson and Rayner's (1920) work, Little Albert learned to fear a white rat when its presence was paired with a very loud noise. According to Mowrer, the child would then engage in behaviors designed to reduce or avoid the anxiety. In some cases these would be realistic coping behaviors, but in other instances they could just as easily be neurotic ones. The point is that whatever worked—that is, reduced anxiety—would be learned. Dollard and Miller (1950) had a similar view. They described anxiety as a painful affective drive state that motivated the learning of behaviors that would reduce the drive.

The Dollard and Miller view of anxiety as a drive state was elaborated by Hull (1943) and Spence (1958). They tried to understand how fear can become attached to a previously neutral stimulus by looking at the number of occasions in which the neutral (conditioned) stimulus and the unconditioned stimulus are paired (i.e., the more often the rat and the loud noise are presented together, the greater is the likelihood that the fear response will occur). Also, a more intense stimulus will be more effective than a relatively weak one. For instance, in the development of a fear of elevators, dropping suddenly five floors before the elevator catches would be more effective than a momentary drop of three feet. Then, too, there are individual differences in emotional responsiveness that will affect the conditioning process.

To provide a way of ordering and conceptualizing these and other factors, Hull (1943) proposed that the strength of the relationship between the conditioned response and the conditioned stimulus was dependent on two basic factors: the habit strength associated with the response and the overall drive level of the organism when the stimulus occurs. These two general variables combine multiplicatively to determine the response potential. Thus:

$$\mathbf{E} \text{ (response potential)} = \mathbf{D} \text{ (drive)} \times \mathbf{H} \text{ (habit strength)}$$

This formula suggests that when people become emotionally aroused by some stimulus, they will perform more intensely those responses that have become habitual or overlearned. For example, we all overlearn the responses of putting our hand on the doorknob, twisting it, pulling on the knob, stepping through the open door, and then pulling it shut behind us. All of us go through the sequence repeatedly every day, and habit strength is high. But what happens when I become very angry just before I have to make an exit? According to the Hull-Spence view, under such emotional arousal (high drive) my door-opening responses will be intensified. I yank on the knob, twist it ferociously, and slam the door. Drive and habit combined to intensify the normal response potential. Of course, there may occasionally be inhibiting factors present that must be subtracted from the $D \times H$ product (e.g., my hand is in a cast, my boss is watching me). As for anxiety specifically, it was Spence's (1958) contention that by knowing a person's anxiety level in a given situation, we could then better predict the speed and effectiveness of classical conditioning.

## Different Conceptions and Measures of Anxiety

The Manifest Anxiety Scale. To predict the effectiveness of classical conditioning, J. A. Taylor (1953) developed the **Manifest Anxiety Scale** (**MAS**) to measure individual differences in chronic levels of anxiety. She selected 50 items from the MMPI for her scale. Table 16-2 presents some of these items. People who receive high scores on the MAS are regarded as chronically anxious. That is, they are high on the trait of anxiety, and this should manifest itself across a variety of situations over time. Hundreds of studies have shown how this trait of anxiety affects behavior. From this research, two generalizations can be made:

1. On simple tasks, participants high in anxiety perform better than participants low in anxiety—a finding consistent with the Hull-Spence drive theory.

## Table 16-2

Examples of MAS Items. The Response in Parentheses After Each Item Indicates Anxiety

| T | F | 4. I have very few headaches. (false) |
|---|---|---|
| T | F | 7. I worry over money and business. (true) |
| T | F | 25. I am easily embarrassed. (true) |
| T | F | 32. I am happy most of the time. (false) |
| T | F | 36. I have sometimes felt that difficulties were piling up so high that I could not overcome them. (true) |

Source: From "A Personality Scale of Manifest Anxiety" by J. A. Taylor, *Journal of Abnormal and Social Psychology*, 1953, *48*, 285–290.

This theory is that in simple tasks, there are relatively few competing responses that are incorrect. Thus, the high-anxiety drive strength combines (multiplies) with the higher habit strength of the correct responses to produce a facilitative effect.

2. On more difficult or complex tasks, participants high in anxiety perform more poorly than participants low in anxiety, particularly in the early stages of the task. As learning proceeds, the performance of highly anxious participants will improve and often surpass that of participants low in anxiety. On difficult tasks, the correct responses are weaker than the competing incorrect responses. The result is that the high drive level activates a larger number of those incorrect tendencies, creating a poorer performance.

**Test Anxiety.**   An alternative explanation of the effect of anxiety on performance comes from the theory of **test anxiety**. Instead of drive theory, the role of interfering thoughts and responses is emphasized. This approach was initially proposed by Mandler and Sarason (1952) and more recently elaborated by I. G. Sarason (1980). It regards anxiety as a response to what is cognitively appraised as a threatening situation. The key here is perception of threat. It is not the objective situation but one's appraisal of it that is crucial. A student who feels well prepared for a test is not likely to approach the test with anxiety even if the preparation has been inadequate. Another student, expecting to do poorly, will experience stress and will react to it in one of three general ways. The student can try to adaptively cope with the stress by studying more, consulting with the instructor, or perhaps practicing on possible test questions. One maladaptive response would be to do nothing and just hope that things will be better on the next test. A maladaptive anxious response would be to worry or to decide that one is stupid or unworthy. Sarason (1980) describes the characteristics of such anxiety as follows:

1. The situation is seen as difficult, challenging, and threatening.
2. The individual sees himself as ineffective, or inadequate, in handling the task at hand.
3. The individual focuses on undesirable consequences of personal inadequacy.
4. Self-deprecatory preoccupations are strong and interfere or compete with task-relevant cognitive activity.
5. The individual expects and anticipates failure and loss of regard by others. (p. 6)

There are individual differences in the way anxiety is experienced and the situations that precipitate it. But the interfering thoughts or debilitating self-preoccupations of the anxious person are probably traceable to a history of experiences that have taught the person that successful coping is unlikely. It should be remembered, however, that "successful coping" is an individually defined matter that also depends on prior experience and the personal standards that have been acquired.

## ⬡ Table 16-3
### Examples of TAS Items. The Response in Parentheses After Each Item Indicates Anxiety

| | | | |
|---|---|---|---|
| T | F | 2. | If I were to take an intelligence test, I would worry a great deal before taking it. (true) |
| T | F | 7. | During tests, I find myself thinking of the consequences of failing. (true) |
| T | F | 15. | When taking a test, my emotional feelings do not interfere with my performance. (false) |
| T | F | 20. | During exams, I sometimes wonder if I'll ever get through college. (true) |
| T | F | 25. | If examinations could be done away with, I think I would actually learn more. (true) |

Source: From "Introduction to the Study of Text Anxiety" by I. G. Sarason. In *Text Anxiety: Theory, Research, and Applications* by I. G. Sarason (ed.) (Hillsdale, N.J.: Erlbaum), 1980. Copyright 1980 by Lawrence Erlbaum Associates. Reprinted by permission.

To measure individual differences in test anxiety, the **Test Anxiety Scale (TAS)** (Sarason, 1978) is commonly used. This is a 37-item scale that measures responses to testing situations. Several illustrative items are shown in Table 16-3. In contrast to the MAS, the TAS measures anxiety as it relates to a specific testing situation. Because of its focus on testing situations, it can be considered a narrow rather than a broad or generalized measure of chronic anxiety.

Research with the TAS suggests that high levels of anxiety impair our ability both to process task information and to perform well on tasks. More specifically, anxiety negatively influences three basic processes: (1) our ability to use correctly the task stimuli necessary for us to do well on a given task, (2) our reactions to our own successes or failures during performance on the task, and (3) our interpretation of our own body state during task performance (Geen, 1980). An anxious person is less likely to pay attention to the appropriate cues during the task. Such an individual is also likely to react poorly as failure is encountered in the initial phases of a difficult task. Finally, worry and emotionality will combine to impede performance further (Sarason, 1984).

### State Versus Trait Anxiety

Anxiety is a construct that can be viewed as both a state and a trait (Chaplin, John, and Goldberg, 1988). As a stable trait, anxiety is a chronic condition that characterizes how a person feels in most aspects of his or her life. As a temporary state, anxiety is the momentary and specific feeling that nearly everyone experiences in certain situations. Cattell and Scheier (1961) were among the first to try to measure these two separate aspects of anxiety. Spielberger (1966) also differentiated between anxiety as a trait and anxiety as a state. By his definition, **trait anxiety (A-Trait)** is an acquired behavioral tendency predisposing the person to perceive a wide range of objectively nonthreatening situations as dangerous. The resultant responses are disproportionate to the real danger. **State anxiety (A-State)** is a more transitory state of emotional arousal; it varies in intensity and fluctuates over time. There are feelings of tension and apprehension accompanied by activations of the autonomic nervous system. This A-State will arise whenever there is an appraisal of threat in a situation.

To measure A-Trait versus A-State, Spielberger, Gorsuch, and Lushene (1970) have developed a questionnaire called the **State-Trait Anxiety Inventory (STAI)**. The STAI A-State scale consists of 20 statements used by subjects to describe how they feel at a certain moment, for example: "I feel tense," "I am jittery," or "I am worried." The 20 items on the STAI A-trait scale include such items as "I lack self-confidence" or "I feel like crying." The A-Trait scale asks people to describe how they generally feel. All items are rated by subjects on a four-point scale. Basically, the A-Trait scale is a measure of individual differences in anxiety proneness. A person high on this scale will respond to psychological stress with a high level of A-State intensity, particularly if the stressful situation involves loss of self-esteem. Anyone, however, will experience an anxiety state if a situation is perceived to be threatening. As a general rule, anxiety as a trait exists in those individuals who respond to a wide range of stimuli as threatening.

A study by Kendall, Finch, Auerbach, Hooke, and Mikulka (1976) illustrates how stress affects changes in A-State for participants who differ in trait anxiety. The participants were college students enrolled in an experimental psychology class. Stress was induced by an examination that was worth 100 points and counted for one third of the final grade. The students filled out the STAI several times during the course, including just before the examinations were handed out and just after the collection of the test booklets. The results of this experiment are shown in Figure 16-1. They indicate that on three separate occasions (prior to the examination day, just before the examination, and afterward), the A-State scores were more extreme for participants high in trait anxiety than they were for participants low in trait anxiety.

## Stress

Regardless of how it is conceptualized and measured, **anxiety** is fundamentally a personality variable. The related construct of **stress** is an environmental variable: it concerns experiences that may result in anxiety or other negative feelings. Of course, what is stressful to one person may not be stressful to another. Thus, there is some circularity in defining stress and anxiety. However, many aspects of the world in which we live would be called stressful by most people. Some examples are crowding, noise, bureaucracies, pollution, indebtedness, and the threat of terrorism. The study of stress, its causes and consequences, and how people cope with it has partially replaced research on anxiety (Lazarus, 1966).

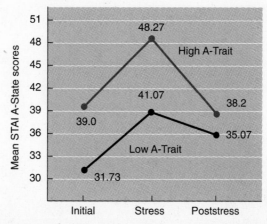

**Figure 16-1** A-state scores for high- and low-A-Trait groups across three situations.

From "The State-Trait Anxiety Inventory: A Systematic Evaluation" by P. C. Kendall, A. J. Finch, Jr., S. M. Auerbach, J. F. Hooke, and P. J. Mikulka, *Journal of Consulting and Clinical Psychology*, 1976, *44*, 406–412. Copyright © 1976 by the American Psychological Association.

## Definitions of Stress

There have been many ideas about the nature of stress, ranging from the biological to the psychosocial (Fleming, Baum, and Singer, 1984). Lazarus (1966, 1969) regards **stress** as an external circumstance that makes unusual or extraordinary demands upon the person. This could be a flood or a tornado, or it could be failure on a major examination, a divorce, or facing combat. But in the assessment of stress, the person's responses to the stressful event must also be considered. For Lazarus, these responses could be (1) emotional, such as fear, anxiety, or anger; (2) motor, such as speech disturbances, tremors, or perspiring; (3) cognitive, such as failures in concentration, or perceptual distortions; or (4) physiological changes, such as changes in heart rate or breathing. Some prefer to distinguish stress as the condition or responses of the organism and **stressors** as those things in the world outside the person (or within the person's mind) that precipitate a stress response (Geen, 1976).

## Phenomenological Appraisal

Theories of stress and coping are generally phenomenological or cognitive. Events will produce stress only when individuals perceive the event as a threat to themselves. A tornado is a threat because it threatens coping strategies. A demanding job induces stress because the person believes that he or she cannot handle it. Thus, it is not the event so much as it is my cognition about the event that makes the event stressful. My job stress may stem less from the objective demands of the job than from childhood experiences in which my father constantly

Stress is common in contemporary society, whether one lives in a rural or an urban area.

reminded me that I was not living up to the family's standards. Of course, some stressors would frighten nearly everyone regardless of their thoughts and perceptions (e.g., natural calamities, nuclear warfare). But even here, it is not likely that the degree of stress would be identical for everyone. This interaction between person and situation has led Lazarus and Folkman (1984) to define stress as "a particular relationship between the person and the environment that is appraised by the person as taxing or exceeding his or her resources and endangering his or her well-being" (p. 19).

Several factors about the event may influence the appraisal process. First, there is the role of familiarity. In general, unfamiliar events are more likely to provoke stress. Second, there is controllability. Being in control tends to lessen our stress. For example, when I am a passenger in a car, I am more likely to be nervous than when I am driving. Predictability is also important. Sudden, unexpected events are appear to be more stressful than predictable or expected events. Many argue that this is why severe earthquakes leave so many psychological scars on people. In contrast, tornadoes, which are often preceded by warnings that allow time for psychological and physical preparation, seem to be more easily forgotten.

## Types of Stressful Events

Stress can result from almost any kind of event, depending on the person and how that person appraises the event. The following are some major types of events that may result in stress.

Daily Hassles.  Although we most often associate stress with major life events and personal tragedies, stress can also result from the minor annoyances that we experience on a daily basis. Recently, the concept of **daily hassles** has emerged (e.g., DeLongis, Folkman, and Lazarus, 1988; Gruen, Folkman, and Lazarus, 1988). These are ordinary, daily kinds of events that create stress in our lives. Lazarus and his colleagues (Kanner, Coyne, Schaefer, and Lazarus, 1981) have developed a scale that measures stress as a result of daily hassles. Ten hassles that were reported most frequently by 100 middle-aged adults are shown in Table 16-4. DeLongis et al. (1988) have found a relation between daily stress and the occurrence of health problems such as the flu, sore throat, headaches, and backaches. Small daily hassles may act cumulatively over time to produce significant difficulties or stress for the person. An example that is beginning to receive research attention is the daily chronic hassles typically experienced by those adults who provide in-home care to disabled persons. Although there are substantial individual differences in how caregivers cope with stress, the degree of stress experienced is mediated by the appraisal process (Stephens and Zarit, 1989).

Major Traumas.  Traumatic events such as earthquakes, tornadoes, accidents, and acts of terrorism are major sources of stress. These are usually powerful, sudden

## Table 16-4
The Ten Most Common Events That Produce Daily Stress

| Item | Times Checked (%) |
| --- | --- |
| 1. Concerns about weight | 52.4 |
| 2. Health of family member | 48.1 |
| 3. Rising prices of common goods | 43.7 |
| 4. Home maintenance | 42.8 |
| 5. Too many things to do | 38.6 |
| 6. Misplacing or losing things | 38.1 |
| 7. Yard work or outside maintenance | 38.1 |
| 8. Property, investment, taxes | 37.6 |
| 9. Crime | 37.1 |
| 10. Physical appearance | 35.9 |

From "Comparison of Two Models of Stress Management: Daily Hassles and Uplifts versus Major Life Events," by Kanner, A. D., et al., *Journal of Behavioral Medicine, Vol. 4*, pp. 1–39 (1981). Reprinted by permission of Plenum Publishing Corporation and the author.

occurrences that often affect large numbers of people. That these events are unpredictable and often result in loss of personal control makes them especially traumatic.

Change. Life changes can be major sources of stress. Indeed, a major theory of stress views *change* as the one feature of an event that is crucial for it to be stressful (Dohrenwend and Dohrenwend, 1981). According to this theory, it is not the negative features of events that cause stress so much as the change and readjustment the event requires. Thus, positive change such as a promotion or buying a new house can promote stress and even precipitate illness or other bodily symptoms. With change there often comes the expectation that we may not be able to successfully handle the new situations. And therein lies the potential for stress.

What types of life events are typically associated with the development of stress reactions? Examining the records of about 5,000 medical patients, Holmes and Rahe (1967) identified a list of events that seemed to have occurred about the time of the onset of their medical problems. These events were then rated by 394 judges for the amount of readjustment the change required. Each event was assigned a value that was the mean of the judges' ratings of the degree of life change entailed by experiencing the event. Table 16-5 shows the resulting **Social Readjustment Rating Scale.** When participants respond to the scale, they usually are asked to indicate which events they have experienced in the last six months to a year. The total of the life-change units for the events checked constitutes the

## ❧ Table 16-5

### The Social Readjustment Rating Scale

| Rank | Life Events | Mean Value (life-change units) |
|---|---|---|
| 1 | Death of spouse | 100 |
| 2 | Divorce | 73 |
| 3 | Marital separation | 65 |
| 4 | Jail term | 63 |
| 5 | Death of close family member | 63 |
| 6 | Personal injury or illness | 53 |
| 7 | Marriage | 50 |
| 8 | Fired at work | 47 |
| 9 | Marital reconciliation | 45 |
| 10 | Retirement | 45 |
| 11 | Change in health of family member | 44 |
| 12 | Pregnancy | 40 |
| 13 | Sex difficulties | 39 |
| 14 | Gain of new family member | 39 |
| 15 | Business re-adjustment | 39 |
| 16 | Change in financial state | 38 |
| 17 | Death of close friend | 37 |
| 18 | Change to different line of work | 36 |
| 19 | Change in number of arguments with spouse | 35 |
| 20 | Mortgage over $10,000 | 31 |
| 21 | Foreclosure of mortgage or loan | 30 |
| 22 | Change in responsibilities at work | 29 |
| 23 | Son or daughter leaving home | 29 |
| 24 | Trouble with in-laws | 29 |
| 25 | Outstanding personal achievement | 28 |
| 26 | Wife begins or stops work | 26 |
| 27 | Begin or end school | 26 |
| 28 | Change in living conditions | 25 |
| 29 | Revision of personal habits | 24 |
| 30 | Trouble with boss | 23 |
| 31 | Change in work hours or conditions | 20 |
| 32 | Change in residence | 20 |
| 33 | Change in schools | 20 |
| 34 | Change in recreation | 19 |
| 35 | Change in church activities | 19 |
| 36 | Change in social activities | 18 |

(continued)

🕉 Table 16-5 (continued)

| Rank | Life Events | Mean Value (life-change units) |
|------|-------------|-------------------------------|
| 37 | Mortgage or loan less than $10,000 | 17 |
| 38 | Change in sleeping habits | 16 |
| 39 | Change in number of family get-togethers | 15 |
| 40 | Change in eating habits | 15 |
| 41 | Vacation | 13 |
| 42 | Christmas | 12 |
| 43 | Minor violations of the law | 11 |

Source: From "The Social Readjustment Rating Scale" by T. H. Holmes and R. H. Rahe, *Journal of Psychosomatic Research*, 1967, *11*, 213–218. Copyright 1967 by Pergamon Press. Reproduced by permission.

participants score. Using the scale, Rahe (1972) was able to predict who would develop an illness and who would remain in good health over the subsequent year. Those who remained healthy received an average score of 150 life-change units, while those who become ill reported up to 300 life-change units. The scale has stimulated numerous studies and shows promise in helping us understand the relationship between stress and the onset of illness.

## Responses to Stress

The responses to environmental stress are complex and fall into a variety of categories ranging from the emotional to the physiological. Figure 16-2 outlines how these reactions follow from objective events and our subjective appraisal of them.

**Emotional Responses.** Unpleasant emotional reactions usually accompany stress. The most common emotions are (1) annoyance, anger, and rage; (2) apprehension, anxiety, fear, and terror; (3) and pensiveness, sadness, and grief (Woolfolk and Richardson, 1978). The relation between stress and negative emotions is illustrated in a study by Caspi, Bolger, and Eckenrode (1987). They had 96 women complete diaries each day in which they listed the stresses and moods that occurred during a 28-day period. Daily fluctuations in mood were correlated with daily fluctuations in stress. In essence, as stress grew so did the unpleasantness of the moods. Other research has also indicated that negative emotions are associated with a broad range of subjective complaints and physical symptoms (Watson and Pennebaker, 1989; Bolger, DeLongis, Kessler, and Schilling, 1989).

**Physiological Responses.** Many years ago, Cannon (1932) argued that threat leads to physiological responses that enable the autonomic nervous system to prepare the organism to either flee or fight. But it was Hans Selye (1956, 1974), one of the founders of stress research, who voiced concerns over the effects of prolonged

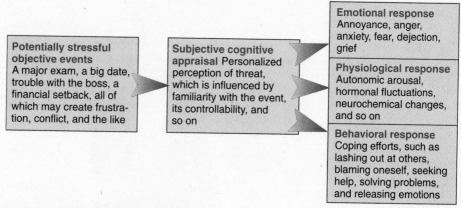

**Figure 16-2** Outline of the stress process.

From *Psychology: Themes and Variations* by Wayne Weiten. Copyright © 1989 by Wadsworth, Inc. Reprinted by permission of Brooks/Cole Publishing Company.

physiological arousal. Selye believed that in reaction to any kind of stress, there is a **general adaptation syndrome.** This is a set of physiological responses that occur in three distinct stages. The initial response to stress is *alarm*, during which the sympathetic nervous system is activated (e.g., heartbeat and respiration increase). Assuming that the stress continues, the second stage—*resistance*—begins. This is a period during which the outward signs of emotion actually decline. Breathing and heartbeat slow down, but an analysis of the blood during this stage will reveal the presence of several hormones normally associated with emotional states. Even though outwardly all now appears well, a long interval of stress will deplete the body's defenses and make one susceptible to diseases such as flu and mononucleosis. If the stress continues for a very lengthy time, the person will enter the third stage: *exhaustion*. And this can, in extreme cases, result in death.

Many of Selye's conclusions were based on animal research, and as always there is some question as to how directly they apply to humans. Lacey (1967) suggests that different types of stress will induce different patterns of physiological responses. In short, there appear to be more individual differences and variety than the general adaptation syndrome would suggest. Then, too, Selye did not seem to take into account adequately the cognitive appraisals that play such an important part in determining what will become a stressor (Lazarus, 1966). However, regardless of the exact details of theories of stress, there can be little doubt that when it becomes chronic it has many harmful effects on health and well-being.

The physiological responses (e.g., increased heart rate, rapid breathing) that occur in response to stressful events are the result of brain signals to the endocrine system. The path is through the autonomic nervous system (Asterita, 1985). A second path is directly between the brain and the endocrine system. The precise mechanisms responsible for physiological reactions are still unclear, but

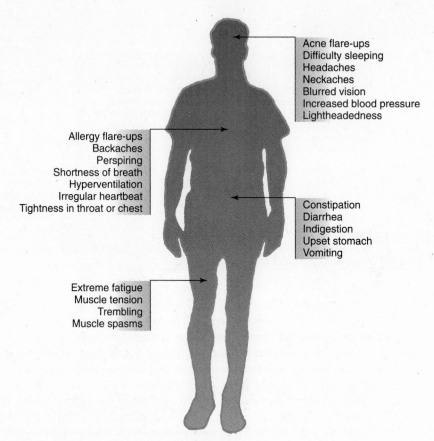

**Figure 16-3** &#x0A7E; Common physical reactions to stress.

From *Exploring Choices: The Psychology of Adjustment* by Donald Meichenbaum, Richard Price, E. Jerry Phares, Naomi McCormick and Janet Hyde. Copyright © 1989 Scott, Foresman and Company.

the effects are pervasive and unmistakable. Figure 16-3 shows common physical reactions that people report they have to stress.

**Behavioral Responses.** A variety of behaviors can follow from the perception of threat and the ensuing stress. For example, the person may respond to frustration with aggression (Dollard et al., 1939). In contrast, another person may respond to stress by giving up. This has come to be referred to as **learned helplessness** (Seligman, 1975). Still others respond defensively. For example, several psychodynamic defense mechanisms such as denial, overcompensation, and intellectualization may be activated. Of course, others may employ more effective coping behaviors in the face of stress.

We noted earlier that impaired performance on tasks is a frequent outcome of anxiety. And we also saw how test anxiety, for example, can interfere with our performance. Similarly, athletes are sometimes said to "choke" in certain games. Baumeister and Steinhilber (1984) checked statistical performance records from numerous championship baseball and basketball games over the years. Contrary to conventional wisdom, they found that home teams are often at a distinct disadvantage in final championship games. Apparently, this is because the pressure is so great for that final game when everything is on the line. This is shown in Table 16-6.

Another example of impaired performance is reflected in the differences in functioning between older and younger individuals, especially when stress is an element. Bäckman and Molander (1986) studied both younger and older miniature golf players who were skilled at the sport. All the players showed an increased heart rate and also rated themselves as more anxious when they moved from training to actual golf competition. Older players also displayed a dropoff in their performance in the competitive phase. The older players in particular, however, were less proficient in coping with the stress of competition. It seems likely that cognitive impairments were responsible here. That is, poor decisions about the speed of one's backswing or misjudging the proper angle for bank shots were probably involved. The results of this study are shown in Figure 16-4.

When prolonged stress is coupled with preexisting personality characteristics, clear pathology can result. This can range from the contemporary phenomenon of **burnout**, which is the loss of motivation or interest in an aspect of one's

## Table 16-6
Outcomes of Championship Games

**Baseball: World Series Results 1924–1982***

| Games | Home | Visitor | Home % |
|---|---|---|---|
| 1 and 2 | 59 | 39 | .602 |
| last game | 20 | 29 | .408 |
| 7 | 10 | 16 | .385 |

*10 series excluded where same team won all games

**Basketball: NBA Championship and Semifinal Results 1967–1982**

| Games | Home | Visitor | Home % |
|---|---|---|---|
| 1–4 | 115 | 49 | .701 |
| last game | 19 | 22 | .463 |
| 7 | 5 | 8 | .385 |

Adapted from Roy F. Baumeister and Andrew Steinhilber, "Paradoxical Effects of Supportive Audiences on Performance Under Pressure: The Home Field Disadvantage in Sports Championships," *Journal of Personality and Social Psychology, Vol. 47*, No. 1, July 1984. Copyright © 1984 by the American Psychological Association. Reprinted by permission of Roy F. Baumeister.

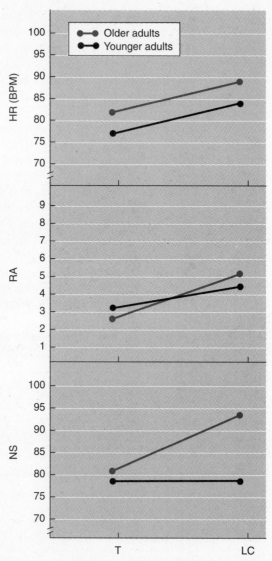

**Figure 16-4** ❧ Mean heart rate (top panel, HR), mean related anxiety (middle panel, RA), and mean number of shots per two rounds (bottom panel, NS) for older and younger adults during training (T), and club championship (LC).

From Bäckman, L., and Molander, B., (1986). Adult differences in the ability to cope with situations of high arousal in a precision sport. *Psychology and Aging, 1,* 133–139.

life such as a job or relationship (Maslach, 1982), to psychiatric disorders such as posttraumatic stress disorders that are associated with the Vietnam conflict and to other persistent severe traumas, alcoholism and drug addiction (Davison and Neale, 1990).

## Type A Behavior Pattern

Anxiety and stress have long been regarded as impacting health, and both of these constructs have been studied by personality psychologists. However, the study of personality and health emerged as a contemporary field of study with the discovery of the **Type A behavior pattern (TABP)**. In 1892 Sir William Osler described the typical coronary patient as neither delicate nor neurotic but robust, keen, ambitious, and vigorous in mind and body. Also of interest was the observation of cardiologists that the fabric on the front edge of the seats of the chairs in their waiting rooms tended to wear out quickly, suggesting that their patients were agitated and high-strung. In 1974, Friedman and Rosenman formally introduced a description of a common pattern of stable behavior observed in coronary patients that they labeled **Type A behavior pattern.** The publication of their work has generated a tremendous amount of research linking personality and health.

### The TABP Construct

Friedman and Rosenman (1974) depicted TABP as "an action-emotion complex that can be observed in any person who is aggressively involved in a chronic, incessant struggle to achieve more and more in less and less time, and if required to do so, against the opposing efforts of other things or persons" (p. 67). The **Type B behavior pattern** refers to the absence of Type A behaviors. This is an individual differences approach to the impact of stress which recognizes that not every life event, stressful or not, has the same impact on everyone under all circumstances (Matthews and Glass, 1981).

A variety of behaviors are often said to characterize Type A individuals (Glass, 1977). Thus, Type A subjects tend to

- Perceive time passing rather rapidly
- Show a deteriorating performance on tasks that require delayed responding
- Work near maximum capacity even when there is not a time deadline
- Arrive earlier for appointments
- Become aggressive and hostile when frustrated
- Report less fatigue and fewer physical symptoms
- Become motivated by intense desires to master their physical and social environments and to maintain control

Wright (1988) has proposed a somewhat different view of TABP in coronary patients. He asserts that the basic ingredients of TABP include

- A sense of time urgency—not over large amounts of time but over seconds (e.g., changing lanes to save a few car lengths)
- A chronic activation level—being keyed up most of the time every day
- A multiphasic quality—the tendency to be engaged in multiple tasks that need to be done at the same time.

There is also some disagreement over the status of TABP as a personality variable. For some, it is a description of a set of overt behaviors that are found in coronary patients, whereas for others it is a dispositional personality trait with causal implications for heart disease (Rodin and Salovey, 1989). Another issue is whether the Type A-B distinction is a typology rather than a dimensional concept (Strube, 1989).

## Measurement of TABP

Both **structured interviews** and questionnaires have been used to assess Type A behavior (Matthews and Glass, 1981). The interview contains questions about, for example, how the person responds when waiting for someone who is slow. The interviewer will also try to provoke the person by interrupting or questioning the interviewee's accuracy. Such a strategy is designed to produce Type A behavior (if it is prone to occur) in the interview itself. The most frequent questionnaire employed is the **Jenkins Activity Survey for Health Prediction (JAS)** (Jenkins, Zyzanski, and Rosenman, 1971). It contains 54 self-report items similar to those asked in the interview.

Unfortunately, the questionnaire and the structured interview do not always converge (Matthews, Krantz, Dembroski, and MacDougall, 1982). For example, Suls and Wan (1989) surveyed a large number of studies that used either questionnaires or interviews to identify TABP. They found that Type A subjects who reported chronic unpleasant emotional states were identified by questionnaires but not by interview techniques. However, Miller et al. (1996) reviewed all published studies that used either questionnaires, structured interviews, or both. He concluded that structured interviews are better than questionnaires as predictors of **coronary heart disease (CHD)**: the variety of pathological processes that affect the heart muscle and coronary vessels. The use of questionnaires to assess TABP in some studies and interviews in others may be responsible for the discrepant findings about the relation between Type A behavior and risk of coronary heart disease.

## TABP and CHD

TABP has now been related to many outcome variables. For example, Kelly and Houston (1985) found that Type A women tend to be in higher, more demanding occupational levels than Type B women. Moreover, they experience more stress and tension. Male Type A individuals who are working on a challenging intellectual task have been shown to become more aroused than Type B individuals. This relation between arousal and task difficulty is shown in Figure 16-5, where arousal is defined in terms of systolic blood pressure. More recently, Contrada (1989) has shown a modest but reliable relation between TABP and elevated blood pressure, although only when TABP was measured by a structured interview but not when questionnaires were used.

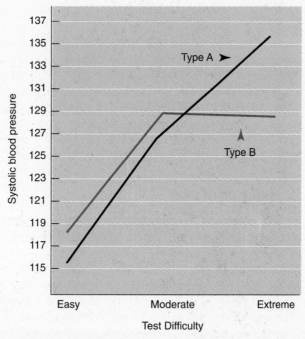

**Figure 16-5** ⚙ Systolic blood pressure of Type A and Type B subjects while working on easy, moderately difficult, and extremely difficult tasks.

From Holmes, D. S., McGilley, B. M. and Houston, B. K., 1984. Task-related arousal of Type A and Type B persons: Levels of challenge and response specificity. *Journal of Personality and Social Psychology, 46,* 1322–1327.

However, the major focus of TABP research has been its hypothesized relation to CHD. Several studies over the years have found that Type A's have at least twice the likelihood of CHD as do Type B's. Matthews and Glass (1981) have suggested several possible explanations for this heightened risk. For example, the specific Type A characteristics of competitive drive and impatience have been linked with the subsequent onset of CHD. These same features have been found to be associated with elevations of systolic blood pressure and heart rate in experimental settings. So it may be that Type A's respond to environmental stress with greater physiological reactions than do their Type B counterparts. Another possibility relates to the self-involvement of Type A individuals. People who focus a great deal on themselves tend to show higher blood pressure levels. Because Type A individuals are acutely aware of themselves, this may explain the **hypertension** (elevated blood pressure) and, ultimately, the development of CHD. A third possibility is based on the Type A person's need to exert personal control over the environment. Some evidence suggests that while the person is coping with stress and thus maintaining control, sympathetic nervous system activity increases and catecholamine neurotransmitters are released, which may elevate blood pressure, increase the rate of arterial damage, and facilitate fatal cardiac arrhythmias. Other research (Humphries, Carver, and Neumann, 1983; Matthews and Brunson, 1979) suggests that Type A's may have a tendency to focus on important events to the exclusion of more peripheral events or stimuli. If such events happen to be frustration or anger, autonomic hyperactivity could result and thus increase the risk of CHD. Finally, TABP has been conceptualized within a person-environment interactional model of personality. Specifically, Type A's do not just respond to challenges or demands; they seek out and create such environments by their own thought processes, actions, and style of interacting with others (Smith and Anderson, 1986). This explanation is presented schematically in Figure 16-6.

## Components of TABP

Evidence has been accumulating that the relation between the Type A pattern and CHD is not as straightforward as the original theory implied (Matthews, 1984). In recent years, several large-scale studies, carried out over periods ranging from three to eight years, have failed to find the customary Type A–CHD relation (e.g., the Multiple Risk Factor Intervention Trial Study sponsored by the National Heart, Lung, and Blood Institute). These failures may, in part, be a symptom of the measurement problems that have plagued this construct. Other investigators have suggested that specific components of the TABP that account for the TABP-CHD relation. In particular, the hostility and the control components have received the most attention.

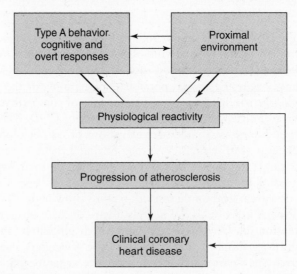

**Figure 16-6** ⚬ From Type A to CHD: an interactional model.

From Smith, T. W. and Anderson, N. B., 1986. Models of personality and disease: An interactional approach to Type A behavior and cardiovascular risk, *Journal of Personality and Social Psychology, 50,* 1166–1173.

**Hostility.** Many investigators who study TABP have turned their attention to a specific component of that construct: **anger and hostility** (Moser and Dyck, 1989). Three elements contribute to this component: having cynical thoughts, feeling anger, and behaving antagonistically towards others (Barefoot, 1992). Evidence has accumulated that although global TABP scores do not always predict coronary heart disease, the anger-hostility component of TABP is generally associated with CHD (Rodin and Salovey, 1989). For example, in the Western Collaborative Group Study, global TABP scores as measured by an interview did not consistently predict CHD, but when the interview was rescored for just the hostility component, those scores were related to CHD (Hecker, Chesney, Black, and Frautschi, 1988). Williams (1994) reported the results of a survey study of hostility in which he found that communities with higher average levels of hostility (for example, Philadelphia) also had higher incidence rates of CHD. Finally, Gidron, Davidson, and Bata (1996) assigned high-hostile males who had recently had a heart attack to either a hostility reduction treatment group or a control group. They found that those in the hostility reduction group reported lower hostility and were observed by others to be less hostile. Most important, the treatment group had fewer **hypertensive** individuals.

Smith (1992) proposed four plausible mechanisms that may serve as mediators of the hostility–CHD association: (1) that hostile individuals experience more stress or have fewer resources such as social support to cope with stress (psychosocial vulnerability), (2) that hostile individuals react more intensely physiologically to psychological stressors (psychophysiological hyperreactivity), (3) that hostile individuals engage in fewer health-promoting behaviors or more health-damaging behaviors (health behavior), and (4) that hostility is a marker in some individuals of an underlying, genetically determined vulnerability to CHD (constitutional vulnerability).

That hostile individuals are more likely to engage in behavior that puts them at higher risk for CHD recurrence is a particularly useful possibility because such behavior could be specifically targeted for intervention. For example, high hostile people might continue to smoke, continue to refrain from exercise, or see physicians less frequently. Further, they may be more resistant to lifestyle or health behavior change when notified of the dangers of such behavior (Leiker and Hailey, 1988). Evidence consistent with these suppositions has been found for both men and women (Houston and Vavak, 1991; Scherwitz, Perkins, Chesney, Hughes, Sidney, and Manolio, 1991). Indeed, Lee et al. (1992) in a multicenter randomized double-blind study of hypertensive white men found that hostility predicted self-reported noncompliance with medical advice.

As with global TABP, the anger/hostility complex has been measured in numerous ways, and there has not yet been any clear consensus on the optimal way to measure this construct (Barefoot, 1992). There is agreement that the anger/hostility complex is multidimensional (Siegman, 1994) and that only some aspects may be coronary-prone (Siegman, Dembroski and Ringel, 1987). The present state of knowledge suggests that a tridimensional view of hostility may be the most productive division of the construct, with three components labeled attitudinal, expressive, and experiential, respectively (Musante, MacDougall, Dembroski and Costa, 1989).

The primary questionnaire used to assess hostility is the **Cook-Medley Hostility Scale** (Cook and Medley, 1954). This scale consists of 50 items from the MMPI that were originally selected for their ability to discriminate between popular and unpopular teachers! This scale assesses the attitudinal component of hostility. The other approach to measuring hostility has used coders to assess the expressive component of hostility from their observation of the TABP structured interview. It appears that the coding of the structured interview is a better predictor of CHD than the Cook-Medley Scale. However, the coding of the interviews is not without it own problems. For example, Davidson, MacGregor, McLean, McDermott, Farqurharson, and Chaplin (1996) recently found substantial differences in the hostility scores from the structured interview depending on whether the coders were male or female.

Control. A second key element in the Type A syndrome is thought to be perceived lack of control (Glass, 1977; Strube and Werner, 1985). Type A individuals feel a strong need to exert control. Their active, dynamic style even makes them look as if they are in control of situations, whether or not they are (Strube, Lott, Heilizer, and Gregg, 1986). Much of their Type A behavior may be thought of as a chronic attempt to regain the control that they continually feel is slipping away from them. It is almost as if they have a set to control everything, followed by an inevitable frustration-hostility reaction when events in their lives elude their grandiose plan of control. They constantly feel challenged, experiencing a great deal of stress as a result. This interpretation is highlighted in a study by Brunson and Matthews (1981). Type A and Type B participants were confronted with a series of insoluble problems (lack of control) and were also asked to verbalize their thoughts as they worked on the task. Eventually, the efforts of Type A participants deteriorated, and they reported that their failures were due to themselves. They also expressed increasing disappointment with themselves, along with a growing pessimism. All of this suggests that lack of personal control over this situation was especially disruptive for Type As.

# Personality Characteristics That Strengthen

The emphasis on anxiety, stress, hostility, and lack of control may imply that personality characteristics have a primarily negative impact on health. However, several personality characteristics appear to strengthen individuals and prevent illness.

## Optimism and Hardiness

Personality characteristics that are associated with positive health outcomes generally have in common an association with **optimism,** flexibility, persistence, and resiliency in response to stress or threat. For example, there is **hardiness,** which is a stress-buffering characteristic that includes a sense of (1) commitment to self, work, and other values; (2) personal control; and (3) challenge—a recognition that change is normal and that it promotes development. Hardiness helps to inoculate the individual against stress-induced illness (Kobasa, Maddi, and Kahn, 1982). Research has seemed to support the relation between hardiness and the avoidance of illness (e.g., Roth, Wiebe, Fillingim, and Shay, 1989). But there are many contradictions in reported findings. For example, Allred and Smith (1989) found support for the presumed "hardy" cognitive style but not for any linkage between hardiness and health. The problem is that hardiness is a composite of a variety of qualities, such as optimism, personal control, and flexibility, and it has proved difficult to identify the particular quality or qualities that are most important for avoiding illness (Funk and Houston, 1987; Hull, Van Treuren, and Virnelli, 1987).

Others, such as Scheier and Carver (1987) believe that a general quality of **optimism** provides a coping style that helps individuals resist a variety of stress-related illnesses. Peterson and Seligman (1987) echo this line of reasoning, as they argue for a dimension of optimism-pessimism that relates to coping effectiveness. Dispositional optimism has also been shown to relate to faster recovery from coronary bypass surgery (Scheier et al., 1989).

## Self-Efficacy

Another variable is **self-efficacy.** Although there is no single dispositional measure of self-efficacy, several studies suggest that perceived self-efficacy affects physiological systems associated with health. For example, Bandura, Taylor, Williams, Mefford, and Barchas (1985) found that phobic individuals who had doubts about their ability to cope produced significant increases in circulating catecholamines, a hormonal sign of stress. As the participants began to gain mastery, the secretions declined. Also, arthritic patients who perceived their own efficacy showed an increase in the number of suppressor T cells, which inhibit the production of antibodies. A variety of other studies have shown a relation between self-efficacy and compliance with health-related regimens such as exercise (e.g., Kaplan, Atkins, and Reinsch, 1984).

## Ego Control and Ego Resiliency

Two other traits that are relevant here are ego control and ego resiliency. **Ego control** refers to the ability to control one's impulses by delaying gratification, inhibiting aggression, and making plans (Funder and Block, 1989). The related concept, **ego resiliency,** involves the ability to adapt to environmental demands by modifying ego control—a kind of "ego elasticity." One of the correlates of these dispositions is the ability to regroup after experiencing stress (Block and Block, 1980). A related idea suggests that there may be a general personality trait that prompts some individuals to behave in a self-assertive fashion. This, in turn, tends to reduce psychological distress (Towbes, Cohen, and Glyshaw, 1989).

## Motives

Recently, McClelland (1989) has reviewed evidence suggesting that motive systems such as power and affiliation are related to physiological systems and ultimately to health and illness. For example, a relaxed or easygoing affiliative syndrome characterizes some types of diabetics. When this affiliative syndrome is aroused there diabetics tend to ignore dictary restrictions which can lead to poorer blood sugar control. Likewise stressed power motive syndrome is related to sympathetic nervous system activation, release of stress hormones, depressed immune functions, and greater susceptibility to infections. In contrast, affiliative trust and sense of efficacy are associated with better health.

## Humor

An effective stress buffer for many people is their **sense of humor,** which is their ability to laugh at themselves and to find the humor in otherwise stressful situations. Dixon (1980) has shown that humor can be adaptive, and as Martin and Lefcourt (1983) have discussed, Freud, Allport, and May all considered humor as healthy and adaptive. Also, Nezu, Nezu, and Blissett (1988) have found that humor can help moderate depression. It was such reasoning that led Rotter and Rafferty (1950) to score humor responses on an incomplete sentences blank as an indication of adjustment tendencies.

## Personal Control

The feeling of not being in control of one's life or future can have profound negative effects upon emotional, cognitive, and physical well-being (Rodin, 1986). However, it also appears that providing people with a sense of control has positive effects on health that go beyond ameliorating the negative effects of lack of control. In recent years there has been a growing trend toward involving patients in their own health care. The case study on page 553, illustrates this movement. For example, Krantz (1980) has argued that providing information to a cardiac patient can help lessen threat and result in a better prognosis. Also, providing patients with options in their lives can likewise reduce the threat, as can arranging the environment to allow patients a measure of personal control.

Not only can threat be reduced by a sense of personal control, depression can also be lessened. For example, in newly diagnosed cancer patients, it has been found that the relation between severity of illness and degree of depression

# CASE STUDY

*Illustrating Personal Responsibility for Treatment*

What exactly are the effects of exerting choice or sensing that personal control and responsibility still exist in our lives? Consider the words of Norman Cousins, formerly editor of the Saturday Review, whose personal bout with a supposedly irreversible illness led him to campaign for the importance of personal responsibility:

> For the past three years I have been studying some forty patients who have recovered from supposedly irreversible illnesses.
>
> A case history from the group may be instructive at this point. It concerns a man, forty-two, married and the father of two children. He had lost his job as an assistant plant manager after sixteen years with the same firm. It was the first time in his life he had been unemployed. He suffered a loss of self-confidence, reflected in increased tensions inside the family. He became morose and found it difficult to approach prospective employers. After three months, he developed a pain in his left hip. It became increasingly severe. Cancer cells were found in the hip. The precise extent of the spread of the cancer could not be determined, but there was no doubt in the mind of the specialist that metastasis had already taken place.
>
> The patient was given an unadorned report. The effect was one of emotional devastation. He knew the cancer was spreading. There was no assurance it could be arrested. The radiation treatment caused his hair to fall out. The chemotherapy produced severe nausea and dizziness. All his savings were rapidly used up by medical and hospital expenses not covered by insurance. He could feel himself falling ever more deeply into a pit.
>
> He decided to find out whether other people recovered under similar circumstances. He read the medical and popular literature. He found his way to a group called "We Can Do," an organization of cancer survivors founded by Barbara Coleman of Los Angeles, herself a cancer sufferer. The most important thing he learned is that members of the group had decided that they wanted to live, that they would not allow themselves to feel defeated, that they were going to experience joy and all the things that made life worth living, and that they were going to prove the experts wrong.
>
> He said he could feel himself breathing more deeply and experiencing a surge of energy just in listening to the "We Can Do" members. He had no difficulty in adopting the same course for himself. This decision had some immediate results. First, when he took the chemotherapy he "programmed" himself for a good result. That is, instead of expecting adverse effects, he visualized the process by which his body would derive maximum benefits from

*(continued)*

Case Study *(continued)*

the medication. He was delighted with the reduced nausea and other adverse effects.

He assured his family that he was now on high ground and would come through. He took genuine pleasure in his family life. He knew that money matters, however pressing, were actually secondary. He forced himself to do physical things. His appetite was better. He was able to sleep through the night. After two months, X-rays confirmed the retreat of his cancer. There is still some pain in the hip but it is significantly less than it was at the time of the original diagnosis and it is diminishing all the time. The oncologist now predicts a sustained remission.

What this case and others like it seem to indicate is that treatment for any disease has twin requirements. One is the availability of the best that medical science has to offer. The other is that the patient himself or herself become fully involved in the recovery effort. Brain research is now turning up evidence that attitudes have biochemical effects. Attitudes of defeat or panic will constrict the blood vessels and have a debilitating effect on the entire endocrine system. Attitudes of confidence and determination activate benevolent and therapeutic secretions in the brain.

Obviously, we can't expect to live forever. We can't expect that every disease will be reversed. But we can get the most out of whatever is possible. We can give it our best shot. Not until then do predictions mean anything. (1982, p. 12)

is weaker in patients who believe they can personally control their health (Marks, Richardson, Graham, and Levine, 1986). However, there are important individual differences in coping strategies. Some people use denial, and these individuals will feel more threatened by too much information about their illness. Other people are fatalistic and are not likely to pay attention to instructions on how to help care for themselves. Thus, not all individuals will benefit from more information about and control over the treatment of their illness. Several scales have been developed to measure individual differences in desire for personal control in health-related matters. The *Krantz Health Opinion Survey* (Krantz, Baum, and Wideman, 1980) was designed to measure preferences for (1) self-treatment and active involvement in one's health care and (2) information about health care. Similarly, Wallston, Wallston, Kaplan, and Maides (1976) have developed the *Health Locus of Control Scale* to better predict health-related behavior. Each of these instruments is based on the premise that recognition of individual differences is important in recommending effective programs. Table 16-7 presents several items from the Krantz Health Opinion Survey.

The personality characteristic of internal locus of control is positively related to good health, primarily because a sense of personal control results in personal health promotion and maintenance. Internals are more likely to show enhanced efforts to maximize their health and well-being and minimize illness. From a re-

## Table 16-7

Sample Items from a Scale Measuring Preferences Regarding Health Care

**From the Krantz Health Opinion Survey:**

I'd rather have doctors and nurses make the decisions about what's best than for them to give me a whole lot of choices.

I usually ask the doctor or nurse lots of questions about the procedures during a medical exam.

It's always better to seek professional help than try to treat yourself.

It is better to rely less on physicians and more on your own common sense when it comes to caring for your body.

Source: From "Assessment of Preferences for Self-Treatment and Information in Health Care" by D. S. Krantz, A. Baum, and M. V. Wideman, *Journal of Personality and Social Psychology*, 1980, *39*, 977–990. Copyright 1980 by the American Psychological Association. Reprinted by permission.

view by Strickland (1979), the following are some of the health-related behaviors or characteristics in which internals have been found to surpass externals:

Information seeking about health maintenance

Precautionary health practices

Greater knowledge of their own illnesses when stricken

More positive attitudes about physical exercise

Greater participation in physical activities

Greater likelihood of refraining from smoking or of having given it up

Some tendency to complete weight reduction, programs more successfully

Lessened susceptibility to essential hypertension and heart attacks

Better prognoses once heart attacks occur

## Critical Issues in Personality and Health

The relation between personality and health has emerged as a major area of research and theory. There is little question that personality can contribute to our understanding of health and to our treatment of physical problems. However, several critical issues need to be addressed as the field continues to develop.

### Mechanisms

There are several potential ways in which personality and disease may be linked (Friedman and Booth-Kewley, 1987): (1) personality features may be the result of disease processes, (2) personality features may lead to unhealthy behaviors that then promote disease, (3) personality may directly affect disease through physiological mechanisms, (4) a third underlying biological variable may be related to both personality and disease, and (5) several different causes and feedback loops may affect the relation between personality and disease.

Personality characteristics are naturalistic variables that generally can not be experimentally manipulated. Thus, it is difficult to distinguish empirically among these possible explanations for any observed relation between personality and health. Krantz and Hedges (1987) have argued for caution in conducting and interpreting research in this area. In particular, they note that much research on personality and health involves correlating measures of traits with measures of disease. Such research, they argue, will likely be difficult to interpret and has often proved difficult to replicate. Their recommended alternative is to conduct research that focuses on testing specific hypothesized mechanisms that link behavior to health.

## Women and Minorities

The vast majority of research on personality and health—particularly research on TABP, stress, hostility, and control—has been conducted on white men. Indeed, most of the large-scale research projects on CHD that have been conducted at major medical centers have used white male subjects. The tendency has been to generalize the results of these studies to women and minorities, but such generalization may be unfounded. For example, the well-known link between high levels of cholesterol and CHD does not appear to be as strong for women (Jacobs et al., 1992); thus, the use of cholesterol lowering drugs with women may not be warranted. Similarly, the widely publicized "aspirin" study, which appeared to demonstrate that taking aspirin daily would lower the risk of CHD, used only male subjects. It appears that for women, daily doses of aspirin are unrelated to CHD. Thus, women who have been taking aspirin on the advice of their physicians may have been misadvised, for aspirin also has negative side effects. The links between hostility, stress, anxiety, and TABP and CHD are also based on research with men. Evidence is accumulating that these links are likely different for women (Davidson, 1991).

For example, women are significantly less prone than men to encounter life-threatening diseases, particularly CHD (Jenkins, 1985). Relative to women, men show a higher incidence of TABP—they tend to exhibit patterns of work overloads, they smoke more frequently, and they manifest a greater willingness to engage in risky behaviors that involve physical danger and illegal activities (Waldron, 1976, 1983). All of this affects health. Likewise, the risk of CHD is 10 to 70 percent higher in the lowest socioeconomic levels. To a large extent this reflects the greater incidence of smoking, obesity, high blood pressure, and hypertensive disease among the less affluent (Jenkins, 1988). Links among socioeconomic status, racial groups, and disease seem largely attributable to factors such as unstable environments and lack of social support along with poor education, poor nutrition, and inadequate health care (Rodin and Salovey, 1989).

It is crucial that research on personality and health include women and minority subjects and that the data be evaluated separately for these different groups (Davidson, Hall, and MacGregor, 1996). Fortunately, there is a strong movement in the field of health psychology to attend to the specific problems and issues in the health of women (Stanton and Gallant, 1995) and minorities (Anderson, 1995).

## Outcome Measures

The fields of health psychology and behavioral medicine are flourishing. One of the reasons for the growing acceptance of these fields by the medical establishment has been the emphasis on biological outcome variables. That is, psychological and social factors are viewed as causal or explanatory of a biological or physiological problem. Recently, this emphasis on biological outcome variables such as cell pathology, blood pressure, blood chemistry (e.g., cholesterol), and other physiological risk factors was criticized by Kaplan (1990). Kaplan argues that these measures are often unreliable and that they do not have a strong relation to outcomes that are important. That is, physiological risk factors are deemed important because of their impact on longevity, behavioral functioning, and quality of life. Yet, the correlation between risk factors and these variables is generally modest. Moreover, lowering risk factors does not always impact these outcomes. For example, it appears that lowering serum cholesterol may reduce mortality from a heart attack but *increase* mortality from all causes (Muldoon and Manuck, 1992).

Kaplan argues that while a person is alive, there are only two relevant health outcome variables, **life expectancy** and **quality of life.** Treatments and treatment decisions may be more meaningful and more thoughtfully applied if these outcomes rather than physiological ones, are focused on.

## Neuroticism and Negative Affectivity

Most of the personality traits related to poor health come from Factor IV (neuroticism) in the Big Five. Costa and McCrae (1987) define neuroticism as "a broad dimension of individual differences in the tendency to experience negative distressing emotions and to possess associated behavioral and cognitive traits" (p. 301). Specifically, *anxiety, hostility, depression, self-consciousness, impulsiveness, and vulnerability* are all facets of this dimension. Watson and Clark (1984) refer to this set of characteristics as **negative affectivity**. Although conceptually these different types of negative affect are distinct, measures of these different characteristics tend to all be positively correlated.

In 1987 Costa and McCrae reported the results of several studies in which they found, consistent with the literature on personality and health, that neuroticism was positively related to reports of physical symptoms. However, neuroticism was not related to mortality. Thus, Costa and Mccrae suggest that the relation between health and anxiety, hostility, depression, and other forms of negative affect reflects a reporting bias. Specifically, people who report being neurotic are also likely to report physical symptoms. However, their ultimate level of health is unrelated to their neuroticism. In 1989 Watson and Pennebaker reported similar results with their measure of negative affect:

> Results indicate that self report health measures reflect a pervasive mood disposition of negative affectivity (NA); self report stress scales also contain a substantial NA component. However, although NA is correlated with health complaint scales, it is not strongly or consistently related to long term health status, and thus will act as a general nuisance factor in health research" (Watson and Pennebaker, 1989, p. 234).

People who report negative feelings on psychological inventories also report negative physical health on medical surveys; neither may have much to do with their long-term health status.

## Summary

- There do not appear to be specific links between psychological problems and physical symptoms. Rather, the relation is a general one.
- There are numerous definitions of anxiety. Most, however, incorporate three elements: a state of physiological arousal, a perception of threat and lack of preparedness, and a disruption of coping behavior. When this pattern occurs in the face of no clearly perceived stimuli, the anxiety is likely to be viewed as neurotic.
- Anxiety as a concept has been identified historically with two broad traditions. The first is the clinical approach. The second tradition springs from the experimental-laboratory perspective, beginning with Pavlov's work on dogs and culminating in the research of Dollard and Miller, who tried to integrate the clinical and experimental traditions.
- The Hull-Spence approach, growing out of the experimental tradition, declared that response potential is determined by drive multiplied by habit strength. This implies that emotional arousal will lead subjects to perform habitual responses more intensely. Thus, by knowing a person's anxiety level we can better predict exactly how classical conditioning will develop.

- The need to measure level of arousal so as to predict conditioning led to the development of Taylor's Manifest Anxiety Scale (MAS), a 50-item self-report inventory.
- Over the years, MAS research has led to the development of two broad generalizations. First, anxiety facilitates learning when the task is easy or when the correct responses are readily available. Second, with complex tasks or in the case of responses with weak habit strength, learning proceeds more slowly in anxious subjects.
- An alternative approach to drive theory has arisen out of the research on test anxiety. The role of interfering thoughts is emphasized here. The participant's appraisal of a situation as one in which failure is likely leads to the perception of threat. These cognitions and preoccupations about failure then interfere or compete with more appropriate problem-solving thoughts and action.
- To pursue the implications of this approach and to identify individual differences in test anxiety, the Test Anxiety Scale (TAS) was developed. Research with this scale suggests that high levels of test anxiety impair one's ability to process task information and to perform well on the task at hand.
- Further work has led to the differentiation of anxiety as both a state and a trait. State anxiety is a more transitory phenomenon, whereas anxiety as a trait refers to an acquired behavioral predisposition. The State-Trait Anxiety Inventory (STAI) has been developed to measure individual differences in these dual aspects of anxiety.
- Whether or not one experiences stress is heavily dependent on how events are appraised. In particular, the elements of familiarity, controllability, and predictability are important.
- Some major kinds of events that often produce stress include frustrations and daily hassles, natural disasters, and life change. The Social Readjustment Rating Scale was described as one prominent measure of stressful life events.
- Our responses to stress are complex, but in general they include emotional reactions (e.g., anger or fear), physiological reactions (e.g., the general adaptation syndrome), and behavioral reactions (e.g., aggression).
- Stress operates to produce health problems in several ways. Some effects are direct and occur through the hormonal, autonomic, or immune systems. Other influences are indirect and operate through our behaviors (e.g., smoking, failure to exercise) and eventually lead to poor health outcomes.
- Some individuals seem to possess psychological characteristics that make them prone to CHD. They have been described as action-oriented people who are chronically engaged in an aggressive struggle against other persons or things to achieve more and more in less and less time. Both a structured inventory and a questionnaire have been devised to identify these so-called Type A individuals.

- Research has indicated that Type A persons have several distinct characteristics. They perceive time as passing rapidly; they perform poorly on tasks requiring patience; they work hard even when it is not necessary; they arrive early for appointments; they react to frustration with aggression and hostility; and they show an intense desire to master their physical and social environments and to maintain personal control.
- The link between Type A behavior and CHD may well be elevated blood pressure. But whether this link is forged through intense competitive needs, hostility, an extreme self-focus, or the chronic desire to control one's environment is still unclear. It certainly appears, however, that the need for personal control over events is a very important element in the Type A pattern.
- There is a growing suspicion that the relationship between the Type A pattern and CHD is not as strong as was once thought. But it may be that specific elements of the Type A pattern, such as anger or hostility, will predict CHD better than global Type A scores.
- Other dispositions such as hardiness, optimism, self-efficacy, ego control, and ego resiliency may help inoculate some individuals against undue stress. Certain motives and a sense of personal control may likewise be important here.
- Several issues need to be addressed as the fields of personality and health develops. These include the mechanisms that underlie the relation, the study of women and minorities, the importance of behavioral as opposed to physiological outcome variables, and the general influence of neuroticism or negative affect on research.

# Chapter 17
# Personality, Occupations, and the Workplace

Personality and Occupational Choice
  Strong Vocational Interest Blank
  Holland's Theory of Vocational Choice
Motivation
  Intrinsic and Extrinsic Motivation
  Psychological Theories of Motivation
  Motivation as a Personality Variable
Leadership
  Theory X and Theory Y
  Specific Theories of Leadership
  Personality Characteristics
Honesty and Integrity
  Polygraphs
  Integrity Tests
  Evaluation of Integrity Tests
Personnel Selection
  Problems with Personality Measures
  Contemporary Personality Assessment
    and Personnel Selection
Summary

Work is a central activity in most people's lives. For nearly everyone, even those who are unemployed, an important component of their self-image is their occupation; one of the first items of information we share with someone is what we do for a living. Finding a job is one of the rites of passage from childhood to adulthood, and failing to find or keep a job generally has devastating effects on a person's self-esteem and psychological and physical health (Kuhnert and Palmer, 1991). For most people, work is not simply a means for earning money to survive and enjoy life but an activity that defines who they are and gives meaning and structure to their lives.

There have long been personality stereotypes associated with different occupations; the stingy and cold-hearted banker, the sly and cunning lawyer, the greedy and manipulative businessperson, the absent-minded professor, and the jolly grocer are a few examples. Each stereotype probably seems accurate to everyone except those who hold that occupation (absent-minded professor, indeed!). However, the relations among personality, interests, motives, and occupational choice has been widely studied, and we will consider that issue in this chapter. The field of personality psychology is also making contributions to other issues relevant to occupational and workplace issues. In particular, personality psychology has contributed to theories and research on **worker motivation, leadership, human relations, employee honesty and integrity,** and **personnel selection.**

## Personality and Occupational Choice

There are some occupations for which a particular type of personality seems logically related to job success. For example, traits of agreeableness, affiliation, and nurturance seem to be important for a counselor. Independence, persistence, and self-confidence would likely be important for an investigative reporter, and orderliness and conscientiousness might be good qualities in an accountant (Shultz and Shultz, 1990). In addition, research on person–environment interactions suggests that individuals will seek out occupations that are consistent with their personalities and that if individuals are in occupations that are inconsistent with their personalities (e.g., an impulsive accountant) they will be dissatisfied (Paunonen and Jackson, 1987).

### Strong Vocational Interest Blank

There is a long history of the use of measures of vocational interests to counsel people in their occupational choices and to place people in positions congruent with their interests once they have been hired. Interest measures can be viewed as a more subtle form of personality assessment (Guion, 1965; Hogan, 1990). The pattern of interests provides an indication of a person's identity and personality, although a theory of how identity and personality become translated into interests has not yet been fully articulated.

The most widely used measure of occupational interests in the United States is the **Strong Vocational Interest Blank (SVIB)** (Strong, 1927). The need for a measure of vocational interests might be questioned. After all, what could be more straightforward than simply asking people if they would like to be doctors, lawyers, police officers, farmers, and so on? The rational view of interest measurement accepts at face value a person's stated preference for an occupation and his or her actual preference. However, people's stated occupational preferences generally correlate only modestly with their scores on interest inventories such as the SVIB. In addition, it is easy to think of people who seem to have made poor career choices. One reason is that people may not have a good idea about what an occupation actually entails. To many people, police work seems adventurous and exciting, involving undercover drug raids, high-speed chases, and gun battles. In fact, much police work involves filling out forms and sitting around a crowded office. Thus, impulsive and sensation-seeking individuals often make for unhappy police officers.

Out of an appreciation for this problem, Strong developed the SVIB on the assumption that stated interests would be valid only in comparison with the preferences of a well-defined occupational group. Moreover, groups' preferences would be useful only if they differed from the preferences of people in general (Strong, 1943). Thus, Strong developed the interest scales empirically, using the strategy of **contrasted groups**, in which items are selected for a scale on the basis of their empirical ability to distinguish between members of the two or more comparison groups. He presented his basic item pool of 400 items to a well-defined occupational group, say lawyers. The items consisted of occupations such as actor, architect, lawyer, mechanical engineer, or research scientist. The group of lawyers indicated for each occupation whether they would like, dislike, or feel neutrally about each occupation. The responses of the lawyers would be compared with those of people in general, and those occupations for which the lawyers expressed preferences that differed from people in general would appear on the lawyer interest scale. For example, if 45 percent of the lawyers indicated that they would like the work of a research scientist and only 10 percent of people in general expressed that preference, the item *research scientist* would appear on the lawyer interest scale. An individual who indicated liking for the work of a research scientist would subsequently receive a point on the lawyer interest scale. The meaning of the individual's preference for this occupation is *not* taken as a direct indication that he or she would like to be a research scientist; rather, that preference is interpreted as indicating that the individual has the same interest as that of lawyers. If the pattern of the individual's likes and dislikes across many occupations is similar to that of lawyers, the individual is assumed to share interests with lawyers and might therefore like to be a lawyer.

## Holland's Theory of Vocational Choice

A major criticism of empirically developed interest inventories is that they offer no theory (other than that "birds of a feather flock together") to explain vocational preferences. In 1966, Holland proposed a psychological theory of vocational choice that combined personality, occupation, and organizational structure. This theory was designed to explain why different types of people would prefer different types of occupations. The theory relies heavily on the concept of **person–environment fit**. An individual prefers those occupations whose job requirements and organizational structure fit the individual's personality.

Holland identified six types of work environments and arranged them in the hexagonal structure shown in Figure 17-1. Some sample occupations are also shown in the structure. Environments that are adjacent to each other, such as *realistic* and *investigative,* are assumed to share some components, whereas environments that are across from each other, such as *artistic* and *conventional,* are assumed to be largely unrelated in their work requirements and employment settings. Holland further proposed that each of these six work environments would attract people with specific personality traits. Moreover, people who found themselves in a work environment that was incompatible with their personality should generally be dissatisfied with their occupation. Table 17-1 presents some of the personality characteristics associated with each type of work environment.

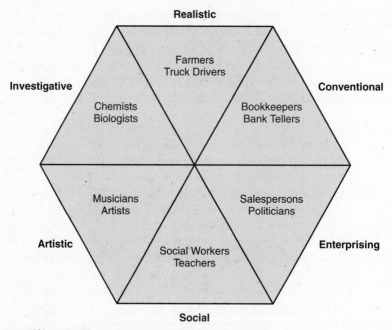

**Figure 17-1** ⊗  Holland's Structural Model of Work Environments.

## Table 17-1
Personality Correlates of Holland's Six Work Environments

**Realistic**

unsociable, mature, masculine, extraverted, persistent

**Investigative**

unsociable, masculine, self-sufficient, introverted, persistent

**Social**

cheerful, adventurous, conservative, feminine, dominant, dependent, responsive, sociable

**Conventional**

conforming, conservative, dependent, masculine, playful, extroverted, responsible

**Enterprising**

sociable, dominant, cheerful, adventurous, conservative, dependent, impulsive, extraverted, playful

**Artistic**

immature, effeminate, paranoid, introverted

Based on Osipow, S. H. (1983). *Theories of Career Development* (*Third Edition*). Englewood Cliffs, NJ, Prentice Hall: p. 88.

Holland's theory has provided a powerful and comprehensive model, which has been used to classify every job in the *Dictionary of Occupational Titles* published by the United States Government. In addition, Holland's theory has received a substantial amount of empirical support. Holland developed two measures of his theoretical constructs: the first, the *Vocational Preference Inventory* (Holland, 1958), was actually developed prior to Holland's formulation of his theory and produces interest scores for the six work environments. The second instrument is the *Self-Directed Search* (Holland, 1985) which is designed to allow the individual to explore his or her interests in a self-directed, personalized format. This instrument also provides scores on the six work environments. By use of these instruments, support for the stability (Holland, 1963), structure (Holland, Whitney, Cole, and Richards, 1969), and personality correlates of the work environment scores (Holland, Gottfredson, and Nafziger, 1975) has been obtained. More recently, Holland's theory has been related to circumplex models of interpersonal behavior (Broughton, Trapnell, and Boyes, 1991) and career scales from other inventories (e.g., Ahadi, 1991; Hansen and Campbell, 1985).

Holland's theory has been found to explain job satisfaction among disabled persons (Jagger, Neukrug, and McAuliffe, 1992), and a recent conceptual elaboration of the theory (Meir, 1993) suggests that its contributions go beyond the hexagonal structural model to providing a complex characterization of impact of the congruence between work environment and personality on satisfaction, performance, and achievement in the workplace.

# Motivation

A central concern of employers is worker motivation. It is also, indirectly, a concern of consumers, because products that are made by unmotivated workers may be flawed and substandard. For optimal job performance it is not enough that an individual has the ability to perform the a job; that individual must also be motivated to perform that job to the best of his or her ability. All of us have had the positive experience of dealing with a motivated salesperson, mechanic, waiter, or professor who paid extra attention to our needs and therefore provided us with optimal service, whether it was finding the right article of clothing, fixing our car efficiently, helping put the baby in the high chair at a restaurant, or individually going over a class project. Unfortunately, we all have experienced the dissatisfaction and frustration that results from dealing with unmotivated workers as well.

## Intrinsic and Extrinsic Motivation

Most psychological theories of motivation distinguish between **extrinsic motivation** and **intrinsic motivation**. Intrinsic motivation concerns the drive to work because the work is itself rewarding. The scientist who conducts research because it is challenging to design studies and analyze data, the stockbroker who finds patterns of investment fascinating, and the author who enjoys finding the right word or phrase are all motivated by the intrinsic rewards of their work. In contrast, extrinsic motivation is the drive to work because of the rewards one receives when the work is completed. The scientist who conducts research to obtain tenure, the stockbroker who studies investment patterns to make money, and the author who writes books to please editors and win the praise of critics are motivated by extrinsic rewards.

A number of individuals have commented on the changes in values and motivation that have occurred in the work force (Yankelovich, 1979; Donovan, 1984). Older workers have been characterized as motivated by extrinsic considerations such as money, promotion, and job security. In contrast, younger workers are characterized as motivated by intrinsic features of the job such as the challenges it poses, the need for creativity, and the opportunities it provides for personal growth and learning. To some extent, these differences may reflect a shift in the requirements of many jobs from physical labor and routine tasks to mental effort and unique applications. An exception to this pattern is provided by modern professional athletes who are young but who have been stereotyped, perhaps unfairly, as motivated by money and endorsements rather than a love of the game. However, regardless of whether motivation is intrinsic or extrinsic, employers have an interest in finding and/or producing motivated employees.

Extrinsic motivation is typically explained through learning principles based on how people respond to different types of external reward structures. Intrinsic motivation has, therefore, been of more interest to personality psychologists because it is used to explain why people engage and persist in tasks for which there are no clear extrinsic rewards (White, 1959).

## Psychological Theories of Motivation

Several psychological theories of motivation have been applied to understanding and promoting worker motivation. Box 17-1 summarizes the major theories and their implications for the workplace.

## Motivation as a Personality Variable

Most research on intrinsic and extrinsic motivation has had a social psychological emphasis on the situational factors that influence an individual's temporary motivational state (e.g., Deci, 1971; Lepper and Greene, 1978). Much of this research that has experimentally manipulated the extent to which an individual is intrinsically or extrinsically motivated in a particular situation has found that extrinsically motivated individuals exhibit several negative side effects relative to intrinsically motivated individuals. For example, extrinsic motivation resulted in less creativity (Amabile, Goldfarb, and Brackfield, 1990), more impatience (Garbarino, 1975), and less learning (McCullers and Martin, 1971).

More recently, several investigators have conceptualized the tendency to be extrinsically or intrinsically motivated as a trait-like disposition rather than an experimentally manipulated state (e.g., Harter, 1981; de Charms, 1976). In 1985, Deci and Ryan proposed the construct of **causality orientation** and introduced the General Causation Orientation Scale to assess three components of causality orientation in adults: autonomy, control, and impersonal. Causality orientation concerns individuals' general preferences for how they like the regulation of reinforcements in their lives to be structured. Among other predictions, Deci and Ryan argued that autonomy-oriented individuals will generally be intrinsically motivated, whereas control-oriented individuals will be extrinsically motivated.

Work Preference Inventory. The most direct and successful attempt to assess the general tendency to be intrinsically or extrinsically motivated has been the work of Amabile and her colleagues. In 1994, Amabile, Hill, Hennessey, and Tighe reported on the development and evaluation of the **Work Preference Inventory (WPI)**. This inventory assesses the major elements of intrinsic motivation, such as self-determination, competence, task involvement, curiosity, enjoyment, and in-

BOX 17-1

## Psychological Theories of Motivation Applied to the Workplace

McClelland's (1985) **need-achievement theory** (discussed in Chapter 13) views the need to achieve in the workplace as a trait. According to this view, organizations do not need to generate motivation; rather, they need to identify high *n* Achievement individuals and provide working conditions that will allow them to achieve.

Maslow's (1970) **needs-hierarchy theory** (discussed in Chapter 7) has influenced managers and executives who have accepted a need for **self-actualization** as an important motivating force. However, this theory has received little empirical support (Wahba and Bridwell, 1976).

**The ERG (existence-relatedness-growth) theory** (Alderfer, 1972) is similar to Maslow's theory, but it has been more specifically linked to the work environment. Employers meet existence needs through the provision of salary, health benefits, a safe working environment, and job security. They meet relatedness needs by providing a structure where workers interact on and off the job, and they meet growth needs by providing the opportunity for challenge, independence, and creativity on the job so as to enhance self-esteem.

**The motivator-hygiene theory** (Herzberg, 1974) also divides needs into existence (hygiene) needs and growth (motivator) needs. However, the failure to satisfy hygiene needs in the workplace results in job dissatisfaction, whereas meeting motivator needs results in job satisfaction. Although this theory has been declining in popularity, it is the basis for the concept of **job enrichment** (Herzberg, 1968), which has had substantial influence on the redesign of many jobs to satisfy motivator needs.

**The job characteristics theory** (Hackman and Oldham, 1976) developed from an analysis of job characteristics that relate to worker satisfaction. However, the theory emphasizes the importance of the worker's phenomenological perceptions of job attributes rather than the objective characterization of the job. The important job characteristics are (1) the skill requirements, (2) whether the job completes tasks or does parts of them, (3) the importance of the job to the business, (4) the degree of autonomy of the employee, and (5) the degree and nature of feedback about job performance. Hackman and Oldham provide suggestions for redesigning jobs on these characteristics to make the jobs more motivating.

**Expectancy theory** (Vroom, 1964) is one of the most popular theories of motivation in the workplace. The theory reflects social learning principles (Chapter 11) and emphasizes that workers will be more motivated as their expectation of being rewarded for good performance increases. The goal of employers is to establish and maintain good expectations.

*(continued)*

BOX 17-1 (*continued*)

**Goal-setting theory** (Locke, 1968) is also related to social learning principles and is perhaps the most thoroughly investigated theory of workplace motivation. The theory is based on the premise that motivation results from a desire to achieve a particular goal. Goals direct attention, mobilize energy and effort, increase persistence, and motivate the development of skills needed to meet the goal.

Adams (1965) proposed **equity theory** from the observation that workers seem more motivated if they perceive that they are being treated equitably. However, there are individual differences in how people respond to perceptions of equity or inequity. **Benevolent individuals** are satisfied if they believe that they are undercompensated and feel guilty when they are over compensated or perhaps even equitably compensated. **Equity-sensitivity persons** believe everyone, including themselves, should be treated fairly. Finally, **entitled persons** believe that they are due everything they can get. Thus, they feel distressed whenever they are undercompensated or even equitably compensated. Equity theory represents a combination of individual difference, situational, and phenomenological variables.

terest, and the major elements of extrinsic motivation, such as competition, evaluation, recognition, money, and constraints. The inventory yields scores on both an intrinsic motivation (IM) and an extrinsic motivation (EM) scale. Some sample items from each scale are presented in Table 17-2.

Consistent with their conceptualization of the WPI as assessing intrinsic and extrinsic motivation as stable traits, Amabile et al. (1994) report that the scores on the two scales are stable across a six-month period with test–retest correlations of .84 and .94 on the IM and EM scales, respectively, in a student sample, and .89 and .80, respectively, in a sample of working adults. Amabile et al. also report that scores on the IM and EM scales are generally correlated with scores on other personality and motivational measures in patterns consistent with theories of intrinsic and extrinsic motivation. For example, the IM scales are positively correlated with measures of creativity, whereas the EM scales correlate negatively with those measures. As you might have guessed by reading the sample items, IM correlates positively with need for cognition (see Chapter 15) and EM correlates negatively with this construct. IM correlates positively with the autonomy scale and negatively with the control and impersonal scales from Deci and Ryan's (1985) Causation Orientation Inventory. The EM scale shows the opposite pattern of correlations with these scales. Finally, the IM scale correlated positively with Holland's investigative (science) occupation preference, which was scored from the Strong Interest Inventory.

&#9901; Table 17-2

Sample Items to Measure Intrinsic and Extrinsic Motivation from the Work Preference Inventory

**Intrinsic Motivation**

1. I enjoy tackling problems that are completely new to me.
2. I prefer to figure things out for myself.
3. Curiosity is the driving force behind much of what I do.
4. I'm more comfortable when I can set my own goals.
5. What matters most to me is enjoying what I do.
6. I want to find out how good I can really be at my work.

**Extrinsic Motivation**

1. To me, success means doing better than other people.
2. I'm less concerned with what work I do than what I get for it.
3. I prefer having someone set clear goals for me in my work.
4. I have to feel that I am earning something for what I do.
5. I'm concerned about how other people are going to react to my ideas.
6. I believe that there is no point in doing a good job if nobody else knows about it.

From Amabile, T. M., Hill, K. G., Hennessey, B. A., and Tighe, E. M. (1994). The Work Preference Inventory: Assessing Intrinsic and Extrinsic Motivational Orientations. *Journal of Personality and Social Psychology, 66*, 950–967.

One of the most interesting findings obtained from the WPI is the empirical independence of the IM and EM scales (correlations of –.08 and –.21 for the working adult and student samples, respectively). Within the motivation literature, intrinsic and extrinsic motivation have typically been viewed as opposites. The more an individual was intrinsically motivated, the less he or she would be extrinsically motivated, and vice versa. This conceptualization implies a substantial negative correlation between scores on the two scales, whereas only a small correlation was obtained. The independence of these two scales means that some individuals may be motivated intrinsically *or* extrinsically, other individuals may be *both* intrinsically and extrinsically motivated, and still others may not be motivated by anything. The traditional social psychological approach to studying motivation through experimental manipulation would have masked the independence of these intrinsic or extrinsic motivations, because only one could have been created at a time. This would make it appear that two types of motivation were opposites, and apparently they are not. Not only does this finding complicate the study of motivation, it illustrates the danger of concluding that we know what people are *naturally* like on the basis of methods that *experimentally* manipulate them to be that way (Hogan and Cheek, 1983).

# Leadership

**Leadership** is a topic of considerable importance in organizations. A central concern of nearly all organizations such as businesses, governmental agencies, universities, nonprofit organizations, and the military is finding and training effective leaders. Rightly or wrongly, failures in these organizations are often blamed on poor leadership. Likewise, success in organizations is often credited to good leadership, and individuals who have the reputation of being good leaders are often recruited with lavish salaries, lucrative stock options, and numerous fringe benefits.

Psychologists have studied leadership in a variety of ways. Theories and research have attempted to specify and identify the characteristics of successful and unsuccessful leaders; the effects of various leadership styles on productivity, worker morale, and motivation have been intensively studied; and a variety of techniques for training individuals to be better leaders have been proposed and evaluated. Personality psychology has considerable relevance to issues of leadership. In general, the behavior of leaders and the manner in which they lead reflects their implicit assumptions about human nature—a topic of central importance in personality psychology. Therefore, formal theories of leadership also concern human nature. In addition, many qualities of good and poor leaders are personality characteristics (Hogan, Curphy, and Hogan, 1994).

## Theory X and Theory Y

During the early part of this century, the dominant philosophy of management and leadership was **scientific management** (Taylor, 1911). The emphasis of this approach was increasing production levels through optimizing the physical work environment. Under this approach, workers were generally viewed as extensions of the machines on which they worked. This theory of leadership was based on an unflattering view of the characteristics of workers. They were regarded as lazy, dishonest, shiftless, and unintelligent. As a result of the famous **Hawthorne experiments** (Roethlisberger and Dickson, 1939), this view of workers and how they should be managed and led changed dramatically.

The Hawthorne experiments concerned how changes in the work environment would affect worker productivity. Originally, the studies, which took place between 1927 and 1932 at the Hawthorne (Chicago) plant of the Western Electric Company, were designed as engineering studies to determine optimal work conditions such as illumination and the timing of rest breaks for worker productivity. However, with the discovery of the **Hawthorne effect,** the studies became more psychologically focused. In essence, the Hawthorne effect refers to increases in worker productivity that occur despite no changes in the physical work environment or even changes that seem counterproductive. For example, the most striking result was an increase in productivity when workers thought that illumination had increased even though it had not. Indeed, productivity was not adversely affected when illumination levels were equivalent to moonlight! The explanation for these results was that simply paying attention to workers and treating them as people rather than machines increased their morale, which increased their productivity regardless of the physical work environment. This interpretation has been a source of considerable controversy (Adair, Sharpe, and Huynh, 1989), and there was some suggestion that the conclusion of the authors was based more on the political motivation of promoting humanistic social policy than on scientific considerations (Jones, 1990). However, the results as they were originally presented spawned the **human relations** approach to leadership, which emphasized the importance of the psychological work environment for productivity. Under this approach, the humanity of workers was recognized and they were regarded as industrious, creative, responsible and capable.

In 1960, MacGregor formalized the scientific management and human relations styles of leadership as **Theory X** and **Theory Y**. Theory X reflected the earlier scientific management approach and was based on three major assumptions about human nature:

1. People generally dislike work and avoid it or minimize it whenever possible.
2. Thus, people must be forced, manipulated, threatened, and punished to make them put forth enough effort to satisfy the company's goals.
3. People prefer to be directed, avoid responsibility, and want security.

According to Theory X, a leader needs to be demanding and dictatorial. Workers must be scolded and treated like children to make them do any work at all.

Theory Y reflects the human relations approach to leadership and is in direct contrast to Theory X. Theory Y is generally consistent with contemporary views of motivation and is based on five assumptions about human nature:

1. People do not dislike work; for many it is a source of satisfaction.
2. Most people display self-discipline in working for organizational goals; they do not need to be threatened.
3. Most people not only accept responsibility but seek it.
4. The ability to be creative, imaginative, and resourceful in solving organizational problems is widely distributed in the population. It is not limited to a few select managers.
5. Reward is the most effective means to make people committed to organizational goals.

Theory Y requires leaders to relate to their workers as people, to give them responsibility, to be sensitive to their needs, and to listen to their insights and suggestions about organizational problems and goals. Theory Y is the basis for the widespread emphasis on **sensitivity training, training groups ("T-groups")**, and communication skills in management education (Fulmer, 1983). Theory Y reflects the influence of humanistic theories of personality, such as those of Abraham Maslow and Carl Rogers, which were discussed in Chapter 7.

## Specific Theories of Leadership

Theory X and Theory Y represent the two extremes of leadership styles. Most contemporary theories of organizational leadership emphasize that effective leadership is a complex function of the characteristics of the leader, the characteristics of the workers, the demands of the work tasks, and the structure of the organization. In addition, leadership style is generally viewed as being on a continuum rather than as purely authoritarian (Theory X) or democratic (Theory Y). Figure 17-2 illustrates this continuum of leadership style.

Fiedler's Contingency Theory. The best known and most thoroughly investigated theory of leadership is Fiedler's (1978) **contingency theory**. According to contingency theory, a leader's effectiveness is a function of the interaction between the leader's personal characteristics and the features of the situation. Leader characteristics are classified as ranging from person-oriented to task-oriented. The important situational variable is the extent to which the leader exercises control

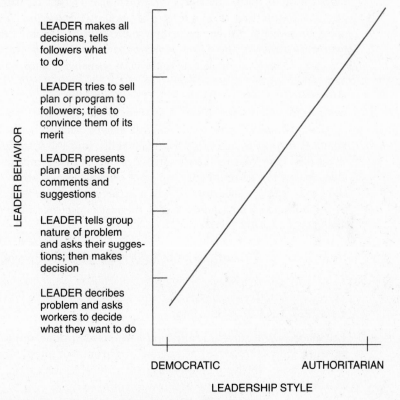

**Figure 17-2**   Authoritarian-democratic leadership continuum.

Adapted from Psychology and industry today: an introduction to industrial and organizational psychology, 5e by Schultz/Schultz. Copyright © 1990 by S. Schultz and D. Schultz.

and can influence the workers and their interactions. To assess the personality of the leader, Fielder developed the **Least-Preferred Co-worker Scale (LPC)** (Fiedler, 1976), which is shown in Figure 17-3. High scorers on the LPC rate even their least preferred co-worker in generally positive terms. Such individuals are viewed as person-oriented and as emphasizing close interpersonal relationships for accomplishing work tasks. Low-scoring LPC managers—those who have a strong negative reaction to people they had trouble working with—are viewed as task-oriented. Situational control is indicated by (1) the support leaders receive from the group, (2) the extent to which leaders know what to do and how to do it to accomplish a task, and (3) the degree of power the leader has in the organization and over his or her subordinates.

Research based on contingency theory suggests that task-oriented leaders function best when their control and influence is either very high or very low. Person-oriented leaders are most effective when their control is moderate. Contingency theory is also the basis for **leader match training.** Leader match training emphasizes changing environments to match a leader's personality. Leaders are taught how to assess their organizational situation in terms of subordinate support, task structure, and power. They are also given the LPC. On the basis of these assessments, leaders determine the extent to which their situation matches their personality; if the match is poor they are given training for changing their situation to make it more consistent with their leadership style. In 1987, Fiedler and Garcia proposed an elaboration of contingency theory that they called **cognitive resource utilization theory.** This theory also considers the interaction between leader characteristics and situational variables as the basis for leader effectiveness. However, the focus of this newer theory is the leader's cognitive abilities, such as intelligence, technical skills, and job knowledge. In addition to situational control, this theory introduces stress as an important workplace variable. According to the theory, an important source of stress for a leader comes from that leader's superiors. When a leader has a stressful relationship with his or her boss, the leader tends to rely on past experience rather than creativity or intelligence to solve problems.

**Other Theories.** Other theories of leadership have been proposed; they are summarized in Box 17-2.

## Personality Characteristics

The theories of leadership reflect different assumptions about human nature and have generally emphasized personality–environment interactions to explain effective leadership. In this section we consider the research on the general personality characteristics of successful and unsuccessful leaders.

**Characteristics of Emergent Leaders.** A common paradigm in early social psychology studies of leadership was the **leaderless discussion group.** Using this method, individuals were formed into groups and asked to discuss a topic. Of interest

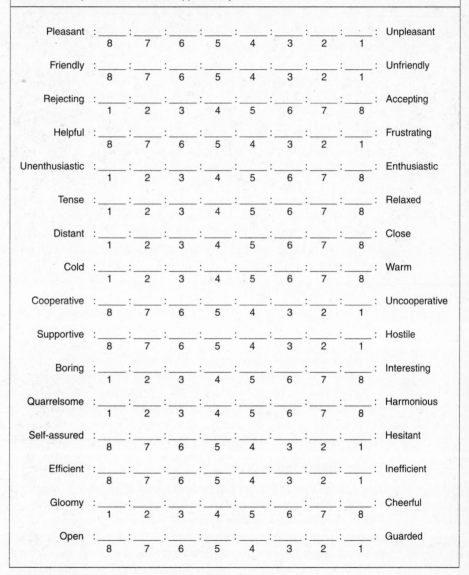

Think of the person with whom you can work least well. He or she may be someone you work with now, or someone you knew in the past. He or she does not have to be the person you like least well, but should be the person with whom you had the most difficulty in getting a job done. Describe this person as he or she appears to you.

| Pleasant | : ___ : ___ : ___ : ___ : ___ : ___ : ___ : ___ : | Unpleasant |
| | 8 7 6 5 4 3 2 1 | |
| Friendly | : ___ : ___ : ___ : ___ : ___ : ___ : ___ : ___ : | Unfriendly |
| | 8 7 6 5 4 3 2 1 | |
| Rejecting | : ___ : ___ : ___ : ___ : ___ : ___ : ___ : ___ : | Accepting |
| | 1 2 3 4 5 6 7 8 | |
| Helpful | : ___ : ___ : ___ : ___ : ___ : ___ : ___ : ___ : | Frustrating |
| | 8 7 6 5 4 3 2 1 | |
| Unenthusiastic | : ___ : ___ : ___ : ___ : ___ : ___ : ___ : ___ : | Enthusiastic |
| | 1 2 3 4 5 6 7 8 | |
| Tense | : ___ : ___ : ___ : ___ : ___ : ___ : ___ : ___ : | Relaxed |
| | 1 2 3 4 5 6 7 8 | |
| Distant | : ___ : ___ : ___ : ___ : ___ : ___ : ___ : ___ : | Close |
| | 1 2 3 4 5 6 7 8 | |
| Cold | : ___ : ___ : ___ : ___ : ___ : ___ : ___ : ___ : | Warm |
| | 1 2 3 4 5 6 7 8 | |
| Cooperative | : ___ : ___ : ___ : ___ : ___ : ___ : ___ : ___ : | Uncooperative |
| | 8 7 6 5 4 3 2 1 | |
| Supportive | : ___ : ___ : ___ : ___ : ___ : ___ : ___ : ___ : | Hostile |
| | 8 7 6 5 4 3 2 1 | |
| Boring | : ___ : ___ : ___ : ___ : ___ : ___ : ___ : ___ : | Interesting |
| | 1 2 3 4 5 6 7 8 | |
| Quarrelsome | : ___ : ___ : ___ : ___ : ___ : ___ : ___ : ___ : | Harmonious |
| | 1 2 3 4 5 6 7 8 | |
| Self-assured | : ___ : ___ : ___ : ___ : ___ : ___ : ___ : ___ : | Hesitant |
| | 8 7 6 5 4 3 2 1 | |
| Efficient | : ___ : ___ : ___ : ___ : ___ : ___ : ___ : ___ : | Inefficient |
| | 8 7 6 5 4 3 2 1 | |
| Gloomy | : ___ : ___ : ___ : ___ : ___ : ___ : ___ : ___ : | Cheerful |
| | 1 2 3 4 5 6 7 8 | |
| Open | : ___ : ___ : ___ : ___ : ___ : ___ : ___ : ___ : | Guarded |
| | 8 7 6 5 4 3 2 1 | |

**Figure 17-3** ⬡ Least preferred co-worker scale.

were the processes through which a leader emerged in the group. In 1948, Stogdill reviewed research using this paradigm that had obtained personality in-formation on the emergent leaders. He found that individuals who became leaders were dominant, extraverted, sociable, ambitious, responsible, trusted, self-confident, emotionally stable, cooperative, and tactful. Hogan, Curphy, and Hogan (1994) translated these characteristics into the Big Five and concluded

BOX 17-2
## Other Theories of Leadership

### Path-goal Theory

Proposed by House (1971), this theory emphasizes the types of behaviors or "paths" leaders should use to help subordinates achieve their goals. Four paths can be used: (1) *directive*, in which the leader tells employees how to achieve their goals, (2) *supportive*, in which the leader shows concern and support for subordinates, (3) *participative*, in which leaders allow subordinates to participate in work decisions, and (4) *achievement-oriented*, in which the leader sets challenging goals for subordinates and emphasizes high standards. Effective leaders are able to apply different paths with different workers and in different situations.

### Normative Decision Theory

This theory (Vroom and Yetten, 1973) focuses on decision making as the crucial component of leadership. The theory emphasizes the degree to which leaders allow subordinates to participate in decisions, ranging from complete autocracy to complete consensus. Effective leadership depends upon (1) the quality of decisions, (2) the acceptance of the decision by subordinates, and (3) the speed at which the decision is reached. Good leadership requires optimizing these three goals through flexibility in decision-making style. For example, a consensual decision style will likely increase employee acceptance but slow down the decision process. The leader must decide which aspect of the decision is more important in a particular situation.

### Vertical Linkage Theory

This theory (Graen, 1976) emphasizes the relationships between leaders and followers. It distinguishes between in-group members whom the leader trusts and views as competent and out-group members who are viewed as incompetent and poorly motivated. Leaders use *supervision*, leadership based on formal authority, with out-group members. Out-group members are assigned low-level tasks, and there is no personal relationship between leaders and out-group members. With in-group members, leaders use *leadership*, which relies on persuasion. In-group members are given responsibility and important tasks, and they typical have a personal relationship with the leader. An effective leader works to increase the amount of leadership and decrease the amount of supervision they employ.

(continued)

BOX 17-2 (continued)

**Situational Leadership Theory**

This theory (Hersey and Blanchard, 1982) characterizes leader-follower relationships along two dimensions: (1) the extent to which leaders organize and direct subordinates' work and (2) the extent to which employers develop and maintain a personal relationship with employees. This conceptualization allows for four combinations of high and low work direction and high and low personal relationships. Thus, a leader can direct work and have personal relationships, direct work and not have personal relationships, and so on. The theory suggest that leaders should have different types of associations with different types of employees.

that people who became leaders of initially leaderless groups were high on Factors I (extroversion), II (agreeableness), III (conscientiousness), and IV (emotional stability). Perhaps it is not surprising that people who are selected as leaders generally have a wide range of desirable personality characteristics. More interesting is that personality variables generally predict emergent leadership as well as, or better than, other variables such as abilities, attitudes, and demographic characteristics (Kenny and Zaccaro, 1983).

Characteristics of Effective Leaders.    Hogan, Curphy, and Hogan (1994) summarized evidence, again using the Big Five, that certain personality characteristics are consistently correlated with effective leadership. For example, Bentz (1990) studied executive selection at the large retail company Sears. The executives promoted to the highest levels were articulate and active (Factor I), hard-working and responsible (Factor III), and independent and self-confident (Factor IV). Bray and Howard (1983; Howard and Bray, 1990) reported similar findings with executives at the communications conglomerate AT&T. The personality traits that best predicted managerial promotion were the desire for advancement and a readiness to make decisions (Factor I), inner work standards (Factor III), resistance to stress and tolerance for uncertainty (Factor IV), and range of interests (Factor V, intellect). Box 17-3 presents information about the personality characteristics of airline pilots.

Characteristics of Leaders Who Fail.    The focus of most research on leadership is on the positive qualities of effective leaders. However, leaders and their teams often fail. There is evidence that otherwise bright, competent, and committed managers fail because of a "dark side" (Hogan et al., 1994) to their personalities. Some of the characteristics of managers who fail include arrogance, vindictiveness, selfishness, emotionality, aloofness, and abrasiveness (e.g., Lombardo, Ruderman, and McCauley, 1988). Leaders who possess these undesirable traits generally have teams that perform more poorly than leaders who do not possess these characteristics. In addition, it appears that subordinates are always aware

BOX 17-3
## Personality Characteristics of Airline Pilots

Chidester, Helmreich, Gregorich, and Geis (1991) and Foushee and Helmreich (1988) studied the relation between a pilot's personality measures and the performance of his or her commercial airline flight crews. Given that breakdowns in team performance are the most common explanation of air transportation disasters, this research has important implications for the selection and training of airline pilots. This research demonstrated a clear relation between the personality of the pilot and the performance of the flight crew. Pilots who were warm, friendly, self-confident, and able to handle stress had crews that made the fewest, and the least significant, errors. In contrast, pilots who were arrogant, hostile, boastful, egotistical, dictatorial, and passive-aggressive had crews who made the largest number of, and the most significant, errors. These findings are especially troubling because personality is not typically considered during the process of airline pilot selection.

of this dark side (Harris and Hogan, 1992). Harris and Hogan (1992) note that these undesirable characteristics are difficult to detect in a hiring situation because, in potential managers, they often occur in the company of good social skills. Thus, in interviews these potential managers do well and their undesirable tendencies become apparent only after they have been hired.

The difficulty of detecting undesirable employee characteristics until after the person has been hired has been a major concern for employers. This issue is particularly salient for the issue of employee honesty and integrity.

## Honesty and Integrity

It is estimated that employee theft results in over $15 billion in losses each year to American business (Shepard and Duston, 1987). As many as 30 percent of all business failures may be due to employee theft (American Management Association, 1977). Although theft is the most obvious problem, other forms of employee dishonesty such as lying about hours worked, deliberately failing to complete jobs or contact customers, and falsely calling in sick also have a negative impact on businesses. Thus, it is not surprising that employers have a strong interest in identifying job applicants who have the potential to behave dishonestly before they are hired and to detect current employees who are dishonest. Historically, **polygraph tests** ("**lie detectors**") were frequently used in employment situations to identify potential and actual dishonest employees. In 1988, the **Em-**

ployee **Polygraph Protection Act** was enacted into law by the United States Congress. This act severely restricted the use of "lie detectors" in employment screening. As a replacement for polygraphs, numerous paper-and-pencil **integrity or "honesty" tests** have been developed.

## Polygraphs

Polygraphs are devices that are designed to detect changes in overall physiological arousal as indicated by changes in heart rate, breathing rate, blood pressure, and **galvanic skin response** (the electrical resistance of the skin that is related to perspiration). Although polygraphs are often referred to as lie detectors, this is misleading. The polygraph has no means for directly showing whether a person has lied. A better name for the polygraph might be "anxiety detector" because it is designed to assess physiological responses that are associated with nervousness, tenseness, and anxiety. The theory on which polygraph testing is based is that a person who answers most questions truthfully (e.g., "Is your name Erica Smith?") but lies on a key question ("Have you ever used illegal "inside" information in trading stocks?") will exhibit more nervous physiological arousal to the lies.

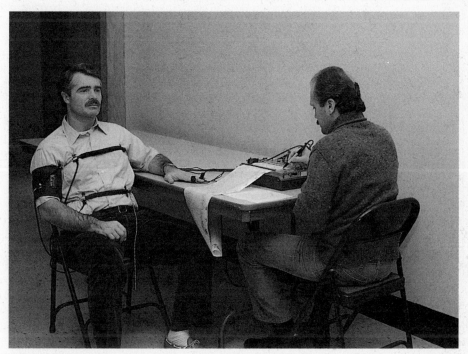

The polygraph test.

The general public and many law enforcement officers and employers view the polygraph as a near-perfect window into the mind of the criminal or dishonest employee. Learning that a suspect has agreed to take a polygraph test makes most of us believe that the person is not guilty; likewise, refusal to take a polygraph test is often viewed as solid evidence of guilt. However, research generally shows that the accuracy of polygraph tests is far from perfect. Between 10 and 15 percent of innocent people appear guilty on the standard lie detector test, and the results of such a test, as well as a person's refusal to take one, are seldom admissible as evidence in court. One form of the polygraph test, the **guilty knowledge test**, does appear to be useful for detecting innocence (Lykken, 1974). Using this test, the polygraph examiner asks a crime suspect questions (e.g., "Did you steal the television around midnight?" "around 3 AM?" "around 6 AM?") to which only the person who committed the crime (and the police) could know the correct answer. Signs of nervousness around the correct answer are interpreted as evidence of guilty knowledge. Innocent people seldom fail this test, although guilty people can occasionally pass it.

In employment screening, the guilty knowledge test is not generally applicable. Instead, general questions about past deeds of dishonesty (e.g., "Have you ever stolen from an employer") or future intentions to be dishonest (e.g., "If I knew I would not be caught I would steal from my employer") might be used. Supporters of polygraph testing (e.g., Fry and Fry, 1988) claim that the results of polygraph tests in such circumstances are more than 90 percent accurate in detecting dishonest potential or current employees. However, several factors are known to reduce the accuracy of polygraph tests for detecting guilty employees. They include tranquilizers, self-inflicted pain, thinking disturbing thoughts, and being able to lie without feeling anxious. Moreover, many people who submit to a polygraph test in these circumstances are found to be "lying" when they are actually telling the truth (Murphy, 1987). A major government study by the Office of Technology Assessment (1983) concluded that the polygraph had *no value* for personnel selection and employee screening. The Employee Polygraph Protection Act was passed on the basis of this evidence and with the support of the American Psychological Association, which provided psychologists as expert witnesses to the government hearings on this issue.

## Integrity Tests

The invalidity of polygraph tests created a strong market for methods that employees could effectively and legally use to detect dishonest employees. The primary alternative to polygraphs is an **integrity test**. Integrity tests are paper-and-pencil, self-report measures that are designed to detect, and therefore screen out, potential employees who may engage in dishonest acts such as theft. Some tests can also be used with current employees in the context of promotion, workforce reduction, or employee assistance decisions.

Hogan (1990) notes that integrity tests are either broad or narrow in focus. Narrow-integrity tests are similar to polygraph test questions in that they ask the respondent specific questions about their attitudes toward theft and other dishonest behavior. Broad-integrity tests view theft and dishonesty as specific examples of the broader class of counterproductive work behaviors that might include drug abuse, malingering, sabotage, and tardiness. Narrow integrity tests are typically **overt tests**, that is, tests whose purpose is clear to the respondent. Broad tests are more **covert** in that their purpose is often disguised. Table 17-3 describes the six major integrity tests that were reviewed in Hogan and Hogan, (1990).

## Evaluation of Integrity Tests

As was the case for polygraphs, integrity tests are a source of controversy in the employment testing literature (Camara and Schneider, 1994; 1995; Lilienfeld, Alliger, and Mitchell, 1995; Ones, Viswesvaran, and Schmidt, 1995; Rieke, and Guastello, 1995). One of the reasons for the controversy is that the narrow criterion that the tests are supposed to predict—theft—is difficult to measure. Although theft occurs frequently in the workplace, the frequency with which employees are caught stealing is low. As a result, it is difficult to assess the validity of these tests. One review (U.S. Congress, 1990) could identify only five studies of integrity tests that obtained measures of theft as a criterion. Most of these

**Table 17-3**
Six Major Integrity Tests

**Broad Focused Tests**

1. *Employee Attitude Inventory*. This inventory assesses six aspects of counterproductive behavior: theft admissions, theft attitudes, theft knowledge, drug use, job burnout, and job dissatisfaction. The inventory is designed to be used with current employees.
2. *PDI Employment Inventory*. This instrument assesses productive (reliable, good work habits, and motivated) and counterproductive (irresponsible, risk-taking, unstable, and dishonest) behavior. It is designed to be used with applicants to predict who will be a productive or counterproductive employee.
3. *Personnel Reaction Blank*. This instrument assesses dependability, conscientiousness, reliability, and social conformity among job applicants.

**Narrow Focused Tests**

1. *Personnel Selection Inventory*. This instrument was specifically designed as a substitute for polygraph tests. It contains specific scales on theft, drug abuse, and violence and is designed to be used as a selection instrument to screen out potential employees who are likely to engage in those behaviors.
2. *Reid Report*. This measure is specifically designed to predict theft. It can be used with current employees or with applicants.
3. *Stanton Survey*. This instrument is designed to predict theft and dishonesty in those jobs where there is considerable opportunity for such behaviors. It is used as a screening device with applicants.

studies were methodologically flawed (Goldberg, Grenier, Guion, Sechrest, and Wing, 1991), and the report concluded that there were insufficient data to scientifically evaluate integrity tests. By use of a broader set of criteria, including a variety of forms of counterproductive behavior, job dissatisfaction, and emotional instability, Goldberg et al. (1991) concluded that "the preponderance of evidence is supportive of the tests predictive validity" (p. 26). Hogan and Hogan (1989) reached a similar conclusion regarding the ability of the broadly focused integrity tests to predict a variety of positive or negative work behaviors.

Construct Validity. The problem with the conclusions of these validity studies is that the construct assessed by integrity tests has shifted from specific forms of dishonesty to a broad constellation of desirable employee characteristics that are related to general job performance. Ones, Viswesvaran, and Schmidt (1995) report that the most effective view of integrity was a combination of conscientiousness, agreeableness, and emotional stability. It is questionable, from an ethical standpoint, to use the pretense of suspected dishonesty to screen out an applicant or terminate an employee, because he or she is unpleasant to be around and has bad work habits. Moreover, as Hogan (1990) notes, such screening may be counterproductive for some occupations. In general, individuals who score high on broad integrity tests tend to be honest and conscientious but also unimaginative and inflexible. Customer service, marketing, and sales jobs, for example, often require some spontaneity and willingness to take risks, and integrity measures will serve to screen out individuals with those qualities. "The exclusive usage of an honesty measure for selection purposes will ultimately yield a work force that is highly reliable and uncreative" (Hogan, 1990, p. 34).

Faking. In a sense, assessing honesty through a self-report measure is a logical contradiction. The situation is similar to the puzzle of interpreting the statement "Everything I say is a lie." For most questions on integrity tests (e.g., "Have you ever stolen from an employer?"), it is easy to determine what the acceptable answer would be. The dishonest applicant who was fired from a previous job from stealing would likely have little difficulty providing the dishonest answer "No" to the question. The honest applicant might think back to the day he or she took a pencil home from work and answer "Yes." In fact, there is good empirical evidence that overt integrity tests can be faked, (Ryan and Sackett, 1987), particularly when the applicant has been taught how to fake his or her responses (Alliger, Lilienfeld, & Mitchell, 1996).

Many integrity tests include a **lie scale** designed to detect dishonest responding. Lie scales generally consist of items in which one response is so unlikely that a person who makes that response is probably lying. For example, a "True" response to the items "I have never argued with anyone" or "I have never had a cold" would be a lie for most of us. Although one or two such responses might be legitimate, or at least honest mistakes, a person who makes many such unlikely responses is probably lying and would have unacceptable test scores. However, because the items on lie scales are generally easy to spot, it is not clear that lie scales would effectively detect a careful dishonest responder. Moreover, one study (Guastello and Rieke, 1991) found a *positive* correlation between scores on integrity tests and lie scales, suggesting that individuals who score higher on integrity tests have a stronger tendency to lie!

Moral Issues. The presumption of integrity testing is that moral behavior is a fixed characteristic that cannot be modified. Yet, this presumption contradicts the position of American culture that moral behavior can be taught, that criminals can be rehabilitated, and that a one-time dishonest person can "go straight." It is not clear that a person who was dishonest in the past and who admits it on an integrity test should be punished for doing so by not being hired. In addition, it is likely that dishonesty has a substantial situational component. Few of us would feel comfortable contemplating our behavior in a situation where a substantial amount of money was left lying about in a relatively deserted office. Perhaps the money that organizations are currently spending on the questionable effort to detect dishonest people would be better spent modifying the workplace to reduce the opportunities for theft and dishonest behavior.

## Personnel Selection

The theories and research on occupational interests, motivation, leadership, and integrity suggest that personality characteristics have a substantial impact on productivity, job satisfaction, and workplace behavior. Thus, measures of personality appear to be a critical component of personnel selection. However, during much of the history of personnel selection, personality measures were often not employed, and when they were used, their predictive power was generally disappointing. As Hogan (1990) notes:

> There is an important difference between what a person can do and what he or she is willing to do; the fact that a person has the capacity for good judgment doesn't mean that he or she will use it. And this, in turn means that a personnel selection program based entirely on measures of cognitive abilities is too narrow and will ignore critical features of human performance. A person's motives, values, needs, goals, and dispositions are all part of what is meant, loosely, by *personality*. It seems intuitively the case that personality should be a major (if not the major) predictor of job performance. Nonetheless, as recently as 1965 the principle reference work on personnel testing (Guion, 1965) made it clear that little persuasive data existed to support the use of personality measures for predicting job performance. (p. 25)

## Problems with Personality Measures

There are several reasons for the historically poor performance of personality measures at predicting employment outcome variables. One was the focus of early personality tests on negative and abnormal characteristics; a second was the view of personality measures as reflecting inner dispositions rather than describing behavior (see Chapters 13 and 14); a third was the susceptibility of personality tests to cheating.

**Personality as Psychopathology.** The earliest personality measures emphasized psychopathology. The forerunner of contemporary personality inventories, The *Woodward Psychoneurotic Inventory*, primarily concerned responses to stress, maladjustment, and neurotic tendencies. Indeed, it was originally designed to screen out potential soldiers who would likely react to combat experience with debilitating psychological problems. The best-known and most widely used personality measure, the Minnesota Multiphasic Personality Inventory (MMPI), was designed as a clinical diagnostic instrument. However, it has been used indiscriminantly to make a host of nonclinical predictions, ranging from graduate school admission to law enforcement officer selection (Scogin et al., 1995).

The focus of many personality measures on such characteristics as psychopathology, distress, neurosis, and low self-esteem provided information about only a limited domain of human personality. Although the knowledge that an individual is susceptible to, or has had, psychological problems can be useful in hiring decisions, knowing that an individual is *not* neurotic or emotionally unstable does not provide much information about the person's strengths, interests, and motives. It is not surprising that predicting positive job characteristics such as creativity, communication skill, leadership, integrity, and reliability from measures of psychopathology was generally not successful.

**Dispositions Versus Descriptions.** In Chapter 13 the scientific problems of viewing personality characteristics as dispositional were discussed. Historically, personality measures in employment settings were designed to assess the inner dispositions of a person that would cause that person to be successful or unsuccessful on the job. Hogan (1990) notes that personality measures based on this conceptualization were generally unrelated to employment behavior. The truism in employment testing is that "past behavior is the best predictor of future behavior." Personality measures that are based on items that summarize past behaviors (e.g., "Tends to talk with co-workers") rather than reveal hidden dispositions (e.g., "Talks with co-workers to hide insecurity") have generally been better predictors of behavior (Jackson, 1971).

**Cheating.** In contrast to ability measures (see Chapter 15), people can easily "cheat" (provide false information) on personality measures. It is not possible to pretend to be smarter than one is (unless one has access to the test answers and memorizes them before the session). However, one can claim to be more friendly, conscientious, or honest than one is by selecting answers that make one appear friendly, conscientious, or honest even if those answers are lies. For example, in applying for a job as a salesclerk in a department store at Christmas, an applicant would be unlikely to answer "true" to the following questions, even if he or she believed that these statements were accurate:

I prefer jobs dealing with computers rather than people.
I feel anxious in crowds.

To the extent that applicants pretend to be something they are not when responding to personality tests, the accuracy of their scores will likely be diminished. The vulnerability of personality tests to cheating has led to the publication of books (e.g., Liebers, 1966) that instruct job seekers how to respond to personality test items to enhance their chance of being hired (see Box 17-4).

## Contemporary Personality Assessment and Personnel Selection

Over the past decade, the use of personality measures in personnel selection has increased dramatically, and research is beginning to support the predictive validity of personality measures in several employment contexts. Hogan (1990) argues that the recent successes of personality assessment can be traced to particular developments, including the development of the **California Psychological Inventory (CPI)** (Gough, 1988), which emphasized normal personality in everyday life; the work of Jackson (1971) on the greater predictive power of descriptive rather than dispositional personality items; and the emergence of the Big Five as a structure of everyday personality description. The Big Five, especially, has provided a framework for guiding the study of personality correlates of job performance variables and a common system for summarizing and communicating previous and ongoing research on personality and the workplace.

There have been many studies demonstrating that various of the Big Five Factors are substantially related (correlations in the range of .40–.60) to different aspects of job performance (Barrick and Mount, 1991; Hough, Barge, Houston, McGue, and Kamp, 1985). Probably the single most important of the Big Five factors, in terms of the breadth of its predictive power, is Factor III (conscientiousness). However, different aspects of job performance are predicted by other Big Five factors as well. The conclusions of Hough et al. (1985) are summarized as follows:

• Factor I (extraversion) is positively related to performance in sales and management.

## BOX 17-4
## How to Cheat on Personality Tests

The important thing to recognize is that you don't win a good score; you avoid a bad one. . . .

By and large, however, your safety lies in getting a score somewhere between the 40th and 60th percentiles, which is to say, you should try to answer as if you were like everybody else is supposed to be. This is not always easy to figure out, of course. . . . When in doubt however, there are two general rules you can follow: (1) When asked for word associations or comments about the world give the most conventional, run-of-the-mill, pedestrian answer possible. (2) To settle on the most beneficial answer to any question, repeat to yourself:

1. I loved my father and my mother, but my father a little bit more.
2. I like things pretty well the way they are.
3. I never worry much about anything.
4. I don't care for books or music much.
5. I love my wife and children.
6. I don't let them get in the way of company work."

[Other bits of advice include]

"Don't be too dominant . . . As always, the middle course is best. Resist the temptation to show yourself as trying to control each situation."

"Choose your neurosis. When you come across questions . . . like . . . 'I often get pink spots all over'—be very much on your guard. Such questions were originally the by-product of efforts to screen mentally disturbed people; they measure degrees of neurotic tendency and were meant mainly for use in mental institutions and psychiatric clinics. The Organization has no business at all to throw these questions at you, but its curiosity is powerful and some companies have been adopting these questions as standard. Should you find yourself being asked about spiders, Oedipus complexes and such you must . . . remain consistent and as much in character as possible—these tests almost always have lie scores built into them. A few mild neuroses conceded here and there won't give you too bad a score. . . . "

From Liebers, A. (1966). *How to pass employment tests* (*Third Edition*). New York: Arco Publishing, pp. 94–98.

- Factor II (agreeableness) predicts supervisor ratings of job performance.
- Factor III (conscientiousness) correlates positively with academic performance and negatively with dishonesty and rule violations.

- Factor IV (emotional stability) predicts upward mobility and leadership status.
- Factor V (intellect or openness to experience) is related to creativity and intellectual ability.

## Summary

- Personality has long been thought to have a strong influence on occupational choice and job satisfaction.
- The most widely used interest inventory is the Strong Vocational Interest Blank. On this measure, a person's interests in occupations are interpreted by comparing them with the interests of people in various occupations.
- Holland proposed a theory of vocational choice that classified work environments into six types. Certain personality characteristics are predicted to be associated with each type, and job satisfaction depends on the congruence of the two.
- Motivation is classified as either intrinsic or extrinsic. Most psychological theories have focused on the situational characteristics that promote intrinsic motivation.
- Intrinsic and extrinsic motivation have also been conceptualized as personality traits. The Work Preference Inventory is designed to assess stable individual differences in motivation.
- Leadership is a crucial element in most organizations. Implicitly, a leader's behavior—and explicitly formal theories of leadership—make assumptions about general human nature.
- The major dimension of human nature is reflected in Theory X (people are lazy and irresponsible) versus Theory Y (people are motivated and trustworthy).
- Contingency theory, and most other theories of leadership, emphasize the importance of person–environment interaction and leader flexibility for effective leadership. The personality of the leader, the characteristics of the followers, and the nature of the work situation must all be considered. No one style of leadership will always be most effective.
- Several studies have found substantial personality correlates with emergent leadership and leader effectiveness. On the negative side, leaders who fail also exhibit predictable personality traits.
- Determining employee honesty is of great concern to businesses. Historically, polygraphs ("lie detectors") were used in employment screening. However, these tests are not generally valid in employment situations, and their use has been curtailed by federal law.
- Integrity or honesty tests have become widely used as an alternative to polygraphs. These tests, particularly when evaluated against a broad criterion of

counterproductive behavior, have some predictive validity. However, the construct of integrity is not well defined, these tests appear to be susceptible to faking, and the morality of their use can be questioned. Thus, these tests are controversial.

- Historically, personality measures did not fare well in personnel selection contexts. This may be due in part to the focus of tests on psychopathology and neurosis, their emphasis on assessing dispositions rather than summarizing past behavior, and their susceptibility to cheating.

- Contemporary personality assessment has largely overcome these problems, and personality measures have been developed that are effective for predicting a variety of job performance criteria.

# Chapter 18
# Personality and Gender Differences

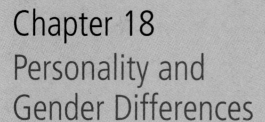

Sex and Gender
Gender Stereotypes
    Description of Gender Stereotypes
    Stereotyping Among Psychologists
    Factors That Promote Stereotypes
    Variations in Stereotypes
Research on Gender Differences
    Prediction Versus Explanation
    Group Versus Individual Differences
    The Politics of Gender Research
Psychoanalytic Theories and Gender
  Differences
Biology and Gender Differences
    Differences in Infants
    Animal Research
    External Versus Chromosomal Sex
    Gender Differences in Brain Structure
Social Cognition and Gender Differences
    Cognitive-Developmental Theory
    Gender Schema
    Flexibility
Behaviorism and Gender Differences

Social Learning and Gender Differences
    Imitation and Differential Attention
    Consistency
    Self-Regulation and Reciprocal
      Determinism
Gender Differences in Personality Structure
  and Description
    Gender Differences and the Big Five
    Androgyny
Summary

P eople differ on a host of variables. The vast number of individual difference variables, and the essentially infinite number of ways they can combine, means that ultimately each person is unique. But one variable is so fundamental to our species and is so salient in every culture that it cannot be overlooked by any serious student of personality and human behavior. Of course, that variable is biological sex.

Probably the first characteristic we notice about someone is whether the person is a woman or a man, and then we automatically make certain inferences about the person that reflect what we believe to be true about men and women. These beliefs are formed at an early age, tend to be stable and consistent within a culture, and have a substantial impact on how we behave toward another person and thus how that person behaves toward us. These beliefs probably have some legitimacy, although as with most stereotypes they are undoubtedly over-applied. In this chapter, we describe gender stereotypes and sex roles in our society and then consider theories of, and research on, gender differences that represent each of the major perspectives on personality discussed in Part II. We conclude by considering masculinity and femininity as well as their androgynous combination as personality characteristics.

## Sex and Gender

The terms **sex** and **gender** are often used interchangeably. However, these two terms have different implications. According to the American Psychological Association (1994) *Publication Manual*, "*Gender* is cultural and is the term to use when referring to men and women as social groups. *Sex* is biological; use it when the biological distinction is predominant. Note that the word *sex* can be confused with *sexual behavior*. *Gender* helps keep meaning unambiguous . . . " (p. 47). To the extent that personality concerns social behavior and is culturally influenced, personality differences between men and women are probably best considered **gender differences** rather than **sex differences**. This view is somewhat at odds with evolutionary personality theory (Buss, 1995), which predicts that men and women will exhibit personality differences primarily in those domains where men and women have faced different adaptive problems relating to their biological differences in sex and reproduction. In labeling personality differences as gender differences rather than sex differences, we do not mean to imply that we reject evolutionary theory as an explanation for them. Instead, this reflects our view that regardless of their origin, personality characteristics are socially constructed phenomena that are not biologically defined in the same way as the physical differences between men and women.

## Gender Stereotypes

A **stereotype** is a summary description of a specified group that is believed to be applicable to all members of that group. **Gender or sex-role stereotypes** concern men and women, with a particular emphasis on how these two groups differ. Definitions of sex-role stereotypes are often thought to imply bias against individuals because of their gender. For example, Unger (1979) defines a sex-role stereotype as "an attitudinal or behavioral bias against individuals in identical situations engaged in identical behaviors because of their membership in some specific sexual group" (p. 27). However, although stereotypes may result in, be the result of, or reflect the, biases against a particular group, stereotypes may be positive or neutral as well as negative.

Critics of traditional sex-role stereotypes have argued that it is often not one's biological heritage that limits one's roles and aspirations. Rather, it is the person's associated **gender identity**, which is the person's expectations about what his or her gender implies about roles and capabilities, that is critical. Thus, if society's stereotypes and individuals' expectations about the capabilities of men and women can change, so too will the roles of men and women in society. Anatomy is destiny only if we believe it is destiny.

### Description of Gender Stereotypes

Although changes in society have shown them to be at least partly inaccurate, gender or sex-role stereotypes remain pervasive, consistent, and influential. Stereotyping begins at an early age: Rubin, Provenzano, and Luria (1974) interviewed parents within one day of the birth of their first child. Male and female infants showed no differences in body length, weight, or activity scores. Yet, daughters were more likely to be described as cute, little, beautiful, or pretty and boys to be characterized as firmer, more alert, or stronger. As a child grows older these stereotypes persist. Much of what we know about sex stereotyping comes from work with college students by Broverman and her colleagues (e.g., Broverman, Vogel, Broverman, Clarkson, and Rosenkrantz, 1972). In most of these studies, students are asked to list the personality characteristics they feel differentiate men and women. Items from such lists are then presented to other students, who are requested to indicate which items would likely apply to a person about whom they know nothing except that he is a male. The students perform the same task for a hypothetical female as well. Results show that there is general agreement between male and female participants about what typical men and women are like. Interestingly, masculine traits are rated as more socially desirable than feminine ones, and it also appears that a greater number of male traits are positively valued than are female traits. The most common positive stereotypic traits that distinguish between men and women are listed in Table 18-1.

##  Table 18-1
Positive Stereotypic Traits for Men and Women

**Positive Traits for Men**

| | |
|---|---|
| Aggressive | Knows the way of the world |
| Independent | Feelings not easily hurt |
| Unemotional | Adventurous |
| Hides emotions | Makes decisions easily |
| Objective | Never cries |
| Easily influenced | Acts as a leader |
| Dominant | Self-confident |
| Likes math and science | Not uncomfortable about being aggressive |
| Not excitable in a minor crisis | Ambitious |
| Active | Able to separate feelings from ideas |
| Competitive | Not dependent |
| Logical | Not conceited about appearance |
| Worldly | Thinks men are superior to women |
| Skilled in business | Talks freely about sex with men |
| Direct | |

**Positive Traits for Women**

| | |
|---|---|
| Does not use harsh language | Interested in own appearance |
| Talkative | Neat in habits |
| Tactful | Quiet |
| Gentle | Strong need for security |
| Aware of feelings of others | Appreciates art and literature |
| Religious | Expresses tender feelings |

Source: From "Sex-Role Stereotypes and Self-Concepts in College Students" by P. Rosenkrantz, S. Vogel, H. Bee, I. Broverman, and D. M. Broverman, *Journal of Consulting and Clinical Psychology*, 1968, *32*, 287–295. Copyright 1968 by the American Psychological Association. Reprinted by permission.

Williams and Best (1990) have undertaken the most extensive and systematic study of gender stereotypes. In their work, they used the set of 300 common person-descriptive adjectives from the *Adjective Check List (ACL)* (Gough and Heilbrun, 1980). The ACL is a widely used, easily administered, self-description measure of personality on which a subject is asked to simply check all of the adjectives in the set that are descriptive of him or her. In their work, Williams and Best modified the instructions to the ACL to obtain descriptions of stereotypes. In one study, Williams and Bennett (1975) asked male and female participants to make a relative judgment about whether the characteristic described by each adjective was more frequently associated with women or men. They found that men and women generally agreed about these relative judgments and so combined the responses of both genders to develop a **sex stereotype index (SSI)** for each adjective (Williams and Best, 1977). This index is based on the percentage of individuals who judged the adjective to be more frequently associated with men relative to the number of individuals who judged the adjective to be more frequently associated with women. An SSI above 500 indicates that the adjective is more stereotypic of males, whereas a score below 500 indicates that the adjective is more stereotypic of females. The adjective most strongly associated with men relative to women was, not surprisingly, *masculine*, with an SSI of 790. This was followed by *aggressive* (SSI 761), *adventurous* (752), and *dominant* (736). For women, the most highly stereotyped adjective was, again not surprisingly, *feminine* (192), followed by *sentimental* (241), *affectionate* (270), and *soft-hearted* (303).

Gender Stereotypes and Self and Other Descriptions.    Williams and Best have used their SSI to evaluate the extent to which people's descriptions of themselves and others reflect sex-role stereotyping. In these studies, participants are asked to use the ACL to describe themselves or other targets. Subsequently, the SSI of the adjectives the participants select are averaged to obtain an overall sex-role stereotyping score for each participant's description. Several interesting finding have emerged from this research:

1. Participant's self-descriptions are not highly sex-role stereotyped. For women, the average SSI for their self-descriptions was 480, whereas for men the average SSI was 495.

2. Men and women show considerable overlap in the sex-role stereotyping of their self descriptions. Over 25 percent of the women had self-descriptions that were more stereotypic of men than the average male stereotype. Likewise, over 25 percent of the men had self-descriptions that were more stereotypic of women than the average women's stereotype.

3. For descriptions of their ideal selves, men and women both indicated a desire to have both typically male and typically female characteristics, with a slight tendency for each ideal self to be tilted toward the same-sex stereotype. The SSI for women's ideal self was 492, whereas for men the ideal was 506.

4. For descriptions of their best friends, the results were different. Men and women both rated their best male friends as more male stereotyped (SSI 513) and their best female friends as more female stereotyped (SSI 474).

5. Finally, for descriptions of their peers in general, the extent of stereotyping was dramatically more pronounced. The average male peer rating had an SSI of 597, and the average female peer rating had an SSI of 398.

All of these results are consistent with general findings regarding the influence of stereotypes on self and other personality descriptions (e.g., Goldberg, 1978). When we describe ourselves, we are much less influenced by stereotypes than when we describe others; moreover, the influence of stereotypes on our descriptions of others tends to increase as we move from targets we know well (such as best friends) to targets with whom we are less well acquainted.

**Cultural Differences in Gender Stereotypes.** Cross-cultural research indicates that the degree of sex role stereotyping differs across cultures. For example, Zammuner (1987) reports that Dutch children differentiate between the sexes less than do Italian children. Lii and Wong (1982) studied sex role stereotyping in Chinese and American college students. The American students described women with more adjectives related to competence and active roles, whereas the Chinese students emphasized more warm and expressive attributes. The authors suggested that these differences reflected the influence of the women's liberation movement on American stereotypes, whereas the Chinese students continued to hold more traditional views.

These cultural differences are also found in an individual's self-perceptions. Crittendon (1991) studied the extent to which female and male university students in Taiwan and the United States provide self-effacing versus self-enhancing attributions for their behavior. She found that the Taiwanese women made more modest and self-effacing attributions than American women. She argued that this pattern conformed with general Chinese cultural values for women. All of this research suggests that learning to stereotype is mediated by cultural and familial factors. It is also probably mediated by a desire to sort people into social roles; stereotyping then becomes a way of rationalizing our biases (Hoffman and Hurst, 1990).

Williams and Best (1990) have applied their methodology to studying sex-role stereotypes in 25 different countries. Their work, again, is the most extensive and systematic study of cultural variation in sex-role stereotypes. Here are some of the most important results from their work:

1. There is a slight tendency for cultures to apply more personality descriptive terms to men than to women. Across the 25 countries, on the average, 53 percent of subjects applied each of the 300 adjectives on the ACL more to men than to women.

2. However, people in different countries varied in the extent to which they saw the adjectives as applying more to men or women. The country whose people saw the highest percentage of adjectives as more descriptive of men than of women was Italy (63.5 percent) followed by India (59.4 percent), Peru (58.8 percent), Bolivia (57 percent), and Brazil (56 percent). The country whose people applied the most adjectives to women was Nigeria (53.7 percent), followed by Trinidad (53.4 percent), Australia (51.6 percent), Malaysia (51 percent) and Canada (50.1 percent).

3. The major religion of the country seems to be related to the extent to which descriptions focus on men or women. Specifically, predominantly Catholic countries have a higher average percentage of adjectives applied to men (56.2 percent) than do the predominantly Protestant countries (51.3 percent).

## Stereotyping Among Psychologists

Psychologists have not been immune from the effects of stereotyping. The negative effects of stereotyping on psychoanalysts' views of women is well documented, and a systematic effort to revise these beliefs has only recently been undertaken (Alpert, 1986). But analysts have not been alone in their tendencies toward stereotyping. A study by Broverman, Broverman, Clarkson, Rosenkrantz, and Vogel (1970) included participants who were psychologists with clinical training, psychiatrists, and social workers. They were asked to alternately describe a man, a woman, and an adult (sex unspecified) who were all healthy, mature, and socially competent. The participants' descriptions differed along sex lines. There was agreement that competence characterized the healthy male more than it did the healthy female. Healthy women, in comparison with healthy males, were also depicted as being more submissive, less independent and adventuresome, less objective and more easily influenced, less aggressive and competitive, more easily excitable in minor crises, more conceited about their appearance, and more prone to having their feelings hurt. These results are not unlike the ratings of college students that were shown in Table 18-1. This illustrates that mental health professionals, both male and female, are as prone to the biases of stereotypes as nonprofessionals. Sex-role stereotyping is a deeply rooted phenomenon in our society.

Gender stereotypes can also affect psychological research. For example, Geis (1993) reviewed gender research on nurturance and aggression and found numerous examples where investigators had ignored or downplayed results showing that men had displayed nurturant behavior and women had acted aggressively. Preexisting beliefs about what men or women are like may create expectancies that impact the conduct and interpretation of research.

## Factors That Promote Stereotypes

As Graham (1975) has shown, our language itself tends to reinforce sex-role stereotypes. For example, the use of qualifiers such as *woman* doctor or career *woman* implies exceptions to what are "normally" male activities. Words such as poet*ess* and suffrag*ette* provide what amounts to an unnecessary qualification or even trivialization of roles. And children get an early start in developing sex-role stereotypes through the books they are given to read. The textbooks they study all too often misrepresent the possibilities and varieties of activities open to women. By presenting examples that describe only the norm in society rather than a range of possibilities, stereotypes are reinforced. A monograph, "Dick and Jane as Victims," was published in 1972 by the National Organization for Women. When 2,760 stories in 134 children's books were examined, it was found that the ratio of boy-centered to girl-centered stories was five to two. Men were three times more likely than women to appear as characters, and biographies of men and boys were six times more frequent than biographies of women and girls. Boys were described as clever 131 times, but girls only 33 times. Sternglanz and Serbin (1974) found much the same pattern in their analysis of male and female role models on 10 popular children's TV programs. Not only were there twice as many male roles as female roles, but the frequency of various kinds of behavior was characteristically different for males and females.

## Variations in Stereotypes

Between the years 1972 and 1976, research suggested that in both student and community samples, there were large and significant shifts of attitudes in the direction of equality between the sexes (Helmreich, Spence, and Gibson, 1982). However, between 1976 and 1980, male students showed no overall change in attitudes, whereas female students showed a small but significant shift back toward the conservative or traditional direction. Helmreich, Spence, and Gibson suggested that these data may signal a leveling off in the trend toward acceptance of sex-role equality.

It is generally believed that sex-role stereotypes promote a negative view of women because women are the more oppressed group in society (Unger and Crawford, 1992). However, recent research that has systematically evaluated the desirability of the traits and behaviors ascribed to women has not found evidence for a general unfavorable perception of women (Eagly and Mladinic, 1994). Indeed, this research suggests that the stereotype of women in the United States and Canada is actually more favorable than the stereotype of men. However, although more desirable, the particular types of positive characteristics ascribed to women concern "niceness" and nurturance, and such qualities may still be used to exclude women from high-status positions (Eagly, 1995).

# Research on Gender Differences

Gender stereotypes are widely shared and have consequences for how people act and think and for how they are treated by others. However, stereotypes are often inaccurate. Although our stereotypes suggest that we generally believe that men and women differ substantially on a variety of characteristics, it is less certain that these beliefs have an empirical basis. In the sections that follow, we consider the scientific evidence generated by the different theoretical traditions reviewed in Part II for gender differences in personality. First, however, three general issues related to research on gender differences will be considered.

## Prediction Versus Explanation

Knowing whether a person is male or female provides a wealth of information about that person's physical characteristics, life experiences, and biological makeup. This means that gender is likely to be a potent and general predictor of many personality variables and other criteria. The problem is that although knowing a person's gender may help us to better predict that person's characteristics and behavior, gender is not a very useful variable for understanding and explaining those characteristics. To say that a person is gentle *because* she is a woman does not really explain gentleness at all. What is it about being a women that leads to gentleness? Among the many possibilities are hormones, socialization, and unconscious motives—or perhaps the person is simply perceived as more gentle because she is a woman. Moreover, unless the correlation between gentleness and gender is perfect (and it is not), then not all women will be gentle, and some men will be. In short, gender may be a powerful predictor variable, but it is next to useless as an explanatory variable (Chaplin, in press).

## Group Versus Individual Differences

The existence of an average difference between men and women as a group does not mean that the difference will characterize all individual men and women. The sex differences that are found will likely be smaller than the ones in our stereotypes. As Unger (1979) has observed, we tend to conceptualize gender as a dichotomy. We use biology to divide the world into two genders and then view the psychology of what are now two worlds in separate ways. Our attention focuses on mean differences rather than on the variability between the two genders. It is a fact that in their behavior, females and males overlap substantially—and this overlap is much greater than the differences between them (Figure 18-1).

## The Politics of Gender Research

It is difficult to be dispassionate about theories and research on group differences in personality. Most research on the differences between men and women seems to be motivated by a political agenda. That agenda may be to maintain the status quo by finding differences that support the traditional and unequal perception and treatment of men and women. Alternatively, the agenda may be to document a lack of differences in an effort to challenge traditional sex roles and support greater equality in the treatment of men and women. In a review of research on gender differences, Eagly (1995) argued that such research has reflected the history of **feminism** as a social and intellectual force in society. Feminism concerns the social, economic, political, and cultural inequities between men and women and the influence of those inequities on the relations between men and women and the behaviors, thoughts, and emotions of the two sexes. In particular, contemporary gender research was influenced by one feminist strategy:

> methodologically sound comparisons of women and men would raise women's status by dispelling people's stereotypes about women . . . . Much feminist research on sex differences was (and still is) intended to shatter stereotypes about women's characteristics and change people's attitudes by proving that men and women are essentially equivalent in their personalities, behavioral tendencies, and intellectual abilities. (Eagly, 1995, p. 149)

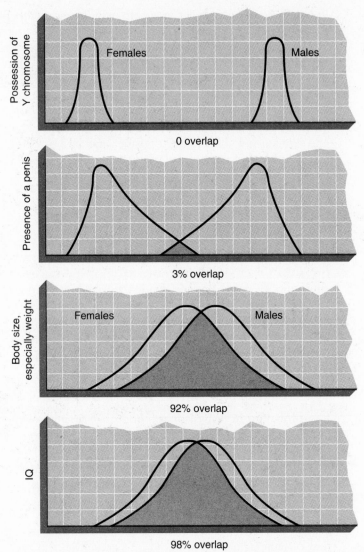

**Figure 18-1** &#x2108; Frequency distributions of selected characteristics related to sex. Frequencies are idealized to illustrate the range of possible overlap in characteristics supposedly dichotomized by sex.
From *Male and Female: Psychological Perspectives* by Rhoda K. Unger.

Eagly focused her review on four claims that are typically made about the results of research on gender differences. These claims are that gender differences are small, difficult to replicate, confounded and artifactual, and inconsistent with gender stereotypes. From her evaluation of quantitative summaries of research on gender differences, Eagly concludes that in direct contrast to these claims, many gender differences are large, often replicated, not the result of methodological confounds, and consistent with gender stereotypes. The political implications of Eagly's conclusions are profound, because they undermine the agenda of some feminist psychologists to disconfirm gender stereotypes as a way of raising women's status. Not surprisingly, Eagly's characterization of research on gender differences, and her conclusions, have been disputed (e.g., Hyde and Plant, 1995; Marecek, 1995).

## Psychoanalytic Theories and Gender Differences

As we saw in Chapters 3 and 4, most psychoanalytic theories explicitly treat men and women differently. Thus, it is not surprising that psychoanalytic theories have been used to explain gender differences. The psychoanalytic concept of **identification** is central to most of these explanations. The identification process works differently for boys and girls. For identification to occur, the child must be dependent on the parent—and this is true for girls and boys alike. The difference for boys and girls lies in the form of identification. Identification in females is called **anaclitic,** which means that the child identifies with a given parent to avoid loss of love. In males, identification is **defensive** in that it occurs as a way of avoiding punishment from an all-powerful parent.

For Freud, the differential identification processes in males and females were biologically determined by a simple fact: boys have a penis and girls do not. However, before their discovery of their anatomical differences, boys and girls share an anaclitic identification with their mothers. Because the mother is most responsible for comforting them, feeding them, and generally providing for their satisfactions, they value her highly. They feel better when they think about her, and to become as close to her as they can, they assume some of her characteristics and values. This helps guard against her potential loss.

This changes during the Oedipal phase and the growing awareness of anatomical differences. Specifically, when children discover that boys have a penis and girls do not, different mechanisms of identification are initiated. The boy wants his mother but fears his father. He also assumes that if he does not heed his father's implicit or explicit admonitions to stop competing for his mother's favors, his penis will be cut off. This becomes a real threat when he observes that girls have no penis; he assumes they were "bad" and that their penis was removed as a result. To avoid this horrible outcome, the boy engages in defensive identification with his father.

In the case of the girl the process is different. She cannot fear castration because she has no penis, but she notices this deficiency and, as a result, develops feelings of personal inferiority as well as a sense of the inferiority of women generally. She also becomes jealous of the male and his penis, and she decides that having a baby will be a good substitute for the missing penis. This desire reinforces her earlier anaclitic identification with the mother by encouraging her to adopt the female sex role and thus ensure that she becomes a mother just like her own mother. Basically, then, little boys adopt the male sex role out of the defensive identification process. They identify with the aggressor (father), avoid retaliation, and at the same time vicariously enjoy the mother. Girls, in contrast, have no reason to employ defensive identification. Their identification remains anaclitic and their self-image one of inferiority.

Many investigators, such as Uri Bronfenbrenner (1960), argue that identification is not a useful concept. Nevertheless, the use of identification as an explanation is common. In some cases, what is said to be valued and thus serve as the basis of identification is not the penis, but status (e.g., Whiting, 1960). Others (e.g., Kagan, 1958) argue that each child observes the same-sexed parent's experience, notes the parent's reactions, and—almost on the basis of empathy—comes to share those reactions (both pleasant and unpleasant ones). Eventually, the child has internalized that parent's reactions to such a degree that it is not necessary to actually observe the parent any longer. Whatever the specific version of identification may be, the concept has proved to be an attractive one for psychologists over the years.

## Biology and Gender Differences

 That men and women differ biologically in important ways is both obvious and inescapable. For some, the fact of biological difference is sufficient to explain all the psychological differences that we observe between men and women. For example, to understand why women are described as more nurturant then men, one need look no further than the biological difference that results in women, and not men, bearing and nursing children. However, this extreme "anatomy is destiny" view is inconsistent with some other observations. For example, the average difference in nurturance does not apply to all individual men and women; some women are less nurturant then some men, and vice versa. Also, the focus on biological difference overlooks the fact that men and women are biologically highly similar. For example, male humans are biologically more like female humans than they are like male pigeons.

Although ascribing all differences between men and women to biology is undoubtedly naive, so too is the failure to consider biological differences as having some impact on some of the differences between men and women. The current climate of "political correctness," in which gender-neutral terms such as sales-*person* as opposed to sales*man* are used, is appropriate to a point. However, the warning sign for a sauna shown in Figure 18-2, in which pregnant *persons*

---

## WHIRLPOOL RULES

The following rules are for your safety and convenience:

- Only enter the whirlpool where there are railings and steps.
- Do not use the whirlpool while under the influence of alcohol, anticoagulants, antihistamines, stimulants, narcotics, or tranquilizers.
- Do not use alone.
- No pets allowed.
- Absolutely no glass containers in the whirlpool area.
- Pregnant persons should not use the whirlpool.
- No running around the whirlpool area.
- Unsupervised use by anyone under 16 is prohibited.
- All persons using the whirlpool do so at their own risk.
- Maximum water temperature 104 degrees.

IN CASE OF EMERGENCY USE THE PHONE MARKED EMERGENCY

---

**Figure 18-2** ⚬⚬ From a sign over a whirlpool in downtown Halifax, Nova Scotia, Canada.

(among others) are advised not to use the facility reflects as naive a perspective as the "anatomy is destiny" one.

## Differences in Infants

One approach to separating the influence of biology from other factors on gender differences is to search for gender differences in infants who have presumably not yet been systematically trained according to sex stereotypes. It has been found that infant girls vocalize more than infant boys (Lewis, 1969). They also smile more and show greater variety in expressions to facial stimuli. For some, these findings suggest a biological basis for subsequent gender differences in tendencies to socialize. Likewise, it is not unusual to find studies that report greater evidence of irritability (crying, fussiness) in male infants than in female infants (e.g., Moss, 1967).

Although it is logical to do research on gender differences in infants before the culture has had an influence, in practice it is not easy. Infant behavior is newly emerging and is unreliable and unstable. For example, a variety of vocalizations may occur one day but not the next. Thus, it is difficult to measure vocalization accurately so that gender differences in that behavior can be assessed. In addition, it is not at all clear what infant behaviors will translate into later in life. It is doubtful that just because an infant moves his or her legs rapidly, a career as a world-class sprinter will follow. Finally, in many studies the observers of infants cannot help but know the sex of the infants they are watching. As a result, it can be all too easy for them to apply gender stereotypes to the behaviors they see. What is seen as sociability in the female infant may be scored as aggressiveness in the male. For all these reasons—and more—research on sex differences in infants has not provided any crystal-clear insights into the biological origins of adult gender differences in behavior. Although behavioral differences between male and female infants are of considerable interest, they must be interpreted with caution.

Furthermore, not all gender differences would be expected to reveal themselves as early as infancy. For example, hormones are often used to account for behavioral differences in adulthood. But the hormone system undergoes many changes during puberty. As a result, differences in such characteristics as aggressiveness or nurturance might be more directly traceable to this stage of maturation. However, by this time the socialization process has been at work so long that it would be extremely difficult to separate the effects of biology from those of learning, stereotyping, and socialization. By the beginning of adolescence, an entire pattern of parent–child interactions has developed. How infants' behavioral characteristics and parental responses might combine to produce distinctly different response patterns later is shown in Box 18-1.

## Animal Research

Another approach for assessing biological influences on gender differences is animal research. Animals can be raised and observed in more carefully controlled environments than can humans. Also, hormonal levels can be monitored more closely and accurately, and they can be experimentally manipulated. There is considerable evidence that sex hormones affect behavior, especially sexual behavior. Sexual responsiveness in male animals is linked to high levels of testosterone, whereas in females, high estrogen and progesterone levels are important.

Altering hormone levels experimentally or changing the levels in young animals can significantly affect sexual behavior. For example, when young female rats are injected with testosterone immediately after birth, they will subsequently exhibit a greater incidence of mounting behaviors (normally characteristic of males) than normal (Levine, 1966). In essence, exposing young rats to altered hormone levels has a direct effect on subsequent sexual behavior.

Similar results have been shown for aggression. For instance, the introduction or androgen to newborn female rhesus monkeys results in patterns of aggressiveness normally characteristic of males (Young, Goy, and Phoenix, 1964). Although it seems clear that testosterone in particular affects aggressiveness and sexual responses, it is less clear how directly applicable these findings are to humans. However, Hines (1982) seems optimistic. She suggests that much animal research is relevant and that even in humans, prenatal hormone levels may be specifically related to gender differences in behavior. But as a rule, the higher a

BOX 18-1

# The Production of Differential Response Patterns in Boys and Girls

| Infant A | Infant B |
|---|---|
| **(More characteristic of a girl)** | **(More characteristic of a boy)** |

### Infant's Characteristics

| | |
|---|---|
| Physically mature | Physically less mature |
| Sleeps a lot | Cries a lot |
| Vocalizes to faces | More active |
| Smiles at faces | |

### Parents' Responses to Above

| | |
|---|---|
| Affectionate | Irritable |
| Responsive when child does cry | Less responsive to child's frequent cries |
| Talks to child | Uses physical restraints and punishment |

### Child's Responses to Parents' Responses

| | |
|---|---|
| Affiliative—comes to like people and expects them to satisfy needs | Aggressive |
| Early vocalization | Expects to satisfy needs through own efforts |

Source: Adapted from *Women and Sex Roles* by I. H. Frieze, J. E. Parsons, P. B Johnson, D. N. Ruble, and G. L. Zellman, 1978, New York: Norton, p. 78.

species is in the evolutionary hierarchy, the less hormones seem to affect behavior directly and the more important learning becomes.

## External Versus Chromosomal Sex

A "natural experiment" that has been used to separate biological effects from socialization effects on human gender differences occurs in those rare cases of humans whose external genital development is inconsistent with their chromosomal sex. For example, the newborn infant may have external male genitals but female internal sex organs. Hampson (1965) investigated 19 such children who were raised on the basis of their external sex characteristics. That is, their sexual and gender socialization was the opposite of their biological sex. In every instance, their gender-role orientation was consistent with the manner in which they had been regarded by their parents and peers.

This finding was replicated by the work of Money and his colleagues (Money, 1965, 1975; Money and Ehrhardt, 1972). An individual with male hormones who has been raised as a girl (clothes, values, outlook, etc.) will grow up to function as a woman. Therefore, important as hormones are, their role cannot be understood without considering the person's experience. The joint influence of hormones and learning is also shown in research by Money and Ehrhardt (1972). Women whose mothers received androgyn as part of their pre-natal treatment were compared to women whose mothers did not receive androgyn. Girls in the treated group showed a higher level of masculine tendencies (toy and clothing preferences) and little interest in feminine things such as infant care. They were more career oriented than most girls of their age, although they still thought about romance, marriage, and having a family.

## Gender Differences in Brain Structure

As we saw in Chapter 5, differences in brain structure such as the connections among neurons, the density of cells, the localization of function, and the dominance of the right or left hemisphere (lateralization) have become a focus of neuroscience research. The idea that the brains of men and women differ is an old one, although the nature of the differences has always been a source of controversy (Shields, 1975). The problem with research in this area is that the human brain is remarkably individualized (Sperry, 1982). Thus, the differences between the brains of individual people will often be as great as the differences between the brains of men and women. Any general conclusions about the average differences between the brains of men and women will often disappear or be reversed in comparisons between individual men or women (Gorski, quoted in Kolata, 1995).

With these cautions in mind, recent research has indicated some differences between the brains of men and women. Shaywitz et al. (1995) used magnetic resonance imaging to scan the brains of 19 men and 19 women while the subjects were processing verbal information. They found that brain activity in the men was confined to the left hemisphere, whereas in over half of the women, activity was found in both hemispheres. This reduced lateralization of function in women's brains is consistent with earlier observations that women exhibit fewer language difficulties following a left hemisphere stroke than do men (McGlone, 1978). Another intriguing finding was reported by Witelsen, Glaser, and Kager (1994), who found from autopsies that women had a higher density of cells in brain areas associated with auditory processing than did men.

Although these differences appear well established, their implications for behavior, and particularly differences between the behavior of men and women, is not well understood. Popular books tend to seize findings such as these and use them to explain such stereotypes as women's intuition, men's interest in sports, women's greater verbal ability, and men's greater spatial ability (see Springer and

Deutsch, 1981). However, at this point, the only legitimate conclusion is that the influence of these differences on the behavior, thought, and emotion of men and women is uncertain but probably complicated (Hoptman and Davidson, 1994).

## Social Cognition and Gender Differences

With their emphasis on the individual person in the present, phenomenological/humanistic theories do not generally address gender differences. Although gender may influence a person's experiences, the focus of these theories is on those experiences and not what caused them. Thus, individuals should be shown the same degree of unconditional positive regard and should be encouraged to grow and become self-actualized regardless of their gender.

### Cognitive-Developmental Theory

Social cognitive theories address more directly how gender differences develop and how they influence social information processing. Kohlberg (1966) developed a cognitive-developmental view of sex-role behavior. Very early, the child comes to a decision about his or her own "maleness" or "femaleness." Indeed, it also appears that children as young as nine months can differentiate the faces (Fagot and Leinbach, 1993) and voices (Poulin-Dubois et al., 1994) of men and women. Anatomical sexual identity reinforces these early judgments so that sexual categorization remains stable. The child has now arrived at a crucial self-judgment. Consequently, that judgment about sexual identity begins to serve as an important organizer of the child's values. Almost automatically, a boy values those objects and activities he associates with the masculine role. The child is, in effect, motivated to accommodate to his or her own physical sexual identity by acquiring, maintaining, and enhancing the appropriate self-image—femininity for females, masculinity for males. In Kohlberg's (1966) words, "I am a boy, therefore I want to do boy things (and to gain approval for doing them)" (p. 89). All of this suggests a drive for cognitive consistency. Children make early judgments about their physical sexual identity. They will then strive to arrange their values and behavior so that the latter are viewed as consistent with their physical characteristics.

### Gender Schema

Once a gender identity has developed as part of the self schema, it guides the individual's attention and action. There is evidence that boys and girls attend differentially to events in their environment associated with sex roles. Perry and Perry (1975) demonstrated that when children view a videotape of an interaction between a man and a woman, children of either sex who have a masculine orientation will recall more about the behavior of the male character than about that of the female. Box 18-2 illustrates how a gender schema influences the processing of sex-typed information and behavior.

Other evidence is supportive of Kohlberg's contention that children strive to behave in ways consistent with their sex-role judgments about themselves. For example, Hartup, Moore, and Sager (1963) found that boys in particular were resistant to playing with "feminine" toys and that this resistance increased with age. Interestingly, these researchers did not find such resistance in girls. It may be that girls' sex-typing is not so rigid as that of boys.

## Flexibility

Phenomenological and social cognitive theories emphasize the importance of the individual's construction of reality. Thus, unlike biological, behavioral, and psychodynamic theories, they provide individuals with some control over how they react in different situations. Specifically, the expectations, goals, and prior knowledge that people bring into a situation will have a substantial impact on their actions in that situation. Thus, as individuals mature they exhibit greater flexibility in how they exhibit gender-related behavior and how they use gender-related abilities to cope with life tasks (Katz and Ksansnak, 1994).

This flexibility is the basis of an influential theory of gender-role behavior developed by Deaux and Major (1987). These investigators noted that gender differences may differ in importance, depending on the nature of particular situations or the personalities of interacting individuals. Deaux and Major focused on the flexibility and variability of gender-related behaviors. They emphasize the importance of the expectations of those interacting in a specific situation for determining the extent to which traditional gender roles are enacted. For example, how I react to a man or a woman is not determined solely by preexisting gender beliefs. My reaction is also influenced by situational factors that activate or do not activate such beliefs, by my expectations about the other person, and by the degree to which the other person is enacting gender-typed roles. These ideas are represented in the model shown in Figure 18-3.

## Behaviorism and Gender Differences

Neither the operant psychology of Skinner nor the stimulus-response theory of Dollard and Miller explicitly address differences between men and women. The principles of learning that are the basis of these theories apply equally to men and women, just as they apply to rats, pigeons, and other organisms. Learning theory is gender neutral.

However, learning theory does provide a direct and simple explanation for the sex-typed differences in the way men and women behave: reinforcement. We do what we are reinforced for doing. The idea is that girls and boys are differentially reinforced by their parents and others. Very early, girls are dressed in pink, boys in blue. This little girl gets a doll and is praised when she plays with it "cor-

# BOX 18-2

## A Gender Schema Illustrating the Encoding and Regulation of Sex-Typed Preferences and Behavior

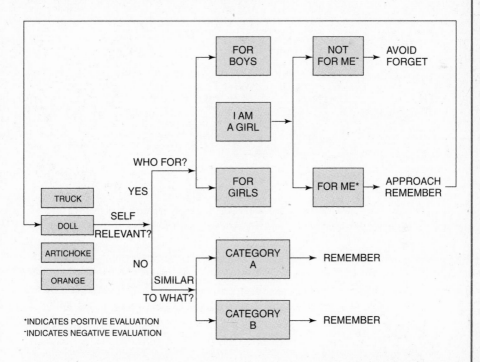

*INDICATES POSITIVE EVALUATION
‾INDICATES NEGATIVE EVALUATION

According to the gender schema or flow chart above, a little girl finds herself in a situation in which she is presented with a doll. On the basis of her gender schema, she will make several decisions that will in turn determine the manner in which she interacts with that doll. First, she will decide that dolls are self-relevant. Next, she will conclude that because she is a girl and that dolls are for girls, she should approach the doll, examine it, perhaps ask questions about it, and then play with it. In the process of playing with it she gains further information about it, which is then elaborated and stored in memory. Should she be confronted with a toy truck, her responses will be different. Trucks are for boys; she is a girl. The decision, in most cases, will be to avoid the truck because it is not self-relevant. As a result of all this, information about it will be largely ignored and poorly remembered. Thus, her cognition and her behavior will be consistent with her schema.

Adapted from "A Schematic Processing Model of Sex Typing and Stereotyping in Children" by Carol Lynn Martin and Charles F. Halverson, Jr., *Child Development*, December 1981. Copyright 1981, The Society for Research in Child Development, Inc. Reprinted by permission.

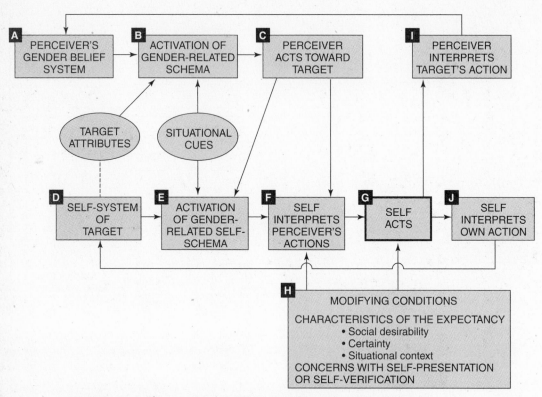

**Figure 18-3** ∞∞  A model of social interaction for gender-related behavior.

rectly." When she expresses the desire to climb trees like the little boy next door, frowns and displeasure may come from the traditional mother.

The use of the word *traditional*, of course, implies that attitudes change. Learning theory can easily account for changes in sex-role behavior across time and cultures. As cultural attitudes change, different behaviors will be reinforced. Likewise, individual men and women may exhibit more or less sex-typed behavior as a function of their learning history. But, though what is regarded as an appropriate sex-typed behavior may change, the role of reinforcement does not. Parents readily admit that they treat their sons differently from their daughters, and children are also aware of the differential treatment (Maccoby and Jacklin, 1974). For example, contrary to earlier views that men are more aggressive than women (e.g., Sears, Rau, and Alpert 1965), it now appears that women and men are equally aggressive (Campbell, 1993). However, men and women learn to exhibit their aggression in different ways; in domestic disputes, women are more verbally abusive, whereas men tend to use more physical aggression (Gelles and Straus, 1988). Likewise, the standard view that women are more nurturant than men is misleading; traditionally, men learn to nurture their families by providing them with food or by dying in wars to protect them. They have learned to exhibit nurturance in different ways (Gilmore, 1990). Learning theory concerns how men and women develop different sex-typed behaviors via the medium of parental, peer, and general cultural reinforcement differentially applied to males and females almost from the moment of birth.

## Social Learning and Gender Differences

 Social learning theory has proven useful for explaining the psychological differences between men and women. Moreover, it provides a basis for understanding why individual men and women differ in the extent to which they exhibit sex-typed behavior. Differential attention and imitation are central to the social learning perspective on gender differences, and these concepts are used to explain specific behaviors as well as emotional reactions and feeling states (Bandura, 1969b).

### Imitation and Differential Attention

Imitation is assumed to occur when the child is more often exposed to same-sexed models than to opposite-sexed ones. Actually, this is a dubious assumption about early childhood, because both boys and girls spend more time with their mothers or other females than with their fathers. But, then, it could be that even under these conditions, the child will pay more attention to same-sexed than opposite-sexed models. An example of this comes from a study by Maccoby and Wilson (1957). Seventh-grade children watched two films. One film presented two boys; the other film involved an interaction between an adolescent boy and an adolescent girl. A week later, all subjects returned, and an assessment was made of what they recalled about the films. Participants of both genders revealed that they identified more with the same-sexed leading character. Also, their memories of the actions and verbalizations of the same-sexed character were greater. Their memories also had a sex-linked quality. Aggressive content was better remembered by boys than by girls, and the girls recalled more male–female interactions involving the leading female character than did the boys.

Such results do suggest differential attentional processes with respect to potential models on the part of boys and girls. Of course, in later childhood the importance of differential attending is not so important because the child has the opportunity to spend more time with same-sexed peers, parents, and other adults. But if it is true that children pay differential attention to potential male

Girls can learn to play softball as easily as they can learn to wear makeup. What each of these girls chooses to do will depend on how her actions are reinforced.

and female models depending on their own gender, the next question is why this should be true. It may simply be that they learn that they are rewarded for doing so. Boys are overtly and subtly rewarded by both their mothers and fathers for paying attention to things masculine; girls, for attending to the feminine. Of course, this learning does not have to be direct. It can also occur vicariously by watching others.

## Consistency

As with the behavioral tradition, social learning theorists deemphasize consistency in sex-role behavior. If there is any traitlike consistency, it occurs because the person repeatedly observes and is reinforced, directly and vicariously, for one particular sex role. Again, the focus shifts from internal states to external reinforcers. Perhaps, argues the social learning theorist, this is why we are now seeing women both engage in and be proud of their accomplishments in what were formerly considered masculine activities (jogging, truck driving, police work, etc.). As they are permitted to be reinforced by the culture for success in such roles, they will continue in them. Such examples also imply the social learning view that sex-role learning is not something that is imprinted on the person at an early age. Sex roles are not inflexible, nor is the learning that underlies them. As the environmental rewards change, so do the behaviors and roles.

For example, the middle-aged man who has had a beard and moustache almost from the time he developed facial hair impulsively decides to shave at age 40. He receives many compliments, and people remark at how much younger he looks. Compliments are such potent reinforcers that he remains clean shaven for the rest of his life.

This latter example also suggests that sex-role learning is not the inevitable province of parent-child interactions. The man did not decide to shave and to remain clean-shaven because of his upbringing. He may have done so because an admired sports hero or TV star recently shaved, or because his wife or friends urged him to. Similarly, children do not learn their sex-typed behaviors only from a same-sexed parent. They learn from peers, teachers, movies, and other sources.

## Self-Regulation and Reciprocal Determinism

Not all boys are alike in their preferences for particular sex-typed behaviors, nor are girls. This means that within a vast array of appropriate possibilities, the child actively regulates what is reinforcing and actively chooses, through reciprocal determinism, his or her situations and behaviors. Similarly, research by Hetherington (1965) indicates that the child's preference for his or her own sex role is affected by the nature of the parent–child relationship. Differences in subjective values, competencies, perceptions, and goals can affect the child's choice of one sex role over another and also the choice of specific behaviors within any given sex role.

# Gender Differences in Personality Structure and Description

Structural models of personality have generally been found to work equally well at organizing the personality descriptions of men and women. Of course, as we saw in our discussion of gender stereotypes, there are substantial differences in the extent to which different traits are characteristic, or at least are thought to be characteristic, of men and women.

## Gender Differences and the Big Five

MacDonald (1995), in his evolutionary analysis of the Big Five, has noted that the system generally minimizes sex differences at the level of the Five Factors. However, at the level of the Big Five hierarchy that emphasizes more specific traits, sex differences are found for all the factors except V, openness to experience. In particular, extraversion (Factor I) is viewed as containing dominance and sensation-seeking, which are aspects of personality typically more common in males, whereas agreeableness (Factor II) emphasizes nurturance and love, which are more typical of females. This view is also consistent with Eysenck's results showing that males typically score higher on his psychoticism dimension. Psychoticism represents the absence of qualities associated with nurturance and love.

## Androgyny

The words *masculine* and *feminine* are generally used as descriptive terms to summarize traits and behaviors that are typically associated with biological sex. Thus, a feminine person is viewed as warm, nurturant, and loving, whereas a masculine person is viewed as dominant, aggressive, and impulsive. Historically, masculinity and femininity were viewed as opposite ends of a single dimension, implying that as a person became more masculine they would necessarily become less feminine and vice versa.

In 1975, Sandra Bem took exception to the polarization of masculinity and femininity and to their equation with biological sex. Instead, Bem introduced the concept of **androgyny** to describe a person, male or female, who could exhibit both masculine and feminine behaviors and traits. This concept has had a powerful influence on the study of the personality of men and women. Androgyny has most often been assessed by either the Bem Sex Role Inventory (BSRI) (Bem,

1974) or the Personal Attributes Questionnaire (PAQ) (Spence, Helmreich, and Stapp, 1975). Although androgyny has offered an appealing alternative to sex-role stereotyping that has often been reinforced by the research literature, the concept of androgyny has been strongly criticized (Locksley and Colten, 1979). In addition, the measurement of androgyny has serious problems (Pedhazur and Tetenbaum, 1979). In particular, the BSRI has not been well received by the psychometric community (Myers and Gonda, 1982).

### Androgyny and Psychological Adjustment.

Androgyny is a concept that is consistent with the contemporary view that women (and men) should behave in ways that are compatible with their abilities and aspirations rather than accepting the constraints of stereotypes dictated by society. According to Bem (1975), androgynous individuals behave in an effective masculine or feminine way depending upon the demand characteristics of the situation. This flexibility, then, confers upon such persons a greater potential for effective problem solving, satisfactions, and psychological adjustment (Wiggins and Holzmuller, 1981). Several investigations have reported a positive relation between androgyny and adjustment. However, some studies have failed to support the hypothesis that androgynous individuals are psychologically healthier than sex-typed individuals (Hall and Taylor, 1985).

Other research has described the characteristics and background of androgynous individuals. Work by Janet Spence and colleagues (1975) reveals that androgynous men and women date more, receive more awards during their school years, and are sick less frequently. Parents of androgynous children have been described as warm, competent, encouraging, and considerate (Kelly and Worell, 1976). As sex roles in our society continue to change and evolve, androgyny may become characteristic of more men and women. As Olds and Shaver (1980) conclude, "traditional sex roles may be easier to transcend if we talk directly about universal standards of competence and health rather than tie these standards to outmoded conceptions of masculinity, femininity, or even androgyny" (p. 340).

### Masculinity and Femininity as Two Processes.

Taylor and Hall (1982) have contended that androgyny should not be viewed as an independent characteristic that certain people have within them. All androgyny signifies is that masculinity and femininity operate simultaneously to influence behavior in some people. Most importantly, this implies that androgyny is not a thing; it is merely two processes—masculinity and femininity—operating in concert within the same person. In this sense, the androgyny hypothesis really refers to the avoidance of a sex-typed self-definition—an avoidance that constitutes a distinctive type of psychological functioning with a variety of positive consequences. Nevertheless, the mere existence of the concept of androgyny reminds us that sex biases and sex-role stereotypes are rampant in our society (Schaffer, 1981).

## Summary

- Gender is probably the most powerful and salient individual difference variable. Numerous beliefs and stereotypes about men and women and the differences between them exist in most cultures, although the specific content of these beliefs differs from culture to culture and has changed over time.
- The term *sex differences* generally refers to biological differences between men and women, whereas the term *gender differences* refers to the psychosocial differences.
- Gender stereotypes are consistent and easily described within a culture. Stereotypes have a stronger influence on the description of others than of ourselves.
- There is a tendency for people to use more terms to describe men than women. However, this tendency differs across cultures.
- Gender undoubtedly exerts a powerful and pervasive influence on behavior, thought, and emotion. However, this is because gender is associated with so many aspects of a person's life. Thus, gender is an excellent predictive variable but a poor explanatory one.
- We need to be aware that average differences between men and women on many characteristics may be small and that there will be substantial overlap between the distributions of men and women on most psychological variables.
- The topic of gender differences is political as well as scientific, and their study is influenced by the values of the investigator. Thus, some psychologists regard gender differences as a topic that should be avoided. However, to avoid discussing gender is to avoid the most salient and influential individual difference.
- The concept of identification is the basis for psychoanalytic explanations of gender differences. Anaclitic identification is characteristic of girls, whereas defensive identification is characteristic of boys. These identification processes are triggered during the Oedipus conflict.
- The existence of biological differences between men and women makes it tempting to use biology to explain any differences that are observed. However, disentangling genetic from environmental and socialization influences is difficult. Studies of infants and animals are often used.
- Natural experiments in which people are raised to be the gender opposite that of their chromosomes suggest that how one is raised is more important than one's biology for determining many gender-related personality characteristics.
- The phenomenological theories of Roger and Maslow focus on the unique individual. Therefore, gender is viewed as but one of many important aspects of the individual.
- The more cognitively oriented approach of Kohlberg suggests that a sense of gender identity develops from the child's discovery that there are two gen-

ders and the subsequent categorization of self into one of them. Gender, then, becomes an organizer for information about the social world.

- Social cognitive theories provide for more flexibility in gender roles. In particular, the specifics of a social interaction, including expectations, self-perceptions, and situational factors, may override the importance of gender roles.

- Learning theory does not devote any special attention to gender differences. Psychological gender differences can be explained by the same principles of learning that apply to all behavior. Specifically, the differences between the behaviors of men and women are a result of the differential reinforcement they received for sex-typed behaviors. Thus, there is nothing inherent about psychological gender differences; change the patterns of reinforcement, and the differences between men and women will change accordingly.

- Social learning theory has provided many explanations for the differences between men and women. Imitation, self-regulation, and reciprocal determinism are all relevant to the development of gender differences.

- Gender differences in personality are typically summarized with the labels *masculine* and *feminine*. These labels reflect dominance/sensation seeking and nurturance/love, respectively.

- The concept of androgyny was introduced to emphasize that masculine and feminine characteristics are not inextricably linked to biological sex and that they need not be treated as polar opposites.

# Glossary

**Ability trait**   For Cattell, a trait that determines a person's effectiveness in the pursuit of goals.

**Absorption**   The ability to become so engaged in an experience that all other stimuli are ignored; considered a stable individual difference that predicts hypnotic susceptibility.

**Absurdity**   For existentialists, a characterization of human beliefs as existing in a meaningless and irrational universe.

**Acquaintance**   A variable that is thought to influence rater agreement. Raters who are well acquainted with a target will agree more about the target than raters who are strangers to the target.

**Acquiescence**   Tendency to respond "true" to each true-false item.

**Acquired motive**   A motive whose value, and means of being satisfied, are learned; varies from person to person.

**Act nomination**   A procedure in the act-frequency approach for generating lists of behaviors that are relevant to a given trait construct.

**Act prototypicality**   The degree to which an act is representative of a trait construct.

**Act Report**   An inventory used in the act-frequency approach to assess whether or not a person has ever performed a particular behavior.

**Act trend**   Within the act-frequency approach, a general tendency for a person to exhibit behaviors (acts) that are consistent with a particular trait.

**Act-frequency theory**   A descriptive theory of traits in which trait terms are viewed as summary descriptions of relevant behaviors; a person's position on a trait dimension is a function of the frequency with which the person exhibits those behaviors.

**Action slip**   The behavioral form of Freudian slip: a person's actions seem to imply a motive that the person would not likely admit.

**Additive genetic effects**   The simplest form of genetic transmission in which the effects of different genes sum to influence a quantitative phenotype.

**Adenine**   A protein that is one of the four base pairs that make up DNA. It is paired with thymine in the double helix DNA strand.

**Adoption study**   A method used by behavior geneticists to estimate genetic and environmental influences on phenotypes. It involves comparing adopted children with both their biological and natural parents.

**Agency**   A component of hope that refers to a person's motivation to cope with a situation.

**Aggression**   Hostile action or behavior. Some people would restrict the definition to physical harm; others would include psychological harm. For Kelly, the result of an attempt to extend one's construct system.

**Alienation**   State in which people feel separate or detached from their existence.

**Alpha press**   According to Murray, an environmental characteristic that effects the individual directly, regardless of how the individual perceives it.

**Altruism**   Pertaining to an act intended solely to benefit another person or group and of no benefit to the person engaging in the act.

**Anaclitic identification**   A situation in which a child identifies with a given parent to avoid loss of love.

**Anal expulsive**   In Freudian theory, a period of psychosexual development (from 6 months to 3 years) when an important source of pleasure is the expulsion of feces.

**Anal retentive** In Freudian theory, a period of psychosexual development (from 12 months to 4 years) when an important source of pleasure is the retention of feces.

**Anal stage** In Freudian theory, the second psychosexual stage, in which pleasure and attention are focused on bowel control along with retention and expulsion of feces.

**Analytic psychology** Term used to describe Jung's personality theory.

**Androgyny** Having both masculine and feminine characteristics.

**Anger-anxiety conflicts** According to Dollard and Miller, conflicts produced in the child when parents punish that child's anger responses.

**Anima and animus** For Jung, archetypes representing the feminine side of men (anima) and the masculine side of women (animus).

**Antipsychotics** Drugs that are used to reduce the frequency and intensity of psychotic symptoms in patients with schizophrenia or other forms of psychosis.

**Anxiety** Unpleasant state of emotional arousal characterized by diffuse fears, physiological arousal, and bodily symptoms such as rapid breathing and accelerated heartbeat. Specific personality theorists each define the concept somewhat differently: for existentialists, an emotion resulting from the failure to be authentic; for Kelly, an awareness that events cannot be construed within one's construct system.

**Approach-approach conflict** Conflict between two positive motives.

**Approach-avoidance conflict** Conflict that results from the desire to satisfy a motive that may produce other negative consequences.

**Archetypes** For Jung, the structural elements of the collective unconscious.

**Assortative mating** The tendency for males and females of a species to be more (or less) similar on a genetic attribute than would be expected by chance.

**Attentional processes** In observational learning, those processes of attention to the model's behavior that permit learning.

**Attitudes** For Cattell, overt expressions of interest marked by a high level of intensity.

**Authenticity** State of expressing who one really is through behavior and emotions.

**Autonomous ego** Term used by ego psychologists to refer to an ego that grew not out of the id, but in accordance with its own predispositions.

**Autonomous self** Kohut's ideal type, characterized by self-esteem, self-confidence, ambition, talents, and skills.

**Autosomes** The 44 out of 46 human chromosomes that are the same for men and women.

**Aversion therapy** Induction of negative feelings or reactions to a stimulus regarded as attractive by the person but viewed as negative by the larger culture (e.g., pairing alcohol with a nausea-inducing drug).

**Avoidance-avoidance conflict** Conflict between two negative motives.

**Bad-me** For Sullivan, the result of negative reactions from the mother and others; helps the child develop a conscience.

**Base pairs** The two pairs of proteins (adenine, cytosine, guanine, and thymine) in DNA that are the foundation for genetic material.

**Basic anxiety** For Horney, the singular motive that impels behavior to cope with threat.

**Behavior** Anything that an organism does involving action and response to stimulation.

**Behavior genetics** The study of the way genetic and environmental factors combine to influence human and animal behavior.

**Behavior potential** In Rotter's theory, the potential for a behavior to occur in a given situation as a way of achieving a particular goal.

**Behavioral activation system (BAS)** A biological system that serves to motive or energize behavior. It is the basis for impulsivity in Gray's system.

**Behavioral data** One of the three major types of data used to study personality. It refers to direct observations of the subject's behavior.

**Behavioral deficit** Situation in which the quantity or quality of any given behavior is lacking in the person's behavioral repertoire.

**Behavioral inhibition system (BIS)** A biological

system that serves to block behavior. It is the basis for anxiety in Gray's system.

**Behavioral medicine** The broad, interdisciplinary field of research, education, and practice that involves health, illness, and related physiological dysfunctions.

**Behaviorism** A general theoretical position that emphasizes direct observation as the only legitimate source of scientific data. Under this system, psychology is limited to the study of the relations between observed behavior and observed environmental variables.

**Being values** According to Maslow, motives to extend our experience and enrich our lives.

**Beta press** According to Murray, an environmental factor that influences behavior because of the way the person perceives it.

**Big five** A structural model of personality description that organizes description into five broad areas: (1) extraversion, (2) agreeableness, (3) conscientiousness, (4) emotional stability, and (5) intellect.

**Binet-Simon Scale** Early intelligence scale developed in France by Binet and Simon; forerunner of the present Stanford-Binet.

**Biochemistry** The study of chemicals that influence biological processes.

**Biofeedback** Feedback provided to the person from various autonomic or somatic systems by means of special equipment; often used to treat headache, hypertension, etc.

**Bivariate research** Research method in which only two variables are considered at a time.

**Burnout** The condition in which a person loses motivation and interest in work or a relationship due to chronic stress.

**California Psychological Inventory (CPI)** A widely used objective measure of normal adult personality that is designed to assess personality characteristics that are well known to both scientists and lay persons.

**Cardinal trait** For Allport, a master motive or ruling passion that affects virtually every aspect of our existence.

**Case study** Research based on the intensive study of a single individual. In this method, the individual case is regarded as unique and interesting in itself, and no effort is made to generalize beyond that case.

**Catharsis** Release of pent-up energy; tendency for the verbal or fantasy expression of an impulse to reduce its likelihood of actual expression; prominent concept in psychoanalytic therapy and theory.

**Causal theory** An explanation for an observed or predicted relation between two variables stipulating that one variable causes the other.

**Causality orientation** A construct related to motivation that concerns an individual's preferences for the way reinforcements are structured and administered.

**Central trait** For Allport, a trait that is less important than a cardinal trait but still exerts widespread influence on a person.

**Chaining** Pairing of a secondary reinforcer with a neutral event, which in turn becomes a secondary reinforcer.

**Chromosomes** The material present in every cell that contains DNA. Each human somatic cell contains 46 chromosomes.

**Classical conditioning** Form of learning emphasized initially by Pavlov in which the response to an unconditioned stimulus (e.g., food) is conditioned to a formerly neutral stimulus (e.g., a noise) by repeated pairings of the two stimuli.

**Cleanliness training** According to Dollard and Miller, the period during which the child learns to control the processes of urination and defecation.

**Clinical method** For Cattell, a research method akin to the multivariate strategy in which the observer notes how variables move in concert.

**Cognitive complexity** A characteristic of personal construct systems that refers to the extent to which the system contains many constructs.

**Cognitive resource utilization theory** A theory of leadership that concerns a leader's cognitive abilities and how those abilities are used to manage work place stress.

**Cognitive restructuring** Broad set of techniques designed to change one's cognitive processes or thoughts and thereby change undesirable behaviors.

**Cognitive simplicity**   A characteristic of personal construct systems that use a small number of constructs and, therefore, emphasize the similarities among people.

**Cognitive style**   The general manner in which one approaches mental tasks and problems.

**Cognitive-affective system theory**   A theory proposed by Mischel and Shoda which provides a reconciliation between the general analysis of personality at the level of traits with the more specific analysis of personality at the level of behavior and cognition.

**Collective unconscious**   According to Jung, the seat of memory from our common ancestral past, including prehuman ancestry.

**Common trait**   For Allport and Cattell, a trait that occurrs frequently among people.

**Communication**   A variable that is thought to influence rater agreement. Raters who communicate with each other about a target will agree more about the target than raters who do not communicate.

**Compensation**   For Adler, the development of physical or mental abilities to overcome feelings of inferiority.

**Competencies**   One of the classes of variables in Mischel's cognitive social learning reconceptualization of personality. Competencies are the person's abilities and knowledge that allow them to behave in certain ways.

**Computerized axial tomography (CAT scan)**   A technique used to provide an image of the brain; is used to locate areas of the brain that are active during psychological experiences such as thinking, feeling, or behaving.

**Concurrent validity**   Extent to which a test score correlates with an existing criterion.

**Conditional description**   A personality description that depends on or is limited to certain situations or circumstances.

**Conditioned response**   A learned response to a conditioned stimulus.

**Conditioned stimulus**   An initially neutral stimulus that elicits a response through the neutral stimulus's association with an unconditioned stimulus.

**Conditions of worth**   Rules in the family that serve as the bases on which the child will receive love, approval, and attention.

**Conflict-free sphere**   Term used by ego psychologists to refer to a part of the ego, the processes of which are not in conflict with the id, superego, or real world.

**Conscience**   In Freudian theory, that part of the superego incorporating moral values and ideals.

**Conscious**   Those sensations, perceptions, experiences, and memories of which one is aware at any given moment.

**Consistency**   The regularity of an individual's behavior and personality across different situations.

**Constitutional trait**   For Cattell, a source trait with a constitutional origin.

**Constellatory constructs**   In Kelly's system, constructs that have wide connections throughout a person's construct system.

**Constitutional psychology**   Sheldon's theory that personality and temperament are related to body type because both are influenced by the same genes.

**Construct**   A theoretical concept that does not exist in reality.

**Construct validity**   General pattern of relationships between a test and relevant behaviors as defined by a particular theory.

**Content analysis**   The theory and techniques used to code qualitative data so that they can be used in quantitative analyses.

**Content validity**   Extent to which test items constitute an adequate sample of the events being measured.

**Contents**   In Guilford's model of intelligence, the dimension that refers to material or information to which the person reacts.

**Contingency theory**   A theory of leadership that focuses on the person-environment fit between the leader's personal characteristics and the demands of the situation.

**Continuous reinforcement**   Reinforcement that

occurs whenever the target response occurs; reinforcement on a 100 percent schedule.

**Contrasted groups** A strategy of scale construction in which items are selected on the basis of their ability to discriminate between two groups of people that differ on the attribute being assessed.

**Control group** Subjects in an experiment who undergo the same conditions as the experimental subjects except for the key factor being studied.

**Controlled field observations** A combination of experimental and naturalistic research in which subjects are observed in a natural setting, but an experimental manipulation is introduced into that setting.

**Convergent thinking** The ability to narrow a set of alternatives down to finding a correct solution to a problem.

**Cook-Medley Hostility Scale** A scale consisting of 50 items from the MMPI that assesses the attitudinal component of hostility.

**Coronary heart disease (CHD)** A variety of pathological processes that affect the heart muscle and coronary vessels.

**Correlation coefficient** Numerical value indicating the strength and direction of the relation between two variables.

**Correlation matrix** An array of correlations among all possible pairs of test scores.

**Counterconditioning** Conditioning of a desirable response that is incompatible with an undesirable one.

**Countertransference** In psychoanalysis, the tendency of the therapist to react to the patient on the basis of the therapist's own needs and conflicts.

**Covert test** A measure whose purpose is disguised from the test-taker.

**Creationism** A theory of how species developed that is based on divine intervention. Creationism is not considered a scientific theory because it cannot be tested.

**Creativity** The ability to come up with new ideas and novel solutions that are useful for solving problems or that provide adaptive new perspectives on events in the world.

**Crises** In Erickson's system, eight critical stages influenced by both biological and psychological factors. Either positive or negative outcomes are possible.

**Criterion analysis** Eysenck's method of testing hypothesis through factor analysis.

**Criterion contamination** Situation in which a subject's standing on a given variable is influenced or corrupted by preexisting related information.

**Criterion validity** Extent to which test scores relate to an agreed-upon behavioral criterion.

**Cross-situational coefficient** A term used by Mischel to describe a correlation coefficient between measures of a person's behavior in two situations.

**Crystallized ability** According to Cattell, a broad kind of intelligence that reflects one's experiences in the culture.

**Cue** Stimulus that determines the particular response a person will make.

**Cue-producing response** A production of similarity or differences among situations by virtue of the cues residing in language.

**Culture-fair test** A test designed to measure intelligence free from the influence of cultural factors.

**Cytosine** A protein that is one of the four base pairs that make up DNA. It is paired with guanine in the double helix DNA strand.

**Daily hassles** A form of stress that emerges from the ordinary, daily events in our lives.

**Daseinsanalysis** In existential psychology, the analysis of the immediate experience of the individual.

**Death instincts (Thanatos)** In Freudian theory, those instincts responsible for the destructive aspects of human behavior.

**Defense mechanisms** The group of styles that individuals may use to protect their egos from threatening thoughts, feelings, and impulses. Individuals typically use only one of the many possible defense mechanisms in a given situation, and each individual may have a generally preferred mechanism

**Defensive identification** A situation in which a child identifies with a given parent in order to avoid punishment from that parent.

**Defensive pessimisim** A strategy for accomplishing life tasks in which a person adopts a pessimistic attitude to diffuse the negative effects of failure and to enhance the positive effects of success.

**Delay of gratification**  The ability to defer immediate, smaller rewards in favor of larger but delayed ones.

**Deoxyribonucleic acid (DNA)**  The material contained in chromosomes consisting of the base pairs that are the basis of genetic transmissions.

**Dependent variable**  Factor in an experiment that may or may not change as a result of manipulation of the independent variable.

**Descriptive theory**  A theory that concerns how personality should be described and how descriptive terms should be structured and organized.

**Descriptive-predictive view of traits**  The position that traits are primarily descriptive, and perhaps predictive, of behavior without being causes of the behavior.

**Deviation scores**  The deviation (difference) of an individual's score on a variable from the mean of the variable. Deviation scores are used in the calculation of the variance.

**Diagnostic council**  A strategy used by Murray in which several observers are brought together to discuss their separate observations of an individual and synthesize them into a personality description.

**Dichotomous construct**  Either-or nature of constructs, according to Kelly.

**Differential heritability**  The tendency for characteristics to differ in the extent to which they are influenced by genes.

**Differential R-technique**  A factor analytic approach to studying change based on the correlations among change scores. The resulting factors indicate which variables exhibit similar patterns of change.

**Disconfirmation**  A characteristic of a scientific theory that allows for it to be tested, and altered according to inconsistent evidence.

**Discrimination of cues**  Process in which the individual pays appropriate attention to those environmental signals relevant to achieving reinforcement.

**Discriminative stimuli**  Stimuli that indicate one response rather than another is likely to be rewarded.

**Dispositional-explanatory view of traits**  A view of traits as being able to explain people's behavior, explicit in the traditional trait theories of Allport, Cattell, Murray, and to some extent Eysenck.

**Dispositions**  The inclinations or tendencies that help direct and energize our behavior.

**Distance**  For Adler, the tendency to establish distance between the self and goals in order to avoid failure.

**Distinctiveness**  The uniqueness of an individual's personality, a result of the overall pattern and combination of his or her feelings, thoughts, and behavior.

**Divergent thinking**  The ability to generate a broad set of alternative ideas and possible solutions to problems.

**Dizygotic (DZ) twins**  Literally, two (di) egg (zygote) twins. Also called fraternal twins, these are twins who came from two separately fertilized eggs. These twins share, on the average, 50 percent of their genetic material, as do regular siblings.

**Dominant gene**  A gene whose characteristic will be expressed even when it is paired with a gene that codes for a different characteristic.

**Double helix**  The description of the structure of DNA, which consists of two strands of genetic material wrapped around each other in a spiral (helix).

**Dread and despair**  For existentialists, emotions of fear, uneasiness, and loss of hope resulting from the person's failure to be authentic.

**Dream analysis**  A form of psychoanalytic interpretation that is applied to a person's dreams.

**Drive**  According to Dollard and Miller, a strong internal stimulus that impels an organism to action.

**Drive-activation method**  Method of studying the unconscious by activating it through subliminal perception.

**Dynamic lattice**  For Cattell, the relations among dynamic traits, ergs, sentiments, and attitudes.

**Dynamic self-concept**  A view of the self as forceful and changing.

**Dynamic trait**  For Cattell, a trait that initiates a person's response in a given situation.

**Early sex training**  A period of learning sexual roles and norms in early childhood that, according to Dollard and Miller, may become a source of conflict and produce chronic anxiety in the child.

**Ego** In Freudian theory, the reality-oriented portion of the personality; utilizes learning, perception, and reasoning to satisfy id impulses in light of real-world constraints. Jung used a similar concept in referring to an "I" feeling.

**Ego control** Ability to control one's impulses by self-delay, inhibition of aggression, and making plans.

**Ego-ideal** In Freudian theory, the part of the superego consisting of standards of perfection which, if realized, bring a sense of pride and self-esteem.

**Ego identity** In Erikson's system, self-perceptions that give one a sense of uniqueness and stability over time.

**Ego psychology** A revision of Freudian theory that occurred in the late 1950s. It emphasized the role of the ego in healthy personalities and did not view the ego as being in constant conflict with the id.

**Ego resiliency** Ability to adapt to environmental demands by modifying ego-control.

**Electra complex** In Freudian theory, the counterpart in girls of the Oedipus complex.

**Eminent person** According to Galton, an individual whose contributions to society are so profound that such an individual will occur only once in 4,000 people.

**Emotional intelligence** The ability to be aware of, and control and channel, one's emotions, needs, and desires in adaptive ways.

**Empirical research** Research based on observations that can be shared and verified.

**Employee Polygraph Protection Act** Legislation passed by the United States Congress that restricts the use of polygraphs in employment situations.

**Enactive attainment** One's performance in a dreaded situation that has an effect on self-efficacy.

**Encoding strategies** One of the classes of variables in Mischel's cognitive social learning reconceptualization of personality, concerning the manner in which people perceive and represent events and people in their lives.

**Encounter groups** A technique to enhance personal growth by allowing the person to encounter his or her feelings through encounters with other people in a controlled and supportive group environment.

**Environmental-mold trait** For Cattell, a source trait developed out of experience with the environment.

**Enzymes** Proteins; the basic genetic material.

**Epigenetic principle** According to Erikson, the theory that the developing personality follows a blueprint that constantly guides it toward broader social interactions.

**Episodic memory** Memory for events or episodes.

**Equal-environments assumption** A crucial assumption in twin study research that MZ and DZ twins are equally similar in their environmental experience.

**Erg** For Cattell, a dynamic constitutional source trait, which is innate, motivates the person, and determines numerous surface traits.

**Erotogenic zones** In Freudian theory, the parts of the body that, if manipulated produce pleasurable sensations.

**Eugenics** A naive view promoted by Galton, later Hitler, and, unfortunately, still by some segments of society today that humankind can be improved by using scientific methods to eliminate undesirable characteristics (negative eugenics) and promote desirable characteristics (positive eugenics) in the human gene pool.

**Evolutionary theory** An explanation of how variability and commonalities developed in species as a result of mutation and natural selection.

**Existentialism** Theory emphasizing freedom of choice, taking responsibility for one's own life, and the achievement of one's full potential.

**Expectancy** In Rotter's theory, a subjectively held probability that a particular reinforcement will occur as the result of a specific behavior.

**Experience sampling method** A research technique in which subjects are asked at various times during the day to record what they are experiencing and answer questions about the experience.

**Experimental control** Eliminating possible confounds in a research setting by nullifying them or making them constant for all subjects in the experiment.

**Experimental hypothesis**  Hypothesis to be tested by means of an experimental procedure.

**Explicit (formal) personality theory**  Theories of personality that are rigorously evaluated through scientific methods.

**Expressive behaviors**  Behaviors that reflect a basic style of responding rather than the function of the response. Thought by Allport to be more useful for assessing personality because these behaviors would be less influenced by situational variables.

**External control**  In Rotter's theory, the belief or expectancy that attaining or failing to attain reinforcements is due to luck, chance, fate, or powerful others; contrasts with internal control.

**Extinction**  Elimination of a learned response following repeated nonoccurrence of reward.

**Extraversion**  For Jung, an orientation toward the outer world, characterized by sociability and friendliness. Term also used by Eysenck.

**Extrinsic motivation**  Motivation derived from external rewards

**Factor analysis**  Mathematical technique of arranging traits or responses into homogeneous groupings within a matrix of intercorrelations.

**Feedback control**  Behavioral control through the continual monitoring of progress toward a goal.

**Feeding situation**  According to Dollard and Miller, the early situation in which the groundwork is laid for many subsequent emotional reactions.

**Feminine protest**  According to Adler, the striving for superiority by adopting feminine and nurturant behavior.

**Feminism**  The concern with the social, political, economic, and cultural inequities between men and women.

**Field-dependence vs. independence**  A cognitive style that concerns the extent to which an individual's thinking about a problem or issue is influenced by the context in which the issue is presented.

**Five-Factor Model**  A version of the Big Five that emphasizes the dispositional properties of traits as opposed to merely their descriptive aspects.

**Fixed-role therapy**  Form of therapy associated with Kelly in which clients play roles for a specified time period.

**Fluid ability**  According to Cattell, the ability determined by one's biological capacity.

**Focus of convenience**  Term often used by Kelly to indicate that each theory is best applied to a particular set of situations or events.

**Four fundamentals of learning**  According to Dollard and Miller, the four components required for learning: drive, cue, response, and reward.

**Free association**  In psychoanalytic therapy, the method whereby the patient verbalizes every thought no matter how irrational, trivial, or threatening it may appear.

**Free descriptions**  Data obtained by allowing subjects to describe themselves or others without any constraints. Neither the characteristics to be described nor the scales on which the characteristics are rated are provided.

**Freedom of movement**  In Rotter's theory, the mean subjective probability that a group of related behaviors will lead to a particular set of goals.

**Frequency-dependent selection**  A form of influence on natural selection; the effect of the relative frequency of phenotypes on their selective advantage.

**Freudian slip**  A misstatement that seems to imply an unconscious motive that the person would not likely admit.

**Fully functioning person**  According to Rogers, an individual who utilizes his or her potential.

**Functional analysis of behavior**  Analysis of behavior designed to show how a behavior covaries with the environmental conditions that control it.

**Functional autonomy**  Allport's idea that adult motives are often independent of their early beginnings (e.g., a man no longer fishes because of the desire for food but because he simply enjoys fishing).

**Galvanic skin response**  A measure of skin conductance used to physiologically assess anxiety or arousal. It is based on changes in the electrical properties of the skin that result from perspiration.

**Gender**   One's psychosexual identity.

**Gender differences**   The psychosocial, as opposed to biological, differences between men and women.

**Gender identity**   The aspects of the self that are related to one's identification with one or another gender.

**Gender- or sex-role stereotype**   Bias against individuals because of their membership in a specific sexual group.

**Gene mapping**   The process of locating the genetic material that codes for a specific characteristic (gene) in a specific area of a specific chromosome.

**Gene pool**   The collection of genes available for mixing in a particular species or group.

**General adaptation syndrome**   Selye's concept of a set of physiological responses to stress that involve several distinct stages, the last of which could be death.

**General factor of intelligence (g)**   According to Spearman, the broad factor underlying all intellectual activity.

**Generalized expectancy**   In Rotter's theory, an expectancy based upon experiences accumulated over a variety of related situations.

**Generalized reinforcer**   Reinforcer whose value does not depend solely on the drive state.

**Genetic engineering**   The process of actively altering human genetic material by inserting or replacing portions of DNA in the chromosomes.

**Genetic independence**   One of the principles Mendel derived from his observation that phenotypes for different characteristics appear in all combinations.

**Genetic segregation**   One of the principles Mendel derived from his observation that some phenotypes are not blends of the parents' phenotypes but are one or the other of the parents' phenotypes.

**Genetic similarity theory**   A theory proposed to account for altruism. According to this theory, individuals will show greater altruism toward individuals or species that are more genetically similar to them.

**Genetic theory**   The general theory of how genes contribute to the origin, maintenance, and transmission of characteristics.

**Genital stage**   In Freudian theory, the final psychosexual stage, in which the mature development of heterosexual impulses and behavior occurs.

**Genotype**   The underlying genetic basis for a phenotype. Phenotypes will not always reflect their underlying genotype because of the effects of the environment on the phenotype.

**Germ cells**   The cells (sperm and egg) involved in reproduction. Unlike most cells, germ cells contain only half the normal number of an organism's chromosomes.

**Global personality ratings**   A compromise between objective personality scales and free descriptions. Subjects are provided with the personality characteristic to be described and a rating scale, but the rating is based on the subjects' global impression of the target rather than on a set of specific behaviors defined by the experimenter.

**Good-me**   For Sullivan, the result of positive reactions received by a child from the mother and others; high self-esteem.

**Goodenough-Harris Drawing Test**   A test of intelligence requiring children to draw pictures of a man, a woman, and themselves.

**Grand unified theory**   A comprehensive set of principles that can explain all phenomena.

**Group factors of intelligence**   According to Thurstone, factors intermediate between g and s factors that affect individual performance.

**Group selection**   The tendency for natural selection to operate on a group of genetically similar organisms.

**Guanine**   A protein that is one of the four base pairs that make up DNA. It is paired with cytosine in the double helix DNA strand.

**Guided participation**   Method by which a patient or subject is helped by assistants to perform a desired behavior.

**Guilt**   A feeling of liability or culpability that, according to Kelly, comes from an awareness that one is not behaving in the manner dictated by one's core constructs.

**Guilty knowledge test** An application of polygraph testing based on asking subjects questions that can be answered only by someone who has knowledge of the event in question.

**Habit** Association between stimuli and responses that develops as a result of rewards.

**Habitual responses** For Eysenck, large numbers of repeatedly performed behaviors that complete a trait.

**Hardiness** Stress-buffering characteristics such as commitment, control, and challenge; said to make individuals resistant to stress-induced illness.

**Hawthorne effect** The finding from the Hawthorne studies that work productivity is influenced more by worker morale than by the physical work environment.

**Hawthorne experiments** A series of studies on factors that affect worker productivity, conducted at the Hawthorne plant of the Western Electric Company in the 1920s and 1930s.

**Head Start** A nationally funded educational program for preschoolers who come from disadvantaged backgrounds, designed to give these children "head start" on their education.

**Health psychology** A field of psychology that emphasizes the application of psychological theory, research, and practice to the maintenance and promotion of physical health.

**Heritability** A statistic that reflects the proportion of phenotypic variance that can be attributed to genetic variance in a particular population.

**Heuristic** A model, assumption, or principle that is used because it clarifies a situation rather than because it is necessarily thought to be true.

**Hierarchical model of intelligence** A model of intelligence that emphasizes the superior role of g factors, which in turn affect s factors.

**Hierarchical structure** An organizational scheme in which some elements are broad and general and contain other narrower and more specfic elements.

**Hope** A life task strategy emphasizing optimism and a sense that one can accomplish the life task at hand.

**Hostility** For Kelly, A state of conflict or opposition that results from a person's attempt to validate a construct that is failing in its task of prediction.

**Human genome project** A worldwide effort to completely map and sequence the human genome.

**Human relations** A theory of leadership that emphasizes fostering employee morale and communication among workers and managers.

**Humanism** Point of view emphasizing the essential goodness of human beings and the optimistic belief in their potential for growth.

**Hypertension** A diagnosis of high blood pressure.

**Id** In Freudian theory, the deep, unconscious part of the personality composed of the biological, instinctual drives; its goal is the immediate gratification of impulses.

**Ideal-self** That which the person would like to feel, be, or experience.

**Identical twins reared apart (study of)** A rare but powerful natural experiment that allows behavior geneticists to study MZ twins raised in separate circumstances, thus combining the advantages of the twin study and the adoption study.

**Identification with the aggressor** During the Oedipal period, a process by which the son resolves his conflict by identifying with his father.

**Identities** The various self-concepts that a person has in different contexts.

**Identity crisis** According to Erickson, the period of life during which a young person struggles to define the "real me."

**Idiographic** Approach emphasizing the intensive study of one individual; contrasts with the nomothetic approach, which focuses on the search for general laws by combining data from many individuals.

**Imaginary standard** One of three types of standards subjects can use to evaluate their own and other's behavior, based on idealized, imagined criteria.

**Implicit (informal) personality theory** Theories of personality based on people's everyday observations of others.

**Inappropriate set of responses** Responses that

appear to the observer as not suited to the nature of the situation.

**Inclusive fitness** The benefit to an organism's genes from an act that is disadvantageous to the organism. Used to explain altruistic behavior.

**Independent variable** The variable that is viewed as causal or predictive of the dependent variable.

**Indicants** Measures or observations that represent (indicate) a construct.

**Individual difference variables** Variables that derive their meaning from their ability to differentiate among individuals.

**Individual psychology** Term used to describe Adler's personality theory.

**Individual superordinate construct** In Kelly's system, a construct that exercises an overriding influence in a person's construct system.

**Inferiority complex** For Adler, strong feelings that one is inadequate compared with others.

**Initial (or innate) response hierarchy** According to Dollard and Miller, the order in which an organism's responses can be arranged in terms of their likelihood of occurrence.

**Innate motives** Biological motives that relate directly to the survival of the individual and the species (e.g., finding food and water).

**Instincts** In Freudian theory, the collections of unconscious wishes that have a source, an aim, and an object; usually divided into the life instincts and the death instincts.

**Instrumental conditioning** Learning to perform a given response as the result of having it reinforced or rewarded; sometimes called operant conditioning.

**Integration learning** For Cattell, the ability to suppress some motives and drives to permit the satisfaction of other motives.

**Integrity ("honesty") tests** Paper-and-pencil self-report measures designed to assess employee integrity and predict employees who will behave dishonestly on the job.

**Intelligence** The ability to apply knowledge to one's environment, or to think abstractly as measured by objective criteria.

**Intelligence quotient (IQ)** At first, defined as one's mental age divided by one's chronological age and multiplied by 100; now refers to one's test performance in relation to age peers.

**Intentions** For Cattell, one's hopes, aspirations, plans, and wishes.

**Interaction effect** The nonadditive combination of two variables to produce an effect that could not be predicted from knowing the effect of each variable by itself.

**Interactionism** The position that human behavior is the result of a nonadditive combination (interaction) between a person's qualities and the nature of the situation.

**Interjudge reliability** Extent to which different observers who are observing the same event make similar judgments about that event.

**Internal consistency reliability** A method for estimating a scale's reliability on the basis of correlations among the items on the scale.

**Internal control** In Rotter's theory, the belief or expectancy that attaining or failing to attain reinforcements is due to one's own efforts or lack of them; contrasts with external control.

**Internal standards** For Bandura, self-regulated criteria that influence our thoughts, actions, and emotions.

**Interpersonal psychology** The label used to describe Harry Stack Sullivan's theory of personality. Although psychoanalytic in origin, it emphasized that the manner in which we are evaluated by others comes to be the manner in which we evaluate ourselves.

**Interpersonal trust** In Rotter's theory, a problem-solving generalized expectancy regarding how trusting one should be of others.

**Intraclass correlation** A statistic designed to assess the relation on a variable between pairs of individuals within a class such as twins or spouses.

**Intraspecies variation** Differences among individuals of the same species.

**Intrinsic motivation** Motivation derived from characteristics of the task and internal rewards.

**Introversion** For Jung, a reserved, withdrawn orientation; interest in ideas rather than sociability. Contrasts with extraversion. Term also used by Eysenck.

**Intuition vs. sensation** The nonrational pair of

styles in Jung's typological system that refers to how a person perceives the world.

**Ipsative standard** One of three types of standards subjects can use to evaluate their own and others' behavior, based on past behavior or behavior in other domains.

**Item-response theory** A set of concepts and techniques that concern the relation between an individual's overt response to an item and the underlying (latent) attribute the item is designed to assess.

**Jenkins Activity Survey for Health Prediction (JAS)** A self-report method for identifying Type A individuals.

**Judgment response** Response to items that can objectively be judged to be correct or incorrect.

**Judgmental error** In contrast to a judgmental mistake, a judgmental error occurs when a subject's judgment departs from a known correct answer in a controlled laboratory setting in which the error is of little consequence to the subject.

**Judgmental mistake** In contrast to a judgmental error, a judgmental mistake occurs when a person makes an error in a real-world setting and the error has consequences to the person.

**Kin selection** Animals' increasing the likelihood that relatives will live to procreate, and thus pass their genes along to succeeding generations, by behaving selflessly.

**Knowledge-acquisition components** One type of component in Sternberg's triarchic theory of intelligence. These components concern the processes through which people obtain information.

**L-data** Data drawn from life records; often associated with Cattell's methods.

**Latency period** In Freudian theory, a period following the phallic stage in which sexual urges lie dormant.

**Law of effect** Thorndike's principle that explains the relation between a stimulus and a response solely on the basis of the reinforcing effect of the response.

**Leader match training** Leadership training based on teaching individuals how to assess their leadership style and the organizational situation, and change the situation if it does not match their style.

**Leaderless discussion group** A method for studying the development of leadership by grouping individuals and asking them to discuss a topic.

**Leadership** The psychological characteristics and abilities that help an individual motivate and persuade others to perform tasks and follow him or her.

**Learned helplessness** Condition resulting from exposure to painful, inescapable stimuli or failure in which helplessness behavior or diminished effort endures even in later circumstances, when escape or success is possible.

**Learning theories** Theories of how an organism learns to respond to its environment.

**Learning theory** The broad set of principles that explain how an organism learns from its environmental experiences.

**Least-Preferred Co-Worker Scale (LPC)** A measure of leadership style developed by Fiedler based on the individual's reactions to the person he or she least prefers to work with.

**Leveling vs. sharpening** A cognitive style that concerns the extent to which a person ignores or emphasizes unusual details in a problem.

**Lexical hypothesis** The foundation for descriptive theories of personality that are based on an analysis of words used to describe people. The hypothesis states that important individual differences will be encoded into the natural language.

**Libido** In Freudian theory, the energy responsible for the life instincts.

**Lie-detector test** A popular and somewhat misleading term for a polygraph misleading because polygraphs do not directly detect lies.

**Lie scale** A set of items designed to detect individuals who are likely to be lying on a personality inventory.

**Life expectancy** One of the major outcome variables in the study of health. It concerns the average length of time that people with certain characteristics and/or undergoing certain treatments are expected to live.

**Life instincts (eros)** In Freudian theory, those instincts responsible for the positive or constructive portions of behavior.

**Life tasks** The challenges and trials that a person faces as he or she goes through life.

**Locus of control**  In Rotter's theory, a generalized problem-solving expectancy regarding the extent to which reinforcement is controlled by self or other factors. Synonymous with *internal-external control of reinforcements.*

**Logical empiricism**  A principle in the philosophy of science that theories would emerge from the careful collection of data.

**Manifest Anxiety Scale**  Developed by Taylor, a true-false test for the measurement of anxiety levels.

**Masculine protest**  According to Adler, the striving for superiority by adopting assertive and dominant behavior.

**Maximum performance tests**  Tests on which a person can not appear to have a higher level of the attribute being assessed than he or she actually possesses; tests that cannot be faked in a positive direction.

**Mediated stimulus generalization**  Tendency for a response learned in one situation to apply to other situations; similarity is based not on physical similarity but on labeling.

**Meiosis**  The process of cell division through which germ cells are formed. Meiosis results in half an organism's chromosomes in the new cell.

**Metacomponents**  One type of component in Sternberg's triarchic theory of intelligence. These components concern how people define problems, organize their steps to solve the problem, and decide when the problem is solved.

**Metamotives**  See being-values.

**Metatheoretical**  Theories or principles about theories. A theory of how a theory should be tested is a metatheory.

**Minimal goal level**  In Rotter's theory, the lowest goal in a hierarchy of goals that is perceived by the individual as reinforcing.

**Minnesota Multiphasic Personality Inventory (MMPI)**  Widely used objective test originally designed to determine appropriate psychiatric diagnosis.

**Mirroring**  A therapeutic technique used in Kohut's self-psychology. It involves reflecting a client's feelings, particularly those of which the client is unaware.

**Mitosis**  The process of cell division through which normal (somatic) cells reproduce. Each new cell has all the chromosomes of the parent cell.

**Moderator variable**  A variable that changes the relation between two other variables.

**Monozygotic (MZ) twins**  Literally, one (mono) egg (zygote) twins. Also called identical twins, these are twins who came from a single fertilized egg. These twins are genetic clones, sharing 100 percent of their genetic material.

**Moral anxiety**  In Freudian theory, an awareness experienced as guilt stemming from the threat of punishment by the superego.

**Motivation**  The forces within us that activate and direct our behavior toward certain goals rather than others.

**Motivational processes**  In observational learning, the processes that determine whether we actually perform behaviors we have learned through observation.

**Motive**  The goal or outcome of a given behavior as it relates to a particular emotional state.

**Motor reproduction**  In observational learning, production of those behaviors exhibited by the model.

**Moving against people**  The strategy of coping with basic anxiety by being aggressive and hostile.

**Moving away from people**  The strategy of coping with basic anxiety by being isolated and withdrawn.

**Moving toward people**  The strategy of coping with basic anxiety by being affectionate and dependent.

**Multiple factor hypothesis**  An explanation to reconcile the inheritance of quantitative characteristics with Mendelian principles. Specifically, quantitative characteristics are the result of multiple genes (factors) that individually segregate independently, but that together appear to blend.

**Multistage testing**  An adaptive testing procedure used in the Stanford-Binet, involving giving the vocabulary subtest to determine the entry point for other subtests.

**Multivariate research**  Research involving taking a variety of measurements on the same person at one time, without experimental manipulation of variables.

**Mutation** The biological process through which genes change from one generation to the next.

**Narcissistic personality disorder** A form of psychopathology that results when the self's innate drive to develop is thwarted.

**Natural categories** Categories that are applied to natural phenomena that have unclear boundaries and graded membership.

**Natural selection** The principle that organisms are "chosen" to survive and reproduce on the basis of their phenotypic advantages; the foundation for evolutionary theory.

**Naturalistic observation** Observations of people or organisms in a natural, as opposed to a controlled experimental, environment.

**Need achievement** According to McClelland, the learned desire to perform well and to strive to attain a standard of excellence.

**Need for affiliation** The desire to seek the company of others and to achieve their friendship.

**Need for cognition** The general tendency to engage in and enjoy thinking.

**Need for power** The desire to exert control over the events that affect our lives.

**Need potential** In Rotter's theory, the mean potential for a group of related behaviors to occur as a way of achieving a particular set of goals.

**Need value** In Rotter's theory, the value of a group of related reinforcements composing a given need.

**Needs** In Murray's system, forces that organize and give direction to feelings, thoughts, and behaviors so that an unsatisfying state of affairs can be overcome.

**Negative affectivity** A general factor that concerns distressing emotional states such as depression, anger, and anxiety.

**Neuroscience** An interdisciplinary field whose goal is to relate the biological functions of the brain and nervous system with the individual's psychological experience of thought, feeling, and action.

**Neurotic anxiety** In Freudian theory, an aware-ness of a threat that unconscious id impulses are seeking expression.

**Neuroticism** A dimension in Eysenck's system that concerns emotional stability.

**Neutral stimulus** A stimulus that elicits no response in the absence of learning.

**Nomological network** A framework that illustrates how theories and constructs can be empirically evaluated through observations of their indicants (measures).

**Nomothetic** Approach focusing on the search for general laws by combining data from many individuals; contrasts with the idiographic approach, which emphasizes the intensive study of one individual.

**Non-additive genetic effects** A more complex form of genetic transmission in which the effects of different genes multiply together to influence a quantitative phenotype.

**Non-conditional description** A personality description that can be applied generally; not dependent on or limited to certain situations or circumstances.

**Non-shared environmental experience** A form of environmental influence on phenotypes that concerns the unique, idiosyncratic experiences of an individual in the context of his or her family or group.

**Non-voluntary responses** Responses that are not under the person's control and that do not require effort.

**Normal curve** A theory of the distribution of variables that requires most observations to hover around the average of the distribution and to taper off symmetrically on both sides.

**Normative standard** The most commonly used of three types of standards subjects can use to evaluate their own and other's behavior, based on the behavior of other people.

**Norms** Average scores from a comparison group used to evaluate a person's responses relative to the responses of other people.

**Not-me** For Sullivan, the result of strong disapproval from the mother or others. Experienced as strong anxiety by the child.

**Object relations theory** A psychodynamic theory

that concerns the way people use internal representations of objects to cope with life transitions.

Object representation   One's internalized image of a significant other object.

Objective personality test   Self-report test in which the subject provides responses to questions about feelings, thoughts, and behavior.

Objective tests   Self-report test in which the subject provides responses to questions about feelings, thoughts, and behavior.

Observational learning   Term often associated with Bandura, referring to learning by means of observing a live or symbolic model; also called *vicarious learning*.

Oedipus complex   In Freudian theory, sexual longing by a boy for his mother; occurs in the phallic stage.

Openness to experience   A label given to Factor V in the Big Five, which concerns curiosity, awareness, and a willingness to consider and try new ideas and experiences.

Operant behavior   Behavior acquired on the basis of instrumental conditioning.

Operations   In Guilford's model of intelligence, the dimension that refers to what the person does.

Optimism   A general quality of anticipating favorable outcomes to situations; said by some to make people resistant to stress-related illnesses.

Oral biting   In Freudian theory, a period of psychosexual development (from birth to eighteen months) when a chief mode of pleasure is biting.

Oral stage   In Freudian theory, the first psychosexual stage, in which the mouth is the prime area of pleasure.

Oral sucking   In Freudian theory, a period of psychosexual development (from birth to eight months) when the chief mode of pleasure is sucking.

Organ inferiority   For Adler, a congenital weakness in a body organ that stimulates feelings of inferiority in that person.

Other-report data   One of the three major types of data used to study personality, referring to ratings from others about the subject's behavior.

Outcome expectancy   The belief that certain results will occur if a certain response is made or if a certain pattern of stimuli is observed.

Overlap   A variable that is thought to influence rater agreement. Raters whose observations of a target occur at the same time or situation will agree more about the target than raters whose observations do not overlap.

Overt test   A test whose purpose is easily recognized by the test-taker.

P-technique   Statistical technique by which a single person's scores on a number of measures are compared from one to another; often associated with Cattell.

Parent effectiveness training   An approach to treating a child's psychological and behavioral problems by teaching the parents more effective ways to interact with and discipline the child.

Parsimonious explanation   A principle of theory development that a good theory is one that offers the simplest (most parsimonious) interpretation of the data.

Partial reinforcement   Less than 100 percent reinforcement of a response, usually increasing that response's resistance to extinction. Sometimes called intermittent reinforcement.

Path diagram   A description of a theory in which paths are drawn among variables to indicate how those variables are related.

Pathways   Knowledge of the plans or means one will use to achieve their goals.

Peak experience   For Maslow, an experience that is intensely fulfilling; often characteristic of self-actualizers.

Pedigree   A depiction of a person's ancestry (family tree) that indicates which relatives had a particular characteristic of interest. Used by geneticists to evaluate how genotypes for a particular phenotype may be transmitted.

Penis envy   In Freudian theory, the girl's desire to have a penis; persists throughout life and is responsible for the wish (in symbolic terms) to have a child, achieve power, etc.

Percept-genetics method   Method of studying the unconscious, using tachioscopic exposure of varying levels of illumination or exposure lengths.

Performance components   One type of component in Sternberg's triarchic theory of intelligence. These components concern the processes people use to solve problems.

**Permeable constructs**  Constructs that can be applied to, and revised in accordance with, an individual's changing experiences.

**Person–environment fit**  The degree to which characteristics of the individual are well suited to the demands of the situation.

**Person-centered therapy**  The approach to therapy based on Rogers' theory, emphasizing the person and the legitimacy of his or her feelings.

**Persona**  For Jung, the archetype representing the public face we put on in response to social demands.

**Personal constructs**  In Kelly's system, constructs that can be applied to events not yet a part of the construct system.

**Personal growth**  An actualizing tendency within individuals; a potential constantly seeking expression.

**Personal self-concept**  Part of the self containing physical, behavioral, and psychological characteristics.

**Personal trait**  For Allport, a trait unique to a given person.

**Personal unconscious**  Jung's concept, which is roughly equivalent to the preconscious of Freud.

**Personality**  Pattern of characteristic thoughts, feelings, and behaviors that distinguishes one person from another and persists over time and situations.

**Personality assessment**  The set of techniques, principles, and theories that concern how to measure personality.

**Personality coefficient**  A term used by Mischel to refer to correlations between measures of personality traits and measures of specific behaviors. The term is pejorative because these correlations are often small.

**Personality theory**  An organized set of assumptions or principles concerning the nature of personality.

**Phallic stage**  In Freudian theory, the third psychosexual stage, in which the genitals become the focus of attention and pleasure.

**Phenomenal field**  Everything experienced by the person at a given moment.

**Phenomenal self**  The part of the phenomenal field designated as the "I" or "me."

**Phenomenology**  Personality approach emphasizing the idea that behavior, emotions, and thoughts are determined by the person's subjective experience or perceptions.

**Phenotype**  The overt (observable) manifestation of a characteristic.

**Phenylketonuria (PKU)**  A genetic disorder that affects metabolism, which in turn can result in severe retardation. Often used to illustrate the difference between genotypes and phenotypes because environmental intervention (diet) can essentially eliminate the effect of the genotype.

**Philosophy of science**  That branch of philosophy that concerns how scientific knowledge originates, how it is maintained, and how it is communicated.

**Physiognomy**  An individual's physical appearance, from which personality characteristics are often (correctly or incorrectly) inferred.

**Placebo**  A substance or treatment that has no known effect on behavior but is administered under the pretense of having effects.

**Placebo effect**  A response to a substance or treatment that is consistent with the response the person expects rather than the actual effect of the substance or treatment

**Pleasure principle**  In Freudian theory, the principle by which the id operates; the seeking for immediate gratification of impulses.

**Polygraph**  A device designed to detect changes in physiological arousal such as blood pressure and heart rate. These changes are monitored in association with questions and changes in arousal are interpreted as signs of lying.

**Positive regard**  For Rogers, a strong need to be well regarded by others that motivates a vast array of human behavior.

**Positive self-regard**  For Rogers, a strong need to think well of oneself.

**Positron-emission tomography (PET scan)**  A technique used to provide an image of the brain. It is used to locate areas of the brain that are active during psychological experiences such as thinking, feeling, or behaving.

**Post-hoc explanation** An explanation that is made up to fit the facts. Post-hoc explanations are generally viewed as weak and of little worth.

**Practical significance** A contrast to statistical significance. Practical significance concerns the size or importance of an observed effect.

**Preconscious** Memories and material that are not immediately conscious but with some effort can be recalled.

**Predictive validity** Extent to which a test can predict to a criterion in the future.

**Preemptive construct** In Kelly's system, a construct that does not permit its elements to belong to any other category.

**Press** In Murray's theory, environmental factors that aid or hinder goal attainment.

**Primary drive** Basic, innate drive such as hunger or thirst.

**Primary needs** For Murray, physiological needs.

**Primary process** In Freudian theory, the id process whereby tension is reduced by forming a mental image of an object that will satisfy a drive.

**Primary reinforcer** Reinforcements such as food or water.

**Principle of aggregation** A general finding in statistics and assessment that combining relevant observations across some dimensions such as time, situations, items, or subjects increases the reliability and validity of the combined observations.

**Products** In Guilford's model of intelligence, the dimension that refers to the form in which information is processed.

**Progressive Matrices** A so-called culture-fair test developed by Raven, which consists of a series of designs.

**Projective test** Test in which personality factors are revealed by the way a subject responds to ambiguous test stimuli; a familiar example is the Rorschach test.

**Proprium** According to Allport, everything in the personality regarded by the person as his or her own.

**Prototype** A characterization of a concept that does not require a single clear definition; instead, a combination of several possible aspects of the concept, none of which is treated as defining.

**Psychic determinism** Belief of Freud that every behavior, thought, and emotion has meaning and purpose.

**Psychoanalytic interpretation** The psychoanalytic explanations offered by a therapist about a client's thoughts, dreams, and behaviors during psychotherapy.

**Psychobiography** The study of individuals, usually from a psychoanalytic standpoint, that attempts both to validate the theory and to understand the individuals in question.

**Psychohistory** Method of inquiry, especially associated with Erickson, in which major themes in a person's life are related to certain historical events.

**Psychological differentiation** A broadening of the cognitive style of field dependence-independence from a perceptual construct to a general personality dimension.

**Psychological situation** The aspect of the situation that the subject perceives and interprets. According to Rotter, situational variables impact behavior according to how a person construes them.

**Psychological types** According to Jung a type concerns the typical manner that a person processes information and relates to the world.

**Psychopharmacology** The study and application of drugs to relieve psychological problems and distress.

**Psychosocial theory** Erikson's theory of ego psychology which emphasizes eight stages of human development.

**Psychosomatic medicine** A field in which certain illnesses are regarded as caused or related to psychological factors.

**Psychoticism** Dimension or type used by Eysenck; at the extreme end, a person would be solitary, without loyalties, uncaring of others, and insensitive.

**Q-data** Self-rating questionnaire data; often associated with Cattell's methods.

**Q-sort** Method of obtaining trait ratings. The subject sorts cards containing traits or other information into a series of piles; these piles are labeled from "very characteristic" to "not at all characteristic."

**Q-sort technique** A method of obtaining trait ratings. The subject sorts cards containing traits or other information into a series of piles; which are subsequently labeled from "very characteristic" to "not at all characteristic."

**Q-technique** Statistical method in which people's scores on several measures are correlated, with the resulting index revealing the similarity among individuals; often associated with Cattell.

**Qualitative characteristics** Characteristics that appear in an all-or-none fashion.

**Quality of life** One of the major outcome variables in the study of health. It concerns how pleasant and rewarding and productive a person's life will be, regardless of how long the person lives.

**Quantitative characteristics** Characteristics that appear along a continuum.

**R-technique** Traditional correlation method in which the scores from a large number of tests administered to many subjects are correlated; often associated with Cattell.

**Radical behaviorism** An extreme form of behaviorism associated with B.F. Skinner that deals exclusively with the observed consequences of behavior for understanding and controlling that behavior.

**Reactive measure** A measure that influences the characteristic it is being used to measure.

**Reality anxiety** In Freudian theory, an awareness of a threat from the environment that has a rational basis.

**Reality principle** In Freudian theory, the principle used by the ego whereby immediate gratification is postponed until appropriate objects or conditions are identified.

**Recessive gene** A gene whose potential influence on a characteristic is masked when it is paired with a gene that is dominant for that characteristic.

**Reciprocal determinism** Term usually associated with Bandura referring to the influence of the situation, the person, and behavior.

**Reflectivity vs. impulsivity** A cognitive style that concerns the extent to which a person carefully

considers options as opposed to jumping at the first solution to a problem.

**Reinforcement value** In Rotter's theory, the degree of preference for one reinforcement rather than others, given the possibility that all are equally likely to occur.

**Reinforcer** According to Skinner, an event or stimulus that follows a response and is then determined to have increased the likelihood of that response.

**Reliability** Consistency with which a test or observational method yields comparable results under the same condition.

**Repression** In psychoanalytic theory, an unconsciously determined defense mechanism in which ego-threatening thoughts and impulses are involuntarily banished to the unconscious. For Dollard and Miller, it refers to "stopping thinking."

**Repressive coping style** A general style of repressing psychological distress as a means of coping with stressful experiences.

**Resistance** In psychotherapy, occurs when the patient becomes anxious over the eruption of unconscious material and responds by attempting to impede therapy in various ways.

**Respondent behavior** Behavior emitted in response to stimulation.

**Response** An act prompted by an internal or external stimulus.

**Response carelessness** A type of response style characterized by haphazard, thoughtless responses.

**Response expectancy** The expectation that a nonvoluntary response will occur in association with certain voluntary behavior or in the presence of a certain pattern of stimuli.

**Response extremeness** A type of response style characterized by scoring at the end points rather than in the middle of a rating scale.

**Response set** Deliberate tendency to respond to personality items to convey a particular impression.

**Response style** Tendency for a subject to respond to an item in a particular way (e.g., agree or disagree) regardless of the item's content.

**Retention processes** In observational learning,

these processes that permit learning through forming mental images and verbal coding of the model's behavior.

**Reward**   According to Dollard and Miller, anything that increases the likelihood of a given response being elicited by a particular stimulus.

**Rod-and-frame test**   A test to determine cognitive style.

**Role**   An individual's expected behavior. For Cattell, a person's role characterizes how he or she perceives a situation or event, and likewise determines how he or she responds.

**Role Construct Repertory Test**   Test devised by Kelly to identify and measure important constructs in a person's construct system.

**Role-playing**   Assessment of therapeutic technique in which individuals act out parts given them.

**Rorschach inkblots**   A projective test based on a person's interpretation of ambiguous inkblots.

**Rotter Incomplete Sentences Blank**   A personality test consisting of 40 sentence stems, requiring subjects to complete the sentences.

**Scatterplot**   Technically, a bivariate frequency distribution. A picture of the relation between two variables obtained by plotting pairs of observations on the variables in two dimensions.

**Schedules of reinforcement**   The various patterns in which reinforcers can be associated with responses. Different patterns of reinforcement have different impacts on behavior.

**Schemas**   Structures of knowledge that reside in memory.

**Scientific management**   A style of leadership in which workers are viewed as mere extensions of machines. The workers' feelings, abilities, and motives are considered unimportant.

**Scripts**   Organized presentations of familiar activities used to perceive and understand events.

**Secondary needs**   For Murray, needs that arise out of primary needs but are not connected with organic processes.

**Secondary process**   In Freudian theory, the principle employed by the ego whereby perceptual skills help prevent the individual from being endangered by the gratification of instinctual needs.

**Secondary reinforcer**   A reinforcer that, by having been paired with a primary reinforcer, comes to serve as a reinforcer in its own right (e.g., money, smiles).

**Secondary trait**   For Allport, a trait that exerts a relatively narrow or specific influence on behavior.

**Seeding theory**   A theory of how species developed that is based on intervention by extraterrestrial aliens. Seeding theory is not considered a scientific theory because it cannot be tested.

**Self**   For Rogers, the perception of oneself and its associated values; the "I" or "me." For Jung, an archetype that promotes a search for unity. For Sullivan, the reflected appraisals of others.

**Self-actualization**   Term associated with both Maslow and Rogers; a tendency or desire to be all that one can become.

**Self-efficacy**   Bandura's concept referring to a person's belief that a given behavior can be successfully executed.

**Self-handicapping**   Defensive strategy in which the person acquires an impediment to successful performance which, in turn, provides an excuse for potential failure.

**Self-ideals**   Aspects of the self as one would like them to be.

**Selfism**   A generalized problem-solving expectancy that emphasizes a focus and reliance on the self and its needs and desires.

**Self-monitoring**   Method of assessment in which subjects monitor their own behavior by keeping records such as diaries.

**Self psychology**   Heinz Kohut's personality theory, which emphasizes the development of the self as the crucial aspect of personality.

**Self-regulation**   The continuous and conscious evaluation and monitoring of progress toward a goal.

**Self-report data**   One of the three major types of data used to study personality, referring to ratings from the subject about his or her own behavior and personality.

**Self-schemata**   Cognitive generalizations about the self, derived from past experience, that organize and guide the processing of self-related information.

**Semantic memory**    An organized store of information about concepts and meaning.

**Sensitivity training**    A form of leadership training based on the human relations model, emphasizing listening and communication skills and the ability to promote positive human interactions between managers and employees.

**Sentiment**    For Cattell, a dynamic source trait arising out of experiences in the culture.

**Sentiment responses**    Responses to items that concern opinions or subjective evaluations, which consequently cannot objectively be judged to be correct or incorrect

**Sequencing chromosomes**    A method for establishing the sequence of base pairs in DNA that code for a particular characteristic.

**Sex**    A person's biological status as a man or woman.

**Sex chromosomes**    The two chromosomes that together genetically determine a person's sex.

**Sex differences**    Differences between men and women that are primarily biological, as opposed to psychosocial, in origin.

**Sex stereotype index (SSI)**    A measure developed by Williams and Best of the extent to which a person-descriptive term is associated with men or women.

**Shadow**    For Jung, the archetype incorporating the unrealized side of human nature.

**Shaping**    In operant conditioning, the gradual molding of behavior into the desired behavior through reward; sometimes called method of successive approximation.

**Shared environmental experience**    A form of environmental influence on phenotypes that concerns the common experiences of members of a family or group.

**Shared meaning**    A variable that is thought to influence rater agreement. Raters who agree about the meaning of a personality construct will agree more about the target's standing on that construct than raters who do not share meaning.

**Sign vs. sample**    Contrasting approaches that deal with test data as signs of underlying processes or as a sample of a larger pool of observations that could be made in other situations.

**Single-subject research**    A research method that applies experimental procedures to a single subject at a time. Such research is often replicated across several subjects.

**Social cognition**    The application of cognitive models to understand how people organize and categorize their social worlds, how people evaluate themselves and others, and how biases and stereotypes operate to influence behavior thought and action.

**Social cognitive theory**    Bandura's version of social learning theory that emphasizes how people acquire or learn the behaviors that they may choose to exhibit in a given situation.

**Social desirability**    Response style characterized by a tendency to give socially acceptable responses to items.

**Social intelligence**    The skills, knowledge, and abilities that people use in social settings.

**Social interest**    For Adler, a predisposition, nurtured by experience, to contribute to a society.

**Social learning theory**    A theory that emphasizes learning in a social context and the role of cognitive processes.

**Social Readjustment Rating Scale**    A scale listing potential stressful life events that may be implicated in the production of illness.

**Social self-concept**    The part of the self referring to how the individual believes he or she is seen by others.

**Sociobiology**    The study of the biological basis of social behavior in animals and humans.

**Somatic cells**    The normal cells in the human body. All cells are somatic cells except the sperm or the egg cells.

**SORC**    Four kinds of variables that the behavioral clinician will assess: stimuli, organismic variables, responses, and the consequences of behavior.

**Source traits**    For Cattell, underlying structures that cause behavior and constitute the core of personality.

**Specific expectancy**    In Rotter's theory, an expectancy based on experience in a specific situation.

**Specific factor (s) of intelligence**    According to

Spearman, a factor underlying performance on specific tasks that require intellect.

**Specific reflexes** Reflexes with which the infant is endowed at birth and that make it responsive to a very narrow range of stimuli.

**Specific responses** For Eysenck, the behavioral elements of habits.

**Specification equation** For Cattell, the formula combining all information about traits to predict a person's behavior in a specific situation.

**Stability** A developmental phenomenon referring to the regularity of a person's behavior and personality across time.

**Stanford-Binet** Intelligence test developed by Terman and based on Binet's early work.

**State** Within a hierarchical view of categories, the level of categorization that is "below" (more specific than) the basic level.

**State anxiety (A-state)** Level of anxiety experienced momentarily in a specific situation; varies in level from time to time and situation to situation.

**State-Trait Anxiety Inventory (STAI)** A self-report inventory designed to assess anxiety at a particular point in time (state anxiety) as well as a general tendency for a person to be prone to anxiety (trait anxiety).

**Statistical analysis** The numerical analysis of data to describe the results and to draw inferences from them.

**Statistical significance** A criteria used in the evaluation of data. It refers to the likelihood of a result under the condition that a particular statistical model is true.

**Stereotype** A summary description of a specified group that is believed to be applicable to all members of that group.

**Stimulus** Any event in the environment that could, under the right conditions, elicit a response.

**Stimulus generalization** Tendency for a response learned in connection with one stimulus to occur in relation to other, physically similar stimuli.

**Stress** A psychological and physiological state produced by a wide variety of unpleasant and sometimes dangerous events.

**Stress inoculation** Method of therapy in which patients are cognitively prepared and then taught to acquire and rehearse the skills necessary to deal with their problems.

**Stressor** An event in the environment that precipitates a state of stress in the person.

**Striving for superiority** For Adler, the desire to overcome feelings of inferiority and to reach the limits of one's abilities.

**Strong Vocational Interest Blank (SVIB)** A widely used measure of occupational preference. This measure is based on matching an individual's stated occupational preferences with the preferences of groups of individuals in a given occupation.

**Structure of intellect model** Model employed by Guilford that classifies intelligence along three dimensions: operations, contents, and products.

**Structured Interviews** An approach to interviewing in which the questions are explicitly organized.

**Style of life** For Adler, the unique pattern of characteristics that distinguishes the behavior of one person from that of another.

**Subjective experience** The way people perceive events and themselves.

**Subjective values** People's personal beliefs and convictions that influence their behavior; one of the classes of variables in Mischel's cognitive social learning reconceptualization of personality.

**Subordinate level** Within a hierarchical view of categories in act-frequency theory, the level of categorization that includes specific behaviors but is more general than the basic level.

**Successive approximation** A method of producing a response in the organism by reinforcing those responses that bring it closer to the desired behavior.

**Superego** In Freudian theory, the conscience representing the ideals and values of society as acquired from the parents.

**Superordinate level** The most abstract level of act-frequency theory, indicating general classes of behavior such as "interpersonal style."

**Surface traits** For Cattell, clusters of observable responses, the elements of which all seem to belong together.

**Symbiosis** Primitive period in which the infant

does not differentiate between the self and, for example, the mother.

**Syntality** For Cattell, the dimensions along which groups of people can be described.

**Systematic desensitization** Behavior therapy technique based on counterconditioning principles in which an incompatible response (often relaxation) is paired with progressively more anxiety-provoking stimuli until the person is able to imagine or be in the presence of such stimuli without anxiety.

**Systematic distortion hypothesis** A hypothesis that personality and behavior ratings are systematically distorted so that the ratings are consistent with the rater's beliefs about what personality characteristics and behaviors go together.

**Systems of constructs** A combination of constructs that combine to describe and explain events in the world.

**T-data** Objective test data; often associated with Cattell's methods.

**T-group** Training group; a group formed for the purpose of sensitivity training, designed to provide a supportive atmosphere for learning communication and interpersonal skills.

**Tachistoscope** An experimental apparatus designed to allow the experimenter to control the duration and illumination of a stimulus. Often used to present stimuli to subjects so quickly or under such poor illumination that the subject cannot consciously report seeing the stimuli.

**Temperament trait** A trait that is thought to cause behavior (at least in part) and therefore can be used to explain that behavior.

**Test anxiety** Anxiety that results from evaluative situations.

**Test Anxiety Scale (TAS)** A thirty-seven-item self-report scale that measures anxiety responses to testing situations.

**Test bias** The degree to which scores on a test systematically reflect factors related to group or individual differences that are irrelevant to the attribute assessed by the test.

**Test-retest reliability** Extent to which a test yields, under the same conditions, similar scores at different times.

**Thema** In Murray's theory, a combination of needs and presses that results in a given outcome.

**Theory** A set of principles that may serve to explain a specific set of phenomena, as well as a specification for how those principles can be tested.

**Theory X** A theory of leadership based on the scientific management view of workers as machines rather than people.

**Theory Y** A theory of leadership based on the human relations view of workers as people with needs, skills, and goals.

**Thinking vs. feeling** The rational pair of styles in Jung's typological system that refers to a person's preferred way of knowing the world.

**Third force** Descriptive term referring to humanistic approaches in personality.

**Threat** An indication of impending injury or damage. For Kelly, an awareness of an imminent change in one's construct system.

**Thymine** A protein that is one of the four base pairs that make up DNA. It is paired with adenine in the double helix DNA strand.

**Time-out** Behavior therapy method in which the individual is briefly removed from situations where positive reinforcement of unwanted behavior is possible.

**Tit-for-tat strategy** A form of strategic competitive behavior in which one member who engages in risky behavior for the group is compensated by another individual who takes the risk the next time.

**Token economy** Operant conditioning approach in which a given behavior earns tokens, which can then be exchanged for specific reinforcements; often used in institutional settings.

**Trait** Enduring personality characteristic that describes some people and not others. For Allport, a neuropsychic structure that influences perceptions of stimuli and gives consistency to modes of response.

**Trait anxiety (A-trait)** A person's chronic or stable level of anxiety.

**Transference** Essential element of psychoanalytic therapy in which the patient responds to the therapist as if the therapist were a parent or some other significant figure from childhood. When issues of transference become paramount in therapy, the term *transference neurosis* is used.

**Triarchic theory of intelligence**  Sternberg's theory that intelligence consists of three basic aspects: componential, experiential, and contextual.

**Twin study method**  A method used by behavior geneticists to separate genetic and environmental influence on a characteristic. It is based on comparing the similarity of MZ twins with the similarity of DZ twins.

**Type**  A personality structure organized around types rather than traits.

**Type A behavior pattern (TABP)**  A pattern related to proneness coronary heart disease that is characterized by competitiveness, aggressiveness, and a desire to do more in less time.

**Type B behavior pattern**  The absence of Type A behaviors.

**Typology**  A set of discrete categories into which people can be sorted.

**Unconditional positive regard**  According to Rogers, total and genuine love and respect given without conditions or strings attached.

**Unconditioned response**  An automatic response to a stimulus that occurs in the absence of learning.

**Unconditioned stimulus**  A stimulus that elicits an unconditioned response.

**Unconscious**  In psychoanalytic theory, the portion of the mind that is largely inaccessible to the ego or conscious thought.

**Unconscious motivation**  In Freudian theory, drives that motivate individuals without their being aware of the source.

**Unique influence**  A variable thought to influence rater agreement. This refers to any influence on ratings that does not come from observations of the rater's behavior.

**Unique traits**  For Cattell, traits not possessed in common with other people.

**Unsystematic observation**  The informal everyday observations that are often the beginning of scientific theories.

**Validated constructs**  Personal constructs that have received empirical support from the person's observations.

**Validity**  Extent to which a test measures what it purports to measure.

**Variable centered approach**  An approach to the study of personality that emphasizes how variables are related to each other rather than to a specific individual's personality.

**Variance**  A basic statistic designed to index the extent to which observations differ on a variable. It is the average of the squared deviation scores on that variable.

**Vicarious conditioning**  Observation of another person being conditioned, increasing the likelihood that the observer will become similarly conditioned.

**Vicarious experience**  In observational learning, watching the performance of others.

**Vicarious reinforcement**  Being reinforced (although less intensely so) by observing a model receive reinforcement.

**Voluntary behavior**  Responses that are under the person's control and require effort.

**Wechsler-Bellevue Intelligence Scale**  An individual test designed by Wechsler to focus on adult-level knowledge.

**Work Preference Inventory (WPI)**  A self report inventory designed to assess both intrinsic and extrinsic motivation.

**X chromosome**  A sex chromosome that when paired with another X chromosome produces a female, and when paired with a Y chromosome produces a male.

**Y chromosome**  A sex chromosome that together with an X chromosome produces a male.

# References

Abelson, R. P. (1994). A personal perspective on social cognition. In P. G. Devine, D. L. Hamilton, & T. M. Ostrom (Eds.), *Social cognition: Impact on social psychology* (pp. 15–39). San Diego, CA: Academic Press.

Adair, J. G., Sharpe, D., & Huynh, C. (1989). Hawthorne control procedures in educational experiments: A reconsideration of their use and effectiveness. *Review of Educational Research, 59,* 215–228.

Adams, J. S. (1965). Inequity in social exchange. In L. Berkowitz (Ed.), *Advances in experimental social psychology (Vol. 2).* New York: Academic Press.

Adams-Weber, J. R. (1979). Personal construct theory: Concepts & Applications. Chichester, England: Wiley.

Adler, A. (1924). *The practice and theory of individual psychology.* New York: Harcourt, Brace.

Adler, A. (1939). *Social interest: A challenge to mankind.* New York: Putnam.

Ahadi, S. A. (1991). The use of API career factors as Holland occupational types. *Educational and Psychological Measurement, 51,* 167–173.

Ahering, R. F., & Parker, L. D. (1989). Need for cognition as a moderator of the primacy effect. *Journal of Research in Personality, 23,* 313–317.

Ahren, F. M., Johnson, R. C., Wilson, J. R., McClearn, G. E., & Vandenberg, S. G. (1982). Family resemblances in personality. *Behavior Genetics, 12,* 261–280.

Alderfer, C. (1972). *Existence, relatedness, and growth: Human needs in organizational settings.* New York: Free Press.

Alexander, F. (1950). *Psychosomatic medicine.* New York: Norton.

Alexander, I. E. (1988). Personality, psychological assessment, and psychobiography. *Journal of Personality, 56,* 265–294.

Alexander, R. D. (1979). *Darwinism and human affairs.* Seattle: University of Washington Press.

Allen, B. P., & Potkay, C. R. (1981). On the arbitrary distinction between states and traits. *Journal of Personality and Social Psychology, 41,* 916–928.

Allen, K. E., Hart, B., Buell, J. S., Harris, F. R., & Wolf, M. M. (1964). Effects of social reinforcement on isolate behavior of a nursery school child. *Child Development, 35,* 511–518.

Alliger, G. M., Lilienfeld, S. O., & Mitchell, K. E. (1996). The susceptibility of overt and covert integrity tests to coaching and faking. *Psychological Science, 7,* 32–39.

Allport, G. W. (1937). *Personality: A psychological interpretation.* New York: Holt.

Allport, G. W. (1961). *Pattern and growth in personality.* New York: Holt, Rinehart & Winston.

Allport, G. W. (1965). *Letters from Jenny.* New York: Harcourt, Brace & World.

Allport, G. W. (1966). Traits revisited. *American Psychologist, 21,* 1–10.

Allport, G. W. (1968). *The person in psychology; selected essays.* Boston: Beacon Press.

Allport, G. W. (1973). *Personality: A psychological interpretation.* New York: Holt.

Allport, G. W., & Odbert, H. S. (1936). Trait-names: A psycholexical study. *Psychological Monographs, 47*(1, No. 211).

Allport, G. W., & Vernon, P. E. (1933). *Studies in expressive movement.* New York: Macmillan.

Allport, G. W., Vernon, P. E., & Lindzey, G. (1960). *A study of values* (3rd ed.). Boston: Houghton Mifflin.

Allred, K. D., & Smith, T. W. (1989). The hardy personality: Cognitive and physiological responses to evaluative threat. *Journal of Personality and Social Psychology, 56,* 257–266.

Almagor, M., Tellegan, A., & Waller, N. G. (1995).The Big Seven Model: A cross-cultural replication and further exploration of the basic dimensions of natural language trait descriptors. *Journal of Personality and Social Psychology, 69,* 300–307.

Alpert, J. L. (Ed.). (1986). *Psychoanalysis and women: Contemporary reappraisals.* Hillsdale, NJ: Analytic Press.

Amabile, T. M. (1983). Social psychology of creativity: A componential conceptualization. *Journal of Personality and Social Psychology, 45,* 357–377.

Amabile, T. M., Goldfarb, P., & Brackfield, S. (1990). Social influences on creativity: Evaluation, coaction, and surveillance. *Creative Research Journal, 3,* 6–21.

Amabile, T. M., Hill, K. G., Hennessey, B. A., & Tighe, E. M. (1994). The Work Preference Inventory: Assessing intrinsic and extrinsic motivational orientations. *Journal of Personality and Social Psychology, 66,* 950–967.

American Management Association. (1977). Summary overview of the "state of the art" regarding information gathering techniques and level of knowledge in three areas concerning crimes against business. Washington, DC: National Institute of Law Enforcement and Criminal Justice, Law Enforcement Administration.

American Psychiatric Association. (1994). *Diagnostic and statistical manual of mental disorders (4th ed.).* Washington, DC: Author.

American Psychiatric Association. (1980). *Diagnostic and statistical manual of mental disorders* (3rd ed.). Washington, DC: Author.

American Psychological Association (1994). *Publication manual of the American Psychological Association (4th ed.).* Washington, DC: Author.

Anastasi, A. (1976). *Psychological Testing* (4th ed.). New York: MacMillan.

Anderson, N. B. (1995). Behavioral and sociocultural perspectives on ethnicity and health: Introduction to the special issue. *Health Psychology, 14,* 589–591.

Angoff, W. H. (1988). The nature-nurture debate, aptitudes, and group differences. *American Psychologist, 43,* 713–720.

Ansbacher, H. L. (1977). Individual psychology. In R. J. Corsini (Ed.), *Current personality theories.* Itasca, IL: Peacock.

Ansbacher, H. L., & Ansbacher, R. R. (eds.). (1956). *The individual psychology of Alfred Adler.* New York: Basic Books.

Armstrong, S. L., Gleitman, L. R., & Gleitman, H. (1983). What some concepts might not be. *Cognition, 13,* 263–308.

Aronoff, J. (1985). *Personality in the social process.* Hillsdale, NJ: Erlbaum.

Asch, S. E. (1946). Forming impressions of personality. *Journal of Personality and Social Psychology, 41,* 258–290.

Asch, S. (1952). *Social Psychology.* New York: Prentice-Hall.

Asch, S. E., & Zukier, H. (1984). Thinking about persons. *Journal of Personality and Social Psychology, 46,* 1230–1240.

Asterita, M. F. (1985). *The physiology of stress.* New York: Human Sciences Press.

Atkinson, J. W. (1957). Motivational determinants of risk-taking behavior. *Psychological Review, 64,* 359–372.

Atkinson, J. W. (1964). *An introduction to motivation.* Princeton, NJ: Van Nostrand.

Avila, C., Molto, J., Segarra, P., & Torrubia, R. (1995). Sensitivity to conditioned or unconditioned stimuli: What is the mechanism underlying passive avoidance deficits in extraverts. *Journal of Research in Personality, 29,* 373–394.

Ayllon, T., & Azrin, N. H. (1968). *The token economy, A motivational system for therapy and rehabilitation.* New York: Appleton-Century-Crofts.

Ayllon, T., & Michael, J. (1959). The psychiatric nurse as a behavioral engineer. *Journal of the Experimental Analysis of Behavior, 2*, 323–334.

Azrin, N. H., & Lindsley, O. R. (1956). The reinforcement of cooperation between children. *Journal of Abnormal and Social Psychology, 52*, 100–102.

Babledelis, G. (1984). *The study of personality.* New York: Holt, Rinehart & Winston.

Backman, L., & Molander, B. (1986). Adult differences in the ability to cope with situations of high arousal in a precision sport. *Psychology and Aging, 1*, 133–139.

Baer, J. S., Holt, C. S., & Lichtenstein, E. (1986). Self-efficacy and smoking reexamined: Construct validity and clinical utility. *Journal of Consulting and Clinical Psychology, 54*, 846–852.

Baldwin, A. (1942). Personal structure analysis: A statistical method for investigating the single personality. *Journal of Abnormal and Social Psychology, 37*, 163–183.

Bandura, A. (1965). Influence of models' reinforcement contingencies on the acquisition of imitative responses. *Journal of Personality and Social Psychology, 1*, 589–595.

Bandura, A. (1969a). *Principles of behavior modification.* New York: Holt, Rinehart & Winston.

Bandura, A. (1969b). Social-learning theory of identificatory processes. In D. A. Goslin (Ed.), *Handbook of socialization theory and research.* Chicago: Rand McNally.

Bandura, A. (1974). Behavior theories and the models of man. *American Psychologist, 29*, 859–869.

Bandura, A. (1977). *Social learning theory.* Englewood Cliffs, NJ: Prentice-Hall.

Bandura, A. (1982). Self-efficacy mechanism in human agency. *American Psychologist, 37*, 122–147.

Bandura, A. (1986). *Social foundations of thought and action: A social cognitive theory.* Englewood Cliffs, NJ: Prentice-Hall.

Bandura, A. (1989). Human agency in social cognitive theory. *American Psychologist, 44*, 1175–1184.

Bandura, A., Adams, N. E., & Beyer, J. (1977). Cognitive processes mediating behavioral change. *Journal of Personality and Social Psychology, 35*, 125–139.

Bandura, A., Adams, N. E., Hardy, A. B., & Howells, G. N. (1980). Tests of the generality of self-efficacy theory. *Cognitive Therapy and Research, 4*, 39–66.

Bandura, A., Blanchard, E. B., & Ritter, B. (1969). Relative efficacy of desensitization and modeling approaches for inducing behavioral, affective, and attitudinal changes. *Journal of Personality and Social Psychology, 13*, 173–199.

Bandura, A., Cioffi, D., Taylor, C. B., & Brouillard, M. E. (1988). Perceived self-efficacy in coping with cognitive stressors and opioid activation. *Journal of Personality and Social Psychology, 55*, 479–488.

Bandura, A., & Kupers, C. J. (1964). The transmission of patterns of self-reinforcement through modeling. *Journal of Abnormal and Social Psychology, 69*, 1–9.

Bandura, A., & Mischel, W. (1965). Modification of self-imposed delay of reward through exposure to live and symbolic models. *Journal of Personality and Social Psychology, 2*, 698–705.

Bandura, A., O'Leary, A., Taylor, C. B., Gauthier, J., & Gossard, D. (1987). Perceived self-efficacy and pain control: Opioid and nonopioid mechanisms. *Journal of Personality and Social Psychology, 53*, 563–571.

Bandura, A., & Rosenthal, T. L. (1966). Vicarious classical conditioning as a function of arousal level. *Journal of Personality and Social Psychology, 3*, 54–62.

Bandura, A., & Schunk, D. H. (1981). Cultivating competence, self-efficacy, and intrinsic interest through proximal self-motivation. *Journal of Personality and Social Psychology, 41*, 586–598.

Bandura, A., Taylor, C. B., Williams, S. L., Mefford, I. N., & Barchas, J. D. (1985). Catecholamine secretion as a function of perceived coping self-efficacy. *Journal of Consulting and Clinical Psychology, 53*, 406–414.

Bandura, A., & Walters, R. (1963). *Social learning and personality development*. New York: Holt, Rinehart & Winston.

Bandura, A., & Wood, R. (1989). Effect of perceived controllability and performance standards on self-regulation of complex decision making. *Journal of Personality and Social Psychology, 56*, 805–814.

Bannister, D. (Ed.). (1970). *Perspectives in personal construct theory*. New York: Academic Press.

Bannister, D. (Ed.). (1985). *Issues and approaches in personal construct theory*. Orlando, FL: Academic Press.

Barefoot, J. C. (1992). Developments in the measurement of hostility. In H. S. Friedman (Ed.), *Hostility, coping, and health*. (pp. 13–31). Washington, DC: American Psychological Association.

Bargh, J. A. (1982). Attention and automaticity in the processing of self-relevant information. *Journal of Personality and Social Psychology, 43*, 425–436.

Barker, R. G., & Wright, H. F. (1951). *One boy's day*. New York: Harper & Row.

Barrick, M. R., & Mount, M. K. (1991). The Big Five personality dimensions and job performance: A meta-analysis. *Personnel Psychology, 44*, 1–26

Barron, F., & Harrington, D. (1981). Creativity, intelligence, and personality. *Annual Review of Psychology, 32*, 439–479.

Barron, F. H. (1968). *Creativity and personal freedom*. New York: Van Nostrand Reinhold.

Barry, H., Child, I., & Bacon, M. (1959). Relation of child training to subsistence economy. *American Anthropologist, 61*, 51–63.

Barsalou, L. W. (1985). Ideals, central tendency, and frequency of instantiation as determinants of graded structure in categories. *Journal of Experimental Psychology: Learning, Memory, and Cognition, 11*, 629–654.

Barsalou, L. W. (1987). The instability of graded structure: Implications for the nature of concepts. In U. Neisser (Ed.), *Concepts and conceptual development: Ecological and intellectual factors in categorization* (pp. 101–140).

Cambridge, England: Cambridge University Press.

Baumeister, R. F. (1987). How the self became a problem: A psychological review of historical research. *Journal of Personality and Social Psychology, 52*, 163–176.

Baumeister, R. F., & Steinhilber, A. (1984). Paradoxical effects of supportive audiences on performance under pressure: The home field disadvantage in sports championships. *Journal of Personality and Social Psychology, 47*, 85–93.

Baumeister, R. F., & Tice, D. M. (1988). Metatraits. *Journal of Personality, 56*, 571–598.

Beach, F. (1975). Behavioral endocrinology: An emerging discipline. *American Scientist, 63*, 178–187.

Beaumont, G. (1990). Adverse effects of antidepressants. *International Clinical Psychopharmacology, 5*, 61–66.

Bechara, A., Tranel, T., Damasio, H., Adolphs, R., Rockland, C., & Damasio, A. R. (1995). Double dissociation of conditioning and declarative knowledge relative to the amygdala and hippocampus in humans. *Science, 269*, 1115–1118.

Bem, D. J., & Allen, A. (1974). On predicting some of the people some of the time: The search for cross-situational consistencies in behavior. *Psychological Review, 81*, 506–520.

Bem, S. L. (1974). The measurement of psychological androgyny. *Journal of Consulting and Clinical Psychology, 42*, 155–162.

Bem, S. L. (1975). Sex-role adaptability: One consequence of psychological androgyny. *Journal of Personality and Social Psychology, 31*, 634–643.

Benet, V., & Waller, N. G. (1995).The Big Seven factor model of personality description: Evidence for its cross-cultural generality in a Spanish sample. *Journal of Personality and Social Psychology, 69*, 701–718.

Bentz, V. J. (1990). Contextual issues in predicting high-level leadership performance: Contextual richness as a criterion consideration in personality research with executives. In K. E.

Clark & M. B. Clark (Eds.), *Measures of leadership* (pp. 131–143). West Orange, NJ: Leadership Library of America.

Berry, J. W. (1967). Independence and conformity in subsistence-level societies. *Journal of Personality and Social Psychology, 7,* 415–418.

Berry, J. W. (1971). Independence and conformity in subsistence-level societies. *Journal of Abnormal and Social Psychology, 7,* 415–418.

Bettelheim, B. (1976). *The uses of enchantment: The meaning and importance of fairy tales.* New York: Knopf.

Bieri, J. (1955). Cognitive complexity-simplicity and predictive behavior. *Journal of Abnormal and Social Psychology, 51,* 61–66.

Binswanger, L. (1963). *Being-in-the-world* (with a critical introduction by J. Needleman, Trans.). New York: Basic Books.

Block, J. (1957). A comparison between ipsative and normative ratings of personality. *Journal of Abnormal and Social Psychology, 54,* 50- 54.

Block, J. (1971). *Lives through time.* Berkeley, CA: Bancroft Books.

Block, J. (1977). Advancing the psychology of personality: Paradigmatic shift or improving the quality of research. In D. Magnusson & N. S. Endler (Eds.), *Personality at the crossroads: Current issues in interactional psychology* (pp. 37–63). Hillsdale, NJ: Erlbaum.

Block, J. (1978). *The Q-sort method in personality assessment and psychiatric research.* Palo Alto, CA: Consulting Psychologists Press.

Block, J., Weiss, D. S., & Thorne, A. (1979). How relevant is a semantic similarity interpretation of personality ratings? *Journal of Personality and Social Psychology, 37,* 1055–1074.

Block, J. (1989). Critique of the act frequency approach to personality. *Journal of Personality and Social Psychology, 56,* 234–245.

Block, J. (1995). A contrarian view of the five-factor appraoch to personality description. *Psychological Bulletin, 117,* 187–215.

Block, J. H., & Block, J. (1980). The role of ego-control and ego-resiliency in the organization of behavior. In W. A. Collins (Ed.), *The Minnesota symposium on child psychology (Vol. 13).* Hillsdale, NJ: Erlbaum.

Bloom, B. (1985). *Developing talent in young children.* New York: Ballantine.

Blum, G. S. (1950). *The Blacky Pictures: A technique for the exploration of personality dynamics.* New York: The Psychological Corporation.

Bolger, N., Delongis, A., Kessler, R. C., & Schilling, E. A. (1989). Effects of daily stress on negative mood. *Journal of Personality and Social Psychology, 57,* 808–818.

Bonarius, J. C. J. (1965). Research in the personal construct theory of George A. Kelly: Role construct repertory test and basic theory. In B. A. Maher (Ed.), *Progress in experimental personality research.* New York: Academic Press.

Bond, M., Gardner, S. T., Christian, J., & Sigal, J. J. (1983). Empirical study of self-rated defense styles. *Archives of General Psychiatry, 40,* 333–338.

Bootzin, R. R., & Acocella, J. R. (1988). *Abnormal psychology: Current perspectives* (5th ed.). New York: Random House.

Boring, E. G. & Lindzey, G. H. (1967). *A history of psychology in autobiography (Vol. 5).* Worcester, MA: Clark University Press.

Boss, M. (1963). *Psychoanalysis and Daseinsanalysis.* New York: Basic Books.

Boss, M. (1977). *Existential foundations of medicine and psychology.* New York: Aronson.

Bottome, P. (1957). *Alfred Adler.* New York: Vanguard.

Botwinick, J. (1984). *Aging and human behavior: A comprehensive integration of research findings* (3rd ed.). New York: Springer.

Bouchard, T.J., Jr., Heston, L., Eckert, E., Keys, M., & Rescind, S. (1981). The Minnesota study of twins reared apart: Project description and sample results in the developmental domain. *Twin Research 3: Intelligence, Personality and Development.* New York: Alan R. Liss.

Bouchard, T. J., Jr. (1994). Genes, environment, and personality. *Science, 264,* 1700–1701.

Bouchard, T. J., Jr., Lykken, D. T., McGue, M., Segal, N. L., & Tellegan, A. (1990). Sources of human psychological differences: The Minnesota study of twins reared apart. *Science, 250,* 223–228.

Bouchard, T. J., Jr., & McGue, M. (1981). Familial studies of intelligence: A review. *Science, 212,* 1055–1059.

Bouchard, T. J., & McGue, M. (1990). Genetics and rearing environmental influences on adult personality: An analysis of adopted twins reared apart. *Journal of Personality, 58,* 263–292.

Bowers, K. S. (1973). Situationism in psychology: An analysis and a critique. *Psychological Review, 80,* 307–336.

Bray, D. W. (1982). The assessment center and the study of lives. *American Psychologist, 37,* 180–189.

Bray, D. W., & Howard, A. (1983). The AT&T longitudinal studies of managers. In K. W. Schaie (Ed.), *Longitudinal studies of adult psychological development* (pp. 112–146). New York: Guilford.

Breger, L., & McGaugh, J. L. (1965). Critique and reformulation of "learning theory" approaches to psychotherapy and neurosis. *Psychological Bulletin, 63,* 338–358.

Breggin, P. (1994). Another view: Talking back to Prozac. *Psychology Today, 27,* 46+.

Bridell, D. W., Rimm, D. C., Caddy, G. W., Krawitz, G., Sholis, D., & Wunderlin, R. J. (1978).The effects of alcohol and cognitive set on sexual arousal to deviant stimuli. *Journal of Abnormal Psychology, 87,* 418–430.

Briggs, S. R. (1992). Assessing the five-factor model of personality description. *Journal of Personality, 60,* 253–293.

Brigham, C. C. (1923). *A study of American intelligence.* Princeton, NJ: Princeton University Press.

Brody, E. B., & Brody, N. (1976). *Intelligence: Nature, determinants, and consequences.* New York: Academic Press.

Broman, S. H., Nichols, P. L., & Kennedy, W. A. (1975). *Preschool IQ: Prenatal and early developmental correlates.* Hillsdale, NJ: Erlbaum.

Brondolo, E., Baruch, C., Conway, E., & Marsh, L. (1994). Aggression among inner-city youth: A biophysical model for school based

evaluation and treatment. *Journal of Social Distress and the Homeless, 3,* 53–80.

Bronfenbrenner, U. (1960). Freudian theories of identification and their derivatives. *Child Development, 31,* 15–40.

Broughton, R., Trapnell, P. D., & Boyes, M. C. (1991). Classifying personality types with occupational prototypes. *Journal of Research in Personality, 25,* 302–321.

Broverman, I. K., Broverman, D. M., Clarkson, F. E., Rosenkrantz, P. S., & Vogel, S. R. (1970). Sex-role stereotypes and clinical judgments of mental health. *Journal of Consulting and Clinical Psychology, 34,* 1–7.

Broverman, I. K., Vogel, S. R., Broverman, D. M., Clarkson, F. E., & Rosenkrantz, P. S. (1972). Sex-role stereotypes: A current appraisal. *Journal of Social Issues, 28,* 59–78.

Brown, J. F. (1940). *The psychodynamics of abnormal behavior.* New York: McGraw-Hill.

Brown, J. S. (1965). A behavioral analysis of masochism. *Journal of Experimental Research in Personality, 1,* 65–70.

Bruch, M. A., Kaflowitz, N. G., & Berger, P. (1988). Self-schema for assertiveness: Extending the validity of the self-schema construct. *Journal of Research in Personality, 22,* 424–444.

Bruner, J. S., & Tagiuri, R. (1954). The perception of people. In G. Lindzey (Ed.), *Handbook of Social Psychology.* Cambridge, MA: Addison-Wesley.

Brunson, B. I., & Matthews, K. A. (1981). The Type A coronary-prone behavior pattern and reactions to uncontrollable stress: An analysis of performance strategies, affect, and attributions during failure. *Journal of Personality and Social Psychology, 40,* 906–918.

Brunswik, E. (1943). Organismic achievement and environmental probability. *Psychological Review, 50,* 255–272.

Bugental, J. F. T. (1989). Guru for the 1960's; Moses for the 1990's. *Contemporary Psychology, 34,* 873–894.

Burger, J. M. (1985). Desire for control and achievement-related behavior. *Journal of Per-*

sonality and Social Psychology, 48, 1520–1533.

Burnham, J.C. (1968). Historical background for the study of personality. In E. F. Borgotta & W. W. Lambert (Eds.), *Handbook of personality theory and research*. Chicago: Rand McNally.

Buss, A. H. (1988). *Personality: Evolutionary heritage and human distinctiveness*. Hiilsdale, NJ: Erlbaum.

Buss, D. M. (1989). Sex differences in human mate preferences: Evolutionary hypotheses tested in 37 cultures. *Behavioral and Brain Sciences, 12*, 1–49.

Buss, D. M. (1990). Toward a biologically informed psychology of personality. *Journal of Personality, 58*, 1–16.

Buss, D. M. (1991). Evolutionary personality psychology. *Annual Review of Psychology, 42*, 459–491.

Buss, D, M. (1994). *The evolution of desire: Strategies of human mating*. New York: Basic Books.

Buss, D. M. (1995). Psychological sex differences: Origins through sexual selection. *American Psychologist, 50*, 164–168.

Buss, D. M., & Craik, K. H. (1980). The frequency concept of dispositions: Dominance and prototypically dominant acts. *Journal of Personality, 43*, 379–392.

Buss, D. M., & Craik, K. H. (1983). The act frequency approach to personality. *Psychological Review, 90*, 105–126.

Buss, D. M., & Craik, K. H. (1986). Acts, dispositions, and clinical assessment: The psychopathology of everyday conduct. *Clinical Psychology Review, 6*, 387–406.

Buss, D. M., & Craik, K. H. (1987). Act criteria for the diagnosis of personality disorders. *Journal of Personality Disorders, 1*, 73–81.

Buss, D. M., & Schmitt, D. P. (1993). Sexual strategies theory: An evolutionary perspective on human mating. *Psychological Review, 100*, 204–232.

Butler, J. M., & Haigh, G. V. (1954). Changes in the relation between self-concepts and ideal concepts consequent upon client-centered counseling. In C. R. Rogers & R. F. Dymond (Eds.), *Psychotherapy and personality change: Coordinated studies in the client-centered approach*. Chicago: University of Chicago Press.

Button, E. (Ed.). (1985). *Personal construct theory and mental health: Theory, research, and practice*. Cambridge, MA. Brookline Books.

Byrne, D., & Kelley, K. (1981). *An introduction to personality* (3rd ed.). Englewood Cliffs, NJ: Prentice-Hall.

Cacioppo, J. T., & Petty, R. E. (1982). The need for cognition. *Journal of Personality and Social Psychology, 42*, 116–131.

Cacioppo, J. T., Petty, R. E., Kao, C. F., & Rodriguez, R. (1986). Central and peripheral routes to persuasion: An individual difference perspective. *Journal of Personality and Social Psychology, 51*, 1032–1043.

Cacioppo, J. T., Petty, R. E., & Morris K. J. (1983). Effects of need for cognition on message evaluation, recall, and persuasion. *Journal of Personality and Social Psychology, 45*, 805–818.

Camara, W. J., & Schneider, D. L. (1994). Integrity tests: Facts and unresolved issues. *American Psychologist, 49*, 112–119.

Camara, W. J., & Schneider, D. L. (1995). Questions of construct breadth and openness of research in integrity testing. *American Psychologist, 50*, 459–460.

Campbell, A. (1993). *Men, women, and aggression*. New York: Basic Books.

Cann, D. R., & Donderi, D. C. (1986). Jungian personality typology and the recall of everyday and archetypal dreams. *Journal of Personality and Social Psychology, 50*, 1021–1030.

Cannon, W. B. (1932). *The wisdom of the body*. New York: Norton.

Cantor, N., & Kihlstrom, J. F. (1985). Social intelligence: The cognitive basis of personality. *Review of Personality and Social Psychology, 6*, 15–33.

Cantor, N., & Kihlstrom, J. F. (1987). *Personality*

*and social intelligence*. Englewood Cliffs, NJ: Prentice-Hall.

Cantor, N., & Kihlstrom, J. F. (1989). Social intelligence and cognitive assessments of personality. In R. S. Wyer & T. K. Srull (Eds.), *Advances in social cognition: Vol. II. Social intelligence and cognitive assessments of personality* (pp.1–59). Hillsdale, NJ: Erlbaum.

Cantor, N., Norem, J. K., Niedenthal, P. M., Langston, C. A., & Brower, A. M. (1987). Life tasks, self-concept ideals, and cognitive strategies in a life transition. *Journal of Personality and Social Psychology, 53*, 1178–1191.

Carlson, R. (1971). Where is the person in personality research? *Psychological Bulletin, 75*, 203–219.

Carlson, R., & Levy, N. (1973). Studies of Jungian typology: I. Memory, social perception, and social action. *Journal of Personality, 41*, 559–576.

Carson, R. C., Butcher, J. N., & Mineka, S. (1996). *Abnormal psychology and modern life* (10th ed.). New York: Harper-Collins.

Carver, C. S., & Scheier, M. F. (1981). *Attention and self-regulation: A control-theory approach to human behavior*. New York: Springer.

Carver, C. S., & Scheier, M. F. (1988). *Perspectives on personality*. Boston: Allyn & Bacon.

Caspi, A., Bolger, N., & Eckenrode, J. (1987). Linking person and context in the daily stress process. *Journal of Personality and Social Psychology, 52*, 184–195.

Casseldon, P. E., & Hampson, S. E. (1990). Forming impressions from incongruent traits. *Journal of Personality and Social Psychology, 59*, 353–362.

Cattell, R. B. (1950). *Personality: A systematic, theoretical, and factual study*. New York: McGraw-Hill.

Cattell, R. B. (1957). *Personality and motivation structure and measurement*. New York: Harcourt Brace Jovanovich.

Cattell, R. B. (1963). Theory of fluid and crystallized intelligence: A critical experiment. *Journal of Educational Psychology, 54*, 1–22.

Cattell, R. B. (1965). *The scientific analysis of personality*. Baltimore, MD: Penguin.

Cattell, R. B. (1971). *Abilities: Their structure, growth, and action*. Boston: Houghton Mifflin.

Cattell, R. B., & Scheier, I. H. (1961). *The meaning and measurement of neuroticism and anxiety*. New York: Ronald Press.

Cattell, R. B., Young, H., & Hundleby, J. (1964). Blood groups and personality traits. *American Journal of Human Genetics, 16*, 397–402.

Chance, J. E. (1959). Generalization of expectancies among functionally related behaviors. *Journal of Personality, 27*, 228–238.

Chaplin, W. F. (1988). Two traditions of personality psychology. *Contemporary Psychology, 33*, 816–817.

Chaplin, W. F. (1991). The next generation of moderator research in personality psychology. *Journal of Personality, 59*, 143–178.

Chaplin W. F. (in press). Personality, interactive relations, and applied psychology. In R. Hogan, J. Johnson, & S. R. Briggs (Eds.), *Handbook of personality psychology*. Orlando, FL: Academic Press.

Chaplin, W. F., & Buckner, K. E. (1988). Self-ratings of personality: A naturalistic comparison of normative, ipsative, and idiothetic standards. *Journal of Personality, 56*, 509–530.

Chaplin, W. F., & Goldberg L. R. (1984). A failure to replicate the Bem and Allen study on individual differences in cross-situational consistencies. *Journal of Personality and Social Psychology, 47*, 1074–1090.

Chaplin, W. F., John, O. P., & Goldberg, L. R. (1988). Conceptions of traits and states: Dimensional attributes with ideals as prototypes. *Journal of Personality and Social Psychology, 54*, 541–557.

Chaplin, W. F., & Panter, A. T. (1993). Shared meaning and the convergence among observers' personality descriptions. *Journal of Personality, 61,* 553–585.

Cheek, J. M. (1982). Aggregation, moderator variables, and the validity of personality tests: A peer rating study. *Journal of Personality and Social Psychology, 43,* 1254–1269.

Chidester, T. R., Helmreich, R. L., Gregorich, S. E., & Geis, C. E. (1991). Pilot personality and crew coordination. *International Journal of Aviation Psychology, 1,* 25–44.

Chodorow, N. (1978). *The reproduction of mothering: Psychoanalysis and the sociology of gender.* Berkely: University of California Press.

Churchland, P. S., & Sejnowski, T. J. (1992). *The computational brain.* Cambridge, MA: The MIT Press.

Cloninger, C. R. (1987). A systematic method for clinical description and classification of personality variants: A proposal. *Archives of General Psychiatry, 44,* 573–588.

Cloninger, C. R. (1991). Brain networks underlying personality development. In B. J. Carroll & J. E. Barrett (Eds.), *Psychopathology and the brain* (pp. 183–208). New York: Raven Press.

Cloninger, C. R., Przybeck, T. R., & Svrakic, D. M. (1991). The Tridimensional Personality Questionnaire: U. S. normative data. *Psychological Reports, 69,* 1047–1057.

Cohen, A. R., Stotland, E., & Wolfe, D. M. (1955). An experimental investigation of need for cognition. *Journal of Abnormal and Social Psychology, 51,* 291–291.

Coles, R. (1970). *Erik Erikson: The growth of his work.* Boston: Little, Brown.

Condrey, J. (1977). Enemies of exploration: Self-initiated versus other-initiated learning. *American Psychologist, 35,* 459–477.

Contrada, R. J. (1989). Type A behavior, personality hardiness, and cardiovascular response to stress. *Journal of Personality and Social Psychology, 57,* 895–903.

Cook, W., & Medley, D. (1954). Proposed hostility and pharasaic-virtue scales for the MMPI. *Journal of Applied Psychology, 38,* 414–418.

Cooley, C. H. (1902). *Human nature and the social order.* New York: Scribner's.

Cooper, A. M. (1989). Drives and desires: Introduction. In A. M. Cooper, O. F. Kernberg, & E. S. Person (Eds.), *Psychoanalysis: Toward the second century.* New Haven: Yale University Press.

Corcoran, D. W. J. (1964). The relation between introversion and salivation. *American Journal of Psychology, 77,* 298–300.

Corrigan, P. W. (1991). Strategies that overcome barriers to token economies in community programs for severe mentally ill adults. *Community Mental Health Journal, 27,* 17–30.

Corsini, R. J. (Ed.) (1977). *Current personality theories.* Itasca, IL: Peacock.

Costa, P. T., & McCrae, R. R. (1976). Age differences in personality structure revisited: Studies in validity, stability, and change. *International Journal of Aging, 8,* 261–275.

Costa, P. T., & McCrae, R. R. (1985). *The NEO Personality Inventory: Manual.* Odessa, FL: Psychological Assessment Resources.

Costa, P. T., Jr., & McCrae, R. R. (1987). Personality assessment in psychosomatic medicine: Value of a trait taxonomy. In T. N. Wise (Ed.), *Advances in psychosomatic medicine.* Switzerland: Karger.

Costa, P. T., & McCrae, R. R. (1988). From catalog to classification: Murray's needs and the five-factor model. *Journal of Personality and Social Psychology, 55,* 258–265.

Craik, K. H. (1986). Personality research methods: An historical perspective. *Journal of Personality, 54,* 18–51.

Crain, W. C. (1980). *Theories of development: Concepts and applications.* Englewood Cliffs, NJ: Prentice-Hall.

Cramer, P. (1987). The development of defense mechanisms. *Journal of Personality, 55,* 597–614.

Cramer, P. (1991a). The development of defense mechanisms: Theory, research, and assessment. New York: Springer-Verlag.

Cramer, P. (1991b). Anger and the use of defense

mechanisms in college students. *Journal of Personality, 59,* 39–55.

Crandall, J. E. (1980). Adler's concept of social interest. Theory, measurement, and implications for adjustment. *Journal of Personality and Social Psychology, 39,* 481–495.

Crandall, J. E. (1982). Social interest, extreme response style, and implications for adjustment. *Journal of Research in Personality, 16,* 82–89.

Crandall, V. C., Good, S., & Crandall, V. J. (1964). Reinforcement effects of adult reactions and nonreactions on children's achievement expectations: A replication study. *Child Development, 35,* 485–497.

Crandall, V. J. (1955). An investigation of the specificity of reinforcement of induced frustration. *Journal of Social Psychology, 41,* 311–318.

Crittendon, K. S. (1991). Asian self-effacement or feminine modesty? Attributional patterns of women university students in Taiwan. *Gender & Society, 5,* 98–117.

Crockett, W. H. (1965). Cognitive complexity and impression formation. In B. A. Maher (Ed.), *Progress in experimental personality research (Vol. 2,* pp. 47–90). New York: Academic Press.

Cronbach, L. (1978). Review of the BITCH test. In O. K. Buros (Ed.), *The eighth mental measurements yearbook* (Vol. 1). Highland Park, NJ: Gryphon Press.

Cronbach, L. J. (1955). Processes affecting scores on "understanding of others" and "assumed similarity." *Psychological Bulletin, 52,* 177–193.

Cronbach, L. J., & Meehl, P. E. (1955). Construct validation in psychological tests. *Psychological Bulletin, 52,* 281–302.

Council, J. R., Kirsch, I., & Grant, D. L. (1996). Expectancy, imagination, and hypnotic susceptibility. In R. Kunzendorf, B. Wallace, & N. P. Spanos (Eds.). *Imagination and hypnosis.* Amityville, NY: Baywood.

Damasio, H., Grabowski, T., Frank, R., Galaburda, A. M., & Damasio, A. R. (1994). The return of Phineas Gage: Clues about the brain from the skull of a famous patient. *Science, 264,* 1102–1105.

Darnton, N. (1991, October 7). The pain of the last taboo. *Newsweek,* pp. 70–72.

Darwin, C. (1872). *The expression of emotions in man and animals.* Chicago: University of Chicago Press.

Darwin, C. R. (1930). *The voyage of the Beagle.* In C. W. Eliot (Ed.). *The Harvard classics, 29.* New York: P. F. Collier.

Davidson, K. (1991). Gender roles and health. In C. R. Snyder & D. R. Forsyth (Eds.), *Handbook of social and clinical psychology* (pp. 179–196). New York: Pergamon Press.

Davidson, K. W. (1993). Suppression and repression in discrepant self-other ratings: Relations with thought control and cardiovascular reactivity. *Journal of Personality, 61,* 669–691.

Davidson, K., & Hall, P. (1995). What does the potential for hostility measure? Gender differences in the expression of hostility. *Journal of Behavioral Medicine, 18,* 233–248.

Davidson, K., Hall, P., & MacGregor, M. W. (1996). Gender differences in the relations between interview-derived hostility scores and resting blood pressure. *Journal of Behavioral Medicine, 19,* 185–201.

Davidson, K., MacGregor, M. W., Maclean, D. R., McDermott, N., Farquharson, J., & Chaplin, W. F. (1996). Coder gender and potential for hostility ratings. *Health Psychology, 15,* 298–302.

Davidson, K., Prkachin, K., Mills, D., & Lefcourt, H. M. (1994). A comparison of three theories relating facial expressiveness to blood pressure in male and female undergraduates. *Health Psychology, 13,* 404–411.

Davis, W. L., & Phares, E. J. (1969). Parental antecedents of internal-external control of reinforcement. *Psychological Reports, 24,* 427–436.

Davison, G. C., & Neale, J. M. (1990). *Abnormal psychology* (5th ed.). New York: Wiley.

Dawkins, R. (1976). *The selfish gene.* London: Oxford University Press.

de Charms, R. (1976). Enhancing motivation: *Change in the classroom.* New York: Irvington.

Deaux, K., & Major, B. (1987). Putting gender

into context: An interactive model of gender-related behavior. *Psychological Review, 94,* 369–389.

Deci, E. L. (1971). Effects of externally mediated rewards on intrinsic motivation. *Journal of Personality and Social Psychology, 18,* 105–115.

Deci, E. L., & Ryan, R. M. (1985). The General Causality Orientation Scale: Self-determination in personality. *Journal of Research in Personality, 19,* 109–134.

DeFries, J. C., & Plomin, R. (1978). Behavior genetics. *Annual Review of Psychology, 29,* 473–515.

deGroh, M. (1989). Correlates of hypnotic susceptibility. In N. P. Spanos & J. F. Chaves (Eds.), *Hypnosis: The cognitive-behavioral perspective* (pp. 32–63). Buffalo, NY: Prometheus.

DeLongis, A., Folkman, S., & Lazarus, R. S. (1988). The impact of daily stress on health and mood: Psychological and social resources as mediators. *Journal of Personality and Social Psychology, 54,* 486–495.

Derry, P. A., & Kuiper, N. A. (1981). Schematic processing and self-reference in clinical depression. *Journal of Abnormal Psychology, 90,* 286–297.

Digman, J. M. (1990). Personality structure: Emergence of the five-factor model. *Annual Review of Psychology, 41,* 417–440.

Disher, D. R. (1959). Improvement without fundamental change. In K. A. Adler & D. Deutsch (Eds.), *Essays in individual psychology: Contemporary application of Alfred Adler's theories.* New York: Grove Press.

Dixon, N. F. (1980). Humor: A cognitive alternative to stress? In I. G. Sarason & C. D. Spielberger (Eds.), *Stress and anxiety* (Vol. 7). Washington, DC: Hemisphere.

Dohrenwend, B. S., & Dohrenwend, B. F. (1981). Life stress and illness: Formulation of the issues. In B. S. Dohrenwend & B. F. Dohrenwend (Eds.), *Stressful life events and their contexts.* New York: Prodist.

Dollard, J., Doob, L. W., Miller, N. E., Mowrer, O. H., & Sears, R. R. (1939). *Frustration and aggression.* New Haven, CT: Yale University Press.

Dollard, J., & Miller, N. E. (1950). *Personality and psychotherapy: An analysis in terms of learning, thinking, and culture.* New York: McGraw-Hill.

Donahue, E. M. (1994). Do children use the Big Five too? Content and structural form in personality description. *Journal of Personality, 62,* 45–66.

Donovan, R. J. (1984). Bringing America into the 1980s. *American Psychologist, 39,* 429–431.

Dugdale, R. L. (1877). *The Jukes.* New York: G. P. Putnam's Sons.

Duke, M., & Nowicki, S., Jr. (1979). *Abnormal psychology: Perspectives on being different.* Monterey, CA: Brooks/Cole.

Dunbar, H. F. (1947). *Mind and body: Psychosomatic medicine.* New York: Random House.

Dunlap, R. L. (1953). *Changes in children's preferences for goal objects as a function of differences in expected social reinforcement.* Unpublished doctoral dissertation, Ohio State University, Columbus, OH.

Dunning, D., & McElwee, R. O. (1995). Idiosyncratic trait definitions: Implications for self-description and social judgement. *Journal of Personality and Social Psychology, 68,* 936–946.

Dweck, C. S. (1975). The role of expectation and attribution in the alleviation of learned helplessness. *Journal of Personality and Social Psychology, 31,* 674–685.

Dworkin, R. H., Burke, B. W., Maher, B. A., & Gottesman, I. I. (1976). A longitudinal study of the genetics of personality. *Journal of Personality and Social Psychology, 34,* 510–518.

Dymond, R. F. (1950). Personality and empathy. *Journal of Consulting Psychology, 14,* 343–350.

Eagly, A. H. (1995). The science and politics of comparing women and men. *American Psychologist, 50,* 145–158.

Eagly, A. H. & Mladinic, A. (1994). Are people prejudiced against women? Some answers from research on attitudes, gender stereotypes, and judgements of competence. In W. Strobe & M. Hewstone (Eds.), *European review of social psychology,* (Vol. 5, pp. 1–35). New York: Wiley.

Ellis, A. (1962). *Reason and emotion in psychotherapy.* New York: Lyle Stuart.

Elms, A. C. (1988). Freud as Leonardo: Why the first psychobiography went wrong. *Journal of Personality, 56,* 19–40.

Emmons, R. A. (1986). Personal strivings: An approach to personality and subjective well-being. *Journal of Personality and Social Psychology, 51,* 1058–1068.

Emmons, R. A. (1987). Narcissism: Theory and measurement. *Journal of Personality and Social Psychology, 52,* 11–17.

Engel, G. L. (1968). A life setting conducive to illness: The giving-up–given-up complex. *Bulletin of the Menninger Clinic, 32,* 355–365.

Entwistle, D. R. (1992). To dispel fantasies about fantasy-based motivation. *Psychological Bulletin, 77,* 377–381.

Epstein, S. (1972). The nature of anxiety with emphasis upon its relationship to expectancy. In C. D. Spielberger (Ed.), *Anxiety: Current trends in theory and research* (Vol. 2). New York: Academic Press.

Epstein, S. (1979a). The stability of behavior: I. On predicting most people much of the time. *Journal of Personality and Social Psychology, 37,* 1097–1126.

Epstein, S. (1979b). Explorations in personality today and tomorrow: A tribute to Henry A. Murray. *American Psychologist, 34,* 649–653.

Epstein, S. (1980). The self-concept: A review and the proposal of an integrated theory of personality. In E. Staub (Ed.), *Personality: Basic aspects and current research.* Englewood Cliffs, NJ: Prentice-Hall.

Epstein, S. (1991). Cognitive-experiential self-theory: An integrative theory of personality. In R. Curtis (Ed.), *The relational self: Convergences in psychoanalysis and social psychology,* (pp. 111–137). New York: Guilford Press.

Epstein, S. (1994). Integration of the cognitive and the psychodynamic unconscious. *American Psychologist, 49,* 709–724.

Epstein, S., & O'Brien, E. J. (1985). The person-situation debate in historical perspective. *Psychological Bulletin, 98,* 513–537.

Erdelyi, M. H. (1992). Psychodynamics and the unconscious. *American Psychologist, 47,* 784–787.

Erdelyi, M. H., & Goldberg, B. (1979). Let's not sweep repression under the rug: Toward a cognitive psychology of repression. In J. F. Kihlstrom & F. J. Evans (Eds.), *Functional disorders of memory* (pp. 355–402). Hillsdale, NJ: Erlbaum.

Erikson, E. H. (1945). Childhood and tradition in two American Indian tribes. In *The psychoanalytic study of the child* (Vol. 1). New York: International Universities Press.

Erikson, E. H. (1958). *Young man Luther.* New York: Norton.

Erikson, E. H. (1963). *Childhood and society* (2nd ed.). New York: Norton.

Erikson, E. H. (1969). *Gandhi's truth.* New York: Norton.

Erlenmeyer-Kimling, L., & Jarvik, L. F. (1963). Genetics and intelligence: A review. *Science, 142,* 1477–1479.

Eron, L. D. (1982). Parent-child interaction, television violence, and aggression of children. *American Psychologist, 37,* 197–211.

Eron, L. D., & Huesmann, L. R. (1984). The control of aggressive behavior by changes in attitudes, values, and the conditions of learning. In R. J. Blanchard & D. C. Blanchard (Eds.), *Advances in the study of aggression* (Vol. 1). New York: Academic Press.

Erskine, N. J. (1981). *An investigation into the construct validity of the Selfism Scale.* Unpublished master's thesis, Kansas State University, Manhattan, KS.

Estabrook, A. H. (1916). The Jukes in 1915. Washington, DC: Carnegie Institution.

Exner, J. E., Jr. (1974). *The Rorschach: A comprehensive system.* New York: Wiley

Eysenck, H. J. (1947). *Dimensions of personality.* London: Routledge & Kegan Paul.

Eysenck, H. J. (1950). Criterion analysis: An application of the hypothetico-deductive method to factor analysis. *Psychological Review, 57,* 38–53.

Eysenck, H. J. (1952). *The scientific study of personality.* London: Routledge & Kegan Paul.

Eysenck, H. J. (1960). The place of theory in psychology. In H. J. Eysenck (Ed.), *Experiments in psychology* (Vol. 2, pp. 303–315). London: Routledge & Kegan Paul.

Eysenck, H. J. (1970). *The structure of human personality* (3rd ed.). London: Methuen.

Eysenck, H. J. (1975). *The inequality of man.* San Diego, CA: Edits.

Eysenck, H. J. (1990). Biological dimensions of personality. In L. A. Pervin (Ed.), *Handbook of personality: Theory and research* (pp. 244–276). New York: Guilford Press.

Eysenck, H. J. (1992).Four ways five factors are not basic. *Personality and Individual Differences, 12,* 773–790.

Eysenck, H. J. & Kamin, L. (1981). *The intelligence controversy: H. J. Eysenck vs. Leon Kamin.* New York: Wiley-Interscience.

Fagot, B. I., & Leinbach, M. D. (1993). Gender-role development in young children: From discrimination to labeling. *Developmental Psychology, 13,* 205–224.

Falbo, T. (1981). Relationships between birth category, achievement, and interpersonal orientation. *Journal of Personality and Social Psychology, 41,* 121–131.

Farmer, R. F., & Nelson-Gray, R. O. (1995). Anxiety, impulsivity, and the anxious-fearful and erratic-dramatic personality disorders. *Journal of Research in Personality, 29,* 189–207.

Fehr, B., & Russell, J. A. (1984). Concept of emotion viewed from a prototype perspective. *Journal of Experimental Psychology: General, 113,* 464–486.

Ferster, C. B., & Skinner, B. F. (1957). *Schedules of reinforcement.* Englewood Cliffs, NJ: Prentice-Hall.

Festinger, L. A. (1954). A theory of social comparison processes. *Human Relations, 7,* 117–140.

Fiedler, F. E. (1976). *Improving leadership effectiveness: The leader match concept.* New York: Wiley.

Fiedler, F. E. (1978). The contingency model and the dynamics of the leadership process. In L. Berkowitz (Ed.), *Advances in experimental social psychology.* New York: Academic Press.

Fiedler, F. E., & Garcia, J. E. (1987). *New approaches to effective leadership: Cognitive resources and organizational performance.* New York: Wiley.

Figueredo, A. J., Cox, R. L., & Rhine, R. J. (1995). A generalizability analysis of subjective personality assessments in the stumptail macaque and the zebra finch. *Multivariate Behavioral Research, 30,* 167–197.

Findley, M. J., & Cooper, H. M. (1983). Locus of control and academic achievement: A literature review. *Journal of Personality and Social Psychology, 44,* 419–427.

Fischer, W. F. (1978). An empirical-phenomenological investigation of being anxious: An example of the meanings of being-emotional. In R. S. Valle & M. King (Eds.), *Existential-phenomenological alternatives for psychology.* New York: Oxford University Press.

Fiske, D. W. (1978). *Strategies for personality research: The observation versus interpretation of behavior.* San Francisco: Jossey-Bass.

Fiske, S. T. (1993). Social cognition and social perception. In M. R. Rosenzweig & L. W. Porter (Eds.), *Annual Review of Psychology, 44,* 155–194.

Fiske, S. T., & Cox, M. G. (1979). Person concepts: The effect of target familiarity and descriptive purpose on the process of describing others. *Journal of Personality, 47,* 136–161.

Fleming, R., Baum, A., & Singer, J. E. (1984). Toward an integrative approach to the study of stress. *Journal of Personality and Social Psychology, 46,* 939–949.

Floderus-Myrhed, B., Pedersen, N., & Rasmuson, I. (1980). Assessment of heritability for personality, based on a short form of the Eysenck Personality Inventory. *Behavior Genetics, 10,* 153–162.

Foushee, H. C., & Helmreich, R. L. (1988). Group interaction and flight crew performance. In E. L. Weiner & D. C. Nagel (Eds.), *Human factors in aviation* (pp. 189–227). San Diego, CA: Academic Press.

Fransella, F., & Thomas, L. (Eds.) (1988). *Experimenting with personal construct psychology.* New York: Routledge & Kegan Paul.

Freud, S. (1938). *The basic writings of Sigmund Freud.* New York: Modern Library.

Freud, S. (1955). Analysis of a phobia in a five-year-old boy. In J. Strachey (Ed. and Trans.), *The standard edition of the complete works of Sigmund Freud* (Vol. 11). London: Hogarth Press. (Original work published 1910)

Freud, S. (1957). Leonardo da Vinci and a memory of his childhood. In J. Strachey (Ed. and Trans.), *The standard edition of the complete works of Sigmund Freud* (Vol. 11, pp. 59–137). London: Hogarth Press. (Original work published 1910)

Freud, S. (1961). Dostoevsky and patricide. In J. Strachey (Ed. and Trans.), *The standard edition of the complete works of Sigmund Freud* (Vol. 21). London: Hogarth Press. (Original work published 1928)

Freud, S. (1964). Moses and monotheism. In J. Strachey (Ed. and Trans.), *The standard edition of the complete works of Sigmund Freud* (Vol. 23). London: Hogarth Press. (Original work published 1939)

Friedman, H. S., & Booth-Kewley, S. (1987). The "disease-prone personality": A meta-analytic view of the construct. *American Psychologist, 42,* 539–555.

Friedman, M., & Rosenman, R. H. (1974). *Type A behavior and your heart.* New York: Knopf.

Frieze, I. H., Parsons, J. E., Johnson, P. B., Ruble, D. N., & Zellman, G. L. (1978). *Women and sex roles.* New York: Norton.

Fromm, E. (1941). *Escape from freedom.* New York: Rinehart.

Fromm, E., & Maccoby, M. (1970). *Social character in a Mexican village.* Englewood Cliffs, NJ: Prentice-Hall.

Frosh, S. (1987). *The politics of psychoanalysis: An introduction to Freudian and post-Freudian theory.* New Haven, CT: Yale University Press.

Fry, E. H., & Fry, N. E. (1988). Information vs. privacy: The polygraph debate. *Personnel, 65,* 57–60.

Fuller, J. F., & Thompson, W. R. (1960). *Behavior genetics.* New York: Wiley.

Fulmer, R. M. (1983). *Practical human relations.* Homewood, IL: Richard D. Irwin, Inc.

Funder, D. C. (1987). Errors and mistakes: Evaluating the accuracy of social judgements. *Psychological Bulletin, 101,* 75–90.

Funder, D. C. (1994). Editorial. *Journal of Research in Personality, 28,* 1–3.

Funder, D. C., & Block, J. (1989). The role of ego-control, ego-resiliency, and IQ in delay of gratification in adolescence. *Journal of Personality and Social Psychology, 57,* 1041–1050.

Funder, D. C., Block, J. H., & Block, J. (1983). Delay of gratification: Some longitudinal personality correlates. *Journal of Personality and Social Psychology, 44,* 1198–1213.

Funder, D. C., & West, S. G. (1993). Consensus, self-other agreement, and accuracy in personality judgment: An introduction. *Journal of Personality, 61,* 457–476.

Funk, S. C., & Houston, B. K. (1987). A critical analysis of the Hardiness Scale's validity and utility. *Journal of Personality and Social Psychology, 53,* 572–578.

Gagnon, J. H., & Davison, G. C. (1976). Asylums, the token economy, and the metrics of mental life. *Behavior Therapy, 7,* 528–534.

Galton, F. (1869). *Hereditary genius.* London: Macmillan.

Galton, F. (1879) Psychometric experiments. *Brain, 2,* 149–162.

Galton, F. (1883). *Inquiries into human faculty and its development.* London: J. M. Dent.

Galton, F. (1887). Good and bad temper in English families. *Fortnightly Review, 42,* 21–30.

Galton, F. (1894). Arithmetic by smell. *Psychological Review, 1,* 61–62.

Ganaway, G. K. (1992). Some additional questions. *Journal of Psychology and Theology, 20,* 201–205.

Gangestad, S. W., & Simpson, J. A. (1990). Toward an evolutionary history of female sociosexual variation. *Journal of Personality, 58,* 69–96.

Garbarino, J. (1975). The impact of anticipated reward upon cross-age tutoring. *Journal of Personality and Social Psychology, 32,* 421–428.

Gardner, H. (1983). *Frames of mind: The theory*

*of multiple intelligences.* New York: Basic Books.

Geen, R. G. (1976). *Personality: The skein of behavior.* St. Louis, MO: Mosby.

Geen, R. G. (1980). Test anxiety and cue utilization. In I. G. Sarason (Ed.), *Test anxiety: Theory, research, and applications.* Hillsdale, NJ: Erlbaum.

Geen, R. G. (1984). Preferred stimulation levels in introverts and extraverts: Effects on arousal and performance. *Journal of Personality and Social Psychology, 46,* 1303–1312.

Geer, J. H. (1965). The development of a scale to measure fear. *Behavior Research and Therapy, 3,* 45–53.

Geis, F. L. (1993). Self-fulfilling prophecies: A social psychological view of gender. In A. E. Beall & R. J. Sternberg (Eds.), *The psychology of gender.* New York: Guilford Press.

Geiwitz, J., & Moursund, J. (1979). *Approaches to personality: An introduction to people.* Monterey, CA: Brooks/Cole.

Gelles, R. J., & Straus, M. A. (1988). *Intimate violence: The causes and consequences of abuse in the American family.* New York: Simon & Schuster.

Gendlin, E. T. (1988). Carl Rogers (1902–1987). *American Psychologist, 43,* 127–128.

Gergen, K. J. (1985). The social constructivist movement in modern psychology. *American Psychologist, 40,* 266–275.

Gergen, K. J., Hepburn, A., & Comer Fisher, D. (1986). Hermeneutics of personality description. *Journal of Personality and Social Psychology, 50,* 1261–1270.

Gidron, Y., Davidson, K., & Bata, I. (1996). Effects of a brief hostility treatment on hostility and short-term health outcomes of CHD patients. Unpublished manuscript, Dalhousie University, Halifax, Nova Scotia.

Gilligan, C. (1982). *In a different voice.* Cambridge, MA: Harvard University Press.

Gilmore, D. D. (1990). *Manhood in the making: Cultural concepts of masculinity.* New Haven, CT: Yale University Press.

Glass, D. C. (1977). *Behavior patterns, stress, and coronary disease.* Hillsdale, NJ: Erlbaum.

Gleser, G. C., & Ihilevich, D. (1969). An objective instrument for measuring defense mechanisms. *Journal of Consulting and Clinical Psychology, 33,* 51–60.

Glisky, M. L., Tataryn, D. J., Tobias, B. A., Kihlstrom, J. F., & McConkey, K. M. (1991). Absorption, openness to experience, and hypnotizability. *Journal of Personality and Social Psychology, 60,* 263–272.

Goddard, H. H. (1912). *The Kallikak family.* New York: Macmillan.

Goldberg, L. R. (1972). Some recent trends in personality assessment. *Journal of Personality Assessment, 36,* 547–560.

Goldberg, L. R. (1978). Differential attribution of trait-descriptive terms to oneself as compared to well-liked, neutral, and disliked others: A psychometric analysis. *Journal of Personality and Social Psychology, 36,* 1012–1028.

Goldberg, L. R. (1981). Language and individual differences: The search for universals in personality lexicons. In L. Wheeler (Ed.), *Review of personality and social psychology* (Vol. 2, pp. 141–165). Beverly Hills, CA: Sage.

Goldberg, L. R. (1990). An alternative "Description of Personality": The Big-Five Factor structure. *Journal of Personality and Social Psychology, 59,* 1216–1229.

Goldberg, L. R. (1993). The structure of phenotypic personality traits. *American Psychologist, 48,* 26–34.

Goldberg, L. R., & Digman, J. M. (1994). Revealing structure in the data: Principles of exploratory factor analysis. In S. Strack & M. Lorr (Eds.), *Differentiating normal and abnormal personality* (pp. 216–242). New York: Springer.

Goldberg, L. R., Grenier, J. R., Guion, R. M., Sechrest, L. B., & Wing, H. (1991). *Questionnaires used in the prediction of trustworthiness in pre-employment selection decisions: An APA task force report.* Washington, DC: American Psychological Association.

Goldberg, L. R., & Rosolack, T. K. (1994). The Big Five factor structure as an integrative framework: An empirical comparison with Eysenck's P-E-N Model. In C. F. Halverson,

Jr., G. A. Kohnstamm, & R. P. Martin (Eds.), *The developing structure of temperament and personality from infancy to adulthood.* New York: Lawrence Erlbaum.

Goldfried, M. R. (1976). Behavioral assessment. In I. B. Weiner (Ed.), *Clinical methods in psychology.* New York: Wiley-Interscience.

Goldfried, M. R., & Davison, G. C. (1976). *Clinical behavior therapy.* New York: Holt, Rinehart & Winston.

Golding, S. L. (1977b). Method variance, inadequate constructs, or things that go bump in the night? *Multivariate Behavioral Research, 12,* 89–98.

Golding, S. L. (1978). Toward a more adequate theory of personality: Psychological organizing principles. In H. London, & N. Hirschberg (Eds.), *Personality: A new look at metatheories.* Washington, DC: Hemisphere Press.

Goldsmith, H. H. (1983). Genetic influences on personality from infancy to adulthood. *Child Development, 54,* 331–355.

Goleman, D. (1995). *Emotional Intelligence.* New York: Bantam Books.

Goodenough, F. L. (1949). *Mental testing.* New York: Rinehart.

Goolsby, L. L., & Chaplin, W. F. (1988). The impact of normative, ipsative, and idiothetic information on feelings about academic performance. *Journal of Research in Personality, 22,* 445–464.

Gottesman, I. I. (1966). Genetic variance in adaptive personality traits. *Journal of Child Psychology and Psychiatry, 7,* 199–208.

Gough, H. G. (1988). *California Psychological Inventory Manual.* Palo Alto, CA: Consulting Psychologists Press.

Gough, H. G., & Heilbrun, A. B., Jr. (1980). *The Adjective Check List manual.* Palo Alto, CA: Consulting Psychologists Press.

Gould, S. J. (1981). *The mismeasure of man.* New York: W. W. Norton.

Gould, S. J. (1994, November). Curveball. *The New Yorker, 28,* 139–149.

Graen, G. (1976). Role-making process within complex organizations. In M. D. Dunnett (Ed.), *Handbook of industrial organizational psychology.* Chicago: Rand McNally.

Graham, A. (1975). The making of a nonsexist dictionary. In B. Thorne & N. Henley (Eds.), *Language and sex: Difference and dominance.* Rowley, MA: Newbury House.

Graham, W., & Balloun, J. (1973). An empirical test of Maslow's need hierarchy theory. *Journal of Humanistic Psychology, 13,* 97–108.

Gray, J. A. (1972). The psychophysiological basis of introversion-extraversion: A modification of Eysenck's theory. In V. D. Nebylitsyn & J. A. Gray (Eds.), *The biological basis of individual behavior* (pp. 182–205). New York: Academic Press.

Gray, J. A. (1981). A critique of Eysenck's theory of personality. In H. J. Eysenck (Ed.), *A model for personality* (pp. 246–276). New York: Springer.

Greenwald, A. G. (1992). New look 3: Unconscious cognition revisited. *American Psychologist, 47,* 766–779.

Greenwald, A. G., & Banaji, M. R. (1989). The self as a memory system: Powerful, but ordinary. *Journal of Personality and Social Psychology, 57,* 41–54.

Greenwald, A. G., & Pratkanis, A. R. (1984). The self. In R. S. Wyer & T. K. Srull (Eds.), *Handbook of social cognition.* (Vol. 3, pp. 129–178). Hillsdale, NJ: Erlbaum.

Gruen, R. J., Folkman, S., & Lazarus, R. S. (1988). Centrality and individual differences in the meaning of daily hassles. *Journal of Personality, 56,* 743–762.

Grusec, J. E. (1992). Social learning theory and developmental psychology: The legacies of Robert Sears and Albert Bandura. *Developmental Psychology, 28,* 776–786,

Gualtieri, C. (1991). *Neuropsychiatry and behavioral pharmacology.* New York: Springer-Verlag.

Guastello, S. J., & Rieke, M. L. (1991). A review and critique of honesty test research. *Behavioral Sciences and the Law, 9,* 501–523.

Guilford, J.P. (1959). *Personality.* New York: McGraw-Hill.

Guilford, J. P. (1967). *The nature of human intelligence.* New York: McGraw-Hill.

Guion, R. M. (1965). *Personnel testing.* New York: McGraw-Hill.

Gur, R. C., Mozley, L. H., Mozley, P. D., Resnick, S. M., Karp, J. S., Alavi, A., Arnold, S. E., & Gur, R. E. (1995). Sex differences in regional cerebral glucose metabolism during a resting state. *Science, 267,* 528–531.

Gurtman, M. B., & Lion, C. (1982). Interpersonal trust and perceptual vigilance for trustworthiness descriptors. *Journal of Research in Personality, 16,* 108–117.

Hackman, J. R. & Oldham, G. R. (1976). Motivation through the design of work: Test of a theory. *Organizational Behavior & Human Performance, 16,* 250–279.

Hall, C. S., & Lindzey, G. (1978). *Theories of personality* (3rd ed.). New York: Wiley.

Hall, J. A., & Taylor, M. C. (1985). Psychological androgyny and the masculinity-femininity interaction. *Journal of Personality and Social Psychology, 49, 429*–435.

Hall, R. V., Lund, D., & Jackson, D. (1968). Effects of teacher attention on study behavior. *Journal of Applied Behavior Analysis, 1,* 1–12.

Hamilton, W. D. (1964). The genetic evolution of social behavior: I and II. *Journal of Theoretical Biology, 7,* 1–52.

Hampson, J. L. (1965). Determinants of psychosexual orientation. In F. A. Beach (Ed.), *Sex and behavior.* New York: Wiley.

Hampson, S. E. (1984). The social construction of personality. In H. Bonarius, G. van Heck, & N. Smid (Eds.), *Personality psychology in Europe: Theoretical and empirical developments.* Lisse, The Netherlands: Swets, & Zeitlinger.

Hampson, S. E. (1988). *The construction of personality: An introduction (2nd ed.).* London: Routledge & Kegan Paul.

Hampson, S. E. (1990). Reconciling inconsistent information: Impressions of personality from combinations of traits. *European Journal of Personality, 4,* 157–172.

Hampson, S. E. (1995, June). *When is an inconsis-*

*tency not an inconsistency?* Paper presented at the Nagshead Invitational Conference on Personality and Social Behavior, Delray Beach, FL.

Hampson, S. E., John, O. P., & Goldberg, L. R. (1986). Category breadth and hierarchical structure in personality: Studies of asymmetries in judgments of trait implications. *Journal of Personality and Social Psychology, 51,* 37–54.

Hansen, J. C., & Campbell, D. P. (1985). *The Strong manual.* Palo Alto, CA: Consulting Psychologists Press.

Harris, B. (1979). What ever happened to Little Albert? *American Psychologist, 34,* 151–160.

Harris, D. B. (1963). *Children's drawings as measures of intellectual maturity: A revision and extension of the Goodenough Draw-a-Man Test.* New York: Harcourt, Brace & World.

Harris, G., & Hogan, J. (1992). *Perceptions and personality correlates of managerial effectiveness.* Paper presented at the 13th Annual Psychology in the Department of Defense Symposium, Colorado Springs, CO.

Harter, S. (1981). A new self-report scale of intrinsic versus extrinsic orientation in the classroom: Motivational and informational components. *Developmental Psychology, 17,* 300–312.

Hartmann, H. (1958). *Ego psychology and the problem of adaptation.* New York: International Universities Press.

Hartmann, H. (1964). *Essays on ego psychology: Selected problems in psychoanalytic theory.* New York: International Universities Press.

Hartshorne, H., & May, M. A. (1928). Studies in the nature of character (Vol. 1). *Studies in deceit.* New York: Macmillan

Hartup, W. W., Moore, S. G., & Sager, G. (1963). Avoidance of inappropriate sex-typing by young children. *Journal of Consulting Psychology, 27, 467*–473.

Hathaway, S. R., & McKinley, J. C. (1951). *The Minnesota Multiphasic Personality Inventory* (revised). New York: Psychological Corporation.

Haugtvedt, C. P., & Petty, R. E. (1992). Personality and persuasion: Need for cognition moderates the persistence and resistance of attitude changes. *Journal of Personality and Social Psychology, 63,* 308–319.

Hawking, S. A. (1988). *A Brief history of time: From the big bang to black holes.* New York: Bantam Books.

Healy, W., Bronner, A. F., & Bowers, A. M. (1930). *The structure and meaning of psychoanalysis.* New York: Knopf.

Heath, A. C., Cloninger, C. R., & Martin, N. G. (1994). Testing a model for the genetic structure of personality: A comparison of the personality systems of Cloninger and Eysenck. *Journal of Personality and Social Psychology, 66,* 762–775.

Hecker, M. W., Chesney, M. A., Black, G. W., & Frautschi, N. (1988). Coronary-prone behaviors in the Western Collaborative Group Study. *Psychosomatic Medicine, 50,* 153–164.

Heckhausen, H., & Beckmann, J. (1990). Intentional action and action slips. *Psychological Review, 97,* 36–48.

Heilbrun, A. B. (1982). Psychological scaling of defensive cognitive styles on the Adjective Check List. *Journal of Personality Assessment, 46,* 495.

Heinsohn, R., & Packer, C. (1995). Complex cooperative strategies in group-territorial African lions. *Science, 269,* 1260–1262.

Helmreich, R. L., Spence, J. T., & Gibson, R. H. (1982). Sex-role attitudes: 1972–1980. *Personality and Social Psychology Bulletin, 8,* 656–663.

Helson , R. (1992). Women's difficult times and the rewriting of the life story. *Psychology of Women Quarterly, 16,* 331–347.

Helson, R., & Moane, G. (1987). Personality change in women from college to midlife. *Journal of Personality and Social Psychology, 53,* 176–186.

Helson, R., & Roberts, B. W. (1994). Ego development and personality change in adulthood. *Journal of Personality and Social Psychology, 66,* 911–920.

Henderson, N. D. (1982). Human behavior genetics. In M. R. Rosenzweig & L. W. Porter (Eds.), *Annual review of psychology, 33,* 403–440. Palo Alto, CA: Annual Reviews.

Hergenhahn, B. R. (1972). *Shaping your child's personality, 33,* 403–440. Englewood Cliffs, NJ: Prentice-Hall.

Hermans, H. J. (1988). On the integration of nomethetic and idiographic research methods in the study of personal meaning. *Journal of Personality, 56,* 785–812.

Herrnstein, R. J., & Murray, C. (1994). *The bell curve: Intelligence and class structure in American life.* New York: The Free Press.

Hersey, P., & Blanchard, K. (1982). *Management of organizational behavior (4th ed.).* Englewood Cliffs, NJ: Prentice-Hall.

Herzberg, F. (1968). One more time: How do you motivate employees? *Harvard Business Review, 46,* 53–62.

Herzberg, F. (1974). Motivator-hygiene profiles: Pinpointing what ails the organization. *Organizational Dynamics, 3,* 18–29.

Hetherington, E. M. (1965). A developmental study of the effects of sex of the dominant parent on sex-role preference, identification, and imitation in children. *Journal of Personality and Social Psychology, 2,* 188–194.

Higgins, E. T. (1987). Self-discrepancy: A theory relating self and affect. *Psychological Review, 94,* 319–340.

Higgins, E. T., Strauman, T., & Klein, R. (1986). Standards and the process of self-evaluation: Multiple affects from multiple stages. In R. M. Sorrentino & E. T. Higgins (Eds.), *Handbook of motivation and cognition: Foundations of social behavior* (pp. 23–63). New York: Guilford Press.

Hilgard, E. R. (1952). Experimental approaches to psychoanalysis. In E. Pumpian-Mindlin (Ed.), *Psychoanalysis as science.* New York: Basic Books.

Hilgard, E. R. (1978). Hypnosis and consciousness. *Human Nature, 1,* 42–49.

Hines, M. (1982). Prenatal gonadal hormones and sex differences in human behavior. *Psychological Bulletin, 92,* 56–80.

Hinkle, D. (1965). *The change of personal con-*

*structs from the viewpoint of a theory of implications.* Unpublished doctoral dissertation, Ohio State University.

Hjelle, L. A., & Ziegler, D. J. (1981). *Personality theories: Basic assumptions, research, and applications* (2nd ed.). New York: McGraw-Hill.

Ho, M-W (1988). On not holding nature still: evolution by process, not by consequence. In Ho, M-W & Fox, S. W. (Eds.). Evolutionary Processor and Metaphors. New York: Wiley.

Hoffman, E. (1988). The right to be human: A biography of Abraham Maslow. Los Angeles: Tarcher.

Hoffman, L. W. (1991). The influence of the family environment on personality: Accounting for sibling differences. *Psychological Bulletin, 110,* 187–203.

Hoffman, C., & Hurst, N. (1990). Gender stereotypes: Perception or rationalization? *Journal of Personality and Social Psychology, 58,* 197–208.

Hofstee, W. K. B., De Raad, B., & Goldberg, L. R. (1992). Integration of the Big-Five and circumplex approaches to trait structure. *Journal of Personality and Social Psychology, 63,* 146–163.

Hogan, J. (1990). Employment tests: History and user considerations. In J. Hogan & R. Hogan (Eds.), *Business and industry testing: Current practices and test reviews* (pp. 1–21). Austin, TX: PRO-ED.

Hogan, J., & Hogan, R. (1989). How to measure employee reliability. *Journal of Applied Psychology, 74,* 273–279.

Hogan, J., & Hogan, R. (1990). *Business and industry testing: Current practices and test reviews.* Austin, TX: PRO-ED.

Hogan, R. (1986). *Hogan Personality Inventory Manual.* Minneapolis, MN: National Computer Systems.

Hogan, R. (1990). What kinds of tests are useful in organizations. In J. Hogan & R. Hogan (Eds.). *Business and industry testing: Current practices and test reviews* (pp. 22–35). Austin, TX: PRO-ED.

Hogan, R., & Cheek, J. M. (1983). Identity, au-

thenticity, and maturity. In T. R. Sarbin & K. E. Scheibe (Eds.), *Studies in social identity* (pp. 339–357). New York: Praeger.

Hogan, R., Curphy, G. J., & Hogan, J. (1994). What we know about leadership: Effectiveness and personality. *American Psychologist, 49,* 493–504.

Holbrook, S. H. (1957). *Dreamers of the American dream.* Garden City, NY: Doubleday.

Holden, C. (1987). The genetics of personality. *Science, 237,* 598–601.

Holland, J. L. (1958). A personality inventory employing occupational titles. *Journal of Applied Psychology, 42,* 336–342.

Holland, J. L. (1963). Explorations of a theory of vocational choice and achievement: II. A four-year prediction study. *Psychological Reports, 12,* 547–594.

Holland, J. L. (1985). *The Self-Directed Search, professional manual.* Odessa, FL: Psychological Assessment Resources, Inc.

Holland, J. L., Gottfredson, G. D., & Nafziger, D. H. (1975). Testing the validity of some theoretical signs of vocational decision making ability. *Journal of Consulting Psychology, 22,* 411–422.

Holland, J. L., Whitney, D. R., Cole, N. S., & Richards, J. M., Jr. (1969). *An empirical occupational classification derived from a theory of personality and intended for practice and research.* (ACT Research Rep., No. 29). Iowa City, IA.

Holmes, D. S. (1990). The evidence for repression: An examination of sixty years of research. In J. L. Singer (Ed.), *Repression and dissociation: Implications for personality theory, psychopathology, and health* (pp. 85–102). Chicago: University of Chicago Press.

Holmes, T. H., & Rahe, R. H. (1967). The Social Readjustment Rating Scale. *Journal of Psychosomatic Research, 11,* 213–218.

Hoptman, M. J., & Davidson, R. J. (1994). How and why do cerebral hemispheres interact? *Psychological Bulletin, 116,* 195–219.

Hormuth, S. E. (1986). The sampling of experiences in situ. *Journal of Personality, 54,* 262–293.

Horn, J. M., Plomin, R., & Rosenman, R. (1976). Heritability of personality traits in adult male twins. *Behavior Genetics, 6,* 17–30.

Horn, J. L. (1968). Organization of abilities and the development of intelligence. *Psychological Review, 75,* 242–259.

Horn, J. L. (1976). Human abilities: A review of research and theory in the early 1970s. *Annual Review of Psychology, 27,* 437–485.

Horn, J. M. (1983). The Texas Adoption Project: Adopted children and their intellectual resemblance to biological and adoptive parents. *Child Development, 54,* 268–275.

Horn, J. M., Loehlin, J. C., & Willerman, L. (1979). Intellectual resemblance among adoptive and biological relatives: The Texas Adoption Project. *Behavior Genetics, 9,* 177–208.

Horney, K. (1937). *Neurotic personality of our times.* New York: Norton.

Horney, K. (1945). *Our inner conflicts.* New York: Norton.

Horney, K. (1967). *Feminine psychology.* New York: Norton.

Hough, L. M, Barge, B. N., Houston, J. S., McGue, M. K., & Kamp, J. D. (1985). *Problems, issues and results in the development of temperament, biographical, and interest measures.* Paper presented at the Annual Meeting of the American Psychological Association, Los Angeles.

House, R. J. (1971). A path-goal theory of leadership effectiveness. *Administrative Science Quarterly, 16,* 321–328.

Houston, B. K., & Vavak, C. R. (1991). Hostility: Developmental factors, psychosocial correlates, and health behaviors. *Health Psychology, 10,* 9–17.

Howard, A., & Bray, D. W. (1990). Predictions of managerial success over long periods of time: Lessons for the Management Progress Study. In K. E. Clark & M. B. Clark (Eds.), *Measures of leadership* (pp. 113–130). West Orange, NJ: Leadership Library of America.

Hull, C. L. (1943). *Principles of behavior.* New York: Appleton-Century-Crofts.

Hull, J. G., Van Treuren, R. R., & Virnelli, S. (1987). Hardiness and health: A critique and alternative approach. *Journal of Personality and Social Psychology, 53,* 518–530.

Humphreys, L. G. (1957). Characteristics of type concepts with special reference to Sheldon's typology. *Psychological Bulletin, 54,* 218–228.

Humphries, C., Carver, C. S., & Neumann, P. G. (1983). Cognitive characteristics of the Type A coronary-prone behavior pattern. *Journal of Personality and Social Psychology, 44,* 177–187.

Huntley, C. W., & Davis, F. (1983). Undergraduate Study of Values scores as predictors of occupation 25 years later. *Journal of Personality and Social Psychology, 45,* 1148–1155.

Hyde, J. S., & Plant, E. A. (1995). Magnitude of psychological gender differences: Another side to the story. *American Psychologist, 50,* 159–161.

Insel, P. M., & Moos, R. H. (1974). Psychological environments: Expanding the scope of human ecology. *American Psychologist, 29,* 179–188.

Jackson, D. N. (1971). The dynamics of structured personality tests: 1971. *Psychological Review, 78,* 229–248.

Jackson, D. N. (1984). *Personality Research Form (3rd ed.).* Port Huron, MI: Research Psychologists Press.

Jackson, D. N., & Messick, S. (1958). Content and style in personality assessment. *Psychological Bulletin, 55,* 243–252.

Jacobs, D., Blackburn, H., Higgins, M. et al. (1992). Report on the Conference on Low Cholesterol: Mortality asociations. *Circulation, 86,* 1046–1060.

Jagger, L., Neukrug, E., & McAaliffe, G. (1992). Congruence between personality traits and chosen occupation as a predictor of job satisfaction for people with disabilities. *Rehabilitation Counseling Bulletin, 36,* 53–60.

James, W. (1890). *The principles of psychology* (Vol. 1). New York: Holt.

Janis, I. L. (1958). *Psychological stress.* New York: Wiley.

Jarvik, L. F., Klodin, V., & Matsuyama, S. S. (1973). Human aggression and the extra Y chromosome: Fact or fantasy? *American Psychologist, 28,* 674–682.

Jenkins, C. D. (1985). The epidemiology of sudden cardiac death: Incidence, clinical features, biomedical and psychological risk factors. In R. E. Beamish, P. K. Singal, & N. S. Dhalla (Eds.), *Stress and heart disease.* Boston: Nijhoff.

Jenkins, C. D. (1988). Epidemiology of cardiovascular diseases. *Journal of Consulting and Clinical Psychology, 56,* 324–332.

Jenkins, C. D., Zyzanski, S. J., & Rosenman, R. H. (1971). Progress toward validation of a computer-scored test for the Type A coronary-prone behavior pattern. *Psychosomatic Medicine, 33,* 193–201.

Jensen, A. R. (1969). How much can we boost IQ and scholastic achievement? *Harvard Educational Review, 39,* 1–123.

Jensen, A. R. (1972). *Genetics and education.* New York: Harper & Row.

Jensen, A. R. (1977). Cumulative deficit in IQ of blacks in the rural South. *Developmental Psychology, 13,* 184–191.

Jessor, R., Carman, R. S., & Grossman, P. H. (1968). Expectations of need satisfaction and drinking patterns in college students. *Quarterly Journal of Studies in Alcohol, 29,* 101–116.

Jogawar, V. V. (1983). Personality correlates of human blood groups. *Personality and Individual Differences, 4,* 215–216.

John, O. P. (1986). How shall a trait be called: A feature analysis of altruism. In A. Angleitner, A. Furnham, & G. van Heck (Eds.), *Personality psychology in Europe: Current trends and controversies* (pp. 117–140). Berwyn, PA: Swets North America.

John, O. P. (1990). The "Big Five" factor taxonomy: Dimensions of personality in the natural language and in questionnaires. In L. A. Pervin (Ed.), *Handbook of personality: Theory and research* (pp. 66–100). New York: Guilford Press.

John, O. P., Hampson, S. E., & Goldberg, L. R. (1991). The basic level in personality-trait hierarchies: Studies of trait use and accessibility in different contexts. *Journal of Personality and Social Psychology, 60,* 348–361.

Johnson, S. M., & Bolstadt, O. D. (1973). Methodological issues and naturalistic observation: Some problems and solutions for field research. In L. A. Hamerlynk, L. C. Handy, & E. J. Marsh (Eds.), *Behavior change: Methodology, concepts, and practice.* Champaign, IL: Research Press.

Jones, E. (1953, 1955, 1977). *The life and work of Sigmund Freud. Vol 1 (1856–1900): The formative years and the great discoveries* (1953); *Vol. 2 (1901–1919): Years of maturity* (1955); *Vol. 3 (1919–1939): The last phase,* (1957). New York: Basic Books.

Jones, E. E., & Berglas, S. (1978). Control of attributions about the self through self-handicapping strategies: The appeal of alcohol and the role of underachievement. *Personality and Social Psychology Bulletin, 4,* 200–206.

Jones, E. E., & Davis, K. E. (1965). From acts to dispositions: The attribution process in person perception. In L. Berkowitz (Ed.), *Advances in experimental social psychology (Vol. 2).* New York: Academic Press.

Jones, M. C. (1924). The elimination of children's fears. *Journal of Experimental Psychology, 7,* 383–390.

Jones, S. R. (1990). Worker interdependence and output: The Hawthorne studies reevaluated. *American Sociological Review, 55,* 176–190.

Josephson, W. L. (1987). Television violence and children's aggression: Testing the priming, social script, and disinhibition predictions. *Journal of Personality and Social Psychology, 53,* 882–890.

Jourard, S. M., & Landsman, T. (1980). *Healthy personality: An approach from the viewpoint of humanistic psychology* (4th ed.). New York: Macmillan.

Jung, C. G. (1928). *Contributions to analytical psychology.* New York: Harcourt, Brace.

Jung, C. G. (1961). *Memories, dreams, reflections.* New York: Random House.

Jung, C. G. (1964). *Man and his symbols.* New York: Dell Publishing.

Kagan, J. (1958). The concept of identification. *Psychological Review, 65,* 296–305.

Kagan, J. (1994). *Galen's prophecy: Temperament in human nature.* New York: Basic Books.

Kahneman, D., Slovic, P., & Tversky, A. (1982). *Judgement under uncertainty: Heuristics and biases.* New York: Cambridge University Press.

Kamin, L. G. (1974). *The science of politics of I.Q.* Potomac, MD: Erlbaum.

Kanfer, A., & Tanaka, J. S. (1993). Unraveling the web of personality judgements: The influence of social networks on personality assessment. *Journal of Personality, 61,* 711–738.

Kanfer, F. H., & Phillips, J. S. (1970). *Learning foundations of behavior therapy.* New York: Wiley.

Kanner, A. D., Coyne, J. C., Schaefer, C., & Lazarus, R. S. (1981). Comparison of two modes of stress management: Daily hassles and uplifts versus major life events. *Journal of Behavioral Medicine, 4,* 1–39.

Kantor, J. R. (1924). *Principles of psychology* (2 vols.). New York: Knopf.

Kaplan, R. M. (1990). Behavior as the central outcome in health care. *American Psychologist, 45,* 1211–1220.

Kaplan, R. M., Atkins, C. J., & Reinsch, S. (1984). Specific efficacy expectations mediate exercise compliance in patients with COPD. *Health Psychology, 3,* 223–242.

Katkovsky, W. (1976). Social-learning theory analyses of maladjusted behavior. In W. Katkovsky & L. Gorlow (Eds.), *The psychology of adjustment: Current concepts and applications* (3rd ed.). New York: McGraw-Hill.

Katz, P. A., & Ksansnak, K. R. (1994). Developmental aspects of gender role flexibility and traditionality in middle childhood and adolescence. *Developmental Psychology, 30,* 272–282.

Kauffman, S. A. (1993). *The origins of order: self organization and selection in evolution.* New York: Oxford University Press.

Kaufman, A. S., Kamphaus, R. W., and Kaufman, N. L. (1985). New directions in intelligence testing: The Kaufman assessment battery for children (K-ABC). In B. B. Wolman (Ed.),

*Handbook of intelligence: Theories, measurements, and applications.* (663–698). New York: Wiley.

Kelley, H. H. (1992). Common-sense psychology and scientific psychology. *Annual Review of Psychology, 43,* 1–23.

Kelly, E. L., & Fiske, D. W. (1951). *The prediction of performance in clinical psychology.* Ann Arbor: University of Michigan Press.

Kelly, G. A. (1955). *The psychology of personal constructs: A theory of personality* (2 vols.). New York: Norton.

Kelly, J., & Worell, L. (1976). Parent behaviors related to masculine, feminine, and androgynous sex role orientations. *Journal of Consulting and Clinical Psychology, 44,* 843–851.

Kelly, K. E., & Houston, B. K. (1985). Type A behavior in employed women: Relation to work, marital, and leisure variables, social support, stress, tension, and health. *Journal of Personality and Social Psychology, 48,* 1067–1079.

Kendall, P. C., Finch, A. J., Jr., Auerbach, S. M., Hooke, J. F., & Mikulka, P. J. (1976). The State-Trait Anxiety Inventory: A systematic evaluation. *Journal of Consulting and Clinical Psychology, 44,* 406–412.

Kenny, D. A. (1991). A general model of consensus and accuracy in interpersonal perception. *Psychological Review, 98,* 155–163.

Kenny, D. A., & Zaccaro, S. J. (1983). An estimate of the variance due to traits in leadership. *Journal of Applied Psychology, 68,* 678–685.

Kenrick, D. T., & Funder, D. C. (1988). Profiting from controversy: Lessons from the person-situation debate. *American Psychologist, 43,* 23–34.

Kenrick, D. T., & Keefe, R. C. (1992). Age preferences in mates reflect differences in human reproductive strategies. *Behavioral and Brain Sciences, 15,* 75–133.

Kenrick, D. T., Sadalla, E. K., Groth, G., & Trost, M. R. (1990). Evolution, traits, and the stages of human courtship: Qualifying the parental investment model. *Journal of Personality, 58,* 97–116.

Kenrick, D. T., & Stringfield, D. O. (1980). Personality traits and the eye of the beholder:

Crossing some traditional boundaries in the search for consistency in all people. *Psychological Review, 87,* 88–104.

Kihlstrom, J. F. (1987). The cognitive unconscious. *Science, 237,* 1445–1452.

Kihlstrom. J. F. (1990). The psychological unconscious. In L. Pervin (Ed.), *Handbook of Personality: Theory and Research* (pp. 445–464). New York: Guilford.

Kihlstrom, J. F., & Cantor, N. (1984). Mental representations of the self. In l. Berkowitz (Ed.), *Advances in experimental social psychology* (Vol. 17, pp. 1–47). New York: Academic Press.

Kileen, P. R. (1994). Mathematical principles of reinforcement. *Behavioral and Brain Sciences, 17,* 105–172.

Kirsch, I. (1985a). Response expectancy as a determinant of experience and behavior. *American Psychologist, 11,* 1189–1202.

Kirsch, I. (1985b). Self-efficacy and expectancy: Old wine with new labels. *Journal of Personality and Social Psychology, 49,* 824–830.

Kirsch, I. (1993). Clinical implications of expectancy research: Activating placebo effects without deception. *Contemporary Hypnosis, 10,* 130–132.

Kirsch, I. & Council, J. R. (1992). Situational & personality correlates of hypnotic susceptibility. In E. Fromm & M. R. Nash (Eds.). *Contemporary Hypnosis Research.* New York: Guilford.

Kissinger, H. (1979). *White House years.* Boston: Little, Brown.

Klein, J. (1993). *Our need for others and its roots in infancy.* London: Routledge & Kegan Paul.

Klein, P. (1987). The experimental study of the psychoanalytic unconscious. *Personality and Social Psychology Bulletin, 13,* 363–378.

Klineberg, O. (1935). *Negro intelligence and selective migration.* New York: Columbia University Press.

Klinger, E. (1977). *Meaning and void: Inner experience and the incentives in people's lives.* Minneapolis, MN: University of Minnesota Press.

Klotz, M. L., & Alicke, M. D. (1989). The effects of schema appropriateness on recall. *Journal of Research in Personality, 23,* 225–234.

Kobasa, S. C., Maddi, S. R., & Kahn, S. (1982). Hardiness and health: A prospective study. *Journal of Personality and Social Psychology, 42,* 168–177.

Kohlberg, L. (1966). A cognitive-developmental analysis of children's sex-role concepts and attitudes. In E. E. Maccoby (Ed.), *The development of sex differences.* Stanford, CA: Stanford University Press.

Kohut, H. (1971). *The analysis of the self.* New York: International Universities Press.

Kohut, H. (1977). *The restoration of the self.* New York: International Universities Press.

Kolata, G. (1995). Man's world, woman's world: Brain studies point to differences. *New York Times* (February 28, 1995), p. C–7

Kolb, D. A. (1965). Achievement motivation for underachieving high-school boys. *Journal of Personality and Social Psychology, 2,* 783–792.

Kramer, P. D. (1993) *Listening to Prozac.* New York: Viking.

Krantz, D. S. (1980). Cognitive processes and recovery from heart attack: A review and theoretical analysis. *Journal of Human Stress, 6,* 27–38.

Krantz, D. S., Baum, A., & Wideman, M. V. (1980). Assessment of preferences for self-treatment and information in health care. *Journal of Personality and Social Psychology, 39,* 977–990.

Krantz, D. S., & Hedges, S. M. (1987). Some causations for research on personality and health. *Journal of Personality, 55,* 351–357.

Kris, E. (1952). *Psychoanalytic exploration in art.* New York: International Universities Press.

Kuhnert, K. W., & Palmer, D. R. (1991). Job security, health, and the intrinsic and extrinsic characteristics of work. *Group and Organizational Studies, 16,* 178–192.

Lacey, J. I. (1967). Somatic response patterning and stress: Some revisions of activation theory. In M. H. Appley and R. Trumbull (Eds.), *Psychological stress.* New York: Appleton-Century-Crofts.

Lachman, R., Lachman, J. L., & Butterfield, E. C. (1979). *Cognitive psychology and information processing.* Hillsdale, NJ: Erlbaum.

Lakoff, G. (1987). *Women, fire, and dangerous*

*things: What categories reveal about the mind.* Chicago: University of Chicago Press.

Lambert, N. (1981). Psychological evidence in *Larry P. v. Wilson Riles:* An evaluation by the witness for the defense. *American Psychologist, 36,* 937–952.

Lameill, J. T. (1981). Toward an idiothetic psychology of personality. *American Psychologist, 36,* 276–289.

Lamiell, J. T. (1987). *The psychology of personality: An epistemological inquiry.* New York: Columbia University Press.

Lamiell, J. T., Foss, M. A., Larsen, R. J., & Hempel, A. M. (1983). Studies in intuitive personality from an idiothetic point of view: Implications for personality theory. *Journal of Personality, 51,* 438–467.

Landfield, A. W., Stern, M., & Fjeld, S. (1961). Serial conceptual processes and change in students undergoing psychotherapy. *Psychological Reports, 8,* 63–68.

Lanning, K. (1988). Individual differences in scalability: An alternative conception of consistency for personality theory and measurement. *Journal of Personality and Social Psychology, 55,* 142–148.

Lasch, C. (1979). *The culture of narcissism: American life in an age of diminishing expectations.* New York: Norton.

Latané, B., & Darley, J. M. (1970). *The unresponsive bystander: Why doesn't he help?* New York: Appleton-Century-Crofts.

Lazarus, A. A. (1961). Group therapy of phobic disorders by systematic desensitization. *Journal of Abnormal and Social Psychology, 63,* 504–510.

Lazarus, A. A. (1971). Where do behavior therapists take their troubles? *Psychological Reports, 28,* 349–350.

Lazarus, A. A., & Wilson, G. T. (1976). Behavior modification: Clinical and experimental perspectives. In B. B. Wolman (Ed.), *The therapist's handbook.* New York: Van Nostrand Reinhold.

Lazarus, R. S. (1966). *Psychological stress and the coping process.* New York: McGraw-Hill.

Lazarus, R. S. (1969). *Patterns of adjustment and human effectiveness.* New York: McGraw-Hill.

Lazarus, R. S., & Folkman, S. (1984). *Stress, appraisal, and coping.* New York: Springer.

Leahey, T. H. (1984). *A history of psychology: Main currents in psychological thought* (2nd ed.). Englewood Cliffs, NJ: Prentice-Hall.

Lecky, P. (1969). *Self-consistency: A theory of personality.* Hamden, CT: Shoe String Press.

Lee, D. J., Mendes de Leon, C. F., Jenkins, C. D., Croog, S. H., Levine, S., & Sudilovsky, A. (1992). Relation of hostility to medications adherence, symptoms complaints, and blood pressure reduction in a clinical trial of antihypertensive medication. *Journal of Psychosomatic Research, 36,* 181–190.

Lee, H. (1960). *To kill a mockingbird.* Philadelphia: Lippincott.

Lee, E. S. (1951). Negro intelligence and selective migration: A Philadelphia test of Klineberg's hypothesis. *American Sociological Review, 61,* 227–233.

Lefcourt, H. M. (Ed.). (1981). *Research with the locus of control construct: Vol. 1. Assessment methods.* New York: Academic Press.

Lefcourt, H. M. (1982). *Locus of control: Current trends in theory and research* (2nd ed.). Hillsdale, NJ: Erlbaum.

Lefcourt, H. M. (Ed.). (1984). *Research with the locus of control construct: Vol. 3. Extensions and limitations.* Orlando, FL: Academic Press.

Leiker, M., & Hailey, B. J. (1988). A link between hostility and disease: Poor health habits? *Behavioral Medicine, 3,* 129–133.

Leith, G. O. M. (1972). The relationships between intelligence, personality, and creativity under two conditions of stress. *British Journal of Educational Psychology, 42,* 240–247.

Lepper, M., & Greene, D. (1978). Overjustification research and beyond: Toward a means-ends analysis of intrinsic and extrinsic motivation. In M. Lepper & D. Greene (Eds.), *The hidden costs of reward* (pp. 109–148). Hillsdale, NJ: Erlbaum.

Lerner, R. M. (1982). Children and adolescents as

producers of their own development. *Developmental Review, 2,* 342–370.

Lerner, R. M., & Lerner. G. V. (1977). Effects of age, sex, and physical attractiveness on child-peer relations, academic performance, and elementary school adjustment. *Developmental Psychology, 13,* 585–590.

Leventhal, H. & Tomarken, A. J. (1986). Emotion: Today's problems. *Annual Review of Psychology, 37,* 565–610.

Levine, S. (1966). Sex differences in the brain. *Scientific American, 214*(4), 84–90.

Levinson, D., Darrow, C., Klein, M., Levinson, M., & McKee, B. (1978). *The seasons of a man's life.* New York: Knopf.

Levy, L. H. (1954). *A study of relative information value in personal construct theory.* Unpublished doctoral dissertation, Ohio State University.

Levy, L. H. (1970). *Conceptions of personality.* New York: Random House.

Lewin, K. (1935). *A dynamic theory of personality.* New York: McGraw-Hill.

Lewis, M. (1969). Infants' responses to facial stimuli during the first year of life. *Developmental Psychology, 1,* 75–86.

Liebers, A. (1966). *How to pass employment tests.* New York: Arco.

Liebert, R. M., & Sprafkin, J. (1988). *The early window: Effects of television on children and youth* (3rd ed.). Oxford, England: Pergamon Press.

Liebert, R. S. (1983). *Michelangelo: A psychoanalytic study of his life and images.* New Haven, CT: Yale University Press.

Lii, S., & Wong, S. (1982). A cross-cultural study on sex-role stereotypes and social desirability. *Sex Roles, 8,* 481–491.

Lilienfeld, S. O., Alliger, G., & Mitchell, K. (1995). Why integrity testing remains controversial. *American Psychologist, 50,* 457–458.

Linville, P. W. (1985). Self-complexity and affective extremity: Don't put all your eggs in one cognitive basket. *Social Cognition, 3,* 94–120.

Linville, P. W. (1987). Self-complexity as a cognitive buffer against stress-related illness and depression. *Journal of Personality and Social Psychology, 52,* 663–676.

Linville, P. W., & Carlston, D. E. (1994). Social cognition and the self. In P. G. Devine, D. L. Hamilton, & T. M. Ostrom (Eds.), *Social cognition: Impact on social psychology* (pp. 144–195). San Diego, CA: Academic Press.

Lipinski, D. P., Black, J. L., Nelson, R. O., & Ciminero, A. R. (1975). Influence of motivational variables on the reactivity and reliability of self-recording. *Journal of Consulting and Clinical Psychology, 43,* 637–646.

Littlefield, C. H., & Rushton, J. P. (1986). When a child dies: The sociobiology of bereavement. *Journal of Personality and Social Psychology, 51,* 797–802.

Liverant, S. (1960). Intelligence: A concept in need of re-examination. *Journal of Consulting Psychology, 24,* 101–110.

Locke, E. A., (1968). Toward a theory of task motivation and incentives. *Organizational Behavior & Human Performance, 3,* 157–189.

Locke, E. A. (1971). Is "behavior therapy" behavioristic? An analysis of Wolpe's psychotherapeutic methods. *Psychological Bulletin, 76,* 318–327.

Locksley, A., & Colten, M. E. (1979). Psychological androgyny: A case of mistaken identity? *Journal of Personality and Social Psychology, 37,* 1017–1031.

Loehlin, J. C. (1992). *Genes and environment in personality development.* Newbury Park, CA: Sage.

Loehlin, J. C., Horn, J. M., & Willerman, L. (1981). Personality resemblance in adoptive families. *Behavior Genetics, 11,* 309–330.

Loehlin, J. C., & Nichols, R. C. (1976). *Heredity, environment, and personality.* Austin, TX: University of Texas Press.

Loehlin, J. C., Willerman, L., & Horn, J. M. (1988). Human behavior genetics. In M. R. Rosenzweig & L. W. Porter (Eds.), *Annual review of psychology, 239,* 101–103. Palo Alto, CA: Annual Reviews.

Loftus, E. F. (1993). The reality of repressed memories. *American Psychologist, 48,* 518–537.

Loftus, E. F., & Klinger, M. R. (1992). Is the unconscious smart or dumb? *American Psychologist, 47*, 761–765.

Lombardo, M. M., Ruderman, M. N., & McCauley, C. D. (1988). Explanations of success and derailment in upper-level management positions. *Journal of Business and Psychology, 2*, 199–216.

Lombroso, C. (1911). *Crime: Its causes and remedies*. Boston: Little, Brown.

Lykken, D. T. (1974). Psychology and the lie detector industry. *American Psychologist, 29*, 725–739.

Lykken, D. T. (1981). *A tremor in the blood: Uses and abuses of the lie detector*. New York: McGraw-Hill.

Maccoby, E. E., & Jacklin, C. N. (1974). *The psychology of sex differences*. Stanford, CA: Stanford University Press.

Maccoby, E. E., & Wilson, W. C. (1957). Identification and observational learning from films. *Journal of Abnormal and Social Psychology, 55*, 76–87.

MacDonald, K. (1995). Evolution, the Five-Factor Model, and levels of personality. *Journal of Personality, 63*, 525–567.

MacKinnon, D. W. (1965). Personality and the realization of creative potential. *American Psychologist, 20*, 273–281.

Maddi, S. R. (1989). *Personality theories: A comparative analysis* (5th ed.). Chicago: Dorsey Press.

Maddux, J. E., Norton, L. W., & Stoltenberg, C. D. (1986). Self-efficacy expectancy, outcome expectancy, and outcome value: Relative effects on behavioral intentions. *Journal of Personality and Social Psychology, 51*, 783–789.

Maher, B. A. (1966). *Principles of psychopathology: An experimental approach*. New York: McGraw-Hill.

Maher, B. (Ed.). (1969). *Clinical psychology and personality: The selected papers of George Kelly*. New York: Wiley.

Mahler, M. S. (1968). *On human symbiosis and the vicissitudes of individuation*. New York: International Universities Press.

Mahony, P. J. (1986). *Freud and the rat man*. New Haven, CT: Yale University Press.

Mahrer, A. R. (1956). The role of expectancy in delayed reinforcement. *Journal of Experimental Psychology, 52*, 101–106.

Maloney, M. P., & Ward, M. P. (1976). *Psychological assessment: A conceptual approach*. New York: Oxford University Press.

Manaster, G. J., & Corsini, R. J. (1982). *Individual psychology*. Itasca, IL: Peacock.

Mandler, G., & Sarason, S. B. (1952). A study of anxiety and learning. *Journal of Abnormal and Social Psychology, 47*, 166–173.

Mann, C. C. (1994). Behavioral genetics in transition. *Science, 264*, 1686–1689.

Marecek, J. (1995). Gender, politics, and psychology's ways of knowing. *American Psychologist, 50*, 162–163.

Marin, P. (1975, October). The new narcissism. *Harper's*.

Marks, G., Richardson, J. L., Graham, J. W., & Levine, A. (1986). Role of health locus of control beliefs and expectations of treatment efficacy in adjustment to cancer. *Journal of Personality and Social Psychology, 51*, 443–450.

Markus, H. (1977). Self-schemata and processing information about the self. *Journal of Personality and Social Psychology, 35*, 63–78.

Markus, H. (1983). Self-knowledge: An expanded view. *Journal of Personality, 51*, 543–565.

Markus, H., & Nurius, P. (1986). Possible selves. *American Psychologist, 41*, 954–969.

Markus, H., & Sentis, K. (1982). The self in social information processing. In J. Suls (Ed.), *Psychological perspectives on the self (Vol. 1)*. Hillsdale, NJ: Erlbaum.

Markus, H., & Wurf, E. (1987). The dynamic self-concept: A social psychological perspective. In M. R. Rosenzweig & L. W. Porter (Eds.), *Annual review of psychology, 38*, 299–337. Palo Alto, CA: Annual Reviews.

Martin, C. L., & Halverson, C. F., Jr. (1981). A schematic processing model of sex typing and stereotyping in children. *Child Development, 52*, 1119–1134.

Martin, N., & Jardine, R. (1986). Eysenck's contribution to behavior genetics. In S. Modgil & C. Modgil (Eds.), *Hans Eysenck: Consen-*

sus and controversy (pp. 13–47). Philadelphia: Falmer Press.

Martin, R. A., & Lefcourt, H. M. (1983). Sense of humor as a moderator of the relation between stressors and moods. *Journal of Personality and Social Psychology, 45,* 1313–1324.

Maslach, C. (1982). *Burnout: The cost of caring.* Englewood Cliffs, NJ: Prentice-Hall.

Masling, J. (Ed.). (1983). *Empirical studies of psycho-analytical theories* (Vol. I). Hillsdale, NJ: Erlbaum.

Masling, J. (Ed.). (1986). *Empirical studies of psychoanalytic theories* (Vol. II). Hillsdale, NJ: Analytic Press.

Maslow, A. H. (1943). Dynamics of personality organization, I and II. *Psychological Review, 50,* 514–558.

Maslow, A. H. (1962). *Toward a psychology of being.* Princeton, NJ: Van Nostrand.

Maslow, A. H. (1970). *Motivation and personality* (2nd ed.). New York: Harper & Row.

Maslow, A. H. (1987). *Motivation and personality* (3rd ed.). New York: Harper & Row. (revised by R. Frager, J. Fadiman, C. McReynolds, & R. Cox).

Masson, J. M. (1985). *The assault on truth: Freud's suppression of the seduction theory.* New York: Penguin Books.

Matarazzo, J. D. (1972). *Wechsler's measurement and appraisal of adult intelligence* (5th and enlarged ed.). Baltimore, MD: Williams & Wilkins.

Mathews, K. E., & Canon, L. K. (1975). Environmental noise level as a determinant of helping behavior. *Journal of Personality and Social Psychology, 32,* 571–577.

Matthews, K. A. (1984). Assessment of Type A, anger, and hostility in epidemiological studies of cardiovascular disease. In A. Ostfield & E. Eaker (Eds.), *Measuring psychosocial variables in epidemiological studies of cardiovascular disease.* Bethesda, MD: National Institutes of Health.

Matthews, K. A., & Brunson, B. I. (1979). Allocation of attention and the Type A coronary-prone behavior pattern. *Journal of Personality and Social Psychology, 37,* 2081–2090.

Matthews, K. A., & Glass, D. C. (1981). Type A behavior, stressful life events, and coronary heart disease. In B. S. Dohrenwend & B. P. Dohrenwend (Eds.), *Stressful life events and their contexts.* New York: Prodist.

Matthews, K. A., Krantz, D. S., Dembroski, T. M., & MacDougall, J. M. (1982). Unique and common variance in structured interview and Jenkins Activity Survey measures of the Type A behavior pattern. *Journal of Personality and Social Psychology, 42,* 303–313.

McAdams, D. P. (1988). Biography, narrative, and lives: An introduction. *Journal of Personality, 56,* 1–18.

McAdams, D. P. (1992). The Five-Factor Model in personality: A critical appraisal. *Journal of Personality, 60,* 175–215.

McAdams, D. P. (1995). What do we know when we know a person? *Journal of Personality, 63,* 365–396.

McArdle, J. J. (1996). Current directions in structural factor analysis. *Current Directions in Psychological Science, 5,* 11–18.

McClelland, D. C. (1961). *The achieving society.* Princeton, NJ: Van Nostrand.

McClelland, D. C. (1975). *Power: The inner experience.* New York: Irvington.

McClelland, D. C. (1980). Motive dispositions: The merits of operant and respondent measures. In L. Wheeler (Ed.), *Review of personality and social psychology,* 1. Beverly Hills, CA: Sage Publications.

McClelland, D. C. (1982). The need for power, sympathetic activation, and illness. *Motivation and Emotion, 6,* 31–41.

McClelland, D. C. (1985). *Human motivation.* Glenview, IL: Scott, Foresman.

McClelland, D. C. (1989). Motivational factors in health and disease. *American Psychologist, 44,* 675–683.

McClelland, D. C., Atkinson, J. W., Clark, R. W., & Lowell, E. L. (1953). *The achievement motive.* New York: Appleton-Century-Crofts.

McClelland, D. C., Clark, R. A., Roby, T. B., and Atkinson, J. W. (1949). The effect of the need for achievement on thematic apperception. *Journal of Experimental Psychology, 37,* 242–255.

McClelland, D. C., Koestner, R., & Weinberger, J. (1989). How do self-attributed and implicit motives differ? *Psychological Review, 96,* 690–702.

McCrae, R. R., & Costa, P. T. (1987). Validation of the five-factor model of personality across instruments and observers. *Journal of Personality and Social Psychology, 52,* 81–90.

McCrae, R. R., & Costa, P. T. (1989). Reinterpreting the Myers-Briggs Type Indicator from the perspective of the five factor model of personality. *Journal of Personality, 57,* 17–40.

McCrae, R. R., & Costa, P. T. (1990). *Personality in adulthood.* New York: Guilford.

McCrae, R. R., Costa, P. T., & Busch, C. M. (1986). Evaluating comprehensiveness in personality systems: The California Q-Set and the five factor model. *Journal of Personality, 54,* 430–446.

McCullers, J. C., & Martin, J. A. G. (1971). A reexamination of the role of incentive in children's discrimination learning. *Child Development, 42,* 827–837.

McGinnies, E. (1949). Emotionality and perceptual defense. *Psychological Review, 56,* 244–251.

McGlone, J. (1978). Sex differences in functional brain asymmetry. *Cortex, 14,* 122–128.

McGregor, D. (1960). *The human side of enterprise.* New York: McGraw- Hill.

McKey, R. H. (1985). *The impact of head start on children, families, and communities.* Washington, DC: U.S. Department of Health and Human Services.

Mead, G. H. (1934). *Mind, self, and society.* Chicago: University of Chicago Press.

Meehl, P. E. (1962). Schizotaxia, schizotypy, and schizophrenia. *American Psychologist, 17,* 827–838.

Meichenbaum, D. (1985). *Stress innovation training.* Elmsford, NY: Pergamon.

Meichenbaum, D. (1992). Evolution of cognitive behavior therapy: Origins, tenets, and clinical examples. In J. K. Zweig (Ed.), *The evolution of psychotherapy: The second conference* (pp. 114–127). New York: Bruner/ Mazel.

Meichenbaum, D. (1993). Changing conceptions of cognitive behavior modification: Retrospect and prospect. *Journal of Consulting and Clinical Psychology, 61,* 202–204.

Meichenbaum, D., Price, R., Phares, E. J., McCormick, N., & Hyde, J. (1989). *Exploring choices: The psychology of adjustment.* Glenview, IL: Scott, Foresman.

Meir, E. I. (1993). Conceptual elaboration of Holland's theory on personality-occupational congruence. *Man and Work, 4,* 59–70.

Miller, N. E. (1948). Theory and experiment relating psychoanalytic displacement to stimulus-response generalization. *Journal of Abnormal and Social Psychology, 43,* 155–178.

Miller, N. E., & Dollard, J. (1941). *Social learning and imitation.* New Haven, CT: Yale University Press.

Miller, T. Q., Smith, T. W., Turner, C. W., Guijarro, M. L., Hallet, A. J. (1996). A meta-analytic review of research on hostility and physical health. *Psychological Bulletin, 119,* 322–354.

Mischel, W. (1966). Theory and research on the antecedents of self-imposed delay of reward. In B. A. Maher (Ed.), *Progress in experimental personality research* (Vol. 3). New York: Academic Press.

Mischel, W. (1968). *Personality and assessment.* New York: Wiley.

Mischel, W. (1972). Direct versus indirect personality assessment: Evidence and implications. *Journal of Consulting and Clinical Psychology, 38,* 319–324.

Mischel, W. (1973). Toward a cognitive social learning reconceptualization of personality. *Psychological Review, 80,* 252–283.

Mischel, W. (1979). On the interface of cognition and personality: Beyond the person-situation debate. *American Psychologist, 34,* 740–754.

Mischel, W. (1984). On the predictability of behavior and the structure of personality. In R. A. Zucker, J. Aronoff, & A. J. Rabin (Eds.), *Personality and the prediction of behavior* (pp. 269–305). New York: Academic Press.

Mischel, W., & Masters, J. C. (1966). Effects of

probability of reward attainment on responses to frustration. *Journal of Personality and Social Psychology, 3,* 390–396.

Mischel, W., & Shoda, Y. (1995). A cognitive-affective system theory of personality: Reconceptualizing situations, dispositions, dynamics, and invariance in personality structure. *Psychological Review, 102,* 246–268.

Mischel, W., Shoda, Y., & Peake, P. K. (1988). The nature of adolescent competencies predicted by preschool delay of gratification. *Journal of Personality and Social Psychology, 54,* 687–696.

Mitchell, C., & Stuart, R. B. (1984). Effect of self-efficacy on dropout from obesity treatment. *Journal of Consulting and Clinical Psychology, 52,* 1100–1101.

Mittleman, W. (1991). Maslow's study of self-actualization: A reinterpretation. *Journal of Humanistic Psychology, 31,* 114–135.

Money, J. (1965). Psychosexual differentiation. In J. Money (Ed.), *Sex research: New developments.* New York: Holt, Rinehart & Winston.

Money, J. (1975). Ablatiopenis: Normal male infant–sex reassigned as a girl. *Archives of Sexual Behavior, 4,* 65–72.

Money, J., & Ehrhardt, A. (1972). *Man and woman, boy and girl.* Baltimore, MD: Johns Hopkins University Press.

Morgan, C. D., & Murray, H. A. (1935). A method for investigating fantasies: The Thematic Apperception Test. *Archives of Neurology and Psychiatry, 34,* 289–306.

Moser, C. G., & Dyck, D. G. (1989). Type A behavior, uncontrollability, and the activation of hostile self-schema responding. *Journal of Research in Personality, 23,* 248–267.

Moss, H. A. (1967). Sex, age, and state as determinants of mother-infant interaction. *Merrill-Palmer Quarterly, 13,* 19–36.

Mowrer, O. H. (1960). *Learning theory and behavior.* New York: Wiley.

Muldoon, M. F., & Manuck, S. B. (1992). Health through cholesterol reduction: Are there unforeseen risks? *Annals of Behavioral Medicine, 14,* 101–108.

Munroe, R. L. (1955). *Schools of psychoanalytic thought.* New York: Dryden Press.

Murphy, D. L., Wright, L., Buchsbaum, M. S., Nichols, A., Costa, J. L., & Wyatt, R. Z. (1976). Platelet and plasma amine oxidase activity in 680 normals: Sex and age differences and stability over time. *Biochemical Medicine, 16,* 254–263.

Murphy, G. (1947). *Personality: A biosocial approach to origins and structure.* New York: Harper.

Murphy, K. R. (1987). Detecting infrequent deception. *Journal of Applied Psychology, 72,* 611–614.

Murray, H. A. (and collaborators). (1938). *Explorations in personality.* New York: Oxford University Press.

Murray, H. A. (1951). Uses of the Thematic Apperception Test. *American Journal of Psychiatry, 10,* 577–581.

Musante, L., MacDougall, J. M., Dembroski, T. M., & Costa, P. T. Jr. (1989). Potential for hostility and dimensions of anger. *Health Psychology, 8,* 343–354.

Mussen, P., & Eichorn, D. (1988). Mary Cover Jones (1896–1987). *American Psychologist, 43,* 818.

Myers, A. M., & Gonda, G. (1982). Empirical validation of the Bem Sex-Role Inventory. *Journal of Personality and Social Psychology, 43,* 304–318.

Myers, I. B. (1975). *Manual: The Myers-Briggs Type Indicator.* Palo Alto, CA: Consulting Psychologists Press.

Myers, L. B., & Brewin, C. R. (1994). Recall of early experiences and the repressive coping style. *Journal of Abnormal Psychology, 103,* 288–292.

Neale, M. C., & Stevenson, J. (1989). Rater bias in the EASI temperament scales: A twin study. *Journal of Personality and Social Psychology, 56,* 446–455.

Neher, A. (1991). Maslow's theory of motivation: A critique. *Journal of Humanistic Psychology, 31,* 89–112.

Neisser, U. (1979). The concept of intelligence. In R. J. Sternberg & D. K. Detterman (Eds.), *Human intelligence: Perspectives on its theory and measurement.* Norwood, NJ: Ablex.

Newcomb, T. M. (1929). *Consistency of certain*

extrovert-introvert behavior patterns in 51 problem boys. New York: Columbia University Teacher's College, Bureau of Publications.

Newman, J. P. (1987). Reactions to punishment in extraverts and psychopaths: Implications for the impulsive behavior of disinhibited individuals. Journal of Research in Personality, 21, 464–480.

Nezu, A. M., Nezu, C. M., & Blissett, S. E. (1988). Sense of humor as a moderator of the relation between stressful events and psychological distress: A prospective analysis. Journal of Personality and Social Psychology, 54, 520–525.

Nicholls, J. G. (1972). Creativity in the person who will never produce anything original and useful: The concept of creativity as a normally distributed trait. American Psychologist, 27, 717–727.

Nilsson-Ehle, H. (1908). Einige Ergebnisse von Kruezungen bei Hafer and Weisen. Botanische Notiser, 1908–1909, 257–294.

Nisbett, R., & Ross, L. (1980). Human inference: Strategies and shortcomings of social judgement. New York: Prentice-Hall.

Nisbett, R. E., & Wilson, T. D. (1977). Telling more than we can know: Verbal reports on mental processes. Psychological Review, 84, 231–259.

Norem, J. K., & Cantor, N. (1986). Defensive pessimism: "Harnessing" anxiety as motivation. Journal of Personality and Social Psychology, 51, 1208–1217.

Norem, J. K., & Illingworth, K. S. S. (1993). Strategy-dependent effects of reflecting on self and tasks: Some implications of optimism and defensive pessimism. Journal of Personality and Social Psychology, 65, 822–835.

Norman, W. T. (1967). 2800 personality trait descriptors: Normative operating characteristics for a university population. Ann Arbor: University of Michigan, Department of Psychology.

Norman, W. T., & Goldberg, L. R. (1963). Raters, ratees, and randomness in personality structure. Journal of Personality and Social Psychology, 4, 681–691.

Novaco, R. W. (1977). Stress inoculation: A cognitive therapy for anger and its application to a case of depression. Journal of Consulting and Clinical Psychology, 45, 600–608.

Nowack, R. (1995). Genome mappers have a hot time at Cold Spring Harbor. Science, 268, 1134–1135.

Nunnally, J. C. (1978). Psychometric theory (2nd ed.). New York: McGraw-Hill.

Office of Technology Assessment, U. S. Congress (1983). Scientific validity of polygraph testing.(OTA-TM-H–15). Washington, DC: U. S. Government Printing Office.

Olds, D. E., & Shaver, P. (1980). Masculinity, femininity, academic performance, and health: Further evidence concerning the androgyny controversy. Journal of Personality, 48, 323–341.

O'Leary, K. D., & Becker, W. C. (1967). Behavior modification of an adjustment class: A token reinforcement program. Exceptional Children, 33, 637–642.

Ones, D. S., Viswesvaran, C., & Schmidt, F. L. (1995). Integrity tests: Overlooked facts, resolved issues, and remaining questions. American Psychologist, 50, 456–457.

Ortony, A., Clore, G. L., & Foss, M. A. (1987). The referential structure of the affective lexicon. Cognitive Science, 11, 341–364.

Osberg, T. M. (1987). The convergent and discriminant validity of the Need for Cognition Scale. Journal of Personality Assessment, 51, 441–450.

Osborne, R. T. (1960). Racial differences in mental growth and school achievement: A longitudinal study. Psychological Reports, 7, 233–239.

Osgood, C. E., Suci, G. J., & Tannenbaum, P. H. (1957). The measurement of meaning. Urbana, IL: University of Illinois Press.

Osipow, S. H. (1983). Theories of career development (3rd ed.). Englewood Cliffs, NJ: Prentice-Hall.

Osler, W. (1892). Lectures on angina pectoris and allied states. New York: Appleton.

OSS Assessment Staff. (1948). Assessment of men: Selection of personnel for the Office of Strategic Services. New York: Rinehart.

Ozer, D. J., & Reise, S. P. (1994). Personality assessment. *Annual Review of Psychology, 45,* 357–388.

Paige, J. (1966). Letters from Jenny: An approach to the clinical analysis of personality structure by computer. In P. Stone (Ed.), *The general inquirer: A computer approach to content analysis.* Cambridge, MA: M.I.T. Press.

Parker, K. C., Hanson, R. K., & Hunsley, J. (1988). MMPI, Rorschach, and WAIS: A meta-analytic comparison of reliability, stability, and validity. *Psychological Bulletin, 103,* 367–373.

Patterson, G. R. (1977). Naturalistic observation in clinical assessment. *Journal of Abnormal Child Psychology, 5,* 307–322.

Paunonen, S. V., & Jackson, D. N. (1987). Accuracy of interviewers and students in identifying the personality characteristics of personnel managers and computer programers. *Journal of Vocational Behavior, 31,* 26–36.

Paunonen, S. V., Jackson, D. N., Trzebinski, J., & Forsterling, F. (1992). Personality structure across cultures: A multimethod evaluation. *Journal of Personality and Social Psychology, 62,* 447–456.

Pavlov, I. P. (1927). *Conditioned reflexes.* London: Oxford University Press.

Peabody, D. (1967). Trait inferences: Evaluative and descriptive aspects. *Journal of personality and social psychology monographs, 7,* (4, Whole No. 644).

Peabody, D., & Goldberg, L. R. (1989). Some determinants of factor structures from personality-trait descriptors. *Journal of Personality and Social Psychology, 57,* 552–567.

Pedersen, N. L., Friberg, L., Floderus-Myrhed, B., McClearn, G. E., & Plomin, R. (1984). Swedish early separated twins: Identification and characterization. *Acta Geneticae Medicae et Gemellologiae, 33,* 243–250.

Pedersen, N. L., Plomin, R., McClearn, G. E., & Friberg, L. T. (1988). Neuroticism, extraversion, and related traits in adult twins reared apart and reared together. *Journal of Personality and Social Psychology, 55,* 950–957.

Pederson, F. A. (1958). *Consistency data on the role construct repertory test.* Unpublished master's thesis, Ohio State University.

Pedhazur, E. J., & Tetenbaum, T. J. (1979). Bem Sex Role Inventory: A theoretical and methodological critique. *Journal of Personality and Social Psychology, 37,* 996–1016.

Perry, D. G., & Perry, L. C. (1975). Observational learning in children: Effects of sex of model and subject's sex role behavior. *Journal of Personality and Social Psychology, 31,* 1083–1088.

Pervin, L. A. (1978). *Current controversies and issues in personality.* New York: Wiley.

Pervin, L. A. (1985). Personality: Current controversies, issues, and directions. In M. R. Rosenzweig & L. W. Porter (Eds.), *Annual review of psychology, 36,* 83–114. Palo Alto, CA: Annual Reviews.

Pervin, L.A. (1989). *Personality: Theory and research (5th ed.).* New York: Wiley.

Peterson, C., & Seligman, M. E. P. (1987). Explanatory style and illness. *Journal of Personality, 55,* 237–265.

Peterson, D. R. (1965). Scope and generality of verbally defined personality factors. *Psychological Review, 72,* 48–59.

Phares, E. J. (1957). Expectancy changes in skill and chance situations. *Journal of Abnormal and Social Psychology, 54,* 339–342.

Phares, E. J. (1962). Perceptual threshold decrements as a function of skill and chance expectancies. *Journal of Psychology, 53,* 399–407.

Phares, E. J. (1972). A social learning theory approach to psychopathology. In J. B. Rotter, J. E. Chance, & E. J. Phares (Eds.), *Applications of a social learning theory of personality.* New York: Holt, Rinehart & Winston.

Phares, E. J. (1976). *Locus of control in personality.* Morristown, NJ: General Learning Press.

Phares, E. J. (1980). Rotter's social learning theory. In G. M. Gazda and R. J. Corsini (Eds.). *Theories of learning: A comparative approach.* Itasca, IL: Peacock.

Phares, E. J. (1988). *Clinical psychology: Concepts, methods, and profession* (3rd ed.). Chicago: Dorsey Press.

Phares, E. J. (1992). *Clinical psychology: Concepts, methods, and profession (4th ed.).* Chicago: Dorsey Press.

Phares, E. J., & Erskine, N. (1984). The measurement of selfism. *Educational and Psychological Measurement, 44,* 597–608.

Phares, E. J., & Lamiell, J. T. (1977). Personality. In M. R. Rosenzweig and L. W. Porter (Eds.), *Annual review of psychology, 36,* 83-114. Palo Alto, CA: Annual Reviews.

Phares, E. J., & Rotter, J. B. (1956). An effect of the situation on psychological testing. *Journal of Consulting Psychology, 20,* 291–293.

Piper, W. E., Wogan, M., & Getter, H. (1972). Social learning theory predictors of termination in psychotherapy. In J. B. Rotter, J. E. Chance, & E. J. Phares (Eds.), *Applications of a social learning theory of personality.* New York: Holt, Rinehart and Winston.

Plomin, R. (1987). *Nature, nurture, and human development.* Washington, DC: Federation of Behavioral, Psychological, Cognitive Sciences.

Plomin, R., Chipuer, H. M., & Loehlin, J. C. (1990). Behavioral genetics and personality. In L. A. Pervin (Ed.), *Handbook of personality: Theory and research* (pp. 225–243). New York: Guilford Press.

Plomin, R., Coon, H., Carey, G., Defries, J. C., & Fulker, D. W. (1991). Parent-offspring and sibling adoption analyses of parental ratings of temperament in infancy and childhood. *Journal of Personality, 59,* 705–732.

Plomin, R., & Daniels, D. (1987). Why are children in the same family so different from each other? *Behavioral and Brain Sciences, 10,* 1–16.

Plutchik, R. (1962). *The emotions: Facts, theories, and a new model.* New York: Random House.

Plutchik, R. (1965). What is emotion? *The Journal of Psychology, 61,* 295–303.

Plutchik, R., & Kellerman, H. (1974). *Emotions Profile Index.* Los Angeles, CA: Western Psychological Services.

Poch, S. (1952). *Study of changes in personal constructs as related to interpersonal prediction and its outcomes.* Unpublished doctoral dissertation, Ohio State University.

Popper, K. R. (1962). *Conjectures and refutations.* New York: Basic Books.

Posner, M. I., & Raichle, M. E. (1994). *Images of the mind.* New York: Scientific American Library/Freeman.

Poulin-Dubois, D., Serbin, L. A., Kenyon, B., & Derbyshire, A. (1994). Infants' intermodal knowledge about gender. *Developmental Psychology, 30,* 436–442.

Powers, W. T. (1973). *Behavior: The control of perception.* Chicago: Aldine.

Privette, G. (1983). Peak experience, peak performance, and flow: A comparative analysis of positive human experience. *Journal of Personality and Social Psychology, 45,* 1361–1368.

Rahe, R. H. (1972). Subjects' recent life changes and their near-future illness susceptibility. In Z. J. Lipowski (Ed.), *Advances in psychosomatic medicine: Vol. 8. Psychosocial aspects of physical illness.* Basel, Switzerland: S. Karger.

Raimy, V. C. (1948). Self-reference in counseling interviews. *Journal of Consulting Psychology, 12,* 153–163.

Rapaport, D. (1959). The structure of psychoanalytic theory: A systematizing attempt. In Koch, S. (Ed.), *Psychology: A study of a science* (Vol. 3). New York: McGraw-Hill.

Raven, J. C. (1938). *Progressive matrices.* London: Lewis.

Reeder, G. D., & Brewer, M. B. (1979). A schematic model of dispositional attribution in interpersonal perception. *Psychological Review, 86,* 61–79.

Rescorla, R. A. (1988). Pavlovian conditioning: It's not what you think it is. *American Psychologist, 43,* 151–160.

Revelle, W., Amaral, P., & Turriff, S. (1976). Introversion/extraversion, time stress, and caffeine: The effect on verbal performance. *Science, 192,* 149–150.

Revelle, W., Humphreys, M. S., Simon, L., & Gilliland, K. (1980). The interactive effect of personality, time of day, and caffeine: A test of the arousal model. *Journal of Experimental Psychology: General, 109,* 1–31

Revelle, W., Anderson, K. J., & Humphreys, M. S. (1987). Empirical tests and theoretical extensions of arousal-based theories of personality.

In J. Strelau & H. J. Eysenck (Eds.), *Personality dimension and arousal* (pp. 17–36). New York: Plenum.

Rhodewalt, F. (1995). Conceptions of ability, achievement goals, and individual differences in self-handicapping behavior: On the application of implicit theories. *Journal of Personality, 62,* 67–85.

Rhodewalt, F., & Morf, C. C. (1995). Self and interpersonal correlates of the Narcissistic Personality Inventory: A review and new findings. *Journal of Research in Personality, 29,* 1–23.

Rieke, M. L., & Guastello, S. J. (1995). Unresolved issues in honesty and integrity testing. *American Psychologist, 50,* 458–459.

Riggio, R. E., Lippa, R., & Salinas, C. (1990). The display of personality in expressive movement. *Journal of Research in Personality, 24,* 16–31.

Ritchie, E., & Phares, E. J. (1969). Attitude change as a function of internal-external control and communication status. *Journal of Personality, 37,* 429–443.

Roberts, A. A. (1985). Biofeedback: Research, training, and clinical roles. *American Psychologist, 40,* 938–941.

Roche, S. M., & McConkey, K. M. (1990). Absorption: Nature, assessment, and correlates. *Journal of Personality and Social Psychology, 59,* 91–101.

Rodin, J. (1986). Aging and health: Effects of the sense of control. *Science, 233,* 1271–1276.

Rodin, J., & Salovey, P. (1989). Health psychology. In M. R. Rosenzweig & L. W. Porter (Eds.), *Annual Review of Psychology, 40,* 533–579. Palo Alto, CA: Annual Reviews.

Rodriguez, M. L., Mischel, W., & Shoda, Y. (1989). Cognitive person variables in the delay of gratification of older children at risk. *Journal of Personality and Social Psychology, 57,* 358–367.

Roe, A. (1953). A psychological study of eminent psychologists and anthropologists, and a comparison with biological and physical scientists. *Psychological Monographs General and Applied, 67*(2, Whole No. 352).

Roethlisberger, F. J., & Dickson W. J. (1939). *Management and the worker: An account of a research program conducted by the Western Electric Company, Chicago.* Cambridge, MA: Harvard University Press.

Rogers, C. R. (1951). *Client-centered therapy.* Boston: Houghton Mifflin.

Rogers, C. R. (1959). A theory of therapy, personality, and interpersonal relationships, as developed in the client-centered framework. In S. Koch (Ed.), *Psychology: A study of a science* (Vol. 3). New York: McGraw-Hill.

Rogers, C. R. (1961). *On becoming a person: A therapist's view of psychotherapy.* Boston: Houghton Mifflin.

Rogers, C. R. (1977). *Carl Rogers on personal power.* New York: Delacorte Press.

Rogers, C. R. (1980). *A way of being.* Boston: Houghton Mifflin.

Rogers, C. R., & Skinner, B. F. (1956). Some issues concerning the control of human behavior. *Science, 124,* 1057–1066.

Rogers, T. B., Kuiper, N. A., & Kirker, W. S. (1977). Self-reference and the encoding of personal information. *Journal of Personality and Social Psychology, 35,* 677–688.

Romer, D., & Revelle, W. (1984). Personality traits: Fact or fiction? A critique of the Scweder and D'Andrade systematic distortion hypothesis. *Journal of Personality and Social Psychology, 47,* 1028–1042.

Rorer, L. G. (1965). The great response-style myth. *Psychological Bulletin, 63,* 129–156.

Rosch, E. (1975). Cognitive representations of semantic categories. *Journal of Experimental Psychology: General, 104,* 192–233.

Rosch, E. (1978). Principles of classification. In E. Rosch & B. B. Lloyd (Eds.), *Cognition and Categorization* (pp. 27–48). Hillsdale, NJ: Erlbaum.

Rosch, E., & Mervis, C. B. (1975). Family resemblances: Studies in the internal structure of categories. *Cognitive Psychology, 7,* 573–605.

Rose, R. J., Koskenvuo, M., Kaprio, J., Sarna, S., & Langinvainio, H. (1988). Shared genes, shared experiences, and similarity of personality. *Journal of Personality and Social Psychology, 54,* 161–171.

Rosen, B. C., & D'Andrade, R. (1959). The psychosocial origins of achievement motivation. *Sociometry, 22,* 185–218.

Rosenbaum, R. (1995, January 15). The great Ivy League nude posture photo scandal. *The New York Times Magazine,* pp. 26–31, 40, 46, 55–56.

Rosenberg, S. (1989). A study of personality in literary autobiography: An analysis of Thomas Wolfe's *Look Homeward Angel. Journal of Personality and Social Psychology, 56,* 416–430.

Rosenberg, S., & Gara, M. A. (1985). The multiplicity of personal identity. In P. Shaver (Ed.), *Review of Personality and Social Psychology, 16,* 87–113.

Rosenberg, S., & Sedlak, A. (1972). Structural representations of perceived personality trait relationships. In A. K. Romney, R. N. Shepard, & S. B. Nelson (Eds.), *Multidimensional scaling: Theory and applications in the behavioral sciences, Vol II, Application* (pp. 133–162).s New York: Seminar Press.

Rosenkrantz, P., Vogel, S., Bee, H., Broverman, I., & Broverman, D. M. (1968). Sex-role stereotypes and self-concepts in college students. *Journal of Consulting and Clinical Psychology, 32,* 287–295.

Rosenzweig, S. (1941). Need-persistive and ego-defensive reactions to frustration as demonstrated by an experiment on repression. *Psychological Review, 48,* 347–349.

Ross, S., & Buckalew, L. W. (1983).The placebo as an agent in behavioral manipulation: A review of problems issues and affected measures. *Clinical Psychology Review, 3,* 457–471.

Roth, D. L., Wiebe, D. J., Fillingim, R. B., & Shay, K. A. (1989). Life events, fitness, hardiness, and health: A simultaneous analysis of proposed stress-resistance effects. *Journal of Personality and Social Psychology, 57,* 136–142.

Rotter, J. B. (1954). *Social learning and clinical psychology.* Englewood Cliffs, NJ: Prentice-Hall.

Rotter, J. B. (1966). Generalized expectancies for internal versus external control of reinforcement. *Psychological Monographs, 80*(1, Whole No. 609).

Rotter, J. B. (1967a). A new scale for the measurement of interpersonal trust. *Journal of Personality, 35,* 651–665.

Rotter, J. B. (1967b). Personality theory. In H. Helson & W. Bevan (Eds.), *Contemporary approaches to psychology.* Princeton, NJ: Van Nostrand.

Rotter, J. B. (1970). Some implications of a social learning theory for the practice of psychotherapy. In D. J. Levis (Ed.), *Learning approaches to therapeutic behavior change.* Chicago: Aldine.

Rotter, J. B. (1971). Generalized expectancies for interpersonal trust. *American Psychologist, 26,* 443–452.

Rotter, J. B. (1981). The psychological situation in social learning theory. In D. Magnusson (Ed.), *Toward a psychology of situations: An interactional perspective.* Hillsdale, NJ: Erlbaum.

Rotter, J. B. (1980). Interpersonal trust, trustworthiness, and gullability. *American Psychologist, 35,* 1–7.

Rotter, J. B. (1982). *The development and application of social learning theory: Selected papers.* New York: Praeger.

Rotter, J. B. (1990). Internal versus external control of reinforcement: A case history of a variable. *American Psychologist, 45,* 489–493.

Rotter, J. B. (1992). Cognates of personal control: Locus of control, self-efficacy, and explanatory style. *Applied and Preventive Psychology, 2,* 127–129.

Rotter, J. B., Chance, J. E., & Phares, E. J. (Eds.). (1972). *Applications of a social learning theory of personality.* New York: Holt, Rinehart & Winston.

Rotter, J. B., & Hochreich, D. J. (1975). *Personality.* Glenview, IL: Scott, Foresman.

Rotter, J. B., & Rafferty, J. E. (1950). *Manual for the Rotter Incomplete Sentences Blank, col-*

*lege form.* New York: Psychological Corporation.

Rotter, J. B., & Wickens, D. D. (1948). The consistency and generality of ratings of "social aggressiveness" made from observations of role playing situations. *Journal of Consulting Psychology, 12,* 234–239.

Rowe, D. (1994). *The limits of family influence: Genes, experience, and behavior.* New York: Guilford.

Rubin, J. Z., Provenzano, F. J., & Luria, Z. (1974). The eye of the beholder: Parents' views on sex of newborns. *American Journal of Orthopsychiatry, 44,* 512–519.

Runyan, W. M. (1988). Progress in psychobiography. *Journal of Personality, 56,* 295–326.

Rushton, J. P. (1988). Race differences in behavior: Testing an evolutionary hypothesis. *Personality and Individual Differences, 9,* 329–333.

Rushton, J. P. (1989). Genetic similarity, human altruism, and group selection (with commentaries and response). *Behavioral and Brain Sciences, 12,* 503–559.

Rushton, J. P. (1990). Sir Francis Galton, epigenetic rules, genetic similarity theory, and human life history analysis. *Journal of Personality, 58,* 117–140.

Rushton, J. P., Russell, R. J. H., & Wells, P. A. (1984). Genetic similarity theory: Beyond kin selection. *Behavior Genetics, 14,* 179–193.

Ryan, A. M., & Sackett, P. R. (1987). Pre-employment honesty testing: Fakeability, reactions of test takers, and company image. *Journal of Business and Psychology, 1,* 248–256.

Rychlak, J. F. (1981). *Introduction to personality and psychotherapy* (2nd ed.). Boston: Houghton Mifflin.

Ryckman, R. M., Robbins, M. A., Thornton, B., & Cantrell, P. (1982). Development and validation of a physical self-efficacy scale. *Journal of Personality and Social Psychology, 42,* 891–900.

Samelson, F. (1980). J. B. Watson's Little Albert, Cyril Burt's twins, and the need for a critical science. *American Psychologist, 35,* 619–625.

Samuda, R. J. (1975). *Psychological testing of American minorities: Issues and consequences.* New York: Harper & Row.

Sarason, I. G. (1978). The Test Anxiety Scale: Concept and research. In C. D. Spielberger & I. G. Sarason (Eds.), *Stress and anxiety* (Vol. 5). Washington, DC: Hemisphere.

Sarason, I. G. (1980). Introduction to the study of test anxiety. In I. G. Sarason (Ed.), *Test anxiety: Theory, research, and applications.* Hillsdale, NJ: Erlbaum.

Sarason, I. G. (1984). Stress, anxiety, and cognitive interference: Reactions to tests. *Journal of Personality and Social Psychology, 46,* 929–938.

Sattler, J. M., & Gwynne, J. (1982). White examiners generally do not impede the intelligence test performance of black children: To debunk a myth. *Journal of Consulting and Clinical Psychology, 50,* 196–208.

Saucier, G. (1992). Openness versus intellect: Much ado about nothing? *European Journal of Personality, 6,* 381–386.

Saucier, G., & Goldberg, L. R. (1996).The language of personality: Lexical perspectives on the Five-Factor Model. In J. S. Wiggins (Ed.), *The Five-Factor Model of personality: Theoretical perspectives* (pp. 21–50). New York: Guilford Press.

Scarr, S., Webber, P. L., Weinberg, R. A., & Wittig, M. A. (1981). Personality resemblance among adolescents and their parents in biologically related and adoptive families. *Journal of Personality and Social Psychology, 40,* 885–898.

Scarr, S., & Weinberg, R. A. (1976). I.Q. test performance of black children adopted by white families. *American Psychologist, 31,* 726–739.

Schachter, S., & Singer, S. E. (1962). Cognitive, social, and physiological determinants of emotional state. *Psychological Review, 69,* 379–399.

Schaffer, K. F. (1981). *Sex roles and human behavior.* Cambridge, MA: Winthrop.

Schank, R. C., & Abelson, R. P. (1977). *Scripts,*

*plans, goals, and understanding.* Hillsdale, NJ: Erlbaum.

Scheier, M. F., & Carver, C. S. (1987). Dispositional optimism and physical well-being: The influence of generalized outcome expectancies on health. *Journal of Personality, 55,* 169–210.

Scheier, M. F., Matthews, K. A., Owens, J. F., Magovern, G. J., Sr., Lefebvre, R. C., Abbott, R. A., & Carver, C. S. (1989). Dispositional optimism and recovery from coronary artery bypass surgery: The beneficial effects on physical and psychological well-being. *Journal of Personality and Social Psychology, 57,* 1024–1040.

Scheinfeld, A. (1944). The Kallikaks after thirty years. *Journal of Heredity, 35,* 259–264.

Scherwitz, L. W., Perkins, L. L., Chesney, M. A., Hughes, G. H., Sidney, S., & Manolio, T. A. (1992). Hostility and health behaviors of young adults: The CARDIA study. *American Journal of Epidemiology, 136,* 136–145.

Schlegel, W. S. (1983). Genetic foundations of social behavior. *Personality and Individual Differences, 4,* 483–490.

Schneider, D. J. (1991). Social cognition. *Annual Review of Psychology, 42,* 527–561.

Scogin, F., Schumacher, J., Gardner, J., & Chaplin, W. (1995). Predictive validity of psychological testing in law enforcement settings. *Professional Psychology: Research and Practice, 26,* 68- 71.

Scott, W. A., & Johnson, R. C. (1972). Comparative validities of direct and indirect personality tests. *Journal of Consulting and Clinical Psychology, 38,* 301–318.

Scroggs, J. R. (1985). *Key ideas in personality theory.* St. Paul, MN: West.

Sears, R. R., Rau, L., & Alpert, R. (1965). *Identification and child rearing.* Stanford, CA: Stanford University Press.

Sechrest, L. (1977). Personal constructs theory. In R. J. Corsini (Ed.), *Current personality theories.* Itasca, IL: F. E. Peacock Publishers, Inc.

Seligman, M. E. P. (1975). *Helplessness: On depression, development, and death.* San Francisco: W. H. Freeman.

Selverston, A. I. (1988). A consideration of invertebrate central pattern generators as computational data. *Neural Networks, 1,* 109–117.

Selye, H. (1956). *The stress of life.* New York: McGraw-Hill.

Selye, H. (1974). *Stress without distress.* Philadelphia: J. B. Lippincott.

Shaw, M. L. G. (Ed.). (1981). *Recent advances in personal construct technology.* New York: Academic Press.

Shaywitz, B. A., Shaywitz, S. E., Pugh, K. R., et al. (1995). Sex differences in the functional organization of the brain for language. *Nature, 373,* 607–609.

Sheldon, W. H., & Stevens, S. S. (1942). *The varieties of temperament: A psychology of constitutional differences.* New York: Harper & Bros.

Sheldon, W. H., Stevens, S. S., & Tucker, W. B. (1940). *The varieties of human physique: An introduction to constitutional psychology.* New York: Harper & Bros.

Shepard, I. I. & Duston, R. L. (1987). *Workplace privacy: Employee testing surveillance, wrongful discharge, and other areas of vulnerability.* Washington, DC: Bureau of National Affairs.

Shields, S. A. (1975). Functionalism, Darwinism, and the psychology of women: A study in social myth. *American Psychologist, 30,* 739–754.

Shoben, E. J. (1954). Theoretical frames of reference in clinical psychology. In L. A. Pennington, & I. A. Berg, (Eds.), *An introduction to clinical psychology* (2nd ed.). New York: Ronald Press.

Shrauger, J. S., & Schoneman, T. J. (1979). Symbolic interactionist view of self-concept: Through the looking glass darkly. *Psychological Bulletin, 86,* 549–573.

Shultz, D. P., & Shultz, S. E. (1990). *Psychology and industry today: An introduction to industrial and organizational psychology (5th ed.).* New York: Macmillan.

Shweder, R. A. (1982). Fact and artifact in trait perception: The systematic distortion hypothesis. In B.A. Maher & W. B. Maher

(Eds.), *Progress in experimental personality research* (Vol. 11, pp. 65–95). New York: Academic Press.

Siegel, S. (1983). Classical conditioning, drug tolerance, and drug dependence. In Y. Israel, F. B. Glaser, H. Kalant, R. E. Popham, W. Schmidt, & R. G. Smart (Eds.), *Research advances in alcohol and drug problems (Vol. 7).* New York: Plenum Press.

Siegler, R. (1983). Information processing approaches to development. In P. H. Mussen (Ed.), *Handbook of child psychology* (4th ed., Vol. 2, No. 1). New York: Wiley.

Siegman, A. W. (1994). From Type A to hostility to anger: Reflections on the history of coronary-prone behavior. In A. W. Siegman & T. W. Smith (Eds.), *Anger, hostility and the heart.* Hillsdale, NJ: Erlbaum.

Siegman, A. W., Dembroski, T. M., & Ringel, N. (1987). Components of hostility and the severity of coronary artery disease. *Psychosomatic Medicine, 49,* 127–135.

Siipola, E. M. (1984). Thematic Apperception Test. In R. J. Corsini (Ed.), *Encyclopedia of Psychology.* New York: Wiley-Interscience.

Silverman, L. H. (1976). Psychoanalytic theory: The reports of my death are greatly exaggerated. *American Psychologist, 31,* 621–637.

Silverman, L. H., & Weinberger, J. (1985). Mommy and I are one: Implications for psychotherapy. *American Psychologist, 40,* 1296–1308.

Simonoff, E., Pickles, A., Hewitt, J., Silberg, J., Rutter, M., Loeber, R., Meyer, J., Neale, M., & Eaves, L. (1995). Multiple raters of disruptive child behavior: Using a genetic strategy to examine shared views and bias. *Behavior Genetics, 25,* 311–326.

Simpson, M. T., Olewine, D. A., Jenkins, F. H., Ramsey, S. J., Zyzanski, S. J., Thomas, G., & Hames, C. G. (1974). Exercise-induced catecholamines and platelet aggregation in the coronary-prone behavior pattern. *Psychosomatic Medicine, 36,* 476–487.

Singer, J. L. (1990). Preface: A fresh look at repression, dissociation, and defenses as mechanisms and as personality styles. In J. L. Singer (Ed.), *Repression and dissociation: Implications for personality theory, psychopathology, and health* (pp. xi-xxi). Chicago: University of Chicago Press.

Skinner, B. F. (1938). *The behavior of organisms.* New York: Appleton-Century-Crofts.

Skinner, B. F. (1948). *Walden two.* New York: Macmillan.

Skinner, B. F. (1953). *Science and human behavior.* New York: Macmillan.

Skinner, B. F. (1969). *Contingencies of reinforcement: A theoretical analysis.* New York: Appleton-Century-Crofts.

Skinner, B. F. (1971). *Beyond freedom and dignity.* New York: Knopf.

Skodak, M., & Skeels, H. M. (1949). A final follow-up of one hundred adopted children. *Journal of Genetic Psychology, 75,* 85–125.

Skodol, A. E., & Perry, J. C. (1993). Should an axis for defense mechanisms be included in DSM-IV? *Comprehensive Psychiatry, 34,* 108–119.

Sloane, K. D., & Sosniak, L. A. (1985). The development of accomplished sculptures. In B. S. Bloom (Ed.). *Developing talent in young people.* New York: Ballantine Books.

Slovic, P. (1995). The construction of preference. *American Psychologist, 50,* 364–371.

Smith, M. L., Glass, G. V., & Miller, T. I. (1980).*The benefits of psychotherapy.* Baltimore: Johns Hopkins University Press.

Smith, E. E., & Medin, D. L. (1981). *Categories and concepts.* Cambridge, MA: Harvard University Press.

Smith, T. W. (1992). Hostility and health: Current status of a psychosomatic hypothesis. *Health Psychology, 11,* 139–150.

Smith, T. W., & Anderson, N. B. (1986). Models of personality and disease: An interactional approach to Type A behavior and cardiovascular risk. *Journal of Personality and Social Psychology, 50,* 1166–1173.

Snyder, C. R. (1995). Conceptualizing, measuring, and nurturing hope. *Journal of Counseling and Development, 73,* 355–360.

Spanos, N. P. (1986). Hypnotic behavior: A social psychological interpretation of amnesia, analgesia, and "trance logic." *Behavioral and Brain Science, 9,* 449–467.

Spanos, N. P., Burnley, M. C., & Cross, P. A. (1993). Response expectancies and interpretations as determinants of hypnotic responding. *Journal of Personality and Social Psychology, 65,* 1237–1242.

Spanos, N. P., Burgess, C. A., DuBreuil, S. C., & Liddy, S. (1995). The effects of simulation and expectancy instructions on responses to cognitive skill training for enhancing hypnotizability. *Contemporary Hypnosis, 12,* 1–11.

Spearman, C. (1923). *The nature of "intelligence" and the principle of cognition.* London: Macmillan.

Spence, J. T., Helmreich, R. L., & Stapp, J. (1975). Ratings of self and peers on sex-role attributes and their relation to self-esteem and conceptions of masculinity and femininity. *Journal of Personality and Social Psychology, 32,* 29–39.

Spence, K. W. (1958). A theory of emotionally based drive (D) and its relation to performance in simple learning situations. *American Psychologist, 31,* 131–141.

Sperry, R. W. (1982). Some effects of disconnecting the cerebral hemispheres. *Science, 217,* 1223–1226.

Spielberger, C. D. (1966). *Anxiety and behavior.* New York: Academic Press.

Spielberger, C. D., Gorsuch, R. L., & Lushene, R. E. (1970). *The State-Trait Anxiety Inventory (STAI) Test Manual for Form X.* Palo Alto, CA: Consulting Psychologists Press.

Springer, S. P., & Deutsch, G. (1981). *Left brain, right brain.* San Francisco: W. H. Freeman.

Spuhler, J. N. (1967). Behavior and mating patterns in human populations. In J. N. Spuhler (Ed.), *Genetic diversity and human behavior* (pp. 241–268). Chicago: Aldine.

Staats, A. W. (1975). *Social behaviorism.* Chicago, IL: Dorsey.

Staats, A. W., & Staats, C. K. (1963). *Complex human behavior.* New York: Holt, Rinehart & Winston.

Stanton, A. L., & Gallant, S. J. (Eds.) (1995). *The psychology of women's health.* Washington, DC: American Psychological Association.

"A star cries incest." (1991, October 7). *People,* pp. 84–88.

Stephens, M. A. P., & Zarit, S. H. (1989). Symposium: Family caregiving to dependent older adults: Stress, appraisal, and coping. *Psychology and Aging, 4,* 387–388.

Stephenson, W. (1953). *The Study of Behavior.* Chicago: University of Chicago Press.

Sternberg, R. J. (1985a). *Beyond the IQ: A triarchic theory of human intelligence.* Cambridge, England: Cambridge University Press.

Sternberg, R. J. (1985b). Implicit theories of intelligence, creativity, and wisdom. *Journal of Personality and Social Psychology, 49,* 607–627.

Sternberg, R. J. (1995). For whom does *The Bell Curve Toll? It tolls for you.* Washington, D. C.: EdPress.

Sternberg, R. J., Conway, B. E., Ketron, J. L., & Bernstein, M. (1981). People's conceptions of intelligence. *Journal of Personality and Social Psychology, 41,* 37–55.

Sternberg, R. J., & Detterman, D. K. (Eds.). (1986). *What is intelligence? Contemporary viewpoints on its nature and definition.* Norwood, NJ: Ablex.

Sternberg, R. J., & Wagner, R. K. (Eds.). (1986). *Practical intelligence: Nature and origins of competence in the everyday world.* New York: Cambridge University Press.

Sternglanz, S. H., & Serbin, L. A. (1974). Sex role stereotyping in children's television programs. *Developmental Psychology, 10,* 710–715.

Stevenson-Hinde, J., & Zunz, M. (1978). Subjective assessment of individual rhesus monkeys. *Primates, 19,* 473–482.

Stoler, N. (1963). Client likability: A variable in the study of psychotherapy. *Journal of Consulting Psychology, 27,* 175–178.

Stone, A. A., Kessler, R. C., & Haythornthwaite, J. A. (1991). Measuring daily events and experiences: Decisions for the researcher. Special Issue: Personality and daily experience. *Journal of Personality, 59,* 575–607.

Strickland, B. R. (1977). Internal-external control of reinforcement. In T. Bass (Ed.), *Personal-*

*ity variables in social behavior*. Hillsdale, NJ: Erlbaum.

Strickland, B. R. (1979). Internal-external expectancies and cardiovascular functioning. In L. C. Perlmuter & R. A. Monty (Eds.), *Choice and perceived control*. Hillsdale, NJ: Erlbaum.

Strickland, B. R. (1989). Internal-external control expectancies: From contingency to creativity. *American Psychologist, 44*, 1–12.

Strong, E. K., Jr. (1927). *Vocational Interest Blank*. Stanford, CA: Stanford University Press.

Strong, E. K., Jr. (1943). *Vocational interests of men and women*. Stanford, CA: Stanford University Press.

Strube, M. J. (1989). Evidence for the *type* in Type A behavior: A taxometric analysis. *Journal of Personality and Social Psychology, 56*, 972–987.

Strube, M. J., Lott, C. L., Heilizer, R., & Gregg, B. (1986). Type A behavior pattern and the judgment of control. *Journal of Personality and Social Psychology, 50*, 403–412.

Strube, M. J., & Werner, C. (1985). Relinquishment of control and the Type A behavior pattern. *Journal of Personality and Social Psychology, 48*, 688–701.

Sullivan, H. S. (1953). *The interpersonal theory of psychiatry*. New York: Norton.

Sullivan, H. S. (1964). *The fusion of psychiatry and social science*. New York: Norton.

Suls, J., and Rittenhouse, J. D. (1987). Personality and physical health: An introduction. *Journal of Personality, 55*, 155–167.

Suls, J., & Wan, C. K. (1989). The relation between Type A behavior and chronic emotional distress: A meta-analysis. *Journal of Personality and Social Psychology, 57*, 503–512.

Sundberg, N. D., Snowden, L. R., & Reynolds, W. M. (1978). Toward assessment of personal competence and incompetence in life situations. In M. R. Rosenzweig & L. W. Porter (Eds.), *Annual review of psychology* (Vol. 29). Palo Alto, CA: Annual Reviews.

Suppe, F. (1977). *The structure of scientific theories*. Urbana: University of Illinois Press.

Swann, W. B. (1984). Quest for accuracy in person perception: A matter of pragmatics. *Psychological Review, 91*, 457–477.

Swede, S.W., & Tetlock, P.E. (1986). Henry Kissinger's implicit theory of personality: A quantitative case study. *Journal of Personality, 54*, 617–646.

Swiezy, N. B., Matson, J. L., & Box, P. (1992). The Good Behavior Game: A token reinforcement system for preschoolers. *Child and Family Behavior Therapy, 14*, 21–32.

Symons, D. (1990). On the use and misuse of Darwinism in the study of human behavior. In J. Barkow, L. Cosmides, & J. Tooby (Eds.), *The adapted mind: Evolutionary psychology and the generation of culture*. New York: Oxford University Press.

Taft, R. (1955). The ability to judge people. *Psychological Bulletin, 52*, 1–23.

Tambs, K., Sundet, J. M., Eaves, L., Solaas, M. H., & Berg, K. (1991). Pedigree analysis of Eysenck Personality Questionnaire (EPQ) scores on monozygotic (MZ) twin families. *Behavior Genetics, 21*, 369–382.

Tanaka, J. S., Panter, A. T., & Winborne, W. C. (1988). Dimensions of the need for cognition: Subscales and gender differences. *Multivariate Behavioral Research, 23*, 35–50.

Tangney, J. P., & Feshbach, S. (1988). Children's television-viewing frequency: Individual differences and demographic correlates. *Personality and Social Psychology Bulletin, 14*, 145–158.

Taylor, F. W. (1911). *Scientific management*. New York: Harper.

Taylor, J. A. (1953). A personality scale of manifest anxiety. *Journal of Abnormal and Social Psychology, 48*, 285–290.

Taylor, M. C., & Hall, J. A. (1982). Psychological androgyny: Theories, methods, and conclusions. *Psychological Bulletin, 92*, 347–366.

Tellegen, A. (1982). Brief manual for the Differential Personality Questionnaire. Unpublished manuscript: University of Minnesota.

Tellegen, A. (1987). Discussion: Hypnosis and absorption. Paper presented at the 38th annual meeting of the Society for Clinical and Experimental Hypnosis, Los Angeles.

Tellegen, A. (1993). Folk-concepts and psychological concepts of personality and personality disorder. *Psychological Inquiry, 4,* 122–130.

Tellegen, A. & Atkinson, G. (1974). Openness to absorbing and self-altering experiences ("absorption"), a trait related to hypnotic susceptibility. *Journal of Abnormal Psychology, 83,* 268–277.

Tellegen, A., Lykken, D. T., Bouchard, T. J., Jr., Wilcox, K.J., Segal, N. L., & Rich, S. (1988). Personality similarity in twins reared apart and together. *Journal of Personality and Social Psychology, 54,* 1031–1039.

Tellegen, A., & Waller, N. G. (1987). Reexamining basic dimensions of natural language trait descriptors. *95th annual meeting of the American Psychological Association.* (abstract).

Tennen, H., Suls, J., & Affleck, G. (1991). Personality and daily experience: The promise and the challenge. *Journal of Personality, 59,* 313–338.

Thomas, A., & Chess, S. (1977). *Temperament and development.* New York: Bruner/Mazel.

Thompson, E. P., Chaiken, S., & Hazelwood, J. D. (1993). Need for cognition and desire for control as moderators of extrinsic reward effects: A person x situation approach to the study of intrinsic motivation. *Journal of Personality and Social Psychology, 64,* 987–999.

Thorndike, E. L. (1905). *The elements of psychology.* New York: A. G. Seiler.

Thorndike, E. L., Bregman, E. O., Cobb, M. V., & Woodyard, E. (1926). *The measurement of intelligence.* New York: Teachers College, Columbia University.

Thorndike, R. L., Hagen, E. P., & Sattler, J. M. (1986). *Guide for administering and scoring the fourth edition of the Stanford-Binet Intelligence Scale.* Chicago: Riverside Publishing Co.

Thorne, A. (1989). Conditional patterns, transference, and the coherence of personality across time. In D. M. Buss & N. Cantor (Eds.), *Personality psychology: Recent trends and emerging directions* (pp. 149–159). New York: Springer.

Thurstone, L. L. (1938). Primary mental abilities. *Psychometric Monographs,* No. 1.

Tice, D. M., & Baumeister, R. F. (1990). Self-esteem, self-handicapping, and self-presentation: The strategy of inadequate practice. *Journal of Personality, 58,* 443–464.

Tomkins, S. S. (1987). Script theory. In J. Aronoff, A. I. Rabin, & R. A. Zucker (Eds.), *The emergence of personality* (pp. 147–216). New York: Springer.

Tomlinson, T. M., & Hart, J. T., Jr. (1962). A validation study of the Process Scale. *Journal of Consulting Psychology, 26,* 74–78.

Tooby, J., & Cosmides, L. (1990). On the universality of human nature and the uniqueness of the individual: The role of genetics and adaptation. *Journal of Personality, 58,* 17–68.

Towbes, L. C., Cohen, L. H., & Glyshaw, K. (1989). Instrumentality as a life-stress moderator for early versus middle adolescents. *Journal of Personality and Social Psychology, 57,* 109–119.

Trivers, R. L. (1972). Parental investment and sexual selection. In B. Campbell (Ed.), *Sexual selection and the descent of man: 1871–1971* (pp. 136–179). Chicago: Aldine.

Truax, C. B. (1966). Reinforcement and nonreinforcement in Rogerian psychotherapy. *Journal of Abnormal Psychology, 71,* 1–9.

Turner, J. A., Deyo, R. A., Loeser, J. D., & Von Korff, M. (1994).The importance of placebo effects in pain treatment and research. *JAMA: Journal of the American Medical Association, 271,* 1609–1614.

Turner, J. H. (1970). Entrepreneurial environments and the emergence of achievement motivation in adolescent males. *Sociometry, 33,* 147–165.

U.S. Congress, Office of Technology Assessment (1990). *The use of integrity tests for pre-employment screening. (OTA-SET–442).* Washington, DC: U. S. Government Printing Office.

Ullmann, L. P., & Krasner, L. (1975). *A psychological approach to abnormal behavior.* Englewood Cliffs, NJ: Prentice-Hall.

Unger, R., & Crawford, M. (1992). *Women and gender: A feminist psychology.* New York: McGraw-Hill.

Unger, R. K. (1979). *Female and male: Psychological perspectives.* New York: Harper & Row.

Vaillant, G. E. (1992). The struggle for empirical assessment of defenses. In G. E. Vaillant (Ed.),

*Ego mechanisms of defense: A guide for clinicians and researchers* (pp. 89–103). Washington, D C: American Psychiatric Press.

Van De Water, D. A., & McAdams, D. P. (1989). Generativity and Erikson's "belief in the species." *Journal of Research in Personality, 23,* 435–449.

van Kaam, A. (1966). *Existential foundations of psychology.* Pittsburgh, PA: Duquesne University Press.

Van Lawick-Goodall, J. (1968). The behavior of free-living chimpanzees in the Gombe Stream Reserve. *Animal Behavior Monograph, 1,* 161–311.

Vandenberg, S. G. (1967). Heredity factors in normal personality traits (as measured by inventories). In J. Wortis (Ed.), *Recent advances in biological psychiatry, 9,* 65–104. New York: Plenum Press.

Vernon, P. E. (1933). Some characteristics of the good judge of personality. *Journal of Social Psychology, 4,* 42–57.

Vockell, E. L., Felker, D. W., & Miley, C. H. (1973). Birth order literature 1967–1972. *Journal of Individual Psychology, 29,* 39–53.

Vroom, V. H. (1964). *Work and motivation.* New York: Wiley.

Vroom, V. H., & Yetten, P. W. (1973). *Leadership and decision-making.* Pittsburgh, PA: University of Pittsburgh Press.

Wagner, K. D., Lorion, R. P., & Shipley, T. E. (1983). Insomnia and psychological crisis: Two studies of Erikson's developmental theory. *Journal of Consulting and Clinical Psychology, 51,* 595–603.

Wahba, M. A., and Bridwell, L. G. (1976). Maslow reconsidered: A review of research on the need hierarchy theory. *Organizational Behavior and Human Performance, 15,* 212–240.

Waldron, I. (1976). Why do women live longer than men? Part I. *Journal of Human Stress, 2,* 2–13.

Waldron, I. (1983). Sex differences in illness incidence, prognosis and mortality: Issues and evidence. *Social Science and Medicine, 17,* 1107–1123.

Wallach, M. A. (1971). *The intelligence/creativity distinction.* Morristown, NJ: General Learning Press.

Wallach, M. A., & Wallach, L. (1983). *Psychology's sanction for selfishness: The error of egoism in theory and therapy.* San Francisco: W. H. Freeman.

Wallen, K. (1992). Evolutionary hypothesis testing: Consistency is not enough. *Behavioral and Brain Sciences, 15,* 118–119.

Wallston, B. S., Wallston, K. A., Kaplan, G. D., & Maides, S. A. (1976). Development and validation of the Health Locus of Control (HLC) Scale. *Journal of Consulting and Clinical Psychology, 44,* 580–585.

Watson, D., & Clark, L. A. (1984). Negative affectivity: The disposition to experience aversive emotional states. *Psychological Bulletin, 96,* 465–490.

Watson, D., Clark, L. A., McIntyre, C. W., & Hamaker, S. (1992). Affect, personality, and social activity. *Journal of Personality and Social Psychology, 63,* 1011–1025.

Watson, D., & Pennebaker, J. W. (1989). Health complaints, stress, and distress: Exploring the central role of negative affectivity. *Psychological Review, 96,* 234–254.

Watson, J. B. (1919). *Psychology from the standpoint of a behaviorist.* Philadelphia: Lippincott.

Watson, J. B. (1930). *Behaviorism* (2nd ed.). Chicago: University of Chicago Press.

Watson, J. B., & Rayner, R. (1920). Conditional emotional reactions. *Journal of Experimental Psychology, 3,* 1–14.

Wechsler, D. (1939). *The measurement of adult intelligence.* Baltimore, MD: Williams & Wilkins.

Wechsler, D. (1949). *Wechsler Intelligence Scale for Children.* New York: Psychological Corporation.

Wechsler, D. (1955). *Manual for the Wechsler Adult Intelligence Scale.* New York: Psychological Corporation.

Wechsler, D. (1967). *Manual for the Wechsler Preschool and Primary Scale of Intelligence.* New York: Psychological Corporation.

Wechsler, D. (1974). *Manual: Wechsler Intelligence Scale for Children* (rev.). New York: Psychological Corporation.

Wechsler, D. (1981). *Manual for the Wechsler*

*Adult Intelligence Scale* (rev.). New York: Psychological Corporation.

Weinberg, R. A. (1989). Intelligence and IQ: Landmark issues and great debates. *American Psychologist, 44*, 98–104.

Weinberger, D. A. (1990). The construct validity of the repressive coping style. In J. L. Singer (Ed.) *Repression and dissociation: Implications for personality theory, psychopathology, and health* (pp. 337–386). Chicago: University of Chicago Press.

Weiss, D. S., & Mendelsohn, G. A. (1986). An empirical demonstration of the implausibility of the semantic similarity explanation of how trait ratings are made and what they mean. *Journal of Personality and Social Psychology, 50,* 595–601.

West, S. G., & Hepworth, J. T. (1991). Statistical issues in the study of temporal data: Daily experiences. Special Issue: Personality and daily experience. *Journal of Personality, 59,* 609–662.

Westen, D. (1995).The clinical-empirical model of personality: Life after the Mischelian ice age and the Neo-Lithic era. *Journal of Personality, 63,* 495–524.

White, R. W. (1959). Motivation reconsidered: The concept of competence. *Psychological Review, 66,* 279–333.

White, R. W. (1976). *The enterprise of living: A view of personal growth* (2nd ed.). New York: Holt, Rinehart & Winston.

White, R. W. (1981). Exploring personality the long way: The study of lives. In A. I. Rabin, J. Aronoff, A. M. Barclay, & R. A. Zucker (Eds.), *Further explorations in personality.* New York: Wiley-Interscience.

Whiting, J. W. M. (1960). Resource mediation and learning by identification. In I. Iscoe & H. W. Stevenson (Eds.), *Personality development in children.* Austin: University of Texas Press.

Whitney, G. (1995). *Presidential address.* At the Annual convention of the Behavior Genetics Association in Richmond, VA.

Widiger, T. A. (1993). The DSM-III-R categorical personality disorder diagnoses: A critique and an alternative. *Psychological Inquiry, 4,* 71–93.

Widiger, T. A., & Trull, T. J. (1992). Personality and psychopathology: An application of the five-factor model. *Journal of Personality, 60,* 363–393.

Wiggins, J. S. (1973). *Personality and prediction: Principles of personality assessment.* Reading, MA: Addison-Wesley.

Wiggins, J. S., & Holzmuller, A. (1981). Further evidence on androgyny and interpersonal flexibility. *Journal of Research in Personality, 15,* 67–80.

Wiggins, J. S., & Pincus, A. L. (1992). Personality: Structure and assessment. *Annual Review of Psychology, 43,* 473–504.

Williams, J. E., & Bennett, S. M. (1975). The definition of sex stereotypes via the Adjective Check List. *Sex Roles, 1,* 327–337.

Williams, J. E., & Best, D. L. (1977). Sex stereotypes and trait favorability on the Adjective Check List. *Educational and Psychological Measurement, 37,* 101–110.

Williams, J. E., & Best, D. L. (1990). *Measuring sex stereotypes: A multination study.(Rev. Ed.).* Newbury Park, CA: Sage.

Williams, R. (1994). Your anger can kill you. *Health Confidential, 8,* 5+.

Williams, R. L. (1972, September). *The BITCH–100: A culture-specific test.* Paper presented at the meetings of the American Psychological Association, Honolulu.

Wilson, D. S., & Sober, E. (1994). Reintroducing group selection to the human behavioral sciences. *Behavioral and Brain Sciences, 17,* 585–654.

Wilson, E. O. (1975). *Sociobiology: The new synthesis.* Cambridge, MA: Harvard University Press.

Wilson, J. J., Chaplin, W. F., Foster, C. W., & White, A. (1996). Non-normative standards of evaluation: Implications for psychological research and personal well-being. Unpublished manuscript, University of Alabama.

Wilson, J. J., Chaplin, W. F., & Thorn, B. E. (1995).The influence of different standards on the evaluation of pain: Implications for assessment and treatment. *Behavior Therapy, 26,* 217–239.

Winnicott, D. W. (1953). Transitional objects and

transitional phenomena. *International Journal of Psychoanalysis, 34,* 89–97.

Winter, D. G., & Stewart, A. J. (1978). The power motive. In H. London & J. E. Exner, Jr. (Eds.), *Dimensions of personality.* New York: Wiley-Interscience.

Witelsen, S. F., Glaser, I. I., & Kiger, D. L. (1994). Sex differences in numerical density of neurons in human auditory association cortex. *Society for Neuroscience Abstracts, 30,* Abstract No. 582.12.

Witkin, H. A., Dyk, R. B., Faterson, H. F., Goodenough, D. R., & Karp, S. A. (1962). *Psychological differentiation.* New York: Wiley.

Witkin, H. A., Lewis, H. B., Hertzman, M., Machover, K., Meissner, P. B., & Wapner, S. (1954). *Personality through perception: An experimental and clinical study.* New York: Harper.

Wittgenstein, L. (1953). *Philosophical investigations.* New York: Macmillan

Wogan, M., & Norcross, J. C. (1982). Sauce for the goose: A response to Wolpe. *American Psychologist, 37,* 100–102. (Comment)

Wolberg, L. R. (1948). *Medical hypnosis: The principles of hypnotherapy* (Vol. 1). New York: Grune & Stratton.

Wolf, M., Risley, T., & Mees, H. (1964). Application of operant conditioning procedures to the behavior problems of an autistic child. *Behavior Research and Therapy, 1,* 305–312.

Wolfe, T. (1929). *Look homeward, angel.* New York: Scribner's.

Wolpe, J. (1958). *Psychotherapy by reciprocal inhibition.* Stanford, CA: Stanford University Press.

Wolpe, J. (1973). *The practice of behavior therapy* (2nd ed.). New York: Pergamon Press.

Wolpe, J. (1981). Behavior therapy versus psychoanalysis: Therapeutic and social implications. *American Psychologist, 36,* 159–164.

Wolpe, J., & Lang, P. J. (1964). A fear survey schedule for use in behavior therapy. *Behavior Research and Therapy, 2,* 27–30.

Wolpe, J., & Lazarus, A. A. (1966). *Behavior therapy techniques.* New York: Pergamon Press.

Woodward, W. R. (1982). The "discovery" of social behaviorism and social learning theory, 1870–1980. *American Psychologist, 37,* 396–410.

Woolfolk, R. L., Novalany, J., Gara, M. A., Allen, L. A., & Polino, M. (1995). Self-complexity, self-evaluation, and depression: An examination of form and content within self-schema. *Journal of Personality and Social Psychology, 68,* 1108–1120.

Woolfolk, R. L., & Richardson, F. C. (1978). *Stress, sanity, and survival.* New York: Sovereign/Monarch.

Wright, E. (1992). *Feminism and psychoanalysis: A critical dictionary.* Cambridge, MA: Blackwell.

Wright, L. (1988). The Type A behavior pattern and coronary artery disease: Quest for the active ingredients and the elusive mechanism. *American Psychologist, 43,* 2–14.

Wright, S. (1921). Systems of mating. *Genetics, 6,* 111–178.

Wright, T. L., Maggied, P., & Palmer, M. L. (1975). An unobtrusive study of interpersonal trust. *Journal of Personality and Social Psychology, 32,* 446–448.

Wrightsman, L. S. (1981). Personal documents as data in conceptualizing adult personality development. *Personality and Social Psychology Bulletin, 7,* 367–385.

Wyer, R. S., & Srull, T. K. (1986). Human cognition in its social context. *Psychological Review, 93,* 322–359.

Wylie, R. (1984). Self-concept. In R. Corsini (Ed.), *Encyclopedia of psychology* (Vol. 3). New York: Wiley-Interscience.

Yankelovich, D. (1979). Work, values, and the new breed. In C. Kerr & J. M. Rosow (Eds.), *Work in America: The decade ahead.* New York: Van Nostrand Reinhold.

Young, W. C., Goy, R. W., & Phoenix, C. H. (1964). Hormones and sexual behavior. *Science, 143,* 212–218.

Zadeh, L. A. (1975). *Fuzzy sets and their application to cognitive and decision processes.* New York: Academic Press.

Zammuner, V. L. (1987). Children's sex-role stereotypes: A cross-cultural analysis. In P. Shaver & C. Hendrick (Eds.), *Sex and gender: Review of Personality and Social Psychology* (Vol. 7). Beverly Hills, CA: Sage.

Zeller, A. (1950). An experimental analogue of repression: II. The effect of individual failure and success on memory measured by relearning. *Journal of Experimental Psychology, 40,* 411–422.

Zigler, E., & Valentine, J. (Eds.) (1979). *Project Head Start: A legacy of the War on Poverty.* New York: Free Press.

Zinbarg, R., & Revelle, W. (1989). Personality and conditioning: A test of four models. *Journal of Personality and Social Psychology, 57,* 301–314.

Zuckerman, M. (1978). Sensation seeking. In H. London & J. Exner (Eds.), *Dimensions of personality.* New York: Wiley.

Zuckerman, M. (1984). Sensation-seeking: A comparative approach to a human trait. *Behavioral and Brain Sciences, 7,* 913–971.

Zuckerman, M. (1992). What is a basic factor and which factors are basic? Turtles all the way down. *Personality and Individual Differences, 13,* 675–681.

Zuckerman, M. (1994). *Behavioral expressions and biosocial bases of sensation seeking.* Cambridge, England: Cambridge University Press.

Zuckerman, M., Ballinger, J. C., & Post, R. M. (1984). The neurobiology of some dimensions of personality. *International Review of Neurobiology, 25,* 391–436.

Zuckerman, M., Bernieri, F., Koestner, R., & Rosenthal, R. (1989).To predict some of the people some of the time: In search of moderators. *Journal of Personality and Social Psychology, 57,* 279–293.

Zuckerman, M., & Como, P. (1983). Sensation-seeking and arousal systems. *Personality and Individual Differences, 4,* 381–386.

Zuckerman, M., Buchsbaum, M. S., & Murphy, D. L. (1980). Sensation seeking and its biological correlates. *Psychological Bulletin, 88,* 187–214.

Zuckerman, M., Kuhlman, M., & Camac, K. (1988). What lies beyond E and N? Factor analysis of scales believed to measure basic dimensions of personality. *Journal of Personality and Social Psychology, 54,* 96–107.

Zuroff, D. C., & Rotter, J. B. (1985). A history of the expectancy construct in psychology. In J. Dusek (Ed.), *Teacher expectancies.* Hillsdale, NJ: Erlbaum.

# Credits

## Text Credits

Page 41   From "Personality Research Methods: An Historical Perspective" by Kenneth H. Craik from *Journal of Personality* 54:1, pp. 18–51, 1986. Copyright © 1986 by Duke University Press. Reprinted by permission.

Page 50   From "Effects of Teacher Attention on Study Behavior" by R. V. Hall, D. Lund, and D. Jackson from *Journal of Applied Analysis,* 1968, 1, 1–12. Copyright © 1968 by Society for the Experimental Analysis of Behavior. Reprinted by permission.

Page 60   *From Personality and Prediction: Principles of Personality Assessment* by J. S. Wiggins. Copyright © 1973 by Alfred A. Knopf, Inc. Used with permission.

Page 73   Redrawn from *The Structure and Meaning of Psychoanalysis* by Healy, W., Bronner, A. F. and Bowers, A. M. Copyright © 1930, renewed © 1958 by Alfred A. Knopf, Inc. Reprinted by permission of the publisher.

Pages 82–83   From *Abnormal Psychology and Modern Life,* 8th Edition by Robert C. Carson, James N. Butcher, and James C. Coleman. Copyright © 1988 Scott, Foresman and Company. Reprinted by permission of Scott Foresman-Addison Wesley.

Pages 97–99   From "Impovement Without Fundamental Change" by D. R. Disher in *Essays in Individual Psychology: Contemporary Application of Alfred Adler's Theories,* ed. Kurt A. Adler and Danica Deutsch. Copyright © 1959 by Grove Press, Inc. Reprinted by permission.

Page 111   From *Personality Theories: A Comparative Analysis* by S. Maddi. Copyright © 1989, 1980, 1976, 1972, 1968 by The Dorsey Press; 1996 by Brooks/Cole Publishing Company, a division of International Thomson Publishing Inc. Reprinted by permission.

Page 135   From "The Development of Defense Mechanisms" by Phebe Cramer from *Journal of Personality* 55:4, December 1987. Copyright © 1987 by Duke University Press. Reprinted by permission.

Page 151   From *Introduction to Behavioral Genetics* by G.E. McClearn and J. DeFries. Copyright © 1973 by W. H. Freeman and Company. Used with permission.

Page 152   "A Normal Female's and Normal Male's Set of 23 Pairs of Chromosomes" by McKusick from *Human Genetics.* Copyright © 1964 by Prentice Hall Publishers. Reprinted by permission.

Page 153   "Schematic Diagram of the Structure of DNA, Showing the Pairing of the Proteins During Replication" from *Biology of the Gene,* 3rd Edition by Louis Levine. Copyright © 1980 by Louis Levine. Reprinted by permission of the author.

# Photo Credits

page 5    Copyright © 1977 by Sidney Harris – "American Scientist" magazine

page 6    Reuters/Bettmann

page 8    Copyright © Robert Brenner/PhotoEdit

page 17    Preuss/The Image Works

page 20    Drawing by Chas. Addams; copyright ©1981 The New Yorker Magazine, Inc.

page 29    Copyright © Spencer Grant/The Picture Cube

page 34    Michael Dwyer/Stock, Boston

page 56    Copyright © Michael Newman/PhotoEdit

page 66    Mary Evans/Sigmund Freud Copyrights

page 67    Corbis/Bettmann

page 69    Freud Museum, London

page 72    Superstock

page 77    Copyright © Arlene Collins/Monkmeyer Press

page 91    AP/Wide World

page 94    Copyright © Elizabeth Crews/The Image Works

page 101    Corbis/Bettmann

page 102    Granger Collection, New York

page 107    Jon Erikson

page 108    Susie Fitzburgh/Stock, Boston Standard Edition (Vol. 10) Hogarth Press (1909)

page 120    Copyright © Nita Winter/The Image Works

page 123    Press Information Bureau/Government of India

page 131    Reproduced by permission of Gerald Blum

page 133    Merim/Monkmeyer Press Photo Service

page 134    Verlag Hans Huber Bern. Copyright © 1921 (renewed 1948)

page 155    Library of Congress

page 196    Hanna Damasio MD, Professor and Director, Human Neuroanatomy and Neuroimaging Laboratory, University of Iowa

page 217    Corbis/Bettmann

page 218    Copyright © Spencer Grant/The Picture Cube

page 222    Peter Menzel/Stock, Boston

page 227    Corbis/Bettmann

page 231    Frederick Bodin/Stock, Boston

page 235    Photo by Ralph Norman. Courtesy of Brendan Mahler

page 291    Corbis/Bettmann

page 295    Goodwin/Monkmeyer Press

page 297    B.F. Skinner

page 307    (t) John Dollard

page 307    (b) Rockefeller University

page 328    Rhoda Sidney/Stock, Boston

# Author Index

Abbott, R. A., 551
Abelson, R. P., 211, 241
Acocella, J. R., 79
Adair, J. G., 572
Adams, J. S., 569
Adams, N. E., 335, 392
Adams-Webber, J. R., 235
Adler, A., 89–90
Adolphs, R., 196
Affleck, G., 44, 50
Ahadi, S. A., 565
Ahering, R. F., 521
Ahren, F. M., 183
Alavi, A., 197–198
Alderfer, C., 568
Alexander, F., 527
Alexander, I. E., 123
Alexander, R. D., 177
Alicke, M. D., 268
Allen, A., 443
Allen, B. P., 469
Allen, K. E., 298
Allen, L. A., 267
Alliger, G., 581
Alliger, G. M., 582
Allport, G. W., 8–9, 415–417, 420,
    448, 455–459, 465
Allred, K. D., 551
Almagor, M., 451, 483
Alpert, J. L., 595
Alpert, R., 608
Amabile, T. M., 518, 567, 569–570
Amaral, P., 193
American Management Association,
    578

American Psychiatric Association,
    528
American Psychological
    Association, 590
Anastasi, A., 474
Anderson, K. J., 470
Anderson, N. B., 548, 557
Anghoff, W. H., 513
Ansbacher, H. L., 91–92
Ansbacher, R. R., 91–92
Armstrong, S. L., 481
Arnold, S. E., 197–198
Aronoff, J., 256
Asch, S. E., 270–271, 277, 521
Asterita, M. F., 541
Atkins, C. J., 551
Atkinson, G., 522
Atkinson, J. W., 438, 440, 475,
    478
Auerbach, S. M., 534–535
Avila, C., 471
Ayllon, T., 324–325, 333
Azrin, N. H., 303, 324–325

Babledelis, G., 16
Bäckman, L., 543–544
Bacon, M., 21
Baer, J. S., 392
Baldwin, A., 456
Ballinger, J. C., 190
Balloun, J., 256
Banaji, M. R., 244
Bandura, A., 335, 364, 366–371,
    390–392, 394–396, 398,
    401, 551, 609

Bannister, D., 235–236
Barchas, J. D., 551
Barefoot, J. C., 549
Barge, B. N., 585
Bargh, J. A., 243
Barker, R. G., 36, 333
Barrick, M. R., 585
Barron, F. H., 518–519
Barry, H., 21
Barsalou, L. W., 481
Baruch, C., 325
Bata, I., 549
Baum, A., 535, 554–555
Baumeister, R. F., 211, 243, 443,
    543
Beach, F., 170
Beaumont, G., 190
Bechara, A., 196
Becker, W. C., 334
Beckmann, J., 121
Bee, H., 592
Begental, J. F. T., 644
Bem, D. J., 443
Bem, S. L., 612, 613
Benet, V., 451
Bennett, S. M., 592
Bentz, V. J., 577
Berger, P., 267
Berg, K., 166
Berglas, S., 243
Bernieri, F., 443
Bernstein, M., 498
Berry, J. W., 21
Best, D. L., 592–594
Bettelhein, B., 120–121

Beyer, J., 335
Bieri, J., 267
Binswanger, L., 230
Blackburn, H., 556
Black, G. W., 549
Black, J. L., 336
Blanchard, D. C., 394
Blanchard, E. B., 371
Blanchard, K., 577
Blanchard, R. J., 394
Blissett, S. E., 552
Block, J., 249, 251, 253–255, 271,
    274, 399–400, 445, 451,
    465, 472, 482, 485, 551–552
Block, J. H., 399–400, 552
Bloom, B., 518
Blu, G. S., 130
Bolger, N., 540
Bolstadt, O. D., 343
Bonarius, J. C. J., 266
Bond, M., 129
Booth-Kewley, S., 555
Bootzin, R. R., 79
Boss, M., 230
Bottome, P., 91
Botwinick, J., 39
Bouchard, T. J., 169
Bouchard, T. J., Jr., 19, 169, 181,
    183–186, 508
Bowers, A. M., 73
Bowers, K. S., 443
Box, P., 325
Boyes, M. C., 565
Brackfield, S., 567
Bradford, D. C., 332
Bray, D. W., 44, 577
Breger, L., 344
Breggin, P., 190
Bregman, E. O., 499
Brewer, M. B., 279
Brewin, C. R., 127
Bridell, D. W., 383
Bridwell, L. G., 568
Briggs, S. R., 483
Brigham, C. C., 158
Brody, E. B., 499
Brody, N., 499
Broman, S. H., 505
Brondolo, E., 325
Bronfenbrenner, U., 600
Bronner, A., 73
Broughton, R., 565
Brouillard, M. E., 392, 395

Broverman, D. M., 591–592, 595
Broverman, I. K., 591, 592, 595
Brower, A. M., 243
Brown, J. F., 121
Brown, J. S., 342
Bruch, M. A., 267
Bruner, J. S., 3, 269
Brunson, B. I., 548, 550
Brunswik, E., 443
Buchsbaum, M. S., 192
Buckalew, L. W., 383
Buckner, K. E., 51, 249, 483
Buell, J. S., 298
Burger, J. M., 385
Burgess, C. A., 384
Burke, B. W., 181
Burnham, J. C., 7
Burnley, M. C., 384
Busch, C. M., 484
Buss, A. H., 174, 202, 204
Buss, D. M., 144, 171, 174,
    176–177, 198, 200–201,
    204, 413, 447, 479–481,
    590
Butcher, J. N., 83
Butcher J. N., 83
Butler, J. M., 252
Butterfield, E. C., 15
Button, E., 235
Byrne, D., 437

Caccioppo, J. T., 521
Caddy, G. W., 383
Camac, K., 483
Camara, W. J., 581
Campbell, A., 608
Campbell, D. P., 565
Cann, D. R., 133
Cannon, W. B., 540
Canon, L. K., 38
Cantor, N., 242–243
Cantrell, P., 401
Carey, G., 183
Carlson, R., 40, 131
Carlston, D. E., 211
Carman, R. S., 388
Carson, R. C., 83
Carver, C. S., 242, 285, 548, 551
Caspi, A., 540
Casseldon, P. E., 271–272, 279
Cattell, R. B., 188, 274, 423, 426,
    429, 460, 464–467, 499, 533
Chaiken, S., 521

Chance, J. E., 380, 402
Chaplin, W. F., 33–34, 41, 51, 53,
    249, 272, 276–277, 280,
    392, 443, 469, 482–483,
    496, 533, 550, 584, 597
Cheek, J. M., 443, 570
Chesney, M. A., 549
Chess, S., 16
Chidester, T. R., 578
Child, I., 21
Chipuer, H. M., 183–185
Chodorow, N., 79
Christian, J., 129
Churchland, P. S., 206
Ciminero, A. R., 336
Cioffi, D., 392, 395
Clark, L. A., 484, 557
Clark, R. A., 438, 475, 478
Clarkson, F. E., 591, 595
Cloninger, C. R., 471–472
Clore, G. L., 482
Cobb, M. V., 499
Cohen, A. R., 521
Cohen, L. H., 552
Cole, N. S., 565
Coles, R., 106
Colten, M. E., 613
Comer Fisher, D., 271
Como, P., 433
Condrey, J., 345
Contrada, R. J., 546
Conway, B. E., 498
Conway, E., 325
Cook, W., 550
Cooley, C. H., 212–213
Coon, H., 183
Cooper, A. M., 110
Cooper, H. M., 385
Corcoran, D. W. J., 434
Corrigan, P. W., 325
Corsini, R. J., 91, 266
Cosmides, L., 171, 199
Costa, J. L., 192
Costa, P. T., 484–485, 522
Costa, P. T., Jr., 550, 557–558
Council, J. R., 384
Cox, M. G., 276
Cox, R. L., 202
Coyne, J. C., 537
Craik, K. H., 40, 413, 447,
    479–481
Crain, W. C., 121
Cramer, P., 129–130, 133, 135

Crandall, J. E., 135
Crandall, V. C., 406
Crandall, V. J., 381–382, 406
Crawford, M., 596
Crittendon, K. S., 594
Crockett, W. H., 267
Cronbach, L. J., 59, 277–278, 515
Croog, S. H., 549
Cross, P. A., 384
Curphy, G. J., 571, 576–577

Damasio, A. R., 193–196
Damasio, H., 193–196
D'Andrade, R., 271, 439
Daniels, D., 186
Darnton, N., 75
Darrow, C., 136
Darwin, C., 201
Darwin, C. R., 161
Davidson, K. W., 127, 549–550,
    556–557
Davidson, R. J., 605
Davis, F., 458
Davis, K. E., 279
Davison, G. C., 304, 323, 325, 328,
    333, 345, 544
Davis, W. L., 45
Dawkinsm R., 174
Deaux, K., 606
de Charms, R., 567
Deci, E. L., 567, 569
DeFries, J. C., 151, 168–169, 183
deGroh, M., 522
DeLongis, A., 537, 540
Dembroski, T. M., 546, 549,
    550
de Raad, B., 450, 484
Derbyshire, A., 605
Derry, P. A., 268
Detterman, D. K., 498
Deutsch, G., 605
Deyo, R. A., 384
Dickson, W. J., 571
Digman, J. M., 462, 483, 522
Disher, D. R., 97, 99
Dixon, N. F., 552
Dohrenwend, B. F., 538
Dohrenwend, B. S., 538
Dollard, J., 307–308, 313,
    315–316, 530, 542
Donahue, E. M., 484
Donderi, D. C., 133
Donovan, R. J., 566

Doob, L. W., 542
DuBreuil, S. C., 384
Dugdale, R. L., 158–159
Duke, M., 300
Dunbar, H. F., 527
Dunlap, R. L., 381
Dunning, D., 276
Duston, R. L., 578
Dweck, C. S., 479, 480
Dworkin, R. H., 181
Dyck, D. G., 268, 549
Dyk, R. B., 519–520
Dymond, R. F., 277

Eagly, A. H., 596–597
Eaves, L., 166, 180
Eckenrode, J., 540
Eckert, E., 19
Ehrhardt, A., 604
Eichorn, D., 322
Ellis, A., 328
Emmons, R. A., 242, 387
Engel, G. L., 527
Entwhistle, D. R., 476
Epstein, S., 40, 44, 129, 211, 284,
    343, 443, 445, 529
Erdelyi, M. H., 125, 127
Erikson, E. H., 105, 122
Erlenmeyer-Kimling, L., 508–509
Eron, L. D., 393
Erskine, N., 387
Erskine, N. J., 274, 387
Exner, J. E., Jr., 133
Eysenck, H. J., 187–188, 415, 430,
    432, 451, 470–471, 509

Fagot, B. I., 605
Falbo, T., 134
Farmer, R. F., 471
Farqurharson, J., 550
Faterson, H. F., 519–520
Fehr, B., 482
Felker, D. W., 134
Ferster, C. B., 299, 339
Feshbach, S., 393
Festinger, L. A., 249
Fiedler, F. E., 573–574
Figueredo, A. J., 202
Fillingim, R. B., 551
Finch, A. J., Jr., 534–535
Findley, M. J., 385
Fischer, W. F., 260

Fiske, D. W., 472
Fiske, S. T., 23, 276
Fjeld, S., 266
Fleming, R., 535
Floderus-Myrhed, B., 182–183
Folkman, S., 537
Forsterling, F., 484
Foss, M. A., 249, 482
Foster, C. W., 249, 496
Foushee, H. C., 578
Frank, R., 193–195
Fransella, F., 264
Frautschi, N., 549
Freud, S., 68, 116–117, 121–122
Friberg, L., 183
Friberg, L. T., 470
Friedman, H. S., 555
Friedman, M., 545
Frieze, I. H., 603
Fromm, E., 104, 122
Frosh, S., 137
Fry, E. H., 580
Fry, N. E., 580
Fulker, D. W., 183
Fuller, J. L., 161
Fulmer, R. M., 572
Funder, D. C., 54, 277–279, 374,
    399–400, 446, 551
Funk, S. C., 551

Gagnon, J. H., 325
Galaburda, A. M., 193–195
Gallant, S. J., 557
Galton, F., 156–157, 167
Ganaway, G. K., 75
Gangestad, S. W., 176, 200
Gara, M. A., 267
Garbarino, J., 567
Garcia, J. E., 574
Gardner, H., 499–500
Gardner, J., 584
Gardner, S. T., 129
Gauthier, J., 392
Geen, R. G., 434, 533, 535
Geer, J. H., 333
Geis, C. E., 578
Geis, F. L., 595
Geiwitz, J., 67, 74
Gelles, R. J., 608
Gendlin, E. T., 217, 223
Gergen, K. J., 271–272
Getter, H., 389
Gibson, R. H., 596

Gidron, Y., 549
Gilligan, C., 79
Gilliland, K., 193–194
Gilmore, D. D., 609
Glaser, I. I., 604
Glass, D. C., 545–547, 550
Glass, G. V., 389
Gleitman, H., 481
Gleitman, L. R., 481
Gleser, G. C., 129
Glisky, M. L., 523
Glyshaw, K., 552
Goddard, H. H., 158–159
Goldberg, B., 125
Goldberg, L. R., 41, 272, 279, 406, 413, 443, 449–451, 462, 469, 482, 484–485, 497, 522, 533, 582, 593
Goldfarb, P., 567
Goldfried, M. R., 328, 331, 336, 345
Golding, S. L., 59, 274, 343, 445
Goldsmith, H. H., 181
Goleman, D., 397, 501
Gonda, G., 613
Goodenough, D. R., 519–520
Goodenough, F. L., 331
Good, S., 406
Goolsby, L. L., 249
Gorski, R., 604
Gorsuch, R. L., 333, 469, 534
Gossard, D., 392
Gottesman, I. I., 181, 511
Gottfredson, G. D., 565
Gough, H. G., 585, 592
Gould, S. J., 158, 505, 507, 512
Goy, R. W., 602
Grabowski, T., 193–195
Graen, G., 576
Graham, A., 595
Graham, J. W., 554
Graham, W., 256
Grant, D. L., 384
Gray, J. A., 432, 471
Greene, D., 567
Greenwald, A. G., 129, 243–244
Gregg, B., 550
Gregorich, S., 578
Grenier, J. R., 582
Grossman, P. H., 388
Groth, G., 200
Gruen, R. J., 537
Grusec, J. E., 359

Gualtieri, C., 190
Guastello, S. J., 581, 583
Guijarro, M. L., 546
Guilford, J. P., 9, 500, 518
Guion, R. M., 582–583
Gur, R. C., 197–198
Gur, R. E., 197–198
Gurtman, M. B., 387
Gwynne, J., 515

Hackman, J. R., 568
Hagen, E. P., 503
Haigh, G. V., 252
Hailey, B. J., 549
Hall, C. S., 32–33, 71, 117, 338, 341, 425, 473
Hallet, A. J., 546
Hall, J. A., 613
Hall, P., 557
Hall, R. V., 49
Halverston, C. F., Jr., 607
Hamaker, S., 484
Hames, C. G., 59
Hamilton, W. D., 174
Hampson, J. L., 603
Hampson, S. E., 269–272, 276, 279, 413, 450, 482
Hansen, J. C., 565
Hanson, R. K., 133
Hardy, A. B., 392
Harrington, D., 519
Harris, B., 292
Harris, D. B., 516
Harris, F. R., 298
Harris, G., 578
Hart, B., 298
Harter, S., 567
Hart, J. T., Jr., 263
Hartmann, D. P., 332
Hartmann, H., 105
Hartshorne, H., 441
Hartup, W. W., 606
Hathaway, S. R., 56
Haugtvedt, C. P., 521
Hawking, S. A., 30
Haythornthwaite, J. A., 50
Hazelwood, J. D., 521
Healy W., 73
Heath, A. C., 472
Hecker, M. W., 549
Heckhausen, H., 121
Hedges, S. M., 556
Heilbrun, A. B., 129

Heilbrun, A. B., Jr., 592
Heilizer, R., 550
Heinsohn, R., 202–203
Helmreich, R. L., 578, 596, 613
Helson, R., 472
Hempel, A. M., 249
Henderson, N. D., 508
Hennessey, B. A., 567, 569–570
Hepburn, A., 271
Hepworth, J. T., 50
Hergenhahn, B. R., 302
Hermans, H. J., 45
Herrnstein, R. J., 19, 158, 495, 505, 507, 511, 513
Hersey, P., 577
Hertzmann, M., 519
Herzberg, F., 568
Heston, L., 19
Hetherington, E. M., 611
Hewitt, J., 180
Higgins, E. T., 212, 249–250
Higgins, M., 556
Hilgard, E. R., 71
Hill, K. G., 567, 569–570
Hines, M., 602
Hinkle, D., 266
Hjelle, L. A., 226, 238
Hochreich, D. J., 32, 353
Hoffman, C., 594
Hoffman, E., 226
Hoffman, L. W., 147, 186
Hofstee, W. K., 450, 484
Hogan, J., 571, 576–578, 581–582
Hogan, R., 451, 570–571, 576–577, 580–585
Holbrook, S. H., 158
Holden, C., 19
Holland, J. L., 564–565
Holmes, D. S., 125, 547
Holmes, T. H., 538, 540
Holt, C. S., 392
Holzmuller, A., 613
Ho, M-W, 172
Hooke, J. F., 534–535
Hoptman, M. J., 605
Hormuth, S. E., 37
Horney, K., 79, 103
Horn, J. L., 499, 518
Horn, J. M., 181, 183, 508–509
Hough, L. M., 585
House, R. J., 576
Houston, B. K., 546–547, 549, 551
Houston, J. S., 585

Howard, A., 577
Howells, G. N., 392
Huesmann, L. R., 393
Hughes, G. H., 549
Hull, C. L., 293, 530
Hull, J. G., 551
Humphreys, L. G., 145
Humphreys, M. S., 193–194, 470
Humphries, C., 548
Hundelby, J., 188
Hunsley, J., 133
Huntley, C. W., 458
Hurst, N., 594
Huynh, C., 572
Hyde, J., 16
Hyde, J. S., 599

Ihilevich, D., 129
Illingworth, K. S. S., 243
Insel, P. M., 333

Jacklin, C. N., 608
Jackson, D. N., 49, 275, 477, 484, 562, 584–585
Jacobs, D., 556
Jagger, L., 566
James, W., 211
Janis, I. L., 275
Jardine, R., 182
Jarvik, L. F., 508–509
Jenkins, C. D., 546, 549
Jenkins, D. C., 556
Jenkins, F. H., 59
Jensen, A. R., 508, 513
Jessor, R., 388
Jogawar, V. V., 188
John, O. P., 272, 413, 449–450, 469, 482–483, 485, 497, 522, 533
Johnson, P. B., 603
Johnson, R. C., 183, 278
Johnson, S. M., 343
Jones, E., 67, 89
Jones, E. E., 243, 279
Jones, M. C., 293
Jones, S. R., 572
Josephson, W. L., 393
Jourard, S. M., 230
Jung, C. G., 99–100, 103

Kaflowitz, N. G., 267
Kagan, J., 430, 600
Kager, D. L., 604

Kahneman, D., 277
Kahn, S., 551
Kamin, L. G., 19, 158, 509
Kamp, J. D., 585
Kamphus, R. W., 516
Kanfer, A., 280
Kanfer, F. H., 275
Kanner, A. D., 537–538
Kantor, J. R., 443
Kao, C. F., 521
Kaplan, G. D., 554
Kaplan, R. M., 551, 557
Kaprio, J., 182, 186
Karp, J. S., 197–198
Karp, S. A., 519–520
Katkovsky, W., 359
Katz, P. A., 606
Kauffman, S. A., 172
Kaufman, A. S., 516
Kaufman, N. L., 516
Keefe, R. C., 174
Kellerman, H., 201
Kelley, H. H., 269
Kelley, K., 437
Kelly, E. L., 472
Kelly, G. A., 30, 232–233, 244, 264, 280
Kelly, J., 613
Kendall, P. C., 534–535
Kennedy, W. A., 505
Kenny, D., 279
Kenny, D. A., 54, 277, 577
Kenrick, D. T., 174, 200, 443, 446
Kenyon, B., 605
Kessler, R. C., 50, 540
Ketron, J. L., 498
Keys, M., 19
Kihlstrom, J. F., 128, 242–243, 523
Kileen, P. R., 341, 349
Kirker, W. S., 243
Kirsch, I., 370, 383–384
Kissinger, H., 6
Klein, J., 109
Klein, M., 136
Klein, P., 127
Klein, R., 249
Klineburg, O., 513
Klinger, E., 242
Klinger, M. R., 128
Klotz, M. L., 268
Kobasa, S. C., 551
Koestner, R., 443, 478
Kohlberg, L., 605

Kohut, H., 110, 387
Kolata, G., 604
Kolb, D. A., 478
Koskenvuo, M., 182, 186
Kramer, P. D., 190, 191
Krantz, D. S., 546, 552, 554–556
Krasner, L., 304
Krawitz, G., 383
Kris, E., 105
Ksansnak, K. R., 606
Kuhlman, M., 483
Kuhnert, K. W., 562
Kuiper, N. A., 243, 268
Kupers, C. J., 369

Lacey, J. I., 541
Lachman, J. L., 15
Lachman, R., 15
Lakoff, G., 481
Lambert, N., 515
Lamiell, J. T., 43, 248–249, 281, 472, 486, 496
Landfield, A. W., 266
Landsman, T., 230
Langinvainio, H., 182, 186
Lang, P. J., 56
Langston, C. A., 243
Lanning, K., 443
Larsen, R. J., 249
Lasch, C., 219
Lazarus, A., 330, 335
Lazarus, A. A., 336, 344
Lazarus, R. S., 529, 534–535, 537, 541
Leahey, T. H., 65
Lecky, P., 213
Lee, D. J., 549
Lee, E. S., 513
Lee, H., 210
Lefcourt, H. M., 385, 552
Lefebvre, R. C., 551
Leiker, M., 549
Leinbach, M. D., 605
Leith, G. O. H., 256
Lepper, M., 567
Lerner, G. V., 144
Lerner, R. M., 144
Leventhal, H., 193
Levine, A., 554
Levine, L., 153
Levine, S., 549, 602
Levinson, D., 136
Levinson, M., 136

Levy, L. H., 30, 33, 266, 314, 408
Levy, N., 131
Lewin, K., 443
Lewis, H. B., 519
Lewis, M., 601
Lichtenstein, E., 392
Liddy, S., 384
Liebers, A., 585–586
Liebert, R. M., 393
Liebert, R. S., 122
Lii, S., 594
Lilienfeld, S. O., 581–582
Lindzey, G., 32–33, 71, 117, 338,
    341, 425, 458–459, 473
Linville, P. W., 211, 267
Lion, C., 387
Lipinski, D. P., 336
Lippa, R., 457
Littlefield, C. H., 174
Liverant, S., 510
Locke, E. A., 344
Locke, E. R., 569
Locksley, A., 613
Loeber, R., 180
Loehlin, J. C., 181, 183–186,
    508–509
Loeser, J. D., 384
Loftus, E. F., 75, 126, 128
Lombardo, M. M., 577
Lombroso, C., 158
Lorion, R. P., 135
Lott, C. L., 550
Lowell, E. L., 438, 475
Lund, D., 49
Luria, Z., 591
Lushene, R., 333, 469, 534
Lykken, D. T., 169, 184, 580

Maccoby, E. E., 608–609
Maccoby, M., 122
MacDonald, K., 200, 612
MacDougall, J. M., 546, 550
MacGregor, M. W., 550, 557, 572
Machover, K., 519
MacKinnon, D. W., 518
Maclean D., 550
Maddi, S. R., 111, 551
Maddux, J. E., 370
Maggied, P., 386
Magovern, G. J., Sr., 551
Maher, B., 235
Maher, B. A., 181, 529
Mahler, M. S., 109

Mahony, P. J., 139
Mahrer, A. R., 37, 397
Maides, S. A., 554
Major, B., 606
Maloney, M. P., 499
Manaster, G. J., 91
Mandler, G., 532
Mann, C. C., 161
Manolio, T. A., 549
Manuck, S. B., 557
Marecek, J., 599
Marin, P., 219
Marks, G., 554
Markus, H., 211, 243–244, 267,
    276
Marsh, L., 325
Martin, C. L., 607
Martin, J. A. G., 567
Martin, N., 182
Martin, N. G., 472
Martin, R. A., 552
Maslach, C., 544
Masling, J., 125
Maslow, A. H., 225, 258, 260, 521,
    568
Masson, J. M., 118
Masters, J. C., 398–399
Matarazzo, J. D., 505
Mathews, K. E., 38
Matson, J. L., 325
Matthews, K. A., 545–548,
    550–551
May, M. A., 441
McAdams, D. P., 124, 136, 413,
    451
McArdle, J., 422
McAuliffe, G., 566
McCauley, C. D., 577
McClearn, G. E., 151, 183, 470
McClelland, D. C., 438–441,
    475–476, 478, 552, 568
McConkey, K. M., 522–523
McCormick, N., 16
McCrae, R. R., 484–485, 497, 522,
    557–558
McCullers, J. C., 567
McDermott, N., 550
McElwee, R. O., 276
McGaugh, J. L., 344
McGilley, B. M., 547
McGinnies, E., 127
McGlone, J., 604
McGue, J. S., 585

McGue, M., 169, 508
McIntyre, C. W., 484
McKee, B., 136
McKey, R. H., 513
McKinley, J. C., 56
McKusick, V. A., 152
Mead, G. H., 212
Medin, D. L., 482
Medley, D., 550
Meehl, P. E., 59, 162
Mees, H., 324
Mefford, I. N., 551
Meichenbaum, D., 16, 327–329
Meir, E. I., 16, 566
Meissner, P. B., 519
Mendelsohn, G. A., 271
Mendes de Leon, C. F., 549
Mervis, C. B., 480
Messick, S., 275
Meyer, J., 180
Michael, J., 333
Mikulka, P. J., 534–535
Miley, C. H., 134
Miller, N. E., 306–308, 313,
    315–316, 530, 542
Miller, T. I., 389
Miller, T. Q., 546
Mischel, W., 7, 278, 343, 373–374,
    397–400, 414, 442–444,
    497, 517
Mitchell, C., 392
Mitchell, K., 581
Mitchell, K. E., 582
Mittleman, W., 260
Mladinic, A., 596
Moane, G., 472
Molander, B., 543–544
Molto, J., 471
Money, J., 604
Moore, S. G., 606
Moos, R. H., 333
Morf, C. C., 387
Morgan, C. D., 57, 132, 473
Morris, K. S., 521
Moser, C. G., 268, 549
Moss, H. A., 601
Mount, M. K., 585
Moursund, J., 67, 74
Mowrer, O. H., 530, 542
Mozley, P. D., 197–198
Muldoon, M. F., 557
Munroe, R. L., 96, 119
Murphy, D. L., 192

Murphy, G., 8, 521
Murphy, K. R., 580
Murray, C., 19, 158, 495, 505, 507, 511, 513
Murray, H. A., 8, 57, 132, 436, 443, 473
Musante, L., 550
Mussen, P., 322
Myers, A. M., 613
Myers, I. B., 103
Myers, L. B., 127

Nafziger, D. H., 565
National Organization for Women, 595
Neale, J. M., 180, 304, 323, 544
Neale, M. C., 180
Neher, A., 256
Neisser, U., 498
Nelson–Gray, R. O., 471
Nelson, R. O., 336
Neukrug, E., 566
Neumann, P. G., 548
Newcomb, T. M., 441
Newman, J. P., 471
Nezu, A. M., 552
Nezu, C. M., 552
Nicholls, J. G., 518
Nichols, A., 192
Nichols, P. L., 505
Nichols, R. C., 181, 184, 186
Niedenthal, P. M., 243
Nilsson-Ehle, H., 149
Nisbett, R. E., 275, 277
Norcross, J. C., 337
Norem, J. K., 243
Norman, W. T., 279, 448, 460
Norton, L. W., 370
Novaco, R. W., 329
Novalany, J., 267
Nowack, R., 151
Nowicki, S., 300
Nunnally, J. C., 273, 496
Nurius, P., 211

O'Brien, E. J., 445
Odbert, H. S., 415, 448, 465
Office of Technology Assessment, 580
Oldham, G. R., 568
Olds, D. E., 613
O'Leary, A., 392
O'Leary, K. D., 334

Olewine, D. A., 59
Ones, D. S., 581–582
Ortony, A., 482
Osberg, T. M., 521
Osborne, R. T., 513
Osgood, C. E., 273
Osipow, S. H., 565
Osler, W., 545
OSS Assessment Staff, 474
Owens, J. F., 551
Ozer, D. J., 483

Packer, C., 202–203
Paige, J., 456
Palmer, D. R., 562
Palmer, M. L., 386
Panter, A. T., 53, 276, 280, 521
Parker, K. C., 133
Parker, L. D., 521
Parsons, J. E., 603
Patterson, G. R., 334
Paunonen, S. V., 484, 562
Pavlov, I. P., 530
Peabody, D., 450, 484–485
Peake, P. K., 399
Pedersen, N. L., 182, 183, 470
Pederson, F. A., 266
Pedhazur, E. J., 613
Pennebaker, J. W., 540, 558
Perkins, L. L., 549
Perry, D. G., 605
Perry, J. C., 130
Perry, L. C., 605
Pervin, L. A., 9, 173, 482
Peterson, C., 551
Peterson, D. R., 489
Petty, R. E., 521
Phares, E. J., 13, 16, 42, 45, 132, 353, 358–359, 362, 382, 385, 387, 402–403, 472
Philips, J. S., 275
Phoenix, C. H., 602
Pickles, A., 180
Pincus, A. L., 449
Piper, W. E., 389
Plant, E. A., 599
Plomin, R., 161, 168–169, 181, 183–186, 470
Plutchik, R., 201
Poch, S., 266
Polino, M., 267
Popper, K. R., 34
Posner, M. I., 197

Post, R. M., 190
Potkay, C. R., 469
Poulin–Dubois, D., 605
Powers, W. T., 242
Pratkanis, A. R., 243
Price, R., 16
Privette, G., 260
Provenzano, F. J., 591
Przybeck, T. R., 471
Pugh, K. R., 604

Rafferty, J. E., 403, 552
Rahe, R. H., 538, 540
Raichle, M. E., 197
Raimy, V. C., 262
Ramsey, S. J., 59
Rapaport, D., 105
Rasmuson, I., 182
Rau, L., 608
Raven, J. C., 515
Rayner, R., 292, 530
Reeder, G. D., 279
Reinsch, S., 551
Reise, S. P., 483
Rescind, S., 19
Rescorla, R. A., 290
Resnick, S. M., 197–198
Revelle, W., 193–194, 271, 470–471
Reynolds, W. M., 281
Rhine, R. J., 202
Rhodewalt, F., 243, 387
Richards, J. M., Jr., 565
Richardson, F. C., 540
Richardson, J. L., 554
Rich, S., 184
Rieke, M. L., 581, 583
Riggio, R. E., 457
Rimm, D. C., 383
Ringel, N., 549
Risley, T., 324
Ritchie, E., 385, 387
Rittenhouse, J. D., 527
Ritter, B., 371
Robbins, M. A., 401
Roberts, A. A., 326
Roberts, B. W., 472
Roby, T. B., 478
Roche, S. M., 522
Rockland, C., 196
Rodin, J., 546, 549, 557
Rodriguez, M. L., 400
Rodriguez, R., 521

Roe, A., 518
Roethlisberger, F. J., 571
Rogers, C. R., 215–217, 221, 223, 256, 258, 259
Rogers, T. B., 243
Romer, D., 271
Roper, B. I., 332
Rorer, L. G., 275
Rosch, E., 447, 480–481
Rosenbaum, R., 147
Rosen, B. C., 439
Rosenberg, S., 38, 267
Rosenkrantz, P. S., 591, 592, 595
Rosenman, R. H., 181, 545, 546
Rosenthal, R., 443
Rosenthal, T. L., 368
Rosenzweig, S., 124
Rose, R. J., 182, 186
Rosolack, T. K., 450
Ross, L., 277
Ross, S., 383
Roth, D. L., 551
Rotter, J. B., 32, 336, 349–351, 353, 356–360, 363, 382, 384–386, 400–403, 443–444, 552
Rowe, D., 147, 186
Rubin, J. Z., 591
Ruble, D. N., 603
Ruderman, M. N., 577
Runyan, W. M., 124
Rushton, J. P., 158, 174
Russell, J. A., 482
Russell, R. J. H., 174
Rutter, M., 180
Ryan, A. M., 582
Ryan, R. M., 567, 569
Rychlak, J. F., 230
Ryckman, R. M., 401

Sackett, P. R., 582
Sadalla, E. K., 200
Sager, G., 606
Salinas, C., 457
Salovey, P., 546, 549, 557
Samelson, F., 292
Samuda, R. J., 513
Sarason, I. G., 532–533
Sarason, S. B., 532
Sarna, S., 182, 186
Sattler, J. M., 503, 515
Saucier, G., 449, 483
Scarr, S., 186, 514

Schachter, S., 192
Schaefer, C., 537
Schaffer, K. F., 613
Schank, R. C., 241
Scheier, I. H., 429, 533
Scheier, M. F., 242, 285, 551
Scheinfeld, A., 160
Scherwitz, L. W., 549
Schilling, E. A., 540
Schlegel, W. S., 188–189
Schmidt, F. L., 581–582
Schmitt, D. P., 200
Schneider, D. J., 23
Schneider, D. L., 581
Schoneman, T. J., 279
Schumacher, J., 584
Schunk, D. H., 396
Scogin, F., 584
Scott, W. A., 278
Scroggs, J. R., 123
Sears, R. R., 542, 608
Sechrest, L., 232–233, 235, 265–266
Sechrest, L. B., 582
Sedlak, A., 267
Segal, N. L., 169, 184
Segarra, P., 471
Sejnowski, T. J., 206
Seligman, M. E. P., 542, 551
Selverston, A. I., 206
Selye, H., 540
Sentis, K., 244
Serbin, L. A., 605
Serbin, L. R., 569
Sharpe, D., 572
Shaver, P., 613
Shaw, M. L. G., 264
Shay, K. A., 551
Shaywitz, B. A., 604
Shaywitz, S. E., 604
Sheldon, W. H., 145
Shepard, I. I., 578
Shields, S. A., 604
Shipley, T. E., 135
Shoben, E. J., 28
Shoda, Y., 399–400, 414, 444
Sholis, D., 383
Shrauger, J. S., 279
Shultz, D. P., 562
Shultz, S. E., 562
Shweder, R. A., 271
Sidney, S., 549
Siegel, S., 383

Siegler, R., 240
Siegman, A. W., 549
Sigal, J., 129
Siipola, E. M., 473
Silberg, J., 180
Silverman, L. H., 128
Simon, L., 193–194
Simonoff, E., 180
Simpson, J. A., 176, 200
Simpson, M. T., 59
Singer, J. E., 535
Singer, J. L., 125
Singer, S. E., 192
Skeels, H. M., 508
Skinner, B. F., 7, 256, 258, 299, 326–327, 339, 341–342
Skodak, M., 508
Skodol, A. E., 130
Sloane, K. D., 518
Slovic, P., 275, 277
Smith, E. E., 482
Smith, M. L., 389
Smith, T. W., 546, 548–549, 551
Snowden, L. R., 281
Snyder, C. R., 243
Sober, E., 174
Solaas, M. H., 166
Sosniak, L. A., 518
Spanos, N. P., 71, 384
Spearman, C., 499, 511
Spence, J. T., 596, 613
Spence, K. W., 530–531
Sperry, R. W., 604
Spielberger, C. D., 333, 469, 533–534
Sprafkin, J., 393
Springer, S. P., 604
Spuhler, J. N., 166
Srull, T. K., 240, 242
Staats, A. W., 325, 407
Staats, C. K., 325, 407
Stanton, A. L., 557
Stapp, J., 613
Steinhilber, A., 543
Stephens, M. A. P., 537
Stephenson, W., 251
Sternberg, R. J., 269, 498–499, 501, 505, 507, 511–512
Sternglanz, S. H., 569
Stern, M., 266
Stevenson-Hinde, J., 201
Stevenson, J., 180
Stevens, S. S., 145

Stewart, A. J., 440
Stogdill, 575
Stoler, N., 263
Stoltenberg, C., 370
Stone, A. A., 50
Stotland, E., 521
Strauman, T., 249
Straus, M. A., 608
Strickland, B. R., 384–385, 555
Stringfield, D. O., 443
Strong, E. K., Jr., 563
Strube, M. J., 546, 550
Stuart, R. B., 392
Suci, G. J., 273
Sudilovsky, A., 549
Sullivan, H. S., 104, 212
Suls, J., 44, 50, 527, 546
Sundberg, N. D., 281
Sundet, J. M., 166
Suppe, F., 23, 27
Svrakic, D., 471
Swann, W. B., 279
Swede, S. W., 6
Swiezy, N. B., 325
Symons, D., 171

Taft, R., 277, 279
Tagiuri, R., 3, 269
Tambs, K., 166
Tanaka, J. S., 280, 521
Tangney, J. P., 393
Tannenbaum, P. H., 273
Tataryn, D. J., 523
Taylor, C. B., 392, 395, 551
Taylor, F. W., 571
Taylor, J. A., 531
Taylor, M. C., 613
Tellegen, A., 169, 184, 451,
    483–484, 522
Tennen, H., 44, 50
Tetenbaum, T. J., 613
Tetlock, P. E., 6
Thomas, A., 16
Thomas, G., 59
Thomas, L., 264
Thompson, E. P., 521
Thompson, W. R., 161
Thorn, B. E., 392
Thorndike, E. L., 293, 499
Thorndike, R. L., 503
Thorne, A., 271, 413
Thornton, B., 401
Thurstone, L., 499

Tice, D. M., 243, 443
Tighe, E. M., 567, 569–570
Tobias, B. A., 523
Tomarken, A. J., 193
Tomkins, S. S., 241
Tomlinson, T. M., 263
Tooby, J., 171, 199
Torrubia, R., 471
Towbes, L. C., 552
Trapnell, P. D., 565
Trivers, R. L., 176
Trost, M. R., 200
Truax, C. B., 224
Trull, T. J., 483
Trzebinski, J., 484
Tucker, W. B., 145
Turner, J. H., 439
Turner, C. W., 546
Turner, J. A., 384
Turriff, S., 193
Tversky, A., 277

Ullmann, L. P., 304
Unger, R., 596
Unger, R. K., 591, 597
U. S. Congress, Office of
    Technology Assessment, 581

Vaillant, G. E., 130
Valentine, J., 513
Vandenberg, S. G., 181, 183
Van De Water, D. A., 136
van Kaam, A., 261
Van Lawick-Goodall, J., 201
Van Treuren, R. R., 551
Vavak, C. R., 549
Vernon, P. E., 277, 457–459, 500
Virnelli, S., 551
Viswesvaran, C., 581–582
Vockell, E. L., 134
Vogel, S., 592
Vogel, S. R., 591, 595
Von Korff, M., 384
Vroom, V. H., 568, 576

Wagner, K. D., 135
Wagner, R. K., 501
Wahba, M. A., 568
Waldron, I., 556
Wallach, L., 219
Wallach, M. A., 219, 518
Wallen, K., 176
Waller, N. G., 451, 483–484

Wallston, B. S., 554
Wallston, K. A., 554
Walters, R., 370
Wan, C. K., 546
Wapner, S., 519
Ward, M. P., 499
Watson, D., 484, 540, 557–558
Watson, J. B., 291–292, 530
Webber, P. L., 186
Weinberger, D. A., 127
Weinberger, J., 128, 478
Weinberg, R. A., 186, 497, 514
Weiss, D. S., 271
Weiten, W., 541
Wells, P. A., 174
Werner, C., 550
Westen, D., 451
West, S. G., 50, 54
White, A., 249, 496
White, R. W., 45, 472, 567
Whiting, J. W. M., 600
Whitney, D. R., 565
Whitney, G., 206
Wickens, D. D., 336
Wideman, M. V., 554–555
Widiger, T. A., 483
Wiebe, D. J., 551
Wiggins, J. S., 60, 275, 449, 474,
    613
Wilcox, K. J., 184
Willerman, L., 181, 183, 508–509
Williams, J. E., 592–594
Williams, R., 549
Williams, R. L., 515
Williams, S. L., 551
Wilson, D. S., 174
Wilson, E. O., 173
Wilson, G. T., 344
Wilson, J. J., 249, 392, 496
Wilson, J. R., 183
Wilson, T. D., 275
Wilson, W. C., 609
Winborne, W. C., 521
Wing, H., 582
Winnicott, D. W., 110
Winter, D. G., 440
Witelsen, S. F., 604
Witkin, H. A., 519–520
Wittgenstein, L., 481
Wittig, M. A., 186
Wogan, M., 337, 389
Wolberg, L. R., 70
Wolfe, D. M., 521

Wolf, M., 324
Wolf, M. M., 298
Wolpe, J., 56, 322, 336–337
Wong, S., 594
Wood, R., 394, 396
Woodward, W. R., 349
Woodyard, E., 499
Woolfolk, R. L., 267, 540
Worell, L., 613
Wright, E., 176
Wright, H. F., 36, 333
Wright, L., 192, 545
Wright, S., 162
Wrightsman, L. S., 456

Wright, T. L., 386
Wunderlin, R. J., 383
Wurf, E., 211, 243–244, 276
Wyatt, R. Z., 192
Wyer, R. S., 240, 242
Wylie, R., 211

Yankelovich, D., 566
Yetten, P. W., 576
Young, H., 188
Young, W. C., 602

Zaccaro, S. J., 577
Zadeh, L. A., 481

Zammuner, V. L., 594
Zarit, S. H., 537
Zeller, A., 125
Zellman, G. L., 603
Ziegler, D. J., 226, 238,
    422
Zigler, E., 513
Zinbarg, R., 471
Zuckerman, M., 190, 192, 433,
    443, 451, 470, 483
Zukier, H., 271
Zunz, M., 201
Zuroff, D. C., 351, 418
Zyzanski, S. J., 59, 546

# Subject Index

Ability traits, 423–424
Absorption, 522
Absurdity, existentialism and, 230–231
Achievement. *See also* n Achievement
  motivation for, 437*t*, 438–440
*The Achievement Motive* (McClelland), 438
ACL. *See* Adjective Check List
Acquiescence, phenomenological assessment and, 275
Acquired motives, 435
Act-frequency approach (AFA), 447–448
  critique of, 482–483
  research on, 479–481
Acting out, as defense mechanism, 82*t*
Action slips, 122
Act nominations, 479
Adaptation, evolutionary forces and, 199–200
Additive genetic effects, 183
Adenine, in DNA composition, 150, 153*f*
Adjective Check List (ACL), 592
  gender stereotypes and, 593
Adjustment, 13
  in Adler's theory, 94–95
  in Allport's theory, 421–422
  androgyny and, 613
  behaviorist perspective on, 13, 304–305
  in Cattell's theory, 428–429
  construct of, 29

in Dollard and Miller's theory, 313–317
environmental objects and, 109–110
in Freudian theory, 81, 84*t*
in Kelly's theory, 238
in Rogers' theory, 221
in social cognitive theory, 370–371
in social learning theory, 13, 359
Adler, Alfred, 67, 89
  biography of, 91
  dream analysis of, 119–120
  psychotherapy of, 96
    case study in, 97–99
  Rotter and, 350
  theories of, 89–95
    deficiencies of, 137
    research on, 134–135
Adolescence, personality development during, 105*t*, 106–108
Adoption study(ies)
  in behavior genetics, 168–169
  heritability estimates based on, 183
  intelligence and, 508–510, 509*t*
Aesthetic and cognitive needs, in Maslow's hierarchy, 228, 228*f*
AFA. *See* Act-frequency approach
Affiliation. *See also* n Affiliation
  and health, 552
  need for, 441
Age
  and anxiety effects, 544*f*
  defense mechanisms and, 130, 135*f*

intelligence testing and, 502–503
personality and, 10
Agency, sense of, 243
Aggregate data analysis, versus single-subject research, 51
Aggregation, principle of, 445
Aggression
  construct inconsistency and, 237
  gender differences in, 608
  observational learning of, 390–394
Aggressor, identification with, 77
Ahistorical position, phenomenology and, 281
Aichhorn, August, 107
Alienation, existentialism and, 230
Allport, Gordon
  biography of, 417
  Goldberg and, 448
  personality assessment and, 455–458, 456*t*
  trait theory of, 415–422, 486–487
Alpha presses, 438
Altruism
  definition of, 173
  evolutionary explanation of, 173–174
Amygdala, functions of, 196
Anaclitic identification, 599
Anal expulsive stage, 76
Anal retentive stage, 76
Anal stage, of personality development, 76
Analytic psychology, 96
Androgyny, 612–613
Anger-anxiety conflicts, 313

Anger, type A behavior and, 549–550
Anima, archetype of, 100–101
Animal personality, 201–203
versus human personality, 202–204, 204*t*
Animal research, 305–307, 338
anxiety and, 530
gender differences and, 602–603
Animus, archetype of, 100–101
Anna O., case of, 65–68
Antidepressant(s), 190–191
Antipsychotics, 188
Anti-semitism
Freud and, 65–67
Jung and, 101
Anxiety, 529–534
construct inconsistency and, 237
coping with, 103
definitions of, 529
drugs for, 190
existentialism and, 230
in Freudian theory, 80
Gray's theory of, 471
and illness, 527
learning theory and, 530–531
measures of, 531–534
moral, 80
neurotic, 80, 527, 529
and performance, 531–532
physiological measures of, 59
reality, 80
Appearance, physical, influence of, 144–145
Approach-approach conflict, 313
Approach-avoidance conflict, 313
representation of, 314*f*
Archetypes, 99–101
dreams and, 120
Aristotle, 7, 414
Arnold, Roseanne Barr, 75
Assertiveness, self-schemata for, 268, 269*f*
Assessment
behavioral. *See* Behavioral assessment
general versus specific, 51–52
of hostility, 550
of intelligence, 500–505
of interpersonal trust, 385–387
of intrinsic motivation, 567–570, 570*t*
of observational learning, 390–394

personality. *See* Personality assessment
of self-efficacy, 392–395
Assortative mating, 166
genetic similarity theory and, 175
A-State, 534
A-Trait, 533–534
Attentional processes, in observational learning, 367
Attitudes, 425
biochemical effects of, 554
political, environment and, 186
in test-taking, 51–53
Attractiveness, physical, 144–145
Authenticity, existentialism and, 230
Autism, 325
Autobiographical data, 11
example of, 12
Autonomous ego, 105
Autonomous self, 111
Autonomy, functional, 419–420, 486–487
Autosomes, 150
Aversion therapy, 322–323
Aversive experiences, self-efficacy and, 392–394, 395*f*
Avoidance-avoidance conflict, 313
Avoidance, social learning theory on, 359–360

Bad-me, 212
Bandura, Albert, 21
biography of, 365
Goldberg and, 449
social cognitive theory of, 363–373, 403
BAS. *See* Behavioral activation system
Base pairs, DNA, 150
Basic anxiety, 103
Basic level, in personality description, 447–448
Behavior(s)
cognition processes and, 242, 327–330
enhancement, 360–362
expressive component of, 457
factors influencing, 33
functional analysis of, 294
personal and environmental variables in, 366, 367*f*
respondent, 296
shaping of, 301–302
stress and, 542–544

Behavioral activation system (BAS), 471
Behavioral assessment, 58–59
methods of, 331–336
social learning theory and, 400–403
strengths of, 339–340
versus traditional assessment, 332*t*
weaknesses of, 343–344
Behavioral Coding System (BCS), 334*f*
Behavioral data, 274
Behavioral deficits, 304
Behavioral engineering, 21
Behavioral inhibition system (BIS), 471
Behavioral medicine, 527, 557
Behavior change
Adlerian theory and, 96
Allport's theory and, 422
Cattell's theory and, 429
Freudian theory and, 81
Kelly's theory and, 238–239
Rogerian theory and, 221–224
self-efficacy and, 392
social cognitive theory and, 371–373
social learning theory and, 362–363
Behavior genetics, 161–169
basic model of, 161–164
biological influences and. *See* Twin study(ies)
Cattell's model of, 467
environmental influences and, 185–187
field of, 19
methods of, 162–169
nature of, 161
personality and, 180–187
tools of, 165, 166*f*
*Behavior genetics* (Fuller and Thompson), 161
Behaviorism, 15, 17*f*, 288–319. *See also* Learning theory(ies)
adjustment and, 13, 304–305
versus cognition, 22–23
definition of, 291
gender differences and, 606–609
Hull and, 293–294
versus humanism, 257–258
Skinner and, 294–305
strengths of, 338–340

Thorndike and, 293
Watson and, 291–293, 292*f*
weaknesses of, 340–345
Behavior potential (BP), 351–353
  predictive formulas for, 356–357
Behavior therapy, 321–326
  evaluation of, method for, 49
  historical perspective on, 337
  strengths of, 340
  weaknesses of, 344–345
Being understood, constituents of,
    261*t*
Being values, self-actualization and,
    229–230
*The Bell Curve* (Herrnstein and
    Murray), 19, 495, 507,
    511
Belongingness and love needs, in
    Maslow's hierarchy, 228,
    228*f*
Bem Sex Role Inventory (BSRI), 612
Benevolent individuals, and work-
    place motivation, 569
Bernays, Martha, 66
Beta presses, 438
Betting techniques, behavioral
    assessment and, 401
*Beyond Freedom and Dignity*
    (Skinner), 326–327
Big Five, 448–451, 450*t*
  alternative interpretations of,
    483–485, 485*t*
  description organization in, 18
  description versus development
    in, 32–33
  gender differences and, 612
  leadership and, 576–577
  personnel selection and, 585–587
  research based on, 483–485
  strengths of, 490
Binet, Alfred, 502
Binet-Simon Scale, 502
Biochemistry
  and personality, 170, 188–193
  weaknesses of, 207
Biofeedback, 326
Biological influences, 143–178. *See
    also* Twin study(ies)
  Cattell's estimate of, 467
  versus environmental influences,
    14–16, 165–169. *See also*
    Behavior genetics
  Eysenck's personality types and,
    430–432, 470–472

Freudian theory and, 89
gender differences and, 600–605
historical overview of, 19
intelligence and, 507–510, 509*t*
limitations of, 180
mechanisms of, 187–198
misunderstanding about,
    176–177
personality theory and, 15, 17*f*
research on, 179–208
source traits and, 423
Birth order
  effects on children, 93–94, 134
  and nonshared environmental
    experiences, 186
BIS. *See* Behavioral inhibition sys-
    tem
BITCH. *See* Black Intelligence Test
    of Cultural Homogeneity
Bivariate research, 459
Black Intelligence Test of Cultural
    Homogeneity (BITCH), 515
Blacky test, 130, 131*f*
Blends, personality terms as, 484
Blood pressure, type A behavior
    and, 547, 547*f*, 549
Blood type, and personality, 188
Bodily self, sense of, 420
Body type, personality and,
    144–147, 187–189
Brain structure, 197*f*
  gender differences in, 604–605
  and personality, 193–198
Breadth
  of psychoanalytic theory, 137
  theories and, 33–34
Breggin, Peter, 161
Breuer, Josef, 65–66, 68, 89
Brezhnev, Leonid, 6
BSRI. *See* Bem Sex Role Inventory
Burnout, phenomenon of, 543–544
Burt, Sir Cyril, 155

Caffeine, and impulsiveness, 193,
    194f
California Psychological Inventory
    (CPI), 181
  personnel selection and, 585
  twin study based on, 182*t*
California Q-set, 253–255
  research with, 254–255,
    254*t*–255*t*
*Canterbury Tales* (Chaucer), 414
Cardinal traits, 418

Case study method, 38–39,
    116–118
  versus single-subject research, 49
  subjectivity of, 124
Castration
  fear of, 77
    case study illustrating, 116–117
  female rationalization of, 78
Categories, in personality descrip-
    tion, 481–482
Catharsis, 68
CAT scan. *See* Computerized axial
    tomography
Cattell, Raymond, 155
  anxiety definition by, 529
  biography of, 424–425
  research methods of, 458–468
  trait theory of, 422–429,
    487–489
Causality orientation, 567
Causality, versus correlation, 46–48
Causal theories, 17*f*
Central traits, 418
Chained reinforcers, 301
Change
  personality, 13–14
    measurement of, 467–468
  and stress, 538–540, 539*t*–540*t*
Characterology, 414
Charcot, Jean, 65
Chaucer, Geoffrey, 414
CHD. *See* Coronary heart disease
Checklists, in behavioral assess-
    ment, 333
*Childhood and Society* (Erikson),
    105
Children. *See also* Infant(s)
  Adlerian treatment of, 96
  fairy tales and, 120–121
  Freudian overemphasis on, 140
  gender stereotype influences on,
    595–596
  ordinal position of, 93–94, 134
  pampered, 92–93
  personality learning by, 3–4
  rejected, 93
Chlorpromazine, 188
Chou En-lai, 6
Chromosomes, 150, 152*f*
Circularity, phenomenology and,
    283–284
Clarity, theories and, 30
Classical conditioning, 290
  anxiety and, 530–531

Classical conditioning (*continued*)
  aversion therapy and, 322
  trait theory and, 428
Cleanliness training, 313
Client-centered therapy, 221–224, 282
Clinical method, 460
Clothing, identity and, 123
Cognition
  as behavior, 327–330
  computer model for, 240, 241f
  context of, 240
  need for, 521
  reinforcement and, 364–366
  social. *See* Social cognition
  study of, 239–245
Cognitive-affective system theory, 444
Cognitive and aesthetic needs, in Maslow's hierarchy, 228, 228f
Cognitive determinants, 15
  historical overview of, 22–23
  personality theory and, 15, 17f
Cognitively complex individual, 267
Cognitively simple individual, 267
Cognitive psychology, unconscious in, 128–129
Cognitive resource utilization theory, 574
Cognitive restructuring, 328
  example of, 329
Cognitive social learning theory, 373–376
  research on, 389–396
Cognitive style, 519–520
Cognitive theory(ies)
  of intelligence, 500
  limitations of, 284–285
Collective unconscious, 99
Colorado Adoption Project, 183
Commission, theories and, 35
Common traits, 419, 426
Comparative-anthropological approach, 122
Compensation, organ inferiority and, 89–90
Competency(ies)
  lack of, and maladjustment, 360
  in Mischel's view, 374
Complexity, of personal construct systems, 267

Computerized axial tomography (CAT scan), 197
Computer model(s), 240, 241f
  limitations of, 284
Concepts, personality, 28
Concurrent validity, 54
  strategies for determining, 55t
Conditional description, 413
Conditioned response, 290t
Conditioned stimulus, 290t
Conditioning
  classical. *See* Classical conditioning
  instrumental. *See* Instrumental conditioning
  operant. *See* Operant conditioning
  principles of, 20–21
  theory of, usefulness of, 30
  vicarious, 368–369
Conditions of worth, 218–220
Conflict(s)
  of needs, 360
  types of, 313–314
Conflict-free sphere, of ego, 105
Conscience, punishment and, 74
Conscientiousness, alternative interpretations of, 484, 485t
Conscious
  Freudian concept of, 69
  subdivision of, 73f
Consistency, 10
  assessment and, 53
  construct-reality, 237
  gender differences and, 611
  implicitly personality theories and, 271–272
  psychoanalytic research and, 117–118
  of self, 220
  theories and, 31
  of traits, 443
Constellatory constructs, 266
Constitutional psychology, 145
  critique of, 145–147
  modern development of, 187–189
Constitutional traits, 423
Construct(s)
  versus biological reality, 206
  constellatory, 266
  as descriptions, 28–29
  dichotomous, 233–235
  focus of convenience and, 30

inconsistency of, 237–238
  in nomological network, 59, 60f
  permeable, 235
  personal. *See* Personal constructs
  preemptive, 236
  reality and, 29
  in Rotter's theory, 350
  superordinate, 266–267
  trait. *See* Trait constructs
  use of term, 28
  validated, 266
Construct validity, 54, 445–446
  integrity tests and, 582
  strategies for determining, 55t
*Contemporary Psychology*, 108
Content analysis, 262–263
Content validity, 54
  strategies for determining, 55t
Contingency theory, of leadership, 573–574
Continuous reinforcement, 299
  versus partial reinforcement, 300
Contrasted groups, strategy of, 563
Control
  ego, 551–552
  feedback, 242
  and health, 552–555
  learning and, 42
  locus of. *See* Locus of control
  origins of, 45
  situational, leadership and, 574
  type A behavior and, 550
Control group, 40
Controlled observation(s), 38, 334–335
Convergent thinking, 518
Cook-Medley Hostility Scale, 550
Cooperation
  development of, 303
  social theory of, 203
Coping strategies, Horney's view of, 103
Coronary heart disease (CHD), 546
  personality and, 545–550
Correlation coefficient, 44
Correlation matrix, 461–462, 462t
  types of, 468
Correlation method, 44–48, 46t
  advantages of, 48
  versus causality, 46–48
Counterconditioning, 321–322
Countertransference, 85
Cousins, Norman, 553

CPI. *See* California Psychological
  Inventory
Creationism, 171
Creativity, 518–519
  basic needs and, 256
  mathematical, personality and,
    255t
Crisis, developmental, 106
Criterion analysis, 430, 470
Criterion contamination, 54
Criterion of internal consistency, in
    psychoanalytic research,
    117–118
Criterion validity, 54
Critical training situations, 312–313
Cross-situational coefficients, 442
Crystallized ability, 423–424, 500
Cue(s), 309
  discrimination of, failure in,
    304–305
Cue-producing responses, 311
Culture. *See also* Environmental
    influences
  and gender stereotypes, 594
  and intelligence, 516
Culture-fair tests, 514–516
Cytosine, in DNA composition,
    150, 153f

Daily hassles, 537, 538t
Darwin, Charles
  on eugenics, 161
  evolution theory of, 147
Daseins-analysis, 231
Data
  autobiographical, 11–12
  behavioral, 274
  collection of, research and, 35
  other-report, 274–275
  personality, types of, 274–275
  qualitative, 259, 262–263
  self-report, 274–275
  sources of, 463–465
  types of, 11
Data analysis, aggregate, versus sin-
    gle-subject research, 51
Death instincts, 72
Defense(s), ego, 80–81, 82t–83t
Defense mechanisms, 80–81,
    82t–83t
  adult expressions and, 84t
  age and development of, 130,
    135f

behavioral analysis of, 315–316
psychosexual stages and, 84t
scientific assessment of, 129–131
sex and, 131
stress and, 542
Defense Preference Inquiry, 130,
    131f
Defensive identification, 599
Defensive pessimism, 243
Delay of gratification, 397–400
  ego control and, 551
  expectancy and, 397–398
  observational learning and,
    398–399
  personality and, 399–400, 400t
  reinforcement value and, 398,
    399f
Denial
  as defense mechanism, 130, 135f
  of reality, 82t
  threat to self and, 220
Deoxyribonucleic acid, 150, 153f
  replication of, and mutation, 172
Dependence
  field, versus independence,
    519–520
  reward, 471
Dependent variable, 39
Depression
  case study in, 97–99
  cognitive complexity and, 267
  drugs for, 190
  schedule of reinforcement and,
    304
Description(s)
  in Big Five, 18, 32–33
  conditional, 413
  constructs as, 28–29
  versus development, 32–33
  versus dispositions, 584
  nonconditional, 413
  personality. *See* Personality
    description
  self, 593
Descriptive theories, 17f, 18. *See
    also* Personality description
  critique of, 482–483
  research on, 479–485
  strengths of, 490
  weaknesses of, 490–491
Despair, existentialism and, 230
Determinant(s)
  behavior, 68

cognitive, 15, 22–23
personality, 14–15
  historical overview of, 18–23
  theories resulting from, 15–18,
    17f
Determinism
  psychic, 68, 137
  in psychological study, 281
  reciprocal, 366, 367f
    gender differences and,
      611–612
Development
  versus description, 32–33
  of personality. *See* Personality
    development
  phenomenological disregard of,
    283
  of self, 212–213
Diagnostic council, 473
Dichotomous construct(s), 233–235
Dictionary of Occupational Titles,
    565
Differential attention, gender differ-
    ences and, 609–611
Differential heritability, 181
  twin studies and, 181–182
Differential R-technique, 468
Direct observation
  in behavioral assessment,
    333–334
  diagnostic council in, 473
Disconfirmation, theories and,
    34
Discrimination
  eugenics and, 158–161
  lack of, 360
Discrimination of cues, failure in,
    304–305
Discriminative stimuli, 297
Disease
  personality and, 526–560
  psychological causes of, 527,
    528t
Displacement, as defense mecha-
    nism, 83t
Disposition(s). *See also* Trait(s);
    Trait theory(ies)
  versus descriptions, 584
Distal goals, 396
Distance, in response to problems,
    95
Distinctiveness, 9–10
Distress, coping with, 127

Diurnal rhythms, caffeine effect and, 193, 194*f*
Divergent thinking, 518
Dizygotic twins, 165–166
DNA. *See* Deoxyribonucleic acid
Dollard, John
behavior therapy and, 321, 338
biography of, 306–307
reinforcement theory of, 305–317
social learning and, 349
Dominant factor, in genetics, 148
Double helix, DNA, 150
Dread, existentialism and, 230
Dream(s)
Adler's view of, 119–120
archetypal, neuroticism and, 133–134
id and, 73–74
Jung's view of, 120
in psychotherapy, 84
Dream analysis, 84
in psychoanalytic research, 119–120
Drinking patterns, expectancies and, 388–389
Drive(s), 309
anxiety as, 530–531
learned, 310
primary, 312
Drive-activation method, 128
Drugs, influence on personality, 188–191
Dynamic lattice, 425–426
example of, 426*f*
Dynamic self-concept, 244–245
Dynamic traits, 424–425
DZ twins. *See* Dizygotic twins

E. See Expectancy(ies)
Early sex training, 313
Ebbinghaus, Hermann, 68–69
Ectomorphy, 145, 146*f*
Ego
Adlerian view of, 99
anxiety and, 80
autonomous, 105
conflict-free sphere of, 105
Freudian view of, 74
Ego control, 551–552
Ego defenses, 80–81, 82*t*–83*t*
Ego-ideal, 74
Ego identity, 107. *See also* Identity
research on, 135–136
versus role confusion, 106–108

Ego psychology, 104–108
research on, 135–136
Ego resiliency, 552
Ego threat, repression and, 126
Electra complex, 78
criticism of, 79
drive-activation method and, 128
Eminence, Galton's study of, 154–157, 156*f*
Emotion(s)
animal personality and, 201
brain structure and, 196, 198
gender differences in expression of, 198
information processing and, 284–285
in response to stress, 540
Emotional insulation, 82*t*
Emotional intelligence, 397
Emotional stability-instability type, 430
Emotions Profile Index (EPI), 201
Empirical research
advantages of, 35–36
example of, 37
observation and, 36–38
Employee Polygraph Protection Act, 578–580
Enactive attainment, self-efficacy and, 373
Encoding strategies, 374
Encounter groups, 224
Rogers and, 282
Endomorphy, 145, 146*f*
Engineered society, 326–327
Enhancement behaviors, 360–362
Entitled persons, 569
Environmental influences
versus biological influences, 14–16, 165–169. *See also* Behavior genetics
Cattell's estimate of, 467
Galton's studies and, 157
historical overview of, 20–22
intelligence and, 510, 511*f*
personality theory and, 15, 17*f*. *See also* Behaviorism
shared versus nonshared, 185–186
studies of, 185–187
Environmental interaction, gene operation and, 162, 164*f*
Environmental-mold traits, 423

Enzymes
genes and, 169
influence on personality, 190, 192
Epigenetic principle, 105
Epinephrine, 192
Episodic memory, 241
EPQ. *See* Eysenck Personality Questionnaire
E'. *See* Specific expectancies
Equal-environments assumption, twin studies and, 184–185
Equity-sensitive individuals, 569
Equity theory, and workplace motivation, 569
Erg, 424
Erikson, Erik
biography of, 106–107
comparative-anthropological approach of, 122
developmental stages of, 105*t*, 105–108
scientific research on, 136
psychohistorical writings of, 122–123
Eros. *See* Life instincts
Erotogenic zones, 71
Errors, judgment, versus mistakes, 277–278
Eskimos, 21–22
Esteem needs, in Maslow's hierarchy, 228, 228*f*
Ethnicity, and intelligence, 512–514
Eugenics, 19, 155, 158–161
versus behavior genetics, 161
Everyday life
idiographic evaluation in, 249–250
psychopathology of, 120–122
Evolutionary theory(ies), 171–176
personality research based on, 198–204
Existentialism, themes in, 230–231
Existential theory. *See also* Phenomenology
empirical investigation of, 260–262
Kelly and, 231–239
Rogers and, 224–225
Expectancy(ies)
definition of, 401
delay of gratification and, 397–398
and drinking patterns, 388–389

measurement of, 401–402
Mischel's classification of, 374–375
outcome, 383
research on, 37
response. *See* Response expectancy
in Rotter's social learning theory, 351, 353–355
self-efficacy and, 370
and termination of psychotherapy, 389
and workplace motivation, 568
Experience. *See also* Environmental influences
openness to, 522–523
Experience sampling method, 37
Experimental hypothesis, 39
Experimentation
balance of approaches to, 44
limitations of, 40–43
method of, 39–44
personality psychology and, 40
popularity of, 43–44
psychoanalytic research and, 124–125
Explicit measures, theories and, 32
Explicitness, theories and, 30
Explicit personality theory. *See* Formal personality theory
Exploitative personality, 104
Expressive behavior, 457
Extension of self, 420
Externals, 45
Extinction, reinforcement and, 309–310
Extrinsic motivation, 566–567
measurement of, 570*t*
Extroversion, 102. *See also* Introversion-extroversion type
alternative interpretation of, 484, 485*t*
caffeine effect and, 193, 194*f*
gender differences and, 612
genetic and environmental transmission of, 165, 166*f*
Gray's reinterpretation of, 471
Eysenck, Hans, 155
biography of, 431
followers of, 471–472
research methods of, 469–470
trait theory of, 429–434

Eysenck Personality Questionnaire (EPQ), 182, 186–187

Factor analysis, 460–461
Cattell and, 458–461, 487
criticism of, 488–489
Eysenck and, 429–430, 470, 487
hypothetical example of, 461–463
intelligence theories and, 499
in trait theory, 422, 424
Factual information processing, brain structure and, 196
Fairy tales, 120–121
Family(ies)
and development of self, 212
variations within, personality development and, 186
Family resemblance studies, heritability estimates based on, 183
Fantasy(ies), 75
as defense mechanism, 82*t*
in psychoanalytic research, 120
Father(s)
attraction to, girls and, 78
identification with, boys and, 77
masculine protest and, 95
Fear(s)
development of, 530
learned, 292–293
reality anxiety as, 80
Fear Survey Schedule, 56, 333
Feedback control, cognition and, 242
Feeding situation, 313
Feeling, versus thinking, 102–103
Female(s)
brain activity patterns in, 197–198, 198*f*
chromosomes in, 150, 152*f*
identification in, 599
mate preferences of, 175–176
personality-health correlations in, 556–557
phallic stage of development in, 78–79
sensation seeking in, 192
sociosexuality of, evolutionary theory and, 200–201
stereotypic traits of, 592*t*, 593
Feminine protest, 95

Feminism, 597
Freudian theory and, 79, 103, 140–141
Field dependence, versus independence, 519–520
Fixation, as defense mechanism, 83*t*
Fixed-role therapy, 239
Fluid ability, 424, 500
Fluoxetine, 190
FM. *See* Freedom of movement
Focus of convenience, 30
Food gathering, and personality, 21
Forgetting, intentional, 68–69
Formal personality theory, 3–5
criticism of, 4–5
versus implicit personality theory, 272–273
personality assessment and, 275–276
value of, 30–31
Fragmented self, 111*t*
Fraternal twins. *See* Dizygotic twins
Free association method
beginnings of, 67
illustration of, 119
in psychoanalysis, 83
in psychoanalytic research, 118
Free description approach, 276
Freedom of movement (FM), 357
failure and, 381, 382*f*
and need value, discrepancy between, 359–360
Free will, versus determinism, 281
Frequency-dependent selection, 199
Freud, Anna, 66
Erikson and, 107
Freudian slips, 120
Freudian theory, 65–68. *See also* Psychoanalytic theory
anxiety in, 80
breadth of, 33
criticism of, 89
defense mechanisms in, 80–81
differential identification and, 599–600
historical context of, 30
illustration of, 86–88
instincts in, 71–72
personality development in, 75–79
personality structure in, 72–75
psychic determinism and, 68
psychotherapy and, 81–85, 116
research on, 125–131

Freudian Theory (*continued*)
strengths of, 137–138
unconscious motivation and, 68–69, 173
weaknesses of, 138–141
Freud, Sigmund, 13, 21
achievements of, 137–138
Adler and, 89, 91
Allport and, 417
anxiety definition by, 529
biography of, 66–67, 89
Jung and, 100–101
psychic determinism and, 68
psychoanalytic theory of. *See* Freudian theory
psychobiographical studies of, 122
research methods of, 116–118, 124
view of human nature, 28
Fromm, Erich, 104, 122
Fully functioning person, 221
Functional analysis of behavior, 294
Functional autonomy, 419–420, 486
conceptual ambiguity of, 487
Future
in psychological study, 281, 283
in trait theory, 419

Gage, Phineas, 193–195
neuroimages of injuries to, 196f
Galton, Francis, 147
biography of, 154–155
contribution of, 205
hereditary theories of, 153–161
twin study method of, 167–168
Galvanic skin response, 128, 579
Gandhi, Indira, 6
*Gandhi's Truth* (Erikson), 123
GE. *See* Generalized expectancies
Gender
meaning of term, 590
stereotypes related to, 591–596, 592t
Gender differences, 589–615. *See also* Female(s); Male(s)
in animal/human personality, 202
behaviorism and, 606–609
biology and, 600–605
in brain activity patterns, 197–198, 198f
in brain structure, 604–605

chromosomes as determinants of, 150
in defense mechanisms, 131
in personality description, 612–613
in personality structure, 612
psychoanalytic theories and, 599–600
research on, 596–599
social cognition and, 605–606, 608f
social learning and, 609–612
Gender identity, 591
Gene(s). *See also* Genetic
forerunners of, 148
influence on personality, mechanisms of, 169–170
Gene mapping, 151
Gene pool, evolution and, 173–174
General adaptation syndrome, stress and, 541
General assessment, versus specific assessment, 51–52
General Causality Orientation Scale, 567
General factor (g) of intelligence, 499
Generality, versus specificity, 33
Generalized expectancies (GE), 354–355
locus of control as, 384
problem solving and, 357–358
research on, 380–381
response and, 384–387
Generalized reinforcers, 301
Genetic effects, additive, 183
Genetic engineering, 151–153
Genetic independence, principle of, 148
Genetics. *See also* Biological influences
behavior. *See* Behavior genetics
historical overview of, 147–161
Genetic segregation, principle of, 147–148, 149f
Genetic similarity theory, 173–174
Genetic theory, 144
Genital stage, 78–79
Genius, heritability of, 154–157
Genotype, 149
Genuineness, client-therapist relationship and, 224
Germ cells, 150

g factor. *See* General factor of intelligence
Global personality ratings, 276–277
accuracy of, 277–278
agreement in, 278–280, 279t
Goal level, minimal, 360
Goal setting
and immediacy of rewards, 395–396
and workplace motivation, 569
Goddard, H. H., 159–160
Goldberg, Lewis R.
Big Five model of, 449–451, 450t
biography of, 448–449
Goodenough-Harris Drawing Test, 516
Good-me, 212
Grand unified theories, 30
Gratification, delay of. *See* Delay of gratification
Greek temperament types, 7, 414, 414t
Eysenck's dimensions of personality and, 433f
Group Embedded Figures Test, 519–520, 520f
Group factors of intelligence, 499
Group selection, 173
Guanine, in DNA composition, 150, 153f
Guided participation, 371–372, 372f–373f
Guilt
construct inconsistency and, 237
as source trait, 423
Guilty knowledge test, 580

Habits
behaviorism and, 293, 305
versus traits, 418
Hallucination
id and, 73–74
negative, posthypnotic, 70
Hardiness, 551
Harlow, John, 195
Harm avoidance, 471
Hawaii Family Study of Cognition, 183
Hawthorne experiments, 571–572
Head Start, 513
Health Locus of Control Scale, 554
Health, personality and, 526–560
Health psychology, 527, 557

Heidegger, Martin, 230
Helson, Ravenna, 254
*Hereditary Genius: An Inquiry into
    Its Laws and Consequences*
    (Galton), 155–156
Hereditary traits, 423
Heredity, Galton's research on,
    153–161
Heritability, 167–168
    calculation of, 168
        adoption studies and, 183
        twin studies and, 182–183
    differential, 181
    of genius, 154–157
    of intelligence, 507–510, 509*t*
    twin studies of, 167–168
        contradictions in, 183–187
Hierarchical models of intelligence,
    499–500, 500*f*
Hippocampus, functions of, 196
Hippocrates, temperament types of,
    414, 414*t*
Hoarding personality, 104
Holland's theory of vocational
    choice, 564*f*, 564–566, 565*t*
Homosexuality, genital stage of
    development and, 78
Honesty, 578–583
Hope, as adaptive strategy, 243
Hormones. *See also specific hor-
    mones*
    gender differences and, 604
    influence on personality, 189–193
    versus situational factors,
        192–193
Horney, Karen, 79, 103
Horse phobia, case study in, 117
Hostility
    construct inconsistency and,
        237–238
    type A behavior and, 549–550
Hull, Clark L., learning theory of,
    293–294, 305
Human genome project, 151
Humanism
    definition of, 225
    idiographic research and, 248
Humanistic theory. *See also
    Phenomenology*
    versus behaviorism, 257–258
    empirical investigation of,
        256–260
    as less systematic theory, 32

Maslow and, 225–230
    Rogers and, 225
Human relations, leadership and,
    572
Humor, and health, 552
Humor(s), and personality, 7, 414*t*
Hypertension, type A behavior and,
    547, 547*f*, 549
Hypnosis
    absorption and, 522
    in psychoanalysis, 65, 67–68,
        70–71
    response expectancy and, 384
Hypothesis
    case study and, 38
    development of, 36
    experimental, 39
    lexical, 449
    moderator, 443
    multiple-factor, 149
    systemic distortion, 271
Hysteria, 65–67

Id, 73–74, 74*f*
Ideal-hungry personality, 111*t*
Ideal-self, 212
    Roger's theory and, 218
    versus self, 251–252, 253*t*
Identical twins. *See* Monozygotic
    twins
Identification
    as defense mechanism, 83*t*,
        130–131, 135*f*
    with father, 77
    gender differences and, 599–600
Identity(ies). *See also* Ego identity
    gender, 591
    search for, 123
    self and, 211
Identity crisis, 107
Idiographic research, 43, 248–255
    Allport's trait theory and,
        455–456, 456*t*
    assessment tools in, 251–255
    criticism of, 487
    humanism and, 248
    nomothetic research and, 45
    phenomenological theories and,
        281
    self-evaluation and, 249–250
    Skinner's operant conditioning
        and, 302–303
Idiographic standards, 249–250

I-E Scale, 403, 404*t*
Imaginary standard, 250
Imaging, as cue-producing response,
    311
Imitation, gender differences and,
    609–611
Implicit personality theory, 3,
    269–273
    characteristics of, 30–31
    features of, 270
    versus formal personality theory,
        272–273
    impact of, 6
    meaning of term, 269–270
    personality assessment and, 276
    uses of, 270
    validity of, 270–272
Impressions, formation of, 270–271
Impulsivity
    caffeine and, 193, 194*f*
    Gray's theory of, 471
    versus reflectivity, 519
Inclusive fitness, 174
Incomplete Sentences Blank (ISB),
    403
Independence
    versus field dependence, 519–520
    principle of, 148
Independent variable, 39
    correlation method and, 44
Indicants, in nomological network,
    59, 60*f*
Individual differences
    behavior genetics models of, 205
    Galton's study of, 157–158
Individuality. *See also
    Distinctiveness*
    behaviorist perspective on, 326
Infant(s). *See also* Children
    basic characteristics of, 312
    gender differences in, 601–603
Inferiority complex, 90
Inferiority, organ, 89–90
Informal personality theory. *See
    Implicit personality theory*
Information, personality, 11
Information processing. *See also
    Cognition*
    computer model for, 240, 241*f*
    emotions and, 284–285
    self-schemata and, 244
Innate motives, 435
Innate response hierarchies, 312

Instincts, 71–72. *See also*
    Unconscious
    id and, 73
Institute for Personality Assessment
    and Research (IPAR), 254,
    472
Instrumental conditioning, 293–
    294
    operant behavior and, 296
    trait theory and, 428
Integration learning, 428
Integrity, 578–583
Integrity tests, 580–581, 581*t*
    evaluation of, 581–583
Intellect, 497
    structure, model of, 500
Intellectualization, 82*t*
Intelligence, 494–525
    alternative interpretations of,
        485, 485*t*
    assessment of, 500–505
    cognitive theories of, 500
    controversial issues associated
        with, 495–496
    versus creativity, 518
    crystallized versus fluid, 423–424
    culture and, 516
    definitions of, 498
    emotional, 397
    ethnic differences in, 512–514
    factors of, 499
    formal theories of, 499–501
    group differences in, 511–517
    heritability of, 507–510, 509*t*
    hierarchical models of, 499–500,
        500*f*
    measures of, versus personality
        measures, 496–497
    nature of, 497–499
    versus need for cognition, 521
    versus openness to experience,
        522
    personality and, 496–497
    prototype approach to, 498–499
    social, 242–243
    triarchic theory of, 501
Intelligence quotient (IQ)
    derivation of, 503
    major correlates of, 505–507
    tests of, 495
Intensive research, 472–474, 489
Intentional forgetting, 68–69
Intentions, 419

Interactionism, trait-situation
    debate and, 443–444
Interdisciplinary research, 473, 489
Interest(s)
    measurement of, 562–563
    social. *See* Social interest
Interjudge reliability, 54
Internal consistency reliability, 53
Internal-external locus of control (I-
    E), 358, 384–385, 386*f*
    measurement of, 403, 404*t*
Internals, 45
Internal standards of behavior, 369
Interpersonal relations, personality
    development and, 104,
    109–110
Interpersonal trust, 357–358
    assessment of, 385–387
*The Interpretation of Dreams*
    (Freud), 67
Interpretation, psychoanalytic, 84
    excess in, 140
Interview(s)
    behavioral assessment and,
        331–333
    hostility assessment and, 550
    personality assessment and,
        56–57
    for type A behavior, 546
Intra-species variation, 147
Intrinsic motivation, 566–567
    assessment of, 567–570, 570*t*
Introversion, 102
    caffeine effect and, 193, 194*f*
    Eysenck's structural model of,
        432*f*
    health and, 554
Introversion-extroversion type, 430,
    432–434
Intuition, versus sensation, 102–103
Inventories
    in behavioral assessment, 333
    objective personality, 275
IPAR. *See* Institute for Personality
    Assessment and Research
Ipsative standard, 250
IQ. *See* Intelligence quotient
ISB. *See* Incomplete Sentences Blank
Item-response theory, 517

Jenkins Activity Survey for Health
    Prediction (JAS), 546
Jensen, Arthur, 512–513

Job characteristics theory, 568
Job enrichment, 568
Jones, Ernest, 67
Jones, Mary Cover, 293, 322
*Journal of Research in Personality*
    (December 1995), 7
Judgment responses, intelligence
    and, 496
Jukes family, 159
Jung, Carl, 67
    analytic psychology of, 96
    archetypes of, 99–101
    biography of, 100–101
    comparative-anthropological
        approach of, 122
    dream analysis of, 120
    personality structure and, 99
    psychological types and, 102–103
    theory of, research on, 131–134
Juvenile delinquency, environment
    and, 186

Kallikak family, 159–160, 160*f*
Kamin, Leon, 431
Kelly, E. Lowell, 448
Kelly, George, 30, 211
    anxiety definition by, 529
    biography of, 234–235
    contributions of, 3282
    personality theory of, 231–239
    Rotter and, 350, 352
Kierkegaard, Sören, 230
Kin selection, 173
Kissinger, Henry, informal person-
    ality theory of, 6
Klein, Josephine, 109
Knowledge, expansion of, theories
    and, 31
Kohut, Heinz, self-psychology of,
    110–112
Koresh, David, 440
Krantz Health Opinion Survey, 554,
    555*t*

Labeling
    cognitive restructuring and,
        328
    as cue-producing response, 311
    unconscious and, 315
Laboratory research. *See*
    Experimentation
Laird, Melvin, 6
Lamarckianism, 172

Language
  cue-producing role of, 311
  of descriptive theories, 490
  gender stereotypes and, 595
  intelligence tests and, 514
  lexical hypothesis, 449
  of phenomenological theory, 284
  of psychoanalytic theory, 139
  in Rotter's theory, 350
  of traits, 11
Latency period, 78
Law of effect, 293
L-data, 463, 464*t*
  in 16 P-F Questionnaire, 466
Leaderless discussion group,
  574–577
Leader match training, 574
Leadership, 571–578
  continuum in styles of, 573*f*
  personality and, 574–578
  theories of, 571–574, 576–577
Learned drives, 310
Learned helplessness, 542
Learning
  aspects of, 309
  Cattell's view of, 428
  control and, 42
  four fundamentals of, 307–309
  integration, 428
  of neurosis, 315–317
  observational. *See* Observational
    learning
  rewards and, 309
Learning theory(ies), 20–21. *See
  also* Behaviorism
  anxiety and, 530–531
  beginnings of, 289–294
  description versus development
    in, 32
  gender differences and, 606–
    609
  historical perspective on, 337
  social. *See* Social learning theory
Least-Preferred Co-worker Scale
  (LPC), 574, 575*f*
Lemon juice demonstration, 434
*Leonardo da Vinci and a Memory
  of His Childhood* (Freud),
  122
*Letters from Jenny* (Allport),
  455–456
Leveling, versus sharpening, 519
Lexical hypothesis, 449

Libido, 71
  Jungian view of, 96
  at oral stage of development, 75
Librium, 190
Lie detectors. *See* Polygraph tests
Life
  everyday. *See* Everyday life
  problems of, response to, 95
  style of, 92
Life instincts, 71
Life tasks, 242
  strategies in pursuit of, 243
*Listening to Prozac* (Kramer), 191
Lithium, 190
Locus of control, 358, 384–385
  measurement of, 403, 404*t*
  research on, 384–385, 386*f*
Logical empiricism, 27
Loneliness, coping with, 104
*Look Homeward, Angel* (Wolfe),
  38
Looking-glass self, 213
Love needs and belongingness, in
  Maslow's hierarchy, 228,
  228*f*
LPC. *See* Least-Preferred Co-worker
  Scale

Male(s)
  brain activity patterns in,
    197–198, 198*f*
  chromosomes in, 150, 152*f*
  identification in, 599
  mate preferences of, 175–176
  phallic stage of development in,
    77, 79
  sensation seeking in, 192
  sociosexuality of, evolutionary
    theory and, 200–201
  stereotypic traits of, 592*t*, 593
Male paranoid prototype,
  California Q-set items from,
  254*t*
Management. *See* Leadership
Manic depression, drugs for, 190
Manifest Anxiety Scale (MAS),
  531*t*, 531–532
Manipulated variable. *See*
  Dependent variable
MAO. *See* Monoamine oxidase
Mao Tse-tung, 6
Marketing personality, 104
MAS. *See* Manifest Anxiety Scale

Masculine protest, 95
Maslow, Abraham, 32, 211
  biography of, 226
  hierarchy of needs, 225–227,
    228*f*
    workplace motivation and, 568
  humanistic theory of, 225–230
    empirical investigation of,
    256–260
  selfism phenomenon and, 219
Mate preferences, evolutionary
  analysis of, 175–176
Mathematical creativity, personality
  and, 255*t*
Maudsley Personality Inventory,
  432
MAVA. *See* Multiple abstract variance analysis
Maximum performance tests, 496
McClelland, David, 438–439
  defense of TAT, 476–477
Mediated stimulus generalization,
  311
Meiosis, 150, 151*f*
Memory
  episodic, 241
  impact on personality, 15
  observational learning and,
    367–368
  self-schemata and, 267–269
  semantic, 241
  structure of, 241–242
Men. *See* Male(s)
Mendel, Gregor, genetic theory and,
  147–149
Mesomorphy, 145, 146*f*
Metabolic activity, of brain, gender
  differences in, 197, 198*f*
Metamotives, 229
Microtheoretical approach, 33
Miller, Neal
  behavior therapy and, 321, 338
  biography of, 306–307
  reinforcement theory of, 305–317
  social learning and, 349
Miltown, 190
Mind, Freud's structural model of,
  73*f*
Minimal goal level, 360
Minnesota Multiphasic Personality
  Inventory (MMPI), 56, 584
Minnesota Study of Twins Reared
  Apart, 184–185

Mirror-hungry personality, 111*t*
Mischel, Walter
　cognitive social learning and,
　　373–376, 404
　delay of gratification theory of,
　　397–400
　reconceptualization of person
　　variables, 444
Mistakes, versus errors of judgment,
　277–278
Mitosis, 150
MMPI. *See* Minnesota Multiphasic
　Personality Inventory
Moderator hypothesis, trait-situa-
　tion debate and, 443
Monoamine oxidase (MAO)
　inhibitors, 190
　and sensation seeking, 190, 192
Monozygotic twins, 19, 165–166
Moral anxiety, 80
Morality, superego and, 74
Mother(s)
　attraction to, boys and, 77
　feminine protest and, 95
　hatred of, girls and, 78
　influences of, 12
Motivation
　achievement, 437*t*, 438–440
　intrinsic versus extrinsic,
　　566–567
　measurement of, 567–570, 570*t*
　in Murray's theory, 434–435
　observational learning and, 368
　as personality variable, 567–570
　psychological theories of,
　　567–569
　in Rotter's theory, 351
　self-monitoring and, 337*f*
　unconscious, 68–71, 137
　workplace, 566–570
Motivation-hygiene theory, 568
Motive(s), 434–435
　acquired, 435
　innate, 435
　metamotives, 229
Motor reproduction processes, in
　observational learning, 368
Moving against people, 103
Moving away from people, 103
Moving toward people, 103
Multidimensional Personality
　Questionnaire, 522
Multidisciplinary research, 473,
　489

Multiple abstract variance analysis
　(MAVA), 467
Multiple-factor hypothesis, 149
Multistage testing, 503
Multivariate research, 459–460
Murray, Henry
　personality assessment and,
　　472–479
　trait theory of, 434–441,
　　489–490
Mutation, genetic, 171–172
Myers-Briggs Type Indicator, 103
MZ twins. *See* Monozygotic twins
n Achievement, 437*t*, 438–440. *See
　also* Achievement
　development of, 439
　model for, 440
　nature of, 439
　social influences and, 439–440,
　　440*f*
　study of, 489
　TAT measurement of, 475–476,
　　476*t*, 478
　teaching of, 478–479, 480*f*
　workplace motivation and, 568
Nader, Ralph, 495
n Affiliation, 441. *See also*
　Affiliation
　TAT measurement of, 475–476,
　　476*t*
Narcissism. *See also* Selfism
　assessment of, 387
　personality disorders associated
　　with, 110–111, 111*t*
　test items for predicting, 52
Narcissistic behavior disorder(s),
　111*t*
Narcissistic personality disorder(s),
　110–111, 111*t*
Natural categories, 481–482
Naturalistic observation, 36–37
Natural selection, 147
　mutation and, 172
　variability and, 199
Nature versus nurture debate,
　14–16
　Galton's studies and, 157, 167
Nazi Germany, eugenics and, 158
Need(s)
　for achievement. *See* n
　　Achievement
　for affiliation. *See* n Affiliation
　conflict of, 360

Maslow's hierarchy of, 225–227,
　228*f*
　empirical investigation of,
　　256–260
　workplace motivation and, 568
　measurement of, TAT and, 475
　Murray's taxonomy of, 436, 437*t*
　for power. *See* n Power
　Rotter's categories of, 359
Need for cognition, 521
Need potential (NP), 357
Need value (NV), 357
　versus freedom of movement,
　　359–360
Negative affectivity, and health,
　557–558
Neo-Freudians, 103–108
NEO (neuroticism, extroversion,
　openness) model, 522
Neuroscience, 170–171. *See also*
　Brain structure
　subdisciplines of, 170*t*
　weaknesses of, 206–207
Neurosis, learning of, 315–317
Neurotic anxiety, 80, 527, 529
Neuroticism
　coping strategies and, 103
　criterion analysis of, 470
　Eysenck's type of, 430, 470
　Gray's reinterpretation of, 471
　and health, 557–558
　Jungian study of, 131–134
Neutral stimulus, 290*t*
Nomological network, 59–60, 60*f*
Nomothetic research, 40
　criticism of, 43
　idiographic research and, 45
　psychological research as,
　　248–249
　self-evaluation and, 249–250
Nonadditive genetic effects, 183
Nonconditional description, 413
Nondirective therapy, 221–224
Nonempirical criteria, for theory
　evaluation, 33–35
Nonmanipulated variable. *See*
　Independent variable
Nonshared environmental experi-
　ence, 185–186
Norenephrine, stress and, 59
Normal curve
　individual characteristics and,
　　157–158
　Q-technique and, 251

Norman, Warren, 448
Normative decision theory, 576
Normative standards, 249–251
Norms, in psychological research, 248
Not-me, 212
Novelty seeking, 471
Noyes, John, 158
NP. *See* Need potential
n Power, 440. *See also* Power
   TAT measurement of, 475–476, 476t
NV. *See* Need value

Objective personality inventories, 275
Objective tests, 56
Objectivity, in psychoanalytic research, 124
Object relations theory, 109–110
Object representations, 109
Observation
   controlled, 38, 334–335
   diagnostic council in, 473
   direct, 333–334
   Freud and, 138–139
   naturalistic, 36–37
   types of, 36–38
   unsystematic, 36
Observational learning, 363, 366–368
   assessment of, 390–394
   delay of gratification and, 398–399
   problems with, 407
   stages in, 367–368
   through guided participation, 371–372
Occupation, personality and, 561–588
Oedipus complex, 77
   Adlerian view of, 95
   case studies in, 87–88, 116–117
   drive-activation method and, 128
Omission, theories and, 35
Oneida Community, 158
Openness to experience, 522–523
   gender and, 612
Operant behavior, 296
Operant conditioning, 294–305
   behavior therapy based on, 324–326
Optimism, 551
   as adaptive strategy, 243

Oral biting period, 76
Oral stage, of personality development, 75–76
Oral sucking period, 75
Organ inferiority, 89–90
Organization
   psychoanalytic theory and, 137
   theories and, 30–31
Organizational effectiveness, self-efficacy and, 394–395, 396f
*Origin of the Species* (Darwin), 154
Other-report(s), 274–275
   phenomenology and, 281
   problems with, 275, 282–283
Outcome expectancy, 383
Overburdened self, 111t
Overcompensation, as defense mechanism, 82t
Overstimulated self, 111t

Pain, self-efficacy and, 392–394, 395f
Pampered child, 92–93
Pappenheim, Bertha, 66. *See also* Anna O.
PAQ. *See* Personal Attributes Questionnaire
Paradox, of personality, 3–4
Parent(s). *See also* Father(s); Mother(s); Parent-child interactions
   behavior of, evaluation of, 45
   sexualized encounters with, 75
   superego and, 74
Parental response, self-psychology and, 111, 111t
Parent-child interactions
   gender differences and, 603, 611–612
   personality and, 16
Parent effectiveness training, 96
Partial reinforcement, 300
   schedules of, 300t
Past
   in psychological study, 281, 283
   in trait theory, 419
Path diagram(s), in behavior genetics, 165, 166f
Path-goal theory, 576
Pathways, life tasks and, 243
Pavlov, Ivan, 289–290
Peak experience, 260
Pearson, Karl, 155
Peckham, Robert, 495

Pelvic opening size, and personality, 189, 189f
Penis envy, 78
Percept-genetics method, 127–128
Perception, impact on personality, 15
Performance
   anxiety and, 531–532
   in Rotter's theory, 351
   stress and, 543, 543t
Permeable construct(s), 235
Persona, archetype of, 100
Personal Attributes Questionnaire (PAQ), 613
Personal constructs, 232
   change in, 266–267
   encoding strategies and, 374
   hierarchy of, 236
   Kelly's theory of, 231–239
   research on, 264–267
   response to inconsistency of, 237–238
   systems of, 233–237
      complexity of, 267
Personal growth, striving for, 216–218
Personality
   and adjustment, 81, 84t
   concept of, 3
   definitions of, 8–9
   delay of gratification and, 399–400, 400t
   intelligence and, 496–497
   introduction to, 2–25
   measures of, versus intelligence measures, 496–497
   mechanisms of influence on, 169–177
   modern view of, 8–10
   as science, 7
*Personality and Assessment* (Mischel), 373–374
Personality assessment, 11, 50–59
   approaches to, 55–59
   versus behavioral assessment, 332t
   definition of, 50
   general versus specific, 51–52
   idiographic approach to, 248–255
   intensive method for, 472–474, 489
   personnel selection and, 584–587
   phenomenology and, 273–281

Personality Assessment (*continued*)
  problems with, 584–586
  specific versus general, 51–52
  standards for, 53–55
  subjectivity in, 53
  test–taking attitudes and, 51–53
  trait theories and, 455–458,
      472–479
  variable centered approach to,
      251
Personality, coefficients, 442
Personality description, 412–413
  Big Five model of, 448–451, 450*t*
  category view of, 481–482
  gender differences in, 612–613
  levels in, 447–448
Personality development, 12–13
  Adlerian theory and, 92–94
  Allport's theory and, 420–421
  animal and human, 202
  Bandura's theory and, 370
  Cattell's theory and, 428
  Dollard and Miller's theory and,
      312–313
  Erikson's stages of, 105*t*,
      105–108
  Freudian theory and, 75–79
  Kelly's theory and, 238
  Rogers' theory and, 218–220
  Rotter's theory and, 359
  Skinner's operant conditioning
      and, 303–304
  social cognitive theory and, 370
  social learning theory and, 359
  Sullivan's theory and, 104
*Personality: Evolutionary Heritage
    and Human Distinctiveness*
    (Buss), 202
16 Personality Factor
    Questionnaire, 466*t*,
    466–467
  intelligence test in, 497
Personality psychology
  experimentation and, 40
  field of, 10–14
  theoretical basis of, 3
Personality Research Form (PRF),
    477
Personality structure
  Adlerian view of, 89–92
  Dollard and Miller's theory and,
      312
  evolution and, 200–201
  Eysenck's model of, 430, 432*f*

Freudian view of, 72–75
  gender differences in, 612
  Jungian view of, 99
  Skinner's operant conditioning
      and, 302
Personality theory(ies)
  applications of, 493–614
  constructs and, 28–30
  determinants and, 15–18, 17*f*
  dimensions of, 32–33
  formal (explicit). *See* Formal per-
      sonality theory
  informal (implicit). *See* Implicit
      personality theory
  in late 1930s, 214
  versus personality description,
      412
  social cognition and, 242–245
  value of, 30–31
Personal self-concept, 212
Personal traits, 419
Personal unconscious, 99
Person-centered therapy, 221–224
Person-environment fit, 564
Personnel selection, 583–587
Person product moment correlation
    coefficient, 45, 46*t*
Person, versus situation, 33
Pessimism, defensive, 243
PET scan. *See* Positron emission
    tomography
16 P-F Questionnaire. *See* 16
    Personality Factor
    Questionnaire
Phallic stage, 76–77
Phenomenal field, 210
  in Roger's theory, 215
Phenomenological standards,
    249–250
Phenomenology, 15, 17*f*
  nature of, 210–211
  personality assessment and,
      273–280
  research methods in, 248
  Rogers and, 214–225
  self in, 211–214
  strengths of, 280–282
  weaknesses of, 282–285
Phenotype, 149
Phenylketonuria (PKU), 149
Philosophy of science, 27
Phobia, development of, 308
Physical environment, effects of,
    21–22

Physiognomy, method of, 414–415
Physiological measures, 59
Physiological needs, in Maslow's
    hierarchy, 227, 228*f*
Physiological responses, to stress,
    540–542, 542*f*
PI. *See* Emotions Profile Index
PKU. *See* Phenylketonuria
Placebo effects, 383–384
Planning, as cue-producing
    response, 311
Pleasure principle, 73
Political attitudes, environment and,
    186
Polygraph tests, 578–580
Positive regard
  need for, 218
  unconditional, 220
    client-therapist relationship
        and, 224
Positive self-regard, need for, 218
Positron emission tomography (PET
    scan), 197
Post-hoc explanation, 31
Power
  and health, 552
  need for. *See* n Power
  will to, 90
Practical significance, versus statisti-
    cal significance, 48–49
Preconscious
  Freudian concept of, 69
  versus personal unconscious, 99
  subdivision of, 73*f*
Prediction, behavior, 356–357
  specific versus general, 358*t*
Predictive validity, 54
  strategies for determining, 55*t*
Preemptive construct(s), 236
Present, in psychological study, 281,
    283
Press(es), 436–437
PRF. *See* Personality Research Form
Primary drives, 312
Primary needs, 436
Primary process
  ego and, 74
  id and, 73
Primary reinforcers, 301
*Principles of Behavior* (Hull), 293
Problems of life, styles in response
    to, 95
Processing, impact on personality,
    15

Process Scale, 263
Productive personality, 104
Progress matrices, 515, 516f
Projection
  behavioral analysis of, 316
  as defense mechanism, 82t,
    130–131, 135f
Projective techniques
  applicability of, 458
  behavioral assessment and, 402
  psychoanalytic assessment and,
    130, 132–133
Projective tests, 57–58
Propriate striving, 421
Proprium, 420
  aspects of, 420–421
  conceptual ambiguity of, 486
Prototype(s), 253
  intelligence and, 498–499
  male paranoid, 254t
  Q-set derivation of, 253–254
Proximal goals, 396
Prozac, 190–191
Psychic determinism, 68
  Freudian theory and, 137
Psychoanalysis
  behaviorist perspective on, 305,
    337
  goals of, 81
  as personality theory, 13
  process of, 85
  resistance to, 85
  set-up for, 83
  techniques of, 83–84
  as therapy technique, 13, 81
Psychoanalyst(s)
  adjustment and, 13
  stereotyping among, 595
Psychoanalytic Abstracts, 108–109
Psychoanalytic interpretation, 84
  excess in, 140
Psychoanalytic theory, 136–141.
    See also Freudian theory
  bases of, 68–72
  beginnings of, 65–68
  contemporary, 108–112
  and gender differences, 599–600
  popularity of, 65
  strengths of, 137–138
  weaknesses of, 138–141
Psychobiography, 122–124
Psychodynamic theory, 15, 17f
Psychogenic needs, 436
Psychohistory, 122–124

Psychological differentiation,
  519–520
Psychological situation, 356
  research on, 382–383
Psychological types. See also
    Type(s)
  Jungian theory of, 102–103
Psychology, personality. See
    Personality psychology
Psychometricians, 53
Psychopathology, 584
Psychopharmacology, 188–191,
  205
  cosmetic, 191
Psychosexual stages, 75–79
  adult expressions and, 84t
  defense mechanisms and, 84t
Psychosis. See also Schizophrenia
  maladjustment and, 221
Psychosocial theory, 105t, 105–
  106
Psychosomatic medicine, 527
Psychotherapy. See also
    Psychoanalysis
  Adler and, 96
  client-centered approaches to,
    221–224
  goals of, 81
  in late 1930s, 214
  learning theory and, 321
  phenomenology and, 281
  termination of, expectancy and,
    389
Psychoticism type, 432
  gender differences and, 612
P-technique, 468
Punishment, 21
  superego and, 74

Q-data, 464, 464t
  in 16 P-F Questionnaire, 466
Q-sort technique, 251–252, 252f,
  468
Qualitative characteristics, genetic
  theory and, 148
Qualitative data, 262–263
  example of, 259
  transformation into quantitative
    data, 262
Quantitative characteristics, genetic
  theory and, 148
Questionnaires, for type A behavior, 546
Quételet, Adolphe, 157

Radical behaviorists, 294
Rank, Otto, 67
  will therapy of, 214–215
Rating accuracy, 278–280
Rating agreement, 278–280
Rating scale(s), 273
  problems with, 275
  semantic differential, 273, 274t
Rational coper, self as, 420–421
Rationalization
  behavioral analysis of, 316
  as defense mechanism, 83t
Reaction formation
  behavioral analysis of, 316
  as defense mechanism, 82t
  Freudian theory and, 138
Reading, shaping of, 302
Reality anxiety, 80
Reality, denial of, 82t
Reality principle, 74
  beginnings of, 76
Receptive personality, 104
Recessive factor, in genetics, 148
Reciprocal determinism, 366, 367f
  gender differences and, 611–612
Recorded therapy sessions, 256
Reductionism, biological perspective and, 206
Reflectivity, versus impulsivity, 519
Regression, as defense mechanism,
  83t
Reinforcement(s), 21
  agents of, 298
  behavior therapy and, 324
  cognition and, 364–366
  definition of, ambiguity in,
    341–343
  delay of, 397–400
  effects of, 298, 299f
  expanded view of, 364
  extinction and, 309–310
  gender differences and, 606–608
  giving and withdrawal of, 49, 50f
  immediate versus delayed, 37
  internal, 369
  role in behavior determination,
    37
  schedules of, 299–301, 339
  secondary, 301
  shaping and, 301–302
  superego and, 74
  vicarious, 368
Reinforcement history, maladjusted
  behavior and, 304–305

Reinforcement theory, 305–317
  basic concepts of, 307–312
Reinforcement value, 355–356
  assessment of, 402
  delay of gratification and, 398,
    399f
  research on, 381–382
Reinforcer(s), 298
  types of, 301
Rejected child, 93
Relationship, client-therapist, 224
Relationship therapy, 214–215
Relations, interpersonal, and per-
    sonality development, 104,
    109–110
Relative utility, theories and, 34–35
Reliability
  of measurement, 53–54
  trait theory and, 445
Religion, and development of self,
    101
Repression, 68, 82t
  behavioral analysis of, 315
  illustration of, 88
  research on, 125–127
Repressive coping style, 127
Reproduction
  and adaptation, 199
  evolutionary analysis of, 175–176
Rep Test, 264–266, 284
Research, 14, 35–50. See also spe-
    cific theory
  animal. See Animal research
  bivariate, 459
  determinants debate and, 23
  empirical, 35–38
  historical trends in, 40, 41f
  idiographic. See Idiographic
    research
  individual variations in, 24
  intensive, 472–474, 489
  interdisciplinary, 473, 489
  laboratory. See Experimentation
  methods of, 14
  multivariate, 459–460
  nomothetic. See Nomothetic
    research
  phenomenological, 248, 280
  psychoanalytic, methods of,
    116–125
  theory and, 35–36
Resistance, 68, 85
Respondent behavior, 296

Response(s), 289
  anxiety and, 530–531
  basic types of, 290t
  conditioned, 290t
  cue-producing, 311
  definition of, ambiguity in,
    341–343
  galvanic skin, 128, 579
  inappropriate set of, 305
  initial hierarchy of, 309
  innate hierarchies of, 312
  judgment, intelligence and, 496
  parental, 111, 111t
  sign versus sample in, 331
  to stress, 540–544
  styles of, phenomenological
    assessment and, 275
  unconditioned, 290t
Response carelessness, phenomeno-
    logical assessment and, 275
Response expectancy, 383–384
  generalized, 384–387
Response extremeness, phenomeno-
    logical assessment and, 275
Response sets, 275
Retention processes, in observation-
    al learning, 367–368
Reward(s). See also
    Reinforcement(s)
  immediacy of, goal setting and,
    395–396
  learning and, 309
Reward dependence, 471
Rod-and-frame test, 519
Rogers, Carl Ransom, 13, 21, 211
  anxiety definition by, 529
  biography of, 216–217
  contributions of, 281–282
  phenomenological theory of,
    214–221
  Q-technique and, 251
  research legacy of, 256
  and selfism phenomenon, 219
  versus Skinner, 257–258
  therapeutic practices of, 215,
    221–224
  therapy session of, 259
  view of human nature, 28
Rogers, William, 6
Role confusion, 106–108
Role Construct Repertory Test. See
    Rep Test
Role(s), in specification equation, 427

Role playing, in behavioral assess-
    ment, 336
Rorschach Inkblots, 122, 132, 134f
  scoring system for, 133
Rotter, Julian, 32, 235
  anxiety definition by, 529
  biography of, 352–353
  needs categories of, 359
  social learning theory of,
    350–363, 403–404
R-technique, 468
  differential, 468

Sadat, Anwar, 6
Safety needs, in Maslow's hierarchy,
    228, 228f
Samples, responses as, 331
Sartre, Jean-Paul, 230
Scatterplot, 46
Schedules of reinforcement,
    299–301, 339
Schema(s), 241
  gender, 605–607
Schizophrenia. See also Psychosis
  diathesis-stress model of, 162
  treatment of, 188, 205
Science
  personality as, 7
  theory in, 27
Scientific management, 571
Scientific method, 35
Scripts, 241
Secondary drives, 310
Secondary needs, 436
Secondary process, ego and, 74
Secondary reinforcement, 301, 310
Secondary traits, 418
Seeding theory, 171
Segregation, principle of, 147–148,
    149f
Selective breeding, 158
Self
  archetype of, 101
  autonomous, 111
  components of, 211–212
  concept of, 211
  development of, 212–213. See
    also Personality development
  extension of, 420
  fragmented, 111t
  functions of, 213–214
  versus ideal self, 251–252, 253t
  as rational coper, 420–421

Roger's view of, 218–220
versus selfism, 219
social cognition and, 243–245
Sullivan's view of, 104
Self-actualization, 225
and being, 229–230
characteristics of, 229t
critique of, 258–260
in Maslow's hierarchy of needs, 228, 228f
workplace motivation and, 568
Self description(s), 593
Self-Directed Search, 565
Self-efficacy, 363–364, 369–370
assessment of, 392–395
aversive experiences and, 392–394, 395f
behavior change and, 372–373
clinical treatment and, 392
definition of, 401
and goal setting, 396
and health, 551
measurement of, 401–402
and organizational effectiveness, 394–395, 396f
Self-esteem, sense of, 420
Self-handicapping, 243
Self-help groups, Rogers and, 282
Self-ideal(s). See Ideal-self
Self-identity, sense of, 420
Self-image, 420
Selfism, 218–219. See also Narcissism
assessment of, 387
Self-monitoring, 336
reactive effects of, 336, 337f
Self-psychology, 110–112
Self-regulation, 369
cognition and, 242
gender differences and, 611–612
systems and plans of, 376
Self-report(s), 56–57, 274–275
behavioral assessment and, 58
phenomenology and, 281
problems with, 275, 282–283
versus TAT, 478
Self-schemata, 243–244
research on, 267–269
Semantic differential rating scale, 273, 274t
Semantic memory, 241
Sensation seeking, 190, 192
Sensation, versus intuition, 102–103

Sensitivity training, 572
Sentiment(s), 424
versus judgment, 496
Sequencing, chromosome, 151
SES. See Socioeconomic status
Sex
external versus chromosomal, 603–604
meaning of term, 590
overlap in characteristics related to, 598f
Sex chromosomes, 150
Sex-role stereotypes, 591–596, 592t
Sex stereotype index (SSI), 593
Sex training, early, 313
Sexuality
evolutionary analysis of, 175–176, 200
and personality development
Adlerian view, 95
Freudian view, 75–79
psychoanalytic theory and, 137–138
s factors. See Specific factors of intelligence
Shadow, archetype of, 101
Shaping, behavior, 301–302
Shared environmental experience, 185–186
Sharpening, versus leveling, 519
Sheldon, W. H., constitutional theory of, 145–147, 415
Sibling styles
birth order and, 93–94, 134
environmental experience and, 186
Significance, theories and, 33
Signs, responses as, 331
Sign versus sample approach to assessment, 58
Similarity. See also Consistency; Stability
of humankind, 3–4, 8
measurement of, 467–468
Simon, Théodore, 502
Simplicity, theories and, 33
Single-subject research, 49–50
versus aggregate data analysis, 51
limitations of, 139
Situation
versus dispositional traits, 441–446
versus person, 33

personality and, 10
psychological, 356
research on, 382–383
in social learning theory, 406
Situational factors, personality and, 192–193
Situational leadership theory, 577
Skinner, B. F., 7, 21
biography of, 296–297
contributions of, 338–339
engineered society of, 326–327
operant conditioning theory of, 294–305
versus Rogers, 257–258
view of human nature, 28
Social cognition, 23
emergence of, 282
and gender differences, 605–606, 608f
meaning of term, 239
personality theories based on, 242–245, 363–373
premises of, 241–242
Social constructivist movement, 272
Social desirability, phenomenological assessment and, 275
Social environment
effects of, 22
personality theories based on, 103–108
Social intelligence, 242–243
Social interest
Adlerian concept of, 90–92
scientific study of, 135
Social learning theory, 15, 17f, 348–378
adjustment and, 13, 359
applications of, 387–389
assessment and, 400–403
Bandura and, 363–373
and behavior change, 362–363
case study using, 361–362
cognitive, 373–376
research on, 389–396
extensions of, 383–384
gender differences and, 609–612
research on, 380–400
Rotter and, 350–363
strengths of, 404–406
as systematic theory, 32
weaknesses of, 406–408
Social Readjustment Rating Scale, 538, 539t–540t

Social self-concept, 212
Society
    and achievement, 439–440, 440f
    and intelligence measures,
        513–514
Sociobiology, definition of, 173
Sociobiology: The New Synthesis
    (Wilson), 173
Socioeconomic status (SES), intelli-
    gence and, 505–507
Somatic cells, 150
SORC (stimuli-organism-response-
    consequences), 331
Soul, and personality, 7
Source trait(s), 423
    hereditary influences and, 423
    identification of, 465–467
Spearman, Charles, 155, 424
Specific assessment, versus general
    assessment, 51–52
Specification equation, 426–427
Specific expectancies (E'), 354–355
Specific factors (s) of intelligence,
    499
Specificity, versus generality, 33
Specific reflexes, 312
Spence, Kenneth, 365
Splitting, as defense mechanism, 82t
SSI. See Sex stereotype index
Stability, 10
STAI. See State-Trait Anxiety
    Inventory
Standard(s)
    for evaluating experience,
        249–250
    idiographic, 249–250
    imaginary, 250
    internal, 369
    ipsative, 250
    normative, 249–251
    for personality assessment, 53–55
    phenomenological, 249–250
Stanford-Binet Test, 502–503, 504f
State(s)
    in specification equation, 427
    versus traits, 429, 469
State anxiety, 534
State-Trait Anxiety Inventory
    (STAI), 333, 534, 535f
Statistical analysis, 48
Statistical significance, 48
    versus practical significance,
        48–49

Statistical techniques, 205
Stereotypes, gender, 591–596
    factors promoting, 595–596
Stimulus/stimuli, 289
    ambiguity in definition of,
        341–342
    basic types of, 290t
Stimulus generalization, 311–312
Stress, 534–544
    anxiety and, 529
    behavioral responses to, 542–544
    causes of, 537–540
    definitions of, 535
    and illness, 527
    leadership and, 574
    and performance, 543, 543t
    phenomenological appraisal of,
        535–537
    physical reactions to, 540–542,
        542f
    process of, 541f
    responses to, 540–544
    self-efficacy and, 392–394, 395f
Stress inoculation, 329–330
Striving, 216–218
Strong Vocational Interest Blank
    (SVIB), 562–563
Structure
    brain. See Brain structure
    of memory, 241–242
    personality. See Personality struc-
        ture
Structure of intellect model, 500
Studies on Hysteria (Breuer and
    Freud), 66
Style of life, 92
Subjective experience
    evaluation of, 249–250
        problems with, 282
    phenomenological research and,
        248, 280. See also Social
        cognition
Subjective value(s), 375
Subjectivity
    in personality assessment, 53
    phenomenological theories and,
        210
    in psychoanalytic research, 124
Sublimation
    as defense mechanism, 83t
    in psychotherapy, 81
Subordinate level, in personality
    description, 447

Successive approximation, rein-
    forcement and, 301
Sullivan, Harry Stack, 104
Superego, 74–75
    beginnings of, 76
    construct of, 29
    versus ideal-self, 218
    moral anxiety and, 80
    phallic stage and, 77
Superiority
    socialization of, 92
    striving for, 90
        sexual urges and, 95
Superordinate constructs, 266–267
Superordinate level, in personality
    description, 447
Surface trait, 423
SVIB. See Strong Vocational Interest
    Blank
Swedish Adoption/Twin Study on
    Aging, 183–184
    personality correlation data from,
        184t
Symbiosis, 109
Symbolic modeling, application of,
    371–372, 372f
Syntality, 428
Systematic desensitization, 322
    application of, 371–372, 372f
    precursor of, 293
    procedures in, 323
Systematic theories, 32
Systemic distortion hypothesis, 271

TABP. See Type A behavior pattern
Tachistoscope
    in interpersonal trust assessment,
        387
    in psychoanalytic research,
        127–128
Taft, Jessie, relationship therapy of,
    214–215
Talking cure, 66
Tardive dyskinesia, 190
TAT. See Thematic Apperception
    Test
T-data, 464–465, 465f
    in 16 P-F Questionnaire, 467
Tellegen Absorption Scale, 522
Temne people of Sierra Leone,
    21–22
Temperament traits, 424
Test anxiety, 532–533

Test Anxiety Scale (TAS), 533, 533*t*
Test bias, 514–517
  evidence of, 516–517
Testosterone, antenatal exposure to, and personality, 189, 189*f*
Test-retest reliability, 53
Test-taking, attitudes in, 51–53
Texas Adoption Project, 183
T-groups, 572
Thanatos. *See* Death instincts
Thema, 438
Thematic Apperception Test (TAT), 57–58, 132, 133*f*
  alternatives to, 477–478
  criticism of, 489–490
  defense mechanism study and, 130
  development of, 473
  McClelland's defense of, 476–477
  procedure in, 475–476
  scoring systems for, 133
  versus self-reports, 478
  social learning theory and, 402
  validation of, 478
Theophrastus, 7, 414
Theory(ies). *See also specific theory*
  choice of, 11
  diversity of, 27–28
  evaluation of
    empirical, 35–50
    nonempirical, 33–35
  limitations of, 30
  personality. *See* Personality theory(ies)
  personality psychology and, 11
  research and, 35–36
  science and, 27
  testing of, 59–60
Theory X, leadership and, 572
Theory Y, leadership and, 572
Therapy. *See also* Psychotherapy
  aversion, 322–323
  behavior. *See* Behavior therapy
  client-centered, 221–224, 282
  fixed-role, 239
  nondirective, 221–224
  relationship, 214–215
  will, 214–215
Thinking
  convergent, 518
  divergent, 518
  versus feeling, 102–103
Third force, in psychology, 225
Thomson, Sir Godfrey, 234

Thorndike, Edward L.
  behaviorism of, 293
  Cattell and, 424
Threat
  construct inconsistency and, 237
  self and, 220
Thymine, in DNA composition, 150, 153*f*
Time-out, 324–325
Time, personality and, 10, 281, 283, 419
Tit for tat strategy, 203
Titian, family of, Galton's analysis of, 156*f*
Toilet training, and personality development, 76
Token economy, 325
Training groups, 572
Trait(s)
  ability, 423–424
  Allport's definition of, 416
  cardinal, 418
  Cattell's classification of, 423–427
  central, 418
  classification of, 418–419
  common, 419, 426
  consistency of, 443
  constitutional, 423
  descriptive-predictive view of, 446–451
  dispositional, 414–415
    versus situational, 441–446
  dynamic, 424–425
  empirical identification of, 465–467
  environmental-mold, 423
  versus habits, 418
  hereditary, 423
  language of, 11
  as needs and motives, 434–435
  personal, 419
  as scientific constructs, 490
  secondary, 418
  source, 423, 465–467
  versus states, 429, 469
  surface, 423
  temperament, 424
  and types, 415
  unique, 426
Trait anxiety, 533–534
Trait constructs, 412–413
  advantages of, 413
  hierarchy of, 413

Trait theory(ies), 17–18, 411–453
  act-frequency, 447–448. *See also* Act-frequency approach
  Allport and, 415–422, 486–487
  Cattell and, 422–429, 487–489
  Eysenck and, 429–434, 487–489
  historical beginnings of, 414–415
  Murray and, 434–441, 489–490
  personality assessment and, 455–458
  research methods in, 458–479
  situation and, 441–446
  strengths of, 486–489
  weaknesses of, 486–490
Transference, in psychoanalysis, 68, 85
Transitional objects, 110
Traumatic events, stress and, 537–538
Triarchic theory of intelligence, 501
Tricyclics, 190
Trust. *See* Interpersonal trust
TV viewing, and aggression, 393–394, 394*f*
Twin study(ies), 167
  behavior genetics and, 19, 165–166, 181–183
  heritability estimates based on, 167–168
    contradictions in, 183–187
  intelligence and, 508, 509*t*
  intraclass correlations in, 182*t*
  rearing conditions and, 183–184, 184*t*
Type(s)
  basic, 430–432, 433*f*
  in dispositional theory, 414
  Eysenck's definition of, 430
  Jungian theory of, 102–103
  and traits, 415
Type A behavior pattern (TABP), 545–550
  and blood pressure, 547, 547*f*
  characteristics of, 545
  components of, 548–550
  coronary heart disease and, 546–548, 548*f*
  measurement of, 546
  physiological measures for assessment of, 59
Type B behavior pattern, 545

Unconditional positive regard, 220
  client-therapist relationship and,
    224
Unconditioned response, 290t
Unconditioned stimulus, 290t
Unconscious, 68. *See also* Instincts
  behavioral analysis of, 314–
    315
  collective, 99
  Freudian concept of, 69
  Murray's concept of, 438
  personal, 99
  psychoanalytic versus cognitive,
    128–129
  scientific study of, 127–129
  subdivision of, 73f
Unconscious motivation, 68–69,
    137
  hypnosis and, 70–71
Understanding, tools of, 26–62
Understimulated self, 111t
Undoing, as defense mechanism, 82t
Uniqueness. *See also* Distinctiveness
  of individuals, 3–4, 8
Unique traits, 426
Unsystematic observation, 36

Validated constructs, 266
Validity
  assessment and, 54–55
  concurrent, 54
  construct. *See* Construct validity
  content, 54
  criterion, 54
  of implicit personality theory,
    270–272
  predictive, 54
  strategies for determining, 55f
Valium, 190

Value(s)
  Allport's assessment of, 458, 459t
  of reinforcement. *See*
    Reinforcement value
  subjective, 375
Van Derber, Marilyn, 75
Variable(s), 39
  correlation method and, 44
Variable centered approach, to per-
    sonality assessment, 251
Variance, 162
  calculation of, 163–164
Variation
  in appearance/personality, 147
  evolutionary mechanisms for,
    199–200
  genetic, origin of, 172
  intra-species, 147
VA Selection Project of Clinical
    Psychologists, 472
Vertical linkage theory, 576
Vicarious conditioning, 368–369
Vicarious experience, self-efficacy
    and, 373
Vicarious reinforcement, 368
Vienna Psycho-Analytical Society,
    89
Viscerogenic needs, 436
Vocational choice. *See also*
    Occupation
  Holland's theory of, 564f,
    564–566, 565t
  personality and, 562–566
Vocational Preference Inventory,
    565

WAIS. *See* Wechsler Adult
    Intelligence Scale
*Walden Two* (Skinner), 326

Watson, John B., 21
  behaviorism of, 291–293, 292f
Wechsler Adult Intelligence Scale
    (WAIS), 505
Wechsler-Bellevue Intelligence Scale,
    504
Wechsler Intelligence Scale for
    Children (WISC), 505
Wechsler Preschool and Primary
    Scale of Intelligence (WPPSI),
    505
Wechsler scales, 504–506
*White House Years* (Kissinger), 6
Wiggins, Jerry, 449
Will therapy, 214–215
Will to power, 90
Wilson, E. O., 173
WISC. *See* Wechsler Intelligence
    Scale for Children
Wolfe, Thomas, 38
Women. *See* Female(s)
Women mathematicians, creativity
    in, research on, 254–255,
    255t
Woodward Psychoneurotic
    Inventory, 584
Workplace, personality in, 561–
    588
Work Preference Inventory (WPI),
    567–570, 570t
World, of person, 215–216
Worth, conditions of, 218–220
WPPSI. *See* Wechsler Preschool and
    Primary Scale of Intelligence
Wundt, Wilhelm, 65

X chromosomes, 150

Y chromosome, 150